FOUNDATIONS OF EVIDENCE-BASED
SOCIAL WORK PRACTICE

FOUNDATIONS OF EVIDENCE-BASED SOCIAL WORK PRACTICE

Edited by

Albert R. Roberts

Kenneth R. Yeager

OXFORD

UNIVERSITY PRESS

2006

OXFORD

UNIVERSITY PRESS

Oxford University Press, Inc., publishes works that further
Oxford University's objective of excellence
in research, scholarship, and education.

Oxford   New York
Auckland   Cape Town   Dar es Salaam   Hong Kong   Karachi
Kuala Lumpur   Madrid   Melbourne   Mexico City   Nairobi
New Delhi   Shanghai   Taipei   Toronto

With offices in
Argentina   Austria   Brazil   Chile   Czech Republic   France   Greece
Guatemala   Hungary   Italy   Japan   Poland   Portugal   Singapore
South Korea   Switzerland   Thailand   Turkey   Ukraine   Vietnam

Published by Oxford University Press, Inc.
198 Madison Avenue, New York, New York 10016

www.oup.com

Oxford is a registered trademark of Oxford University Press

Library of Congress Cataloging-in-Publication Data
Foundations of evidence-based social work practice / edited by Albert R. Roberts, Kenneth R. Yeager.
   p. cm.
   Summary: "Concise introduction to evidence-based social work that introduces the issues and methods
most frequently encountered while preparing for evidence-based social work practice"—Provided by
publisher.
   ISBN-13 978-0-19-530594-4; 978-0-19-530558-6 (pbk.)
   ISBN 0-19-530594-9; 0-19-530558-2 (pbk.)
   1. Evidence-based social work.   2. Human services—Research—Methodology.   3. Psychiatric social
work.   I. Roberts, Albert R.   II. Yeager, Kenneth.
   HV41+
   362.2'0425—dc22   2005021938

Printed in the United States of America
on acid-free paper

Preface

For social work students as well as practitioners, this book provides the critically needed framework and foundation knowledge base in order to understand and conduct evidence-based practice. This volume, featuring chapters by prominent evidence-based research professors, includes how-to application chapters demonstrating the latest key elements, operational definitions, critical issues, concepts, and strategies in the application of evidence-based social work assessment measures and interventions.

This is the condensed companion volume and update to Roberts and Yeager's *Evidence-Based Practice Manual: Research and Outcome Measures in Health and Human Services*, a 104-chapter major reference text. The latter volume was published in 2004 and is multidisciplinary in scope. The current volume was specially prepared for evidence-based social workers and their students. It includes two specially written new chapters on step-by-step question formulation and how to conduct systematic reviews of the evidence with co-occurring disorders. It also includes 23 evidence-based social work articles reprinted from two special issues of the *Brief Treatment and Crisis Intervention* journal in 2004, which focused on evidence-based mental health, or the *Evidence-Based Practice Manual*.

The goal of this textbook is to improve understanding, enhance at-risk clients' well-being and quality of life, and facilitate recovery from mental disorders, while preventing further harm. This goal can be facilitated by the acquisition of evidence-based knowledge and the application of evidence-based social work practice.

This book provides answers to the 15 most frequently asked questions by novice as well as experienced evidence-based social workers. The detailed answers to each of the following questions are provided by carefully reading the chapters in this book:

1. What is evidence-based practice?
2. How does the reader design, search for, find, and implement evidence-based social work studies?
3. What is the nature and extent of evidence for and against evidence-based practice?
4. What are the necessary sequential components in formulating evidence-based questions in social work?
5. How does the reader implement best practices and expert consensus procedures?
6. What are the concise standards of evidence-based practice?
7. What are the standard levels in the hierarchy of evidence?
8. What are the similarities and differences regarding the extent of implementing practice guidelines and evidence-based treatment by psychiatrists, psychologists, and social workers?
9. What are the common indicators and outcome measures used in the delivery of evidence-based mental health treatment?
10. What are the specific steps and methods used in developing a systematic evidence-based search plan for a client with comorbidity?
11. Which assessment measures and treatment modality is most likely to reduce suicide risk based on evidence-based studies?
12. What are the elements of evidence-based practice with children and adolescents with a range of the most prevalent mental disorders?
13. What are the evidence-based treatments and interventions most likely to be effective with adults diagnosed with obsessive-compulsive disorders (OCD), depressive disorders, anxiety disorders, PTSD, and/or other disorders?
14. What are the most effective evidence-based treatments for persons suffering with comorbid substance dependence, suicide ideation, and schizophrenia?
15. What are the most effective evidence-based supported employment programs for the seriously mentally ill based on longitudinal research?

Social workers need to know what the most effective practice guidelines, treatment plans, and intervention methods are before they can decisively help their clients.

It is our hope that this evidence-based knowledge and skills textbook will provide the necessary foundation and stimulation for social work students and practitioners. We are lifelong learners and we invite the readers to join us on our preparatory journey for the future. We also encourage all readers to share their suggestions on chapters we should add to the next edition. Please e-mail us at: *prof.albertroberts@comcast.net* and *kyeager@adelphia.net*

The medical profession led the way with evidence-based studies in the early 1990s at McMaster University in Canada, the evidence-based articles published in JAMA between 1993 and 2004, and the Institute of Medicine report on 93,000 medical errors. Social workers have begun to follow the important lead of medical scholars and practitioners. In recent years, social workers have embraced evidence-based practice and are establishing clinical care pathways and practice guidelines based on a synthesis and analysis of the evidence. Social workers have always been concerned with improving the quality of life and restoring psychosocial and family functioning for all clients, and in some cases saving lives. Therefore, given the growing emphasis on best practices and judicious and conscientious decision-making in social work practice, it is imperative for social workers to be prepared with the latest evidence-based practice protocols and research exemplars. We owe it to our clients and the social work profession to only use interventions that have systematic evidence of their effectiveness and efficacy.

This primer provides foundation skills, directions, and exemplars of evidence-based best practices, randomized controlled studies, outcome studies of manualized treatment protocols, systematic studies of mental health interventions, and cost-effectiveness studies. This book is also intended to provide practical guidance to those embarking on their first evidence-based systematic review. We are reasonably confident that this book includes the necessary tools and application chapters to inspire graduate students as well as seasoned practitioners to understand and be able to conduct evidence-based outcome studies. We hope this book serves as a catalyst to all social work students and practitioners in their quest for effective and efficacious evidence-based social work treatment in the important years ahead.

We sincerely appreciate the encouragement and guidance given by Dr. Phyllis Solomon (University of Pennsylvania School of Social Work), Dr. Ed Mullen (Columbia University School of Social Work), Dr. Elizabeth Plionis (Catholic University National School of Social Services), and Dr. David Springer (University of Texas School of Social Work at Austin). These evidence-based professor-scholars suggested a condensed version of the *Evidence-Based Practice Manual* and were instrumental in deciding which 25 chapters to include in this evidence-based social work primer. Finally, our editor Maura Roessner deserves special acknowledgment for her full support in facilitating an Oxford contract, launching this text, and reminding us about deadlines.

Contents

Contributors

EDITORS

Albert R. Roberts, Ph.D., B.C.E.T.S., D.A.C.F.E., is Professor of Criminal Justice
and Social Work, Interdisciplinary Criminal Justice Program in the Faculty of
Arts and Sciences, Livingston College Campus at Rutgers, the State University
of New Jersey in Piscataway. He has been a tenured professor at Rutgers University since 1989, prior to which he taught at Indiana University School of
Social Work, Seton Hall University, Brooklyn College of CUNY, and the University of New Haven. Dr. Roberts has 30 years full-time university teaching
experience, including 15 years of administrative experience (ten years as Chair,
and five years as a Program Director). Dr. Roberts received an M.A. degree in
Sociology from the Graduate Faculty of Long Island University in 1967 and a
D.S.W. in 1978 (which became a Ph.D. in 1981) from the School of Social Work
and Community Planning at the University of Maryland in Baltimore. In addition, his doctoral studies at the University of Maryland included a double spe-
cialization in research methods and criminology. Dr. Roberts is the founding
Editor-in-Chief of the *Brief Treatment and Crisis Intervention* journal (Oxford
University Press, www.brief-treatment.oupjournals.org for abstracts on all articles and guidelines for contributing authors), and he was an Editorial Advisor
to Oxford's Professional Book Division in New York City (1999–2005). For
updates on Dr. Roberts's recent publications see his website: www.crisisinter
ventionnetwork.com

Dr. Roberts is a member of The Board of Scientific and Professional Advisors and a Board Certified Expert in Traumatic Stress for The American Academy of Experts in Traumatic Stress. He is also a Diplomate of the American College of Forensic Examiners. Dr. Roberts is the founding and current Editor of the 42-volume Springer Series on Social Work (1980 to present), and the 10-volume Springer Family Violence Series. He is the author, co-author, or editor of over 200 scholarly publications, including numerous peer-reviewed journal articles and book chapters and 27 books. His recent books and articles include: *Crisis Intervention Handbook: Assessment, Treatment and Research, 3rd edition* (OUP, 2005); *Evidence-Based Practice Manual: Research and Outcome Measures in Health and Human Services* (OUP, 2004, co-edited by Kenneth R. Yeager); *Juvenile Justice Sourcebook* (OUP, 2004); *Handbook of Domestic Violence Intervention Strategies* (OUP, 2002); *Social Workers' Desk Reference* (OUP, 2002, co-edited by Gilbert J. Greene); and *Battered Women and Their Families: Intervention Strategies and Treatment Approaches*, 2nd edition (1998).

Dr. Roberts recent current projects include: continuing to teach courses on Crisis Intervention, Domestic Violence, Research Methods, Program Evaluation, Evidence-Based Practice, Special Topics, Victimology, and Victim Assistance, and Juvenile Justice at Rutgers University; training crisis intervention workers and clinical supervisors in crisis assessment and crisis intervention strategies; training police officers and administrators in domestic violence policies and crisis intervention. He is a lifetime member of the Academy of Criminal Justice Sciences (ACJS), has been a member of the National Association of Social Workers (NASW) since 1974, and has been listed in *Who's Who in America* since 1992 and Who's Who in Medicine and Healthcare, and Who's Who Among Human Service Professionals. Dr. Roberts was the recipient of the Teaching Excellence Award by Sigma Alpha Kappa Chapter of the National Criminal Justice Honors Society in both 1997 and 1998 and is a charter member of the Gamma Epsilon Chapter of Alpha Delta Mu National Social Work Honors Society at Indiana University.

Kenneth R. Yeager Ph.D., LISW is the Director of Quality and Operational Improvement for OSU and Harding Behavioral Healthcare and Medicine and Director of OSU and Harding Behavioral Healthcare and Medicine Outpatient Psychiatric Clinics. For the past eight years Dr. Yeager has served as adjunct professor in the Ohio State University College of Social Work. He is also Clinical Assistant Professor of Psychiatry in the Department of Psychiatry of The Ohio State University. Dr. Yeager completed his doctoral degree at The Ohio State University, College of Social Work. He has more than fifteen years experience in mental health and substance dependence treatment as both administrator and clinician. Currently, he is a Treating Clinician for the National Football League Program for Substances of Abuse. Areas of research interest include development of quality metrics, implementation of quality improvement processes within medical and psychiatric healthcare settings, impact of comorbid diagnosis on rehospitalization rates, substance dependence with mentally ill chemical abusers, and processes of addiction and recovery with resistant populations. Dr. Yeager is an active member of the editorial board for the *Journal of Brief Treatment and Crisis Intervention.*

CONTRIBUTORS

Jonathan S. Abramowitz, M.D.
Mayo Clinic
Rochester, MN

William Bacon, Ph.D.
Research Associate, Columbia
   University
School of Social Work and
Owen Consulting Inc. Brooklyn,
   NY

Bernard Bloom, Ph.D.
Professor Emeritus
Department of Psychology
University of Colorado
Boulder, CO

Patrick Bordnick, Ph.D.
Assistant Professor
School of Social Work
University of Georgia
Athens, GA

Kevin Corcoran, Ph.D., J.D.
Professor, Graduate School
   of Social Work
Portland State University
Portland, OR

Sophia F. Dziegielewski, Ph.D.
Professor and Director
School of Social Work
University of Cincinatti
Cincinatti, OH

Anne E. Fortune, Ph.D.
Professor
School of Social Welfare
University at Albany

State University of New York
Albany, NY

Leonard Gibbs, Ph.D.
Professor
Department of Social Work
University of Wisconsin
Eau Claire, WI

Ken Graap, M.Ed.
Doctoral Student
Department of Psychology
Emory University
Atlanta, GA

Robin J. Jacobs, MSW
Doctoral Candidate
School of Social Work
Florida International University
Miami, FL

Ellen P. Lukens, Ph.D.
Associate Professor
Columbia University
School of Social Work
New York, NY

William McFarlane, M.D.
Director of Research
Department of Psychiatry
Maine Medical Center
Portland, ME

Edward J. Mullen, Ph.D.
Distinguished Professor and
   Director
NIMH Mental Health Services
   Research Doctoral Training
   Program

Columbia University
Graduate School of Social Work
New York, NY

Carlton E. Munson, Ph.D
Professor
University of Maryland
School of Social Work
Baltimore, MD

Scott Okomoto, Ph.D.
Assistant Professor
School of Social Work
Arizona State University
Tempe, AZ

Enola K. Proctor, Ph.D.
Frank J. Bruno Professor of Social
   Work
Research
Dean for Research
George Warren Brown School of
   Social Work
Washington University
St. Louis, MO

Charles Ray, M.Ed.
CGR & Associates
President and Chief Executive
   Officer
National Council for Community
   Behavioral
Healthcare
Rockville, MD

William J. Reid, DSW†
Distinguished Professor Emeritus
School of Social Welfare
The University at Albany
State University of New York
Albany, NY

† Deceased

Aaron Rosen, Ph.D.
Barbara A. Bailey Professor
   Emeritus of Social Work
Washington University St. Louis
St. Louis, MO

Richard N. Rosenthal, M.D.
Professor of Clinical Psychiatry
Columbia University College
   of Physicians and Surgeons
Chairman, Department of
   Psychiatry
St. Luke's Roosevelt Hospital
   Center
New York, NY

Stephanie A. Schwartz, Ph.D.
Post Doctoral Fellow
Mayo Clinic
Rochester, NY

Aron Shlonsky, Ph.D.
Assistant Professor
Faculty of Social Work
University of Toronto
Toronto, Canada

Phyllis Solomon, Ph.D.
Professor and Research Director
University of Pennsylvania
School of Social Work
Philadelphia, PA

David W. Springer, PhD,
Professor and Associate Dean
   of Academic Affairs
The University of Texas at Austin
School of Social Work
Austin, TX

Victoria Stanhope, M.S.W.
Doctoral Candidate
University of Pennsylvania
School of Social Work
Philadelphia, PA

David L. Streiner, Ph.D.
Assistant V. P., Research
Director, Kunin-Lunenfeld Applied
  Research Unit
Baycrest Centre for Geriatric Care
Professor, Department of
  Psychiatry
University of Toronto
Toronto, Ontario, Canada
Co-editor, *Evidence-Based Mental
  Health Journal*

Gregory Teague, Ph.D.
Associate Professor
Department of Mental Health Law
  and Policy
Louis la Parte Florida Mental
  Health Institute
University of South Florida
Tampa, FL

Bruce A. Thyer, Ph.D.
Professor
School of Social Work
Florida State University
Tallahassee, FL

Barbara Thomlison, Ph.D.
Professor
School of Social Work
Florida International University
Director, Institute for Children and
  Families at Risk
Miami, FL

Tom Trabin, Ph.D.
Vice President The Partnership for
  Behavioral Healthcare Central
  Link
Lead Consultant, Carter Forum
  Initiative
Tiburon, CA

Vikki L. Vandiver, M.S.W., Dr.P.H.
Associate Professor
Graduate School of Social Work
Portland State University
Portland, OR
Book Review Editor, *Community
  Mental Health Journal*

M. Elizabeth Vonk, Ph.D., LCSW
Associate Professor and Director
Part-time M.S.W. Program
University of Georgia
School of Social Work
Athens, GA

Marjorie Weishaar, Ph.D.
Clinical Professor
Department of Psychiatry and
  Human Behavior
Brown University Medical School
Providence, RI

Craig Winston LeCroy
Professor
Arizona State University
School of Social Work
Tempe, AZ

Section I

Overview, Definitions, Practice Guidelines, and Critical Issues

1

Bridging Evidence-Based Health Care and Social Work

How to Search for, Develop, and Use Evidence-Based Studies

ALBERT R. ROBERTS

KENNETH YEAGER

CHERYL REGEHR

Social workers are often at the forefront of providing guidance to clients and their families regarding a wide range of health, mental health, and social service options. While social workers obviously do not provide medical or psychiatric advice, they are required to be knowledgeable about health and mental health treatments and issues so that they can assist clients and their families to access required information from health care providers and make informed decisions. Further, in providing social work services social workers can no longer rely on best intentions but are obligated to ensure that the interventions they employ are informed by the available research evidence. The overriding objective of this volume is to bridge and augment health and social work practices with scientific research inquiry.

We live in a scientific age in which new medical and social science advances are reported almost daily, and the pace of change is breathtaking. In the midst of this, health and social services consumers are bombarded with information about medications, surgeries, alternative health care approaches, and psychosocial interventions that are "guaranteed" to ease their burden and enhance their lives each time they open their e-mail, turn on the TV, or go to the mailbox. Individuals are faced with choices of herbal remedies, gadgets, intrusive physical interventions, and intriguingly named psychological treatments, for example, eye movement desensitization and reprocessing (EMDR), to manage everything from life-threatening illness to unappealing aspects of their appearance. While some view this as the age of the educated consumer, few individuals have the ability to sift through the available data and make informed decisions. Rather, many of those seeking and requiring treatment turn to health care and mental health professionals with the expectation that these professionals will have the knowledge base to determine which treatment methodology is going to result in the most positive outcome with the least cost in terms of suffering, time, and money. As a result of the trust placed in them, health care and mental health professionals have a fiduciary duty to acquire the knowledge required to answer the question "What do you recommend?" based on the best available scientific information.

The overriding objective of this volume is to bridge and augment health and social work practices with scientific research inquiry. Toward the end of the 20th century, there was a consistent trend toward bridging practice and research. In the early 21st century, evidence-based practice is beginning to proliferate world-wide in major universities, medical centers, mental health centers, schools, and family treatment centers. From empirical and evidence-based outcome studies conducted within these centers and in the community, best practice guidelines and treatment protocols are emerging that allow practitioners to provide the optimal treatment or intervention to any individual, family, or group seeking assistance. This book attempts to consolidate state-of-the-art evidence-based knowledge so that graduate students and practitioners in social work and other human services professions have all of the latest research and evaluation guidelines, research exemplars, and evidence-based protocols available in one volume.

Our primary goal in compiling and editing the *Evidence-Based Practice Manual* is to make the latest evidence-based protocols, practice-based research designs and exemplars, evaluation research, and assessment tools and measures accessible to all medical, public health, and social work professionals. The secondary goal in developing this volume is to provide clinical research and program evaluation models to facilitate agency and consumer accountability on the part of health and human service professionals. The editors firmly believe that medical and psychosocial diagnosis, treatment plans, and service delivery need to be based on a scientific epistemology. Specifically, all professionals need to have easy access to the latest evidence-based research findings on medical and psychosocial treatment effectiveness, longitudinal follow-up of behavior change and mental health recovery following intervention, outcomes of health and social work programs, and cost-benefit studies.

This volume contains two sections totaling 25 chapters. The first section presents the current issues in evidence-based practice, the rationale behind the development of evidence-based practice, and the controversies that have arisen in the area. Further, the means for conducting evidence-based reviews and the implementation of evidence-based reviews into direct practice are discussed. The second section provides examples of evidence-based practice reviews in action. These provide both specific guidelines for workers in areas such as anxiety disorders, conduct disorders, and PTSD, and exemplars of the means by which evidence-based reviews are conducted and applied to practice.

This overview chapter will systematically introduce and integrate the different operational definitions of evidence-based practice, practice-based research, assessment tools and measures, and evaluation research. The 25 chapters of this volume methodically examine the following:

1. The steps in formulating a problem and selecting the research question
2. The process of determining the appropriate research method
3. Specific methodological issues such as randomization, reliability and validity, and outcome measurement
4. The steps in obtaining research funding
5. The process of conducting program and service evaluations and determining performance indicators
6. Technological issues such as use of computer technology, statistical analysis, and electronic medical records
7. Standards and guidelines for evidence-based practice or best practice

DEFINING EVIDENCE-BASED PRACTICE

It is important to begin with a common understanding of the similarities and differences between evidence-based practice and practice-based research. We asked three esteemed professors to identify and discuss their definitions and the similarities and differences between evidence-based practice (EBP) and practice-based research (PBR).

According to Dr. Edward J. Mullen, professor and director of the National Institute of Mental Health (NIMH) Mental Health Services Research Doctoral Training Program at Columbia University Graduate School of Social Work:

Evidence-based practice (EBP) and practice-based research (PBR) have similarities and differences in meaning. Both phrases refer to the relationship between research and practice. EBP places emphasis on the practitioner's use of scientifically validated assessment, intervention, and evaluation procedures, as well as the practitioner's use of critical thinking when making practice decisions that matter to service recipients. However, a frequently heard criticism of EBP is that there is little relevant research available regarding most questions that a practitioner asks. Further, it is often said that much of the research that is available is of little use because so many scientific studies are conducted in contexts that have little resemblance to realistic practice situations.

Accordingly, many are now calling for finding new ways to bridge this gap between practice and research by supporting efforts to conduct research that will be of direct relevance to practitioners and which will be usable in service systems. Such applied practice-based research can take at least two forms. On the one hand, translational research is looked to since this is a form of research that seeks to take basic research findings from one field or from highly controlled contexts and adapt the findings to realistic practice contexts. Alternatively, another approach is to foster researcher and practitioner partnerships in the conduct of practice research so as to enhance relevance. This is a two-way street in which one can move from research findings to practice contexts or, alternatively, begin with realistic practice problems as the stimulus for research. The phrase *practice-based research* can be used to signify efforts to bridge this gap between practice and research. In turn, findings from such efforts can be used to support EBP.

According to Dr. David L. Streiner, professor of psychiatry at the University of Toronto Medical Center and assistant vice-president and research director for Kunin-Lunenfeld Applied Research Unit at Baycrest Centre for Geriatric Care:

> The link between practice and research is a two-way street. Good clinical practice must be informed by the best available evidence regarding treatment and diagnosis (evidence-based practice). However, in order for this research to be clinically relevant and useful, it must be both well executed and informed by actual clinical practice (practice-based research). This may consist of carefully done case histories, documentation of symptom clusters, or, ideally, N of 1 studies. The clinician cannot be divorced from what is being found in labs and studies with patients, nor can the researcher be isolated from what problems patients are presenting with, and how they are currently being treated.
>
> An example of the usefulness of careful clinical observation of a small number of cases was recently, and unfortunately, provided by the outbreak of sudden acute respiratory syndrome (SARS) in Toronto. After "only" two deaths, it was possible to both identify this new syndrome and to trace all of the other cases to close contact with these two people, resulting in measures (e.g., screening all hospital visitors, quarantines, protective clothing, and mandatory hand washing of all people entering hospitals) that quickly broke the cycle of infections.

According to Dr. Phyllis Solomon, Professor of Social Work and affiliated Professor of Medicine at the University of Pennsylvania:

> Evidence-based practice has two components. One component is basing practice decisions on empirically based evidence as to the interventions or intervention strategies that are likely to produce the desired outcomes. In other words, employing interventions that have empirically been determined to be effective for the particular problem being targeted, including the findings being applicable to the characteristics of the client or client system to be served. The second aspect is to evaluate the implementation of these interventions to ensure that they are being implemented as intended and that the intended outcomes are achieved, with no unintended negative consequences. Whereas practice-based research is scientifically investigating issues related to practice, which may or may not specifically address questions of practice effectiveness. There is clearly some overlap between these two areas, for engaging in evidence-based practice means that practice-based research is being undertaken. The caveat here is that evaluation research must be considered within the domain of research. The arena of practice-based research includes a host of research questions beyond questions of effectiveness of interventions, but still retains the expectation that knowledge gained from this research will result in more effective practice. It is important to note that both evidence-based practice and practice-based research contribute to the development of empirically-based practice knowledge.

EBP has been defined as the conscientious, explicit, and judicious use of the best available scientific evidence in professional decision making (Sackett, Richardson, Rosenberg, & Haynes, 1997). More simply defined, it is the use of treatments for which there is sufficiently persuasive evidence to support their effectiveness in attaining the desired outcomes (Rosen & Proctor, 2002). In chapter 8 of this book,

Rosen and Proctor suggest that evidence-based practice is comprised of three assertions: (a) intervention decisions based on empirical, research-based support; (b) critical assessment of empirically supported interventions to determine their fit to and appropriateness for the practice situation at hand; and (c) regular monitoring and revision of the course of treatment based on outcome evaluation.

Evidence-Based Social Work

Evidence-based [social work] dictates that professional judgments and behaviors should be guided by two distinct but interdependent principles. First, whenever possible, practice should be grounded on prior findings that demonstrate empirically that certain actions performed with a particular type of client or client system are likely to produce predictable, beneficial, and effective results. . . . Secondly, every client system, over time, should be individually evaluated to determine the extent to which the predicted results have been attained as a direct consequence of the practitioner's actions. (Cournoyer & Powers, 2002, p. 799)

In general, decision making using evidence-based methods is achieved in a series of steps (Gibbs & Gambrill, 2002; Hayward, Wilson, Tunis, & Bass, 1995). The first step is to evaluate the problem to be addressed and formulate answerable questions. These questions can include: What is the best way of assisting an individual with these characteristics who suffers from depression? or Which group treatment method is most effective in reducing recidivism among batterers?

The next step is to gather and critically evaluate the evidence available. Evidence is generally ranked hierarchically according to its scientific strength. It is understood that various types of intervention will have been evaluated more frequently and rigorously by virtue of the length of time they have been used and the settings in which they are used. Thus, for newer treatments, only Level 4 evidence may be available (see Table 1.1). In such cases, practitioners should use the method with caution, continue to search for evidence of its efficacy, and

Table 1.1   Levels of Evidence

Level	Description
1	Meta-analysis or replicated randomized controlled trials (RCT) that include a placebo condition/control trial or are from well-designed cohort or case control analytic study, preferably from more than one center or research group, or national consensus panel recommendations based on controlled, randomized studies, which are systematically reviewed.
2	At least one RCT with placebo or active comparison condition, evidence obtained from multiple time series with or without intervention, or national consensus panel recommendations based on uncontrolled studies with positive outcomes or based on studies showing dramatic effects of interventions.
3	Uncontrolled trial or observational study with 10 or more subjects, opinions of respected authorities, based on clinical experiences, descriptive studies, or reports of expert consensus.
4	Anecdotal case reports, unsystematic clinical observation, descriptive reports, case studies, and/or single-subject designs.

be prepared to evaluate the method's efficacy in their own practice. The final steps involve applying the results of the assessment to practice or policy and then continuously monitoring the outcome.

In the past several years considerable controversy has arisen over the perception that evidence-based practice prescribed that practitioners should become slaves to the pursuit and application of "evidence" narrowly defined as randomized controlled trials (Upshur & Tracy, 2004; Webb, 2001; Goodacre, 2003; Gibbs & Gambrill, 2002). This has led to an expanded definition of evidence-based practice beyond that originally proposed by Sackett and colleagues in 1997. The expanded definition states "Evidence based medicine (EBM) is the integration of best research evidence with clinical expertise and patient values" (Centre for Evidence-Based Medicine, 2004). Social work scholars have added that practitioners are required to seek and consider multidimensional sources of knowledge including (1) quantitative and qualitative studies, (2) consumer wisdom, and (3) professional wisdom (Petr & Walter, 2005). It has thus been suggested that the process of implementing evidence-based practice in social work involves the following steps:

1. Convert your practice problem into an answerable question.
2. Locate the best available evidence with which to answer that question.
3. Together with your client, critically appraise the evidence.
4. Use your clinical judgment and your client's preferences to apply that evidence to the present circumstance.
5. Evaluate the performance of your intervention according to the objectives you and your client had set out. (Barber, 2005)

We would add that the nature of the organization in which the practitioner works, the constraints imposed by resources in the organization and the mandate of the organization is a further element that must be considered in the implementation of evidence-based practice. For instance, a child welfare organization charged with protecting the rights and safety of vulnerable children may need to consider an intervention approach that ensures that the mandate is fulfilled. The revised model therefore would be as follows:

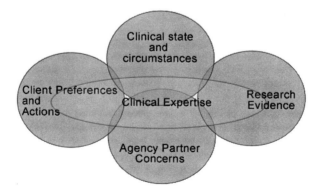

Figure 1.1   Evidence-Based Practice Model. From Regehr, Barber, Trocme, Hart & Knoke, 2005.

Evidence-Based Practice in Health Care

Evidence-based health care "takes place when decisions that affect the care of patients are taken with due weight accorded to all valid, relevant information" (Hicks, 1997, p. 8).

> Evidence-based practice (EBP) is an approach to health care wherein health professionals use the best evidence possible, i.e. the most appropriate information available, to make clinical decisions for individual patients. EBP values, enhances and builds on clinical expertise, knowledge of disease mechanisms, and pathophysiology. It involves complex and conscientious decision-making based not only on the available evidence but also on patient characteristics, situations, and preferences. It recognizes that health care is individualized and ever changing and involves uncertainties and probabilities. Ultimately EBP is the formalization of the care process that the best clinicians have practiced for generations." (McKibbon, 1998, p. 396)

MEDICINE AND EVIDENCE-BASED PRACTICE

A catalyst to the expansion and increased utilization of Evidence-Based Medicine seems to be both the Users' Guides series of articles published in the *Journal of the American Medical Association* (JAMA) between 1993 and 2000, and the outstanding edited book based on 33 articles compiled by Doctors Gordon H. Guyatt and Drummond Rennie (2002). The strength of Guyatt and Rennie's (2002) *Users' Guides to the Medical Literature* is that it is compact and in paperback format, with a CD-rom included. The primary objective of this handbook is to improve clinical decision-making through an awareness, systematic literature search, and critical evaluation of the evidence, and its application to particular patient problems.

The leading discipline in the application of evidence-based practice is the field of medicine. This may be in part due to the critical and sometimes lifesaving nature of decision-making processes within the medical field. There may be additional contributing factors such as the quantitative nature of medical science lending itself well to the application of evidence-based treatment.

The practice of evidence-based medicine begins with a comprehensive systematic review of the literature. The next step is an open-minded and rigorous evaluation of evidence presented. Physicians are challenged to examine three elements critical to the successful implementation of evidence-based medicine. First, the evidence must connect to the treatment and to the ideal overall health outcomes. Second, there must be a control group. Third, the research design must account for any possible confounding factors that could affect the outcomes independently of the treatment. Once the evidence has been evaluated (see Table 1.1), the physician's next task is to determine if the evidence demonstrates the effectiveness, benefit, and value of the treatment for its stated application. When the evidence has been thoroughly reviewed by the physicians and review groups with full understanding of the analysis, a set of recommendations should be made based on the efficacy of the procedure found within the literature. For example:

1. It is advised that this be done in a periodic health examination *or* a diagnostic procedure should be done, *or* treatment of a medical problem should be given. There is good evidence (Level 1) to support the recommendation.
2. This may be done in periodic health examination, *or* a diagnostic procedure may be done, *or* treatment of a medical problem may be given.
3. It should be done in most cases. There is fair evidence (Level 2) to support the recommendation.
4. It should not be done in most cases. There is poor evidence (Level 3) regarding the recommendation, which may be made on other grounds.
5. It is advised that this not be done in a periodic examination, *or* a diagnostic procedure should not be done, *or* treatment of a medical problem should not be given. There is good evidence (Level 1) to support the recommendation that this not be done.

There are numerous ways in which physicians can participate in the practice of evidence-based medicine. All begin with the realization and appreciation that medicine has become far too complicated for physicians to make treatment decisions without a systematic review of evidence. Therefore, many physicians rely on practice guidelines and additional decision-making support tools that are based on principles of evidence to assist with their decision-making process. Nevertheless, we fully appreciate the fact that the decision to follow practice guidelines requires a delicate balance of reviewing the weight of evidence for a particular intervention and the individualized needs of the patient. Medical care in the real world is different from the type of medicine practiced in clinical trials. In the real world populations served are often older than those in clinical trials, with multiple diagnoses requiring multiple integrated treatments, while those in controlled studies suffer only from the condition under investigation. Clinical trials will tell us what treatments are effective but will not provide information regarding which patients should receive them. Therefore, it must be accepted that clinical guidelines and evidence-based medicine provide only guidelines for care, that medical practice and other forms of human care must be inclusive of opinion and collaborative decision making and must always be tailored to meet the individualized need of the patient combined with the treatment team's best judgment in order to obtain the best outcome.

PSYCHOLOGY AND EVIDENCE-BASED PRACTICE

Evidence-based psychotherapy emerged in the early 1990s, and by 1993 the concept of evidence-based psychotherapy had grown sufficiently in scope to warrant the American Psychological Association's publication of established empirically validated treatments (Chambless, 1993; Chambless, 1996a; Chambless, 1996b; Chambless et al., 1996). However, publication of the guidelines was not met with universal enthusiasm, and in the ensuing debates the term *empirically validated* was softened to *empirically supported* treatments. The semantic change alone did not end the controversy, which led to longstanding divisions among American psychologists. Many argued that the publication of such a list was unhelpful and scientifically unjustified because the criteria for evidence-based practice excluded clinical judgment from the scientific assessment of effectiveness. Additionally it was believed that the listing of empirically supported treatments failed to take into account evidence supporting rival hypotheses of factors that influenced the outcome of treatment, including the strong evidence for the centrality of the therapeutic alliance.

In the United Kingdom an alternative strategy for achieving evidence-based practice was implemented that permitted psychotherapists to further develop innovative approaches that built on practice wisdom. From this foundation, psychotherapeutic processes were then formally evaluated through a process of random controlled studies. This process facilitated a balance between research evidence and clinical consciousness that would support and expand clinical practice through the establishment of clinical practice guidelines.

Psychologists have developed evidence-based guidelines for specific populations within multidisciplinary organizations. One example is the *Practice Guidelines* from the International Society for Traumatic Stress Studies, edited by Foa, Keane, and Friedman (2000), that reviews the evidence and suggests guidelines for working with various populations suffering from post-traumatic stress disorder (PTSD). In addition, by virtue of their methodological rigor, psychologists have contributed significantly to the conduct of research on practice efficacy through the development of research methods and specific tools for measuring characteristics and change. David Streiner, for example, has provided an invaluable service to medical, psychology, and social work colleagues through his series of books, book chapters, and articles describing research and statistical methods and identifying their application to practice situations.

Although these efforts in both North America and the United Kingdom have had a substantial impact on the development of evidence-based practice within the practice of psychotherapy, this progress seems to have been relatively slow in comparison to the progress made within the field of medicine. Within the fields of psychotherapy, psychology, and many other disciplines there has been a fundamental distrust of practice guidelines and evidence-based practice. This distrust stems from professional training and skill formulation of practitioners who have been taught to emphasize the uniqueness of individuals and who frequently reject the medical metaphor of a prescriptive approach to psychotherapy.

If the tension between the prescriptive nature of practice guidelines and the traditionally more individualized practice of psychotherapy is not sufficient to slow the establishment of evidence-based practice, there are additional concerns for many therapists that the research evidence is incomplete, misleading, unfairly biased, and detrimental to the highly individualized practice of psychology. Nevertheless, examination of evidence within the field of psychology continues to progress, practice guidelines are established, and practitioners are moving forward with an awareness of the problems and limitations that may be presented through the application of evidence-based practice. This has been fostered in no small part through the development of national guidelines issued by the National Institutes of Health and National Institute of Mental Health in combination with evidence-based sources such as the Campbell and Cochrane collaborations, providing resources for practitioners. The Campbell collaboration is an international organization designed to prepare and disseminate systematic reviews of high-quality controlled studies on the effectiveness of educational criminology and social practices and policies. The Cochrane collaboration and the Cochrane library in Oxford, England, have produced databases summarizing the best and most current evidence available through controlled studies of interventions and treatment protocols for health care and human services.

SOCIAL WORK AND EVIDENCE-BASED PRACTICE

The social work field has experienced similar tensions regarding evidence-based practice. On one hand there is a push primarily by those in academic settings to evaluate practice and establish practice guidelines and on the other hand a reticence by practitioners to read and integrate research into their practices. Supporting this reluctance is another group of academics who criticize evidence-based approaches as reductionistic and mindless empiricism.

Social work has a history related to evidence-based practice dating back to the 1970s and the work of Mullen and Dumpson (1972), Fischer (1973), and Jayaratne and Levy (1979).

The point of departure is Mullen and Dumpson's classic book *Evaluation of Social Intervention* (1972). This book examines 16 field experiments testing the effects of social work interventions including social casework, social group work, and community organization. The volume included all of the known field experiments conducted through 1971 that examined social work interventions. Fifteen internationally recognized social work experts critically assessed these findings and discussed implications for social work practice and education. At the time, Edward Mullen was the director of research and evaluation at the Community Service Society of New York and an associate professor at Fordham University. James R. Dumpson was the dean of the Fordham University Graduate School of Social Service. Contributing authors included Werner Boehm, Edgar Borgatta, James Breedlove, Donald Feldstein, Ludwig Geismar, Wyatt Jones, Harold Lewis, Carol Meyer, Helen Harris Perlman, Simon Slavin, John Turner, Walter Walker, and Gene Webb. The editors convened a national conference to discuss the studies and the book chapters. This conference was attended by 125 representatives of most of the U.S. graduate schools of social work and was held at Fordham University in 1971. This was the first major call for a move toward evidence-based practice in social work.

In his classic article, "Is Casework Effective?: A Review," Joel Fischer (1973) underscored the critical importance of carefully conducted research in order to determine whether or not casework was effective. Fischer reviewed the serious limitations of 11 studies that were supposed to determine the effectiveness of casework services. His book led to a strident debate on the role of research in social work practice. The debate has continued for more than 30 years, and the profession of social work has slowly come to realize the importance of research in measuring treatment effectiveness.

Jayaratne and Levy provided a description of "empirical clinical practice" in their 1979 text. In this text, the authors advocated for practitioners to seek evidence, measure client progress, and document treatment outcome in order to provide objective rather than subjective data to guide clinical practice.

The debate over establishing practice guidelines became most heated in 1997 with an article written by Myers and Thyer that raised the question "Should social work clients have the right to effective treatment?" In this article, they asserted that social work codes of ethics should include the clients' right to effective treatment and social workers' obligation to be educated about and provide such treatments. In the ensuing war of letters, critics countered that such a suggestion ignores the complexity of individual problems, ignores clinical expertise, is merely a cost-cutting measure, and is impossible (see Gibbs & Gambrill, 2002). Nevertheless, many social work researchers, educators, and practitioners have continued to strive toward evidence-based practice. The premise that social work practice must be based on empirically tested and verified knowledge is now widely accepted and endorsed by leaders and social work organizations (Rosen, Proctor, & Staudt, 2003). Concern still exists, however, that research evidence is not easily accessed by practitioners and is not readily translated into practice (Gambrill, 2000; Howard, McMillen, & Pollio, 2003). Thus, considerable time and effort is being directed toward the establishment of practice guidelines (Rosen et al., 2003) and in determining methods for teaching best practices based on empirical evidence to trainees in the field (Howard et al., 2003).

However, it is the scope of social work practice—which spans a multitude of service areas and treatment modalities including behavioral therapy, supportive counseling, marital or family treatment, family and children services, mental illness treatment, health care, gerontology, and many more—that has led to difficulties in defining contemporary evidence-based treatment in social work. It is also social work's unique contribution to the holistic care approach to the individual that has led the profession to an appreciation of the need for evidence-based practice. Within the past decade social workers have been given increased responsibilities in the form of care management, interdisciplinary communication, treatment planning, and resource management, all within the context of a managed care environment. These trends have highlighted the need for social workers to practice intervention with manualized treatment protocols and strategic plans that effectively meet the needs of individuals, families, groups, programs, and organizations.

For those disciplines embracing evidence-based care, social work has become an integrated component, synthesizing and analyzing evidence currently available in the literature and working to establish clinical care pathways and practice guidelines within many care delivery systems. In addition, social workers have a history of gathering data and monitoring the outcome of the population served. It is the goal of agencies such as the National Center for Social Work Research, the National Association of Social Workers, and the Society for Social Work and Research to continue to establish and develop evidence-based practice through the application of ongoing quantitative and qualitative evaluation of outcomes. The social work profession in conjunction with other professional disciplines represents a remarkable resource of scientific measurement and practitioner's talent able to contribute greatly in the area of practice-based research, thus moving forward the goals of evidence-based practice. Evidence of social work's involvement in evidence-based practice is found in this volume in the chapters by Proctor and Rosen, Gibbs and Gambrill, and Mullen and Bacon, which outline the processes by which evidence can be translated into practice. In addition, social work scholars have contributed multiple submissions on measures for evaluating practice and creating new evidence for the assessment of others.

Social work professor Eileen D. Gambrill (2003) at the University of California at Berkeley incisively underscores the potential of EBP:

"Professionals have an obligation to inform clients about services found to be effective and to avoid harm. Concerns that practitioners were continuing to use methods found to be harmful was a key reason for the development of EBP. . . . EBP calls for candid descriptions of limitations of research studies and use of research methods that critically test questions addressed. . . . (The critical question is): How effective have we been in maximizing the flow of knowledge that contributes to helping clients and minimizing the flow of misleading, inaccurate material that diminishes opportunities to help clients and may result in harm" (Gambrill, 2003, pp. 5, 6, and 18).

OPERATIONALIZING AND INTEGRATING PRACTICE-BASED RESEARCH WITH EVIDENCE-BASED PRACTICE

The concept of integrated evidence-based practice is not new. This concept has a very long history dating to the early 1900s in the writings of Joseph Rowntree, who discussed rigor in the assessment of problems and the development of solutions. Mary Richmond in 1917 and Richard Cabot in 1933 followed this work. Evidence-based medicine has a longstanding tradition. In the broadest sense this includes the scientific tradition that has brought medicine to its current status of practice. Narrowing the scope somewhat, evidence-based medicine involves aspects of medicine requiring the burden of proof. This includes the use of hypothesis testing and calculation of statistical significance to interpret clinical research. An example is the Food and Drug Administration's criteria for new drug approval, which includes providing acceptable evidence of effectiveness and safety factors associated with the drug being tested.

As the concept of evidence-based medicine has expanded so has the idea of evidence-based practices. Areas of recent focus have included pharamacological and psychosocial treatment of mental illness, neurocognitive disorders, and substance dependence (Brink, 2003). However, to date, there has been a lack of integration regarding the application of evidence-based practice both within disciplines and across disciplines. Variation in practice-based research approaches, bottlenecks in communication of emerging best practice methods, and the failure to embrace research methodologies that harness the potential of collaborative user interfaces slow the advancement of evidence-based care. The purpose of this chapter is to explore and elaborate on the potential for multidisciplinary collaborations within the application of evidence-based practice.

So what exactly is the difference between practice-based research and evidence-based practice? Naturally, there are overlaps, but generally speaking practice-based research serves as the springboard for the development of evidence-based practice. Practice-based research:

- includes the application of rigorous, systematic, and objective procedures to obtain reliable and valid knowledge relevant to direct clinical practice, education, activities, and programs;
- involves research that employs systematic, empirical methods demonstrating valid and reliable measurement across evaluators, practitioners, and observers among multiple studies by the same or different investigators yielding replicated results, while maintaining awareness of individualized variance in response to interventions and care plans;
- analyzes and evaluates data through experimental or quasi-experimental methods, examining individuals, entities, programs, and interventions within a variety of settings across a variety of conditions with appropriate controls to evaluate the effects of the condition of interest. Controlled and randomized studies are preferable;
- provides sufficient detail and clarity to permit replication or at minimum the opportunity to build systematically on previous study findings;
- is published in peer-reviewed journals or approved by panels of independent experts through a process of rigorous and objective scientific review.

What then is the basis for variance present within the understanding and operational definitions of evidence-based practice?

- First, there are differences both within and between disciplines when addressing various approaches to similar problems with evidence-based care.
- Second, source data contributing to the evidence-based practice foundation does not currently lend itself to the infusion of new knowledge gained from practice settings.

Practice-based research in fact is the foundation for evidence-based care. Therefore, the goal of this book is to present an integrated model showing examples of practice-based research that will serve as a tool for practitioners to bridge the gap between practice, research, and emergent best practices within evidence-based practice. Multidisciplinary or interdisciplinary teams are essential to the integration and development of practice-based research. According to Dziegielewski (2003) in the multidisciplinary team professionals from multiple disciplines work together, each having clear roles and responsibilities designed to assist the client. Within the interdisciplinary team, however, although these professionals from different disciplines continue to work together, they often share roles and responsibilities, often completing tasks not considered traditional for their particular fields. For example, the social worker is expected to know about medications and the effects they can have on intervention outcomes, even though social workers have traditionally not been specifically trained in this area.

Therefore, in health care, whether services are provided through multidisciplinary or interdisciplinary teams, evidence-based practice has come to be equated with practice effectiveness. The examples presented in the chapters of this book are designed to equip practitioners with additional strategies for dealing with the rapidly changing environment where the acquisition of new knowledge and innovative practice is an essential ingredient for innovation in caregiving. We believe when research-based practice principles are appropriately applied, practice-based research will result—thereby fueling the establishment, refinement, and integration of evidence-based practice.

IMPLEMENTATION OF AN INTEGRATED MODEL OF EVIDENCE-BASED PRACTICE AND PRACTICE-BASED RESEARCH

Adoption of practice-based research and evidence-based practice requires utilization of the inherent knowledge of multidisciplinary or interdisciplinary teams. The basis for this is taking the understanding and experience of each individual practitioner and joining it with that of the research-practitioner to better assist the populations to be served. The knowledge acquired by these practitioners has become a part of a growing "toolbox" of practice-based strategies to be further explored, invented, or refined through more traditional approaches to research. When this knowledge is mixed with the skills of the practitioner-researcher, evidence-based research evolves. In essence, this combination approach capitalizes on and creates an entirely logical progression of informal research questions and methods for answering these questions, testing practice methods, and measuring outcomes as applied to issues of direct relevance to the field of interest.

Establishment of practice-based research requires practitioners to make use of their inherent knowledge, understanding, and experiences with the population served through their interactions and informal research processes. The emphasis is on descriptive, historical, and naturalistic approaches. This process information is then available for scrutiny through the rigors of scientific or social science methodology conducted by persons whose professional training has prepared them to conduct such analysis. This method, which utilizes the combination of skill and professional energy, serves to recognize how important it is for practice not to be conducted in a laboratory but rather within the practice setting, providing a necessary feedback loop for further exploration. Thus, practice-based research will accomplish the following important collaborative goals:

- Providing equal representation from all disciplines.
- Providing access for input from a variety of practitioners' groups and users of research generated.
- Promotion of new and innovative approaches to high-risk populations.
- Keeping pace with rapidly changing population needs.
- Addressing questions of importance to the discipline and the population served.
- Capitalizing on the synergistic effectiveness of collaborative approaches.
- Continually improving the quality of care provided.
- Working to minimize bias in research.
- Establishing communication for dissemination of information/knowledge gained.
- Ensuring an atmosphere of growth recognizing parallel application of practice within similar or same populations.

Currently, practitioners are challenged with unprecedented choices in theoretical approaches, community options, medications, and practice approaches. At the same time the challenge exists of providing services and treatment in the most cost-effective manner. The relevance of Senge's ideas (1995) and a growing number of others including those affiliated with the Institute of Medicine is reflective of the need for organizations to invoke their own research strategies and evidence-based practice approaches as a basis for advancing scientific knowledge-building in health care.

Today more than ever it is important for practitioners to be aware of the rapidly changing environment in which care is provided as well as the increasing number of new treatment approaches, processes, and technological advancements available. Practice-based research provides a powerful tool based on the principle that the experience, wisdom, and insight of the practitioner form the structure that can facilitate identification and framing of research questions that are relevant to practice and can improve practice methods. In turn, the research results should be ones that are in theory more easily assimilated into everyday practice. Essential skills necessary for the development of practice-based research include but are not limited to the following:

- Experience in raising research questions from practice.
- Developing or adapting appropriate research methodologies to address practice-based research questions.
- Application of the research methodology within a practice context.
- Development of methods for the generation, evaluation, and application of relevant professional knowledge in practice settings.
- Flexibility in development of methodology to facilitate maximizing input of multidisciplinary team members in the care design/clinical pathway or algorithm of best practice.

In refining practice-based research skills, teams attempt to provide a sense of how this approach can be applied within a multitude of professional settings and visualize what promise this can bring to the complex human interactions faced within the practice environment. The basis of practice-based research is that of the team coming from a "need-to-know" stance. This will require reframing of the hierarchical system approach generally adopted by our (Western) science.

The concept of practice-based research is inclusive in part of the concept of "organizational sensemaking" contained in the work of Weick (1996) on the understanding of organizational science. In a learning, researching multidisciplinary team all members are actively involved in identifying, analyzing, and solving problems, enabling the discipline to further advance and improve its capabilities, knowledge base, and understanding of the impact of multiple systems involved. Within such a learning/research environment there is no preconceived model for knowing. However, there is an overarching philosophy or attitude about the nature of practice. In establishing such an environment the learning and adaptive capability of the entire discipline is greatly enhanced. The group will find that it is able to adapt more rapidly and to manage issues in a more efficient manner, embracing change in a progressively evolving, scientific, medical, and social approach.

One resource that can help the practitioner find the best available evidence is a series of secondary journals: *Evidence-Based Mental Health* (*EBMH*), *Evidence-Based Nursing*, and *Evidence-Based Medicine* (*EBM*). The oldest, *EBM*, has been around for about 10 years and the youngest, EBMH, for five. For each of the journals an experienced team scans up to 200 journals, applying rules to select only those articles that meet rigorous methodological standards for both quantitative and qualitative research. They then prepare a summary of the article, which takes up about two-thirds of a page. The remainder of the page is taken up by a commentary, written by a research-oriented clinician, that places the article in the context of previous research and current clinical practice. In this way the reader gets the bottom line for the best current articles about treatments, diagnosis, etiology, and natural history.

CONCLUSION

This volume provides direction to health, mental health, and human service professionals based on collective wisdom emanating from the practice experience and empirical research of the multidisciplinary contributors. It is intended to inspire professionals to take up the challenges of evidence-based practice and practice-based research in the form of systematic program evaluations, outcome studies of manualized treatment protocols, randomized controlled studies, epidemiological studies, survey research, consumer satisfaction studies, and cost-effectiveness studies. It is also intended to provide practical guidance to those embarking on this process both in terms of steps to achieve the outcomes and tools required in the journey. We are confident that practitioners, when provided with the necessary skills and tools, will produce compelling evidence that will direct the continued development of effective treatment and intervention approaches. In the next edition of this book we look forward to publishing an increasing number of chapters containing the research and practice guidelines produced by frontline practice researchers, epidemiologists, clinicians, and university professors.

REFERENCES

Barber, J. (2005). Evidence-based practice. *Institute for Evidence-Based Social Work. http://www.socialwork.utoronto.ca*

Brink, L. (2003). Integrating evidence based practice with quality management (Special report: Evidence-based practices). *Behavioral Healthcare Tomorrow, 12,* 17–21.

Centre for Evidence-Based Medicine. (2004). EBM: What is it? *http://www.cebm .utoronto.ca/intro/whatis.htm*

Chambless, D. L. (1993). Task force on promotion and dissemination of psychological procedures. A report adopted by the Division 12 Board, October 1993. Washington, DC: American Psychological Association.

Chambless, D. L. (1996a). Identification of empirically supported psychological interventions. *Clinician's Research Digest,* (Suppl. 14), 1–2.

Chambless, D. L. (1996b). In defense of dissemination of empirically supported psychological interventions. *Clinical Psychology, 3,* 230–235.

Chambless, D. L., Sanderson, W. C., Shoham, V., Bennett Johnson, S., Pope, K. S., Crits-Christoph, P., Baker, M., Johnson, B., Woody, S. R., Sue, S., Beutler, L., Williams, D. A., & McCurry, S. (1996). An update on empirically validated therapies. *The Clinical Psychologist, 49,* 5–18.

Cournoyer, B., & Powers, G. (2002). Evidence-based social work: The quiet revolution continues. In A. R. Roberts & G. J. Greene (Eds.), *Social Workers' Desk Reference* (pp. 798–807). New York: Oxford University Press.

Dziegielewski, S. F. (2003). The changing face of health care practice: Professional practice in managed behavioral health care (2nd ed.). New York: Springer.

Fischer, J. (1973). Is casework effective?: A review. *Social Work, 28,* 5–30.

Foa, E., Keane, T., & Friedman, M. (2000). *Effective Treatments for PTSD: Practice Guidelines for the International Society for Traumatic Stress Studies.* New York: Guilford Press.

Gambrill, E. (2000). Evidence-based practice: An alternative to authority-based practice. *Families in Society, 80*(4), 341–350.

Gambrill, E. (2003). Editorial: Evidence-based practice: Sea change or the Emeror's new clothes? *Journal of Social Work Education, 39*(1), 1–18.

Gibbs, L., & Gambrill, E. (2002). Evidence based practice: Counterarguments to objections. *Research on Social Work Practice, 12*(3), 452–476.

Goodacre, S. (2003). Research methods: Beyond the clinical trial. *Annals of Emergency Medicine, 42*(1), 56–65.

Guyatt, G., & Rennie, D. (2002). *Users' guide to the medical literature: Essentials of evidence-based clinical practice.* Chicago, IL: American Medical Association Press.

Hayward, R., Wilson, M., Tunis, S., & Bass, E. (1995). User guides to evidence based medicine. *Journal of the American Medical Association, 274*(20), 1630.

Hicks, N. (1997). Evidence based healthcare. *Bandolier, 4*(39), 8.

Howard, M., McMillen, C., & Pollio, D. (2003). Teaching evidence-based practice: Toward a new paradigm for social work education. *Research on Social Work Practice, 13*(2), 234–259.

Jayaratne, S., & Levy, R. L. (1979). *Empirical Clinical Practice.* New York: Columbia University.

Kleiber, C., & Titler, M. G. (1998). *Journal of Nursing Quality Assurance, 2*(1), 21–27.

McKibbon, K. A. (1998). Evidence based practice. *Bulletin of the Medical Library Association, 86*(3), 396–401.

Muir Gray, J. A. (1997). *Evidence-based healthcare: How to make health policy and management decisions.* London: Churchill Livingstone.

Mullen, E. J., & Dumpson, J. R. (Eds.). (1972). *Evaluation of social intervention* (1st ed.). San Francisco: Jossey-Bass.

Myers, L., & Thyer, B. (1997). Should social work clients have the right to effective treatment? *Social Work, 42*(3), 288–298.

Petr, C., & Walter, U. (2005). Best practices for inquiry: A multidimentional, value-critical framework. *Journal of Social Work Education, 41*(2), 251–267.

Regehr, C., Barber, J., Trocme, N., Hart, S., & Knoke, D. (2005). Towards an evidence-based model for risk assessment in child welfare: Concept paper. Ottawa: Social Sciences and Humanities Research Council of Canada.

Rosen, A., & Proctor, E. (2002). Standards for evidence-based social work practice. In A. R. Roberts & G. J. Greene (Eds.), *Social Workers' Desk Reference* (pp. 743–747). New York: Oxford University Press.

Rosen, A., Proctor, E., & Staudt, M. (2003). Targets of change and interventions in social work: An empirically based prototype for developing practice guidelines. *Research on Social Work Practice, 13*(2), 208–233.

Sackett, D., Richardson, W., Rosenberg, W., & Haynes, R. (1997). *Evidence-based medicine: How to practice and the EBM.* New York: Churchill Livingston.

Senge, P. (1995). Building learning organizations. In N. O. Graham (Ed.), *Quality in healthcare: Theory, application and evolution.* Gaithersberg, MD: Aspen.

Upshur, R., & Tracy, C. (2004). Legitimacy, authority, and hierarchy: Critical challenges for evidence-based medicine. *Brief Treatment and Crisis Intervention 4*(3), 197–204.

Webb, S. (2001). Some considerations on the validity of evidence-based practice in social work. *British Journal of Social Work, 31*, 57–79.

Weick, K. E. (1996). Speaking to practice. *Journal of Management Inquiry, 5*, 251–258.

2

The Evidence For and Against Evidence-Based Practice

EDWARD J. MULLEN

DAVID L. STREINER

Over the years, there have been many developments and changes in the way that social interventions and clinical treatments have been delivered, including the introduction of behavioral and cognitive-behavioral therapies (e.g., Lazarus, 1971; Thomas, 1967), the move toward time-limited, task-structured interventions (Mullen, Dumpson, & Associates, 1972; Reid & Epstein, 1972), and the use of manuals that guide what practitioners can and cannot do (Luborsky & DeRubeis, 1984). Each in its time generated considerable debate, some of it quite heated. However, it is probably safe to say that no innovation has generated as much argument and heat as the introduction of evidence-based practice (EBP) and policy. EBP has been both heralded as one of the major advances in health care, education, criminal justice, and the human services, promising to revolutionize both policymaking and practice (e.g., Gambrill, 1999; Gibbs & Gambrill, 2002; Gray, 2001; Macdonald, 1999; Marshall, 1995; Sackett, Richardson, Rosenberg, & Haynes, 1997), and excoriated as a development that will reduce professionals to mindlessly (and soullessly) following recipe books for the betterment of insurance companies (e.g., Grahame-Smith, 1995; Morgan, 1995). It has led, on the one hand, to a number of journals, texts, and centers based on its principles (e.g., *Evidence-Based Mental Health, Evidence-Based Medicine, Evidence-Based Nursing, ACP Journal Club*; Gibbs, 2003; Gray, 2001; Sackett, Straus, Richardson, Rosenberg, & Haynes, 2000), and on the other, to articles in leading journals holding it up to ridicule (e.g., Britton, Evans, & Potter, 1998; CRAP Writing Group, 2002; Webb, 2001).

21

Where we stand on this can probably best be summed up by the old joke of the couple who come to see their rabbi. The man begins with a long litany of complaints about his wife, to which the rabbi replies, "You're right, you're right." The wife then gives her long list of complaints about her husband, to which the rabbi again replies, "You're right, you're right." After the couple leave, the rabbi's wife yells at him, "How can you tell them both that they're right? One of them must be wrong!"; to which the rabbi replies, "You're right, you're right." Both of us are believers in EBP (one in fact is a coeditor of *Evidence-Based Mental Health*), but we temper this with a healthy dose of skepticism. EBP has, in our view, done much to advance the field, with its insistence that assessment and intervention methods be based on the best available evidence and that the opinions of experts are just that—opinions, rather than proven verities. By the same token, EBP cannot, in and of itself, answer all of the questions that arise in policy and practice. In evidence-informed policy, few would discount the role of public opinion, political expediency, and ideology as shaping even the most rational use of research evidence (Grayson & Gomersall, 2003). In clinical practice, why do not even the best practices achieve a 100% cure rate, or come even close to this? Why do some people improve but others do not or may even deteriorate? What characteristics determine who will respond to one form of treatment but not to others? Why do some people suffer from severe stress reactions to trauma, while others appear to shrug off its effects? Why do some interventions that work well for those who enjoy middle-class status not work for those who are poor or less educated?

In two issues of *Brief Treatment and Crisis Intervention* (vol. 4, nos. 2, 3), many experts in the area, and from a number of disciplines—social work, social policy, psychology, education, psychiatry, family medicine, internal medicine—will discuss the history, practice, and teaching of EBP, as well as some of the problems it faces and possible alternatives. In this chapter, we will set the scene by looking at some of the objections to EBP as well as some arguments in favor of it. But first, we describe what we mean by EBP.

THE MEANING OF EVIDENCE-BASED PRACTICE

The contributors to this special issue present various descriptions of EBP reflecting its evolving character. Some describe EBP as applying only to clinical forms of practice, whereas others describe policy and management applications. In the United Kingdom it is customary to refer to both *evidence-based policy and practice* (e.g., Gray, 2001; Solesbury, 2001), whereas in the United States, reference is more typically made to *evidence-based practice*, focusing on clinical issues (Gibbs, 2003). For us, EBP encompasses policy, management, and direct or clinical practice. The field needs evidence-based policies, evidence-based management, and evidence-based direct services. However, the articles in this special issue are focused primarily on what would be considered clinical or direct practice applications. This is not meant to imply that evidence-based policy and management are less important.

While the shift toward EBP first emerged in medicine and health care, EBP is quickly taking hold in mental and behavioral health, education, criminal justice, and social work. Although EBP is most prominent in the United Kingdom, Canada, and the United States, it is now popular in many northern European countries, including Sweden, Finland, Norway, Denmark, and the Netherlands, where outcomes measurement and effectiveness in public services are increasingly seen as important by governments and citizens (Mullen, in press; Mullen, 2003a, 2003b). Indeed, there are indications that EBP will be required in the not-too-distant future by many governmental authorities, insurers, and accreditation bodies. In spite of this rapid movement toward EBP, we find a wide range of associated meanings. As described in the literature, EBP ranges in meaning from, on the one hand, some recognition of the need to use research findings to aid in practice decision making to, on the other hand, a paradigm shift (Gambrill, 2003). We take the position that EBP requires a major philosophical and technological change for the field, rather than simply an incremental increase in the use of research in decision making. Accordingly, we consider EBP to encompass both evidence-based practices as well as an *evidence-based process*. For us an *evidence-based practice* is any practice that has been established as effective through scientific research according to a clear set of explicit criteria (Drake et al., 2001). For example, in 1998 a Robert Wood Johnson Foundation consensus panel concluded that its review of research findings supported identification of several evidence-based psychosocial practices for the treatment of persons with severe mental illness: assertive community treatment, supported employment, family psychoeducation, recovery skills training and illness self-management, standardized pharmacological treatment, and integrated dual-disorder treatment. To be considered EBP, four selection criteria were used: (1) the treatment practices had been standardized through manuals or guidelines, (2) the treatment practices had been evaluated with controlled research designs, (3) important outcomes were demonstrated through the use of objective measures, and (4) the research was conducted by different research teams (Torrey et al., 2001). Accordingly, we can say that EBPs were identified for the treatment of persons with severe mental illness through efficacy trials meeting these four criteria.

As a process, EBP has been defined in medicine as "the conscientious, explicit and judicious use of current best evidence in making decisions about the care of individual patients" (Sackett, Rosenberg, Gray, Haynes, & Richardson, 1996, p. 71) and the "integration of best research evidence with clinical expertise and patient values" (Sackett et al., 2000, p. 1). In the United Kingdom, *social care EBP* has been described as "the conscientious, explicit and judicious use of current best evidence in making decisions regarding the welfare of service-users and carers" (Sheldon, 2003, p. 1). In the United States, *social work EBP* is described as follows: "Placing the client's benefits first, evidence-based practitioners adopt a process of lifelong learning that involves continually posing specific questions of direct practical importance to clients, searching objectively and efficiently for the current best evidence relative to each question, and taking appropriate action guided by evidence" (Gibbs, 2003, p. 6). *Evidence-based health care* has been described as "a discipline centred upon evidence-based decision-making about groups of patients, or populations, which may be manifest as evidence-based policy-making, purchasing or management" (Gray, 2001, p. 9). In all of these descriptions EBP is seen as a decision-making process in which policymakers, managers, or practitioners make decisions. Accordingly, we consider EBP to be a way of doing practice which involves an individualized, thoughtful process of using evidence to make collaborative decisions with actual or potential service users. Because evidence can play a strong or weak role in this process, some prefer to use alternate terms such as *evidence-informed practice or evidence for practice and policy* (Grayson & Gomersall, 2003; Nutley, 2003). Here, we describe politicians and policy analysts as using "evidence" for decision making.

When we describe EBP this way to audiences and to our students, typically the first response is that the approach has obvious, reasonable merit. We have been asked how anyone could object to it. In turning to a discussion of this question, we draw from prior analyses of arguments for and against EBP (Gambrill, 1999, 2001, 2003; Gibbs & Gambrill, 2002; Pawson, 2002; Sackett et al., 2000; Straus & McAlister, 2000; Webb, 2001).

THE ARGUMENTS AGAINST EVIDENCE-BASED PRACTICE

The arguments against EBP are now well established and fully discussed in the literature, based on a careful review of which Straus and McAlister (2000) developed a classification of criticisms of evidence-based medicine (EBM) which apply equally well to applications in other EBP fields. Since their classification has been used by most other reviewers, we outline the criticisms before we discuss some of them specifically in more detail. Straus and McAlister grouped the criticisms as addressing either *limitations or misperceptions* of EBM. Two types of limitations were identified: those applying to medical practice in general (shortage of coherent, consistent scientific evidence; difficulties in applying evidence to the care of individual patients; and barriers to the practice of high-quality medicine) and those applying specifically to EBM (the need to develop new skills; limited time and resources; and paucity of evidence that EBM works). Criticisms resulting from misperceptions of EBM were identified as being that it (1) denigrates clinical expertise, (2) ignores patients' values and preferences, (3) promotes a "cookbook" approach to medicine, (4) is simply a cost-cutting tool, (5) is an ivory-tower concept, (6) is limited to clinical research, and (7) leads to therapeutic nihilism in the absence of evidence from randomized trials (p. 838). These criticisms have been repeated and discussed by most subsequent reviewers (Gambrill, 2003; Gibbs & Gambrill, 2002; Sackett et al., 2000). Others have criticized EBP on philosophical grounds, arguing that an evidence-based, rational model of decision making does not fit the realities of individualized, contextualized practice, especially nonmedical practice, wherein problems are less well defined

(Webb, 2001). Some have called attention to limitations in the methodology of systematic reviews, such as meta-analysis, which provide the evidence for use in EBP (Pawson, 2002). Concern has been expressed about how evidence-based policy is possible when so many competing factors enter into policymaking, such as public opinion, resource constraints, and ideology (Grayson & Gomersall, 2003; Nutley, 2003).

The contributors to two special issues in *Brief Treatment and Crisis Intervention* address many of these criticisms. We comment next on those we consider most pressing.

Limitations of Evidence-Based Practice

The Shortage of Evidence

EBP, as the term implies, is predicated on the belief that what we do as professionals should be based on the best available evidence. Generally, the best evidence comes from well-designed and-executed randomized controlled trials (RCTs) or, better yet, meta-analyses of a number of RCTs (Egger, Smith, & O'Rourke, 2001). Studies of prognoses require inception cohorts (that is, groups of people who enter the study at equivalent points in their natural history), relatively complete follow-up (around 85% of the sample), and a sufficient duration to ensure that all of the people could have reached the end point, whether it be developing the disorder under study or achieving remission of symptoms (Fletcher, Fletcher, & Wagner, 1988). Assessment and diagnostic studies must involve blinding of raters who complete one test to the results of the other test, as well as demonstration of the reliability and validity of the instruments (Streiner, 2003).

The question that faces proponents of EBP is whether there are enough high-quality studies so that evidence-based decisions can be made. Surprisingly for a field that places a high premium on research, few studies have examined this. Ellis, Mulligan, Rowe, and Sackett (1995) looked at the decisions that were made regarding 109 medical inpatients. They found that 53% of the treatment decisions were based on the results of RCTs and that for an additional 29% of the patients, there was unanimous agreement that good nonexperimental evidence existed. Using similar methods, Geddes, Game, Jenkins, and Sackett (1996) found that for 40 psychiatric inpatients, evidence from RCTs or meta-analyses supported the treatment decisions 65% of the time. So the conclusion at this point, based on just a few studies, is that there are still many decisions that are made that are not based on good evidence, but the picture is not nearly as bleak as opponents of EBP would have us believe. Professionals must remember that when they make decisions for which little or no evidence exists, they should exercise caution and perhaps be even more vigilant in monitoring outcomes.

Applying the Results to Individuals

The results of RCTs are analyzed by comparing the mean score of the experimental group against that of the placebo or control group (or some comparable summary statistic). However, this masks the fact that there is always individual variability around the means, as well as overlap in the distributions of scores for the two groups. The result of this is that a proportion of people in the experimental group actually do worse than some in the control group, and conversely some in the comparison group improve more than some people in the active treatment group. The implication is that practitioners cannot blindly apply a "proven" procedure and assume that a particular individual receiving that procedure will benefit (Seeman, 2001). This has led some critics to reject the whole notion of EBP, stating that results of trials are incapable of being applied at the level of the individual (e.g., Persons & Silberschatz, 1998) and that the primary determinant should be the practitioner's judgment (Garfield, 1998).

There are a number of ways of responding to this valid criticism. The first is that we are at least able to quantify the probability with which an individual person will respond to a given procedure. This value is called the *number needed to treat* (NNT) (Laupacis, Sackett, & Roberts, 1988), which is the number of people who must be treated in order for there to be one additional success. For example, based on a study by Wood, Trainor, Rothwell, Moore, and Harrington (2001), which was aimed at reducing the risk of deliberate self-harm, the staff at *Evidence-Based Mental Health* calculated an NNT of 4. This means that in order to reduce by one the number of adolescents who harmed themselves, four had to be seen in therapy. For the other three, either therapy did not work or, more likely, they would not have harmed themselves again even if they had not been seen in treatment. While this may sound disappointing—as we would like to believe that every person benefits from therapy—it is typical of treatments in this area, and actually compares very favorably with many medical interventions. For example, a class of drugs called the statins have been hailed as lifesavers because they control cholesterol levels. In one study (LIPID Study Group, 1998), the NNT was 44 for patients with coronary heart disease, and has been reported to be at least four times higher for those without heart problems (Hebert, Gaziano, Chan, & Hennekens, 1997). For a new (and very expensive) drug that lowers the risk of stroke, the NNT was 115 over a 3-year period compared with just taking aspirin (CAPRIE Steering Committee, 1996).

A second response to the criticism is that the alternative to using evidence-based interventions—with their known rate of failure—is to use unproven procedures, based only on the hope that they may work, but without any real knowledge of how often they do or do not, except our recall of successful cases. However, memory is a slippery thing. We do very well in recalling our successes, but very poorly in remembering our failures—what has been called the "denominator problem."

A third response is that EBP does not mean only applying the results of large randomized trials conducted by others. Practitioners can and should view each person as an "$N = 1$" study (Barlow & Hersen, 1984). That is, EBP also involves using techniques such as interrupted time series, multiple baseline assessments, before-after designs, and the like, combined with objective measures of functioning, with every person seen (Lueger et al., 2001; Streiner, 1998).

Training, Time, and Resources

In addition to the need for evidence, EBP requires that professionals be trained in the skills necessary to find and critically use evidence. It also means that, once trained, they have the time to do computer-based searches, and therefore that computers and access to search engines are available. Training does not appear to be a problem. Both of us have found our students to be eager and engaged learners of EBP. Articles in this series discuss highly successful programs with students in psychology, social work, nursing, premedicine, communication disorders, special education, public relations, and health care administration (Shlonsky and Gibbs) and psychiatry residents (Bilsker and Goldner in special issues cited on page 22). These reports correspond with our experiences that students and practitioners are avid learners eager to master the skills, given the opportunity. Each new generation (where in this context a generation is no more than about 5 years) is more comfortable and proficient with computers than the last, and searching the Web for information is second nature to them.

Searching for evidence is becoming easier each year. Organizations in which human service and health care professionals work can provide access to original articles by subscribing to services such as PsycINFO (the American Psychological Association's database of abstracts), CINAHL (Cumulative Index to Nursing and Allied Health Literature), Ovid, ERIC (Educational Resources Information Center), and *AARP Ageline*. More importantly, people can log on to *Evidence-Based Medicine, Clinical Evidence, ACP* [American College of Physicians] *Journal Club, Evidence-Based Mental Health*, the *U.K. National Health Service Database of Abstracts of Reviews of Effects*, the *Cochrane Database of Systematic Reviews*, the *Campbell Collaboration Reviews of Interventions and Policy Evaluations*, and other sites that select articles for their methodological rigor and provide meta-analyses, summarizing the results of RCTs. National and regional centers are being established to disseminate evidence through the Web to policymakers, practitioners, caregivers, and users (e.g., the Social Care Institute for Excellence in Great Britain, the Nordic Campbell Center in Copenhagen). As computers become less and less expensive, some organizations are able to place them within each unit, so that it is no longer necessary for practitioners to find time to go to a central library.

In order to save time for practitioners and researchers, Roberts and Yeager (2004) have compiled a major desktop reference book, consisting of 104 original chapters (including 56 flowcharts) on every facet of conducting EBP as well as numerous research exemplars. This landmark practical reference volume was reviewed in the special issue of *Brief Treatment and Crisis Intervention*.

Time, though, remains a problem. For the practitioner rushing from one person to the next, sometimes finding even 5 minutes to do a search may not always be feasible. Time spent doing a search may save many hours later, because effort is not spent on a procedure that hasn't been shown to be effective, but we recognize that though this may seem reasonable in the abstract, it may not be practicable in reality. We would argue, however, that it may be worthwhile in these circumstances to save questions about the effectiveness of an intervention or the utility of an assessment procedure to the end of the day, and to spend 15 or 30 minutes reviewing the evidence. Also, organizations will need to consider how such information can be distributed best in their particular contexts. For larger organizations this may mean expanded responsibilities for a centralized informatics department. For smaller organizations one or more individuals may need to be designated as information experts. In nearly all cases the process can benefit from teamwork and collaborative sharing.

Misperceptions About Evidence-Based Practice

It Denigrates Professional Expertise

One argument against EBP is that it is "cookbook" practice, replacing professional judgment with recipe-like, manualized procedures. It portrays EBP as saying: *For condition A, you must use procedure X; while for condition B, procedure Y must be used*, ignoring the experience and expertise of the practitioner and disregarding his or her knowledge of the individual. However, most views of EBP propose a process that is highly individualized, relying on practitioner discretion. For example, part of Sackett et al.'s (1996) definition of EBM is that it "means integrating individual clinical expertise with the best available external clinical evidence from systematic research" (p. 71). In other words, rather than depreciating expertise, EBP explicitly builds it into the equation. Evidence is like a map outlining a trip: It will show alternative ways of getting from one place to another, but the choice the driver makes depends on a number of factors, such as the trade-off between speed and scenery. In a similar manner, the professional is the person who must determine whether the evidence in the literature is applicable to a particular individual or policy question, bearing in mind unique circumstances, history, and the like.

It Ignores the Clients' Values and Preferences

This is a similar argument to the one above, but focusing on the perspective of the client, as opposed to that of the professional. Again quoting Sackett et al. (1996), EBM also involves "the more thoughtful identification and compassionate use of individual patients' predicaments, rights, and preferences in making clinical decisions about their care" (p. 71). That is, just as the professional's expertise cannot be left out of the picture, neither can the client's wishes. For example, there are two possible treatments for cancer of the larynx: surgery and radiation. The evidence clearly shows that surgery is better for prolonging life expectancy, but it leaves patients with a hole in their throats through which they must eat and drink; they must learn how to speak through the hole; and activities such as swimming are severely curtailed or prohibited. On the other hand, many patients opt for radiation therapy, because they feel that the quality of their lives is more important than the quantity of time remaining to them. This choice can be made only by the patient; the clinician can outline the options, the consequences that flow from each, and the evidence behind them but cannot override the desires of the individual.

EBP Is Simply a Cost-Cutting Tool

Especially with the growth of externally managed care in much of the Western world (even in social welfare states), there is a very real danger that EBP will be used by governments, insurance companies, and other payers as a means of imposing the fastest, least expensive form of intervention. However, this would be a gross distortion of the way EBP should be used, for two reasons. First, as mentioned previously, the choice between or among competing procedures is dictated not only by their respective effectiveness, but also by taking into consideration the practitioner's expertise and the client's wishes. Second, cost is only half of what should be examined; the other half is benefit, or effectiveness. That is, a proper criterion (although, as we have said, never the sole criterion) should be the cost-benefit or cost-effectiveness of the intervention (for a discussion of the differences, see Drummond & Mooney, 1981; Torrance, Stoddart, Drummond, & Gafni, 1981); how much of the outcome does $1 buy? A given procedure may be relatively inexpensive to deliver, but if its results are limited, its cost/benefit ratio may actually be higher than a more expensive but much more effective procedure. For example, cognitive-behaviorial therapy is more costly than medication for treating depression. However, because it is far more effective in preventing relapse and rehospitalization, it is actually more cost effective than medication by itself in treatment-resistant patients (Scott, Palmer, Paykel, Teasdale, & Hayhurst, 2003).

EBP Leads to Research and Therapeutic Nihilism

As we mentioned above, and as a number of articles in this series illustrate, it is relatively easy to teach critical appraisal skills and the evidence-based approach to students and staff. Because effectiveness studies are done in the real world, where compromises must be made between rigor and reality and individuals are not nearly as compliant as undergraduate psychology students or white mice in adhering to research protocols, it is very easy to find flaws with all studies. It is much more difficult, though, to teach people to differentiate between limitations and fatal flaws; that is, to judge whether the problems are serious enough to jeopardize the results or should simply be interpreted with a modicum of caution. Without this judgment, it is easy to become nihilistic, feeling that no study can be believed and therefore that there is little or no evidence upon which to base EBP (which also provides a good excuse to avoid the necessity of keeping up with the literature).

However, EBP means being guided by the best *available* evidence. This means that in the absence of RCTs with no design flaws (if any exist), trials with limitations are better than no evidence at all. Most importantly, professionals and the users of professional services can at least proceed with due caution about probable risks and benefits when the evidence base for a decision is made explicit, even if this means that there is no or limited evidence supporting alternative choices. And, yes, when important gaps in the evidence base are identified, this can and should lead to new research so that future decisions can be better informed.

EBP Is at Philosophical Odds
With the Realities of Practice

This criticism is reminiscent of the decades-old debate in the social and behavioral sciences about positivistic versus subjectivist approaches to knowledge. There is no easy resolution to such debates. In this context EBP is criticized as being a positivistic and mechanistic application of technical rationality, serving new managerialist strategies seeking to advance a performance culture that strips practitioners of their professional judgment and discretion (Webb, 2001). In contrast to EBP, it is alleged that "real practice" decision making is "indeterminate, reflexive, locally optimal at best and based on a limited rationality" and that "cognitive heuristic devices are the determinants of decision making and not evidence," such that "real practice" decision making relies more on common sense than scientific, rational processes (Webb, 2001, p. 57; for a critical analysis of the heuristic view, see Mullen, 1985). We think that this criticism is correct in noting that evidence-based practitioners are concerned with outcomes, effectiveness, and performance and that they rely on clear reasoning about the best evidence available. Evidence-based practitioners do think that their actions probably will affect outcomes. However, EBP excludes neither complex decision making nor values, preferences, inclinations, and commonsense considerations. Rather, the process is expansive, requiring careful reasoning on the part of the practitioner. And while it may be true that commonsense approaches prevail in the average practitioner's decision making, professional educational programs have as a goal preparing professional practitioners with knowledge and skills that go beyond common sense. It is correct that evidence-based practitioners are expected to use more than common sense in making important decisions with clients.

SUMMARY

The history of all innovations has been described as going through three stages. Opponents first say that the new discovery won't work. Once it has been shown to work, the criticism changes to, "OK, but it's not new." Acceptance finally comes when the critics say, "It's new, and I invented it." Within the context of the length of time that the helping professions have existed, the history of EBP is quite short, probably somewhere between the first and second of these phases. As with many innovations, it stormed onto the scene, raising antibodies among many practitioners because of the brashness of some of its claims and the perception that it was trying to elbow aside established practice. But, as with all adolescents, EBP too matures and gains wisdom and judgment. For example, the original claims that practice *must* be based on the conclusions of RCTs and only RCTs have been softened in the face of reality to the use of the best *available* evidence. We are sure that over the next decade, not only will the reaction of practitioners change, but also the practice of EBP. Many of the articles in this series point to some of the directions that this may take; after all, EBP must be based on both evidence and practice.

AN INVITATION TO READERS

This book and the two special issues of *Brief Treatments and Crisis Intervention* comprise a wide range of articles pertaining to EBP. We are confident that a careful reading of these contributions will be a rewarding and enlightening experience for the reader. We trust that these articles will add to the rapidly growing literature supporting the field's evolution toward evidence-based policy and practice (cf. Roberts & Yeager, 2004). We invite readers to send comments in response to the chapters in this book to Professor Albert Roberts @comcast.net editor-in-chief of the journal *Brief Treatments and Crisis Intervention*.

NOTE

REFERENCES

Barlow, D. H., & Hersen, M. (1984). *Single case experimental designs: Strategies for studying behavior change* (2nd ed.). New York: Pergamon.
Britton, B. J., Evans, J. G., & Potter, J. M. (1998). Does the fly matter? The CRACKPOT study in evidence based trout fishing. *British Medical Journal, 317*, 1678–1680.
CAPRIE Steering Committee. (1996). A randomised, blinded, trial of clopidogrel versus aspirin in patients at risk of ischaemic events (CAPRIE). *Lancet, 348*, 1329–1339.
CRAP [Clinicians for the Restoration of Autonomous Practice] Writing Group. (2002). EBM: Unmasking the ugly truth. *British Medical Journal, 325*, 1496–1498.
Drake, R. E., Goldman, H., Leff, H. S., Lehman, A. F., Dixon, L., Mueser, K. T., et al. (2001). Implementing evidence-based practices in routine mental health service settings. *Psychiatric Services, 52*, 179–182.
Drummond, M., & Mooney, G. (1981). Economic appraisal in health care: 1. A

guide to the methodology of economic appraisal. *Hospital & Health Services Review*, 77, 277–282.

Egger, M., Smith, G. D., & O'Rourke, K. (2001). Rationale, potentials, and promise of systematic reviews. In M. Egger, G. D. Smith, & D. G. Altman (Eds.), *Systematic reviews in health care: Meta-analysis in context* (2nd ed., pp. 3–19). London: BMJ Books.

Ellis, J., Mulligan, I., Rowe, J., & Sackett, D. L. (1995). Inpatient general medicine is evidence based. *Lancet, 346*, 407–410.

Fletcher, R. H., Fletcher, S. W., & Wagner, E. H. (1988). *Clinical epidemiology: The essentials* (2nd ed.). Baltimore: Williams & Wilkins.

Gambrill, E. (1999). Evidence-based practice: An alternative to authority-based practice. *Families in Society: The Journal of Contemporary Human Services, 80*, 341.

Gambrill, E. (2001). Social work: An authoritybased profession. *Research on Social Work Practice, 11*(2), 166.

Gambrill, E. D. (2003). Evidence-based practice: Sea change or the emperor's new clothes? *Journal of Social Work Education, 39*, 3–23.

Garfield, S. L. (1998). Some comments on empirically supported treatment. *Journal of Consulting and Clinical Psychology, 66*, 121–125.

Geddes, J. R., Game, D., Jenkins, N. E., & Sackett, D. L. (1996). What proportion of primary psychiatric interventions are based on randomised evidence? *Quality in Health Care, 5*, 215–217.

Gibbs, L. E. (2003). *Evidence-based practice for the helping professions: A practical guide with integrated multimedia*. Pacific Grove, CA: Brooks/Cole—Thompson Learning.

Gibbs, L., & Gambrill, E. (2002). Evidence-based practice: Counteragruments to objections. *Research on Social Work Practice, 12*, 452–476.

Grahame-Smith, D. (1995). Evidence based medicine: Socratic dissent. *British Medical Journal, 310*, 1126–1127.

Gray, J.A.M. (2001). *Evidence-based healthcare* (2nd ed.). New York: Churchill Livingstone.

Grayson, L., & Gomersall, A. (2003). *A difficult business: Finding the evidence for social science reviews*. Unpublished draft manuscript, ESRC onomic and Social Research Council UK Centre for Evidence Based Policy and Practice, London.

Hebert, P. R., Gaziano, J. M., Chan, K. S., & Hennekens, C. H. (1997). Cholesterol lowering with statin drugs, risk of stroke, and total mortality: An overview of randomized trials. *Journal of the American Medical Association, 278*, 313–321.

Laupacis, A., Sackett, D. L., & Roberts, R. S. (1988). An assessment of clinically useful measures of the consequences of treatment. *New England Journal of Medicine, 318*, 1728–1733.

Lazarus, A. A. (1971). *Behavior therapy and beyond*. New York: McGraw-Hill.

LIPID [Long-Term Intervention with Pravastatin in Ischaemic Disease] Study Group. (1998). Prevention of cardiovascular events and death with pravastatin in patients with coronary heart disease and a broad range of initial cholesterol levels. *New England Journal of Medicine, 339*, 1349–1357.

Luborsky, L., & DeRubeis, R. J. (1984). The use of psychotherapy treatment manuals: A small revolution in psychotherapy research. *Clinical Psychology Review, 4*, 5–14.

Lueger, R. J., Howard, K. I., Martinovich, Z., Lutz, W., Anderson, E. E., & Grissom, G. (2001). Assessing treatment progress of individual patients using expected treatment response models. *Journal of Consulting and Clinical Psychology, 69*, 150–158.

Macdonald, G. (1999). Evidence-based social care: Wheels off the runway? *Public Money & Management, 19*, 25–32.

Marshall, T. (1995). Letter to the editor. *Lancet, 346*, 1171–1172.

Morgan, W. K. C. (1995). Letter to the editor. *Lancet, 346*, 1172.

Mullen, E. J. (1985). Methodological dilemmas in social-work research. *Social Work Research & Abstracts, 21*(4), 12–20.

Mullen, E. J. (2003a). *Evidence-based practice*. Unpublished manuscript, Danish University of Education, Copenhagen.

Mullen, E. J. (2003b). *Evidence-based practice and social work professionals: Implications for social work's future*. Unpublished manuscript, Verwey-Jonker Instituut, Utrecht, Netherlands.

Mullen, E. J. (in press). *Evidence-based practice in a social work context: The United States case*. Helsinki, Finland: STAKES [National Research and Development Center for Welfare and Health].

Mullen, E. J. (in press). Facilitating practitioner use of evidence-based practice. In A. R. Roberts & K. Yeager (Eds.), *Desk reference for evidence-based practice in healthcare and human services*. New York: Oxford University Press.

Mullen, E. J., Dumpson, J. R., & Associates. (1972). *Evaluation of social intervention*. San Francisco, CA: Jossey-Bass.

Nutley, S. (2003, April). *Bridging the policy/research divide: Reflections and lessons from the UK*. Keynote paper presented at the National Institute of Governance conference "Facing the Future: Engaging Stakeholders and Citizens in Developing Public Policy," Canberra, Australia.

Pawson, R. (2002). Evidence-based policy: In search of a method. *Evaluation, 8*, 157–181.

Persons, J. B., & Silberschatz, G. (1998). Are results of randomized controlled trials useful to psychotherapists? *Journal of Consulting and Clinical Psychology, 66*, 126–135.

Reid, W. J., & Epstein, L. (1972). *Task-centered casework*. New York: Columbia University Press.

Roberts, A. R., & Yeager, K. (Eds.). (2004). *Evidence-based practice manual: Research and outcome measures in health and human services*. New York: Oxford University Press.

Sackett, D. L., Richardson, W. S., Rosenberg, W., & Haynes, R. B. (1997). *Evidence-based medicine: How to practice and teach EBM*. New York: Churchill Livingstone.

Sackett, D. L., Rosenberg, W. M., Gray, J. A., Haynes, R. B., & Richardson, W. S. (1996). Evidence based medicine: What it is and what it isn't. *British Medical Journal, 312*, 71–72.

Sackett, D. L., Straus, S. E., Richardson, W. S., Rosenberg, W., & Haynes, R. B. (2000). *Evidence-based medicine: How to practice and teach EBM* (2nd ed.). New York: Churchill Livingstone.

Scott, J., Palmer, S., Paykel, E., Teasdale, J., & Hayhurst, H. (2003). Use of cognitive therapy for relapse prevention in chronic depression: Cost-effectiveness study. *British Journal of Psychiatry, 182*, 221–227.

Seeman, M. V. (2001). Clinical trials in psychiatry: Do results apply to practice? *Canadian Journal of Psychiatry, 46*, 352–355.

Sheldon, B. (2003). *Brief summary of the ideas behind the Centre for Evidence-Based Social Services.* Retrieved October 22, 2003, from http://www.ex.ac.uk/cebss/introduction.html

Solesbury, W. (2001). *Evidence based policy: Whence it came and where it's going* (Working Paper No. 1). London: ESRC [Economic and Social Research Council] UK Centre for Evidence Based Policy and Practice.

Straus, S. E., & McAlister, F. A. (2000). Evidence-based medicine: A commentary on common criticisms. *Canadian Medical Association Journal, 163*, 837–841.

Streiner, D. L. (1998). Thinking small: Research designs appropriate for clinical practice. *Canadian Journal of Psychiatry, 43*, 737–741.

Streiner, D. L. (2003). Diagnosing tests: Using and misusing diagnostic and screening tests. *Journal of Personality Assessment, 81*, 209–219.

Thomas, E. J. (Ed.). (1967). *The socio-behavioral approach and applications to social work.* New York: Council on Social Work Education.

Torrance, G. W., Stoddart, G. L., Drummond, M. F., & Gafni, A. (1981). Cost-benefit analysis versus cost-effectiveness analysis for the evaluation of long-term care programs. *Health Services Research, 16*, 474–476.

Torrey, W. C., Drake, R. E., Dixon, L., Burns, B. J., Flynn, L., Rush, A. J., et al. (2001). Implementing evidence-based practices for persons with severe mental illnesses. *Psychiatric Services, 52*, 45–50.

Webb, S. A. (2001). Some considerations on the validity of evidence-based practice in social work. *British Journal of Social Work, 31*, 57–79.

Wood, A., Trainor, G., Rothwell, J., Moore, A., & Harrington, R. (2001). Randomized trial of group therapy for repeated deliberate self-harm in adolescents. *Journal of the American Academy of Child and Adolescent Psychiatry, 40*, 1246–1253.

3

What Is Evidence-Based Practice?

BRUCE A. THYER

WHAT IS EVIDENCE-BASED PRACTICE?

Evidence-based practice (EBP) is receiving considerable attention within the general field of human services and within the disciplinary literatures of specific professions, such as medicine, psychiatry, psychology, social work, marital and family therapy, chiropractic, and nursing, among others. Although it may be premature to label this movement a revolution, it is evident that something serious is afoot, as well as something compellingly different from precursor initiatives.

Various perspectives are associated with EBP, including such terminology as *empirical, science-based, evidence, practice guidelines, systematic reviews, meta-analyses, Cochrane Collaboration, Campbell Collaboration, empirically supported treatments,* and so forth. It is the purpose of this article to set forth, as clearly as possible, the essential features of real evidence-based practice and to relate this movement (whether enduring or not) to the subject matter of this journal, brief treatment and crisis intervention.

The current magnum opus of evidence-based practice is the second edition of the book aptly titled *Evidence-Based Medicine: How to Practice and Teach EBM,* by Sackett, Straus, Richardson, Rosenberg, and Haynes (2000). In it, evidence-based medicine is simply defined as "the integration of best research evidence with clinical expertise and patient values" (p. 1). Definitions are provided for *best research evidence, clinical expertise, and patient values;* and the authors claim that "when these three elements are integrated, clinicians and patients form a diagnostic and therapeutic alliance which optimizes clinical outcomes and quality of life" (p. 1). They explicitly note that EBP is not a static state of knowledge but rather represents a constantly evolving state of information: "New evidence from clinical research both invalidates previously accepted diagnostic tests and treatments and replaces them with new ones that are more powerful, more accurate, more efficacious and safer" (p. 1). Thus, practitioners continually have an obligation to keep themselves abreast of these developments in clinical research and to incorporate such developments into daily care.

To conduct EBP, one needs to perform the following five steps:

1. Convert one's need for information into an answerable question.
2. Track down the best clinical evidence to answer that question.
3. Critically appraise that evidence in terms of its validity, clinical significance, and usefulness.
4. Integrate this critical appraisal of research evidence with one's clinical expertise and the patient's values and circumstances.
5. Evaluate one's effectiveness and efficiency in undertaking the four previous steps, and strive for self-improvement.

It is worth noting (somewhat ironically) that evidentiary support is almost nonexistent for the assertion that EBP improves clinical outcomes, although some preliminary tests do corroborate the hypothesis (Faul, McMurtry, & Hudson, 2001; Slomin-Nevo & Anson, 1998). However, the face validity of EBP is by itself sufficiently compelling to convince most practitioners that the approach has clear merit and is worth testing in the context of routine clinical care. Let's review the five steps in a little more detail.

Step 1: Convert One's Need for Information Into an Answerable Question

An answerable question simply involves a question root that combines a word such as who, what, where, when, how, or why with a verb and a disorder or some other client circumstance. Examples of answerable questions include the following:

- What brief treatments are most effective in alleviating the symptoms of post-traumatic stress disorder?
- What are the effects of critical-incident stress debriefing on clients exposed to terrorist acts?
- Is EMDR more effective than cognitive-behavioral treatment in treating adult survivors of childhood sexual abuse?
- What is the validity of using anatomically correct dolls in the identification of children who have been sexually abused?
- Does journaling help elicit the repressed memories of real episodes of childhood sexual abuse that were consciously forgotten?

To be sure, answerable questions are those that are at the forefront of the concerns of practicing clinicians. They are both practical and (at least potentially) answerable, and the answers will have meaningful applications to treatment.

Step 2: Track Down the Best Clinical Evidence to Answer That Question

Books and Journals

It is sad but true that the conventional resources most of us relied on in graduate school are now relatively thin reeds on which to base practice decisions. Not only books but even professional journals can be years out of date by the time they see print. For example, it is not uncommon for articles appearing in social work journals to be published some three or four years following their date of submission. It also turns out that the majority of articles published in journals do not provide answers to answerable questions. A relative minority of articles either report the results of empirical evaluations of practice in the human services or detail studies on the reliability and validity of assessment methods. Among the more disciplinary outlets that do focus on publishing evidence-based articles are the journals *Archives of General Psychiatry, Brief Treatment and Crisis Intervention, Journal of Consulting and Clinical Psychology, Research on Social Work Practice, and Evidence-Based Mental Health*. EBP suggests that these more pragmatic journals be consulted more often than those disciplinary outlets that focus on theory testing or on knowledge development for its own sake.

Books (especially textbooks) usually rely published journal articles and are even more stale in terms of providing genuinely contemporary information relevant to researching answerable questions. Fortunately, one can turn to several particularly reliable Web-based resources for information on answering answerable questions, namely, the Web sites maintained by the Cochrane Collaboration and the Campbell Collaboration.

World Wide Web

The Cochrane Collaboration, founded in 1992, is an international group of clinical researchers who, among other activities, are dedicated to designing and conducting systematic reviews of well-crafted scientific literature that deals with issues related to the assessment and treatment of various health problems, including mental health issues. Similar in scope and method is the Campbell Collaboration. Founded in 2000, it focuses on the fields of social welfare, education, and criminal justice. Social workers interested in learning about the most up-to-date information pertaining to the assessment and treatment of various health matters can turn to the Cochrane Collaboration Web site (www .cochrane.org) and the Campbell Collaboration Web site (www.campbell

collaboration.org.) for analogous research findings pertinent to social welfare, with systematic reviews that are periodically updated.

Evidence-Based Practice Guidelines

Evidence-based practice guidelines (PGs) consist of the concrete and specific steps needed to implement various interventions (medical or psychosocial) that credible research indicates are first-choice treatments for particular problems or areas of concern. PGs are also referred to as *practice protocols, treatment algorithms,* or *clinical pathways.* PGs have been around in various forms for decades, but the past ten years or so have seen an explicit interdisciplinary commitment to develop these in a manner consistent with the highest canons of scientific research. They are available for all major mental-health problems; for the field of substance abuse; and for an array of additional areas closely relevant to social work practice, such as physical or sexual abuse. (See Howard & Jensen, 1999, for a special issue of the journal *Research on Social Work Practice* that was devoted to the topic of practice guidelines and for which they guest-edited; see also, Rosen & Proctor, 2003.)

Some practice guidelines are discipline-specific—for example, those targeting practitioners in health care, with a set of practice guidelines for the delivery of intravenous therapy. But the best guidelines are those that are interdisciplinary in both audience and literary sources. Few psychosocial problems are the unique purview of a single discipline. Clients who are depressed, for example, are provided care by psychiatrists, social workers, psychologists, marriage and family therapists, counselors, and so forth. Research on effective treatments for depression has been conducted by practitioners in many disparate fields, and it would be the height of foolishness to devise a so-called practice guideline that drew solely on the research contributions authored by members of a single discipline. Rather, the developers of PGs would be better advised to seek out, critically evaluate, and include all relevant scientific investigations, regardless of the disciplinary affiliations of the authors. Similarly, it would make no sense to provide, say psychologists, with PGs that offer guidance on treating clients with panic disorders; to provide a separate set of PGs for social workers focused on the same clinical problem; and yet to offer another set for nurses, psychiatrists, marriage and family therapists, and so on. Problem-focused interdisciplinary PGs that do draw on interdisciplinary-derived research and that are aimed at multiple types of practitioners are available and should be familiar to practitioners active in diverse fields.

Step 3: Critically Evaluate That Evidence

In science, information derived from certain forms of systematic inquiry is given greater credence than other forms. Although this does not completely avoid mistaken conclusions, it does render erroneous knowledge more detectable, and it reduces the chances that serious errors will be perpetuated. In the long run, errors created on the basis of systematically conducted and published research can be uncovered when efforts to replicate a finding become unavailing. In general, a finding that cannot be replicated by other researchers tends to be dismissed by the scientific community. What follows is a review of the types of evidence that can help to produce answers to answerable questions, beginning with the lowest level of research evidence and moving up the hierarchy of credibility.

Anecdotal case reports enjoy a long and justifiably venerable history as a valued method of research inquiry, a method especially valuable in the initial stages of investigating answerable questions. Simply put, a clinician who is providing care to clients makes a novel or replicative observation regarding etiology, diagnosis, or response to treatment. This can be written up as a letter to the editor in a professional journal, as a stand-alone article, or perhaps even as an entire book. Sigmund Freud, for example, authored a number of books based on his individual cases, helping to establish an entirely new field based, in part, on anecdotal case reports. Such observations derived from routine clinical care can indeed report legitimate conclusions. For example, say the first published report on a given antibiotic finds that its administration seemingly produced rapid relief and cure for a patient with a known bacterial illness, leading the author to conclude that this new antibiotic helps to cure this disorder. If said drug really does cure this illness, then this case report has yielded a true conclusion. What case reports do not do is provide sufficiently strong evidence to sort out erroneous conclusions from valid ones. Some problems remit with the simple passage of time (e.g., certain types of stress reactions), have varying courses, or readily respond to placebo influences. It is easy for a clinician to be deceived in the face of an apparently positive response. Its inherent inability to sort out valid conclusions from invalid ones is a serious limitation of anecdotal case reports' producing legitimate conclusions.

Correlational studies can also be quite compelling. For example, a strong correlation exists between smoking and the incidence of lung cancer, which has lead science to conclude, with other evidence, that smoking increases the risk of cancer. But correlational associations can also produce inaccurate causal inferences. Say that it has been determined that the incidence of reported rapes is positively correlated with the sales of ice cream cones in a given community. One would not want to conclude that the consumption of ice cream causes sexual assaults. What is more likely operative is some third variable, as in time of year or outside temperature (reported rapes do decline during colder months). Again, correlational studies can assist in deriving correct inferences, but such studies must be interpreted cautiously.

Single-subject research designs (N-of-1 trial) are exceedingly useful in evaluating the effectiveness of treatments when one has access to a limited number of clients. This approach has only two prerequisites. The first is that the client's situation or problem must be amenable to repeated, reliable and valid assessment. The second is that the clinician must repeatedly assess the client's problem or situation using this valid measure. If this is done during and after treatment, one can confidently conclude whether a client has changed, at least along the dimensions measured. If this is done before, during, and after treatment, one can make tentative conclusions regarding the client's response to treatment, particularly if the pretreatment, or baseline, measures are stable and long-standing. If circumstances permit or dictate that treatment be introduced and removed, and if a client's functioning is observed to systematically co-vary with the implementation and removal of treatment, then one may make legitimate causal inferences regarding treatment effects in this one client. If one can replicate a finding across a number of clients who have the same problem and who receive the same intervention, then the generalized conclusion is strengthened—for example, This intervention is *effective for many clients with this problem, not just the first one.*

Suppose a client meets the criteria for post-traumatic stress disorder (PTSD). A valid measure of PTSD symptoms is completed weekly. After several weeks, the client receives some form of formal treatment (an antianxiety drug, a psychosocial intervention, etc.), and within two weeks, symptoms dramatically decline. Owing to the vicissitudes of therapy, the treatment is stopped after two weeks. During the next two treatment-free weeks, symptoms exacerbate to baseline levels. If treatment resumes and symptoms promptly decline, then this pattern of response can be quite compelling in arguing that the new treatment is causally responsible for improvements. But other potentially confounding factors (such as placebo responses) preclude a completely uncritical acceptance of the conclusion that the treatment caused the changes. Nevertheless, N-of-1 trials can be a quite useful way to systematically evaluate the effects of interventions with individual clients (see Barlow & Hersen, 1984; Thyer, 2001b).

Uncontrolled clinical trials involve validly assessing many clients one or more times before providing them with an intervention; in other words, clients are assessed during the pretest (designated as O1) before beginning the intervention (designated as X). They are assessed again after treatment (known as the *posttest,* or O2), using the same approach as before. Simple inferential statistics are usually used to evaluate changes in the aggregated level of a client's functioning, comparing posttreatment assessment scores with the pretreatment measures. Schematically, this can be depicted as an O1-X-O2 group research design, and this approach is extremely useful both at documenting client changes in large groups and in testing the hypothesis of whether clients changed or were harmed by exposure to treatment. Again, a wide array of potentially confounding factors—such as the passage of time, the placebo responses, a desire to please the assessor, and so on—usually prevent one from concluding that the specific X caused the clients to improve. Nevertheless, initial investigations into new treatments are often tested in a research program using the O1-X-O2 designs.

Quasi-experimental controlled clinical trials attempt to compare the functioning of clients exposed to differing treatment conditions. Say an agency assigns some clients, based on the availability of clinical resources, to short-term treatment provided one-to-one and assigns other clients to the same short-term treatment but delivered in small groups. Sometimes, as in this example, two different genuine treatments can be compared in this approach. Other times, real treatment can be compared to a wait-listing condition or to an entirely different treatment. If clients assessed at pretest are functioning equivalently, some then get treatment X and others get treatment Y; and if it is found at posttest that those who received X have improved more that those who got Y, then the tentative conclusion is that X is a more effective treatment than Y. If those who received X are functioning equivalently posttest to those who got Y, then the tentative conclusion is that X and Y are equivalent therapies. Such conclusions are at best tentative, however. There may be some reasons why clients were assigned to differing treatments, and it may be these reasons that explain why outcomes differ, not the differences in how X and Y affect clients (see Cook & Campbell, 1979).

In an *individual randomized controlled clinical trial* (RCT), large numbers of clients with similar problems are randomly assigned to differing conditions, say X and Y, following a pretest. Using random assignment to determine what treatment a client receives helps to control for systematic differences between the characteristics of the two groups. If posttreatment assessment finds that the clients who received X have enhanced functioning relative to those who received Y, then a relatively stronger conclusion can be make as to whether X is a better treatment than Y. More complicated variations of RCTs can randomly assign clients to a no-treatment condition; a placebo treatment condition; or to a number of alternative, legitimate treatments. Follow-up assessments conducted over longer periods of posttreatment can be used to test the durability of improvements. Other methodological refinements involve using strong and comprehensive outcome measures; having assessments conducted by individuals unconnected with the delivery of service and unaware (or "blind") to the treatment condition the client was assigned to; and, in really well-done RCTs, selecting clients for overall participation in the study using some form of random selection from a larger population of interest (although this is rarely possible). RCTs are obviously more ambitious and usually much more expensive than other ways to investigate answerable questions, but they do permit stronger conclusions.

It is not uncommon for a new treatment to be investigated by a given researcher or by a research team closely associated with the development of the new treatment. This occurs with pharmacological treatments (e.g., by scientists funded by drug companies) and in psychosocial treatments (e.g., by practitioners who develop, market, and provide expensive training programs in the new intervention). Thus, it is important that any conclusions derived from a single RCT be replicated by independent scientists with no financial or personal investment in the new treatment, ideally through the use of a *multi-site randomized controlled clinical trial,* using several independent research teams located at different centers across the country (or even involving multiple countries) and involving diverse client populations. If conclusions based on a single RCT holds up to such strenuous testing, then this is pretty much as good as it gets in terms of having confidence in an answer to an answerable question.

Sometimes, however, multiple RCTs produce disparate results, clouding the ability to make a firm conclusion; or the RCTs are uneven in terms of quality, perhaps owing to an array of outcome measures or a relatively small samples of clients. As RCTs pertinent to answering an answerable question accumulate, the ultimate research analysis becomes possible, an approach known as a *systematic review* (SR). In an SR, independent and unbiased researchers carefully search for every published and unpublished report available that deals with a particular answerable question. These reports are then critically analyzed, and—whether positive or negative, whether consistent or inconsistent—all results are assessed, as are factors such as sample size and representativeness, whether the outcome measures were valid, whether the interventions were based on replicable protocols or treatment manuals, what the magnitude of observed effects were, and so forth. Differential weight is usually given to RCTs, as opposed to the less-rigorous research methods. In some circumstances, a quantitative form of the SR can be applied. Better known as the statistical approach called *meta-analysis* (MA), this method can be used to mathematically aggregate the results obtained across separate outcome studies using differing outcome measures. Typically, MAs include only RCTs, and they ignore findings based on other forms of research (e.g., quasi- and preexperimental outcome studies; correlational, single-subject, and anecdotal case studies). Systematic reviews, however, do usually include these latter forms of research.

This hierarchy of preference research methodologies is admittedly not uncontroversial (Priebe & Slade, 2002). Some believe that the epistemological privileging of RCTs and SRs is unjustifiable, given the supposedly evanescent nature of human relationships and the view that these methods form too blunt an instrument to investigate human affairs. But the alternatives proposed, usually some form of qualitative inquiry, possess their own disadvantages, and arguments remain generally unconvincing.

The Cochrane Collaboration and Campbell Collaboration Web sites are among the best sources for clinicians to locate contemporary systematic reviews and meta-analyses, as are the Web sites Centre for Evidence-Based Medicine (whttp://www.cebm.net) and PubMed (produced by the U.S. National Library of Medicine, http://www.ncbi.nlm.nih.gov/PubMed).

Step 4: Integrate This Critical Appraisal of Research Evidence With Clinical Expertise and Client's Values and Circumstances

Let us suppose that you have searched and located the available systematic reviews, metaanalyses, and RCTs dealing with effective methods to treat clients with serious depression. Let us suppose further that you have uncovered five evidence-based interventions—namely, selected pharmacological agents, cognitive-behavioral treatment, cognitive therapy, interpersonal psychotherapy, and behavior analysis. Let us further stipulate that all seem to produce roughly equivalent long-term results. EBP suggests that you obtain the training and clinical expertise to effectively deliver at least one of these interventions, for even the nonphysician mental health professional needs to be familiar with not only the circumstances indicating the need for medication but also the signs and symptoms of the medication's various agents (including the symptoms of overdose), inasmuch as clients may often be on concurrent drug therapy. Options include participating in stand-alone training workshops, attending professional conferences that offer such training, returning to graduate school, and (if still a student) asking that the program provide training for evidence-based interventions (in fact, this is now an accreditation requirement of professional training programs in clinical and counseling psychology, as well as a somewhat less-stringent expectation of graduate social work training). You may also opt to obtain suitable supervision from a practitioner qualified in the delivery of the evidence-based intervention. It is generally not realistic to try to learn to acquire sophisticated clinical skills from independent study.

Your past training may provide you with some edge in terms of learning selected EBP. For example, interpersonal psychotherapy (IP) draws more from psychodynamic theory than from learning theory, and if your background is strong in psychodynamic therapy, then IP may be a more congenial approach for you to learn. Conversely, those knowledgeable in learning theory would likely be able to more readily acquire skills in behavior analysis or cognitive behavioral treatments. Again, this assumes that these differing approaches enjoy a similarly strong evidentiary foundation.

Integrating your own skills in EBP with the client's values and preferences can begin with describing the treatment options you are capable of providing, with estimates of duration and cost and of the commonly encountered effects and side effects. This, of course, is approached cautiously, with no pretense of making any form of promise regarding individual outcomes. Often a useful practice is to provide clients with written descriptions of these treatment options, perhaps for them to take home and review at leisure or to discuss with others before scheduling a follow-up session with you. Potential medication treatments carry their own considerations. Some types of medications cannot be taken concurrently, and side effects can often be adverse, not minor. Referral options are also important to present. For example, suppose that your client expresses a strong preference for insight oriented psychotherapy, yet your critical appraisal of the research reveals no scientifically credible evidence that this approach helps clients like yours. If evidence-based alternatives are available, then it would be unethical for you to provide such a non-evidence-based treatment. You would be obliged to provide the client with accurate information about treatment alternatives; at best (and even this may be ethically questionable), you could offer to refer the client to a practitioner who provides insight-oriented psychotherapy.

There is nothing within EBP that is at variance with the ethical standards of the various helping professions. EBP does not insist that scientific considerations be the only factors given weight when deciding on a choice of treatments. What it does insist is that such considerations be considered within one's clinical expertise and with the client's values and preferences in mind. There is very little role for authority that is unsubstantiated by credible scientific evidence; theoretical considerations are also minimally considered, in favor of empirical ones.

Step 5: Evaluate One's Own Effectiveness

Clearly, the more experience you gain in EBP, the less time you need to spend investigating the evidence. For instance, if you followed the steps outlined here to care for a depressed client last month, it will require less effort to search the literature for significant updates and developments applicable to a depressed client seen today. Once you have located and acquired the skills to validly access client functioning in a given area (and perhaps kept on file the pencil-and-paper rapid assessment instruments most useful in that area), then that is work that need not be repeated with each new case (although periodically consulting the literature for updates is of course important). To the extent that your practice focuses on one or on a few circumscribed clinical problems, you will find that it becomes more feasible to develop in-depth skills in evidence-based assessment and intervention. As EBP develops, the concept of the generalist practitioner becomes a less-feasible undertaking, as highly specific interventions requiring detailed and intense training focused on particular problems demand more and more of clinicians' time.

You need to evaluate not only your ability to provide evidence-based interventions but also your skills in searching the scientific literature to research answerable questions. It also is really crucial that practitioners be able to read, understand, and critically evaluate published research studies. The world is fraught with bogus therapies and exaggerated claims, and the best protection from being duped by the charlatans and self-deceived is in your own ability to assess the evidence made in support of assertions regarding effective treatments. Personal testimonials by the financially invested (e.g., the purveyors of expensive continuing education programs) are a weak foundation for the practitioner seeking to be guided by evidence-based knowledge. Rather, the important skills include understanding what constitutes an acceptable outcome measure, knowing what the characteristics are of an internally valid research design, and finding a replicable treatment protocol.

Considerable attention has been paid in the social work, psychological, educational, and counseling literatures on how individual practitioners can evaluate the outcomes of their own interventions with individual clients. Integral to EBP are the N-of-1 research designs specifically discussed and recommended by Sackett et al. (2000). It is not sufficient that the clinician learn about and apply evidence-based treatments in their practice; EBP also mandates that we systematically evaluate our own service outcomes.

CONCLUSION

We are fortunate in that a growing number of brief treatments and interventions used in crisis situations are being rigorously tested in wellcrafted N-of-1 and group research designs and are providing evidence of their effectiveness. Short-term treatments have been discussed and practiced in the human services for over 50 years (e.g., Scherz, 1954) and are now being tested using rigorous RCTs (e.g., Evans et al., 2003). Among those short-term treatments that have provisional evidence to suggest usefulness are, among others, interpersonal psychotherapy, for depression; cognitive-behavior therapy, for depression and anxiety disorders; exposure therapy, for panic disorder, agoraphobia, morbid grief, pathological jealousy, obsessive-compulsive disorder, and social and specific phobias; task-centered practice, for school problems; bibliotherapy and computer-based treatments, for anxiety disorders (see Dattilio & Freeman, 2000; Dziegielewski, Shields, & Thyer, 1998).

The policy implications of EBP are considerable (see Grey, 2001); in fact, the model can be applied in nonclinical situations, including community practice (Thyer, 2001a) and managerial practice. EBP is being adopted, to a certain extent, in other countries as well (see Thyer & Kazi, 2004). It is particularly well developed in Great Britain, where the Cochrane Collaboration was founded.

Practitioners in the fields of brief treatment and crisis intervention have the opportunity and the challenge to avail themselves of this emerging knowledge base and of the developing philosophy and approach to service delivery known as evidence-based practice. This is both scientifically tenable and ethically incumbent. EBP builds and expands on prior initiatives in various disciplines, such as the 50-year-old Boulder model of scientist-practitioner training and the empirically supported treatments of the last decade—both of which are found in clinical psychology. EBP also builds on social work's empirical clinical-practice model and is highly congruent with the traditions of applied behavior analysis. EBP presents considerable challenges and opportunities, not only to those of us in the academy who are charged with developing and maintaining state-of-the-science and state-of-the-art clinical-training programs, but also to those providing clinical supervision to practitioners of brief treatments and to those who are health care providers themselves.

NOTE

REFERENCES

Barlow, D. H., & Hersen, M. (1984). *Single-case experimental designs: Strategies for studying behavior change* (2d ed.). New York: Pergamon.

Cook, T. D., & Campbell, D. T. (1979). *Quasiexperimentation: Design and analysis issues for field settings*. New York: Pergamon.

Dattilio, F. M., & Freeman, A. (Eds.). (2000). *Cognitive-behavioral strategies in crisis intervention* (2d ed.). New York: Guilford.

Dziegielewski, S. F., Shields, J. P., & Thyer, B. A. (1998). Short-term treatment: Models, methods, and research. In J. B. W. Williams & K. Ell (Eds.), *Advances in mental health research* (pp. 287–309). Washington, DC: NASW Press.

Evans, M. E., Boothroyd, R. A., Armstrong, M. I., Greeenbaum, P. E., Borwn, E. C., & Kuppinger, A. D. (2003). An experimental study of the effectiveness of intensive in-home crisis services for children and their families. *Journal of Emotional and Behavioral Disorders, 11*(2), 93–104.

Faul, A. C., McMurtry, S. L., & Hudson, W. W. (2001). Can empirical clinical practice techniques improve social work outcomes? *Research on Social Work Practice, 11*, 277–299.

Grey, J. A. Muir (2001). *Evidence-based healthcare: How to make health policy and management decisions.* New York: Churchill-Livingstone.

Howard, M., & Jensen, J. (1999). Clinical practice guidelines: Should social work develop them? *Research on Social Work Practice, 9*, 283–301.

Priebe, S., & Slade, M. (Eds.). (2002). *Evidence in mental health care.* New York: Brunner-Routledge.

Rosen, A., & Proctor, E. (Eds.). (2003). *Developing practice guidelines for social work interventions: Issues, methods and research agenda.* New York: Columbia.

Sackett, D. L., Straus, S. E., Richardson, W. S., Rosenberg, W. & Haynes, R. B. (2000). *Evidence-based medicine: How to practice and teach EBM* (2nd ed.). New York: Churchill-Livingstone.

Scherz, F. H. (1954). *The intake process: Six papers on intake procedures and short-term treatment.* New York: Family Service Association of America.

Slomin-Nevo, V., & Anson, T. (1998). Evaluating practice: Does it improve treatment outcome? *Social Work Research, 22*, 66–74.

Thyer, B. A. (2001a). Evidence-based approaches to community practice. In H. Briggs & K. Corcoran (Eds.), *Social work practice: Treating common client problems* (pp. 54–65). Chicago: Lyceum.

Thyer, B. A. (2001b). Single-case designs. In B. A. Thyer (Ed.), *Handbook of social work research methods* (pp. 239–255). Thousand Oaks, CA: Sage.

Thyer, B. A., & Kazi, M. A. F. (Eds.). (2004). *International perspectives on evidence-based practice in social work.* London: Venture Press.

4

A Practical Approach to Formulating Evidence-Based Questions in Social Work

KENNETH R. YEAGER
ALBERT R. ROBERTS

Leonard Gibbs (2002) in his chapter in Oxford's *Social Workers' Desk Reference* eloquently underscores the harm-reducing importance of formulating specific, well-built questions as a critical element in evidence-based clinical reasoning:

> The history of the helping professions provides many vivid examples of dedicated "helpers" who were harming . . . those whom they sought to help. Beyond any doubt, those professionals cared deeply about the children, aged persons, and clients whose troubled lives they sought to aid, but such caring, though vital and necessary, does not provide sufficient footing to assure success. Learning how to pose specific, well-built questions [e.g. related to adolescent suicide potential, child abuse risk assessment, etc.] as part of an evidence-based approach to practice can provide one approach to avoiding harm. . . . If we can learn how to pose specific questions from practice, we have a chance to find a specific answer, and conversely, if we do not learn how to pose specific questions from practice, how can we ever find specific answers? As Yogi Berra once said, "You've got to be careful if you don't know where you're going cause you might not get there." . . . In summary, caring is a necessary but not a sufficient condition to avoid harm. Practitioners who learn how to pose specific questions about their practice, and who resolve to avoid common errors in practice reasoning, may better avoid harming those to whom they have dedicated their professional lives. Such practitioners can avoid consigning their clients to endure effects of repeated failure. (pp. 752, 755–756)

On any given day, social workers engage in complex interactions with persons who present with unique mental health needs and problems in social functioning. Each clinical encounter will generate questions regarding the care of the individual, family, or group. Many of these questions will be difficult and beyond the means of the social worker to readily answer. Complex questions relating to specific needs of patients/clients as framed by their circumstance, illness, or environment may well require the application of an evidence-based approach. Social workers frequently work with high-risk, vulnerable, and special needs clients. As a result, social workers need the most up-to-date information about these high-risk and vulnerable populations (e.g., refugees with language and cultural barriers who need mental health services; suicidal individuals with comorbid psychiatric disorders, unemployed persons with no health insurance; homeless mentally ill, etc.). Evidence-based social work practice begins by formulating a researchable question—based on a diagnostic assessment of the client being completed. The next critical step is examining existing health system/organization/agency approved electronic practice guidelines, or initiating a systematic search based on all relevant key words for the intervention that has the greatest probability of succeeding.

All important questions are researchable as long as they are expressed in a manner that allows for evidence-based investigation. Questions need to be able to conceptualize ideas clearly in terms of observable phenomena that are testable or measurable. Evidence-based questions are explicated through nominal terms and operational definitions of variables.

Specific evidence-based questions place primary emphasis on the client's benefits. It involves a systematic and continual process of posing specific and well-built questions that have central importance and immediate practical value to clients and their social workers. Each question should include the type of client (i.e., an adolescent with obsessive-compulsive disorder [OCD], or a battered women with major depression), the proposed course of action (i.e., the start of a medication trial with an SSRI, followed within 4 weeks by 10 weeks of exposure-response prevention), and the pertinent findings (i.e., reduction in OCD symptoms as measured by the Yale-Brown Obsessive-Compulsive [Y-BOC] pre and post scores).

Sample Questions

1. If young adult females with OCD receive exposure-response prevention treatment plus an SSRI medication (e.g. Prozac, Luvox, Celexa, or Zoloft) or SSRI medication only, will there be any difference on the Y-BOC scores and the amount of symptom reduction?
2. If abused women who recently left an emergency shelter attend a professional social worker-led twice-weekly group therapy sessions, will they experience a reduction in mental health symptoms after the sixth week of group treatment as measured by the Derogatis Brief Symptom Checklist (SCL-30)?

3. If a middle-aged married man is brought to a hospital-based mental health intake unit soon after banging his head against the wall, telling his wife that his testicles have disappeared and that life is not worth living so he is going to hang himself, should the intake worker administer the Beck Depression Inventory (BDI) or systematically search for and find the most reliable and valid measures and tools for assessing the nature and risk level of suicide lethality? (American Psychiatric Association, 2003; Roberts & Jennings, 2005; Weishaar, 2004)

Every profession relies upon scholarly and critical inquiry, and the social work profession is no exception. Building scholarly knowledge to better inform practice decisions is based on evidence-based studies. This systematic gathering of the latest practice guidelines and research findings all begins with the formulation of evidence-based questions. This chapter addresses the process of formulating questions in a way that leads the social worker to the best available evidence. It will focus on questions regarding direct practice, including the person within the environment, as well as addressing questions related to the individual's illness or social environment; the latter is by nature more general, and answers will be easily found within social work literature (McKibbon et al., 2002; Roberts & Yeager, 2004; Sackett Straus, Richardson, Rosenberg, & Haynes, 2000).

The development of evidence-based social work practice questions should be considered from two perspectives, background and foreground. Background questions have their basis in fact, and they are best answered by reference books, text books, practice manuals and the like. There are two parts of a background question. First, is the subject at hand, e.g., what is Cognitive Behavioral Therapy. The second part of the background question addresses inquiry concerns of who, what, where, when and why. Examples of background questions are:

- What is dialectical behavioral therapy?
- What are the signs and symptoms of drug addiction?
- What are the criteria for involuntary inpatient psychiatric admission?
- What are the criteria for determining high risk of suicide?
- What constitutes domestic violence?

In most cases, a social worker can easily conceptualize his or her question and simply add a consideration of: who, what, where, when, and why. In doing so, the social worker will seek to answer the two components of a background question.

Foreground questions are more complex. They address concerns regarding the most current, strongest evidence and information on illness, diagnosis, social situations and community problems. Questions of this type are best answered by systematically searching the current professional literature. Foreground questions are easily identified by their examination of the person combined with the person's individualized need and social situation. These are the types of questions social workers ask and address daily.

CONCEPTUALIZING EVIDENCE-BASED
QUESTIONS

Within evidence-based practice, it is common practice to divide the question you would like to answer into four parts. The question should consider: the client or problem of interest; the intervention you are considering; inclusion of a comparison group, either implicit or explicit as applied to the population; and the outcome of interest, either positive or negative (Badenoch & Heneghan, 2002pay, 2002; McKibbon et al., 2002; Roberts & Yeager, 2004; Sackett et al., 2000).

In the application of evidence-based practice, practitioners do have time to ask specific questions, with each case addressed if they are familiar with the process of asking the right question. Social workers will face situations where the questions asked become an important component in developing the most appropriate course of action within a given case. As a clinician, you will experience numerous cases that leave you wondering what is the correct thing to do next—particularly where the individual in question is experiencing multiple issues and is not functioning as well as you believe he or she could function. There are other times when you have a case where the individual is functioning very well but you need to give him or her that little boost to move them into optimal functioning. You want to make the right move, but you have only one shot. What will you do? What is the next right thing to do?

You begin the four-part question process by addressing the individual problem of interest. How specifically you ask this question will impact not only your ability to find the right answer to the question but also the applicability of this answer to the individual's unique needs. Your description of the individual is the starting point for the question; therefore, it should be as specific as possible. For example: if you are interested in bipolar disorder in geriatric populations, phrasing your question as "geriatric anxiety disorder" will be more effective then searching "patients with anxiety disorder." On the other hand, if your question is too specific, you will have little luck finding sufficient information to address the question at hand. For example, searching for "83-year-old females with anxiety, diabetes, and little home support."

The intervention and comparison portion of the four-part question can address a treatment, diagnostic test, and social intervention or support program. In most cases, the intervention portion of the question should be combined with a comparison component. That is, the intervention is compared with another intervention or "treatment as usual." There are also diagnostic questions; these address a particular diagnostic test, rating scale or assessment measure. In cases of diagnostic questions, you will want to compare against whatever test is identified as "the gold standard" or, in the absence of a gold standard test, against a screening instrument that is commonly accepted and has demonstrated high levels of validity and reliability in similar situations. Etiology questions address the intervention. In this case, the comparison can be a risk factor—for example, the comparison can be the presence or absence of a risk factor against the population without this risk factor, e.g., the potential for relapse on alcohol or drugs. Prognosis questions may have either three or four parts. Three part questions address the prognosis of patients with a particular illness, such as a first-time depressive disorder. A four-part question will ask if the presence of an individual characteristic or complicating factor may alter the prognosis of the patient. For example, in persons who have an emergent depressive disorder and are chemically dependent but abstinent from all mood-altering substances, are such persons at a greater or less risk for relapse? As social workers develop skills in the application of evidence-based practice questions, several interventions may be considered, such as the impact of social support programs in combination with medication management and a particular therapeutic approach.

An example of a four-part question follows.

Part 1. *Patient or problem of interest: Determine the patient issue or problem area to research.* Who are you working with? What are the individual's unique characteristics or individual needs. This may come in the form of a unique patient issue or a specific problem area. To effectively apply evidence-based practice, you will need to formulate a question that fits the patient issue or problem area.

For example: *In patients with schizophrenia who abuse illegal drugs (substance abuse, drug addiction), what is the most effective therapeutic approach?*

This process enables the clinician to address the patient's unique needs within a searchable answerable question. This question will need to be sufficiently clear to lead to a successful search.

Part 2. *Intervention.* The second part of our question builds on part 1. In this case, in patients with schizophrenia, you are looking for an intervention to enhance the care provided to the patient. Your addition to the question will need to focus on a specific intervention. That intervention must be one that has sufficient documentation in literature to search for effectiveness.

For example: *Does the addition of cognitive behavioral therapy (CBT) to usual care improve outcome within the population of schizophrenic individuals who are also substance abusers?*

Now your question is building in specifics. You are now seeking to answer your question with a very clear, measurable direction. The determination to search the efficacy of the addition of cognitive behavioral therapy may come from a suggestion from a peer or simply from a hunch. Nevertheless, the reason for your search, the application of the evidence-based approach, will strengthen your approach with the individual as actions become informed by the literature. Your question may seek to inform the effectiveness of the treatment when added to the current approaches taken. In the process of treatment, alternative treatments may emerge that increase the likelihood of improvement. In most cases, it is important to search for rival approaches with similar levels of effectiveness. Seldom is there a single approach that is best for all patients treated. Therefore, you will want to consider one or more alternative treatments. This then takes us to part 3.

Part 3. *Control or alternative treatment.* In this section, you are simply asking the question of one intervention in addition to treatment as usual or seeking to answer a question of efficacy of alternative treatments, using the phrase "When compared to usual care alone." Your question is now beginning to read a way that will lead you to a specific literature-informed approach:

For example: *In patients with schizophrenia who are substance abusers, does the addition of cognitive behavioral therapy (CBT) to usual care improve outcome, when compared to USUAL care alone?*

Part 4. *Outcome of interest.* It is important to have an outcome in mind for the individual or population being treated. The outcome is usually prestated by the individual, his or her family, or the treatment team. It should be an agreed-upon outcome with a specific measure of success. Within the treatment population defined, that is, persons with schizophrenia who are substance abusers, one issue frequently stands out: the issue is the issue of relapse prevention. Frequently, the ongoing abuse of mood-altering substances within the schizophrenic population leads to eventual breakdown of functioning levels and relapse of the mental illness. In this case, the outcome of interest becomes: *how to prevent relapse.*

Now the evidence-based question has been formulated completely, and reads: *In patients with schizophrenia who are also substance abusers, does the addition of cognitive behavioral therapy (CBT) to usual care improve outcome by preventing relapse, when compared to usual care alone?*

CASE EXAMPLE

Sam (not a real person) has been admitted to the inpatient psychiatric facility following emergence of an acute psychotic episode. A 26-year-old African American male, Sam is well known to the inpatient psychiatric staff. Sam has a history of alcohol, cannabis, and cocaine dependence. Recently, Sam has experienced numerous hospital admissions. Staff members are becoming frustrated with this case and report feeling helpless to put a plan into place that is effective for Sam. Thomas, a young resident and Sue, a social worker, begin discussing an evidence-based approach to this case.

They begin with an etiology/harm question: *Among those with schizophrenia who are also substance abusers, does the drug of choice impact the risk of readmission?* Thomas and Sue begin a literature search; what they find is cocaine may present as a greater risk, but all mood-altering substances contribute to destabilization in schizophrenic patients. Next, the clinicians begin to examine what might be the most effective approach to relapse prevention. As they interview Sam, they become aware of his frustrations with the side effects he has experienced. Thomas and Sue ask a different type of question related to harm, this time with an explicit comparison group. *In African American male patients with schizophrenia does receiving medication therapy with the antipsychotic medication risperidone have less risk of developing tardive dyskinesia than those receiving olanzapine?* In this case, the patients are African American males with schizophrenia, the treatment of interest is risperidone, the comparison is olan-zapine, and the outcome is the development of side effects, specifically tardive dyskinesia. The literature showed no remarkable difference in the emergence of side effects within the comparison group. Therefore, Sam's medications remained the same.

Next, Thomas and Sue begin examining questions related to prognosis. They asked: *Do African American males with schizophrenia have better outcomes when exposed to programs that develop social and vocational functioning?* Thomas and Sue found evidence supporting the effectiveness of vocational and social support services. The treatment team for Sam began development of a treatment plan based in evidence, designed with the prevention of relapse in mind. The evidence suggested introduction of social skills training in combination with supportive employment. Once Sam demonstrated stability on the inpatient unit, he transitioned to the day treatment program. Following 2 weeks of day treatment, Sam began vocational training and working with the supported employment team. Sam demonstrated good skills working with a facility that built electronic auto rearview mirrors.

Sam transitioned from day treatment to a community-based treatment team. In doing so, he was provided with a team of social workers, psychiatrist, and nurses to provide ongoing care. Sam continued in the vocational training. He was also attending an ongoing support group developed by the community mental health center to enhance social skills in those with severe and persistent mental illness. Sam found his family was supportive of his participation in this program. Sam now attends the social support meetings with his grandmother, sister, and cousin, with whom he lives. In addition to vocational rehabilitation and social skills training, the community team introduced participation in local "double-trouble meetings," a community based "A.A." format for persons with substance dependence as well as mental health issues. In this group, Sam is able to practice the social skills he is learning. He has reduced his use of mood-altering substances to the point of demonstrating sustained partial remission of his substance dependence. Sam has not used cocaine for 6 months. He has used cannabis on two occasions in the past 6 months. He reports having an occasional beer, although his grandmother doesn't like for him to drink. In all Sam, has avoided hospitalization for 1 year and 3 months.

CASE EXAMPLE FROM COURNOYER AND POWER (2002)

The following case example illustrates that even with highly complex clients who have multiple diagnoses, rational and informed decisions can best be made through evidence-based practice. It all starts with an initial clinical assessment and descriptive summary that takes about 60 to 90 minutes to complete and is then formulated into a searchable question.

The client is referred to a clinical social worker who conducts an initial intake interview at a community mental health center:

> Referred by an emergency room physician after an attempted suicide, she arrives for the meeting dressed in a short skirt and low-cut blouse. A 28-year-old, twice-divorced woman, Lisa describes her concerns and situation as she alternately rubs the white bandages that cover both wrists. She reports that she has attempted suicide on at least four previous occasions and sometimes cuts on her arms, legs, or stomach when she feels upset and desperate. She has had numerous romantic relationships. All have ended in a disappointing fashion. A breakup with her most recent boyfriend led to the current suicide attempt. She also describes her work history as off and on. She reports that she has had more than 20 jobs over the course of the past five years. She says that she finds it easy to find employment, but the jobs become boring or her bosses become unreasonable, and she usually ends up quitting in the midst of a loud argument.
>
> When asked about her family history, she reports that her mother was alcoholic, often left her alone for days at a time, and sometimes beat her with a leather strap. She states that her mother was a "slut" who had men over all the time. She also reports that one of her mother's boyfriends raped her when she was 10 years old.
>
> As the meeting draws to a close, you make arrangements to ensure Lisa's safety and reduce the risk of another suicidal attempt. You also schedule another meeting for the next day. Following the interview, however, you realize that you need much more information about how to provide high-quality service to this new client. You decide to look for intervention approaches that reflect evidence of effective outcomes when applied to people such as Lisa. (Cournoyer & Powers, 2002, p. 801)

On the basis of the foregoing case description, a searchable evidence-based question might be something like the following.

> What does the practice effectiveness research suggest is the best intervention approach for effective service to young adult women who report being abused and raped as children, currently engage in self-mutilating behavior, periodically attempt suicide, have difficulty maintaining relationships or employment, and appear to meet several of the criteria of the DSM-IV diagnosis of borderline personality disorder (BPD)? (p. 801)

The second step in an evidence-based social work inquiry is to carefully examine the question and identify the key words, descriptors, and synonyms and then enter them as search terms into all of the relevant electronic databases. Guided by the foregoing question, you would be likely to come up with key words such as *alcoholic parent, child abuse, child sexual abuse, self-mutilation, suicide attempt, suicide ideation, suicide, rape*. Other key terms related to practice research and practice effectiveness may well include *effectiveness, efficacy, research, study, outcome measures, program evaluation, intervention,* or *suicide prevention.* Descriptors may well include *young adult, females, occupation* or *employment status, race,* and *relationship status.* Diagnostic terms may well include *borderline personality disorder, posttraumatic stress disorder, suicide ideation,* or *rape trauma syndrome.* For a review of each of the sequential steps in conducting systematic reviews of the evidence on a particular target clientele or target group, see Corcoran and Vandiver (chapter 5) and Rosenthal (chapter 6).

Gibbs (2003) has aptly enumerated a specific type of direct practice search question that he defines as a *client-oriented practical evidence search* (COPES) question.

Client-oriented practical evidence search questions emanate directly from social work practice situations. These types of question have three general features:

- First, they are questions from daily practice, posed by practitioners, that really matter to the client's welfare—they're client oriented. They concern issues that are central to the welfare of the client and to those whose lives are affected by the client.
- Second, COPES questions have practical importance in several ways:
  - If they concern problems that arise frequently in everyday practice
  - If they concern the mission of the agency
  - If knowing the answer concerns something within the realm of possibility; so knowing the answer could result in effective use for their answer
- Third, COPES questions are specific enough to guide an electronic evidence search. (Gibbs, 2003)

Gibbs (2003, p. 59) identifies several types of questions that can be asked in evidence-based direct practice:

- *Questions about how to enhance effectiveness of an intervention.* If disoriented aged persons who reside in a nursing home are given reality orientation therapy or validation therapy, which will result in better orientation to time, place, person?
- *Questions about how to prevent a social problem from occurring.* If sexually active high school students at high risk for pregnancy are exposed to Baby-Think-It-Over or to didactic material on proper use of birth control methods, then will they have fewer pregnancies during an academic year, have knowledge of birth control methods, use birth control methods?
- *Questions about how to best conduct a client assessment.* If aged residents of a nursing home who may be depressed or may have Alzheimer's disease or dementia are administered depression screening tests or a short mental status examination tests, which measure will be the briefest, most inexpensive, valid and reliable screening test to discriminate between depression and dementia?
- *Questions about how best to describe a practice relevant situation.* If family members of children diagnosed with a learning disorder meet in a support group to receive information and support from staff and other families, what aspects of the support group will they find most helpful?
- *Questions about how to assess risk for a social problem.* If crisis line callers to a battered women shelter are administered a risk assessment scale by tele-

phone or we rely on practical judgment unaided by a risk assessment scale, then will the risk assessment scale have higher reliability and predictive validity regarding future violence?

Note that in each of these examples, five common elements are included:

- The type of client
- The client problem
- What the practitioner is considering doing
- An alternative course of action against which the contemplated action is compared
- What the practitioner seeks to accomplish

Gibbs recommends that a well-built question should include these five elements if it is to guide a social worker's search and decision-making (Gibbs, 2003).

CONCLUSION

In summary, this chapter was planned in order to delineate and discuss the rationale, components, and step-by-step method of formulating searchable evidence-based social work questions based on specific client problems and target groups. We firmly believe that evidence-based practice begins with a solid point of departure when a well-conceived and well-built clinical research question is formulated. We also contend that our ethical obligations as social workers and educators can best be met by facilitating the use and dissemination of research-based evidence. The National Association of Social Workers emphasizes how very important it is for all social workers to base practice decisions on empirically based knowledge and practice-based research evidence.

Every day social workers and other mental health professionals encounter complex and critical decisions requiring advanced knowledge of difficult medical, emotional, and social problems. For most complex client problems, the application of an evidence-based four-part question will facilitate a greater understanding of what is most effective, given specific components of the individual case. By examining the patient or problem of interest, a greater understanding of the intervention of interest (e.g., diagnostic test, treatment, risk factor, or prognostic factor) can be attained. Examination of comparisons (implicit or explicit) will sharpen the clinician's understanding of potential impacts on the outcome of interest.

Some will argue that there is not time in the day to complete this process for each and every case encountered. We agree, but the fact is that graduate social work education and continuing education seminars have demonstrated effectiveness in many of the cases you will encounter on a day-to-day basis. There will, however, be a growing number of individual cases where the social worker will need to go beyond traditional training to improve the outcomes with specific target and vulnerable populations.

In doing so, the social worker will be building on the basis of evidence-based treatment. Evidence-based approaches to social work provide the backdrop for exciting opportunities to improve the outcomes for populations served by social workers. The systematic application of an evidence-based approach combined with practice-based research will over time strengthen social work as a profession and provide a sense of how evidence-based practice can be applied in a multitude of professional settings. Within the learning, researching, and clinical environment members of the interdisciplinary team are equally active participants, identifying, measuring, analyzing, and solving problems within the population served. In this process, evidence-based practice will continue to sharpen the skills of social workers and to advance positive outcomes within the at-risk populations served.

REFERENCES

American Psychiatric Association. (2003). Practice Guideline for the assessment and treatment of patients with suicidal behaviors. *American Journal of Psychiatry*, 160, 1–50.
Badenoch, D., and Heneghan, C. (2002). *Evidence-based medicine toolkit*. London: BMJ Books.
Centre for Evidence-Based Social Services. (1998). Evidence-based social care. *Newsletter of the Centre for Evidence-based Social Services,1*(1). Available: www.ex.ac.uk/cebss/newsletter_one.html.
Cournoyer, B., & Powers, G. T. (2002). Evidence-based social work: The quiet revolution continues. In A. R. Roberts & G. Greene (Eds.), *Social Workers' Desk Reference* (pp. 798–807). New York: Oxford University Press.
Drake, R. E., Goldman, H., Leff, H. S., Lehman, A. F., Dixon, L., & Mueser, K. T. (2001). Implementing evidence-based practices in routine mental health service settings. *Psychiatric Services, 52*(2), 179–182.
Gambrill, E. (1999). Evidence-based practice: An alternative to authority-based practice. *Families in Society, 80*(4), 341.
Gambrill, E. D. (2003). Evidence-based practice: Sea change or the emperor's new clothes? *Journal of Social Work Education, 39*(1), 3–23.
Gibbs, L. E. (2002). How social workers can do more good than harm: critical thinking, evidence-based clinical reasoning and avoiding fallacies. In A. R. Roberts & G. Greene (Eds.), *Social Workers' Desk Reference* (pp. 752–756). New York: Oxford University Press.
Gibbs, L. E. (2003). *Evidence-based practice for the helping professions*. Pacific Grove, CA: Thompson Learning.
Goisman, R. M., Warshaw, M. G., & Keller, M. B. (1999). Psychosocial treatment prescriptions for generalized anxiety disorder, panic disorder, and social phobia, 1991–1996. *American Journal of Psychiatry, 156*, 1819–1821.
Gray, G. E. (2002). Evidence-based medicine: An introduction for psychiatrists. *Journal of Psychiatric Practice 8*:5–13.
Gray, J.A.M. (2001). *Evidence-based healthcare* (2nd ed.). New York: Churchill Livingstone.
Green, L. W. (2001). From research to "best practices" in other settings and populations. *American Journal of Health Behavior, 25*(3), 165–178.

Howard, M. O., McMillen, C. J., & Pollio, D. (2003). Teaching evidence-based practice: Toward a new paradigm for social work education. *Research on Social Work Practice, 13,* 234–259.

McKibbon, A., Hunt, D., Richardson, W. S., Hayward, R., Wilson, M., Jaeschke, R., Haynes, B., Wyer, P., Craig, J., & Guyatt, G. (2002). In G. Guyatt & D. Rennie (Eds.), *Finding the evidence. A manual for evidence-based clinical practice* (pp. 13–47). AMA Press.

Mullen, E. J. (2004). Facilitating practitioner use of evidence-based practice. In A. R. Roberts & K. Yeager (Eds.), *Evidence-based practice manual: Research and outcome measures in healthcare and human services* (pp. 205–209). New York: Oxford University Press.

Mullen, E. J., & Bacon, W. (2004). A survey of practitioner adoption and implementation of practice guidelines and evidence-based treatments. In A. R. Roberts & K. Yeager (Eds.), *Evidence-based practice manual: Research and outcome measures in healthcare and human services* (pp. 210–218). New York: Oxford University Press.

Mullen, E. J., & Bacon, W. F. (2003). Practitioner adoption and implementation of evidence-based effective treatments and issues of quality control. In A. Rosen & E. K. Proctor (Eds.), *Developing practice guidelines for social work interventions: Issues, methods, and a research agenda.* New York: Columbia University Press.

National Health Services Centre for Reviews and Dissemination, University of York. (1999). Getting evidence into practice. *Effective Health Care Bulletin 5* (1). February 1999.

Roberts, A. R., & Jennings, T. (2005, August). Hanging by a thread: How failure to conduct an adequate lethality assessment resulted in suicide. *Brief Treatment and Crisis Intervention, 5*(3), 251–260.

Roberts, A. R., & Yeager, K. (Eds.). (2004). *Evidence-based practice manual: Research and outcome measures in healthcare and human services.* New York: Oxford University Press.

Sackett, D. L., Rosenberg, W.M.C., Gray, J.A.M., Haynes R. B., Richardson W. S. (1996). Evidence based medicine: What it is and what it isn't—It's about integrating individual clinical expertise and the best external evidence. *British Medical Journal, 312*(7023), 71–72.

Sackett, D. L., Straus, S. E., Richardson, W. S., Rosenberg, W., & Haynes, R. B. (2000). *Evidence-based medicine: How to practice and teach EBM* (2nd ed.). New York: Churchill Livingstone.

Sheldon, B. (2002). *Brief summary of the ideas behind the Centre for Evidence-Based Social Services.* Available: ww.ex.ac.uk/cebss.

Torrey, W. C., Drake, R. E., Dixon, L., Burns, B. J., Flynn, L., Rush, A. J., Clark, R. E., & Klatzker, D. (2001). Implementing evidence-based practices for persons with severe mental illnesses. *Psychiatric Services, 52*(1), 45–50.

Weishaar, Majorie, E. (2004). A cognitive-behavioral approach to suicide risk reduction in crisis intervention. In A. R. Roberts & K. Yeager (Eds.), *Evidence-based practice manual: Research and outcome measures in healthcare and human services* (pp. 749–757). New York: Oxford University Press.

Weissman, M. M., & Sanderson, W. C. (2002). Problems and promises in modern psychotherapy: The need for increased training in evidence based treatments. In B. Hamburg (Ed.), *Modern psychiatry: Challenges in educating health professionals to meet new needs.* New York City: Josiah Macy Foundation.

5

Implementing Best Practice and Expert Consensus Procedures

KEVIN CORCORAN
VIKKI L. VANDIVER

EVIDENCE-BASED PRACTICE AND THE EMERGENCE OF SCIENTIFIC THOUGHT

Evidence-based practice (EBP) reflects the continuum in the development of the scientific revolution. Prior to the scientific revolution, methods of answering questions were paramount to the accuracy of the answer (Dear, 2001). The scientific revolution, in contrast, improved the soundness of the methods in order to increase the likelihood of more accurate observations. Improved methods tended to provide more persuasive evidence.

Evidence-based practice is generally this same scientific revolution. It is a process of utilizing a variety of databases to find an appropriate guide to an intervention for a particular diagnostic condition (Vandiver, 2002; Vandiver & Corcoran, 2002). The goal is to select the most accurate, valid if you will, information derived from the best available methods. This may, as is often the case for theory development, be an in-depth description of a single case or a few cases, for example, Piaget's small children, J. B. Watson's Baby Albert, Skinner's few pigeons and only daughter, and, yes, even Freud's cases. While the accuracy of these examples varies considerably, what is common to them all is that social scientists have used more rigorous methods to test, support, refute, and revise these and other areas of case assessment in the behavioral and social sciences.

WHAT IS EVIDENCE-BASED PRACTICE?

Evidence-based practice is a way for clinicians to select from the corpus of the available evidence the most useful information to apply to a particular client who has sought services. Utilizing evidence-based practice approaches is currently considered the industry standard in many helping disciplines, from medicine to managed mental health care. It is as if we had just gotten comfortable with the notion of *best practices* and now use a more contemporary term. As a consequence, the very definition of evidence-based practice has become more illusive, if not ambiguous. Some restrict the term to systematic reviews using meta-analytic procedures. Others use a wider scope in determining evidence-based practice that may include less rigorous studies and influential cases studies. Additionally, there is the evidence delineated by a group of experts in an area or intervention, who in turn produce guidelines (i.e., expert consensus guidelines). These guidelines possess varying degrees of accuracy. This source of evidence-based practice may—by design—have less restrictive inclusion criteria in order to be a broader source of information. Presumably, the experts will have incorporated the same sources considered in the systematic reviews resulting in the same breadth of studies and use of quantitative synthesis.

KEY SOURCES OF EBP

For the practitioner who routinely sees clients several times a day and who frequently faces an unfamiliar and challenging case, it is useful to consider three sources of information on how to deliver the best intervention available that is also the most useful. The three general sources are (a) systematic reviews, (b) practice guidelines, and (c) expert consensus guidelines (see Figure 5.1).

Systematic Reviews

For the typical practitioner the critical concern is not simply the best intervention available, but also the one that is most useful for the client's circumstances. This is reflected in Gibbs and Gambrill's (2002) review of evidence-based practice, which asserts that "evidence applies to the client(s) at hand" in the context of "the values and expectations of the clients" (p. 453).

The chief source of systematic reviews is the Cochrane Library, which contains more than 1,500 systematic reviews of medical, nursing, and health procedures. In the behavioral and social sciences the Campbell Collaboration provides systematic reviews in the areas of crime and delinquency, education, and social welfare. Reviews are also frequently available through professional journals. This is nicely illustrated by Wilson, Lipsey, and Soydan (2003), who published a systematic review of juvenile justice with minority youth the very week this chapter was written. Additionally, many journals such as *Brief Treatment and Crisis Intervention, Evidence-Based Mental Health, Journal of Clinical Psychology,* and

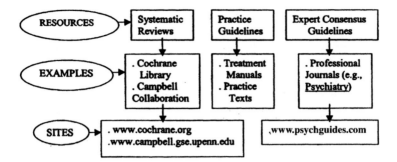

Figure 5.1   Resources for Implementing Evidence-Based Practice
Approaches

Research on Social Work Practice are committed to publishing systematic reviews.

Other critical sources of such evidence are the cutting-edge articles published first in a leading peer-reviewed journal. These articles are not only the most up-to-date information available, but also will eventually be incorporated into future systematic reviews. Staying abreast of the best research in the field still means the well-read practitioner is likely to stay ahead in the field.

As may be suggested from the number of sources of systematic reviews, the quality of the review itself may vary. In fact, the reviews will vary in quality and thoroughness. Additionally, the quantitative methods of data synthesis are not without controversy (Fischer, 1990), and this controversy is not terribly new (Glass & Miller, 1978). Inevitably, resulting uncertainties regarding data synthesis methods give rise to the same concern in applying *any* evidence on which to build a practice, namely, the veracity of the data. Is the evidence persuasive for this particular client whose problem is similar in some ways and different in many others? What would the reasonable and prudent practitioner in the same situation do with this evidence?

Practice Guidelines

Another source for evidence-based practice is the use of practice guidelines. These are also known as treatment manuals and include expert consensus guidelines. These sources are distinguishable from systematic reviews not only by the method of integrating the available evidence, but also by the fact that the practice guidelines are reflective of earlier times when practice was guided by authority (Gambrill, 1999). Practice guidelines and expert consensus guidelines are readily available to a wide audience of practitioners in a variety of disciplines. Additionally, many guidelines and manuals are very practical and direct in facilitating session-to-session therapeutic activities.

Practice guidelines also refer to statements and recommendations for conducting an intervention. Terms associated with practice guidelines include *treat-*

ment protocols, standards, options, parameters, preferred practice, and *best practice.* There are, of course, important distinctions such as standards that are considered a prerequisite to all competent practice, guidelines that are more like suggestions, and options that are other approaches to consider when appropriate (Havinghurst, 1991).

A valuable source of this form of evidence-based practice is practice texts (e.g., Corcoran, 2000), handbooks (e.g., Roberts & Greene, 2002), and manuals (e.g., LeCroy, 1994; Steketee, 1999). Roberts and Greene's *Desk Reference* (2002) has no less than 33 chapters that are relevant to some definition of evidence-based practice. Most textbooks in production and under contract are likely to delineate evidence-based practice while others may find the need for an updated edition. What is striking about these sources is their variety. Some publishers are committed to producing treatment manuals, such as New Harbinger Publications, which has eight diagnosis-specific manuals in production. Texts such as Corcoran's (2000) may focus more on intervention while others are more diagnostic related (Roth & Foragny, 1996), age specific, (Simpson, 1998), or setting specific, such as juvenile justice (e.g., Roberts, 2004). Thus, we see that the clinician attempting to integrate evidence-based practice must inevitably consider the value of that evidence as it relates to the client. Again, judging the veracity of the evidence is a crucial task.

Expert Consensus Guidelines

Expert consensus guidelines are distinguishable from practice guidelines in that they are typically developed by a broad-based panel of experts. For example, McEvoy, Scheifler, and Thomas's *Practice Guidelines for Schizophrenia* (1999) surveyed more than 300 experts from a variety of disciplines and family and advocacy groups. Despite the wide scope of experts that potentially strengthens expert consensus guidelines, these guidelines are limited and rarely consider cultural differences. Frequently, consensus guidelines are marketed by professional organizations. Professional journals such as *Psychiatry* and the *Journal of Clinical Psychology* frequently publish expert consensus guidelines. A useful Web site for guidelines on a number of psychiatric conditions is *www.psychguides.com.*

ELEMENTS OF EVIDENCE-BASED
TREATMENT PLANS

Evidenced-based treatment plans reflect an intervention selected from the best available information appropriate to the values and preferences of a particular client. An evidence-based treatment plan should include seven elements or steps: (a) a biopsychosocial assessment using standardized instruments; (b) an accurate and up-to-date diagnosis using all five axes of the DSM; (c) valid behavioral descriptions of the identified problems or focus of treatment; (d) relevant goals and observable description of the planned target of change; (e) selection of a diagnostic, specific, evidence-based guideline derived from systematic reviews, practice guidelines, or expert consensus guidelines and delineation of a particular/specific treatment plan; (f) repeated administration of outcome measures of the problem, the goals of treatment, or both; and (g) monitoring of client change over the course of treatment and critical evaluation of the treatment outcome. The most critical component of the treatment plan is that the intervention is guided by evidence and delineated in a systematic manner for targeted and observable outcomes.

In the previous section, we discussed the three kinds of resources that the practitioner can draw from to develop an evidence-based treatment plan. Using the seven elements or steps of a treatment plan, the Figure 2.2 illustrates where EBP resources are most often used. There are four main elements or steps where EBP resources are utilized: diagnosis, problem identification, intervention, and outcome.

GUIDELINES FOR IMPLEMENTING EBP

When thoughtfully applied, evidence-based practice will likely strengthen a treatment plan and, in turn, will increase the likelihood of client change and goal attainment. In other words, an intervention derived from evidence-based practice is likely to enhance treatment effectiveness. Vandiver (2002) suggests four summary guidelines for implementing evidence-based knowledge into practice settings: (a) let the assessment be the guide to selecting the appropriate diagnosis, practice guideline, and intervention; (b) use information from all three sources (i.e., systematic reviews, expert consensus guidelines, and practice guidelines) as a guide for determining the most appropriate interventions; (c) if no guideline is available for a particular diagnostic category (e.g., schizoaffective disorder), a

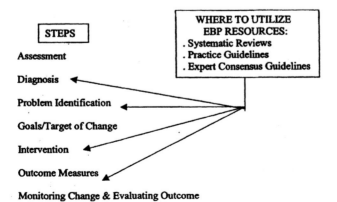

Figure 5.2   Using EBP Resources to Guide Steps for Implementing Treatment Plan

review of the professional literature for cutting-edge research or practice articles is in order; and (d) practice guidelines are guides, supplements if you will, and will never substitute for sound clinical and professional judgment.

CAVEATS FOR IMPLEMENTING EBP

Applying evidence-based practice is the end stage of the search for a practice approach to guide a particular intervention with a unique client. It is never as easy as the article suggests or the manual directs, including the suggestions from this chapter. The results of a search for evidence-based procedures will likely provide several to select and adapt to one's client. Thus, the clinician must sift through more information than less in developing a treatment intervention for the actual client. One's own client (the one who may be late or overly hostile or affected by the weather or the traffic) is seemingly never as uniform as those in the systematic reviews or the description by experts. Such is the variability of clinical practice. It is more difficult than we want to admit. We believe that one of the first steps in applying evidence-based practice is whether the clinician has carefully considered the credibility of the evidence that will guide the procedures.

As summarized by Vandiver (2002), much more successful work has been done on developing evidence-based interventions than has occurred in disseminating guidelines and protocols or seeing that they are easily available and integrated into routine practice. Advances in using evidence-based interventions have had limited success in some managed mental health care settings. For evidence-based practice to be successful it must first be accessible and then applied. This is greatly facilitated by those interventions that are manualized (e.g., LeCroy, 1994), are structured in a step-by-step format (Steketee, 1990), or contain treatment protocols such as those from the Cochrane Library that provide practical steps and procedures for facilitating client change. All too often, however, evidence-based practice requires that the practitioner structure the intervention into a workable treatment plan, which means that the session-by-session planning is unique and appropriate for the particular client condition.

CONCLUSION

In summary, what we consider a predictable continuum in the scientific revolution has, we believe, a Janus face. One side is designed to disseminate the best available knowledge to guide practice while the other side is marked by the lack of centralized and readily available information that is easily applied. This reflects the problem noted above—that there has been more success in developing evidence-based practice information than in dissemination. The challenges of using evidence-based practice are increased because the information that is available itself has variability in accuracy and utility and therefore must be weighed by the practitioner to determine its application. Add to all of this the fact that the field of available information that is, in fact, evidence for practice is growing so rapidly that keeping up is a formidable task even for the most committed practitioner who sees clients daily, whether in an independent practice, a clinic, hospital, or community setting. In the end, isn't improvement in treatments and procedures one of the targets and benefits of the scientific revolution in the first place?

For a detailed discussion of evidence-based practice concepts, databases to guide treatments, and the 5 steps to EBP clinical decisions in medical settings, see chapter 3 in this book.

REFERENCES

Corcoran, J. (2000). *Evidence-based social work practice with families.* New York: Springer.
Dear, P. (2001). *Revolutionizing the sciences: European knowledge and its ambitions, 1500–1700.* Princeton, NJ: Princeton University Press.
Fenley, M. A., Gaiter, J. L., Hummett, M., Liburd, L. C., Mercy, J. A., O'Carroll, P. W., Onwuachi-Saunders, C., Powell, K. E., & Thornton, T. N. (1993). *The prevention of youth violence: A framework for community action.* Atlanta, GA: Center for Disease Control and Prevention.
Fischer, J. (1990). Problems and issues in meta-analysis. In L. Videka-Sherman & W. Reid (Eds.), *Advances in clinical social work research* (pp. 297–325). Silver Spring, MD: National Association of Social Workers.
Gambrill, E. (1999). Evidence-based practice: An alternative to authority-based practice. *Families in Society, 80,* 341–350.
Gibbs, L., & Gambrill, E. (2002). Evidence-based practice: Counterarguments to objections. *Research on Social Work Practice, 12,* 452–476.
LeCroy, C. W. (1994). *Handbook of children and adolescent treatment manuals.* New York: Lexington.
Roberts, A. R. (Ed.) (2004). *Juvenile justice sourcebook: Past, present, and future.* New York: Oxford University Press.
Roberts, A. R., & Greene, G. J. (Eds.) (2002). *Social workers' desk reference.* New York: Oxford University Press.
Roth, A., & Fonagy, P. (1996). *What works for whom? A critical review of psychotherapy research.* New York: Guilford Press.
Simpson, J. S., Koroloff, N., Friesen, B. J., Gac, J. (Vol. Eds.) (1999). *Promising practices in family-provider collaboration: Vol. 2. Systems of care: Promising practices in children's mental health, 1998 series.* Washington, DC: Center for Effective Collaboration and Practice, American Institutes for Research.
Steketee, G. (1999). *Overcoming obsessive-compulsive disorder: A behavioral and cognitive protocol for the treatment of OCD.* Oakland, CA: New Harbinger Publications.
Vandiver, V. L. (2002). Step-by-step practice guidelines for using evidence-based practice and expert consensus in mental health settings. In A. R. Roberts & G. J. Greene (Eds.), *Social workers' desk reference.* New York: Oxford University Press.
Vandiver, V. L., & Corcoran, K. (2002). Guidelines for establishing effective treat-

ment goals and treatment plans with axis I disorders. In A. R. Roberts & G. J. Greene (Eds.), *Social workers' desk reference*. New York: Oxford University Press.

Wilson, S. J., Lipsey, M. W., & Soydan, H. (2003). Are mainstream programs for juvenile delinquency less effective with minority youth than majority youth? A meta-analysis of outcomes research. *Research on Social Work Practice, 13*, 3–26.

6

Overview of Evidence-Based Practice

RICHARD N. ROSENTHAL

INTRODUCTION AND OPERATIONALLY DEFINING EVIDENCE-BASED PRACTICE

In the good old days clinicians defined best practices from the guild's platform, and then the public tacitly accepted them. When the doctor ordered something, it was accepted as correct; if a specialist offered it, it was implicitly accepted as the best approach (Kramer & Glazer, 2001). Without detracting from the role of clinical experience and mentoring for the honing of clinical judgement in trainees, today's Dr. Welby is faced with the unlikely proposition of having to read an estimated 19 articles a day in his or her field just to keep up with the advances in clinical research. As such, without higher-level strategies to organize and evaluate qualitatively the increasing torrent of information, the knowledge base of any clinician is likely to drift away from the center or be doomed to become ever more specialized and restricted over time. Although there is a clear place for individual expertise, it has become apparent that expert intuitions and opinions are not necessarily correspondent with the results of systematic reviews of high quality research. Even the most experienced clinicians need help from reliable studies and other sources of statistical data in order to complement their clinical experience with accurate estimates of benefit and harm (Donald, 2002). Given the rapid pace with which practice is evolving, "without current best evidence, practice risks becoming rapidly out of date, to the detriment of patients" (Sackett, Rosenberg, Gray, Haynes, & Richardson, 1996).

Evidence-based practice (EBP) in behavioral health means the use of clinical interventions for a specific problem that has been (a) evaluated by well-designed clinical research studies, (b) published in peer-reviewed journals, and (c) consistently found to be effective or efficacious upon consensus review. The intention is to improve the process and outcome of care. Evidence-based practice has its roots in evidence-based medicine (EBM), the philosophic underpinnings of which emanate from 19th century France and which, more recently, Cochrane (1972) proposed as the set of methods needed to understand the effectiveness and efficiency of specific clinical interventions. The term *evidence-based medicine* was coined in the 1980s as a term for the clinical learning strategy developed at McMaster Medical School in Canada in the 1970s (Rosenberg & Donald, 1995). In order to clarify the nature of EBP, which is essentially an extension of EBM to disciplines beyond medicine, I will first describe the underlying process of EBM. According to Sackett and colleagues (1996), EBM is the conscientious explicit and judicious use of current best evidence in making decisions about the care of individual patients. This is done by asking questions, finding and appraising relevant data, and harnessing that information in the form of reliable estimates of benefit and harm for everyday clinical practice (Rosenberg & Donald, 1995). This approach to clinical problem solving requires integrating individual clinical expertise with the best available clinical evidence from systematic research.

EBM is the process of systematically finding, appraising, and using contemporaneous research findings as the basis for clinical decisions. This process is generally described as having five well-defined steps (Rosenberg & Donald, 1995; Sackett et al., 1996):

1. Format a structured, clear, and answerable clinical question from a patient's problem or information need.
2. Search the literature for relevant clinical articles that might answer the question.
3. Conduct a critical appraisal on the selected research articles and rank the evidence for its validity and usefulness (clinical applicability).
4. Formulate and apply a clinical intervention based on the useful findings, or "best evidence."
5. Conduct clinical audits to determine if the protocol was implemented properly (identify issues/problems).

Format a Structured, Clear, and Answerable Clinical Question

Evidence-based medicine can be initiated by questions related to diagnosis, prognosis, treatment, iatrogenic harm, quality of care, or health economics (Rosenberg & Donald, 1995). However, most of the time it pertains to finding the best treatment of a particular problem in the context of conditions that obscure the best clinical decision, that is, where the proper clinical intervention is not easily intuited but where making one choice or another will have significant meaning and consequence to the patient (Donald, 2003). Refining the question to one, which will yield a robust set of studies from the literature, takes some practice.

Search the Literature for Relevant Clinical Articles

Armed with a well-formed question, the clinician must construct a search for studies among electronic databases that is broad enough to include all relevant articles but not so broad that there is too much information to process. Another way to frame this is that high sensitivity of searching methodology will tend to reduce the specificity of the product, thus including many clearly unrelated articles in the search result.

Conduct a Critical Appraisal and Rank the Evidence for Validity and Usefulness

Conducting a critical appraisal requires specifying which outcome variables will be examined, the inclusion criteria to be used (e.g., randomized clinical trial), finding studies that meet these criteria, determining effect sizes for each of the outcome variables in the selected studies, and combining effect sizes across the selected studies and subjecting the result to tests for bias (Ziguras, Stuart, & Jackson, 2002). Clinical decision making is a complex process. Apart from evidence from research, clinical decisions are based on the context of a patient's current situation and his or her desires and values, as well as the values and clinical experience of the clinician. Having selected the studies with the most valid evidence, one must then weigh benefits and risks of applying the best practice versus the costs and inconveniences of alternatives in the context of the patient's values (Guyatt et al., 2000). A treatment's effectiveness and the clinician's decision to use that treatment must not automatically be determined solely by efficacy but rather by a decision as to the appropriateness of the intervention. A patient with a terminal illness and severely restricted quality of life may reasonably choose to reject cardiopulmonary resuscitation in the event of cardiac arrest, even though that intervention may be effective in restoring a heartbeat.

Formulate and Apply a Clinical Intervention Based on the Useful Findings, or "Best Evidence"

Having determined the relative benefits and harms of a specific intervention, established its suitability for the identified patient, and decided that the system of care can properly support the intervention, the clinician implements the protocol.

Conduct Clinical Audits to Determine If the Protocol Was Implemented Properly

Generating information about intervention process and outcome in the context of care delivery is the domain of practice-based research, which will be discussed in later sections of this book. The intention supported by this step is to provide feedback both to the practitioner and, if he or she works within a network, to the network in the form of positive reinforcement if the intervention was effective for the patient or information from which to derive corrective action if it wasn't. This can be done either as a quality improvement protocol or can be generated by practitioners or delivery systems as a formal research study.

Part of the evolving art in EBP revolves around how one accesses studies and systematic reviews and determines the highest quality evidence in order to answer the clinical questions. The next section of this chapter examines two domains that affect that process. The first area is that of the key concepts such as methodological quality and related levels of evidence that must guide any process of critical appraisal or systematic review. The second domain is the concept of the hierarchy of information resources, which allows one to interact with research-based information at ever higher levels of extraction.

KEY CONCEPTS AND DATABASES TO GUIDE TREATMENTS THAT FACILITATE POSITIVE CLIENT CHANGE

Key Concepts 1: Levels of Evidence, Methodological Quality

In the United States, levels of evidence are a well-known concept in the legal system, where the potential impact on the defendant dictates the standard level of evidence required. These levels move from the "preponderance of evidence" in deciding simple civil cases to a standard of "clear and convincing" evidence, and finally to requiring evidence based on certitude "beyond a reasonable doubt" in criminal cases. The development of a systematic approach to evaluating the strength of scientific evidence is a more recent development. EBM and EBP rest on an underlying postulate about a hierarchy of evidence to guide clinical decision making; thus, the evidence-based practitioner must be able to assess the quality of evidence in research studies, systematic reviews, and practice guidelines (Guyatt et al., 2000).

Methodological quality answers the question of how well are systematic bias, nonsystematic bias, and inferential error protected against in the design, conduct, and analysis of any study (Lohr & Carey, 1999). That is, how valid overall is the evidence? Validity has two main domains with respect to its use in evaluating the results of clinical studies. Internal validity is the extent to which outcome differences between comparison groups in the study are truly attributable to the clinical intervention (i.e., how correct are the results?). External validity is the extent to which the results can be generalized to populations outside the particular group studied (i.e., how will this intervention work for my patient?).

Randomization of subjects into studies tends to reduce allocation bias, that is, it lowers the risk of confounding variables in comparison groups and increases internal validity. However, the gain in internal validity is often at the expense of external validity, which is reduced when potential subjects are not included in the research, whether through narrow inclusion criteria, local unavailability of the research study, or patient decisions not to participate. For example, in testing psychotropic medications in randomized controlled trials (RCTs) for new drug applications to the Food and Drug Administration (FDA), the pharmaceutical industry has tended to conduct efficacy trials on narrowly defined samples of patients in order to maximize the differential benefit (effect size) in treated subjects as compared to controls. However, the broader the mix of subjects with problem x included in a study, the more likely a true positive result of the study intervention will be of benefit for any other person in the population with problem x. Compared to efficacy research that typically has highly restricted inclusion criteria and subjects with homogeneous characteristics, this is the focus of effectiveness research in behavioral health. As such, one can augment external validity by broadening inclusion criteria, offering the study at multiple sites, and supporting patient participation (McKee et al., 1999).

In order to evaluate the clinical literature for the best evidence to be used in constructing an EBP, one must understand that the strength of evidence presented in a study can be rated according to established standards. Guyatt and colleagues (2000) suggest that evidence in clinical studies can be broadly defined as any empirical observation about the apparent relationship between events. Early attempts by the Canadian Task Force on the Periodic Health Examination (1979) to identify and assess studies according to methodological quality have evolved into several hierarchically based systems developed to rate the strength of scientific evidence in clinical studies. Although there has been continuing differentiation and digression in the levels of evidence in recent years (e.g., see http://www.cebm.net/toolbox.asp), the main demarcations have remained explicit and stable, having been driven mostly by differences in internal validity among the study designs. Fortunately, most hierarchically based systems follow a similar pattern of ranking strength of evidence, starting with the highest level of evidence in multipatient studies:

1. Systematic reviews or meta-analysis of multiple, well-designed controlled studies
2. Well-designed individual experimental studies (randomized, controlled)
3. Well-designed quasi experimental studies (nonrandomized, controlled)
4. Well-designed nonexperimental studies (nonrandomized, uncontrolled)
5. Case series and clinical examples, expert committee reports with critical appraisal
6. Opinions of respected authorities, based on clinical experience

A simpler "A-B-C" system, based on the rating system used by the Agency for Healthcare Research and Quality (AHRQ, formerly AHCPR [Agency for Healthcare Policy and Research]) in developing its depression guidelines (Depression Guideline Panel, 1993), is the consensus panel decision process used by the guidelines development work group at the Texas Medication Algorithm Project (Gilbert et al., 1998). The A-B-C system fits evidence from a broad range of sources into three categories and may be somewhat reductionistic as compared to the levels of evidence from the Center for Evidence-Based Medicine at Oxford University (2001). However, this formal system is an active attempt to form consensus based on the strength of evidence from scientific studies, as opposed to relying on expert opinion or clinical consensus (Suppes et al., 2002). This system rates as A-level evidence to support a recommendation as that evidence which comes from randomized, placebo-controlled studies with raters blinded to study hypotheses and subjects' group membership. Obviously, high-grade evidence from systematic reviews and meta-analyses of randomized, controlled trials also fall into the A category. The B-level data are those from either very large case studies or unblinded controlled studies. This level therefore includes both well-designed quasi-experimental (not randomized) and nonexperimental (neither controlled nor randomized) studies. The C level of evidence is generated from pilot studies, case series, and case reports.

A well-designed individual RCT can provide strong evidence, particularly if there is a large sample size and the target population is diverse and geographically distributed, as in a multisite clinical trial. Observational studies such as cohort studies offer less reliable evidence than RCTs because they cannot plainly control for confounding variables between the groups studied, increasing the risk of selection bias. In addition, observational or nonexperimental studies have been described as tending to overestimate or underestimate treatment effects in an idiosyncratic fashion, making them less valid than RCTs; however, there has been some recent dispute about this (Benson & Hartz, 2000; Concato, Shah, & Horwitz, 2000; McKee et al., 1999). In addition, there are conditions where nonrandomized, uncontrolled studies can provide powerful evidence—for example, when an intervention yields the obvious, consistent, and dramatic result that the introduction of penicillin treatment did in the 1940s (Concato, Shah, & Horwitz, 2000). Generally, unsystematic clinical observations provide the weakest level of evidence from studies because they are typically made in a small number of patients, and there are no safeguards against scientific bias. Without a control group against which to compare outcomes, case studies have low internal validity. Because of small numbers of participants, these studies tend to have low external validity. For those wanting a short primer to help in understanding the different types of research methods, the EBM tutorial website at the State University of New York (SUNY) Health Sciences Center at Brooklyn gives a brief and lucid set of descriptions (http://servers.medlib.hscbklyn.edu/ebm/toc.html).

Key Concepts 2: Hierarchy of Information Resources

Clearly, it is more time-efficient and preferable for clinicians to read one systematic review about a topic than to spend many hours searching for and reading all of the primary literature (Williamson, German, Weiss, Skinner, & Bowes, 1989). Searching, appraising, and selecting from the primary literature is usually beyond the scope of busy individual practitioners. Still, the evidence-based practitioner must have core skills in interpreting statistical results and levels of evidence as well as access to evidence-based resources (Donald, 2002). In dealing with the problem of time limitations on busy clinicians for conducting evidence-based practice, Guyatt and colleagues (2000) offer the mnemonic 4S to describe the hierarchy of information resources available to clinicians. This hierarchy of information preprocessing offers increasing efficiencies in finding an evidence base for treating specific disorders in specific patients: (a) primary *Studies*, where the process is the methodical selection of only well-designed, highly relevant studies; (b) *Summaries* or systematic reviews; (c) *Synopses* of studies or systematic reviews; and (d) *Systems* of information.

Systematic reviews provide an overview of all available evidence pertaining to a specific clinical question. Evidence is located, evaluated, and synthesized using a strict scientific design that must also be reported in the review. Systematic reviews, as compared to traditional narrative reviews, attempt to reduce bias through the inclusiveness and reproducibility of the search process as well as the selection process for studies that are included (AHRQ, 2002). In addition, systematic reviews apply a rigorous critical appraisal compared to narrative reviews and are typically generated in answer to a narrow clinical question (Cook, Mulrow, & Haynes, 1997). As such, the results can be used with more confidence than narrative reviews for decision making about delivery of health care. A meta-analysis is a particular type of systematic review that uses statistical methods to combine and summarize the results of several primary studies, but it can only be done properly with RCT as the study design (Cook, Mulrow & Haynes, 1997). Systematic reviews derived from broad and comprehensive searches also provide another strength—they can reveal what is not known at a particular level of evidence. Compared to systematic reviews, the risk of relying on narrative reviews is that the selection of studies may be idiosyncratic, incomplete, or inaccurate, such that outdated or ineffective clinical directions may continue to be promoted whereas new and effective ones may not be recommended (Antman, Lau, Kupelnick, Mosteller, & Chalmers, 1992).

Synopses provide a further extraction of key methods and results of individual studies or systematic reviews for use in clinical decision making. The typical format of an evidence-based synopsis is the structured abstract, which is specifically designed to quickly reveal information about the validity of results and about applying these results to practice. These abstracts are often found in the newer secondary journals, which select papers from other journals based on whether the studies are of high methodological quality. Systems of information provide a linkage of related high-grade summaries that expands the narrow orientation of evidence-based practice from specific clinical problems into broader approaches to disease management. These may appear as practice guidelines, treatment algorithms, or decision-support software (Guyatt et al., 2000). An important caveat, however, is that systems for rating the strength of a body of evidence are currently much less uniform than those for rating the quality of a given study (AHRQ, 2001).

Rating scales and checklists have been generated that offer a standard approach to rating the strength of evidence in an individual study or a whole body of evidence. In particular, the best scales take into account the design of the study being examined. For example, the main risk for an invalid conclusion from ob-servational studies is the presence of confounding variables between groups in addition to the variable being tested. Therefore, appropriate scales for rating observational studies ask explicit questions about how much information is avail-able to assure the suitability of the comparison groups in addition to rating the quality of the exposure or intervention, the measurement of outcomes, and the statistical analysis (AHRQ, 2002; Goodman, Berlin, Fletcher, & Fletcher, 1994). A good source for finding various scales and checklists that can be used to assess the strength of scientific evidence in systematic reviews, RCTs, and observational studies is the AHRQ Evidence Report number 47, "Systems to Rate the Strength of Scientific Evidence" (2002), which can be found at www.ahrq.gov/clinic/ epcix.htm.

Because EBM involves routine use of research evidence, it was not possible prior to the introduction of large electronic research databases in the early 1990s (Donald, 2002). The years following have produced an increasing torrent of information. The types of clinical questions that EBM is best suited to answer are questions about treatment, risk factors, diagnostic tests, and epidemiology (Donald, 2003). Where there is much research, the search can be limited to RCTs. If observational studies (cohort, retrospective, cross-sectional, or nonran-domized) are going to be used, one should probably only include those that at least incorporate a control group (Benson & Hartz, 2000). Conference proceed-ings, technical reports, and discussion papers (known as *gray literature*) are not typically indexed on the main databases, yet they should be accessed when pos-sible from specialist libraries and databases in order to reduce publication bias. However, the validity of results reported in conference proceedings should be assessed before including them in the review.

LIMITATIONS

Limitations in Determinations of Quality

The concept of research quality measurement is relatively straightforward; how-ever, the actual quality determined may vary depending on the instrument used to measure it. In behavioral health there is neither consensus about the most valid process measures, such as proper dosage of medications or psychotherapy sessions, nor about the most valid outcomes metrics, such as quality of life or change in symptoms (Kramer & Glazer, 2001).

Limitations in EBP Approaches

EBM and EBP have theoretical and practical limits. EBM addresses questions about the probabilities of benefit or harm to people rather than answering ques-tions about underlying mechanisms of pathology or cure. As such, the domain of EBM/EBP is constrained to a subset of questions in clinical practice and policy that can assist the clinician in choosing whether to treat with a certain intervention or not, but EBM/EBP will not answer questions about what is actually wrong with the depressed patient's mood or dopamine receptors (Donald, 2002). Like any machine, EBP methods can only accomplish what they are designed to do. A related limitation is that even with a well-formed question the best evidence for a particular problem will be of questionable value if the problem has not been framed correctly or the diagnosis is wrong. This is why increasing diagnostic validity through a best-efforts approach to diagnosis or problem identification is so important.

The EBM approach will inevitably expose the gaps in the evidence, especially in mental health where there are many disorders with a scanty empirical research base. However, evidence alone is not sufficient to appropriately treat patients; neither is it likely that externally derived evidence will become a substitute for clinical judgment. Both individual clinical expertise and the best available external evidence are necessary for good clinical practice. "Without clinical expertise, practice risks becoming tyrannized by evidence, for even excellent external evidence may be inapplicable to or inappropriate for an individual patient" (Sackett et al., 1996). Clinicians must always weigh the risks and benefits of a particular intervention in a specific patient, regardless of the evidence base supporting that intervention, because patients may have characteristics related to compliance, age, comorbidity, and so on, that affect the estimates of benefit and risk that come from critical appraisals of the literature. If EBM is applied in an uncritical or non-patient-centered way, the results may be harmful (Naylor, 1995). As such, the issue of relevance is as important as the strength of evidence when attempting to apply results.

The critical appraisal process will generate different outcomes depending on the problem being solved, which limits its generalizability (Rosenberg & Donald, 1995). Because individual answers to clinical questions can be idiosyncratic, there should be some opportunity to generate a higher-level set of approaches that are more generic, that have greater external validity. As such, this rationale becomes one's motivation to discover the best practices, which are really about effectiveness, or how well a treatment works when given to a heterogeneous community sample of persons with a particular disorder.

Another practical limit in implementing EBP is external to the query and search process. Rather, it is located in systems of care as the lack of support structures needed for sustained evidence-based decision making. Furthermore, feasibility of evidence-based practice is constrained by lack of institutional commitment to EBP principles and insufficient skills for interpreting evidence-based information (Donald, 2002).

Limitations in Hierarchies of Evidence

Although empiricism serves as the philosophical foundation of evidence-based science, there is criticism that being overly dependent on empiricism will unnecessarily constrain the conceptual framework of psychiatry (Harari, 2001). Because processes used during the conduct of randomized controlled trials are the best at reducing confounding variables and other sources of bias, the RCT method, originally developed from bench models of empirical science, generates the most reliable evidence with the highest internal validity. However, this paradigm has essentially created a tyranny of this form of evidence in psychiatry and behavioral health. The AHRQ suggests separating out magnitude of effect from the quality of evidence, as the effect size and its positive (benefit) or negative (harm) impact is a different matter from the quality of the data. Evans (2003), in a critique of relying solely on efficacy as the indicator of the evidence quality, proposes a hierarchy of evidence that adds two independent dimensions of appropriateness and feasibility to the formal evaluation. Appropriateness does not rest solely with providers or provider systems because patient acceptance has a key role in whether or not an intervention will be useful. For example, naltrexone is highly efficacious at blocking opioid receptors, but its use in opioid dependent persons to treat addiction without other psychosocial interventions is severely limited by nonadherence with the medication regimen.

Limitations in Implementation

Feasibility can and should be evaluated in a systematic fashion, and results generated through systematic reviews and multicenter studies offer the best evidence for evaluating an intervention's feasibility (Evans, 2003). Simply because a particular intervention is effective does not mean it will be broadly implemented. Stakeholders in programmatic approaches that are not evidence-based tend not to cease providing that type of treatment simply because other evidence-based formats have been discovered. Their resistance to adoption of newer, evidence-based practices is typically composed of intellectual, economic, social, and philosophical components working in concert (Corrigan, Steiner, McCracken, Balser, & Barr, 2001). Action research is a strategy that uses a variety of quantitative and qualitative scientific methods to elucidate and address in situ problems in the care environment (Meyer, 2000). As such, action research that explores the relationships between attitudes and aspects of care or barriers to implementation of new practices can provide good quality evidence about an intervention's feasibility (Evans, 2003).

MOVEMENT TOWARD THE DEVELOPMENT OF PRACTICE GUIDELINES AND EXPERT CONSENSUS GUIDELINES

Best Practices

EBM and EBP are bottom-up approaches, starting with a specific question that derives from the problems in setting effective and appropriate treatment for a specific patient. In contrast, best practice is a top-down approach defined as the measurement, benchmarking, and identification of processes that result in better outcomes (Kramer & Glazer, 2001). Whereas the traditional point of view about mental health practice has been the individual clinician or individual clinic, the perspective of best practice requires an organizational approach to assessing variations in practice from the individual level up through groups such as hospitals and provider agencies and through regions (Glazer, 1998). The components necessary to establish best practices are data collection systems, systemic quality improvement processes, and systems of health care providers. Much of what has recently served as the basis of best practices has been gleaned from analysis and benchmarking of pooled provider data, which is often of low quality (e.g., low-resolution clinical information from hospital financial encounter data and billing records). More recently agencies such as AHRQ and the Joint Commission on Accreditation of Healthcare Organizations have created quality indicators that are driving health care provider systems toward the acquisition of better-quality clinical data for their performance improvement initiatives. When a provider organization is given feedback against benchmarks, it tends to drive the quality process. This is not only true at the macrolevel but also on the individual level, for example, when subjecting research papers to peer review (Goodman et al., 1994). However, over and above the specific contributions to individual treatment decisions made through EBM, EBM provides professional bodies with fair and scientifically rigorous means to make best-practice decisions and develop guidelines and standards (Donald, 2002). This point is important because most clinical guidelines have not been constructed using high-grade evidence (Shaney-felt, Mayo-Smith, & Rothwangl, 1999). This may be especially true of behavioral health guidelines, where issues of practice have traditionally been viewed from the perspective of the individual practitioner (Glazer, 1998).

Guidelines Development

Though originally developed through the integration of expert clinical judgment (consensus guidelines), practice guidelines as currently defined are clinical decision rules that have been systematically developed with critical assessment and evaluation of the existing literature using the best available evidence (evidence-based guidelines). This shift from expert consensus to evidence-based consensus is partly due to the increasing recognition, using critical appraisal and systematic review, that expert opinion has relatively low validity as scientific evidence when compared to meta-analyses or systematic reviews. A practical application of evidence-based approaches to clinical guidelines development is the Texas Medication Algorithm Project (TMAP). Medication treatment algorithms have been suggested as a strategy to provide uniform care at predictable costs. TMAP is a three-phase study designed to provide solid data on the usefulness of medication algorithms. In the initial phase, medication algorithms for the treatment of several severe mental disorders were developed. Then a feasibility study of these algorithms was conducted in the next phase. Finally, having demonstrated the feasibility of using these algorithms, a validation phase was implemented. This study compared the outcome and costs of using a combination of an algorithm matched to a specific disorder in one group to another group using

Table 6.1 Evidence-Based Resources

Tool kit sites
New York Academy of Medicine: *http//www.ebmny.org/teach.html* Oxford University: *http://cebm.jr2.ox.ac.uk/docs/toolbox.html* University of Alberta: *http://www.med.ualberta.ca/ebm/ebm.htm* University of Toronto Centre for Evidence-Based Medicine, Canada: *http://www.cebm.utoronto .ca/teach/* Health Information Research Unit (HIRU), McMaster University, Canada: *http://hiru.mcmaster .ca/*

Systematic reviews of the literature
National Health Society Centre for Reviews and Dissemination: *http://www.york.ac.uk/inst/crd/ centre.htm* Centre for Evidence-Based Medicine, Oxford: *http://cebm.jr2.ox.ac.uk/docs/prospect.html* Swedish Council on Technology Assessment in Health Care (SBU): *http://www.sbu.se/sbu-info .html* Cochrane Collaboration database of systematic reviews: *http://cochrane.mcmaster.ca/* Health Services/Technology Assessment Text (HSTAT), U.S. National Library of Medicine: *http://hstat.nlm.nih.gov/hq/Hquest/screen/HquestHome/s/49321* Abstracts of SBU reports: *http://www.sbu.se/abstracts/abstracts.html* The *Bandolier* newsletter on evidence-based health care

treatment as usual including a mismatched algorithm, then to a third group using typical treatment and no use of algorithms to drive treatment (Shon et al., 1999).

CONCLUSION

EBP is a powerful technology-based methodology that can support clinical decisional process, but it must start with a valid diagnosis or problem properly framed into a specific question. The well-described and standardized process entails grading studies on the strength of evidence, necessitating in those conducting EBP a working knowledge of the general standards of the hierarchies of evidence. Once a critical appraisal of the broadly screened literature results in the best evidence for action, the intervention must be weighed in context of its acceptability to the patient's desires and values and the system's capacity to successfully implement it. Limitations intrinsic to the process are that EBP is necessary but not sufficient to drive proper clinical decision making for specific patients. The patient's clinical state and values render an evidence-based intervention suitable or not suitable. Limitations to EBP found within care systems tend to be at the level of diminished implementation due to poor conceptual buy-in, deficient knowledge, or systemic inertia.

REFERENCES

Agency for Healthcare Research and Quality (AHRQ). (2002). *Systems to rate the strength of scientific evidence: Summary.* (Evidence Report/Technology Assessment No. 47, AHRQ Pub. No. 02-E015). Washington, DC: U.S. Department of Health and Human Services, Public Health Service. Retrieved February 13, 2003, from www.ahrq.gov/clinic/epcix.htm.

Agency for Healthcare Research and Quality (AHRQ). (2001). *Current methods of the U.S. preventive services task force: A review of the process.* Retrieved February 13, 2003, from www.ahcpr.gov/clinic/ajpmsuppl/harris/1.htm.

Antman, E. M., Lau, J., Kupelnick, B., Mosteller, F., & Chalmers, T. C. (1992). A comparison of results of meta-analyses of randomized control trials and recommendations of clinical experts: Treatments for myocardial infarction. *Journal of the American Medical Association, 268,* 240–248.

Benson, K., & Hartz, A. J. (2000). A comparison of observational studies and randomized, controlled trials. *New England Journal of Medicine, 342,* 1878–1886.

Canadian Task Force on the Periodic Health Examination. (1979). The periodic health examination. *Canadian Medical Association Journal, 121,* 1193–1254.

Center for Evidence-Based Medicine at Oxford University. (2001). *Levels of Evidence.* Retrieved January 2, 2003, from http://www.cebm.net/toolbox.asp.

Cochrane, A. L. (1972). *Effectiveness and efficiency: Random reflections on health services.* London: Nuffield Provincial Hospitals Trust.

Concato, J., Shah, N., & Horwitz, R. I. (2000). Randomized, controlled trials, observational studies and the hierarchy of research designs. *New England Journal of Medicine, 342,* 1887–1892.

Cook, D. J., Mulrow, C. D., & Haynes, R. B. (1997). Systematic reviews: Synthesis of best evidence for clinical decisions. *Annals of Internal Medicine, 126,* 376–380.

Corrigan, P. W., Steiner, L., McCracken, S. G., Balser, B., & Barr, M. (2001). Strategies for disseminating evidence-based practices to staff who treat people with serious mental illness. *Psychiatric Services, 52,* 1598–1606.

Depression Guideline Panel. (1993). *Depression in primary care: Vol 1. Detection and diagnosis* (Clinical Practice Guideline No. 5, AHCPR Pub. No. 93-0550). Rockville, MD: U.S. Department of Health and Human Services, Agency for Health Care Policy and Research.

Donald, A. (2002). Evidence-based medicine: Key concepts. *Medscape General Medicine, 4*(2) http://www.medscape.com/viewpublication/122_index.

Donald, A. (2003). How to practice evidence-based medicine. *Medscape General Medicine, 5*(1), http://www.medscape.com/viewpublication/122_index.

Evans, D. (2003). Hierarchy of evidence: A framework for ranking evidence evaluating healthcare interventions. *Journal of Clinical Nursing, 12,* 77–84.

Gilbert, D. A., Altshuler, K. Z., Rago, W. V., Shon, S. P., Crismon, M. L., Toprac, M. G., et al. (1998). Texas Medication Algorithm Project: Definitions, rationale, and methods to develop medication algorithms. *Journal of Clinical Psychiatry, 59*(7), 345–351.

Glazer, W. M. (1988). Defining best practices: A prescription for greater autonomy. *Psychiatric Services, 49,* 1013–1016.

Goodman, S. N., Berlin, J., Fletcher, S. W., & Fletcher, R. H. (1994). Manuscript quality before and after peer review and editing at *Annals of Internal Medicine.* *Annals of Internal Medicine, 121,* 11–21.

Guyatt, G. H., Haynes, R. B., Jaeschke, R. Z., Cook, D. J., Green, L., Naylor, C. D., et al. (2000). Users guide to the medical literature XXV. Evidence-based medicine: Principles for applying the users guides to patient care. *Journal of the American Medical Association, 284,* 1290–1296.

Harari, E. (2001). Whose evidence? Lessons from the philosophy of science and the epistemology of medicine. *Australia and New Zealand Journal of Psychiatry, 35,* 724–730.

Kramer, T. L., & Glazer, W. N. (2001). Our quest for excellence in behavioral health care. *Psychiatric Services, 52,* 157–159.

Lohr, H. N., & Carey, T. S. (1999). Assessing "best evidence": Issues in grading the quality of studies for systematic reviews. *Joint Commission Journal on Quality Improvement, 25,* 470–479.

McKee, M., Britton, A., Black, N., McPherson, K., Sanderson, C., & Bain, C. (1999). Interpreting the evidence: Choosing between randomised and non-randomised studies. *British Medical Journal, 319,* 312–315.

Meyer, J. (2000). Using qualitative methods in health related action research. *British Medical Journal, 320,* 178–181.

Naylor, C. D. (1995). Grey zones of clinical practice: Some limits to evidence-based medicine. *Lancet, 345,* 840–842.

Raine, R., Haines, A., Sensky, T., Hutchings, A., Larkin, K., & Black, N. (2002). Systematic review of mental health interventions for patients with common somatic symptoms: Can research evidence from secondary care be extrapolated to primary care? *British Medical Journal, 325,* 1082–1093.

Rosenberg, W., & Donald, A. (1995). Evidence based medicine: An approach to clinical problem solving. *British Medical Journal, 310,* 1122–1126.

Sackett, D. L., Rosenberg, W. M. C., Gray, J. A. M., Haynes, R. B., & Richardson, W. S. (1996). Evidence based medicine: What it is and what it isn't. *British Medical Journal, 312,* 71–72.

Shaneyfelt, T. M., Mayo-Smith, M. F., & Rothwangl, J. (1999). Are guidelines following guidelines? The methodological quality of clinical practice guidelines in the peer-reviewed medical literature. *Journal of the American Medical Association, 281,* 1900–1905.

Shon, S. P., Crismon, M. L., Toprac, M. G., Trivedi, M., Miller, A. L., Suppes, T., et al. (1999). Mental health care from the public perspective: The Texas Medication Algorithm Project. *Journal of Clinical Psychiatry, 60*(Suppl. 3), 16–20; discussion, 21.

Suppes, T., Dennehy, E. B., Swann, A. C., Bowden, C. L., Calabrese, J. R., Hirschfeld, R. M., et al. (2002). Report of the Texas Consensus Conference Panel on medication treatment of bipolar disorder 2000. *Journal of Clinical Psychiatry, 63*(4), 288–299.

Williamson, J. W., German, P. S., Weiss, R., Skinner, E. A., & Bowes, F., III. (1989). Health science information management and continuing education of physicians: A survey of U.S. primary care practitioners and their opinion leaders. *Annals of Internal Medicine, 110,* 151–160.

Ziguras, S. J., Stuart, G. W., & Jackson, A. C. (2002). Assessing the evidence on case management. *British Journal of Psychiatry, 181,* 17–21.

7

Implementation of Practice Guidelines and Evidence-Based Treatment

A Survey of Psychiatrists, Psychologists, and Social Workers

EDWARD J. MULLEN
WILLIAM BACON

Evidence-based practice and the associated use of practice guidelines have become important emphases in recent years within social work, psychology, and psychiatry (e.g., Gibbs, 2003; Weissman & Sanderson, 2001). These emphases stress practitioner use of methods that have been empirically demonstrated to be effective. This movement within the human service professions is a reaction to the widespread use of methods that have not been empirically tested, as well as the variability in practice of methods used.

Clinical practice guidelines have been described by the Institute of Medicine as "systematically developed statements to assist practitioner and patient decisions about appropriate health care for specific clinical circumstances" (Field & Lohr, 1990). Professional organizations and governmental agencies have formulated practice guidelines for various clinical conditions (e.g., American Academy of Child and Adolescent Psychiatry, 1994; American Psychiatric Association, 1993, 1994, 1997). These guidelines prescribe how clinicians should assess and treat clients. Sometimes the guidelines are based on research findings. Sometimes research is not available, and, therefore, the guidelines are based on professional consensus. Although practice guidelines have been promoted for several decades in medicine, this topic has received attention in social work only recently (e.g., Mullen, 2002a, 2002b; Mullen & Bacon, 2002; Rosen & Proctor, 2002; Sackett, Straus, Richardson, Rosenberg, & Haynes, 2000). Not examined is the question of how agencies and practitioners view this development. Prior research has indicated that practitioners are not likely to use research in practice (Kirk, Os-

81

malov, & Fischer, 1976; Kirk & Reid, 2002, Chapter 8). Little is known about the use of guidelines in social work practice and how social work practitioners view the use of guidelines (Sanderson, 2002). Accordingly, this chapter presents findings of one of the few studies examining practitioner attitudes toward and use of practice guidelines and other aspects of evidence-based practice (Addis & Krasnow, 2000).

We conducted a survey examining practitioner awareness of practice guidelines, specification of guidelines known about and used by individual practitioners, practitioner attitudes toward the use of guidelines, and their preferences for guidelines based on expert consensus or based on empirical research findings. In addition, the survey examined a variety of aspects of research use for practice. The survey was conducted in a large, urban, nonprofit social agency.

METHOD

The agency surveyed is among the largest of its type in the United States. It is noted for the high quality of its services and training programs. Master's-level social workers are the primary providers of service, although the staff is multi-disciplinary, including psychologists, psychiatrists, and other mental health professionals. At the time of the survey, the agency employed a professional staff of 697. Of this number, 500 were engaged in provision of clinical services, including 42 psychiatrists, 53 psychologists, 386 social workers, and 19 other mental health professionals. This was the population surveyed. The organization provided a list of all professional staff employed by the agency at the time of the survey, August 1999. A questionnaire was sent by the organization to each staff member addressed to his or her home. A cover letter from the agency executive director stressed the importance of the survey and asked for cooperation. The cover letter explained that the study was seeking information regarding clinical practice and that it was being conducted by a university-based social work research center. Respondents were asked not to write their names on the questionnaire. They were assured that their questionnaires and responses would be anonymous. The questionnaires were to be returned to the research center. Questions were to be directed to the center rather than to the employing organization. Because of the assurance of anonymity and the methods employed, we assume that practitioners provided honest answers.

SAMPLE CHARACTERISTICS

Of the 500 questionnaires mailed to the practitioners' homes, 124 usable ones were returned (24.8%). Of these 124 respondents, 65.3% (81) were social workers, 12.9% (16) were psychologists, 13.7% (17) were psychiatrists, and 8.1% (10) were other mental health professionals (e.g., art therapists). Relative to the population distribution, social workers were somewhat less likely to have responded to the survey (21%, 81 of 386) than the other professions (38%, 43 of 114). With an overall return rate of approximately 25%, one cannot be confident that the respondents are representative of the total population of clinicians at the agency. It is reasonable to suppose that on average respondents were more favorably disposed to research than their nonresponding colleagues. One might also assume that respondents were less likely to be those who felt overburdened by paperwork and administrative demands. The number of respondents who were psychologists or psychiatrists was especially small, and conclusions pertaining to those professions must be made with caution. Because the 10 respondents classified as "other mental health professionals" are from a range of professions, it is not possible to treat them as a homogeneous professional group. Accordingly, they are excluded in the following analyses; subsequently, we report on a total set of 114 respondents. While no claim of representativeness can be made, the findings do provide initial information regarding an important and unresearched area of pertinence to practice. Nevertheless, the low response rate must be recognized as a serious limitation, and generalizations from this sample to professional groups can be made only with extreme caution.

Nearly three fourths (71.9%, $N = 82$) of the respondents reported their highest academic degree to be a master's degree, 14.9% ($N = 17$) reported an MD, and 13.2% ($N = 15$) reported a PhD or its equivalent (13.2%, $N = 15$). All social workers and one psychologist held the master's degree as the highest degree. Of the 112 respondents providing information, the large majority of respondents were employed in an outpatient clinic (61.6%, $N = 69$) or a residential facility (23.2%, $N = 26$). Other reported locations were scattered-site facility (3.6%, $N = 4$), day treatment program (5.4%, $N = 6$), school-based program (1.8%, $N = 2$), and other type of facility (4.5%, $N = 5$). Nearly all the respondents (95.6%, $N = 109$) were engaged in direct practice, and some were also engaged in clinical supervision, clinical training, and administration of clinical services. Most of the respondents reported full-time employment (63.2%, $N = 72$). The length of time employed by this agency ranged from 2 months to 40 years. The median was 3 years, whereas the mode was 1 year. Approximately 28% (28.6%, $N = 15$) of the respondents had worked for the organization 1 year or less, whereas 25% ($N = 36$) had worked at the organization for 6 or more years. The number of years since licensure or certification ranged from 1 to 49. The median was 7 years, whereas the mode was 1 to 2 years. About a quarter (24.6%) of the respondents had received licensure or certification within the past 2 years, whereas 26.4% had received licensure or certification 16 or more years earlier.

ABOUT PRACTICE GUIDELINES

We asked about the practitioners' knowledge of and attitudes toward practice guidelines. As an introduction to these questions, we provided a brief description of what we meant by practice guidelines. Because we found that there were systematic differences among the professions, the findings are presented by profession.

Heard About Practice Guidelines

We asked the respondents if they had ever heard of practice guidelines before this survey. Nearly all of the psychiatrists (94.1%) had heard about practice guidelines, and the overwhelming majority of psychologists (81.3%) had also heard about guidelines, but fewer than half of the social workers had heard of them (42.3%).

Know of a Particular Guideline

When asked if they were aware of a particular guideline, most psychiatrists said they were aware of at least one (87.5%), but relatively few psychologists (12.5%) or social workers (18.4%) reported awareness of even one guideline. For those who said that they were aware of a guideline, we asked them to specify the organization that had developed the guideline and/or what disorder or situation it addressed. Fourteen of the 17 psychiatrists said they knew of a particular guideline, and 12 of these listed the American Psychiatric Association and the American Academy of Child and Adolescent Psychiatry. Just 2 of the 16 psychologists reported knowing a guideline, and no psychologist actually listed an organization. Only 14 of the 81 social workers reported knowing a particular guideline, and just 3 of these listed organizations.

Twelve of the 17 psychiatrists responded that they were aware of guidelines pertaining to a range of mental disorders, including schizophrenia, substance abuse, eating disorders, bipolar disorder, major depression, dementia, anxiety disorders, panic disorder, and borderline personality disorders. Eight of 81 social workers listed disorder-specific or situation-specific guidelines. These were guidelines pertaining to child abuse and neglect reporting, suicide intervention, depression therapy, trauma assessment, posttraumatic stress disorder, how to treat and transfer juvenile sex offenders, teenagers in residential care with conduct disorders, borderline personality disorder, and treatment of depression in residential treatment centers. One of the 16 psychologists indicated awareness of a guideline pertaining to depression evaluation for medication.

Used Guideline

Respondents were asked if they had ever used any practice guideline to help them plan treatment. The majority of psychiatrists (64.3%) said they had, only one psychologist (6.3%) had, and about one in five social workers (18.7%) had used a guideline. For those who said they had used a guideline, we asked what the guideline was and what their experience had been with the guideline's use. For those who said they had not used a guideline, we asked why they had not used one. Most of the social workers who had used a guideline reported vague comments about why a guideline had been used. Only three of the comments could be classified as indicating that the guideline was considered to have been useful to improve treatment. Two indicated that the reason for use was that the guideline was required. One psychologist who had used a guideline commented, "I followed a guideline and have found it helpful." Three guideline-using psychiatrists provided vague or neutral comments, and one commented that it improved treatment ("I have used the dementia guidelines to look for treatment options for family members with a particular client").

Among social workers who had *not* used a practice guideline, the majority of the comments related to being unaware of the existence of guidelines. Some social workers provided vague or neutral comments. Two expressed a lack of need for guidelines ("I have followed the guidance of supervisors & colleagues who have extensive knowledge working with clients experiencing depression"; "agency administrative guidelines from beginning contact with a client to discharge have been clear—changed and/or modified in time and work well"). One said guidelines were not relevant ("sometimes it seems like guidelines don't incorporate culturally relevant issues + what to do"). No social worker volunteered a strongly negative opinion of guidelines' potential usefulness, a sentiment expressed frequently by psychologists ("I don't like following a formula if it doesn't feel right for the patient"; "I am mistrustful of guidelines that seem to encourage cost-saving procedures, or exclude patient/clinician from decision"; "I'm very much a believer in the complexity of development, individual difference, and the fact that the same symptom/syndrome meant very different things in different people—and thus required different intervention"). Among other psychologists' responses, some pertained to guideline irrelevance ("didn't feel that such guidelines were relevant to the cases I was treating"; "didn't apply to the population working with"). Only one psychologist mentioned not being aware of guidelines, and three provided vague or neutral comments as to lack of use. Four psychiatrists commented on reasons for not using guidelines ("I have read the guidelines but don't necessarily look them up for each and every case"; "haven't had enough time or opportunities to use yet"; "Already had information"; "not needed").

Inclination to Use Guidelines

We asked whether respondents were inclined to use guidelines, regardless of whether they had used them in the past. Most psychiatrists (86.7%) and social workers (81.4%) were inclined to use guidelines, whereas about half of the psychologists were so inclined (54.5%). When asked to say why they were or were not inclined to use guidelines, several reasons were common. For social workers who were inclined to use guidelines, the most common type of response (10 of 24 responses) related to guidance. These respondents indicated that they thought guidelines would help them in conceptualizing or planning treatment. Two others specifically mentioned that guidelines would increase their knowledge or skills. Four said that guidelines would improve treatment. Four social workers mentioned or implied that they were attracted to practice guidelines because of their research basis. The remaining comments made reference to willingness to use guidelines if they were not burdensome and if they were easily accessible.

Four psychologists commented on why they would be inclined to use guidelines. They referred to guidance ("if clear and helpful"), their research base ("I'm interested in effective techniques based on empirical data"), and other qualifications ("contingent on the care and guideline restrictions"; "I nevertheless reserve the right to use my clinical judgment in specific cases"). Six psychiatrists commented on why they would use guidelines, mostly making reference to their value in providing guidance ("for reference and guidance"; "They are helpful in approach to patient case"; "standardized consensus"; "as a guide to my own thinking"; "useful in client planned treatment"; "Only because they comply with my practice").

Among social workers who were *not* inclined to use practice guidelines, explanatory comments were usually vague rather than expressing concern about the validity of practice guidelines. On the other hand, psychiatrists and psychologists were more likely to describe a specific objection to practice guidelines.

Guideline Preference

Respondents were asked which type of guideline they would be more inclined to use: those based on research findings or those based on professional consensus (whether or not research supported the consensus). A number of the respondents selected both answer choices (43.8% of psychiatrists, 13.4% of social workers, and 7.1% of psychologists). Of those who selected only one choice, psychiatrists most often said they would be most inclined to use those supported by research (50% for research-only; 6.3% for consensus-only), whereas both social workers and psychologists said they would be most inclined to use those based on professional consensus (social workers: 50.7% for consensus-only vs. 35.8% for research-only; and for psychologists 50.0% for consensus-only vs. 42.9% for research-only).

Practice Conforms to Guidelines

We asked respondents if they thought their current practice conformed to what existing guidelines prescribe. All of the psychologists and most psychiatrists (85.7%) responded affirmatively, whereas about three fourths of social workers (74.1%) thought this. When asked why they thought that their practice did or did not conform, they gave a range of answers. Those who thought their practice did not conform mentioned that the guidelines probably were not promulgated by other social workers, that guidelines probably emphasized short-term treatments, or that practice guidelines are not generally consulted for treatment planning. For those who believed that their practice probably did conform to practice guidelines, most made general statements about their professional competence or the apparent effectiveness of their work.

OTHER INDICATORS OF EVIDENCE-BASED PRACTICE

We asked about other indicators of an evidence-based approach to practice, including frequency of reading professional publications, especially research publications; use of single-subject designs; use of assessment instruments in practice; and seeking consultation from the literature, supervisors, and colleagues regarding research evidence for practice decisions.

Reading or Referring to Journal Articles

We asked how often respondents read or referred to journal articles in their field. The modal responses were strikingly different across professions: one or two times a month for social workers, about once a week for psychologists, and a few times a week for psychiatrists. The response distribution is shown in Table 7.1 under the columns labeled *Articles*.

Reading Other Professional Literature

We also asked how often they read professional literature other than journal articles (e.g., books, newsletters). These responses are shown in Table 21.1 under the columns labeled *Other*.[1] Nearly one quarter of social workers replied that they did this less than once or twice a month (24.6%), with 9.8% reporting doing this once or twice a year or less. About half (51.8%) reported reading or referring to other professional literature at least weekly. No psychiatrist reported such low frequency, with nearly half saying they did this daily or a few times a week (47.0%). Nearly three quarters (70.5%) reported reading or referring to other professional literature at least weekly. Psychologists reported a pattern somewhere in between, with somewhat more than half (56.3%) responding about once a week or once or twice a month and more than one third (37.5%) responding at least weekly.

Table 7.1   Reading or Referring to Publications

Frequency	Social Workers				Psychologists				Psychiatrists			
	Articles		Other		Articles		Other		Articles		Other	
	N	%	N	%	N	%	N	%	N	%	N	%
Daily or nearly so	5	6.3	7	8.6	0	0.0	0	0	3	17.6	3	17.6
A few times a week	11	13.8	17	21.0	3	18.8	4	25.0	7	41.2	5	29.4
About once a week	14	17.5	18	22.2	6	37.5	2	12.5	3	17.6	4	23.5
Once or twice a month	26	32.5	19	23.5	5	31.3	7	43.8	4	23.5	4	23.5
Several times a year	13	16.3	12	14.8	1	6.3	3	18.8	0	0.0	1	5.9
Once or twice a year	7	8.8	4	4.9	1	6.3	0	0.0	0	0.0	0	0.0
Less than once a year	4	5.0	4	4.9	0	0.0	0	0.0	0	0.0	0	0.0

Table 7.2   Reading or Referring to Research Journal Articles

Number of Types Read	Social Workers		Psychologists		Psychiatrists	
	N	%	N	%	N	%
0 (none)	23	29.1	3	18.8	3	17.6
1 (reads 1 type)	17	21.5	1	6.3	7	41.2
2 (reads 2 types)	16	20.3	4	25.0	3	17.6
3 (reads 3 types)	23	29.1	8	50.0	4	23.5

Reading or Referring to Research Journal Articles

We asked what types of articles respondents read. Listed were case studies, clinical theory, research articles on populations or clinical problems, research articles on clinical assessment or interventions, and research articles on outcomes or effectiveness of particular therapeutic techniques. We report here on their responses about research articles only, combining the three types of research articles into a single measure. Accordingly, a respondent who reported reading all three types of research articles would receive a score of 3, if two types a score of 2, if one type a score of 1, and if none a score of 0. As shown in Table 7.2, the modal responses were 3 for psychiatrists, 1 for psychologists, and bimodal for social workers, with approximately 29% reporting 0 and 29% reporting 3. There was considerable variation among social workers, whereas the other professionals tended to be less varied in their responses.

Using Research Literature for Practice Decisions

We asked if the practitioners ever consulted the research literature when they needed to make a decision about how to proceed in treating a particular case. Most of the psychiatrists (94.1%) and psychologists (87.5%) said they did, but only 64.6% of the social workers said this. For those who said they did consult the research literature, we asked how often they did so. The modal response for all professionals was "several times a year" (32% of social workers, 50% of psychiatrists, and 42.9% of psychologists). Of those social workers who responded that they did consult the research literature, 24.5% said they did this at least weekly, whereas only 14.3% of the psychiatrists consulted this frequently and none of the psychologists reported this frequency.

Using Research Methods in Practice

We asked about the practitioners' use of single-subject designs and assessment instruments in their own practice during the preceding 2 years. No psychologist reported conducting a single-subject design study, and only about 1 in 10 of the social workers (11.3%) and psychiatrists (11.8%) reported doing so. Of those saying they had conducted such studies, the number of studies conducted during the 2-year period was almost always one.

Practitioners were asked if they had used the results from any standardized assessment instrument to help them assess a client's symptoms or response to treatment. Psychologists almost always responded that they had (87.5%), nearly three fourths of the psychiatrists said they had (70.6%), but somewhat less than a third of the social workers said they had (30.4%). Of those who said they had, we asked if they themselves had administered any of these instruments. Nearly all of the psychologists (90.9%) and psychiatrists (100%) said they had, whereas only a little over half of the social workers said they did (58.3%). Of those who said they had used standardized assessment instrument results, we asked them to name those instruments they had used most often. Social workers and psychiatrists most frequently cited simple symptom checklists such as the Beck Depression Inventory. Multisymptom instruments such as the Achenbach were also relatively common. Psychologists were much more likely to employ personality tests such as the Rorschach, along with cognitive and achievement tests.

Reasons for Changing Practice

We asked practitioners if research findings of favorable or unfavorable outcomes with a certain technique ever caused them to change their practice, such as starting or stopping a particular treatment technique with some or all of their clients. We also asked if such changes had ever been brought about by their own experience of what works and what doesn't work or by demands of administration or the mental health care marketplace. If they said any of these three had caused a change, we asked them to specify what the change was and when the most recent change had occurred.

Almost all psychiatrists said that research findings had changed their practice (93.8% or 15 of 16), whereas 42.9% of psychologists (6 of 14) and 40.6% of social workers (26 of 64) said this. In contrast, demands of administration or of the mental health care marketplace were said to have changed practice for approximately three quarters of social workers (76.8%) and psychologists (73.3%) but for only about half of the psychiatrists (56.3%). Nearly all reported that their own experiences had changed their practice (87.1% of social workers, 93.8% of psychologists, and 94.1% of psychiatrists).

Regarding what aspect of their practices had been changed by research findings, all the psychiatrists who answered the question ($N = 6$) mentioned medications. Social workers and psychologists gave a much wider variety of answers, most mentioning particular techniques or treatment modalities that they had begun to use, such as behavioral techniques for learning disabilities or eating disorders, cognitive techniques for anger management, or eye movement desensitization and reprocessing for trauma.

Using Supervisors and Colleagues for Practice Decisions

As noted previously, we had asked if the practitioners ever consulted the research literature when they needed to make a decision about how to proceed in treating a particular case. We also asked if, when needing to make a decision about how to proceed in treating a particular case, they ever consulted with a supervisor or colleague. Respondents were then asked to estimate the degree to which their consultations were directed at the consultant's knowledge of research findings, knowledge of clinical theory, clinical wisdom or experience, or knowledge of administrative requirements. With the exception of a few psychiatrists, all respondents reported using consultation. Most social workers (80.6%) said they sought consultation a few times a week (32.5%), weekly (24.7%), or one or two times a month (23.4%). By contrast, the majority of psychiatrists said they did so only several times a year (57.1%), and none reported more often than once a week. Psychologists' modal response was one or two times a month. Consultation was sought at least weekly by 70.1% of social workers, 50% of psychologists, and 21.4% of psychiatrists.

One third of the respondents (41 of 124) said they sought the consultant's knowledge of research findings. The distribution differed little among the professions. Sixty-nine percent of the respondents said they sought the consultant's knowledge of clinical theory (85 of 124). This was true for approximately three quarters of social workers and psychologists but only 41% of the psychiatrists. Seeking consultation regarding administrative requirements was common for all professionals (67.9% of social workers, 50.0% of psychologists, 41.2% of psychiatrists). With few exceptions, respondents also sought the consultant's clinical wisdom and experience.

IMPLICATIONS

These findings have implications for developing and using practice guidelines and evidence-based practice in social work. Viewed from the perspective of how practitioners working in organizations such as the one surveyed in this study think of practice guidelines and other aspects of evidence-based practice, we draw a number of conclusions. The three mental health professions represented in this survey were strikingly different in their knowledge of practice guidelines. Psychiatrists appeared to be relatively well informed about relevant practice guidelines, whereas social workers were poorly informed, typically not even aware of the meaning of practice guidelines. Psychologists were somewhere in between. Once told what practice guidelines were, social workers were inclined to be open to their use.

Social workers generally were not using research findings or research methods in their practice. Psychiatrists and, to a lesser extent, psychologists were using findings and methods of assessment. Many social workers did not often read the research literature or even other professional literature. Psychiatrists read this literature frequently. Social workers were heavy users of consultation, much more so than the other professionals, who functioned more autonomously. Social workers frequently sought guidance and direction from supervisors and other consultants, who were viewed as repositories of knowledge based on experience and as spokespersons for organizational policy.

Given the low use of research methods and infrequent reading of professional literature, it is not likely that social work practitioners will be influenced significantly through these routes. Rather, supervisors and consultants seem to be the most promising conduit for knowledge regarding practice guidelines and other forms of evidence-based practice for social workers. Social workers appeared to be open to guidelines, so long as they are perceived as helping them improve practice, but their preference was for guidelines that represent professional consensus rather than research evidence. A few social work practitioners deviated from this norm, appearing to function more autonomously through behaviors more like those of the psychiatrists in the sample. These social workers expressed preference for evidence-based guidelines, and they have higher frequencies of reading research articles and professional publications. It is likely that they use supervisors and consultants differently as well. These types of social workers may be important resources for dissemination of evidence-based practice knowledge within social work organizations. It is likely that their training has provided them with research skills of relevance to practice.

The reported findings have implications for technologies needed to assist practitioners in identification and use of evidence-based practice guidelines, for quality control and accountability, and for education. Future work is needed to develop and test technologies that can facilitate the use of evidence-based practice. Because of the crucial role played by social work supervisors regarding information, dissemination research is needed to further understand how this resource can be better used to advance evidence-based practice in social work. Also, research is needed to better understand the characteristics of those social workers who are high users of research, as well as how these types of social workers might be used as agents of research dissemination in social work organizations. Finally, because the study reported here is limited to one agency, studies are needed examining additional practitioners in a wide range of settings to determine how representative our findings are of the larger group of human service practitioners and to identify characteristics of situations wherein evidence-based practice and empirically based practice guidelines have been adopted.

NOTE

1. Missing information is excluded from the tabulated results in Tables 7.1 and 7.2, accounting for variation in the sample sizes shown.

REFERENCES

Addis, M. E., & Krasnow, A. D. (2000). A national survey of practicing psychologists' attitudes toward psychotherapy treatment manuals. *Journal of Consulting and Clinical Psychology, 68*(2), 331–339.

American Academy of Child and Adolescent Psychiatry. (1994). Practice parameters for the assessment and treatment of children and adolescents with schizophrenia. *Journal of the American Academy of Child and Adolescent Psychiatry, 33*, 616–635.

American Psychiatric Association. (1993). Practice guideline for major depressive disorder in adults. *American Journal of Psychiatry, 150*(Suppl. 4), 1–29.

American Psychiatric Association. (1994). Practice guideline for treatment of patients with bipolar disorder. *American Journal of Psychiatry, 151* (12), 1–36.

American Psychiatric Association. (1997). Practice guideline for the treatment of patients with schizophrenia. *American Journal of Psychiatry, 154*(12), 1–63.

Field, M. J., & Lohr, K. N. (Eds.). (1990). *Clinical practice guidelines: Directions of a new program.* Washington, DC: National Academy Press.

Gibbs, L. E. (2003). *Evidence-based practice for the helping professions: A practical guide with integrated multimedia.* Pacific Grove, CA: Brooks/Cole–Thompson Learning.

Kirk, S. A., Osmalov, M., & Fischer, J. (1976). Social workers' involvement in research. *Social Work, 21*, 121–124.

Kirk, S. A., & Reid, W. J. (2002). *Science and social work: A critical appraisal.* New York: Columbia University Press.

Mullen, E. J. (2002a). *Evidence-based knowledge: Designs for enhancing practitioner use of research findings.* Paper presented at the fourth International Conference on Evaluation for Practice, University of Tampere, Tampere, Finland.

Mullen, E. J. (2002b). *Evidence-based social work—theory & practice: Historical and reflective perspective.* Paper presented at the fourth International Conference on Evaluation for Practice, University of Tampere, Tampere, Finland.

Mullen, E. J., & Bacon, W. F. (2003). Practitioner adoption and implementation of evidence-based effective treatments and issues of quality control. In A. Rosen & E. K. Proctor (Eds.), *Developing practice guidelines for social work interventions: Issues, methods, and a research agenda.* New York: Columbia University Press.

Research on Social Work Practice. (1999). *9*(3).

Rosen, A., & Proctor, E. (Eds.). (2003). *Developing practice guidelines for social work interventions: Issues, methods, and a research agenda.* New York: Columbia University Press.

Sackett, D. L., Straus, S. E., Richardson, W. S., Rosenberg, W., & Haynes, R. B. (2000). *Evidence-based medicine: How to practice and teach EBM* (2nd ed.). New York: Churchill Livingstone.

Sanderson, W. C. (2002). Are evidence-based psychological interventions practiced by clinicians in the field? *Medscape Psychiatry and Mental Health: A Medscape eMed Journal, 7*(1). Retrieved from http://www.medscape.com/viewarticle/414948

Steketee, G. (1999). Yes, but cautiously. *Research on Social Work Practice, 9*, 343–346.

Weissman, M. M., & Sanderson, W. C. (2001). *Promises and problems in modern psychotherapy: The need for increased training in evidence based treatments.* Unpublished manuscript.

8

Concise Standards for Developing Evidence-Based Practice Guidelines

ENOLA K. PROCTOR

AARON ROSEN

The central challenge now confronting the profession of social work is ensuring and demonstrating that its services are effective. In our view, agencies and individual practitioners can best enhance their effectiveness by using treatment approaches that are evidence-based. Practicing on the basis of scientifically tested evidence is responsible, consistent with social work's values and commitment to client welfare and improvement, and responsive to societal expectations and National Association of Social Workers (NASW) aspirations for effective and accountable practice. Yet we recognize the many challenges inherent in the application of evidence-based approaches in day-to-day practice. Our chapter addresses some of those challenges and lays out steps through which practitioners' ability to apply evidence-based practice can be enhanced.

MEANING OF EVIDENCE-BASED PRACTICE

Evidence-based practice (EBP) has been described in terms of a number of attributes. Most simply, it is the use of treatments for which there is sufficiently persuasive evidence to support their effectiveness in attaining the desired outcomes (Rosen & Proctor, 2002). Consistent with but not exhaustive of definitions by others (Gambrill, 1999; Gonzales, Ringeisen, & Chambers, 2002), we emphasize here three attributes of evidence-based practice: (a) Empirical, research-based support for the effectiveness of interventions is the most persuasive evidence for practice decisions (Rosen, 2002); (b) empirically supported interventions must be critically assessed for their fit to and appropriateness for the practice situation at hand and must be supplemented or modified according to the practitioner's experience and knowledge; and (c) practice should be regularly monitored, and revisions to the course of treatment should be based on a recursive process of outcome evaluation (Proctor & Rosen, in press; Rosen, 2002).

BACKGROUND AND CONTEXT

Evidence-based practice originated as evidence-based medicine (EBM) and subsequently influenced clinical psychology and social work as EBP. Within social work, EBP was first and more widely embraced in Great Britain. Although practitioners have long been urged to apply research in their day-to-day practice and to use approaches with demonstrated effectiveness, the work of Eileen Gambrill (e.g., 1999) could be credited with advancing the concept of EBP in social work in the United States. Evidence-based practice is lodged within broader, longstanding premises about social work practice. First, EBP is consistent with the expectations that practitioners need to identify, explicate, and provide a persuasive rationale for their practice decisions. In evidence-based practice, those decisions must be based, to the fullest extent possible, on the best available and most appropriate research evidence. While managed care accelerated practitioners' need to describe and justify their treatment plans, practitioners have long been encouraged to systematize their treatment plans and provide a rationale for their decisions (Rosen, Proctor, & Livne, 1985; Rosen, Proctor, Morrow-Howell, & Staudt, 1995).

Evidence-based practice is also consistent with a long-standing emphasis within social work on testing and demonstrating practice effectiveness. Research on effective social work practices has grown markedly (Reid & Fortune, in press), increasing the supply of evidence-based practices for practitioners' selection and use (cf. Thyer & Wodarski, 1998). Another recent trend supporting the application of EBP is the increased use of treatment manuals (Fraser, in press). Treatment manuals detail the interventions that have been found to be effective in research studies. Their clear and detailed descriptions of the relevant worker actions and behavior facilitate the application of EBP.

Evidence-based practice is further lodged within an assumption that social work practice should be focused on outcomes and its success evaluated in terms of actually attaining the desired outcomes (Rosen & Proctor, 1978, 1981). As such, it is important that the research upon which practice is based clearly demonstrates the linkages between interventions and the outcomes toward which they are directed (Rosen & Proctor, 2002). Finally, EBP is consistent with the movement to develop and make available guidelines for practice or constellations of practice approaches that, based on current evidence, are deemed to be most effective in addressing certain problems or attaining certain targeted outcomes.

Although practitioners have long been exhorted to use the findings of research, proponents of evidence-based social work practice have grown in number and strength. A fundamental challenge for EBP is practitioners' acceptance of pretested, standardized, empirically supported treatments (ESTs) as a legitimate foundation for practice. This chapter identifies and addresses the steps necessary to identify, select, and apply in day-to-day practice those interventions that have a base of empirical support.

STRATEGIES FOR IMPLEMENTING EVIDENCE-BASED PRACTICE

Although our chapter focuses on the selection, modification, and application of interventions, the treatment process begins with assessment. Vandiver (2002) describes a process for applying practice guidelines, commencing with assessment, making a diagnosis, identifying problems, and deciding the goals or targets of change, which we refer to as treatment outcomes (Proctor & Rosen, in press; Rosen & Proctor, 2002). The reader is encouraged to refer to Vandiver's (2002) discussion, for our strategies commence at the point in the treatment process where assessment, diagnosis, and problem formulation have resulted in designating the desired ultimate and intermediate outcomes to be pursued through intervention. It is important to underscore the point that practice should focus on outcome. The purpose of intervention is to achieve desired outcomes, and interventions should be selected for their potential to attain the outcomes.

Once problem assessment and formulation of desired outcomes are accomplished, the use of empirically tested knowledge necessitates four types of actions: (a) identify potential empirically supported treatments (ESTs) that are relevant to the outcomes to be pursued; (b) select the best-fitting intervention (EST) in view of the client problems, situation, and outcome; (c) supplement and modify the EST as needed, drawing on practitioner experience and knowledge; and (d) monitor and evaluate intervention effectiveness.

Step 1:   Locate evidence-based interventions relevant to the outcomes for pursuit.

The first challenge in implementing EBP is identifying and obtaining information about interventions that have been empirically tested and supported. In the search for EBPs, practitioners should use as their point of departure the outcomes they are striving to achieve with and for a given client. For example, when working to achieve an outcome "to increase client's skills of conflict resolution," the practitioner should search for interventions for which there is research evidence as to their effectiveness in attaining this outcome. The practitioner should seek to identify not just one intervention but rather a repertoire or set of alternative interventions that have solid empirical support for attaining the outcome.

Identifying relevant evidence-based interventions is made challenging by the fact that much of the practice literature is written and organized around problems addressed, not necessarily outcomes sought. That is, while research may report on interventions for the client's relevant population, presenting problem(s), or both, the practitioner must look closely to ascertain that effectiveness was assessed in terms of the outcomes that are actually being pursued.

Where can such evidence be found? First, and in our view ideally, practice guidelines can be a valuable source of empirically supported interventions (Proctor & Rosen, in press). Various practice, professional, and public health organizations have approved and published guidelines and treatment recommendations for a variety of problems and outcomes. Guidelines have a number of advantages: They are well focused around particular practice issues, are oriented to practitioners, may refer to specific client populations or practice conditions, and are worded specifically enough to offer practitioners clear guidance and direction as to the steps to be taken in treatment. To the extent that guidelines are based on empirical research, they offer the considerable advantage of having already been subjected to extensive guideline-development processes that weighed and compared evidence and selected the most effective approaches. Guidelines thereby ease this burden for practitioners. However, at present, three factors may serve to limit the usefulness of some guidelines for social workers. First, some extant guidelines may not be based on empirical support but instead on a consensual process that integrates and summarizes accumulated practice wisdom and expertise in a particular area. To the extent that they are not based on research, their use may not advance evidence-based practice. Second, as noted previously with regard to research studies, some guidelines are not outcome focused but rather address diagnostic categories, probably leaving unclear the specific outcome for which the intervention can be appropriately used. Third, some medicine- and psychiatry-oriented guidelines may emphasize pharmacological treatment.

However, guidelines increasingly contain interventions relevant to social work, including psychosocial, behavioral, and family system interventions. Proctor and Rosen (in press) present a model of practice guidelines for social work and the organizational, professional, and research efforts needed to foster their development. Examples of research-based guidelines with high relevance to social work practice can be found at a number of Internet Web sites. The National Guideline Clearinghouse at http://www.guidelines.gov. lists practice guidelines, organized by problem/disorder or treatment/intervention. This site lists 46 psychotherapy guidelines, such as for the treatment of school-age children with attention-deficit/hyperactivity disorder, depression treatment, and treatment of sexual dysfunction. The American Psychological Association Web site also provides recommendations and information about empirically supported treatments (ESTs) (http://www.apa.org/divisions/div12/rev_est/), including for anxiety disorder, posttraumatic stress disorder, obsessive-compulsive disorder, and stressful events. Finally, the National Institute of Drug Abuse's (NIDA) Web site provides EBP recommendations for treating a variety of addictions (http://www.drugabuse.gov/TXManuals/).

Systematic critical reviews of intervention studies in a given area are a second valuable source of empirically supported interventions. For the practitioner, critical reviews have several advantages: The relevant research literature has been carefully canvassed, the goodness of the evidence has already been assessed systematically and carefully, and the findings are succinctly summarized. However, as with practice guidelines, practitioners must carefully ascertain the fit between the outcomes they target for pursuit and the outcomes evaluated in the research studies. Systematic reviews of research supporting interventions are widely published in psychology, and their number is growing in social work. The Campbell Collaboration provides an umbrella for the conduct of systematic reviews of research in the areas of criminal justice, education, and social welfare, and it summarizes the information in a relatively consumable form (http://www.campbellcollaboration.org/Fralibrary.html). Critical reviews are currently being prepared on such topics as the impact of welfare reform on family structure, cognitive and behavioral interventions for sexually abused children, psychosocial interventions for adolescents with anorexia nervosa, and group-based parent training programs.

Journal articles reporting the results of studies testing the effectiveness of interventions are a third source of evidence-based practices. For practitioners needing guidance about how to treat a particular case, the tasks of locating relevant studies and evaluating their scientific merit and validity may be very challenging. However, agencies and individual practitioners engaged in highly specialized areas of practice, with routine access to research-based journals and time to read them, might avail themselves of knowledge about interventions with a high degree of research support, even before that knowledge is included in systematic reviews and practice guidelines. The Program on Assertive Community Treatment (PACT model) is an example of an intervention program whose effectiveness has been supported in a number of research studies. Indeed, PACT's solid base of evidence has earned it the endorsement of the National Association for the Mentally Ill (NAMI) as the treatment of choice.

Textbooks and edited volumes containing chapters about practice are a fourth source of evidence-based practices. Many such books are based on and also provide detail about the extent of empirical support. For example, Thyer and Wodarski (1998) have published a two-volume book organizing evidence-based interventions around various social problems and psychiatric diagnoses. Reid and Fortune (in press) overview the extent of support for 130 social work intervention programs that were studied in the decade of the 1990s. And in the area of marriage and family therapy, a recent book compiles empirically supported interventions for the problems frequently addressed by family therapists (Sprenkle, 2002).

Practitioners can increasingly find treatment manuals that detail and behaviorally specify interventions and their components, formulated on the basis of a systematic program of research and testing. Treatment manuals facilitate implementation and consistent application across clients and practitioners. The National Association of Social Workers (NASW) Press has begun publishing manuals and handbooks that provide specific guidance on practice strategies. The first such manual addresses social problem-solving skills for use with children

(Fraser, Nash, Galinsky, & Darwin, 2000). To the extent that these manuals are evidence-based, they provide an excellent tool by which practitioners can select and use empirically tested interventions. The National Institute of Drug Abuse Web site (http://www.drugabuse.gov/TXManuals/) provides manuals for a variety of evidence-based interventions in the area of addictions.

Individual practitioners and social work agencies can facilitate the evidence-based practices with some preparation and resource gathering. It is advantageous to develop an in-house collection or compilation of empirically supported interventions for the outcomes most frequently pursued in their settings. Handbooks, research journals, and computers with "bookmarks" to Internet sites containing relevant guidelines or manuals can enhance practitioners' access to ESTs relevant to their practice.

> Step 2:   Select the best fitting intervention in view of the particular client problems, situation, and outcomes.

Even when well specified in treatment manuals, interventions studied and found effective through research remain generalized formulations that have been tested with samples of clients. The practitioner's own client is not likely to share with the clients in the research samples all the characteristics that are relevant to the effective intervention. Hence, having a solid foundation of empirical support does not guarantee that a given intervention will meet the needs of a particular client. Thus, after identifying an array of alternative interventions with empirical support, the practitioner must select from that array the intervention most appropriate to the client and practice task at hand. The second step in evidence-based practice, then, is to select the best fitting intervention from a repertoire of interventions with a solid evidence base. This task requires the practitioner to critically assess the fit between each of the alternative (evidence-based) interventions, on the one hand, and the client's needs and goals on the other hand.

Using assessment skills and critical thinking, the practitioner must bring to the task of selecting the most appropriate intervention from within an array familiarity with the client and circumstances; appreciation of the problem's duration, severity, and co-occurring conditions; knowledge of resources available for implementing the intervention; appreciation of client strengths and preferences; and knowledge of the circumstances that will bear on the implementation of the intervention. Client personal qualities and context, culture, preferences for process, and the service environment and its culture must all be assessed and understood. All that knowledge and understanding is then juxtaposed against the characteristics of the samples and circumstances of the research through which the interventions were supported, and then the practitioner must gauge their similarity to the client and practice context at hand. This assessment and comparison process should enable the practitioner to select from among the alternative interventions the evidence-based intervention that is most appropriate for the task at hand.

> Step 3:   Supplement and modify the most appropriate and best supported treatments, drawing on practitioner experience and knowledge.

Even with a careful assessment of intervention appropriateness, it is unrealistic to expect a perfect fit between an empirically supported, standardized intervention and the needs of a particular client. If the practitioner doubts the goodness of fit of an evidence-based treatment to the needs of the client and situation at hand, a third critical step in EBP is supplementing or modifying the chosen intervention. That is, the best research-based knowledge must be applied in relation to the particular client and be attuned to "local knowledge" (Stricker & Trierweiler, 1995), knowledge of the agency and community setting, prior experience, and theory. Although sometimes given short shrift, local knowledge is an important complement to research-based knowledge.

When the selected empirically based interventions require adaptation, the practitioner's task will involve modifying the intervention by supplementing or revising it in accordance with local knowledge to create a new "blended" or "composite" intervention. This task is likely to be facilitated by the degree of specification typical of empirically supported interventions; specification may be related to their components, recommended order, dosage, and intensity. This level of detail of ESTs would enable the practitioner to discern what elements need to be modified in relation to a particular practice situation. This process of adapting empirically supported treatments to the needs of particular clients and practice situations relies on practitioners' best judgment, as informed by their knowledge and practice experience.

The practitioner should carefully assess the similarity between the conditions under which the EST was tested and shown to be effective and the conditions characterizing the particular practice situation in which the EST is to be applied. Differences between these two sets of conditions do not necessarily preclude application of the EST, nor do they signal the necessity of modifying the EST in order to apply it. Among the differences between the conditions that might signal a need for modifying the standardized, evidence-based interventions are that (a) the client's problem configuration, personal characteristics, or situation differs from the samples that were studied in testing the ESTs; (b) the specific outcomes pursued with the client, while within the same general category, differ somewhat from the outcomes that were tested (for example, the empirically supported treatment was tested in relation to enhancing assertiveness with colleagues at work, whereas the practitioner is working toward enhancing the client's assertiveness with a spouse); and (c) the EST was tested in a different practice setting or with different types of practitioners than those characterizing the practice situation at hand.

When the practice situation differs from the context in which the supporting research was conducted, the following elements in the EST may require modification: (a) intermediate outcomes may need to be added or omitted; (b) the frequency, intensity, or duration of the treatment inputs may need to be altered; (c) changes to the tasks given to clients, such as homework assignments, may be called for; and (d) because many manualized ESTs do not specify procedures for establishing and maintaining a facilitative helping relationship, the practitioner may need to supplement an EST with his or her own knowledge and skills in developing a good relationship with the client. The particular modification to be made depends, of course, on the practitioner's knowledge and the reasons for undertaking the modification.

Modification of established evidence-based treatments carries two risks. First, as practitioners are aware, there is the risk of overcommitting to standardized interventions, applying them "as is" without considering the issue of fit to the client. Doing so may be "taking the easy way out." Second, there is risk associated with changing empirically standardized treatments. Our encouragement to modify and revise ESTs should not be taken as a call to freely change the intervention. Rather, modifications must be careful and well reasoned, or the practitioner could not assume that the modified intervention would retain the effectiveness of the EST. Therefore, both adherence to and modification of evidence-based treatments should always be accompanied by ongoing evaluation, as we discuss later. However, it is critical to recognize that any modification of the original empirically supported intervention introduces substantial change that therefore may affect its effectiveness. Hence ongoing evaluation, as addressed in Step 4, is very important.

Step 4: Monitor and evaluate the effectiveness of the intervention.

Fundamentally, evidence-based practice means that practice decisions should be made on the basis of the best evidence available. In this discussion, we have implicated two types of evidence. First is the evidence on the basis of which practitioners evaluate and select the appropriate intervention to use, as discussed previously. The second type of evidence is that for deciding whether the intervention implemented is having its predicted results, whether it should be further modified or abandoned, or whether treatment has reached its desired outcome. This type of evidence is contained in the feedback that has to be obtained from evaluation of treatment.

Evaluation is especially critical when empirically supported treatments have been modified. When some of the ingredients of the original intervention have been changed, the practitioner cannot assume that the modified intervention retains the effectiveness of the original EST. Accordingly, feedback from evaluation must be used to inform further modification and all other treatment decisions. Recognizing the importance of practicing on the basis of feedback from systematic evaluation, the Council on Social Work Education requires that professional social work education must include training in practice evaluation.

A number of sources provide good information pertaining to practice evaluation. Among them are Roberts and Green's *Social Workers' Desk Reference* (2002), particularly Part 13, and what is by now the classic textbook by Bloom, Fischer, and Orme (1999). Recognizing the limited scope of our discussion here, we underscore three points that are critical in evaluation. First, all the outcomes being pursued need to be defined operationally and assessed as specifically as possible by clinically meaningful indicators. Second, when available, clinically relevant standardized measures with acceptable reliability and validity should be used (cf. Fischer & Corcoran, 1994). Third, although some outcomes are categorical in nature (e.g., obtaining housing, avoiding pregnancy, finding employment), the attainment of many commonly pursued outcomes can be appropriately measured by continuous scales. Such measurement affords a more discriminating evaluation of change and enables assessment of outcome attainment over time—including comparisons of treatment with pretreatment status, assessment of progress during and maintenance of change after treatment, and other comparisons of interest. Constant monitoring and recursive evaluation and revision of treatment should lessen practitioner concern that EBPs may be insensitive to clients and their needs.

CONCLUSION

Increased research activity in social work is yielding a growing number of treatments that meet criteria of effectiveness and appropriateness, address a broader range of issues confronting practitioners, and have been tested in settings that serve more diverse and varied client groups. Concomitantly, considerable progress is evident in distilling research knowledge and packaging and communicating this information for better retrieval and application by practitioners. In this chapter, however, we focused mostly on practitioners and the challenges they face in attempting to apply evidence-based treatments to their individual clients. Undoubtedly, the successful application of EBPs will be greatly affected by the knowledge, skills, and critical judgment of the practitioner. A major factor that we have not addressed that should nonetheless be mentioned here is the auspices under which practice is conducted. As Mullen and Bacon (in press) have suggested, agency administrators and supervisors have a distinct and necessary role in creating an agency culture that encourages, supports, and lends legitimacy to practitioners' efforts to use EBP.

REFERENCES

Bloom, M., Fischer, J., & Orme, J. G. (1999). *Evaluating practice: Guidelines for the accountable professional* (3rd ed.). Englewood Cliffs, NJ: Prentice Hall.
Fischer, J., & Corcoran, K. (1994). *Measures for clinical practice* (2nd ed.). New York: Free Press.
Fraser, M. W. (in press). Intervention research in social work: A basis for evidence-based practice and practice guidelines. In A. Rosen & E. K. Proctor (Eds.), *Developing practice guidelines for social work intervention: Issues, methods, and research agenda.* New York: Columbia University Press.
Fraser, M. W., Nash, J. K., Galinsky, M. J., & Darwin, K. M. (2000). *Making choices: Social problem-solving skills for children.* Washington, DC: National Association of Social Workers.
Gambrill, E. (1999). Evidence-based practice: An alternative to authority-based practice. *Families in Society, 80,* 234–259.
Gonzales, J. J., Ringeisen, H. L., & Chambers, D. A. (2002). The tangled and

thorny path of science to practice: Tensions in interpreting and applying "evidence." *Clinical Psychology: Science & Practice, 9*(2), 204–209.

Mullen, E. J., & Bacon, W. F. (in press). Practitioner adoption and implementation of practice guidelines and issues of quality control. In A. Rosen & E. K. Proctor (Eds.), *Developing practice guidelines for social work intervention: Issues, methods, and research agenda*. New York: Columbia University Press.

Proctor, E. K., & Rosen, A. (in press). The structure and function of social work practice guidelines. In A. Rosen & E. K. Proctor (Eds.), *Developing practice guidelines for social work interventions: Issues, methods, and research agenda*. New York: Columbia University Press.

Reid, W. J., & Fortune, A. E. (in press). Empirical foundations for practice guidelines in current social work knowledge. In A. Rosen & E. K. Proctor (Eds.), *Developing practice guidelines for social work intervention: Issues, methods, and research agenda*. New York: Columbia University Press.

Roberts, A. R., & Green, G. J. (2002). *Social workers' desk reference*. New York: Oxford University Press.

Rosen, A. (2002). *Evidence-based social work practice: Challenges and promise.* Invited address at the Society for Social Work and Research, San Diego, CA.

Rosen, A., & Proctor, E. K. (1978). Specifying the treatment process: The basis for effectiveness research. *Journal of Social Service Research, 2*(1), 25–43.

Rosen, A., & Proctor, E. K. (1981). Distinctions between treatment outcomes and their implications for treatment evaluation. *Journal of Consulting and Clinical Psychology, 49,* 418–425.

Rosen, A., & Proctor, E. K. (2002). Standards for evidence-based social work practice: The role of replicable and appropriate interventions, outcomes, and practice guidelines. In A. R. Roberts & G. J. Greene (Eds.), *Social workers' desk reference* (pp. 743–747). New ford University Press.

Rosen, A., Proctor, E. K., & Livne, S. (1985). Planning and direct practice. *Social Service Review, 59,* 161–167.

Rosen, A., Proctor, E. K., Morrow-Howell, N., & Staudt, M. (1995). Rationale for practice decisions: Variations in knowledge use by decision task and social work service. *Research on Social Work Practice, 5,* 501–523.

Sprenkle, D. H. (2002). A therapeutic Hail Mary. In D. A. Baptiste (Ed.), *Clinical epiphanies in marital and family therapy: A practitioner's casebook of therapeutic insights, perceptions, and breakthroughs* (pp. 20–28). New York: Hawarth Press.

Stricker, G., & Trierweiler, S. J. (1995). The local clinical scientist: A bridge between science and practice. *American Psychologist, 50*(12), 995–1002.

Thyer, B. A., & Wodarski, J. S. (1998). First principles of empirical social work practice. In B. A. Thyer & J. S. Wodarski (Eds.), *Handbook of empirical social work practice* (pp. 1–21). New York: John Wiley & Sons.

Vandiver, V. L. (2002). Step-by-step practice guidelines for using evidence-based practice and expert consensus in mental health settings. In A. R. Robert & G. J. Greene (Eds.), *Social workers' desk reference* (p. 131). New York: Oxford University Press.

9

Will the Real Evidence-Based Practice Please Stand Up?

Teaching the Process of Evidence-Based Practice
to the Helping Professions

ARON SHLONSKY
LEONARD GIBBS

Suppose a practitioner at an agency serving children and families encounters a 15-year-old, female client who discloses that she is suicidal. What methods of assessment and treatment are most effective for working with this youth? Where does this knowledge come from?—experience? training? Is clinical expertise enough to guide casework decisions? If knowledge is gained from research, is the information up-to-date? Is it of sufficient rigor? Is it inclusive of all knowledge or is it selective?

Evidence-based practice (EBP) is a systematic *process* that blends current best evidence, client preferences (wherever possible), and clinical expertise, resulting in services that are both individualized and empirically sound. Applicable to all forms of practice, EBP is particularly relevant to crisis intervention, where, given the gravity of problems faced by clients and the short amount of time in which to act, approaches taken must be both effective and efficient. This *process* is distinguished from other types of practice, whereby "best practices," "evidence-based practices," or "practice guidelines" are identified and promoted for use with clients. There is a concern that such practice guidelines and standards are top-down (that is, subject to being authority based), may become quickly obsolete, and may or may not be sufficiently transparent in how they were developed. While guidelines and standards may have some merit if truly effective services are identified, the *process* of EBP is bottom-up and begins and ends with the client, moving well beyond a one-size-fits-all model and encompassing clients' unique experience with their presenting prob-

103

lems. In addition, since information is continually updated, EBP practitioners avoid obsolescence.

THE DEVELOPMENT OF EVIDENCE-BASED PRACTICE

In this paper, EBP will be defined by concept, operation, and example. The term *evidence-based*, as applied to the helping professions, appears to have been coined by a Canadian medical group at McMaster University in Hamilton, Ontario (Evidence-Based Medicine Working Group, 1992). They contend that "[evidence-based medicine] is the integration of best research evidence with clinical expertise and patient values" (Sackett, Straus, Richardson, Rosenberg, & Haynes, 2000, p. 1). This integration is perhaps best illustrated with the Venn diagram in Figure 9.1.

In the figure, it is the intersection of current best external evidence, client values and expectations, and practitioner expertise that defines EBP. Contrary to some criticisms of the EBP model, action is not dictated by current best evidence operating in a vacuum. None of the three core elements can stand alone; they work in concert by using practitioner skills to develop a client-sensitive case plan that utilizes interventions with a history of effectiveness. In the absence of relevant evidence, the other two elements are weighted more heavily, whereas in the presence of overwhelming evidence the best-evidence component might be weighted more heavily.

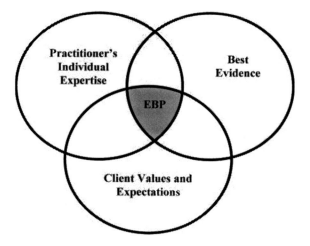

Figure 9.1   EBP Model.

CONCEPTUAL DEFINITIONS OF
EVIDENCE-BASED PRACTICE

In the human services context, EBP has been defined by Gibbs (2003): "Placing the client's benefits first, evidence-based practitioners adopt a process of lifelong learning that involves continually posing specific questions of direct practical importance to clients, searching objectively and efficiently for the current best evidence relative to each question, and taking appropriate action guided by evidence" (p. 6). As with any important advance, controversy and misunderstandings will inevitably arise among competent professionals of goodwill (e.g., the role of *Helicobacter pylori* bacteria in stomach ulcers [Blaser, 1996]). The advent of EBP is no exception. Seven years ago, Sackett, Rosenberg, Gray, Haynes, and Richardson (1996) refuted the argument that "everyone is already doing [evidence-based medicine]" by citing striking variations among clinicians regarding how they integrated client preferences into their practice and kept abreast of advances in the medical literature. Sackett and colleagues also made the point that evidence-based medicine is not a set of external guidelines to be followed slavishly, a sort of "cookbook" approach, but rather a flexible, bottom-up approach that integrates client preferences, practice experience, and the current best evidence (see Figure 9.1). Eileen Gambrill (2003), referring to EBP in social work, makes essentially the same points.

Since its inception, EBP has been misrepresented and misunderstood in medicine and social work, but nevertheless, its innovation will come. Advances in information technology and access to that technology make this inevitable for the following reasons:

Widespread Access to Practice Information. According to survey data, 97% of members of the National Association of Social Workers have access (at either work or home) to the Internet (O'Neill, 2003). Anyone who has access to the Internet can access many useful bibliographic databases for free (e.g., PubMed, ERIC [Education Resources and Information Center], Cochrane Library abstracts [but not full reviews], Campbell Collaboration, the National Criminal Justice Reference Service [NCJRS]). Agencies that have the funds can subscribe to many of the most useful databases through single-source vendors such as Ovid (http://www.ovid.com/site/index.jsp).

Increasing Speed of Access to Practice Information. The National Science Foundation's TeraGrid project has sent information between Los Angeles and Chicago at the rate of 40 gigabits (billion bits) per second, which is about a million times the speed of a dial-up network and four times faster than existing research networks (Science Blog, 2003). The speed of access to practice information will undoubtedly increase over time.

Questions Addressed in Continually Updated Systematic Reviews. Emerging methods for synthesizing studies make it easier to stay current with the best evidence regarding vital practice questions. These procedures employ rigorous methods for locating published and unpublished studies and synthesizing them with respect to their methodological rigor, findings, and implications for practice.

The leading sources in this area are the Cochrane Library (http://www.update
-software.com/abstracts/mainindex.htm) and Campbell Collaboration (http://
www.campbellcollaboration.org).

Improvements in Practical EBP Techniques. Improved techniques for posing
relevant and answerable questions, searching efficiently and effectively, and critically appraising and applying what is found will go a long way toward making
EBP the gold standard for treating clients. Resources for learning these skills can
be found in books (Gibbs, 2003; Sackett et al., 2000), as well as on the Web at
the Evidence-Based Medicine Resource Center (http://www.ebmny.org/teach
.html).

AN OPERATIONAL, STEP-BY-STEP DEFINITION
OF EVIDENCE-BASED PRACTICE

EBP is a process that all practitioners can follow, right in the office, if they have
access to electronic databases. Sackett et al. (2000, pp. 3–4) propose the following steps:

1. Converting the need for information (about prevention, diagnosis, prognosis, therapy, causation, etc.) into an answerable question
2. Tracking down the best evidence with which to answer the question
3. Critically appraising that evidence for its validity (closeness to the truth),
   impact (size of the effect), and applicability (usefulness in clinical practice)
4. Integrating the critical appraisal with clinical expertise and with the patient's
   unique biology, values, and circumstances
5. Evaluating effectiveness and efficiency in executing Steps 1 through 4 and
   seeking ways to improve them both for the next time

This method outlines how an individual practitioner can incorporate research
into daily decision making. As a bottom-up approach, it empowers the parties
to the treatment because decisions can arise out of the active collaboration between individual practitioners and clients.

Ideally, the model extends past practitioners to administrators in human service agencies. Administrators should create a culture of inquiry whereby practitioners are given the time and resources to search for relevant information. Yet
this is a process not only for keeping up with the literature, but of cultural change
within the agency. The search for current best evidence will necessarily prompt
agencies to find ways in which they can integrate new findings into the service
milieu. Errors made with clients must serve to inform clinical expertise in a
proactive rather than reactive manner. Client values and preferences must be
heeded in more than comforting words; they must be truly integrated into service
plans.

DEFINITION BY EXAMPLE

Before giving an example of EBP from practice, some background may be helpful regarding specific techniques. The process begins with a well-built question, one that might be called a *client-oriented*, practical evidence search (COPES) (Gibbs, 2003). Such a question directly concerns the interests of the client. The example below from corrections is *client-oriented* because it concerns risk and the need to consider risk carefully to both protect the community and not restrict the client's freedom more than absolutely necessary. It is *practical* in that it refers to the idea that knowing the answer to the question could result in action. Questions are not posed if answering them would not result in constructive action (i.e., considerations of unethical treatment such as castration, intense punishment, deception, and methods and measures too costly to apply). And, finally, the question needs to be posed specifically enough to guide an evidence search. While the term "COPES" seems more appropriate for social workers, these ideas have been called *patient-oriented evidence that matters* (POEM) in medicine (Slawson & Shaughnessy, 1997). As described by Sackett, Richardson, Rosenberg, and Haynes (1997), well-built COPES questions comprise the four elements of evidence search questions: client type, course of action, alternate course of action, and what you intend to accomplish.

In addition to posing specific and vital questions, EBP requires mastering new skills and technology. Searching efficiently in real time, as problems arise in practice, requires having access to electronic databases from the office, knowing how to identify terms that mark the topic, planning a search for maximum efficiency using methodological filters (terms that locate the best evidence regarding specific question types [Gibbs, 2003; McKibbon, Eady, & Marks, 1999]), knowing which professional databases to search for specific topics, and being able to critically appraise evidence for its quality and utility as a guide to action. For a quick electronic introduction to posing questions and searching, see http://www.evidence.brookscole.com; and for critical appraisal, see the CASP (Critical Appraisal Skills Programme) Web site at http://www.phru.nhs.uk/~casp/casp.htm.

Student Example

Melissa Candell followed the EBP process in her work with high-risk sex offenders on probation and parole. Her example, though competently done, may not represent the best possible solution and is reported (with permission) in order to illustrate a real-practice scenario (M. Candell, personal communication, October 16, 2003). She and her social work field instructor, Bridget Rumphol at the Wisconsin Division of Community Corrections Chippewa Falls Office, worked with adults charged with first-, second-, and third-degree sexual assault, disorderly conduct, and lewd and lascivious behavior. Their work required them to do pre-sentence investigations whereby they recommended either prison sentences or probation for these offenders. Ms. Candell became interested in risk assessment for sex offenders when weighing the rights of citizens in the community versus those of offenders.

Implementing Step 1 in the Sackett et al. (2000) model, she posed this well-built risk/prognosis question: If convicted sex offenders on probation or parole were administered the Rapid Risk Assessment of Sex Offender Recidivism (RRA-SOR) or the Minnesota Sex Offender Screening Tool—Revised (MnSOSTR), which of these instruments would be the most accurate in predicting whether a sexual offender would reoffend? Her experience illustrates how steps in the EBP process may proceed concurrently, not always progressing in sequential order. She posed her question relative to two sex-offender screening tools partly because they were used in neighboring counties and partly because she conducted an electronic search that revealed them to be commonly referenced.

Implementing Step 2, she kept a log of her electronic search in the ERIC, PsycINFO (the the American Psychological Association's database of psychological abstracts), SWAB (Social Work Abstracts), and NCJRS databases to record the number of documents for each database and search terms used in each. From the question, concept terms were derived, such as (sex offender* OR sexual offender*) AND (assessment scale* OR risk scale* OR assessment* OR reoffend OR risk) and combined with several risk/prognosis methodological filters, such as: validation sample OR gold standard OR positive predictive value OR negative predictive value OR predictive validity OR risk reduction OR estimating risk OR risk estimation OR prediction study. The latter filters have been termed *methodology-oriented locators for evidence searching* (Gibbs, 2003), or "MOLES," because, regardless of the bibliographic database, these terms will dig for the studies with the most rigorous methodology.

Based on her search results, Ms. Candell implemented Step 3: She obtained and evaluated the results from the comparison of the RRASOR versus the MnSOST-R using a client assessment and risk evaluation (CARE) form (Gibbs, 2003), which includes criteria specific to evaluating risk in practice. Her comparison demonstrated that the RRASOR scored 11 of 19 criteria on the CARE and that the MnSOST-R scored only 3 of the 19 criteria.

Implementing Steps 4 and 5, she administered both measures to six of her clients in order to gain experience with these instruments. She reported on her experiences with the instruments, summarized her search and critical appraisal of the evidence, and demonstrated how to search the NCJRS homepage (http://www.ncjrs.org) for various agency staff. Although the agency did not begin administering the RRASOR to its clients, it did consider her results when referring to local consultants for risk assessment.

LESSONS LEARNED IN TEACHING EVIDENCE-BASED PRACTICE

The process of EBP requires a substantial shift in the way services are negotiated and delivered to clients. Instruction of students in EBP is critical if the model is to be followed correctly, and our experience in teaching this method to students from a wide range of disciplines within the helping professions has informed our process as well. Certainly, there are several key elements that must be stressed and many pitfalls to avoid.

Misinterpreting the Mission of Evidence-Based Practice

Students often say they want to find evidence to support a particular position in order to advocate for it (e.g., intervention method, assessment method, problem prevalence). One student stated that she had heard the following argument from a professional: "Evidence-based practice is useless, because you can always find a study to support your conclusion." In response to such arguments, we point out that if one searches only for studies that support a given premise, then all one winds up with is an artfully concealed lie. We tactfully point out that it may not help clients, or might even harm them, to advocate for services built on false premises. We argue that in order to approach the truth—we find no absolutes—those doing EBP need to search as diligently for disconfirming evidence as they do for evidence that supports their hunches. Likewise, students and practitioners need to weigh the quality of the evidence and present their formulation to clients in terms that make sense to them, such as *number needed to treat* (Bandolier, 2004; Cordell, 1999).

Posing Well-Built COPES Questions

Posing a question that can be answered by a database is no small task and is the foundation upon which EBP is built (Gibbs, 2003, ch. 3). Simply put, a database must be given information in a format and language that it can interpret, and this is often quite different than the normal phrasing of questions in everyday practice. Separating the question into its four distinct elements (client type and problem, what might be done, alternative course of action, outcome desired) sets the stage for identifying key concepts (Sackett et al., 1997). Questions are then categorized into five domains: effectiveness, prevention, risk/prognosis, assessment, and description. These domains inform the selection of methodological filters, or MOLES, to be used in the subsequent search. Real examples of student questions from each of the domains are presented in Table 9.1. However, it should be noted that none of these questions was initially posed as presented here.

Posing an answerable question often requires many iterations until key concepts are clearly identified and properly separated into their respective categories and domains. Unfortunately, many practitioners seem to struggle with this simple but difficult stage of the process. Our experience has identified some common pitfalls:

- Asking questions that are irrelevant to the client in terms of outcomes sought or resources available (e.g., asking about an intervention that cannot be offered or that the client would refuse).
- Asking questions that are vague in terms of the concept being searched, in-

Table 9.1. COPES Questions from Students at the University of Wisconsin-Eau Claire School of Social Work and the Columbia University School of Social Work

Name of Student	Type of Question	Client Type and Problem	What You Might Do	Alternate Course of Action	What You Want to Accomplish
Laila Salma*	Effectiveness	If African American juvenile delinquent males ages 11–15 who have committed one criminal act	become involved in an afterschool tutoring and mentoring program	compared with those who do not	will they be less likely to commit a second criminal act?
Zayani Lavergne-Friedman*	Prevention	Will high-risk, very young children in urban areas	who participate in an Early Head Start program	compared with those who do not	have better literacy skills and better behavior in kindergarten?
CariLyn Imbery**	Risk/prognosis	For parents or guardians of children who have been found to have abused their child	which risk-assessment scale		would most accurately and inexpensively Identlfy those who would reabuse their child?
Melissa Johnson**	Assessment	For elderly residents of a nursing and rehabilitation home who show signs of depression but may also have a dementia-related illness	is there a depression measure		that briefly and accurately differentiates between depression and dementia?
Tami Wilson**	Description	If patients in a hospital who are scheduled for surgery	are given discharge planning options prior to surgery	as opposed to after surgery	will patient satisfaction be higher in the former group

Note: COPES = client-oriented, practical evidence search.

*Students at the Columbia University School of Social Work.
**Students at the University of Wisconsin-Eau Claire School of Social Work.

tervention(s) applied, or outcome(s) sought. This is probably the most common pitfall. Practitioners tend to pose questions as if they were in a conversation with a person (where context can be understood), rather than attempting to communicate with a computer. Key concepts, interventions, and outcomes must be carefully considered and clearly articulated. Asking students to critically think about and discuss their questions seems to bring about greater clarity (i.e., What are alternative hypotheses? How will you know if an outcome is attained? In what specific ways might this intervention help or harm your client? What, exactly, do you mean by "better functioning"?). Other sources of terms to more accurately mark topics can be found in database thesauri (e.g., MeSH [Medical Subject Heading] terms in Medline, mapping to subject headings in the Ovid database) as well as known articles that address the topic.

- Asking incomplete questions. For example, asking effectiveness or prevention questions that do not include an alternate intervention. Doing nothing is an alternative course. However, not specifying an alternative implies that whatever is done will be better than nothing, which may not be the case.
- Incorrectly labeling a problem, procedure, or outcome. Lay terminology and clinical jargon are often absent in databases and should be used as supplemental search terms rather than primary search terms.
- Asking two or more questions within one question. Practitioners often get excited and put too many items into a single question, making it unwieldy. Better to hone a number of good questions.

Learning How to Search Efficiently

Another example of a student question, posed by CariLyn Imbery, illustrates the process by which reliable and valid decision aids can be obtained and used in the field. CariLyn works as an intern in the Child Protective Services Intake Unit at the Eau Claire (Wisconsin) County Department of Human Services. She and her supervisor were interested in finding ways to prevent maltreated children from having to reexperience the trauma of abuse. They decided that an accurate risk-assessment instrument offered the best opportunity for identifying those parents who were most likely to reabuse their children. Using the COPES method, CariLyn posed the question: For parents or guardians of children who have, by investigation, been found to have abused their child, which risk-assessment scale would most accurately, reliably, and inexpensively identify those who would reabuse their child? Separating this question into the four categories further clarified it and formed the basis for a subsequent search (Table 9.2). Key concepts were distilled from each part of the question. For example, "For parents or guardians of children who have, by investigation, been found to have abused their child" was broken down into the conceptual terms "parent," "guardian," "child abuse," and "child maltreatment." Given that searches should move from the general to the specific, several of these terms would likely have proven to be too specific to begin with. These were italicized to mark them for later use here if the number of hits in the database needed to be decreased.

From here, identified terms should be translated into terms as they appear in the database. This is generally done through interfacing with the database's thesaurus or mapping feature. For instance, entering "child abuse" into Ovid's version of PsycINFO and mapping the term to its subject heading brought up the subject heading Child Abuse with 12,845 entries, a major subject heading containing all forms of child abuse (physical, sexual, neglect, etc.), and a major related subheading, Child Welfare. Exploration of this subheading revealed the

Table 9.2.   Search Planning Worksheet for CariLyn Imbery's COPES Question

	Client Type and Problem	What You Might Do	What You Want to Accomplish
Question	For parents or guardians of children who have, by investigation, been found to have abused their child	which risk-assessment scale	would most accurately and reliably identify those who would reabuse their child?
Concepts	*Parent, Guardian* Child abuse Child maltreatment	Risk assessment	Valid and reliable scale
Equivalent concepts in language of the database	Child abuse Child welfare Child protective services Foster care	Risk assessment Risk analysis	Use MOLES
Final concept search terms	Child abus* Child Welfare Child protective service* Foster care	Risk assessment* Risk analys*	Use MOLES
Combination of concept search terms	(Child abus* OR Child Welfare OR Child protect* service* OR Foster care) AND (Risk OR Risk assessment* OR Risk analys*)		
MOLES	(Predictive validity OR reliab* OR Valid OR Predictive value OR Test valid* OR Receiver operat* OR ROC OR Sensitivity OR Specificity OR False positive* OR False negative* OR Prognosis)		
Final combination of search terms	[(Child abus* OR Child Welfare OR Child protect* service* OR Foster care) AND (Risk OR Risk assessment* OR Risk analys*)] AND [(Predictive validity OR reliab* OR Valid* OR Predictive value OR test valid* OR Receiver operat* OR ROC OR Sensitivity OR Specificity OR False positive* OR False negative* OR Prognosis)]		

Note: COPES = client-oriented, practical evidence search; MOLES = methodology-oriented locators for evidence searching.

terms "protective services" and "foster care," which looked promising as keyword searches. Next, the term "risk assessment" was mapped to the relevant terms "risk assessment" and "risk analysis." Subject headings and question constructs were then entered into the next row along with other important concepts to be searched as key words. In this step, wildcards are essential: These are modifiers, usually placed at the end of a word, that make the letters to the left of the wildcard a root term that can have any ending. For instance, the * in child abus* includes *child abuse, child abuser,* and *child abusing*. Risk analys* includes the terms *risk analysis* and *risk analyses*. Wildcards both expand search options and speed up the process, but practitioners should be aware that wildcards may have different rules for use across databases (e.g., a $ or # might be used instead of a *). The database's help file should be consulted until familiarity is achieved.

The last steps before beginning to search involve the correct combination of Boolean operators and the application of MOLES. Many students seem to get confused at this point, so careful consideration must be given. Terms that ab-solutely must be present in concert should be grouped and linked with an "AND" operator, while terms that may or may not be present in all documents sought should be grouped and linked by an "OR" operator. In CariLyn's search, the child abuse concept was grouped by "OR" operators (Child abus* OR Child Welfare OR Protective service* OR Foster care), as was the risk assessment group (Risk assessment* OR Risk analys*). These meta-concepts were then linked with AND statements, meaning that both meta-concepts had to be present in each citation.

At this point, if background information is desired, key-word terms need to be validated, or if there are only likely to be a few hits, this search can be run. However, if there is a great deal of research in this area and/or the practitioner wishes to cull the very best from the literature without poring over a full set of results, MOLES can be applied to further narrow the findings. In this case, since CariLyn clearly posed a risk/prognosis question, MOLES geared toward risk were applied and combined with the previous search (see Gibbs, 2003, p. 100, for a list of MOLES by question type). Using PsycINFO, a total of 24 articles were found. Among these, several compared the reliability and validity of various risk-assessment tools being used in practice (Baird & Wagner, 2000; Baird, Wag-ner, Healy, & Johnson, 1999; Camasso & Jagannathan, 1995, 2000; Fanshel, Finch, & Grundy, 1994; Lyons, Doueck, & Wodarski, 1996; Milner, 1989; Na-suti, 1991; Nasuti & Pecora, 1993; Reid, 1998). Two studies (Baird & Wagner, 2000; Baird et al., 1999) compared three widely used child abuse risk-assessment instruments (two consensus based, one actuarial), finding that the actuarial risk-assessment model (a data-driven instrument that optimally weights risk factors) appears to have the greatest predictive power for detecting those parents who will reabuse their children. CariLyn is now in the process of obtaining this in-strument and will introduce it to her agency for possible adoption in the field.

Some cautions are in order. All databases are not created equal, nor are all search strategies. In order to be safe, the practitioner should query several rele-vant databases before deciding that enough information has been obtained. When should searching cease? That is a difficult question. Searching is somewhat of an art form. The inclusiveness of the words chosen, the combinations applied, the databases chosen—each step in the process may change the results obtained. However, the likelihood of finding good evidence is fairly high when this method is coupled with an intense commitment to provide the very best services to cli-ents. Sometimes, though, no evidence will be found. While disheartening, this is the state of affairs in the field. The client should be fully informed, and more emphasis should be placed on client values and clinical expertise.

One of the methods we have found that works for teaching this process is to create and maintain a culture of critical inquiry within the classroom. Students are encouraged to question many of the basic tenets of their profession as well as their own thinking. Struggling with difficult questions is modeled, even re-quired, throughout the course. Socratic methods are used early and often. Arti-cles are assigned with contradictory opinions or findings. Connections are made between disparate sources of information. In essence, students are taught to be critical consumers of the information they receive in both the classroom and the field. This is a difficult role for the instructor, who may feel immediately obligated to provide authoritative answers to questions raised in the classroom. But students will not be in the classroom forever and must learn to think critically from the very beginning.

Another part of the process is to cultivate a sense of investment in the posing and answering of questions. By linking COPES questions to their own or another's client, practitioners can give their questions a sense of urgency. The search process can also dovetail nicely into literature review sections of final papers. Familiarizing students with the online library system and taking them through a number of live searches are also essential. Simply reading about how to search is too abstract, and many of the pitfalls have the potential to cause frustration and increase search time.

Learning How to Critically Appraise Evidence

Once sources are acquired—hopefully, sources obtained electronically as full text documents—the next problem is to critically appraise evidence for its methodological quality and implications for practice. Practitioners may not have enough time to get original articles before action is required, but our students are required to get the original sources in order to practice critical appraisal. Gibbs (2003) has developed rating forms to assess the quality of sources specific to each of the five question types (including qualitative). Some of these forms to rate study quality and treatment effect size can be completed with reasonable interrater agreement by undergraduates (Gibbs, 1989). Still, students with more research training may be better able to understand how to apply criteria on the rating forms. A brief overview of basic statistics and study designs used in articles can help students become more informed consumers of information. At the very least, students who become familiar with the constructs contained in the forms will be able to identify key indicators of quality in any article they read.

THE BENEFITS AND CHALLENGES OF EVIDENCE-BASED PRACTICE

One of the major benefits of EBP is its potential for improving interdisciplinary understanding and cooperation. One of our EBP courses contains eight different majors (social work, psychology, public relations, premedicine, nursing, communication disorders, special education, and health care administration). Students in this course each solicit a question from a practitioner in their respective disciplines. They then do exercises in the course to clarify their questions; share their questions; help each other search for evidence regarding each fellow-student's question; practice critically appraising each others' evidence; and present a brief written and oral summary of their findings. A major component of this course is to increase cross-discipline teamwork by providing a common approach to defining questions and answering them, as well as facilitating an understanding of the kinds of problems that confront colleagues in other disciplines. Other benefits include:

- More informed beginnings with clients. Practitioners have both the responsibility and the flexibility to consider the diversity of client backgrounds, conditions, preferences, and values when planning and implementing treatment interventions.
- Assuming the best about trained helpers. That is, this method believes in and relies on the intelligence and skills of practitioners to effectively search, evaluate, and apply current best evidence.
- Increasing the likelihood that effective interventions will be used.

Despite these benefits, some challenges remain. Critics of EBP contend that practitioners are simply too busy to undertake lengthy searches and that effective searching and appraisal techniques require advanced training and skills (Sackett et al., 2000). While much has been made of these limitations, the tools outlined here minimize such concerns. After learning the basics, high-quality searches need not take more than a few minutes. Further, once information is gathered, practitioner knowledge is continually enhanced (with respect to both client conditions and effective search techniques), making future searches even more efficient. Challenges may also exist for practitioners attempting to use this method with insufficient equipment and funding for database access (including access to full text articles) and a lack of evidence in certain areas. Steps should continue to be taken to improve search skills, increase access to databases, and expand the body of knowledge used to make key clinical decisions.

CURRENT STATE AND FUTURE DIRECTIONS

EBP appears to be gaining momentum in the helping professions, but trends in its use may be uneven across disciplines. A search for the number of documents with the term *evidence-based* was conducted in six discipline-specific databases for the years 1990–2002 (Figure 9.2).

Beginning in 1995, an elbow upward appears for medicine (Medline) and then for nursing (CINAHL) in 1996. This trend is followed by an awakening in psychology (PsycINFO) in 1997 and, perhaps, the beginning of a trend in social services (SSAB), education (ERIC), and social work (SWAB). However, the sheer number of hits is at least partially a function of the number of articles contained in each database. Therefore, a proportional representation of articles using the term evidence-based was constructed using these same databases (Figure 9.3). This resulted in substantial differences. As a proportion of studies using the term evidencebased, nursing (CINAHL) and social services (SSAB) ended highest, followed by social work (SWAB), psychology (PsycINFO), medicine (Medline), and

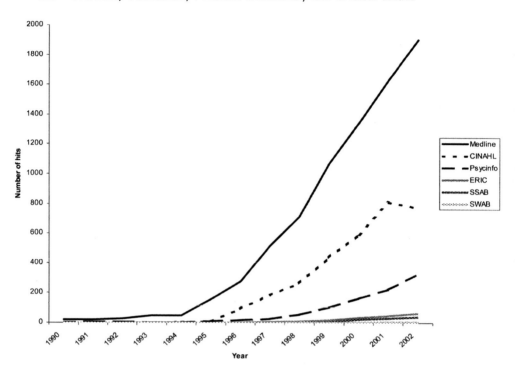

Figure 9.2   Number of "evidence-based" hits by discipline: 1990–2002.
Note: Databases searched: Medline (medicine); CINAHL = Cumulative Index to Nursing and Allied Health Literature (nursing); PsycINFO (psychology); ERIC = Educational Resources and Information Center (education); SSAB = Social Services Abstracts (social services); and SWAB = Social Work Abstracts (social work). Search was conducted in October 2003 using the key-word term evidence-based (including title, abstract, and subject headings) for each year (1990–2002). Searches were limited to studies involving human subjects.

education (ERIC). Using this method, all groups showed strong upward trends by 1998.[1]

Yet the term *evidence-based* may not be an indication of the proportional increase in articles that meet the criteria of current best evidence as identified by methodological filters. Applying MOLES to these same databases and stratifying by year, a search was conducted for studies that had a higher likelihood of answering effectiveness or prevention questions using the key-word terms: random* assign* OR control* clinical trial* OR random* control* trial* OR clinical trial* OR meta anal* OR metaanal* OR metaanal* OR systematic review* OR synthesis of studies OR study synthesis (Figure 9.4). Overall, the proportion of studies using true experimental designs (i.e., random assignment) or systematic review techniques has been steadily increasing since 1990 in almost all fields of practice. The sole exception is ERIC, the education database. Proportional in-

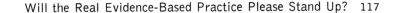

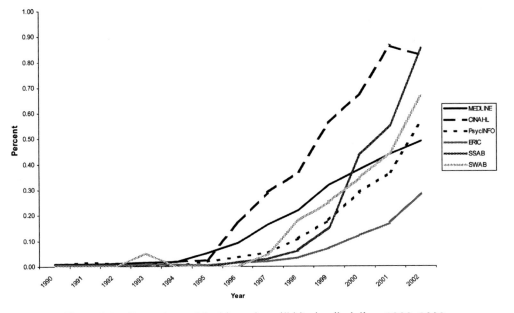

Figure 9.3   Percentage of "evidence-based" hits by discipline: 1990–2002.
Note: Databases searched: Medline (medicine); CINAHL = Cumulative Index to Nursing and Allied Health Literature (nursing); PsycINFO (psychology); ERIC = Educational Resources and Information Center (education); SSAB = Social Services Abstracts (social services); and SWAB = Social Work Abstracts (social work). Search was conducted in October 2003 using the key-word term "evidence-based" (includes title, abstract, and subject headings). Searches were limited to studies involving human subjects.

creases over the 12-year span were greatest for CINAHL (from 1% to almost 5%) and SSAB (from 0.5% to 4.5%). In 2002, Medline (4.4%) and CINAHL (4.9%) had the highest percentage of such studies, and ERIC (0.5%) had the lowest (remaining fairly stable throughout the observation period). SWAB, while showing overall increases, peaked in 1997 with 1.28%, decreasing to 1.13% in 2002. This was the only database that showed somewhat of a reversal in this area, leading to further exploration.

There may be several reasons for the SWAB lag other than a lack of high-quality, empirical studies being conducted and reported by social workers. For instance, there may be a trend among quantitative social work scholars to publish outside of mainstream social work journals, choosing instead to publish in more prestigious psychology or public health journals. A more detailed search of faculty publications in allied fields might reveal such a trend. Added to this possibility is the prospect that social work scholars are undertaking and publishing more qualitative research. A search of these same databases was conducted using the MOLES qualitative study OR qualitative analys* OR in depth interview*

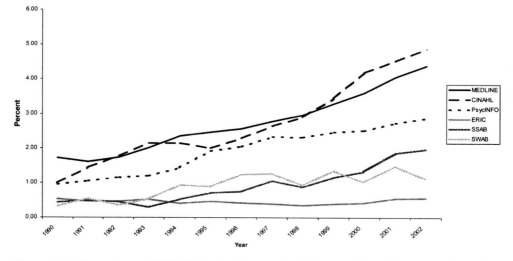

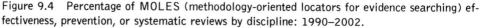

Figure 9.4   Percentage of MOLES (methodology-oriented locators for evidence searching) effectiveness, prevention, or systematic reviews by discipline: 1990–2002.

Note: Databases searched: Medline (medicine); CINAHl = Cumulative Index to Nursing and Allied Health Literature (nursing); PsycINFO (psychology); ERIC = Educational Resources and Information Center (education); SSAB = Social Services Abstracts (social services); and SWAB = Social Work Abstracts (social work). Search was conducted in October 2003 using the following command for each year (1990–2002): random* assign* OR control* clinical trial* OR random* control* trial* OR clinical trial* OR meta anal* OR meta-anal* OR metaanal* OR systematic review* OR synthesis of studies OR study synthesis. Searches were limited to studies involving human subjects.

OR in-depth interview* OR participant observation OR focus group*. Although all databases showed an increasing proportion of qualitative studies, SWAB and SSAB far outpaced other disciplines in this respect.

While qualitative studies are indispensable for understanding and explaining human behavior, as well as for generating hypotheses, the generally lower proportion of studies employing random assignment in the professional literature of social work and social services may point to a deficit of information needed by practitioners to make crucial treatment decisions. At the very least, these disciplines must extend beyond their own boundaries to find current best evidence for effectiveness and prevention studies.

SUMMARY AND CONCLUSIONS

Though often misrepresented and misunderstood across the helping professions, EBP is a process, not a cookbook set of guidelines and standards imposed from above, not what we have been doing all along under another name, and not

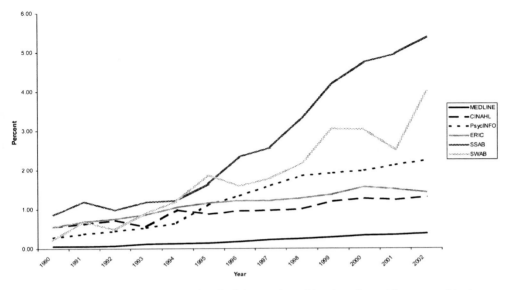

Figure 9.5   Percentage of MOLES (methodology-oriented locators for evidence searching) qualitative study hits by discipline: 1990–2002.

Note: Databases searched: Medline (medicine); CINAHL = Cumulative Index to Nursing and Allied Health Literature (nursing); PsycINFO (psychology); ERIC = Educational Resources and Information Center (education); SSAB = Social Services Abstracts (social services); and SWAB = Social Work Abstracts (social work). Search was conducted in October 2003 using the following command for each year (1990–2002): (qualitative study) or (qualitative analys*) or (in depth interview*) or (in-depth interview*) or (participant observation) or (focus group*). Searches were limited to studies involving human subjects.

something that can be mastered quickly without learning new skills and new technology. EBP assumes a predisposition to inquiry as well as the impetus to pose specific questions. It assumes a fair-minded approach that eschews selling a particular position. Clients are served first, foremost, and always by identifying accurate assessment procedures and effective interventions, and by integrating them with client preferences and values. By searching equally hard for disconfirming evidence as well as for evidence that confirms a notion, and by objectively applying critical appraisal of evidence specific to each client (in real time, as events unfold), evidence-based practitioners may be able to integrate research into their daily practice as never before.

NOTES

   1. Though it should be noted that even the databases with the highest proportion of hits contained such studies less than 1% of the time.

REFERENCES

Baird, C., & Wagner, D. (2000). The relative validity of actuarial- and consensus-based risk assessment systems. *Children and Youth Services Review, 22,* 839–871.

Baird, C., Wagner, D., Healy, T., & Johnson, K. (1999). Risk assessment in child protective services: Consensus and actuarial model reliability. *Child Welfare, 78,* 723–748.

Bandolier. (2004). (Website). Retrieved February 4, 2004, from http://www.jr2.ox.ac.uk/bandolier Blaser, M. J. (1996). The bacteria behind ulcers. *Scientific American, 274,* 104–107.

Camasso, M. J., & Jagannathan, R. (1995). Prediction accuracy of the Washington and Illinois risk assessment instruments: An application of receiver operating characteristic curve analysis. *Social Work Research, 19,* 174–183.

Camasso, M. J., & Jagannathan, R. (2000). Modeling the reliability and predictive validity of risk assessment in child protective services. *Children and Youth Services Review, 22,* 873–896.

Cordell, W. H. (1999). Number needed to treat (NNT). *Annals of Emergency Medicine, 33,* 433–436.

Evidence-Based Medicine Working Group. (1992). Evidence-based medicine. A new approach to teaching the practice of medicine. *Journal of the American Medical Association, 268,* 2420–2425. For current information from this group, see: http://www-hsl.mcmaster.ca/ebm

Fanshel, D., Finch, S. J., & Grundy, J. F. (1994). Testing the measurement properties of risk assessment instruments in child protective services. *Child Abuse & Neglect, 18,* 1073–1084.

Gambrill, E. (2003). Evidence-based practice: Sea change or the emperor's new clothes? *Journal of Social Work Education, 39,* 3–23.

Gibbs, L. E. (1989). Quality of study rating form: An instrument for synthesizing evaluation studies. *Journal of Social Work Education, 25,* 55–67.

Gibbs, L. E. (2003). *Evidence-based practice for the helping professions: A practical guide with integrated multimedia.* Pacific Grove, CA: Brooks/ Cole—Thomson Learning.

Lyons, P., Doueck, H. J., & Wodarski, J. S. (1996). Risk assessment for child protective services: A review of the empirical literature on instrument performance. *Social Work Research, 20,* 143–155.

McKibbon, A., Eady, A., & Marks, S. (1999). *PDQ evidence-based principles and practice.* Hamilton, Ontario: B. C. Decker.

Milner, J. S. (1989). Applications and limitations of the Child Abuse Potential Inventory. *Early Child Development and Care, 42,* 85–97.

Nasuti, J. P. (1991). A test of internal consistency and interrater reliability of the Utah Risk Assessment Instrument. *Dissertation Abstracts International, 51*(12A, Pt 1), 4278. (UMI No. 9112748)

Nasuti, J. P., & Pecora, P. J. (1993). Risk assessment scales in child protection: A test of the internal consistency and interrater reliability on one statewide system. *Social Work Research & Abstracts, 29,* 28–33.

O'Neill, J. V. (2003). Nearly all members linked to Internet. NASW [National Association of Social Workers] *News, 48,* 9.

Reid, R. A. (1998). Content validity and inter-rater reliability of a Hopi child abuse risk assessment instrument (Doctoral dissertation, University of North Dakota, 1998). *Dissertation Abstracts International, 59*(3B), 1413.

Sackett, D. L., Richardson, W. S., Rosenberg, W., & Haynes, R. B. (1997). *Evidence-based Medicine: How to practice and teach EBM.* New York: Churchill Livingstone.

Sackett, D. L., Rosenberg, W. M., Gray, J. A., Haynes, R. B., & Richardson, W. S. (1996). Evidence-based medicine: What it is and what it isn't. *British Medical Journal, 312,* 71–72.

Sackett, D. L., Straus, S. E., Richardson, W. S., Rosenberg, W., & Haynes, R. B. (2000). *Evidencebased medicine: How to practice and teach EBM* (2nd ed.). Edinburgh: Churchill Livingstone.

Science Blog. (2003, October 17). World's fastest network launched to connect Teragrid sites. Retrieved February 3, 2004, from http://www.scienceblog.com/community/article1151.html

Slawson, D. C., & Shaughnessy, A. F. (1997). Obtaining useful information from expert based sources. *British Medical Journal, 314,* 948–949.

10

Health Care Evidence-Based Practice

A Product of Political and Cultural Times

SOPHIA F. DZIEGIELEWSKI
ALBERT R. ROBERTS

We firmly believe that practice accountability through quality assurance measures and operational improvement, utilization of outcome measures, systematic research, and evidence-based practice will become the dominant challenge for all health care and human service professionals in the current decade. "Increasingly federal, state, and foundation funding sources will demand proof of the effectiveness of specific service interventions" (Austin & Roberts, 2002, p. 826) in health care and human service agencies. We predict that there will be intense pressures on professionals in mental health and substance abuse treatment managed care programs to document and measure quality of service, program, and client outcomes. Effectiveness and outcome data will come from rapid assessment measures, case observations, case records, and multiple methodologically rigorous, randomized clinical research trials in different settings.

In the area of health care practice, managed behavioral health care, first introduced in the early 1990s, presents a type of health care delivery never before experienced. As the chapters in this book reinforce, health care professionals are expected to show that the services provided are both short term and evidence-based. If this stance is not adopted, health care professionals will be replaced with other professionals who do adopt this stance. In current health care practice, it is crucial to realize that effectiveness must go beyond just helping the client (Dziegielewski & Holliman, 2001). For evidence-based practice to occur, it must also involve validation that the greatest concrete and identifiable therapeutic gain was achieved, in the quickest amount of time, and with the least amount of financial and professional support. This means that not only must the interventions that professional practitioners provide be socially acknowledged as necessary but also they must be therapeutically effective (Franklin, 2002), specific, and individualized to guide all further intervention efforts (Maruish, 2002). In addition, these services must be professionally competitive with other disciplines that claim similar treatment strategies and techniques. This has led to the rebirth of all efforts for client betterment to be evidence-based in order to be acknowledged as effective (Donald, 2002).

EVOLUTION OF EVIDENCE-BASED PRACTICE

Health care practice has changed dramatically over the years. In addition, the clarity of a definition of what the health care professionals do has been further complicated by basic changes in the health care environment that include scope of practice, the roles served, and the expectations within the client–practitioner relationship. Furthermore, this definition, along with the focus of care, is shifting (Dziegielewski, 2002). Health care practice is changing from a focus on "inpatient acute, tertiary, and specialty/subspecialty care, to ambulatory and community-based care, and to physician's offices, group practices and health maintenance organizations" (Rock, 2002, p. 13). This focus-shifting environment requires that health care practitioners constantly battle "quality-of-care" issues versus "cost-containment" measures, while securing a firm place as a professional provider in the health care environment. Barry Rock (2002) aptly recommends an evidence-based agenda for social workers under the primary care and managed health care environment:

1. Develop job descriptions and skill/knowledge/task inventory for primary care–based social work practice.
2. Develop refined, concise high-risk screening instruments for biopsychosocial assessment, treatment, and outcome measurement.
3. Create treatment protocols—much in demand by managed health and managed behavioral health organizations—linking psychosocial and medical comorbidities, such as diabetes with depression and hypertension with anxiety, in systematic treatment guidelines.
4. Establish psychosocial and medical outcome linkages.
5. Further refine screening tools, assessment instruments, and high-risk indicators appropriate for value-added psychosocial intervention. (Rock, 2002, p. 13)

Today, the health care worker has become essential as the professional "bridge" that links the client, the multidisciplinary or interdisciplinary team, and the environment. For future marketability and competition, it is believed that all health care professionals will need to move beyond the traditional definition and subsequent roles occupied in the past (Dziegielewski, 2002). In the area of clinical practice and as emphasized in each section of this book, new or refined methods of service delivery need to be established and used. By joining the researcher and the practitioner together, the models of evidence-based practice described in this book become manageable.

BECOMING MARKETABLE IN UNCERTAIN TIMES

Many events over the last 15 years have truly transformed health care delivery and the professional expectations of health care workers. For survival in this environment, Dziegielewski (2002) suggests several steps: (a) All health care professionals need to continue to market the services they provide and link them to cost–benefit measurement; (b) all practitioners need to present themselves as essential team members on the health care interdisciplinary and multidisciplinary teams; (c) all health care workers should never forget the importance of anticipating the environment and the role that political and social influences can have on service delivery; and (d) all health care professionals need to adopt a researcher–practitioner stance that looks beyond traditional expectations and assumptions historically noted as clinical professional practice.

This requires all methods of service delivery to incorporate new and innovative ideas and methods that allow for rethinking foundation issues in terms of human growth and development (Farley, Smith, Boyle, & Ronnau, 2002), while applying these concepts in an evidence-based framework (Wodarski & Dziegielewski, 2001). In evidence-based practice, new and revitalized models to guide practice are needed to remain competitive in today's health care environment. Therefore, health care remains a changing environment that requires resilient professionals willing to ebb and flow with the changes.

ROLES AND STANDARDS FOR ALL HEALTH CARE PRACTITIONERS

All health care workers, whether in the role of clinical practitioner, supervisor, administrator, or advocate, have been challenged to anticipate our current health care system. Incremental changes involve compromising and implementing service agreements that are based on the needs and wishes of various political forces. For all health care workers, evidence-based practice must entail some degree of controlling the rising health care costs, whether they have the ultimate power to control this trend or not.

Responsibility for high-quality service delivery in this cost-containment climate has placed greater emphasis on macropractice. This means that health care workers must take an active role in ethical practice while advocating for social action and social change (Strom-Gottfried & Dunlap, 1999). For evidence-based practice to be effective, there must also be advocacy that seeks to help society understand, while controlling and regulating the health care industry. Therefore, regardless of the health care setting, all health care workers must help to develop and present a format for approaching problems in the current system and establishing means for addressing them.

CONCEPTS ESSENTIAL TO CLINICAL PRACTICE

In health care, the behaviorally based biopsychosocial approach continues to be the model of choice to integrate the biomedical and the psychosocial approaches to practice. In this approach, health care professionals such as social workers are considered leaders regarding understanding and interpreting the "behavioral," "psycho," and "social" factors in a client's condition. Teamwork and collaborative efforts are now required in health care service delivery (Abramson, 2002). Practicing professionals on interdisciplinary teams not uncommonly encounter blurred definitions and diffused boundary distinctions (Dziegielewski, 1996). This does not have to be viewed as problematic. Abramson (2002) identifies and discusses the typology of physician–social worker teams that she developed with Terry Mizrahi in 1994. Typologies provide useful frameworks for comparing professional roles of different professions, allocation of control over decision making, opening up of active communication patterns, facilitating a clinical focus and shared responsibility for patient care, and utilizing information from the team meetings (Abramson, 2002). To creative practitioners, it can be viewed as a way to expand roles and services as part of the team. To exemplify this concept, health care practitioners are encouraged to become leading professionals in the quality review process. It is also recommended that efforts toward solid evidence-based practice must highlight the issues related to informed consent that stipulate that health care providers reveal to clients the nature of the medical treatments as well as potential risks and benefits. Practice-based research with solid research designs should be strongly encouraged in order to study the impact of health care teams on patient outcomes (Abramson, 2002). Evidence-based practice can guide this process, while ensuring that high-quality care services are provided.

PRINCIPLES FOR EVIDENCE-BASED PRACTICE

Prior to the publication of this book, there were no specific guidelines that were entirely comprehensive and inclusive of the different health care disciplines. For the first time, this inclusive desk reference addresses the formulation and execution of evidence-based practice, the different levels of evidence-based practice, quantitative and qualitative practice research exemplars, and empirically based guidelines that have recently been developed. For an understanding of the components, definitions, and step-by-step methods of evidence-based practice, see Chapters 1, 2, and 3 in this book.

It is crucial to remember that when creating these guidelines all the resulting practice principles must include three primary sources: (a) information from the client, (b) information from informed sources of practice, and (c) information based on the latest available research. This will require constant evaluation and reevaluation for practical and scientific rigor, as well as sensitivity to the needs of the individual client being served.

For the researcher–practitioner developing these principles and guidelines, the Centre for Health Evidence (2003) suggests considering the following questions:

Were all important options and outcomes clearly identified?

Was an explicit and sensible process used to identify, select, and combine evidence?

Was an explicit and sensible process used to consider the different outcomes?

Is the guideline likely to account for recent developments?

Has the guideline been subjected to peer review and testing?

Furthermore, according to the Centre for Health Evidence (2003), in examining the results the following questions should always be considered:

Can practical, clinically important recommendations be made on the information that was gathered?

How strong are the recommendations that are being made?

What is the impact or the uncertainty associated with the evidence gathered from the use of these guidelines?

In addition, these authors suggest that the following questions be added to ensure that a comprehensive and client-centered approach is conducted.

Does the particular problem being addressed by the client seem to be best addressed by the standardized protocol developed?

If not, what needs to be added to assist the client in terms of self-empowerment, thereby maximizing self-determination?

CHANGING THE HEALTH CARE ENVIRONMENT: DOCUMENTATION, QUALITY ASSURANCE, AND EVIDENCE-BASED PRACTICE

For the worker in health care practice, the process of recording needs to go beyond the traditional bounds of documentation. Documentation to support and justify evidence-based practice is pivotal. Systematically coordinating research and practice yields the type of record keeping employed in the medical setting to facilitate quality assurance. This mix should consider the need to achieve both high-quality service and cost-effectiveness. Although this union may, at times, be an awkward one, the combination is essential to ensure delivery of efficient and effective services.

The health care environment is changing rapidly, and with the tremendous increase in allied health professionals (Flood, Shortell, & Scott, 1994), it is thought that only the strongest will survive. Not only is this survival important for the professions of health care social work, nursing, and medicine but also it is essential for the clients who are served. Each day and with every task the health care specialist completes, the client's lifestyle and expectations are influenced. Health care professionals help to make their clients better able to relate to their environments. To continue to adequately address the client–environment match in the health care setting, there is no choice—practice and research must be one. When practice and research combine, evidence-based practice results (Dziegielewski, 2002; Wodarski & Dziegielewski, 2001). It is this type of evidence-based practice that will be best suited to withstand the rigor and instability of the managed care practice environment in which the health care professional must survive.

Today, the concept of behaviorally based managed care services is creating a whole new practice revolution, in which the provision of research-based practice leading to evidence-based interventions is germane (Bolter, Levenson, & Alverez, 1990; Dziegielewski, 1997). For a strategic practice approach, attention might best be on intermittent or crisis-oriented treatment as a form of brief intervention in which each session stands alone and is conducted as if it is the only client contact that will occur (Dziegielewski, 2002; Roberts, 2000). Crisis intervention, health maintenance organizations, and employee assistance programs generally favor highly structured brief forms of intervention, and as they continue to proliferate, so will use of the time-limited models they support (Roberts, 2000; Wells, 1994). To take this a step further, it is suggested that health care practitioners will need to continue to learn and use psychosocial education in achieving behavioral outcomes.

Furthermore, the goal for insight-oriented intervention and cure-focused therapy seems to have given way to the acquisition of outcomes-based behavioral change that is considered more realistic and practical (Dziegielewski, 2002). This becomes evident since most health care providers (similar to physicians) generally do not cure the problems clients suffer from. What is expected, however, is to help clients realize and use their own strengths to diminish or alleviate symptoms or states of being that cause discomfort or dysfunctional patterns. Emphasis on evidence-based practice and outcomes-based behavioral changes should be not only expected but also mandated for state-of-the-art practice.

The need for time-limited practice strategies has been clearly established, and the models and methods of service delivery, such as those presented throughout this book, only begin to open the door on evidence-based practice and what is yet to come. Practice environments crisp with managed health care policies, capitation, and so on will continue. Evidence-based practice must demonstrate effectiveness and cost containment (Gibelman, 2002). It is important for all health care practitioners to realize, whether they like it or not, that professional survival dictates change. In general, no matter what the setting, the health care worker needs to embrace a more eclectic approach to practice—in which allegiance to one particular model or method is discouraged (Colby & Dziegielewski, 2001). In closing, (a) evidence-based practice approaches need to include a time-limited intervention approach; (b) such approaches must always stress mutually negotiated goals and objectives; (c) all practice should include efforts to make it evidence-based, and objectives should be behaviorally linked, outcomes-based, and measurable; (d) there should always be an emphasis on client strengths and self-development; (e) the focus of intervention should always be concrete, realistic, and obtainable; and (f) it should be changeable, based on the needs and desires of the client being served—not the preference of the practitioner (Dziegielewski, 2002).

CONCLUSION

Rapid change in health care delivery is well under way. Now physicians, nurses, and social workers must decide whether we want to take an active part in the controversial and adversarial evidence-based practice debate or whether we just want to sit at the "gate" and make sure the other business managers or hospital administrators get through and become the ultimate patient care decision makers. If we decide that the role of the health care specialist is essential to the delivery of competent, effective, and efficient health care services, we will have to strongly advocate for it. By building coalitions and strong advocacy efforts, we believe that we will benefit our clients and ourselves as a profession. If we decide not to advocate for ourselves and assume a position of hesitance and apathy for too long, the importance and strength of the evidence-based physician or social worker as a crucial member of the health care delivery team will go untold, and more assertive professions will be free to claim what once was our turf.

REFERENCES

Abramson, J. S. (2002). Interdisciplinary team practice. In A. R. Roberts & G. J. Greene (Eds.), *Social workers' desk reference* (pp. 44–50). New York: Oxford University Press.
Austin, D. M., & Roberts, A. R. (2002). Clinical social work research in the 21st century: Future, present, and past. In A. R. Roberts & G. J. Greene (Eds.), *Social workers' desk reference* (pp. 822–828). New York: Oxford University Press.
Bolter, K., Levenson, H., & Alverez, W. (1990). Differences in values between short-term and long-term therapists. *Professional Psychology, 21,* 285–290.
Centre for Health Evidence. (2003). *Users' guides to evidence-based practice.* Retrieved June 15, 2003, from http://www.cche.net/usersguides/main.asp
Colby, I., & Dziegielewski, S. F. (2001). *Social work: The people's profession.* Chicago: Lyceum.
Donald, A. (2002). Evidence-based medicine: Key concepts. *Medscape Psychiatry & Mental Health eJournal, 7*(2), 1–5. Retrieved June 15, 2003, from http://www.medscape.com/viewarticle/430709

Dziegielewski, S. F. (1996). Managed care principles: The need for social work in the health care environment. *Crisis Intervention and Time-Limited Treatment, 3,* 97–110.

Dziegielewski, S. F. (1997). Should clinical social workers seek psychotropic medication prescription privileges? Yes. In B. A. Thyer (Ed.), *Controversial issues in social work practice* (pp. 152–165). Boston: Allyn & Bacon.

Dziegielewski, S. F. (2002). *DSM-IV-TR in action.* New York: Wiley.

Dziegielewski, S. F., & Holliman, D. (2001). Managed care and social work: Practice implications in an era of change. *Journal of Sociology and Social Welfare, 28*(2), 125–138.

Farley, O. W., Smith, L. L., Boyle, S. W., & Ronnau, J. (2002). A review of foundation MSW human behavior courses. *Journal of Human Behavior and the Social Environment, 6*(2), 1–12.

Flood, A. B., Shortell, S. M., & Scott, W. R. (1994). Organizational performance: Managing for efficiency and effectiveness. In S. M. Shortell & A. D. Kaluzny (Eds.), *Health care management: Organizational behavior and design* (3rd ed., pp. 316–351). Albany, NY: Delmar.

Franklin, C. (2002). Developing effective practice competencies in managed behavioral health care. In A. R. Roberts & G. J. Greene (Eds.), *Social workers' desk reference* (pp. 1–9). New York: Oxford University Press.

Gibelman, M. (2002). Social work in an era of managed care. In A. R. Roberts & G. J. Greene (Eds.), *Social workers' desk reference* (pp. 16–22). New York: Oxford University Press.

Maruish, M. E. (2002). *Essentials of treatment planning.* New York: Wiley.

Roberts, A. R. (Ed.). (2000). *Crisis intervention handbook: Assessment, treatment and research* (2nd ed.). New York: Oxford University Press.

Rock, B. (2002). Social work in health care in the 21st century. In A. R. Roberts & G. J. Greene (Eds.), *Social workers' desk reference* (pp. 10–16). New York: Oxford University Press.

Strom-Gottfried, K., & Dunlap, K. M. (1999). Unraveling ethical dilemmas. *The New Social Worker, 6*(2), 8–12.

Wells, R. A. (1994). *Planned short-term treatment* (2nd ed.). New York: Free Press.

Wodarski, J., & Dziegielewski, S. F. (2001). *Human behavior and the social environment: Integrating theory and evidence-based practice.* New York: Springer.

11

Toward Common Performance Indicators and Measures for Accountability in Behavioral Health Care

GREGORY B. TEAGUE

THOMAS TRABIN

CHARLES RAY

In this chapter we describe an initiative that focuses broadly on organizations and systems of care. Other chapters in this volume focus on implementing specific evidence-based practice models or on developing or using measures to inform clinical practice, together offering practitioners an inviting array of diverse alternatives oriented to the clinical needs of particular groups of clients. Here, in contrast, is a plan to bridge this diversity of measurement by formulating common performance indicators and measures and promoting their widespread use across a wide array of service settings. The Adult Mental Health Workgroup (AMHW) of the Forum on Performance Measures in Behavioral Health and Related Service Systems (Forum) is a nationally representative group that has formulated and now proposes broad adoption of a few organizational performance measures for accountability and quality management in behavioral health care. The measures were carefully selected to reflect key aspects of care—access, quality/appropriateness, and outcomes—in essentially all settings providing mental health services to adults. Although the focus of the AMHW and consequently of this chapter is adult mental health services, the AMHW is working in conjunction with other Forum workgroups with corresponding initiatives in performance measurement for prevention and treatment of mental health and substance use disorders for all age groups.

130

THE NEED FOR COMMON PERFORMANCE MEASUREMENT

Underlying the movement toward common measurement are two compelling motivations: efficiency and quality. First, the proliferation of reporting requirements compromises efficient delivery of services. Numerous performance measurement systems were developed during the 1990s as services were increasingly provided through large systems or health plans and as computer technology made routine reporting increasingly feasible.[1] In general, these systems were intended to serve as mechanisms for both accountability and quality improvement at organizational and systems levels, as distinct from outcomes management or practice-based research at the client level, but any one system might include data that could serve multiple purposes. However, providers have typically been required to report via several systems as a condition of reimbursement. The duplication imposed by redundant but largely incompatible systems came to impose a significant resource burden on the service delivery system; in response, several initiatives were put forward in hopes of consolidation.[2] These efforts advanced the debate regarding consolidation of redundant reporting requirements and laid some of the groundwork for common measurement but thus far have yielded no tangible impact.

A second and more crucial motivation for common measurement is to help elevate the role of service quality in decisions about resource allocation and to make the overall system more accountable for delivering high-quality services. As in general health care, cost rather than quality often dominates behavioral health care resource decisions, in part because the field lacks consensus on how to demonstrate the overall quality of care, including the attainment of desirable outcomes (Manderscheid, 1998). To be sure, quality is much more difficult to define and demonstrate than cost; ironically, one impediment to promoting quality is the great diversity in measurement systems intended for quality management. While there are significant areas of agreement and overlap in indicators, the lack of common measures means that behavioral health organizations and systems of care cannot be effectively compared, and the resulting fragmentation limits the capacity of the field as a whole to speak with clarity and authority on the issue of quality. In the absence of generally accepted evidence of quality, it is difficult to counter effectively the proposition that cheaper is better, and the result is a continuing drain of resources from behavioral health care (Lutterman & Hogan, 2000). Consistent use of even a small set of common indicators and measures across large segments of the field would help to establish the credibility of claims about quality of care and in so doing would place behavioral health in a more equitable position in debates about the allocation of health care and other societal resources. Perhaps more important, comparable data derived from common measures would extend the utility of benchmarking for quality improvement and decision support.

KEY CONCEPTS OF A COMMON MEASUREMENT INITIATIVE

Indicators and Measures

In discussing performance measurement it is important to maintain the distinction between indicators and measures. An *indicator* is a quantitative specification, typically expressed as a ratio (e.g., percentage) of a selected aspect of performance. A *measure*—consistent with the use of this term in research— represents the methodology for deriving and calculating quantitative results used in an indicator. For any one indicator, there may be many alternative sets of specifications for source data and calculations, each producing its own set of results. Some earlier plans for shared indicator sets stopped short of recommending common measures, leaving to implementers the detailed decisions about how performance would actually be measured (American College of Mental Health Administration [ACMHA], 1998). Although this approach would present potential users with minimal requirements for adaptation and thus more easily lead to consensus and wide participation in a common framework, the inevitable variation in instrumentation across settings or populations would make comparisons between groups less precise and therefore largely speculative. Performance measurement systems using unique measures are inevitably local systems, and the AMHW has taken up the necessary if challenging pursuit of commonality of measures.

Inclusion, Not Replacement

The proposed common indicators and measures are intended to complement rather than replace current measurement systems. The plan calls for use of a small number of carefully selected performance indicators and corresponding measures across essentially all settings providing mental health services to adults. For those indicators measured through consumer self-report surveys, the proposal is to include certain specific items within all relevant performance measurement systems rather than to use a single uniform consumer survey instrument. Performance measurement systems reflecting the core needs of specific types of organizations, health care plans, consumer populations, or treatment of specific disorders are vital and should remain in use.

Distinction Between Common and Core

A key distinction for the AMHW's initiative on common performance indicators and measures is the difference between the concepts of *core* and *common*. An organization or group that pays significant attention to performance in service settings could have key or core indicators—that is, indicators representing areas of performance that are central to its mission or fundamental concerns. Because of differences in mission, population, and so on, views of the relative importance of particular areas of substantive performance typically differ across groups. For example, some advocates for adult consumers with serious mental illness focus intensively on reducing use of seclusion and restraint; some advocates for adults with co-occurring disorders focus on integration of care; and some advocates for children focus on increasing family involvement in treatment planning. Each of these groups sees the core issues for the other groups as being relevant but for various reasons not quite as important as their own, and their respective choices of core performance indicators would differ.

Nonetheless, it is also clear that some interests and concerns are important to virtually everyone and are thus held in common, even if these concerns are only a small subset for any one group. For example, whatever else may be a core issue for any group, it is critical that the population of interest be able to gain access to needed care. Access is thus a domain within which one or more common indicators can be defined. Similarly, there are widely shared concerns within the other domains of quality/appropriateness and outcome. Indicators are defined as common if they are both feasible to measure and shared as indicators across a wide range of stakeholder groups. This focus on a number of common indicators is not intended to suggest that core indicators and measures for specific segments of the field have less value or importance in context. In any given setting, core indicators may have more consequence for improving specific aspects of treatment, but common measures offer the capacity to link findings about practice across settings and impact quality of care more widely.

IDENTIFYING AND OVERCOMING PROBLEMS AND OBSTACLES TO COMMON MEASUREMENT

In the face of an ambitious initiative such as widespread adoption of new measurement practices there are inevitably numerous potential objections and impediments. Although most of them represent real challenges, they are also largely surmountable, depending on environmental incentives and other factors.

Measurement Concerns

The general resistance to quantitative measurement of mental health practices in field settings has—at least overtly—diminished, the publication of this volume being a case in point. However, important methodological and substantive concerns remain and can contribute to resistance if they are not satisfactorily answered.

Concerns about psychometric quality are always in order. The methodological work done in developing the measures proposed here is reassuring in that it grounds the proposed survey items in the most thorough empirical investigation on this topic to date (Eisen et al., 1999; Shaul et al., 2001). However, proponents of item response theory (IRT) would argue that the work done on these measures, like the majority of current mental health measures based on classical test theory

(CTT), have inherent limitations that can be ameliorated by exploiting the strengths of more theoretically sophisticated methods (Embretson, 1996). In particular, the interest in embedding a small set of specific items in a wide range of surveys could be significantly supported by having the kind of item-specific and population-independent information that IRT methods generate. Future Forum-sponsored work on surveys may incorporate use of these methods.

Some stakeholders may have concerns about content or perspective. One concern might focus on the scope of measurement. The proposed common measures capture only a few key constructs of care; because they do not constitute a comprehensive measurement model, they would by themselves provide only a partial view of the services and experiences they measure and would therefore ideally be used in conjunction with other measures oriented to quality improvement. At a deeper level there remains considerable variance of opinion among professionals about the value of information obtained from consumers in evaluating practice. Historically, attitudes within the professional community have tended to devalue the views of patients in contrast to professional judgment, and this outlook may weigh against a positive view of the proposed common measures based on consumer surveys. To counter this concern those who encourage use of the proposed common measures in the field will need to convey information about the emerging understanding of the recovery process and the importance of the consumer perspective (Campbell, 1997; Burt, Duke, & Hargreaves, 1998).

Strategic Risk

The proposed indicators and measures are designed to serve both accountability and quality improvement purposes. Few individuals or organizations voluntarily offer themselves up for external accountability, and the mere possession of standardized data that could be used in this way might seem to present risks to those whose services are measured, even if no current plans or mechanisms exist for such use. Such perceived risks could reinforce resistance to adopting common measures, even for exclusively internal use; the earlier industry-wide resistance to the proposal from the Joint Commission on Accreditation of Healthcare Organizations (JCAHO) for such data requirements illustrates this sensitivity. Widespread adoption of common measures will require assurances in the form of clearly defined protocols to ensure proper confidentiality for organizations, reliable and valid data, and appropriate analysis and reporting of comparisons. These and other assurances will also have to be coupled with the acceptance of the common measures by a few regulatory or accrediting bodies that have the authority to override local risk aversion in the service of a more general interest in concerted quality improvement.

Prior Commitments

The process of undertaking a common project would be much simpler if all participants were starting from scratch. To the contrary, most behavioral health organizations and provider groups have already committed themselves to measurement frameworks, determined their measurement priorities, and invested in measurement systems that are or appear partially inconsistent with participation in a common effort. To that extent, any effort such as the one presented in this chapter faces the same kinds of challenges that have become so vividly apparent in efforts to disseminate evidence-based practices (Drake et al., 2001). The Forum's outreach model, discussed later in this chapter, reflects awareness of both the forces underlying reluctance to change and the dynamics through which change can occur (Rogers, 1995).

Financial commitments are typically identified as primary obstacles. The cost of implementing even minor conversions of information systems that are used on a large scale can be daunting. Depending on the amount of methodological rigor desired, the cost of new data collection—for example, via surveys—could discourage participation. With appropriate incentives, however, the reinvestment could seem worthwhile. As in the case of overcoming risk aversion, widespread adoption of common measurement will likely require endorsement by those organizations whose reporting requirements serve as conditions for access to the material and regulatory benefits their members seek.

An important resource that will significantly defray the cost of revising prior measurement commitments for many organizations is Decision Support 2000+ (DS2K+), a national decision support service for both clinical and management decision making that is being developed through support by the Center for Mental Health Services at the U.S. Substance Abuse and Mental Health Services Administration (SAMHSA). Policy makers, data experts, clinicians, consumers, organizational leaders, and software vendors are collaborating to identify data standards and develop a Web-based plug-in system designed to receive and analyze data against appropriate benchmarks and report back comparative results to the requesting organization. Different types of information for decision support will also be available to individual clinicians and consumers. Measures resulting from the work described in this chapter will be included as available components within DS2K+, making implementation of common measures significantly more useful and affordable for organizations using this system.

Collective Action in a Market Environment

In the context of the U.S. health care market environment, collective action is difficult to orchestrate. At one level, the obstacles to common measurement invoke the classic problem of the common: what seems good for the individual (minimizing risk and expense and maximizing market advantage) may not lead to good for the group (optimizing opportunity for collective quality improvement). Since the proposed common indicators and measures do not typically include the core concerns for specific groups, the gain from using them at the individual level is modest, and thus the intrinsic incentive to adopt them is also modest. As indicated, what will be required is that key opinion leaders and organizations in a position to redefine incentives and reframe perceptions of interest endorse both the underlying assumptions and an initial starting point for common measurement. In this regard, it may be important to bear in mind the general tractability of overt objections. What can be perceived or presented at one point as insurmountable obstacles can be transformed by alternative incentives into readily manageable challenges. The AMHW suggests that the potential benefits of common measurement justify attempting such a transformation.

THE FORUM ON PERFORMANCE MEASURES: HISTORY AND PURPOSE

The AMHW's initiative for common measurement in adult mental health care is presented under the auspices of the Forum on Performance Measures in Behavioral Health and Related Service Systems (Forum). The Forum was established in response to the consensus recommendation of a large group of leaders in the field who attended the Consensus Forum on Mental Health and Substance Use Performance Measures in March 2001 at the Carter Center in Atlanta, Georgia. Sponsored by SAMHSA and growing out of the planning efforts of several groups,[3] the meeting included representatives and stakeholders from the full range of the behavioral health field. The meeting's purpose was to assess the progress made to date on the development and implementation of performance measures in health care and related service systems. It highlighted the considerable efforts made to date by a variety of public and private groups in the development of empirical measures of access, quality/appropriateness, and outcomes of care and also made explicit the tremendous overlap in both content and process that has guided these efforts to date. The meeting concluded with a consensus recommendation that the forum be formally constituted to provide ongoing support, enhancement, and coordination of performance measurement efforts in behavioral health. The three SAMHSA centers agreed to collaborate on furthering this initiative and funding its activities. The resulting Forum articulated a mission with suitable scope and focus:

> The mission of the Forum is to improve the delivery of behavioral health treatment and prevention services by supporting the development and adoption of broadly applicable indicators and measures to assess organizational performance and consumer outcomes. These indicators and measures should be designed to serve the needs of both external accountability as well as internal quality improvement. The Forum will provide an ongoing venue for collaboration, coordination, and communication between the various initiatives, both public and private, which are already working separately to measure service access and delivery, quality, and outcomes. The Forum will foster the sharing of information and experiences of provider, government, employer, consumer, and accreditation groups in implementing performance and outcome measurement practices and initiatives. (AMHW, 2003)

Although the Forum's initial vision had allowed for articulation of comprehensively common indicators and measures spanning all age groups and behavioral health treatments, substantive differences in priorities and practices for major subpopulations led to a decision to pursue the Forum's goals initially through five workgroups. They are oriented respectively to adult mental health treatment, adult substance abuse treatment, child and adolescent mental health treatment, child and adolescent substance abuse treatment, and substance abuse prevention. All of the workgroups are articulating indicators and measures within a commonly agreed-upon framework, described later in this chapter. They are finding considerable agreement on the indicators they have formulated, but they differ at the level of measure specifications because of the concerns of the different subpopulations and settings they seek to address.

Each of the five workgroups has adapted its activities to the specific challenges of its focal area. With support from SAMHSA's Center for Mental Health Services, the AMHW has refined a specific set of recommended indicators and measures for adult mental health. On behalf of the Forum this group has also developed a broad outreach strategy for reengaging key groups and individuals in the field to encourage implementation. These products will be described in detail in the remainder of this chapter. The Adult Substance Abuse Workgroup is continuing the agenda laid out by the Washington Circle Group (McCorry, Garnick, Bartlett, Cotter, & Chalk, 2000) and supported by SAMHSA's Center for Substance Abuse Treatment. The long-term goal is refinement and promulgation of a set of indicators and measures for the four domains of alcohol and other drug services representing prevention/education, recognition, treatment, and maintenance; the initial focus is on indicators of identification, treatment initiation, and treatment engagement (Garnick et al., 2002). The Child and Adolescent Mental Health Workgroup is functioning as a corollary effort of the Outcomes Roundtable for Children and Families (1998), supported by SAMHSA's Center for Mental Health Services. They have facilitated movement to consensus on measurement priorities by the diverse set of stakeholders in this field and are currently testing the applicability of the identification, treatment initiation, and treatment engagement measures to child and adolescent mental health services. Similarly, the Child and Adolescent Substance Abuse Treatment Workgroup is working in concert with the Adult Substance Abuse Workgroup to customize measure specifications for applying these indicators to child and adolescent substance abuse treatment services. The Substance Abuse Prevention Workgroup is adapting indicators excerpted from the Core Measures Initiative sponsored by SAMHSA's Center for Substance Abuse Prevention and is supported by that Center. Supporting and linking these five substantive groups within the Forum are a coordinating committee and an executive committee, as well as several task forces that help to integrate and further refine workgroup products to ensure consistency of proposed terminology and credibility of proposed measurement methods.

In addition to these components, a new, crosscutting Forum workgroup is being formed: the Modular Consumer Survey Workgroup (MCSW). This workgroup will use the products of the AMHW along with input from the Forum workgroups and other experts to articulate preliminary specifications for modular sets of consumer survey items. The concepts underlying this effort are discussed in more detail later in the chapter. Many of the products of the MCSW will be incorporated into the next version of the SAMHSA-sponsored Mental Health Statistics Improvement Program (MHSIP) Consumer Survey, which will be modular in design rather than being a single survey instrument. The close relationship between MHSIP and the Performance Partnership Grants, the primary federal funding mechanism for state behavioral health programs, provides an additional avenue for broad implementation of these proposed common measures. The importance of these linkages is reflected in the fact that both the MCSW and MHSIP are represented on the Forum's executive committee.

SELECTING PERFORMANCE MEASURES

The processes used by the Forum workgroups for identifying common indicators and measures included substantial input from consumers, providers, payers, and purchasers of behavioral health care services. Workgroup members representing these key stakeholder groups carefully reviewed the work of previous groups addressing similar tasks (ACMHA, 1998; 2001 Center for Mental Health Services [CMHS], 1996; Teague et al., 1997; National Association of State Mental Health Program Directors [NASMHPD], 1998). Selection of indicators focused on fundamental concerns within a common framework and was informed by a set of underlying core values and technical criteria.

Fundamental Concerns Within a Common Framework

As components of the Forum, all of the workgroups are working to articulate indicators and measures for their specific combinations of population and service sector within a two-dimensional common framework. One dimension of this framework covers the domains, or content areas, of common performance measurement: access, quality/appropriateness, and outcome. These three domains together reflect a fundamental set of underlying values, critical questions, and expectations about performance:

- Are people in need able to get services?
- Are the services that people receive the ones they need and are these services being provided the way they should be?
- Are services effective in producing the results that people need and in maintaining or improving the mental status of the population?

The second dimension in the common framework is the data source. Data to support identified indicators should come from both administrative databases and primary sources of consumer perceptions and self-report. The potential to use administrative data continues to increase as computing hardware and software expand coverage and enhance technical capability. Large-scale systems relying on such data have been in use for several years, albeit using different reporting systems and under different authorities;[4] the technical challenges here are principally in standardization and integration. There is also increasingly widespread acceptance of the need to consider the consumer perspective as a fundamental component in evaluating the effectiveness of behavioral health care services. Recognition of the central role of consumers' perceptions and choices in treatment is reflected in the surgeon general's report on mental health (U.S. Department of Health and Human Services, 1999), the Institute of Medicine's (IOM) report on the "quality chasm" in health care (IOM, 2001), and in discussions about the interpersonal context of evidence-based practice (Drake et al., in press). Reliable methods to gather primary data from consumers are increasingly available; over the past decade many studies have defined and collected this kind of information, resulting in a number of separate but sound measures of consumer perceptions of important aspects of care across populations, organizational settings, and plans (Teague, 2000).

Technical Criteria

Each indicator proposed by the AMHW met three general criteria, which were derived from or consistent with criteria used in performance measurement efforts by other national organizations and policy groups:

- *Meaningfulness*: Does the proposed indicator address a dimension that relates to a critical aspect of care, has value for consumers and other stakeholders in services, and can differentiate among persons or organizations or over time?
- *Measurability*: Can reliable, accurate, and valid information be obtained to support the proposed indicator?
- *Feasibility*: Can the proposed indicators be used at a reasonable cost using data currently available or readily obtainable?

An additional requirement for any common indicator is that it should have *relevance* across diverse consumer populations as well as across differing types of provider and managed care organizations. Finally, fundamental to any performance indicator is the criterion of *actionability*: Does the indicator measure a construct that is susceptible to identifiable corrective action?

Setting Measurement Priorities

The work of selecting indicators and measures was carried out in several phases. Because common measures will impose at least a modest burden on users, parsimony has been of high value throughout. This is particularly the case for the consumer survey, where a large number of survey items would discourage its adoption. At each point, parsimony was challenged by the value of ensuring adequate coverage of important aspects of care; the AMHW's recommendation of 21 items demonstrates a balance between these two values. Nonetheless, anticipating that the MCSW and other organizations may find 21 items too many to adopt, the AMHW has taken the additional step of identifying the most critical content within each indicator, distinguishing between 12 higher-priority and 9 lower priority items. Further details about the items and their respective priority levels are provided in the measure overview later in the chapter as well as in the appendix.

Collaboration Among Forum Workgroups

Initially much of the Forum's work was carried out separately by the workgroups. Nevertheless, the Forum retained its underlying commitment to identify more broadly based common indicators that might be applicable across the different population settings addressed by each of the workgroups. Consequently, the workgroups sought successfully to identify commonalities between their proposed indicators, even though specifications at the measurement level had to be customized for differing treatment contexts or populations. Instances of this form of commonality were identified for both administrative data–based and consumer survey–based indicators.

The exploratory work on measures for identification, initiation, and engagement in treatment represents a prominent example of the effort to find commonality, in this case using administrative data–based indicators. These measures were initially defined and tested for adult substance abuse treatment. Slight modifications have been made to the original measures to adapt them to the requirements for adult mental health and child/adolescent treatment populations, and they are currently being tested in a variety of administrative datasets.

The pending modular measure development represents another important integrative initiative within the Forum, in this case focusing on consumer survey-based data. Some of the modules will have items measuring content shared across multiple behavioral health care sectors. Even before the MCSW has begun its work, the executive committee has identified at least four of the AMHW consumer survey–based indicators as having this wider commonality—three across all treatment populations and one across both treatment and prevention. These designations are noted in the appendix.

OVERVIEW OF THE AMHW'S PROPOSED
INDICATORS AND MEASURES

Common Indicators

A table showing recommended indicators and sample items by domain and data source is located in the appendix to this chapter; the following is a brief overview of content. The first indicators we discuss here are based on measures that have already been tested and validated in the field. In the access domain, an indicator of "timeliness of access to treatment services" is generated by data from consumer survey item responses and indicators of "service use" and "treatment duration" are generated via administrative data. In the quality/appropriateness domain consumer survey data support four indicators: "quality of interaction with counselors and clinicians," "information provided by counselors and clinicians," "perceived overall quality of treatment services," and "perceived cultural sensitivity of treatment services." Another quality/appropriateness indicator is generated from administrative data: "follow-up after hospitalization." In the outcome domain, a single indicator of "perceived improvement" is derived from consumer survey data. In the prioritization of indicators derived from the consumer survey, the outcome indicators were top ranked, followed by the access indicator; the quality/appropriateness indicators were somewhat lower ranked. Each indicator had some high-priority item content, so no indicators were considered to have low priority.

The following indicators are currently under evaluation. Given strong individual and societal interests in employment, there is a consumer survey indicator of "work functioning improvement." There are also three indicators using administrative data corresponding to the common indicators proposed for substance abuse treatment, identification, initial engagement in "treatment," and "continuing engagement in treatment."

Common Measures

The workgroup recognized that only parsimonious scales or other measures tapping general dimensions would be acceptable for widespread implementation, so it relied heavily on material developed and validated in multiple service settings and sectors.

Consumer Survey–Based Measures

A number of proposed survey items are taken from the Experience of Care and Health Outcomes (ECHO) survey (Eisen et al., 1999), which was designed to integrate the best aspects of two national consumer survey measures for evaluating behavioral health care from the perspective of consumers, oriented respectively to private and public sectors. Members of the workgroup participated with developers of the two original surveys in development and extensive testing to optimize the fit between ECHO items and the recommended indicators. Selection of specific items was based on research findings of main item groupings, or factors, from the survey instrument (Shaul et al., 2001) as well as on the preliminary list of target concerns that the precursor to the AMHW had generated prior to the first Carter Center Forum. Next, we briefly describe item content for each survey-generated indicator, with higher and lower priorities indicated.

For the access indicator, the high-priority item asks about timeliness of urgent care; lower-priority items ask about timeliness of regular appointments and availability of help by telephone. For the quality of interaction indicator, higher priority items are used to assess whether practitioners listen carefully and explain things understandably and whether consumers have been sufficiently involved in their treatment; lower priority items ask whether practitioners demonstrate respect for what the consumer says and spend enough time with the consumer and whether consumers feel safe with them. For the information indicator, higher priority questions ask whether practitioners have provided information about medication side effects, treatment options, and illness self-management; lower-priority items ask whether information has been provided about self-help groups and patient rights. The perceived overall quality of treatment indicator is calculated using a single global rating item. The cultural sensitivity indicator is also calculated from a single item, in this case preceded by a screener question designed to elicit responses only from consumers who deem the issue important. The perceived improvement scale asks for comparison of consumers' current status with their earlier status in four areas: higher priority items tap level of problems and symptoms and ability to deal with daily problems; lower priority items tap respondents' ability to accomplish things they want to do and ability to deal with social situations. The primary question for the work functioning improvement indicator addressing ability to perform paid work is structurally identical to the perceived improvement items and is likely to be included in the latter scale in future analyses.

Administrative Data–Based Measures

The measures based on administrative data are a combination of established and developing measures. The measures of "persons with mental health problems using services" (equivalent to measures of penetration), treatment duration, and time until follow-up after hospitalization are already standard in the field and seeing extensive use. They are consistent with definitions and data in one or more of such influential measurement reporting sets as the National Committee for Quality Assurance's (NCQA) Health Employer Data Information Set (HEDIS) (Druss, Miller, Rosenheck, Shih, & Bost, 2002), those advanced by the National Association of State Mental Health Program Directors (NASMHPD, 1998), and the federal Center for Mental Health Services' (CMHS) Uniform Reporting System (URS).

The three additional measures of identification, initial engagement, and continuing engagement are still in development and testing. These are adaptations of the treatment phase–specific measures put forward by the Washington Circle Group for adult substance abuse treatment in managed care settings (Garnick et al., 2002). They address respectively the rate at which persons having specific conditions of interest are newly identified in claims data; the rate at which these persons receive a subsequent service promptly, indicating that they have been initially engaged in treatment; and the rate at which they receive two additional services in due course, indicating that treatment has continued. Although these concerns have not had the same relative prominence in the mental health field as some of the concerns highlighted in the AMHW indicators of quality/appropriateness and outcome, the importance of access and continuity, particularly for persons with serious mental illness, in combination with historically low performance for this population in both of these areas, warrants widespread application of these measures.

Methods

Use of rigorous, standardized methods for data collection are recommended but not necessarily required of all who might use the measures. The workgroup makes the assumption that there are trade-offs between coverage and rigor: if measures are to be widely used, there will inevitably be great variance in capacity and will to commit resources to data collection. For both consumer survey and administrative data, users may opt to conform to existing standards for collection and analysis, and data voluntarily provided in this way can be used in developing norms. Alternatively, users may opt to use the measures in less standardized but nonetheless internally useful ways.

PLANNED NEXT STEPS

The Forum increasingly has come to realize its role as an ongoing manager and coordinator of key efforts to develop common measures. Its placement and membership enable it, both directly and through its components, for example, the AMHW, to facilitate crucial linkages and to speed up development and implementation of common measures. The project of expanding and evaluating the Washington Circle Group measures of identification, initiation, and engagement in other populations is a case in point. Three important tasks are forthcoming: developing modular measures that build on the AMHW's proposed consumer survey–based measures, thereby extending common measurement across other behavioral health care sectors; convening representatives of selected national organizations to share information about the Forum's progress and map out specific implementation steps; and conducting additional outreach to the field as an initial step toward implementation. Following are brief descriptions of these three tasks.

Modular Survey

When the Forum was first established, the challenge of articulating common ground across the full range of behavioral health care seemed premature, and the separate workgroups were formed to make initial progress on a more manageable scale. At this point, attention has returned to the task of integrating separate areas through the creation of a new workgroup, the MCSW, charged with the responsibility of developing a modular survey approach. The vision is that it will be possible to achieve a balance between the unifying vision of common measurement and the substantial variation in populations and treatment concerns represented within the Forum. For this purpose the context is the four primary treatment populations defined respectively by the intersections of two age categories, adult and child/adolescent, and two behavioral disorder categories, mental health and substance use. The premise is that critical performance measurement content has some overlap, however small, across adjacent pairs of these groups as well as across all four groups. The goal is to identify measurement modules that will be used in a unique combination for each of the primary populations. Thus, for example, the total common measurement set for adult mental health would include the content of three separate modules: items unique to adult mental health, items shared with adult substance abuse but not used elsewhere, and items used with all populations.

At this stage, the agenda for the MCSW can be outlined only generally. Products and priorities of the current Forum workgroups will serve as critical input. Critical constructs for each treatment population and corresponding items will be identified and if necessary revised over time to optimize the balance among individual modules. As noted, it is already apparent that several AMHW indicators are relevant outside of adult mental health, but it is not yet clear which of the proposed AMHW measures will be applicable to which of the four modules relevant to adult mental health because overlap with other populations at the level of items has not yet been determined. The goal of developing modular measures will entail achieving a significant degree of measurement utility and efficiency, so it is anticipated that use of methods derived from IRT may be helpful in this work.

Outreach

On behalf of the Forum, the AMHW has identified critical elements in a strategy for taking tested and refined common performance indicators and measures back to the field that, through its representatives at the initial consensus meeting, had provided encouragement to undertake the effort. This important step entails disseminating the Forum's work to major constituencies in behavioral health care, inviting feedback, engaging in dialogue, and obtaining endorsement. National organizations to be contacted are of five types: research and policy organizations that influence opinions and that have some interest in using the data derivable from widespread use of the indicators and measures; consumer advocacy groups; professional associations representing individual clinicians; trade associations representing provider and managed care organizations that are likely to be required to collect, analyze, and report on data from these measures; and public and private purchasers of behavioral health care benefits and accrediting organizations that are in positions to require implementation of these measures.

In view of the considerable effort required both to revise the data infrastructure and to reorient behavior, communications in this outreach process will need to do the following:

- Present a compelling argument for the value of this endeavor and the advantages to organizations of implementing the recommended common measures.
- Provide reassurance to people and organizations that the proposed common measurements are intended to supplement, not supplant, their own unique organizational measurement needs and possible proprietary measurement interests.
- Describe the highly inclusive, multiconstituent consensus process by which proposed common indicators and measures were identified, thus helping to establish the credibility and momentum of the enterprise.
- Portray the current common set in the context of a multiphase, incremental, and continuously improving initiative spanning several years, rather than as completed work. Such a perspective invites participation in the larger, ongoing initiative and helps to allay fears of pressure to employ measures beyond their useful life.
- Assess each organization's readiness and willingness to play a role in supporting their own and others' implementation of the measures. Indicators and measures will adapt and become more refined over time, and ongoing feedback will be needed, but there must be general commitment to going forward with an initial set to get the work started.
- Convey a final point about the level of resources behind this initiative that may be critical to persuasion: SAMHSA is committing ongoing support and intends to encourage the field's use of data derived from widespread adoption of common measures for benchmarking and decision support, for example, through such mechanisms as DS2K+.

Consensus Forum

As initial impetus to this distributed outreach dialogue, the second national Consensus Forum on Mental Health and Substance Abuse Performance Measures will be convened. The meeting itself will serve as an important part of the outreach effort, providing representatives of important stakeholders a setting for collective engagement with the now mature Forum to understand the benefits and opportunities of common measurement. While representatives from all of the types of aforementioned stakeholder groups will be invited, there will be a particular emphasis on inviting those organizations that are in positions either to directly require or implement the common measures. Specific products from Forum workgroups will be featured, including work in progress on modular consumer survey measures and the family of identification, initiation, and engagement measures that have been customized for use with specific populations. Conversely, the meeting will also provide Forum representatives the opportunity to refresh their familiarity with the diversity of contexts to which common measures must be adequately adapted and with the related needs of those who will ultimately carry out common measurement.

CONCLUSION

In this chapter we have outlined the rationale, plan, and substance of a proposal to establish a small number of common indicators and measures of key aspects of performance in adult mental health care. This initiative is part of a larger plan for implementation of common performance measurement throughout behavioral health care for the purpose of improving quality and accountability. The plan calls for incorporation of selected indicators and measures within existing systems rather than replacement of current efforts. Indicators and measures have been selected on the basis of broad applicability to services and populations, technical merit, empirical validation, and capacity to reflect the shared values and concerns of a wide range of stakeholders. It is anticipated that widespread implementation of common measures and indicators would yield several benefits, including

- generating compatible performance measurement efforts across all organizations to facilitate appropriate comparisons for accountability to consumers and purchasers;
- providing more informed decision support for consumers and purchasers selecting treatment and/or health plans;
- facilitating collaboration for benchmarking and quality improvement purposes;
- providing guidance on critically important dimensions of performance to those behavioral health care organizations that are in early stages of measuring performance; and
- reducing redundancy in requirements for performance data by accreditation, regulatory, and purchaser organizations, thereby increasing efficiency and reducing costs.

It is premature at this stage to gauge the degree of success of this effort. Additional refinement and actual implementation still lie ahead. Although the proposal is for modest change in any one setting, the industry-wide impact is potentially substantial, and large systems are difficult to move in concert. However, the Forum and its workgroups represent leadership at the intersection of several crucial spheres: public and private, mental health and substance abuse, and treatment and prevention across the life span. There is therefore reason for optimism, at least about significant progress; even if common measures are less widely implemented than envisioned here, the scope of engagement already visible will surely provide a basis for broader consensus at a later stage.

APPENDIX

Common Indicators, Measures, and Data Sources

Domain Data	Indicator	Abbreviated Description or Items
Access		
Consumer survey	Timeliness of access to treatment services[1]	*In the last [ ] months,* when you needed to get counseling or treatment **right away,** how often did you see someone as soon as you wanted?[2]
		In the last [ ] months, how often did you get an **appointment** for counseling or treatment **as soon as you wanted?**
		In the last [ ] months, how often did you **get the professional help or advice** you needed **over the phone?**
Admin. database	Identification[1]	Percent of persons in enrolled/eligible population with major depression, schizophrenia, schizoaffective disorder, or bipolar disorder who have had at least one mental health service during the year.
Admin. database	Persons with mental health problems using services	Percent of persons in enrolled/eligible population with at least one mental health service, broken out by defined categories of age, gender, race/ethnicity, diagnosis, and level of care.
Quality Appropriateness		
Consumer survey	Quality of interaction with counselors and clinicians	*In the last [ ] months,* how often did the people you went to for counseling or treatment **listen carefully to you?**[2]
		In the last [ ] months, how often did the people you went to for counseling or treatment **explain things in a way you could understand?**[2]
		In the last [ ] months, how often were you **involved as much as you wanted** in your counseling or treatment?[2]
		In the last [ ] months, how often did the people you went to for counseling or treatment **show respect for what you had to say?**
		In the last [ ] months, how often did the people you went to for counseling or treatment **spend enough time** with you?
		In the last [ ] months, how often did you **feel safe** when you were with the people you went to for counseling or treatment?
Consumer survey	Information provided by counselors and clinicians	*(Screener) In the last [ ] months, did you take any prescription medications as part of your treatment?*
		(If yes . . .) In the last [ ] months, were you told what **side effects of those medications to watch for?**[2]
		In the last [ ] months, were you given information about **different kinds of counseling or treatment** that are available?[2]
		In the last [ ] months, were you given as much information as you wanted about **what you could do to manage your condition?**[2]
		In the last [ ] months, were you told about **self-help or support groups,** such as recipient-run groups or 12-step programs?
		In the last [ ] months, were you given information about **your rights as a patient?**

Common Indicators, Measures, and Data Sources (*continued*)

Domain Data	Indicator	Abbreviated Description or Items
Consumer survey	Perceived overall quality of treatment services[1]	Using any number from 0 to 10, where 0 is the worst counseling or treatment possible and 10 is the best counseling or treatment possible, what number would you use to rate the counseling or treatment you received in the last 12 months?[2]
Consumer survey	Perceived cultural sensitivity of treatment services[1]	*(Screener) Does your* **language, race, religion, ethnic background, or culture** *make any difference in the kind of counseling or treatment you need?* *(If yes . . .) In the last [ ] months,* was the care you received **responsive to those needs?**[2]
Admin. database	Treatment duration	Mean length of service during the reporting period for persons receiving services in each of three levels of care: inpatient/24-hour, day/night structured outpatient programs, and ambulatory.
Admin. database	Follow-up after hospitalization	Percent of persons discharged from 24-hour mental health care who receive follow-up ambulatory or day/night mental health treatment within 7 (30) days.
Admin. database	Initiation of treatment[1] for mental health problems	The percent of persons identified during the year with a new episode of major depression, schizophrenia, schizoaffective disorder, or bipolar disorder who have had *either* an inpatient encounter for treatment of that disorder *or* a subsequent treatment encounter within 14 days after a first outpatient encounter.[3]
Admin. database	Engagement in treatment[1] for mental health problems	The percent of persons identified during the year with a new episode of major depression, schizophrenia, schizoaffective disorder, or bipolar disorder who have had *either* a single inpatient encounter *or* two outpatient treatment encounters within 30 days after the initiation of care.[3]
Outcome		
Consumer survey	Perceived improvement[4]	*Compared to [ ] months ago,* how would you rate your **ability to deal with daily problems** *now?*[2] *Compared to [ ] months ago,* how would you rate your **problems or symptoms** *now?*[2] *Compared to [ ] months ago,* how would you rate your **ability to deal with social situations** *now?* *Compared to [ ] months ago,* how would you rate your **ability to accomplish the things you want to do** *now?*
Consumer survey	Work functioning improvement	*Compared to [ ] months ago,* how would you rate your **ability to perform paid work** *now?*[2, 3]

1. Indicators common to all treatment perspectives
2. Consumer survey-based items designated as having higher priority
3. Measures undergoing development
4. Indicators common to all treatment perspectives as well as prevention
Additional details may be found at the website for the Adult Mental Health Workgroup of the Forum on Performance Measures in Behavioral Health and Related Service Systems, http://mindicators.org/.

NOTES

1. Performance measurement systems: Digital Equipment Corporation's (DEC) Performance Measurement System for HMOs under contract to provide behavioral health care services; National Association of Psychiatric Health Systems (NAPHS)/ Association of Behavioral Group Practices (ABGP) performance indicator study; National Committee for Quality Assurance's (NCQA) Health Plan and Employer Data Information Set (HEDIS); Mental Health Statistics Improvement Program's (MHSIP) Consumer-Oriented Report Card; Mental Health Corporation of America (MHCA) consumer survey and performance indicator set; American Managed Behavioral Healthcare Association's (AMBHA) Performance Measurement System (PERMS); Joint Commission on Accreditation of Healthcare Organizations' (JCAHO) Oryx Requirements.

2. Consolidation efforts: Council for Accreditation of Rehabilitation Facilities' (CARF) Performance Measurement Advisory Council; National Association of State Mental Health Program Directors' (NASMHPD) review of state mental health program performance measures and its subsequent multistate studies using selected performance measures; American College of Mental Health Administration's (ACMHA) multiyear initiative in collaboration with the major accrediting organizations serving the mental health care field to produce a consensus document of recommended common performance indicators (ACMHA, 2001).

3. Planning groups for consensus conference: the Summit Planning Group, which worked closely with and built on related initiatives, particularly the ACMHA-hosted Workgroup of Accrediting Organizations; the Washington Circle Group, which focused on substance abuse treatment measures; the Experience of Care and Health Outcomes (ECHO) consumer survey development team; and the Child and Adolescent Outcomes Roundtable.

4. See note 1.

REFERENCES

American College of Mental Health Administration (ACMHA). (1998). *Summit 1997: Preserving quality and value in the managed care equation.* Pittsburgh, PA: The American College of Mental Health Administration. Retrieved July 21, 2003, from http://www.acmha.org/summit_1997_1.htm.

American College of Mental Health Administration (ACMHA) (2001). *A proposed consensus set of indicators for behavioral health.* Pittsburgh, PA: The American College of Mental Health Administration. Retrieved July 21, 2003, from http://www.acmha.org/files/acmha_20.pdf.

Adult Mental Health Workgroup (AMHW). (2003). *Mission.* Retrieved July 21, 2003, from http://mhindicators.org/.

Burt, M. R., Duke, A., & Hargreaves, W. A. (1998). The program environment scale: Assessing client perceptions of community-based programs for the severely mentally ill. *American Journal of Community Psychology, 26*(6), 853–879.

Campbell, J. (1997). How consumers/survivors are evaluating the quality of psychiatric care. *Evaluation Review, 21*(3), 357–363.

Center for Mental Health Services (CMHS). (1996, April). *The final report of the*

Mental Health Statistics Improvement Program Task Force on a Consumer-Oriented Mental Health Report Card. Washington, DC: Center for Mental Health Services, SAMHSA. Retrieved July 21, 2003, from http://www.mhsip.org/reportcard/reportcard.html.

Drake, R. E., Goldman, H. H., Leff, H. S., Lehman, A. F., Dixon, L., Mueser, K. T., et al. (2001). Implementing evidence-based practices in routine mental health service settings. *Psychiatric Services, 52*(2), 179–182.

Drake, R. E., Rosenberg, S. D., Teague, G. B., Bartels, S. J., & Torrey, W. C. (in press). Fundamental principles of evidence-based medicine applied to mental health care. In Evidence-based practices in mental health. *Psychiatric Clinics of North America.*

Druss, B. G., Miller, C. L., Rosenheck, R. A., Shih, S. C., & Bost, J. E. (2002). Mental health care quality under managed care in the United States: A view from the health employer data and information set (HEDIS). *American Journal of Psychiatry, 159*(5), 860–862.

Eisen, S. V., Shaul, J. A., Clarridge, B., Nelson, D., Spink, J., & Cleary, P. D. (1999). Development of a consumer survey for behavioral health services. *Psychiatric Services, 50*(6), 793–798.

Embretson, S. E. (1996). The new rules of measurement. *Psychological Assessment, 8*(4), 341–349.

Garnick, D. W., Lee, M. T., Chalk, M., Gastfriend, D., Horgan, C. M., McCorry, F., et al. (2002). Establishing the feasibility of performance measures for alcohol and other drugs. *Journal of Substance Abuse Treatment, 23*, 375–385.

Institute of Medicine (IOM) Committee on the Quality of Health Care in America. (2001). *Crossing the quality chasm: A new health system for the 21st century.* Washington, DC: National Academy Press.

Lutterman, T., & Hogan, M. (2000). State mental health agency controlled expenditures and revenues for mental health services, FY 1981 to 1997. In R. W. Manderscheid & M. J. Henderson (Eds.), *Center for Mental Health Services. Mental Health, United States, 2000* (DHHS Publication No. SMA 01-3537). Washington, DC: U.S. Government Printing Office. Retrieved July 21, 2003, from http://www.mentalhealth.org/publications/allpubs/sma01—3537/chapter16.asp.

Manderscheid, R. (1998). From many into one: Addressing the crisis of quality in managed behavioral health care at the millennium. *Journal of Behavioral Health Services and Research, 25*(2), 233–236.

McCorry, F., Garnick, D. W., Bartlett, J., Cotter, F., & Chalk, M. (2000). Developing performance measures for alcohol and other drug services in managed care plans. *Journal on Quality Improvement, 26*(11), 633–643.

National Association of State Mental Health Program Directors (NASMHPD). (2000). *Recommended operational definitions and measures to implement the NASMHPD Framework of mental health performance indicators.* Alexandria, VA: National Association of State Mental Health Program Directors Research Institute. Retrieved July 21, 2003, from http://nri.rdmc.org/PresidentsTaskForce2001.pdf.

Outcomes Roundtable for Children and Families (1998). *Fitting the pieces together: Building outcome accountability in child mental health and child welfare systems.* Washington, DC: Center for Mental Health Services, SAMHSA.

Rogers, E. M. (1995). *Diffusion of innovations* (4th ed.). New York: Free Press.

Shaul, J. A., Eisen, S. V., Clarridge, B. R., Stringfellow, V. L., Fowler, F. J., et al. (2001). *Experience of Care and Health Outcomes (ECHO™) survey field test report: Survey evaluation.* Retrieved July 21, 2003, from http://www.hcp.med .harvard.edu/echo/home.html.

Teague, G. B. (2000). Patient perceptions of care measures. In A. J. Rush, H. A. Pincus, First, M. B., Zarin, D. A., Blacker, D., Endicott, J., et al. (Eds.), *Handbook of Psychiatric Measures.* Washington, DC: American Psychiatric Association.

Teague, G. B., Ganju, V., Hornik, J. A., Johnson, J. R., & McKinney, J. (1997). The MHSIP mental health report card: A consumer-oriented approach to monitoring the quality of mental health plans. *Evaluation Review, 21*(3), 330–341.

U.S. Department of Health and Human Services. (USDHHS). (1999). *Mental health: A report of the surgeon general.* Rockville, MD: U.S. Department of Health and Human Services, Substance Abuse and Mental Health Services Administration, Center for Mental Health Services, National Institutes of Health, National Institute of Mental Health. Retrieved July 21, 2003, from http://www .surgeongeneral.gov/library/mentalhealth/home.html.

12

Facilitating Practitioner Use of Evidence-Based Practice

EDWARD J. MULLEN

This chapter discusses ways to support social work practitioners in their attempts to use evidence-based practice to assess, intervene with, and better understand clients. Although social work practitioners report little use of evidence-based practices, many express a desire to use methods that are considered to be valid (Drake et al., 2001; Mullen & Bacon, 2000, 2003; U.S. Department of Health and Human Services, 1999). There is an emerging literature addressing implementation of evidence-based practices in organizations, but little attention has been given to how individual practitioners can be helped to use evidence-based practice (Addis & Krasnow, 2000; Torrey et al., 2001). While implementation strategies that seek system change by focusing on specific service delivery systems or organizations are important, there are limitations to such efforts. The sheer number of organizations defies any attempt to change them one by one. Also, many practitioners provide services outside such organizational settings, such as in private practice. Accordingly, in addition to implementation strategies directed at service systems and organizations, attention needs to be paid to how practitioners themselves can be helped to implement evidence-based practices. This is the focus of this chapter. This chapter describes evidence-based practice, approaches to dissemination and implementation of best practices that can be of benefit to practitioners, organizational and environmental supports needed for practitioners to function as evidence-based practitioners, and suggestions for training social work practitioners in evidence-based practice.

EVIDENCE-BASED PRACTICE

An *evidence-based practice* is considered to be any practice that has been established as effective through scientific research according to a set of explicit criteria (Drake et al., 2001). For example, in 1998 a Robert Wood Johnson Foundation consensus panel concluded that research findings identify six evidence-based treatment practices for the treatment of persons with severe mental illness: assertive community treatment (ACT), supported employment, family psychoeducation, skills training, illness self-management, and integrated dual-disorder treatment. To be considered an evidence-based practice, four selection criteria were used: the treatment practices had been standardized through manuals or guidelines; the practices had been evaluated with controlled research designs; through the use of objective measures, important outcomes were demonstrated; and the research was conducted by different research teams (Torrey et al., 2001). Accordingly, we can say that evidence-based practices or best practices were identified for the treatment of persons with severe mental illness through efficacy trials meeting these four criteria.

The term *evidence-based practice* is used also to describe a way of practicing, or an approach to practice. For example, evidence-based medicine has been described as "the conscientious, explicit and judicious use of current best evidence in making decisions about the care of individual patients" (Sackett et al., 1996, p. 71). Evidence-based medicine is further described as the "integration of best research evidence with clinical expertise and patient values" (Sackett, Straus, Richardson, Rosenberg, & Haynes, 2000, p. 1). Sheldon described evidence-based social care as "the conscientious, explicit and judicious use of current best evidence in making decisions regarding the welfare of service-users and carers" (Sheldon, 2002). Accordingly, evidence-based practice is a decision-making process in which judgments are made on a case-by-case basis by using best evidence. In addition, evidence-based social work practice would incorporate the following characteristics:

- Rather than a relationship based on asymmetrical information and authority, in evidence-based practice the relationship is characterized by a sharing of information and of decision making. The practitioner does not decide what is best for the client, but rather the practitioner provides the client with up-to-date information about what the best evidence is regarding the client's situation, what options are available, and likely outcomes. With this information communicated in culturally and linguistically appropriate ways, clients are supported to make decisions for themselves whenever and to the extent possible.
- There is a focus on fidelity in implementation of client-chosen interventions rather than an assumption that selected interventions will be provided as intended. Fidelity of implementation requires that the specific evidence-based practice be provided as it was tested when research supported its effectiveness. Too often serious distortion occurs during implementation.
- There is a critical, inquisitive attitude regarding the achievement of valued outcomes and unintended negative effects rather than an unquestioning belief

that only intended outcomes will be achieved (and therefore a failure to secure information about actual outcomes, or permitting prior expectations to
color achievements).

- Rather than relying on static prior beliefs, practitioners aggressively pursue
new information about outcomes. This new information is derived from researching what occurs when interventions are implemented and new research
findings promulgated by others.
- Ongoing knowledge revision is based on this new information, which in turn
is communicated to clients.
- A relative weighing of information occurs, placing information derived from
scientific inquiry as more important than information based on intuition,
authority, or custom.

Social work practitioners need to know what has been identified as best practices,
and they need to be prepared to be evidence-based practitioners. Social workers
can benefit greatly from clear identification of interventions that work, through
such efforts as seen in the systematic reviews conducted and disseminated
through the Cochrane and Campbell Collaborations, as well as the work of the
many evidence-based practice centers around the world. These collaborations
and centers are using systematic reviews to identify effective interventions. What
is learned through such reviews needs to be effectively disseminated and made
available to practitioners (Eisenstadt, 2000; Nutley & Davies, 2000b; Nutley,
Davies, & Tilley, 2000; Torrey et al., 2001). Dissemination and implementation
of evidence-based practices present special challenges when the intended users
are social work practitioners and their clients.

TWO APPROACHES TO DISSEMINATION AND
IMPLEMENTATION OF EVIDENCE-BASED
PRACTICE

As noted by Nutley and Davies, two major approaches to dissemination and
implementation of best practices have been used, namely, *macro* and *micro*, or
what I call *top-down* and *bottom-up* strategies (Nutley & Davies, 2000a).[1] In
top-down strategies, findings are disseminated for use by frontline practitioners
through agency directives, guidelines, manualized interventions, accreditation requirements, algorithms, tool kits, and so forth. Top-down or macro strategies
can serve to get the word out about what works or what those in authority favor,
but such methods do not guarantee adoption of best practices on the front lines.
To increase the likelihood of adoption, a bottom-up approach is needed. In contrast to the top-down approach, social work practitioners need to be prepared
to engage in a process of critical decision making with clients about what this
information means when joined with other evidence, professional values and
ethics, and individualized intervention goals. A bottom-up approach recognizes
the importance of engaging the practitioner and the client in a critical, decision-
making process.

ORGANIZATIONAL AND ENVIRONMENTAL SUPPORTS NEEDED FOR PRACTITIONERS TO FUNCTION AS EVIDENCE-BASED PRACTITIONERS

Implementation of evidence-based practice in social work organizations depends on many parts fitting together into a coherent whole (National Health Service Centre for Reviews and Dissemination, 1999). The team for the Implementing Evidence-Based Practices for Severe Mental Illness Project developed a model for achieving organizational change by using implementation tool kits (Torrey et al., 2001). This model provides steps to address a range of stakeholders, including funders, administrators, clinicians, and consumers and their families. Nevertheless, as Sackett and others have noted, there may be insurmountable barriers to implementing evidence-based practice guidelines in individual circumstances (Sackett et al., 2000, pp. 180–181). For successful implementation, a number of components need to be in place, including:

- Organizational culture, policies, procedures, and processes must provide opportunities and incentives supporting evidence-based practice (e.g., financial incentives, funding, openness to change, workload adjustments, information technology supports, and legal protection).
- The organization's external environment must provide similar opportunities and incentives supporting evidence-based practice (e.g., national, regional, and local authorities; funders and accrediting groups).
- Applied practice research and evaluation must provide scientific evidence about assessment, intervention, and outcomes pertinent to the organization's practice domain.
- Systematic reviews that synthesize research findings must be conducted to assess the weight of the evidence generated by current research and evaluation studies.
- Prescriptive statements based on these syntheses must be developed and communicated in user-friendly forms (e.g., practice guidelines, manuals, and tool kits).
- Organizational procedures need to be put in place to assure fidelity of implementation of these prescriptions.
- Systematic, structured evaluation processes capable of providing timely feedback to various stakeholders as to the fidelity of implementation and outcomes must be designed and implemented as an ongoing process.
- The organization must have social workers available who are trained as evidence-based practitioners capable of functioning in evidence-based practice organizations.

TRAINING FOR EVIDENCE-BASED PRACTICE

Unless social work practitioners are trained for evidence-based practice, it is unlikely that organizations will be capable of providing such services to clients

(Goisman, Warshaw, & Keller, 1999; Mullen & Bacon, 2000, 2003; Weissman & Sanderson, 2001). Furthermore, as accountable professionals, social workers must be prepared to engage in evidence-based practice even when working in organizations and environments without such supports, as well as when working in nonorganizational environments, such as in private practice.

Unfortunately, for the most part, social work practitioners are currently not engaged in evidence-based practice (Mullen & Bacon, 2000, 2003; Sanderson, 2002; Weissman & Sanderson, 2001), nor are social work educational programs currently training students for evidence-based practice (Weissman & Sanderson, 2001). In health care there has been much discussion of evidence-based education and how it differs from traditional education (Gray, 2001; Sackett et al., 2000; Willinsky, 2001). We are only beginning to have this discussion in social work (Gambrill, 2003; Howard, McMillen, & Pollio, 2003).

The future of evidence-based practice in social work rests on the profession's capacity and willingness to provide current practitioners and future generations of practitioners with training in evidence-based practice. In the immediate future, evidence-based practice training will need to be provided both for new social work students and for professional social workers already in practice. For the latter group, social workers who are engaged in practice, employing organizations need to make training opportunities available if the organizations are to adopt evidence-based practice. They will need to make a large investment in continuing education and other in-service training programs. Furthermore, especially for private practitioners and others not working in organizational settings conducive to evidence-based practice training, continuing education in such practice methods will need to be put in place. But, for practitioners in training, educational programs will need to provide a foundation in evidence-based practice content and methods. Regrettably, such training is generally absent from current educational programs. As noted by Weissman and Sanderson in discussing training for psychotherapy:

> One major obstacle to the use of evidenced-based treatments is their near absence in many training programs for psychologists and social workers and in residency training programs for psychiatrists. This lag may be due in part to the recency of the evidence, although some is due to ideologic differences. Training efforts are more vigorous in Canada, Great Britain, Holland, Iceland, Germany and Spain where calls for workshops, individual training and supervision in EBT by psychiatrists, general practitioners (in Canada) and psychologists have been overwhelming. (Weissman & Sanderson, 2001, p. 18)

They also note:

> Clinicians trained ten years ago are unlikely to be up-to-date with the newer, evidence-based psychotherapies, since the data supporting EBTs have appeared in the past 10 to 15 years. Continuing Education (CE) Programs have the potential to fill this void. (Weissman & Sanderson, 2001, p. 23)

Because few social work educational programs in the United States now provide training in evidence-based practice, a major curricular challenge lies ahead

(Weissman & Sanderson, 2001). Nevertheless, there are indications that this situation may be changing. For example, the George Warren Brown School of Social Work at Washington University in St. Louis has recently adopted evidence-based practice as one of two approaches to graduate education (Howard et al., 2003). Leonard Gibbs has published the first evidence-based social work practice text, which builds on his many years of experience in teaching evidence-based practice (Gibbs, 2003). Gambrill's writings provide useful suggestions for teaching evidence-based practice, with special emphasis on critical thinking skills (Gambrill, 1999, 2003). In the years ahead, the profession needs to experiment with innovative evidence-based practice curricula. Practitioners need to be prepared to engage in a process of information gathering, analysis, and decision making with clients about what would be a best practice for a given client situation. This idea is in agreement with Lawrence Green's notion that it is *best processes* rather than *best practices* that should be advocated in public health promotion (Green, 2001).

Students preparing for evidence-based practice will need training in critical thinking skills (Gambrill, 1999); evidence-based practice as a framework for and requirement of contemporary social work practice; practice guidelines, manuals, tool kits, and other forms currently used to translate evidence into practice prescriptions; information retrieval and critical assessment skills; systematic review methods, data syntheses, and meta-analytic procedures; methods of social intervention research as a process for developing, testing, refining, and disseminating scientifically validated social work practices; foundations of scientific thinking; research and evaluation methods, as well as quantitative and qualitative modes of inquiry and analysis; and skills for adapting general research findings and guidelines to individualized client circumstances, preferences, and values (Mullen, 1978; Mullen & Bacon, 2003).

CONCLUSION

This chapter has discussed ways to support social work practitioners in their attempts to use evidence-based knowledge to assess, intervene with, and better understand clients. While there is an emerging literature addressing implementation of evidence-based practices in organizations, little attention has been given to how individual practitioners can be helped to use evidence-based knowledge in everyday practice. Accordingly, in addition to dissemination and implementation strategies directed at service systems and organizations, attention needs to be paid to how practitioners themselves can be helped to implement evidence-based practice. This chapter has provided suggestions toward that end.

NOTES

This chapter is adapted from Mullen, E. J. (2002). Evidence-based knowledge: Designs for enhancing practitioner use of research findings. Paper presented at the fourth

International Conference on Evaluation for Practice, University of Tampere, Tampere, Finland.

1. The Cochrane Effective Practice and Organization of Care Group (EPOC) focuses on what has been learned through research about effective dissemination and implementation interventions (Cochrane Effective Practice and Organization of Care Group. 2000). Retrieved July 26, 2003, from http://www.epoc.uottawa.ca.

REFERENCES

Addis, M. E., & Krasnow, A. D. (2000). A national survey of predicting psychologists' attitudes toward psychotherapy treatment manuals. *Journal of Consulting and Clinical Psychology, 68*(2), 331–339.

Drake, R. E., Goldman, H., Leff, H. S., Lehman, A. F., Dixon, L., Mueser, K. T., et al. (2001). Implementing evidence-based practices in routine mental health service settings. *Psychiatric Services, 52*(2), 179–182.

Eisenstadt, N. (2000). Sure start: Research into practice; practice into research. *Public Money & Management, 20*(4), 6–8.

Gambrill, E. (1999). Evidence-based practice: An alternative to authority-based practice. *Families in Society: The Journal of Contemporary Human Services, 80*(4), 341–350.

Gambrill, E. D. (2003). Evidence-based practice: Sea change or the emperor's new clothes? *Journal of Social Work Education, 39*(1), 3–23.

Gibbs, L. E. (2003). *Evidence-based practice for the helping professions: A practical guide with integrated multimedia*. Pacific Grove, CA: Brooks/Cole–Thompson Learning.

Goisman, R. M., Warshaw, M. G., & Keller, M. B. (1999). Psychosocial treatment prescriptions for generalized anxiety disorder, panic disorder, and social phobia, 1991–1996. *American Journal of Psychiatry, 156*, 1819–1821.

Gray, J. A. M. (2001). *Evidence-based healthcare* (2nd ed.). New York: Churchill Livingstone.

Green, L. W. (2001). From research to "best practices" in other settings and populations. *American Journal of Health Behavior, 25*(3), 165–178.

Howard, M. O., McMillen, C. J., & Pollio, D. E. (2003). Teaching evidence-based practice: Toward a new paradigm for social work education. *Research on Social Work Practice, 13*(2), 234–259.

Mullen, E. J. (1978). Construction of personal models for effective practice: A method for utilizing research findings to guide social interventions. *Journal of Social Service Research, 2*(1), 45–63.

Mullen, E. J., & Bacon, W. F. (2000, May 3–5). *Practitioner adoption and implementation of evidence-based effective treatments and issues of quality control.* Paper presented at the Evidence-Based Practice Conference: Developing Practice Guidelines for Social Work Interventions—Issues, Methods, & Research Agenda, George Warren Brown School of Social Work, Washington University, St. Louis, MO.

Mullen, E. J., & Bacon, W. F. (2003). Practitioner adoption and implementation of evidence-based effective treatments and issues of quality control. In A. Rosen & E. K. Proctor (Eds.), *Developing practice guidelines for social work interven-*

tions: Issues, methods, and a research agenda. New York: Columbia University Press.

National Health Services Centre for Reviews and Dissemination, University of York. (1999). Getting evidence into practice. *Effective Health Care Bulletin* 5(1). Retrieved July 26, 2003, from www.york.ac.uk/inst/crd/ehcb.htm.

Nutley, S. M., & Davies, H. T. O. (2000a). Making a reality of evidence-based practice. In H. T. O. Davies, S. M. Nutley, & P. C. Smith (Eds.), *What works? Evidence-based policy and practice in public services.* Bristol: Policy Press.

Nutley, S., & Davies, H. T. O. (2000b). Making a reality of evidence-based practice: Some lessons from the diffusion of innovations. *Public Money & Management, 20*(4), 35–42.

SECTION II

Evidence-Based Practice Interventions
and Applications

13

Developing a Systematic Evidence-Based Search Plan for a Client With Co-occurring Conditions

BARBARA THOMLISON

ROBIN J. JACOBS

When you do an evidence-based practice (EBP) search, you are trying to find the most useful research in the shortest possible time for a practice situation. An evidence-supported practice is a treatment or intervention protocol that has at least some empirical research evidence for its efficacy with its intended target problems and populations. To be useful to practitioners, evidence-based practices consider three elements: (1) client values and preferences; (2) the clinical expertise and abilities of the professional; and (3) the best available research evidence (Petr & Walter, 2005). Practitioners want research that is *useful* (i.e., clinically appropriate to the client's conditions), *relevant* (pertinent to the clinical context), and *valid* (derived from sound research methods). Practitioners will want the best available evidence where the outcome findings consistently show the interventions actually help clients change and improve (Thomlison & Corcoran, in press).

Why should you engage in evidence-based practice? In the years after you graduate, keeping your knowledge and skills up to date is important and necessary if you are to remain a good practitioner or become a better one. As a practitioner, you should refrain from using untested or potentially dangerous treatments. You need to stay on top of new developments, new interventions, and practice frameworks as they occur. It is not your job to know everything, even in your area of expertise, but it is your job to be able to find the information, when you and your clients need it. Clients have a right to receive effective treatment, and evidence-based practice provides you with the tools to do this (Thyer, 2002). Three elements are necessary to keeping your skills up to date:

(1) you need to learn how to formulate clear, specific clinical practice questions regarding client problems; (2) you need to know how to systematically, strategically, and productively plan an electronic search to improve the probability of finding the current best practice-relevant evidence regarding your practice questions; and (3) you need to critically appraise the evidence for application of best practice to your situation. However, in reality, most practitioners do not know what this process is and how to conduct a basic research strategy to determine the current state-of-the-art approaches, models, and interventions for a given client problem and target population. This chapter outlines the steps for identifying evidence-based research to obtain best practices for a clinical problem. A hypothetical case scenario of a young Hispanic man with obsessive-compulsive characteristics and depression as a co-occurring condition is used to illustrate the process of developing a systematic evidence-based search plan. The case below summarizes the client information. The evidence-based practice model and the steps to finding evidence-based practices as applied in the case of an individual with obsessive-compulsive disorder are presented.

Case Scenario: Obsessive-Compulsive Disorder (OCD) With Co-occurring Conditions

Marc is a 25-year-old Hispanic male who lives with his girlfriend. Marc attends the university where, until recently, he has been a good student. He came to the Mental Health Center to address for his fears of contamination, excessive washing behavior, and his anxiety about contracting diseases. He experiences fear when he leaves his apartment. These behaviors and recurrent thoughts are seriously affecting his relationships and his ability to study. Marc has had anxiety-related problems for years. During the preceding 3 months, however, he has become increasingly anxious, waking earlier each day to wash-and-clean behaviors before going to classes. He fears that he will be contaminated with germs and this may lead to contracting cancer. Marc is aware intellectually there is no link between cleanliness and cancer, but whenever someone or something he considers dirty touches him or his belongings, he obsesses about disease. He also feels depressed. He increasingly exhibits cognitive distortions such as "I'll never improve" and "I'll never reach my goals so why bother trying" and "Nobody cares if I do improve." These obsessions and depressive symptoms have come to negatively affect every aspect of Marc's functioning.

EVIDENCE-BASED PRACTICE MODEL

Before you begin, make sure you understand the evidence-based model. According to Mullen, Shlonsky, Beldsoe, and Bellamy (2005), information gathered in search of best practice for a problem or condition and its application to clinical practice requires the "synergistic combination of best evidence, client values and expectations, and the practitioners' clinical expertise" (p. 65). The integration of these three perspectives, illustrated in the model developed by Haynes, Devereaux, and Guyatt (2002) is used here. Figure 13.1 shows how clinical expertise requires a blending of the client's situation, preferences, desires, and values such as cultural barriers or strengths, the clinical state and circumstances as appropriate for client-practitioner compatibility, and the evidence from the research.

APPLYING THE MODEL TO PRACTICE

Client Preferences, Values, and Actions

Acceptability of social work interventions involves paying attention to the clients' values, preferences, and expectations. Include cultural and diversity considerations and attend to interests of specific diverse groups. While factors such as poverty and socioeconomic status, language barriers, and other environmental factors account in part for these differences among clients, practitioners must

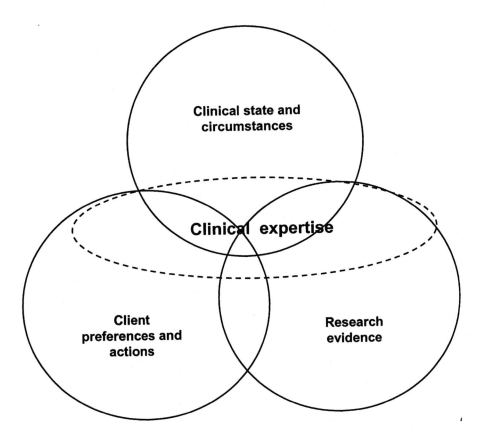

Figure 13.1   The Evidence-Based Practice Model
Note: From Mullen, E.J., Shlonsky, A., Beldsoe, S.E., & Bellamy, J.L. (2005). From concept to implementation: challenges facing evidence-based social work. *Evidence & Policy*, 1(1), 65.

also be aware of the potential impact of prejudice, discrimination, and racism. Mistrust of mental health providers, help-seeking behavior, and medication issues are cultural factors that affect a client's decision to accept treatment. Other non-specific issues to consider when deciding on intervention are age, gender, education level, and race. Any of these factors may affect adherence to medication and interventions, and acceptability and intensity of a treatment (Abramowitz & Schwartz, 2004). Interventions should be selected bearing in mind that "best practice" might not work crossculturally. Evidence-based practice stresses the need to respect people and recognize that their choices may influence assessment, planning, intervention, and research approaches (Gibbs, 2003).

Clinical State and Circumstances

Consider the appropriateness of the intervention for the client's context and specific situation. Begin with a careful assessment of the client's strengths, goals, and objectives. Provide the client with appropriate information about what is currently available. This will help you determine where you plan to do the intervention, and the format the intervention may take, such as a community-based context, brief intervention in the home and in clinic-based settings, using individual and group approaches, with services from a mental health organization (public or private). Geographic location, type of agency, and duration of treatments can affect the options. These are factors influencing the intervention context. Determine if there are any challenges in the clinical context that may impact availability and acceptability of the intervention to the client.

BEST RESEARCH EVIDENCE

After locating research on your problem, the criteria for judging a treatment include the following five elements.

1. *Theoretical basis.* Is it sound, novel, reasonable, or unknown?
2. *Clinical or anecdotal literature.* Is it substantial or limited?
3. *General acceptance or use in clinical practice.* Is it widely used?
4. *Risk.* Do the benefits outweigh the risk for harm? (look for cohort studies)
5. *Level of empirical support.* All research evidence is not the same. An ordinal ranking of research methods, from high to low levels is used to assess their validity and ability to directly inform practice (Chambless & Hollon, 1998; Roberts & Yeager, 2004b). Level 1 is the highest, and level 4 is the lowest.

(For a more detailed review of evidence-based levels, see chapters 1–7 here, and Chambless & Hollon, 1998; McNeece & Thyer, 2004; Mullen, Shlonsky, Beldsoe, & Bellamy, 2005; Roberts & Yeager, 2004b.)

There may be no evidence for some problem situations. Chapter 4 by Yeager and Roberts in this book reviews the levels of evidence and the hierarchy of evidence provides a detailed discussion. A brief outline of the level of evidence for a therapeutic approach follows.

Level 1. Metaanalyses/systematic reviews
- Positive evidence from more than one metaanalysis of randomized clinical trial
- Positive evidence from more than two randomized clinical trials

Level 2. Randomized controlled trials (RCTs)
- Positive evidence from at least one RCT with placebo or comparison condition
- Positive evidence from more than two quasi-experimental studies

Level 3. Comparative studies or observational study
- Positive evidence from comparative studies, correlation studies, and case-control and cohort studies. Preexperimental group studies (no control groups; posttest only)
- Surveys and expert consensus reports

Level 4. Qualitative studies
- Anecdotal case reports, case studies, single-subject designs

Even if you locate studies and rank them against the foregoing criteria, your client will rarely match the clients in a research study exactly. He or she may be older or younger, may have additional health or social problems, and will certainly have his or her own views and values about preferred choice for treatment. Since we do not live in a perfect world in which each evidence-based treatment fits every client and his or her condition, the practitioner must integrate relevant scientific information and appraise the "goodness of fit" with his or her clinical expertise, and then make a professional judgment with the preferences of the client (Howard, McMillen, & Pollio, 2003). In other words, it is up to the practitioner, in consultation with the client, to judge how applicable the interventions are to the client's problem and to the abilities of that practitioner.

Clinical expertise. Evidence-based practice comes together with the expertise and abilities of the practitioner. The practitioner, applying clinical expertise, can assess the benefits or risk of using the intervention and identify available resources for the client. Clinical expertise is also used to identify the client's personal strengths and cultural preferences, and assess the effectiveness of various tools for assessment (e.g., American Psychiatric Association, *Diagnostic and Statistical Manual of Mental Disorders* [1994], Anxiety Disorders Interview Schedule [ADIS], depression inventories, observational measures, or self-report measures) and the intervention service approach (e.g., individual cognitive behavior treatment, group cognitive behavioral treatment, pharmacological treatment, or combinations of interventions and treatments and type of setting such as inpatient or outpatient sites) and the acceptability of the interventions to the client.

STEPS TO FINDING THE BEST PRACTICE FOR A CLIENT WITH OBESSIVE-COMPULSIVE DISORDER AND CO-OCCURRING DEPRESSION

Several researchers (Gibbs, 2003; Rosenberg & Donald, 1995; Sackett, Rosenberg, Gray, Haynes, & Richardson, 1996; Sackett, Straus, Richardson, Rosenberg, & Haynes, 2000) have suggested variations on the steps shown in the EBP model in Figure 13.2 for systematically executing the search protocol, while simultaneously blending the three elements of the EBP model.

Following the step-by-step strategy of Figure 3.3, you can obtain evidence-based research, expert guidelines, and treatment approaches to obsessive-compulsive disorder (OCD) and co-occurring depression for Marc's clinical problem, described in the earlier case study.

THE CLINICAL PROBLEM

Who is the client, what is critical about the client's problem, and what factors are critical to the search? (see chapter 4 in this book). Using the search engine

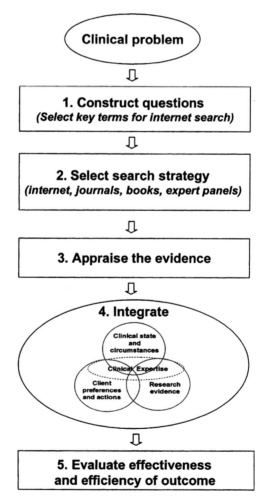

Figure 13.2   Steps to Finding the Best Practice for a Clinical Problem

Google (www.google.com) the following terms were entered exactly as follows: *evidence-based practice obsessive-compulsive disorder*. The first site, the website of the University of Buffalo School of Social Work Children, Youth, and Families Mental Health Evidence Base Practice (EBP) Project (http://www.socialwork .buffalo.edu/centers/CFCS/OMH/EBP/diagnosis/ocd.htm) produced the diagnostic criteria, prevalence rates, and EBP treatment approaches. To further consider the diagnosis by symptoms and intervention, for a second set of searches, using Google, (www.google.com) the name of the database "Pubmed" was entered in the search box, followed by several different combinations of terms, as shown in table 13.1.

Finally, using Google (www.google.com) *treatment of obsessive-compulsive* was then entered, yielding an array of websites; the website of the Online Psychological Services (http://www.psychologynet.org/index.html) provided a listing of disorders; *obsessive-compulsive* was chosen, and then *social phobia,* to obtain assessment, and *treatment guidelines* were entered, to confirm the client has obsessive-compulsive disorder and co-occurring social phobia and underlying depression.

> The client is a 25-year-old Hispanic male experiencing symptoms of obsessive-compulsive disorder and depression that interferes with daily activities of living and academic performance. Symptoms: (1) reoccurring or constant thoughts, images of contamination that interfere with social/interpersonal skills; (2) repetitive behaviors and rituals and preoccupations of cleaning, distractibility and impaired concentration that interfere with ability to leave the home environment; and (3) distorted thinking, periods of isolation, and persistent negative thoughts that interfere with academic performance, as evidenced by fears of leaving the home.

STEP 1: CONSTRUCT GOOD QUESTIONS

Questions about the clinical problem, about what treatment, if any, to give Marc, and what the outcomes of different treatment options might be are posed to

Table 13.1.   Pubmed Search

Search #	Search history	Results
1	Obsessive compulsive	8,729
2	Obsessive compulsive systematic reviews	34
3	Obsessive compulsive social phobia	759
4	Obsessive compulsive social phobia systematic reviews	3
5	Obsessive compulsive social phobia depression reviews	63
6	Obsessive compulsive social phobia cohort studies	61
7	nos. 1 and 4	34

provide a framework for the evidence-based literature search. Good questions are action oriented, clear, and succinct. Formulate questions about: obsessive-compulsive symptoms; Marc's specific situation (e.g., other diagnoses, gender, age, ethnicity), and which interventions would reduce/ameliorate obsessive-compulsive symptoms, improve interpersonal and social interaction, enhance individual functioning, and improve academic performance.

Construct a well-formulated, answerable, and searchable question (derived from an individualized assessment). A full discussion of types of questions is presented in chapter 4 of this book raise the research question in a way that best facilitates the literature search. Gibbs (2003) identifies five types of question practitioners need information on: assessment, effectiveness, prevention, description, and risk factors.

Examples follow.

1. Assessment questions
   a. For persons suspected of having OCD, which rapid assessment measure will most quickly, reliably, and validly discriminate persons with OCD from other diagnoses?
   b. Which assessment or diagnostic procedure will provide the most valid and reliable detection that Marc has OCD?

Using the search engine Google (www.google.com) we entered the database of the Expert Consensus Guideline Series (www.psychguides.com/gl_treatmentof _obsessive-compulsive_disorder.html) to obtain the treatment for OCD.

2. Effectiveness questions
   a. Among young adult males with OCD, will an individual cognitive behavioral intervention program compared to a group cognitive behavioral intervention effectively reduce the obsessive-compulsive symptoms? Improve social and academic functioning? Increase Marc's self-reported happiness?
   b. Is medication alone effective compared to cognitive behavioral intervention and medication for OCD in young adult males?

Using Google, (*www.google.com*) enter the terms *systematic reviews meta-analyses obsessive-compulsive disorders,* and many sites will appear. We chose the website of the National Electronic Library for: Mental Health (www.nelmh .org/page_view.asp?c=20&did=2628&fc=006005030); we also consulted the website of eMedicine: Instant Access to the Minds of Medicine (www .emedicine.com/ped/topic2794.htm).

3. Prevention questions
   a. What is the likelihood that Marc will experience the recurrence of obsessive-compulsive symptoms after treatment?
   b. What is the most effective way to educate Marc about OCD to prevent the recurrence?
4. Descriptive questions:
   a. At what age do symptoms of OCD first appear?
   b. What causes OCD?

    c. When do complications of OCD usually occur?

    d. In clients with OCD, how many have other psychological conditions?

Using Google (*www.google.com*) we entered the name "social work abstracts" to look for evidence-based books. We found Roberts and Yeager (2004) and located "Evidence-based Treatments for Obsessive Compulsive Disorder" by Abramowitz and Schwartz (2004), which complemented the research studies and expert guidelines but added the integrative perspective.

STEP 2: SELECT SEARCH STRATEGIES

The purpose of a search is to obtain an accurate answer. Journals are not your first choice, unless they emphasize results of empirical outcome studies. Prioritize the approach to searching resources. Start with reference sources and research reviews; identify model programs or treatment guidelines, journals for the topic area, and government and other agency websites for conferences reports and presentations. The most useful databases available on the internet are MED-LINE, Cochrane Database of Systematic Reviews, Silver Platter (includes ERIC, Psych Info, Sociological Abstracts, Social Work), OVID, InfoTrac, Cambridge Journals, Biblioline, Web of Science, and Science Direct.

The most useful internet searches are: Google (www.google.com) (using combinations of key words such as *obsessive-compulsive, depression, anxiety disorders*), Psychguides.com by the Expert Consensus Guidelines Series, U.S. Department of Health and Human Services, the CRISP database of the U.S. National Institutes of Health, and the U.S. Centers for Disease Control. For an expanded list of evidence-based resources see Appendix in Roberts & Yeager, 2004, pp. 961–969.

Evaluate websites by relevance, timeliness, bias, and authority. Clarify the clinical problem and decide on search terms. Before starting the search, you must have a clear idea of the type of information you are looking for. Answer the following questions and write them down. The key elements will become search terms in your online search. First, what is the description of your client (e.g. age, sex, ethnicity, sexual orientation)? Second, what is the problem, clinical diagnosis or condition?

    Then:

- Conduct online searches for the terms and combine them appropriately using *and, or,* and *not.* Use *and* to restrict the results of the previous step to the type of research that applies (e.g. randomized controlled trials *and* cohort studies). The type of studies you look for will depend on how you classified the problem. Use *or* to widen your search. Use *not* to filter out irrelevant concepts or terms.
- View and print out the results of the studies you retrieved to keep track of which seem useful and relevant.
- Carefully review the research design methods used in the studies you selected. (Use the evaluation methods described later in this chapter.)
- Draw your conclusions and apply them to your client.

Search Options

Search engines present a list of links to websites containing the work or topic searched. *Examples:* Google, AltaVista.

Websites have interconnected pages or documents available via the Internet, offered by groups, organizations, and individuals. *Example*: the website of the National Institute of Mental Health, available on the Internet at: http://www .nimh.nih.gov/

Databases are collections of records, journals, books, abstracts, bibliographies, and full-text articles. *Example*: PubMed, PsychINFO, HighWire, Ebsco-Retrieval systems.

Collections of databases, grouped by subject, may or may not require a subscription. *Example*: Social Work Abstracts, HighWire, Ebsco, Academic Premier, SAGE (your university or college library may have a subscription, but Google (*www.google.com*) takes you to most).

Table 13.1 shows how the "Boolean operators"(for an explanation of Boolean Searching on the internet see http://library.albany.edu/internet/boolean.html *and*, *or*, and *not* can be applied in a search on obsessive-compulsive disorder and depression. (The University of Michigan website is extremely helpful [www.lib .umich.edu/socwork/rescue/ebsw.html;]ew).

STEP 3: APPRAISE THE RESEARCH

Critically appraise the evidence for its validity (closeness to the truth), impact (size of the effect), and applicability (usefulness). Applicability involves matching the current client to the participants in the studies (e.g., by ethnicity, age, gender, condition, circumstances) to avoid "generalizing" the research evidence. Figure 13.3 can guide you in your appraisal of the quality of the research studies for your client's situation.

Table 13.2   Examples for Finding Primary Sources: Boolean Operators *and, or, not*

Connector	Result	Use
Obsessive compulsive disorder **and** *depression* **and** *adults*	"What do we know about OCD and depression in adults?"	***And*** is used to narrow your search. More variables will always result in less records.
Obsessive compulsive disorder **and** *(depression* **or** *mood disorder)*	"What do we know about OCD and depression or mood disorder in adults?"	***Or*** is used most frequently to search for words that are synonyms or close in definition.
Obsessive compulsive disorder **and** *depression* **and** *(metaanalysis* **or** *randomized clinical trial)* **not** *survey*	"Are there metaanalyses or RCT research on adults with OCD who also have a depression problem?"	***Not*** is used to take out words that are irrelevant to your search.

Adapted from University of Michigan Social Work Library (2005). Retrieved on June 10, 2005, from http:// www.lib.umich.edu/socwork/rescue/ebsw.html

STEP 4: INTEGRATION

Integrate critical appraisal with your clinical experience and client's strengths, values, culture, and circumstances. Identify biases or inconsistencies in current best practices. Take into account social work values, ethics, or mandates.

STEP 5: EVALUATION

Evaluate effectiveness and efficiency to determine if the protocol was implemented as described in steps 1–4. Identify biases, gaps, or inconsistencies of current best practices to Marc's situation.

WHEN YOU CANNOT FIND ANY EVIDENCE

What happens in the unlikely but possible event that you cannot find any evidence, even at the lowest level in the hierarchy, pertaining to your client's problem or condition? Ideas are first communicated informally. Call or email colleagues, scholars, experts in the field, and other service agencies or organizations that treat the client's condition, and ask what their experience has revealed as "best practice." Go to the bottom of the publication chain to locate earliest sources of a new topic by accessing electronic discussion lists and information interviews. Early stages of publications are newsletters, conference proceedings, preprints of articles, and articles. These can be found in professional association newsletters, conference summaries, or by contacting authors. Then try locating conference proceedings and dissertations in electronic databases, by checking journals for conference announcements, or ask university professors. Remember that journal articles begin to appear about 1–2 years after topic initiation. They

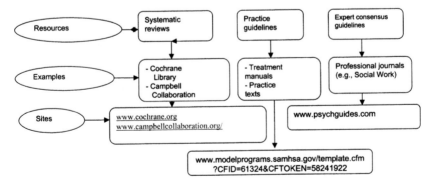

Figure 13.3   Search Strategies for Finding Evidence-Based Research
Adapted from Corcoran, K. & Vandiver, V. L. (2003). Implementing best practice and expert consensus procedures. In A. Roberts & K. Yeager (Eds.) *Evidence-based practice manual: Research and outcomes measures in health and human services* (pp. 19–19). New York, NY: Oxford University Press.

are found by using indexes, abstracts, and electronic databases. Books begin to appear 2–5 years later and can be found in catalogs and electronic databases as well (Social Work Library, 2004).

Primary Literature (Single Studies)

Primary data analysis consists of research reports, abstracts, summaries, and syntheses of original research. Authors analyze and report the findings of the data. The reliability or validity of research based on primary data analysis may be ascertained by looking at citations of its subsequent empirical articles and literature reviews relating to the study.

Secondary Literature (Multiple Studies)

Secondary literature is a good strategy for capturing the best of primary studies. It synthesizes the results of numerous studies and puts them in narrative review form (e.g. look for secondary data analysis reports, metaanalyses, and systematic reviews). You will find Cochrane Database of Systematic Reviews through OVID, direct as Cochrane Collaboration; also ACP Journal Club through OVID; and Clinical Evidence summarizes evidence for common clinical questions. This helps mitigate bias while creating a consensus about best practice in the behavioral sciences. A good website for secondary literature is the University of Michigan Social Work Library (www.lib.umich.edu/socwork/rescue/ebsw.html).

KEY DATABASES FOR BEST PRACTICE

The appendix identifies selected key resources to databases, websites, and centers of evidence-based practices. Do not consider this resource guide exhaustive.

Do I Have the Time for Evaluating the Evidence?

It is unrealistic to think you will have the time to check every possible flaw in a study or verify all the statistics. On the other hand, you don't want to base your decision for client care on inaccurate or misleading results. Evaluation of the evidence will depend on (1) the availability of secondary sources; (2) the severity and duration of the problem and how often it presents itself in your practice; (3) the extent to which the results of the study are aligned with your own experience; (4) how much bias you think is present; and (5) the time available.

How Do I Evaluate Metaanalyses?

First, the author should describe in detail how the search for the studies was conducted and how the authors decided which to include. Many authors conduct a search of several databases, then add any relevant articles quoted in the studies, and ask the authors if there are unpublished studies that address the question.

Authors of metaanalyses include unpublished studies so as to avoid publication bias. Second, look for similar results between studies. Results are more reliable (good study design, homogeneous populations) the more similar the results are between studies.

CONCLUSION

Evidence-based practice is an essential for every practitioner who wants to maintain effective interventions with individual, family, group, and community practice. Although the focus of this chapter is on individual practice, the methodology for a search is the same with other practice areas. Evidence-based practice helps practitioners to find new and important research easily, and to determine its usefulness for a problem and target population. Knowledge is continually expanding, and ongoing research is creating a dynamic foundation for improving practice at every level. This chapter briefly outlined the steps to finding practical research right from your office Internet connection. There is a huge world of databases and information to support your practice and build your ongoing knowledge; you can go from novice to expert on any number of topics.

APPENDIX: ANNOTATED BIBLIOGRAPHY AND RESOURCE GUIDE

The resources listed here were identified by using first Google and then Google advanced search, entering terms such as *evidence-based practice, best practices,* and *centers of evidence-based practice.* From there we explored the schools of social work links and compiled the following list.

- Level 1 Evidence Search Strategy: Example of search terms: *systematic* OR *quantitative* OR *evidence* OR *trials* AND *review* AND *obsessive compulsive disorder*
- Level 2 Evidence Search Strategy: Example of search terms: *randomized controlled trial* OR *controlled clinical trial* AND *obsessive compulsive disorder*
- Level 3 Evidence Search Strategy: Example of search terms: *comparative study* OR *cases* OR *review of reported cases* AND *obsessive compulsive disorder* NOT *children* NOT *youth*
- Level 4 Evidence Search Strategy: Example of search terms: *cases* OR *anecdotes of reported cases* AND *obsessive compulsive disorder* NOT *children* NOT *youth*

Databases, Websites, and Retrieval Systems

Database of Abstracts of Reviews of Effectiveness (DARE)
   NHS Centre for Reviews and Dissemination, University of York, UK. Systematic reviews and metaanalyses extracted from MEDLINE.
www.york.ac.uk/inst/crd/darehp.htm

MEDLINE 1966–2004

Good choice for simple searching. Searches broadly and sensitively. May not provide best results for complex topic or a finely honed search.

www.ncbi.nlm.nih.gov/entrez/query.fcgi?holding=emorylib

PubMed Clinical Queries Database

Provided by the National Institute of Health; contains over 14 million literature citations. This is the National Library of Medicine (NLM) a subset of MEDLINE, offering health information for consumers, physicisans, and other, containing randomized controlled trials, and so on. One can choose therapy, diagnosis, etiology, prognosis categories.

www.ncbi.nlm.nih.gov/entrez/query/static/clinical.shtml

Social Work Abstracts (SWAB)

SWAB is hosted by the National Association for Social Workers and includes abstracts from over 400 international and domestic academic journals. You can access empirical research on social welfare, crime, psychology, child welfare, mental health, health care, substance abuse, and public health.

http://www.lib.ku.edu/robohtml/libmenu1Social_Work_Abstracts_SWAB.html

Synopses and Abstracts of Cochrane Reviews

The Cochrane Collaboration. Results only. See OVID for full-text systematic reviews.

www.cochrane.org/index0.htm

The Campbell Collaboration Library and Database

This site posts a searchable database of randomized controlled clinical trials and systematic reviews of social, psychological, education, and criminological research. All research presented on the website has met rigorous methodological standards and is designed to provide researchers, policy-makers, and practitioners with critical reviews of current research. It is designed to to assist users in making well-informed decisions regarding the effects of interventions in the social, education, criminology, and behavioral arenas.

www.campbellcollaboration.org/

Homepage (has database) of the Social Care Institute for Excellence (SCIE), London

This website provides a free online library with an extensive collection of social care knowledge, including practice information, skills tutorials, research, and several thousand abstracts related to EBP. Monthly research and mainly British policy updates are included, as well as helpful links to the Be Evidence Based website and research search engine and other evidence-based initiatives.

www.scie.org.uk/index.asp

Substance Abuse and Mental Health Services Administration (SAMHSA) and Center for Substance Abuse Prevention (CSAP), CITY: MD: Model Programs and National Registry of Effective Programs

The website provides information about substance abuse and mental health programs tested in communities, schools, social service organizations, and workplaces in the United States. Nominated programs are reviewed by research teams who rate the programs primarily on methodological quality but also consider other factors, such as theoretical development and community involvement. Programs are rated in increasing order of quality as either *promising*, *effective*, or *model*.

www.samhsa.gov/index.aspx

http://modelprograms.samhsa.gov/template.cfm?page=default

Expert Consensus Guideline Series

Gives examples of good practice where it has been identified. The Guides provide a series of topic-based sites that bring together information, research, and current good practice.

www.psychguides.com

National Institute on Drug Abuse (NIDA), CITY: D: Clinical Trials Network

This website provides information about drug abuse-related research studies and contact information for regional research "nodes" currently carrying out studies and trainings related to research-based practice.

www.nida.nih.gov/CTN/Index.htm

National Library of Medicine (NLM)

NLM is part of the National Institutes of Health and is the world's medical library. This site provides free access to several databases, including PubMed, ClinicalTrials, and ToxNet. Information is organized by health subject.

www.nlm.nih.gov

Centers and Organizations

Centre for Evidence Based Medicine

This site provides information and resources for every level and every stage of EBM.

www.cebm.net/

Centre for Evidence Based Mental Health

Among other things, this site has a very useful quick links section under Dissemination Links.

www.cebm.net/

Centre for Evidence Based Social Services

The Centre's mission is to ensure that decisions at all levels of social services are grounded in good research. Also see the Be Evidence Based website: www.be-evidence-based.com/

www.cebss.org/index.html

The Cochrane Collaboration

An international not-for-profit organization, providing up-to-date information about the effects of health care.

www.cochrane.org

Evidence-Based Psychiatry Center

Housed at the Nagoya City, Japan University Department of Psychiatry, the Center aims to accumulate and disseminate clinical evidence of use to practicing psychiatrists.

www.ebpcenter.net/ I checked and this site is now under construction—we can delete but I think it will be up soon

Center for Mental Health Quality and Accountability Evidence-Based Practices

The Center promotes quality and accountability in state mental health systems by providing support in the development and implementation of evidence-based practices, performance measurement, and quality improvement processes.

http://nri.rdmc.org/Center/Center1.html

Center of Health Evidence

Promotes evidence-based health care by presenting knowledge-based resources to health professionals in ways that facilitate their optimum use.

www.cche.net/usersguides/main.asp

Centers for Disease Control and Prevention

Information on health topics, data and statistics, and current health concerns; provides many links to research reports and specialty websites on health and mental health issues.

www.cdc.gov

Books

Briggs, H. E., & Rzepnicki, T. L. (Eds.). (2004). *Using evidence in social work practice: Behavioral perspectives.* Chicago: Lyceum Books.

Corcoran, J. (2003). Clinical applications of evidence-based family interventions. Oxford: Oxford University Press.

Cournoyer, B. R. (2004). *Evidence-based social work skills book.* Needham, MA: Allyn and Bacon.

Gibbs, L. (2003). *Evidence-based practice for the helping professions: A practical guide with integrated media.* Pacific Grove, CA: Wadsworth.

Formulating Answerable Questions Using COPES: www.evidence.brookscole.com/copse.html

Gray, J.A.M. (1997). *Evidence-based healthcare.* New York: Churchill Livingstone.

Rosen, A., & Proctor, P. K. (Eds.). (2003). *Developing practice guidelines for social work intervention: Issues, methods, and research agenda.* New York: Columbia University Press.

Roberts, A. R., & Yeager, K. R. (Eds.). (2004). *Evidence-based practice manual: Research and outcome measures in health and human services.* New York: Oxford University Press.

Journals

Brief Treatment and Crisis Intervention. New York: Oxford University Press. Two special issues of this journal, in May and September 2004, are dedicated to

evidence-based practice. Topics include EBP, teaching EBP, implementation issues, and finding evidence in difficult practice areas. Available online at: http://
brief-treatment.oupjournals.org.
*Journal of Evidence-Based Social Work: Advances in Practice, Programming, Re-
search and Policy.* New York: Haworth Press. Focused on the use of EBP in
everyday care. Designed to help the reader toward understanding and developing his or her own research, outcomes measures, performance measures, quality
improvement strategies, and practice guidelines, as well as assessments and interventions. Available online at: www.haworthpressinc.com/web/JEBSW/.

REFERENCES

Abramowitz, J. S., & Schwartz, S. A. (2004). Evidence-based treatments for
obsessive-compulsive disorder. In A. Roberts & K. Yeager (Eds.), *Evidence-
based practice manual: Research and outcome measures in health and human
services* (pp. 274–281). New York: Oxford University Press.
American Psychiatric Association. (1994). *Diagnostic and statistical manual of
mental disorders* (4th ed.). Washington, DC: Author.
Chambless, D. L., & Hollon, S. D. (1998). Defining empirically supported therapies. *Journal of Consulting and Clinical Psychology, 66*(1), 7–18.
Corcoran, K., & Vandiver, V. L. (2004). Implementing best practice and expert
consensus procedures. In A. Roberts & K. Yeager (Eds.), *Evidence-based practice manual: Research and outcome measures in health and human services*
(pp. 15–19). New York: Oxford University Press.
Gibbs, L. (2003). *Evidence based practice for the helping professions: A practical
guide with integrated multimedia.* Pacific Grove, CA: Thompson Learning.
Haynes, R. B., Devereaux, P. J., & Guyatt, G. H. (2002). Editorial: clinical exper-
tise in the era of evidence-based medicine and patient choice. *APC Journal
Club, 136*, A11–14.
Howard, M. O., McMillen, C. J., & Pollio, D. E. (2003). Teaching evidence-based
practice: Toward a new paradigm for social work education. *Research on Social
Work Practice, 13*(2), 234–249.
McNeece, C. A., & Thyer, B. A. (2004). Evidence-based practice and social work.
Journal of Evidence-Based Social Work, 1(1), 7–25.
Mullen, E. J., Shlonsky, A., Beldsoe, S. E., & Bellamy, J. L. (2005). From concept
to implementation: Challenges facing evidence-based social work. *Evidence and
Policy, 1*(1), 61–84.
Petr, C. G., & Walter, U. M. (2005). Best practices inquiry: A multidimensional,
value-critical framework. *Journal of Social Work Education, 41*(2), 251–267.
Roberts, A. R., & Yeager, K. R. (2004). Systematic reviews of evidence-based stud-
ies and practice-based research: How to search for, develop, and use them. In A.
Roberts & K. Yeager (Eds.), *Evidence-based practice manual: Research and out-
come measures in health and human services* (pp. 3–14). New York: Oxford
University Press.
Roberts, A. R., & Yeager, K. R. (2004). *Evidence-based practice manual: Research
and outcome measures in health and human services.* New York: Oxford University Press.
Rosenberg, W., & Donald, A. (1995). Evidence based medicine: An approach to
clinical problem solving. *British Medical Journal, 310*, 1122–1126.

Sackett, D. L., Richardson, W. S., Rosenberg, W., & Haynes, R. B. (1997). *Evidence-based medicine: How to practice and teach EBM*. New York: Churchill-Livingstone.

Sackett, D. L., Rosenberg, W.M.C., Gray, J.A.M., Haynes, R. B., & Richardson, W. S. (1996). Evidence-based medicine: What it is and what it isn't. *British Medical Journal, 312*, 71–72.

Sackett, D. L., Straus, S. E., Richardson, W. S., Rosenberg, W., & Haynes, R. B. (2000). *Evidence-based medicine: How to practice and teach EBM* (2nd ed.). New York: Churchill Livingstone.

Social Work Library. (2004, September). From idea to knowledge consensus: The publication chain. Available: www.lib.umich.edu/socwork/rescue/publicationchain.html.

Thomlison, B., & Corcoran, K. (in press). *Evidence-based field work: Resources for social workers and criminal justice students*. New York: Oxford University Press.

Thyer, B. A. (2002). Evidence-based practice and clinical social work. *Evidence-Based Mental Health, 5*(1), 6–9.

14

A Cognitive-Behavioral Approach
to Suicide Risk Reduction
in Crisis Intervention

MARJORIE E. WEISHAAR

Working with suicidal patients can be anxiety-provoking for even the most experienced clinician because of the perceived responsibility for another person's life, the difficulty predicting the likelihood and timing of an individual's suicide based on population models, and the particular reliance on the therapy relationship when collaboration may be difficult.

Suicide is the 11th leading cause of death overall in the United States (Minino, Arias, Kochanek, Murphy, & Smith, 2002). Among adolescents, it accounts for a greater proportion of deaths than for the nation as a whole (McIntosh, 2000). Despite these facts, there is a paucity of well-designed research on treatments to reduce *suicidality* (i.e., suicide, suicide attempts, and suicide ideation; Linehan, 1997). Clinicians need empirically validated treatments or will continue to rely methods that are unproven and perhaps ineffective. This chapter presents a summary of the research literature on randomized controlled trials to reduce suicide risk, descriptions of cognitive-behavioral treatments that have demonstrated efficacy, and guidelines for implementing cognitive and behavioral interventions with suicidal individuals.

KEY CONCEPTS AND DATABASES

The low base rate of suicide makes it statistically unpredictable on an individual basis, particularly because the database is limited primarily to cross-sectional studies (Clark & Fawcett, 1992). Despite the apparent differences between those who suicide and those who attempt it repeatedly (Clark & Fawcett, 1992; Linehan, 1986, 1993a), those who contemplate and attempt suicide are the available groups to study and reasonable proxies. Attempting suicide remains one of the most powerful risk factors for eventual suicide (Fawcett et al., 1990; Goldstein, Black, Nasrallah, & Winokur, 1991; Harris & Barraclough, 1997; Steer, Beck, Garrison, & Lester, 1988). A history of nonfatal attempts confers an elevated risk for eventual suicide that is five to six times greater than that for the general population (Clark & Fawcett, 1992). Similarly, reducing suicide ideation is presumed to break a pathway to overt suicidal behavior (Dieserud, Roysamb, Ekeberg, & Kraft, 2001). Much suicide research has focused on reducing the clinical (e.g., depression) and cognitive (e.g., hopelessness, poor problem solving; see Weishaar, 1996, for a review) risk factors associated with suicide. As Shea (1999) points out, a risk factor of a large sample does not accurately predict the chance of imminent suicide for an individual client, but knowledge of risk factors alerts the clinician to suspect increased risk and directs specific lines of questioning to assess risk for that client. Thus, research on treatments to reduce suicide risk targets suicide attempts and other parasuicidal behavior, suicide ideation and intent, and risk factors associated with suicide.

Suicide research has developed several assessment tools that are also very useful clinically, such as the Scale for Suicide Ideation (SSI; Beck, Kovacs, & Weissman, 1979; Beck & Steer, 1991); the Suicide Intent Scale (SIS; Beck, Schuyler, & Herman, 1974); the Beck Hopelessness Scale (BHS; Beck, Weissman, Lester, & Trexler, 1974); and various forms of the Reasons for Living Inventory (Jobes & Mann, 1999; Linehan, Goodstein, Nielson, & Chiles, 1983; Westefeld, Cardin, & Deaton, 1992). These assessment tools can structure a clinical interview to determine a particular individual's risk. A person's suicide risk should never be based on a score from a single scale.

Suicide intent, the intensity and pervasiveness of one's wish to die (Beck, 1986), is a key concept in working with suicidal individuals. High intent distinguishes suicide attempts from other *parasuicidal behavior* (i.e., intentional, acute self-injury with or without suicidal intent; Linehan, Armstrong, Suarez, Allmon, & Heard, 1991). Suicide intent cannot be inferred by the lethality of the attempt unless the patient has an accurate conception of the lethality of his or her chosen means (Beck, Beck, & Kovacs, 1975). That means the clinician has to ask the person how much he or she wished to die. In addition to self-report, which might be less than candid, questions on the SIS identify behavioral markers that indicate intent, such as having taken precautions against being discovered (Beck & Lester, 1976; Beck, Steer, & Trexler, 1989).

Suicide ideation is a target in both outcome studies and clinical treatments because it is a precursor to suicidal behavior. It is especially important for clinicians treating outpatients to ask about ideation at its worst point, for that is most closely linked to eventual suicide (Beck, Brown, Steer, Dahlsgaard, & Grisham, 1999). It is likely that for inpatients, the time of hospitalization is the worst point. Understanding the frequency, duration, power, and context of the suicidal thoughts, as well as the attitudes, purpose, and planning concerning an attempt, guides treatment. For example, someone who has thoughts of suicide when drinking alcohol might receive therapy that treats substance abuse as well as suicide. Someone who is shocked or dismayed by suicidal thoughts is more likely to collaborate with the therapist to challenge them than is someone who is comforted by images of death or convinced that suicide is the only solution to problems.

METHODOLOGICAL ISSUES AND RESEARCH LIMITATIONS

A number of methodological issues have hampered clinical research on suicide. Many suicidal individuals are screened out of or dropped from studies in which suicidality is a comorbidity because of risk-averse criteria. For example, 90% of suicide victims have had a psychiatric or substance abuse disorder, but there are few clinical trials aimed at treating psychopathology or substance abuse that also address suicidality (Fisher, Pearson, Kim, & Reynolds, 2002). Further, in studies of suicidal persons, *high-risk* subjects (i.e., those with a history of attempts, those who suffer mood disorders with concurrent ideation, and those abusing alcohol episodically with concurrent ideation; Maris, Berman, Maltsberger, & Yufit, 1992) are also often excluded for reasons of perceived liability to individual researchers and institutions (Fisher et al., 2002). Thus, one limitation on suicide research has been a reluctance to test treatments for suicidality with randomized clinical trials.

The notion of a control group raises issues for randomized clinical trials in suicide research because a no-treatment control group is unethical. The common solution is the treatment as usual (TAU) control group. However, TAU means different things in different studies, and sometimes even within the same study if some patients return to their primary-care physician while others are given referrals, phone contact, or lesser forms of follow-up. In some recent studies, all patients received more monitoring and more intensive care than would be available outside the study (Fisher et al., 2002). This is called enriched care plus treatment as usual and is the control condition for the current studies by Beck (2002). This EC+TAU condition provides more safety for research participants and is an effort to improve the standard of treatment across practice settings, as well as to reduce attrition from studies. However, there may be treatment effects from this control condition that reduce the power to detect differences between the control group and the experimental group (Fisher et al., 2002).

Difficulty detecting treatment effects due to small sample sizes has plagued randomized controlled trials (Arensman et al., 2001; Fisher et al., 2002; Hawton et al., 1998; Linehan, 1997; Rudd, 2000). Large, multisite studies are recommended in order to have sufficient statistical power to show treatment effects. Other methodological issues have been poor definitions of treatments and how they were applied, lack of standard measures of outcome, lack of information on whether treatment resulted in changes in the targets of treatment (e.g., improved problem solving, emotion regulation, or interpersonal skills; Arensman et al., 2001), and limited follow-up monitoring to evaluate lasting change (Rudd, 2000).

TREATMENT OUTCOME STUDIES TO REDUCE SUICIDE RISK

Recent reviews of the literature (Hawton et al., 1998; Linehan, 1997; Rudd, 2000; Rudd, Joiner, & Rajab, 2001) have identified only 16 randomized or controlled studies of psychotherapeutic treatments for suicide; 14 of them are short-term, and 2 are long-term. Four of the brief (less than 1 year) studies investigated the effectiveness of some intensive follow-up and crisis support in addition to TAU. The outcomes of these studies were generally negative. The remaining 10 studies were some variety of cognitive-behavior therapy (CBT), and all had a core component of problem-solving therapy. (Since those reviews, Guthrie and colleagues, 2001, et al., found that a brief psychodynamic treatment significantly reduced suicide ideation and repeated attempts at 6-month follow-up.) Eight of the 10 CBT studies reported decreases in psychological risk factors for suicidal behavior such as suicide ideation, hopelessness, and depression. Two of the studies (McLeavey, Daly, Ludgate, & Murray, 1994; Salkovskis, Atha, & Storer, 1990) found significant decreases in the frequency of suicide attempts. In the Salkovskis et al. (1990) study of high-risk attempters, the treatment group improved significantly more than the TAU control group in terms of depression, hopelessness, suicide ideation, and target problems at the end of treatment and at 1-year follow-up. The difference in frequency of repeat attempts between treatment and control groups was found at 6-month follow-up but not at 1 year. In the McLeavey et al. (1994) study, which excluded high-risk patients, the reduction in suicide attempts persisted to 12 months after treatment. Thus, brief psychological interventions can be successful in reducing subsequent suicidal behaviors, at least over the short term.

The two long-term studies yielded mixed results. Allard, Marshall, and Plante (1992) examined the role of intensive follow-up across several therapeutic modalities but did not test a specific psychotherapy. Methodological problems compromised the results. In contrast, Linehan and colleagues (1991) tested a very specific form of CBT, dialectical behavior therapy (DBT; Linehan, 1993a, 1993b), to treat parasuicidal behavior in women with borderline personality disorder. After 1 year of treatment, those receiving DBT had fewer incidences of parasuicide, less medically severe parasuicides, fewer inpatient psychiatric days, and a greater chance of remaining in therapy than those in the TAU control group. No between-group differences were found on measures of depression, hopelessness, suicide ideation, reasons for living, or the proportion of parasuicides classified as suicide attempts by the subjects. The superiority of DBT for reducing parasuicidal acts was maintained throughout the 1-year follow-up but not during the

18- to 24-month follow-up (Linehan, Heard, & Armstrong, 1993). Nevertheless, DBT was successful in reducing parasuicidal behavior in a group of severely dysfunctional, chronically suicidal subjects with limited use of hospitalization, thus demonstrating that outpatient treatment of high-risk patients can be safe and effective.

The emergence of CBT as an efficacious modality for the treatment of suicide risk highlights the role of skills training, particularly problem solving. DBT conceptualizes parasuicidal behaviors as maladaptive attempts at problem solving, the primary problem being unbearable emotional distress (Linehan, 1993a). The problem-solving training used in CBT studies is represented by the work of Nezu, Nezu, and Perri (1989) and by Hawton and Kirk (1989), for example. Linehan has a manualized treatment for DBT (Linehan, 1993a, 1993b) that targets suicidal behaviors, therapy-interfering behaviors, skills acquisition (e.g., mindfulness, interpersonal skills), emotion regulation and distress tolerance, posttraumatic stress, self-respect, and individual goals. Short-term adaptations of DBT have been used in studies that did not find significant differences in suicide attempts at the end of treatment, but some of these are preliminary or pilot studies (Evans et al., 1999; Koerner & Linehan, 2000; Rathus & Miller, 2002).

Based on a review of the treatment outcome literature, particularly the success of DBT, and an investigation of personality types and suicidal behavior (Rudd, Ellis, Rajab, & Wehrly, 2000), it has been argued that patients with severe personality pathology and *chronic suicidality* (i.e., unremittingly high suicide ideation, frequent threats of suicide, and difficulty articulating reasons for living; Linehan, 1999) require intensive treatment, closer follow-up monitoring to ensure treatment compliance, treatments to address specific skill deficits, such as CBT, and long-term treatment (Rudd et al., 2000). Short-term CBT appears effective in reducing suicide ideation, depression, and hopelessness in periods up to 1 year (Rudd, 2000). However, a study is currently under way to see whether short-term cognitive therapy immediately following an attempt can effectively reduce suicide attempts in a group of attempters (73% have made more than one attempt) who also have psychiatric and/or substance disorders and significant Axis II pathology (Beck, 2002).

As part of a large-scale investigation, Beck (2002) recently completed preliminary studies of a cognitive therapy treatment for suicidal behavior in a sample of urban, minority suicide attempters who are socially and economically disadvantaged and who present with serious psychopathology. Participants were recruited at the time of their hospitalization for a suicide attempt but were treated on an outpatient basis. The 10-week treatment included cognitive therapy for depression, hopelessness, and substance abuse, as well as cognitive and behavioral interventions specifically for suicidal behavior, including problem solving and focusing on the problem associated with their attempt. The primary outcome variables were the number and timing of suicide attempts following the index attempt, for the risk of a repeat attempt is highest within 3 years of an index attempt (Hawton & Fagg, 1988; Morris, Kovacs, Beck, & Wolffe, 1974). A secondary goal was to determine if cognitive therapy immediately following a suicide attempt reduces the severity of the risk factors depression, hopelessness, and suicide ideation.

Preliminary results show that patients who received cognitive therapy had decreases in depression that were significantly greater than the control group and significantly fewer hospitalizations. To date, it appears that the cognitive therapy intervention reduces the frequency of subsequent suicide attempts and prolongs the time before an individual makes another suicide attempt (Beck, 2002). Patients will be followed for 2 years.

MOVEMENT TOWARD THE DEVELOPMENT OF PRACTICE GUIDELINES

Practice guidelines are available for the legal and clinical care of suicidal patients (Bongar, 2002; Bongar, Maris, Berman, & Litman, 1992; Bongar et al., 1998). Among the clinical guidelines are lists of suicide risk variables, both acute and chronic, as determined by longitudinal studies (Beck, Brown, Berchick, Stewart, & Steer, 1990; Beck, Steer, Kovacs, & Garrison, 1985; Fawcett et al., 1990; Goldstein et al., 1991). Outpatient practice guidelines based on the research literature are presented by Rudd and his colleagues (Rudd, Joiner, Jobes, & King, 1999). Linehan (1999) also presents guidelines for treating chronically suicidal patients. In addition to these standardized guidelines for clinical care, Maltsberger (1986) identifies specific components necessary in formulating one's clinical judgment of suicide risk.

A study of imminent risk based on data from therapists who lost patients to suicide identifies three factors in a suicide crisis: (a) a precipitating event, (b) one or more intense affective states other than depression, and (c) at least one of three behavioral patterns, namely, speech or actions suggesting suicide, deterioration in social or occupational functioning, and increased substance abuse (Hendin, Maltsberger, Lipschitz, Haas, & Kyle, 2001).

Manualized treatments for suicide risk may be thought of as developments toward treatment guidelines when the therapies have demonstrated efficacy. Linehan's manual for DBT (Linehan, 1993a, 1993b), the cognitive-behavioral formulation by Rudd et al. (2001), and Choosing to Live (Ellis & Newman, 1996), which is part of Beck's research protocol, document cognitive-behavioral strategies to reduce suicide risk.

STEPS FOR USING CBT PRACTICE GUIDELINES

In CBT, suicidal behavior is viewed as a maladaptive coping behavior. Regardless of theoretical differences, all forms of CBT for suicide are active, directive, and problem focused. The following steps in assessing and treating suicidal thoughts and behavior are drawn from Beck's cognitive therapy. Throughout the CBT treatment literature, the quality of the therapy relationship is emphasized, so although these steps are presented in a formulaic manner, they are applied with great sensitivity, for the goals are to first understand the patient's view before challenging it and to build collaboration during a very stressful experience. The reader is referred to Shea's (1999) book on interviewing suicidal patients for more guidance.

Acute or Immediate Goals

1. Eliminate access to lethal means and assess need for hospitalization, type of therapy needed (e.g., Does the family need therapy?), presence of clinical risk factors.
2. Intervention begins with assessment: assess suicide ideation, intent, purpose of attempt, and hopelessness.
3. Reduce hopelessness and shake rigid conclusions that things cannot improve. Convey that hopelessness is a viewpoint and not an accurate reflection of the facts. Get a list of all the things the patient feels hopeless about. Are these situational stressors or indicative of a core belief (e.g., "I am a loser.")? Reduce cognitive distortions that complicate the picture.
4. Examine reasons for living and reasons for dying. Tip the balance in favor of living by undermining reasons for dying now and bolstering reasons for living (e.g., ask for details of positive reasons for living, add to the list). Make sure the patient considers consequences of dying for self and others. Reduce distortions that romanticize death. Make a list of deterrents in addition to positive reasons for living.
5. Assess the person's attitude toward suicide ideation and situations in which it occurs. If an attempt has been made, do a behavioral or functional analysis of the situation, thoughts, and emotions that preceded the attempt. Identify alternative thoughts and behaviors. Get descriptions of all other attempts and plans for future attempts.
6. Assess the patient's sense of control over ideation or action. In what situations are the controls effective or ineffective? What types of self-control strategies does the patient utilize?
7. What coping skills or psychological buffers does the patient have (e.g., coping beliefs, reasons for living, frustration tolerance, positive feelings of competence, ability to use distraction or to dispute suicidal ideas, ability to utilize social supports)?
8. Assess problem-solving skills and cognitive deficits that might interfere with problem solving (e.g., rigid or dichotomous thinking).
9. Construct a suicide emergency kit as early as possible. This is a written plan, which the patient can carry, to save oneself when having suicide ideation. It can be elaborated as therapy progresses. An example of a kit for a depressed, suicidal person appears in Table 14.1. The purpose of distraction from suicidal thoughts is to break the focus on negative thinking. Suicidal thoughts can be challenged with the help of the therapist, but not all patients are able to dispute them early in treatment without help. As therapy progresses, the patient can write negative thoughts with their rebuttals on the card along with the suicide emergency kit.

Table 14.1 Suicide Emergency Kit

---

1. Recognize that the thoughts you are having are part of depression. (Note: Substitute whatever the patient identifies as his or her affective state—anxiety, anger.)

2. Recognize that the thoughts go away when you feel better.

3. You have had these thoughts x (patient supplies the number) times before and they have gone away.

4. These thoughts are time-limited and should not be responded to.

5. It is important not to act on these thoughts because they are part of depression (anxiety, anger, frustration, loneliness).

6. Do not focus on losses in the past or imagine losses in the future.

7. Focus on activities and distractions, the more active the better.

List of activities (Note: This list should be individualized for each person. Consider activities to do with other people or alone, daytime or nighttime. Add to the list as therapy progresses): walk or play with the dog, call Laura or Rick, shoot pool with Danny or another friend, visit Diana, call my therapist.

Short-Term to Long-Term Goals

1. Teach skills to identify and modify thoughts leading to suicidal behavior. Examine thoughts and beliefs logically and with behavioral experiments such as asking family members how they would feel if the person died rather than mind reading or assuming what others think.

2. Teach problem-solving skills and reduce cognitive distortions that interfere with each step. Start with problems associated with a suicide attempt, hopelessness, or suicide ideation. The steps in problem solving are as follows:
   a. Accepting problems as a normal part of life.
   b. Properly defining the problem.
   c. Generating alternative solutions.
   d. Anticipating the consequences (for self and others) of various courses of action.
   e. Considering the advantages and disadvantages ("pros and cons") of each alternative.
   f. Choosing an alternative to try first and withholding judgment about its success until it has been given an adequate trial.
   g. Evaluating the outcome with reasonable criteria (e.g., achieving degrees of success, doing a behavior correctly, but there being an outcome out of one's control).
   h. Tolerating the anxiety and frustration that are part of solving problems.

3. Reduce other cognitive risk factors that might predispose the patient to future suicidal episodes. These include the following:
   a. Hopelessness: View hopelessness as a point of view and not an accurate reflection of the situation. List all the problems making the patient hopeless. Reduce cognitive distortions to clearly define problems. Share optimism about finding solutions. Do problem-solving training and skills training (e.g., communication skills, assertiveness, frustration tolerance) to implement solutions.

    b. Impulsivity: Teach the patient to do a functional or behavioral analysis to see the process by which he or she loses control. Review the steps in problem solving. Identify lower levels of emotion. Break all-or-nothing thinking. Use relaxation, "time-out," or a "waiting period" to postpone action.

    c. Low self-concept: Is the negative view of oneself about specific flaws, or is it global? Is rigid thinking operating? Focus on success experiences and positive qualities. Reframe negative labels such as "sensitive" or "dependent."

    d. Dysfunctional assumptions: Gather evidence that supports the dysfunctional belief and that challenges the belief. Look for distortions, inaccuracies, and biases in evidence that support the negative assumption. What would you like to, realistically, believe? Gather evidence for that positive assumption.

    e. Cognitive rigidity: Treat beliefs as hypotheses to be tested and test them logically and with safe behavioral experiments. Build a continuum between extreme points of view and use "shades of gray" or percentages to break rigid judgments if dichotomous thinking is operating. Brainstorm solutions for someone else's problems. Role-play with role reversal to increase flexibility in generating alternatives. Look for exceptions to the client's rules.

    f. View of suicide as desirable: List the reasons for dying and solutions. List the reasons for living. List the advantages and disadvantages of su-

---

Table 14.2   Coping Card

---

1. Warning signs for my suicidality
   a. I feel different, defective
   b. I feel overwhelmed; everything seems to be a problem
   c. I get very self-critical ("I'm a failure. I can't do anything right.")

2. My plan for dealing with suicidal thoughts (like Suicide Emergency Kit)
   a. Call friends—list names and numbers
   b. Exercise—"crunches," running, dancing, step aerobics
   c. Relax with a shower or listen to music (e.g., Stevie Wonder, Beatles)
   d. Read therapy notes and see how far I've come since the worst point

3. List my reasons to live
   a. What were my reasons to live when I was happier? Might they be true in the future? What new reasons to live have I found?
   b. Write a positive statement that rings true: "It would be a shame to kill myself today if I were to feel better in the future."

4. Write my old beliefs and new ideas that contradict them.
   a. Old idea: My life will never get better. New idea: I'm learning new things in therapy to change.
   b. Old idea: I'm a failure. New idea: On any given day, I'm a partial success and a partial failure at anything I try. The idea is to find what I like to do.
   c. Old idea: I am a burden to my family and friends. New idea: My family says they will never get over it if I die. My friends say they depend on me just like I depend on them.
   d. Old idea: I'm a loser. New idea: If I die, I'll never know what it feels like to win something. I don't want to lose my chances, my life.

---

icide relative to other solutions. Correct cognitive distortions and mis-information about the perceived advantages of dying.
3. Construct coping cards to deal with suicide ideation and relapse. An ex-ample of a coping card appears in Table 14.2.

CONCLUSION

The research literature on randomized controlled trials of psychotherapeutic treatments to reduce suicidality supports the use of CBT. Both short-term treat-ments and long-term therapies emphasize problem solving as a key component. Cognitive risk factors may be conceived of as both acute and chronic. Therefore, therapy should target these risk factors throughout treatment, even after the suicidal crisis has passed. If not, they could well predispose the individual to future suicidal episodes.

REFERENCES

Allard, R., Marshall, M., & Plante, M. (1992). Intensive follow-up does not de-crease the risk of repeat suicide attempts. *Suicide and Life-Threatening Behav-ior, 22*, 303–314.
Arensman, E., Townsend, E., Hawton, K., Bremner, S., Feldman, E., Goldney, R., Gunnell, D., Hazell, P., Van Heeringen, K., House, A., Owens, D., Sakinofsky, I., & Traskman-Bendz, L. (2001). Psychosocial and pharmacological treatment of patients following deliberate self-harm: The methodological issues involved in evaluating effectiveness. *Suicide and Life-Threatening Behavior, 31*, 169–180.
Beck, A. T. (1986). Hopelessness as a predictor of eventual suicide. *Annals of the New York Academy of Sciences, 487*, 90–96.
Beck, A. T. (2002, December). *An early cognitive intervention for suicide attempt-ers.* Paper presented at the first annual conference of Treatment and Research Advancements Association for Personality Disorders, Bethesda, Maryland.
Beck, A. T., Beck, R. W., & Kovacs, M. (1975). Classification of suicidal behaviors: I. Quantifying intent and medical lethality. *American Journal of Psychiatry, 132*, 285–287.
Beck, A. T., Brown, G., Berchick, R. J., Stewart, B. L., & Steer, R. A. (1990). Rela-tionship between hopelessness and ultimate suicide: A replication with psychiat-ric outpatients. *American Journal of Psychiatry, 147*, 190–195.
Beck, A. T., Brown, G. K., Steer, R. A., Dahlsgaard, K. K., & Grisham, J. (1999). Suicide ideation at its worst point: A predictor of eventual suicide in psychiatric outpatients. *Suicide and Life-Threatening Behavior, 29*, 1–9.
Beck, A. T., Kovacs, M., & Weissman, A. (1979). Assessment of suicidal intention: The Scale for Suicide Ideation. *Journal of Consulting and Clinical Psychology, 47*, 343–352.
Beck, A. T., & Lester, D, (1976). Components of suicidal intent in completed and attempted suicides. *Journal of Psychology, 92*, 35–38.
Beck, A. T., Schuyler, D., & Herman, I. (1974). Development of suicidal intent

scales. In A. T. Beck, H.C.P. Resnik, & D. Lettieri (Eds.), *The prediction of suicide* (pp. 45–56). Bowie, MD: Charles Press.

Beck, A. T., & Steer, R. A. (1991). *Manual for the Beck Scale for Suicide Ideation.* San Antonio, TX: Psychological Corporation.

Beck, A. T., Steer, R.A., Kovacs, M., & Garrison, B. (1985). Hopelessness and eventual suicide: A ten-year prospective study of patients hospitalized with suicidal ideation. *American Journal of Psychiatry, 142,* 559–563.

Beck, A. T., Steer, R. A., & Trexler, L. D. (1989). Alcohol abuse and eventual suicide: A five to ten year prospective study of alcohol abusing suicide attempters. *Journal of Studies on Alcohol, 50,* 202–209.

Beck, A. T., Weissman, A., Lester, D., & Trexler, L. (1974). The measurement of pessimism: The Hopelessness Scale. *Journal of Consulting and Clinical Psychology, 42,* 861–865.

Bongar, B. (2002). *The suicidal patient: Clinical and legal standards of care* (2nd ed.). Washington, DC: American Psychological Association.

Bongar, B., Berman, A. L., Maris, R. W., Silverman, M. M., Harris, E. A., & Packman, W. L. (1998). *Risk management with suicidal patients.* New York: Guilford Press.

Bongar, B., Maris, R., Berman, A. L., & Litman, R. E. (1992). Outpatient standards of care and the suicidal patient. *Suicide and Life-Threatening Behavior, 22,* 453–478.

Clark, D., & Fawcett, J. (1992). An empirically based model of suicide risk assessment for patients with affective disorders. In D. Jacobs (Ed.), *Suicide in clinical practice* (pp. 55–73). Washington, DC: American Psychiatric Press.

Dieserud, G., Roysamb, E., Ekeberg, O., & Kraft, P. (2001). Toward an integrative model of suicide attempt: A cognitive psychological approach. *Suicide and Life-Threatening Behavior, 31,* 153–168.

Ellis, T. E., & Newman, C. F. (1996). *Choosing to live: How to defeat suicide through cognitive therapy.* Oakland, CA: New Harbinger Publications.

Evans, K., Tyrer, P., Catalan, J., Schmidt, U., Davidson, K., Dent, J., Tata, P., Thornton, S., Barber, J., & Thompson, S. (1999). Manual-assisted cognitive-behavioural therapy (MACT): A randomized controlled trial of a brief intervention with bibliotherapy in the treatment of recurrent deliberate self-harm. *Psychological Medicine, 29,* 19–25.

Fawcett, J., Schefter, W. A., Fogg, L., Clark, D. C., Young, M. A., Hedeker, D., & Gibbons, R. (1990). Time-related predictors of suicide in major affective disorder. *American Journal of Psychiatry, 147,* 1189–1194.

Fisher, C. B., Pearson, J. L., Kim, S., & Reynolds, C. F. (2002). Ethical issues in including suicidal individuals in clinical research. *IRB: Ethics and Human Research, 24* (4), 9–14.

Goldstein, R. B., Black, D. W., Nasrallah, A., & Winokur, G. (1991). The prediction of suicide: Sensitivity, specificity, and predictive value of a multivariate model applied to suicide among 1906 patients with affective disorders. *Archives of General Psychiatry, 48,* 418–422.

Guthrie, E., Kapur, N., Mackway-Jones, K., Chew-Graham, C., Moorey, J., Mendel, E., Marino-Francis, F., Sanderson, S., Turpin, C., Broddy, G., & Tomenson, B. (2001). Randomised controlled trial of brief psychological intervention after deliberate self-poisoning. *British Medical Journal, 323,* 1–5.

Harris, E. C., & Barraclough, B. (1997). Suicide as an outcome for mental disorders: A meta-analysis. *British Journal of Psychiatry, 170,* 205–228.

Hawton, K., Arensman, E., Townsend, E., Bremner, S., Feldman, E., Goldney, R., Gunnell, D., Hazell, P., Van Heeringen, K., House, A., Owens, D., Sakinofsky, I., & Traksman-Bendz, L. (1998). Deliberate self-harm: Systematic review of efficacy of psychosocial and pharmacological treatments in preventing repetition. *British Medical Journal, 317,* 441–447.

Hawton, K., & Fagg, J. (1988). Suicide, and other causes of death, following attempted suicide. *British Journal of Psychiatry, 152,* 359–366.

Hawton, K., & Kirk, J. W. (1989). Problem solving. In K. Hawton, P. M. Salkovskis, J. Kirk, & D. M. Clark (Eds.), *Cognitive behaviour therapy for psychiatric problems: A practical guide* (pp. 406–426). Oxford: Oxford University Press.

Hendin, H., Maltsberger, J. T., Lipschitz, A., Haas, A. P., & Kyle, J. (2001). Recognizing and responding to a suicide crisis. *Suicide and Life-Threatening Behavior, 31,* 115–128.

Jobes, D. A., & Mann, R. E. (1999). Reasons for living versus reasons for dying: Examining the internal debate of suicide. *Suicide and Life-Threatening Behavior, 29,* 97–104.

Koerner, K., & Linehan, M. M. (2002). Dialectical Behavior Therapy for patients with borderline personality disorder. *Psychiatric Clinics of North America, 23,* 151–167.

Linehan, M. M. (1986). Suicidal people: One population or two? In J. J. Mann & M. Stanley (Eds.), *Annals of the New York Academy of Sciences: The psychobiology of suicidal behavior* (pp. 16–33). New York: New York Academy of Sciences.

Linehan, M. M. (1993a). *Cognitive behavioral treatment of borderline personality disorder.* New York: Guilford Press.

Linehan, M. M. (1993b). *Skills training manual for treating borderline personality disorder.* New York: Guilford Press.

Linehan, M. M. (1997). Behavioral treatments of suicidal behaviors: Definitional obfuscation and treatment outcomes. In D. M. Stoff & J. J. Mann (Eds.), *Annals of the New York Academy of Sciences: The neurobiology of suicide from the bench to the clinic* (pp. 302–328). New York: New York Academy of Sciences.

Linehan, M. M. (1999). Standard protocol for assessing and treating suicidal behaviors for patients in treatment. In D. G. Jacobs (Ed.), *The Harvard Medical School guide to suicide assessment and intervention* (pp. 146–187). San Francisco: Jossey-Bass.

Linehan, M. M., Armstrong, H. E., Suarez, A., Allmon, D., & Heard, H. (1991). Cognitive-behavioral treatment of chronically parasuicidal borderline patients. *Archives of General Psychiatry, 48,* 1060–1064.

Linehan, M. M., Goodstein, J. L., Nielson, S. L., & Chiles, J. A. (1983). Reasons for staying alive when you are thinking of killing yourself: The Reasons for Living Inventory. *Journal of Consulting and Clinical Psychology, 51,* 276–286.

Linehan, M. M., Heard, H., L., & Armstrong, H. E. (1993). Naturalistic follow-up of a behavioral treatment for chronically parasuicidal borderline patients. *Archives of General Psychiatry, 50,* 971–974.

Maltsberger, J. T. (1986). *Suicide risk: The formulation of clinical judgment.* New York: New York University Press.

Maris, R. W., Berman, A. L., Maltsberger, J. T. & Yufit, R. I. (Eds.), (1992). *Assessment and prediction of suicide*. New York: Guilford Press.

McIntosh, J. L. (2000). Epidemiology of adolescent suicde in the United States. In R. W. Maris, S. S. Canetto, J. L. McIntosh, & M. M. Silverman (Eds.), *Review of suicidology 2000* (pp. 3–33). New York: Guilford Press.

McLeavey, B. C., Daly, R. J., Ludgate, J. W., & Murray, C. M. (1994). Interpersonal problem-solving skills training in the treatment of self-poisoning patients. *Suicide and Life-Threatening Behavior, 24,* 382–394.

Minino, A. M., Arias, E., Kochanek, K. D., Murphy, S. L., & Smith, B. L. (2002). *Deaths: Final data for 2000*. National Vital Statistics Reports, 50(15). Hyattsville, MD: National Center for Health Statistics.

Morris, J. B., Kovacs, M., Beck, A. T., & Wolffe, A. (1974). Notes toward an epidemiology of urban suicide. *Comprehensive Psychology, 15,* 537–547.

Nezu, A. M., Nezu, C. M., & Perri, M. G. (1989). *Problem-solving therapy for depression: Theory, research, and clinical guidelines*. New York: Wiley.

Rathus, J. H., & Miller, A. L. (2002). Dialectical Behavior Therapy adapted for suicidal adolescents. *Suicide and Life-Threatening Behavior, 32,* 146–157.

Rudd, M. D. (2000). Integrating science into the practice of clinical suicidology: A review of the psychotherapy literature and a research agenda for the future. In R. W. Maris, S. S. Canetto, J. L. McIntosh, & M. M. Silverman (Eds.), *Review of Suicidology 2000* (pp. 47–83). New York: Guilford Press.

Rudd, M. D., Ellis, T. E., Rajab, M. H., & Wehrly, T. (2000). Personality types and suicidal behavior: An exploratory study. *Suicide and Life-Threatening Behavior, 30,* 199–212.

Rudd, M. D., Joiner, T. E., Jobes, D. A., & King, C. A. (1999). The outpatient treatment of suicidality: An integration of science and recognition of its limitations. *Professional Psychology: Research and Practice, 30,* 437–446.

Rudd, M. D., Joiner, T., & Rajab, M. H. (2001). *Treating suicidal behavior: An effective, time-limited approach*. New York: Guilford Press.

Salkovskis, P. M., Atha, C., & Storer, D. (1990). Cognitive-behavioral problem solving in the treatment of patients who repeatedly attempt suicide: A controlled trial. *British Journal of Psychiatry, 157,* 871–876.

Shea, S. C. (1999). *The practical art of suicide assessment: A guide for mental health professionals and substance abuse counselors*. New York: Wiley.

Steer, R. A., Beck, A. T., Garrison, B., & Lester, D. (1988). Eventual suicide in interrupted and uninterrupted attempters. A challenge to the cry-for-help hypothesis. *Suicide and Life-Threatening Behavior, 18,* 119–128.

Weishaar, M. E. (1996). Cognitive risk factors in suicide. In P. M. Salkovskis (Ed.), *Frontiers of cognitive therapy* (pp. 226–249). New York: Guilford Press.

Westefeld, J. S., Cardin, D., & Deaton, W. L. (1992). Development of the College Student Reasons for Living Inventory. *Suicide and Life-Threatening Behavior, 22,* 442–452.

15

Task-Centered Practice

An Exemplar of Evidence-Based Practice

WILLIAM J. REID

ANNE E. FORTUNE

The task-centered model (TC) is a short-term, problem-solving approach to social work practice (Doel & Marsh, 1992; Reid, 1992, 2000; Reid & Epstein, 1972; Reid & Fortune, 2002). Originally designed for practice with individuals and families, the model has been adapted for work with groups (Fortune, 1985; Garvin, 1974) and larger systems (Tolson, Reid, & Garvin, 2003).

THE DEVELOPMENT OF TC AS A RESEARCH-BASED FORM OF PRACTICE

The task-centered approach was developed as a form of research-based practice. It originated from a randomized experiment conducted in the mid-1960s that suggested that brief intervention might provide a more efficient means of helping individuals and families with many problems than conventional, long-term forms of practice (Reid & Shyne, 1969). Using that brief service approach as a starting point, Reid and Epstein (1972) collaborated on developing a more comprehensive, systematic, and effective model of short-term intervention. The research orientation of the model was expressed in several ways. Preference was to be given to methods and theories tested and supported by empirical research. Hypotheses and concepts about the client system were to be grounded in case data obtained through such means as client self-report, observation, and rapid assessment instruments. Speculative theorizing about the client's problems and behavior was to be avoided. Assessment, process, and outcome data were to be systematically collected and recorded for each case. This conception fits well with current definitions of evidence-based practice (Thyer, 2001).

The intent was to create an approach to practice that would evolve in response to continuing research and to developments in research-based knowledge and technology consonant with its basic principles. The model was designed to be an open, pluralistic practice system that would integrate theoretical and technical contributions from diverse sources. In keeping with this design, the model did not adopt a particular theory of human functioning or any fixed set of intervention methods. Rather, it provided a core of values, theory, and methods that could be augmented by compatible approaches.

We launched a program of research that has continued to the present, research to which numerous investigators worldwide have contributed. Early studies suggested that more flexible time limits, 8 to 12 interviews within a 4-month period, may work better than a fixed number of sessions (Reid & Epstein, 1972). A subsequent controlled experiment established the effectiveness of a set of methods in the session for preparing the client to undertake actions or tasks outside the session (Reid, 1975).

Additional controlled experiments have demonstrated the efficacy of the model for treating problems of psychiatric outpatients and children at risk of school failure (Gibbons, Butler, & Bow, 1979; Reid, 1976; Reid & Bailey-Dempsey, 1995; Reid, Epstein, Brown, Tolson, & Rooney, 1980). A number of other studies have shown the model to be promising for work with a variety of other populations, including parents in child welfare settings (Rooney, 1981; Rzepnicki, 1985), delinquents (Larsen & Mitchell), and people who are frail and elderly (Dierking, Brown, & Fortune, 1980; Naleppa & Reid, 1998).

As it has matured, the model has integrated methods from other approaches, notably behavioral, cognitive-behavioral, cognitive, and family structural therapies. The pluralistic, integrative nature of TC enables it to incorporate almost any empirically supported approach that focuses on client action as a means of change. In sum, TC is an evidence-based model in three senses: (a) It is in itself a well-tested model of practice, (b) it provides a framework for incorporating other empirically supported methods, and (c) it makes use of case data as a means of providing feedback to practitioners and clients about progress toward problem resolution.

In the sections to follow, we will summarize the steps of TC as it is used with individuals and families, giving particular attention to the use of evidence-based principles and procedures. Fuller explication of TC for individuals and families, as well as variations for work with groups and other systems, can be found in Tolson, Reid, and Garvin (2003). For a tutorial and a comprehensive bibliography, visit the TC Web site at http://www.task-centered.com.

INITIAL PHASE: PROBLEM EXPLORATION, ASSESSMENT, AND THE SERVICE CONTRACT

Client-acknowledged target problems, usually up to a limit of three, are explored and assessed. If the client is nonvoluntary, the practitioner discloses the reason for the referral and then determines if there are issues the client wants to work on. The social worker's role is to enable the client to express the problem in terms that he or she can comprehend and agree with. Assessment data are obtained on the frequency and severity of the problem for a retrospective baseline period, and current manifestations of the problem are spelled out in specific, measurable terms. Factors that may be contributing to the difficulty are examined collaboratively with the client. The social worker and client also consider resources and strengths that may aid in its resolution. In case management variations (Naleppa & Reid, 2003; Reid & Bailey-Dempsey, 1995), problems may be further explored and assessed by a team consisting of the client(s), the social worker, and others.

The practitioner makes use of research or research-based theory to enhance understanding of the client and his or her problems, as well as to ascertain the most effective means of establishing a therapeutic alliance. For example, in work with a suicidal adolescent, the social worker would make use of empirical knowledge of indicators of suicidal intent (Ivanoff & Reidel, 1995). If the client is a substance abuser "in denial," the social worker, guided by research on reactance (Brehm & Smith, 1986; Rooney, 1992) and engagement of substance abusers (Miller, Andrews, Wilbourne, & Bennett, 1998), would avoid a confrontational approach and make clear that the client had a choice about whether to accept treatment.

The client and practitioner form a revisable service contract that covers the problems to be addressed, the kind of intervention to be used, the number of sessions, and the duration of service. Research on the relative efficacy of planned short-term treatment for a wide range of problems has been an important source of evidence in the use of TC (Bloom, 2000). An effort is made to discriminate between those problems for which there is empirical support for use of brief service (e.g., Reid & Shyne, 1969) and those for which there is not, for example, the adjustment problems of persons with schizophrenia (Hogarty et al., 1997).

From its beginnings, TC has encouraged sharing of information with clients, a characteristic of the model that fits well with the emphasis in evidence-based practice on involving clients as informed decision makers (Gambrill, in press). In using TC the social worker shares with the client evidence that might be important to consider in collaborative decisions concerning the service contract. For example, if the client presented with a problem of chronic grief, the social worker might suggest, as one option, the use of "guided mourning" (Artelt & Thyer, 1998). The social worker would then inform the client about the nature of the intervention, especially its use of sustained exposure to grief-invoking stimuli, which might cause the client some discomfort, and discuss evidence about its effectiveness (which is largely positive). Other options, and evidence for them, would also be considered. The final decision about what option to use would be the client's.

The baseline characteristics of each of the client's problems are recorded on a target problem schedule. Progress on each problem is recorded weekly. Additional assessment data may be obtained through rapid assessment instruments, structured observation, and client self-monitoring devices.

MIDDLE PHASE: TASK PLANNING AND IMPLEMENTATION

The core of TC is helping clients select and carry out tasks that address their problems. A key intervention is the task planning and implementation sequence (TPIS), a set of systematic procedures designed to facilitate the client's task work. The client is helped to select a task, plan it in appropriate detail, anticipate any obstacles to its implementation, and rehearse or practice it, if indicated. Tasks that are successful in alleviating the client's problem are repeated; those that are less successful may be revised or replaced. Frequently, however, it is more strategic to resolve obstacles preventing task accomplishment than to change the task. Thus another major emphasis in the model involves the resolution of obstacles. In this process a variety of methods may be used, including practitioner intervention in the environment (if the obstacle is external) or cognitive-restructuring or insight-oriented techniques (if the obstacle is internal).

The use of an evidence-based approach is incorporated into task selection. Tasks are developed collaboratively with the client (rather than "assigned"). Both clients and practitioners suggest ideas for tasks. In making their suggestions, practitioners give first priority to possible client actions that have research support. This process is facilitated by using task planners, which provide menus of client tasks for a wide variety of clinical problems. One such resource is Reid (2000), which contains task planners for more than 100 frequently encountered problems. Task planners have been developed for specific populations, such as frail elderly people (Naleppa & Reid, 2003) and families receiving temporary financial assistance (TANF) (Reid & Kenaley, 2001). Task planners incorporate empirically supported tasks when such tasks can be located. For example, in a task planner on problems of anger control in children, tasks such as use of self-verbalizations to control angry reactions were drawn from empirically supported cognitive-behavioral programs, with a brief summary of the research support for these programs.

The extraction of tasks from such programs rather than the use of the entire program raises some issues because the evidence of effectiveness applies to the program and not to specific components. However, the extracted tasks are part of an effective program, which gives them priority over tasks lacking any research evidence. Moreover, in practice, social workers usually do not have access to full intervention protocols and, even when they do, are selective in what they draw from them (Richey & Roffman, 1999). Task planners are only one source of evidence-based tasks. Practitioners may have other research-based knowledge or can search for it by using information retrieval procedures, such as those outlined by Gibbs (2002). Most empirically supported interventions are compatible with a task-centered framework.

Once the client has agreed to a task, the details of its implementation are planned. Collaboration between practitioner and client continues in the planning process. The result should be a task plan that is customized to fit the client's abilities, one that should result in progress toward problem alleviation but is not so difficult as to make success unlikely. Possible obstacles to the plan are then considered through "what if" questions. For example, Jon agrees to ask his partner to help him remain sober. The practitioner might ask, "What if she starts to lecture you about your drinking?" Such questions enable the client to anticipate complications that might occur in carrying out the task and to develop ways of handling them.

When appropriate, tasks are rehearsed and practiced in the session through role plays or in vivo exercises. The latter are used extensively in work with couples and families and may take the form of in-session problem solving, communication training, or conflict resolution. Essentially, clients interact, with the practitioner serving as a facilitator. Such tasks draw on evidence-based methods tested in a range of couples and family programs (Robin, Bedway, & Gilroy, 1994; Stern, 1999).

In-session work on tasks (including those involving couple or family interaction) is then followed by clients' implementation in their life situations. Each task is reviewed in the session following its attempt. Progress is recorded on a 4-point task review scale, which specifies if the task has been completely, substantially, partially, or not achieved. The scale may be completed by the practitioner, the client, or both together. This scale, and the one measuring problem change, provides both practitioner and client with a record of progress on each task and its related problem. The information can be used as a guide to case evaluation and planning. When aggregated across cases, the data can provide insight into the relative success of the model with different types of problems and shed light on which types of tasks work best for particular kinds of problems (Reid, 1994). The model's emphasis on tracking problems and tasks also lends itself to the use of case data in agency information systems (Benbenishty & Ben-Zaken, 1988).

Task reviews may identify obstacles preventing task accomplishment. The obstacles may then become the focus of intervention. In helping clients analyze and resolve obstacles, social workers may, as noted, make use of a wide variety of methods. Again, preference is given to those with empirical support. A well-tested method for internalized obstacles is cognitive restructuring (Kuehlwein, 1998). The obstacle is first identified as occurring within the client's cognitive functioning. Through the practitioner's questioning and comments, cognitive distortions are clarified, and the client is helped to develop more functional cognitions. Thus Tom was unable to complete his task of using his wheelchair in a public place because he didn't want others pitying him. Cognitive restructuring helped him to see that people might not necessarily view him that way, given the positive images in the media of people in wheelchairs (e.g., athletes completing in special Olympics) and that he might apply those images to himself. External obstacles may involve individuals in the client's social network, organizations, or lack of resources, among other possibilities. Use is made of the modest research literature on interventions addressed to the client's environment, including research on task-centered methods of linkage (Weissman, 1977), advocacy (Fellin & Brown, 1989), and case management (Madden, Hicks-Coolick, & Kirk, 2002; Naleppa & Reid, 1998).

In TC, methods used to help clients overcome obstacles, whether internal or external, are centered on helping them move ahead with tasks. In this way TC can draw on a wide range of interventions while still maintaining focus on the client's actions as a means of problem resolution.

Practitioners as well as clients can take on tasks to effect changes in the client's environment. Calling such activities *tasks* provides a concrete expression of the collaborative nature of the relationship—both client and practitioner have tasks and are accountable to each other for carrying them out. When a case management team is used, all members, including service providers and peers, may take on tasks.

TERMINATION

The termination phase takes place in the last session or last two sessions. The client and practitioner review changes in target problems and the client's overall problem situation, identify successful problem-solving strategies, discuss ways of maintaining and generalizing client gains, and consider strategies for resolving remaining problems. In some cases, there may be need for further service. If the client requests further help and there is reason to suppose that additional progress can be made, extensions are normally made, usually for time-limited periods, to accomplish specific goals. The client's feelings about the loss of a relationship are dealt with, but these are less likely to occur in short-term than in long-term treatment (Fortune, 2002). The evidentiary base of work in the termination phase includes studies of client reactions to termination (Fortune, 1987; Fortune, Pearlingi, & Rochelle, 1992), of the role of treatment duration on outcome (Howard, Kopta, Krause, & Orlinsky, 1986), and of methods of promoting maintenance and generalization (Karoly & Steffen, 1980; Luiselli, 1998).

CASE ILLUSTRATION

Josie, age 12, was referred by her English teacher to an agency-based case management TC program serving a middle school. Josie was failing English and math and was frequently truant. Initial interviews with the child and her parents were held to explore the problem and develop a tentative service contract. The service typically consisted of meetings with a case management team and concurrent family sessions. The child and parents decided who was to be on the team. In Josie's case, the team was Josie, the social worker, Sarah (Josie's mother, a single parent), Josie's math teacher, and a peer who was not in difficulty in school. Josie and Sarah agreed to work on the problems of Josie's poor academic performance and attendance. In addition, another problem was identified: conflict between Josie and Sarah about Josie's friends (most of whom Sarah considered to be a bad influence).

The TC case management program was developed through a systematic program of studies that began with preliminary tests of the model and culminated in a randomized trial (Bailey-Dempsey & Reid, 1996). In that trial, families assigned to the case management program ($N = 33$) surpassed families assigned to a no treatment control ($N = 38$) and to an alternative monetary incentives condition ($N = 41$) (Reid & Bailey-Dempsey, 1995).

After preparatory interviews with the referring teacher and the math teacher selected for Josie's team, the initial case management team meeting was held. In conducting the session, the social worker used guidelines developed through a process study of case management meetings (Reid & Bailey-Dempsey, 1994). In this and subsequent (twice-monthly) meetings, the team worked together to understand the basis for Josie's problems and to develop possible solutions. Team members undertook tasks to implement the solutions. For example, because Josie had difficulty communicating with her English teacher, the math teacher on the team agreed to talk to the English teacher about a plan for Josie to make up work in that class. Josie and Sarah agreed to set up a structured homework program for both the English and math classes. The peer on the team (who lived close to Josie) agreed to the task of going to Josie's home in the morning and riding with her on the bus, as a way of helping her avoid the temptation to cut classes. Elements of the TPIS were used to help participants formulate and plan the tasks.

Between the case management meetings, the social worker met with Josie and Sarah. The structured homework task had gone well for a few days but broke down after Josie and Sarah began to quarrel over Josie's taking calls from friends and "spending her homework time gabbing." Such interruptions of Josie's homework were taken up as an obstacle to the task. After some discussion, Josie agreed to let her mother answer the phone during her homework period and advise callers that Josie would call them back. A task relating to the truancy problem (suggested by *The Task Planner* [Reid, 2000]) was developed and planned with Josie and her mother. Josie contracted with Sarah that she would miss no more than one class during the week. If Josie was able to do this, Sarah would allow her to choose the programs they would watch on TV during the weekend. Finally, the conflict concerning Josie's friends was worked on through in-session problem solving by Josie and Sarah. With the social worker's help, they worked out an agreement. Josie would stop seeing the individual that Sarah objected to the most, but in exchange Sarah would stop nagging Josie about her other friends and would allow her to invite them over. The agreement was used as a basis for tasks that they both carried out during the following week.

The practitioner worked with Josie and Sarah over a 14-week period (until the end of the school year). The final assessment of the three problems they had worked on was based on client self-report and school records and summarized on 10-point scales. Josie was able to raise her grades in math and English at least to a passing level, and her attendance improved moderately. The conflict between Josie and Sarah over Josie's friends had been largely resolved, and their relationship was on the whole better. Assessment of their overall situation revealed no new problems in other areas.

The case can be considered successful in that all three target problems showed improvement, accompanied by positive contextual change (e.g., the improved mother–daughter relationship). Findings from controlled studies can be used to help evaluate progress in such cases. Thus the limited improvement in grades and attendance becomes more significant, given evidence that untreated children at risk of failure are likely to show declines on such measures (Reid & Bailey-Dempsey, 1995).

REFERENCES

Artelt, T. A., & Thyer, B. A. (1998). Treating chronic grief. In B. A. Thyer & J. S. Wodarski (Eds.), *Handbook of empirical social work practice: Vol. 1* (pp. 341–356). New York: Wiley.

Bailey-Dempsey, C., & Reid, W. J. (1996). Intervention design and development: A case study. *Research on Social Work Practice, 6*(2), 208–228.

Benbenishty, R., & Ben-Zaken, A. (1988). Computer-aided process of monitoring task-centered family interventions. *Social Work Research and Abstracts, 24,* 7–9.

Bloom, B. L. (2002). Planned short-term psychotherapies. In C. R. Snyder & R. E. Ingram (Eds.), *Handbook of psychological change* (pp. 429–454). New York: Wiley.

Brehm, S., & Smith, T. (1986). Social psychological approaches to psychotherapy and behavior change. In S. L. Garfield & A. E. Bergin (Eds.), *Handbook of psychotherapy and behavior change* (pp. 69–116). New York: Wiley.

Dierking, B., Brown, M., & Fortune, A. E. (1980). Task-centered treatment in a residential facility for the elderly: A clinical trial. *Journal of Gerontological Social Work, 2,* 225–240.

Fellin, P., & Brown, K. S. (1989). Application of homelessness to teaching social work foundation content. *Journal of Teaching in Social Work, 3*(1), 17–33.

Fortune, A. E. (1987). Grief only? Client and social worker reactions to termination. *Clinical Social Work Journal, 15*(2), 159–171.

Fortune, A. E. (2002). Terminating with clients. In A. R. Roberts & G. J. Greene (Eds.), *Social workers' desk reference* (pp. 458–463) New York: Oxford University Press.

Fortune, A. E., Pearlingi, B., & Rochelle, C. (1992). Reactions to termination of individual treatment. *Social Work, 37*(2), 171–178.

Gambrill, E. (2000). Evidence-based practice: Implications for knowledge development and use in social work. In A. Rosen & E. Proctor (Eds.), *Developing* practice guidelines for social work intervention: Issues, methods, and research agenda. New York: Columbia University Press.

Gibbons, J., Butler, J., & Bow, I. (1979). Task-centered casework with marital problems. British Journal of Social Work, 8, 393–409.

Gibbs, L. E. (2003). Practice for the helping professions. Pacific Grove, CA: Brooks/ Cole.

Hogarty, G., Greenwald, D., Ulrich, R., Kornblith, S., DiBarry, A., Cooley, S., et al. (1997). Three-year trials of personal therapy among schizophrenic patients living with or independent of family. American Journal of Psychiatry, 154, 1514–1524.

Howard, K. I., Kopta, S. M., Krause, M. S., & Orlinsky, D. E. (1986). The dose-effect relationship in psychotherapy. American Psychologist 41, 159–164.

Ivanoff, A., & Riedel, M. (1995). Suicide. In R. Edwards et al. (Eds.), Encyclopedia of social work (19th ed., pp. 2358–2372). Washington, DC: NASW Press.

Karoly, P., & Steffen, J. J. (Eds.). (1980). Improving the long-term effects of psychotherapy: Models of durable outcome. New York: Gardner.

Kuehlwein, K. T. (1998). The cognitive therapy model. In R. Dorfman (Ed.), Paradigms of clinical social work: Vol. 2 (pp. 125–148). New York: Brunner/Mazel.

Luiselli, J. K. (1998). Maintenance of behavioral interventions. Mental Health Aspects of Developmental Disabilities, 1(3), 69–76.

Madden, L. L., Hicks-Coolick, A., & Kirk, A. B. (2002). An empowerment model for social welfare consumers. Lippincott's Case Management, 7, 129–136.

Miller, W. R., Andrews, N. R., Wilbourne, P., & Bennett, M. E. (1998). A wealth of alternatives. In W. R. Miller & N. Heather (Eds.), Treating addictive behaviors (pp. 203–216). New York: Plenum Press.

Naleppa, M. J., & Reid, W. J. (1998). Task-centered case management for the elderly: Developing a practice model. Research on Social Work Practice, 8, 63–85.

Naleppa, M., & Reid, W. J. (2003). Gerontological social work: A task-centered approach. New York: Columbia University Press.

Reid, W. J. (1975). A test of a task-centered approach. Social Work, 20, 3–9.

Reid, W. J. (1994). Field testing and data gathering on innovative practice interventions in early development. In J. Rothman & E. J. Thomas (Eds.), Intervention research (pp. 245–264). New York: Haworth.

Reid, W. J. (2000) The task planner. New York: Columbia University Press.

Reid, W. J., & Bailey-Dempsey, C. (1994). Content analysis in design and development. Research on Social Work Practice, 4, 101–114.

Reid, W. J., & Bailey-Dempsey, C. (1995). The effects of monetary incentives on school performance. Families in Society, 76, 331–340.

Reid, W. J., & Epstein, L. (Eds.). (1972). Task-centered casework. New York: Columbia University Press.

Reid, W. J., Epstein, L., Brown, L. B., Tolson, E. R., & Rooney, R. H. (1980). Task-centered school social work. Social Work in Education, 2, 7–24.

Reid, W. J., & Kenaley (2001). Task planners for TANF families. Prepared under contract for the Professional Development Program, University at Albany, State University of New York.

Reid, W. J., & Shyne, A. (1969). Brief and extended casework. New York: Columbia University Press.

Richey C. A., & Roffman, R. A. (1999). On the sidelines of guidelines: Further thoughts on the fit between clinical guidelines and social work practice. *Research on Social Work Practice, 9,* 311–321.

Robin, A. L., Bedway, M., & Gilroy, M. (1994). Problem-solving communication training. In C. W. LeCroy (Ed.), *Handbook of child and adolescent treatment manuals* (pp. 92–125). New York: Lexington Books.

Rooney, R. H. (1981). A task-centered reunification model for foster care. In A. N. Malluccio & P. A. Sinanoglu (Eds.), *The challenge of partnership: Working with parents of children in foster care* (pp. 101–116) New York: Child Welfare League of America.

Rooney, R. H. (1992). *Strategies for work with involuntary clients.* New York: Columbia University Press.

Rzepnicki, T. L. (1985). Task-centered intervention in foster care services: Working with families who have children in placement. In A. E. Fortune (Ed.), *Task-centered practice with families and groups* (pp. 172–184). New York: Springer.

Stern, S. B. (1999). Anger management in parent-adolescent conflict. *The American Journal of Family Therapy, 27,* 181–193.

Thyer, B. (2002). Principles of evidence-based practice and treatment development. In A. R. Roberts & G. J. Greene (Eds.), *Social workers' desk reference* (pp. 739–747). New York: Oxford University Press.

Tolson, E. R., Reid, W. J., & Garvin, C. D. (2003). *Generalist practice: A task-centered approach.* New York: Columbia University Press.

Weissman, A. (1977). In the steel industry. In W. J. Reid & L. Epstein (Eds.), *Task-centered practice* (pp. 235–241). New York: Columbia University Press.

16

Evidence-Based Practice and Manualized Treatment With Children

SCOTT K. OKAMOTO

CRAIG WINSTON LeCROY

In social work and allied disciplines, there has been a growing interest in identifying psychosocial treatments for children and adolescents that have demonstrated clinical efficacy and effectiveness. This chapter focuses on illustrating various treatments that have been shown through rigorous, controlled research to be efficacious for child and adolescent mental health problems. Additionally, this chapter focuses on recent literature that addresses the movement of these clinical research studies into the "real world," or what has been described as *transportability* (Schoenwald & Hoagwood, 2001), *diffusion of innovation* (Henggler & Lee, 2002), or *effectiveness* (APA Task Force on Psychological Intervention Guidelines, 1995). While there has been much progress in identifying "what works" with children and adolescents, the issue of implementing these studies into practice remains a challenge for the field of child and adolescent therapy.

HISTORY

Evidence-based treatments for children and adolescents began to garner attention in the mid to late 1990s. For example, during this time period, comprehensive reviews of effective school-based programs (Derzon, Wilson, & Cunningham, 1999) and violence prevention programs (Tolan & Guerra, 1994) were published in efforts to identify the best practices for children and adolescents. Concurrently,

204

organizations such as the Center for the Study and Prevention of Violence (CSPV, 2002) and the Center for Substance Abuse Prevention (CSAP, n.d.) began to examine the research literature to identify model programs for children and adolescents. One of the arguably most careful examinations of evidence-based practices, however, was conducted in 1995 by the Division 12 Task Force on Promotion and Dissemination of Psychological Procedures. Using the rubric of "empirically validated" treatments, this task force published a report that outlined (a) the minimum criteria for a psychosocial treatment to be considered "well established" or "probably efficacious" and (b) a comprehensive list of treatments (including child and adolescent treatments) that met their strict criteria within these categories. "Well-established" treatments are primarily manualized treatments that have been shown to be superior to a psychological placebo or to another treatment in at least two studies conducted by different investigative teams. "Probably efficacious" treatments are primarily those that have been shown to be more effective than a control group in at least two studies, but they do not necessarily have to be manualized or to have been evaluated by two different investigative teams (see Task Force on the Promotion and Dissemination of Psychological Procedures, 1995, for review). Since the publication of the 1995 report, several updates have been published (Chambless et al., 1996, 1998), and articles have identified and discussed specific programs that meet the task force's criteria for child and adolescent externalizing disorders, such as conduct problems (Brestan & Eyberg, 1998), and internalizing disorders, such as anxiety disorders (Ollendick & King, 1998) and depression (Kaslow & Thompson, 1998). Most recently, several books (e.g., Christophersen & Mortweet, 2001; Corcoran, in press; Rapee, Wignall, Hudson, & Schniering, 2001) and Web sites (e.g., Campbell Collaboration, 2002; Cochrane Library, 2002) have sought to direct practitioners in their use of empirically supported treatments.

EFFICACY

The focus of this section is on several clinical practices with children and adolescents that have met the strict criteria of Division 12 for "well-established" or "probably efficacious" treatments (Task Force, 1995). Several of these programs have been included in other published lists of model programs (e.g., Chorpita et al., 2002; CSAP, n.d.; CSPV, 2002). This section examines evidence-based practices for both internalizing disorders (e.g., anxiety disorders and depression) and externalizing disorders (e.g., conduct disorder, attention-deficit/hyperactivity disorder).

Internalizing Disorders

Anxiety

Evidence-based practices for the treatment of child and adolescent anxiety disorders (e.g., separation anxiety disorder, social phobias) include cognitive behavioral therapy and exposure therapy. For example, Barrett (1998) and Silverman et al. (1999) both compared cognitive behavioral therapy (CBT) conducted in a group format with accompanying parent training sessions against waitlist control groups. In both studies, significantly fewer youth in the therapy group than in the control group were diagnosed with an anxiety disorder at posttest and at 12-month follow-up. Silverman's treatment protocol is 12 sessions in which participants develop fear hierarchies and reward contingencies for achieving goals (sessions 2 and 3); conduct group in-session exposure, using the group to provide feedback, modeling, and reinforcement (sessions 4–11); and identify faulty cognitions (session 7). Parent–child contingency management and contracting are used in the early stages of treatment to facilitate the child's exposure to increasingly anxiety-provoking situations (Silverman & Kurtines, 1996; Silverman et al., 1999). The findings from these studies suggest that group CBT for anxiety disorders may be a cost-effective and time-efficient alternative to individual CBT for youth.

Depression

Evidence-based practices for the treatment of adolescent depression or dysthymia include cognitive behavioral or relationship enhancement approaches. Cognitive behavioral therapy for depression typically focuses on changing adolescents' pessimistic or negative thoughts, depressotypic beliefs and biases, and negative causal attributions (e.g., blaming oneself for failures but not taking credit for successes). Reinforcement schedules are used to eliminate behaviors that support these thoughts (Lewinsohn, Clarke, Rohde, Hops, & Seeley, 1996). The adolescent coping with depression (CWD-A) program is one example of an empirically supported treatment for depression (Chorpita et al., 2002). Components of this program incorporate social skills training, relaxation training, and cognitive therapy that focuses on identifying, challenging, and changing negative thoughts and irrational beliefs (Clarke, Lewinsohn, & Hops, 1990; Lewinsohn et al., 1996). Efficacy research on CWD-A indicates that it yields higher depression recovery rates and a greater reduction in self-reported depression than waitlist control groups (Clarke, Rohde, Lewinsohn, Hops, & Seeley, 1999; Lewinsohn, Clarke, Hops, & Andrews, 1990).

Relationship enhancement therapies, such as interpersonal psychotherapy (IPT-A; Mufson, Moreau, & Weissman, 1996; Mufson, Moreau, Weissman, & Kerman, 1993), emphasize the interpersonal nature of depression and actively attempt to change adolescents' communication, affect, and social skills. IPT-A incorporates three phases of treatment. In the initial phase, problem areas and depressive symptoms are addressed, and a treatment contract is developed. The middle phase of treatment focuses on effective strategies to attack the problem by using techniques such as role play to address issues related to communication, affect, and social skills. The termination phase of treatment focuses on establishing a sense of competence to deal with future problems (Mufson et al., 1996). Compared with a waitlist control group, one study found that youth who received IPT-A reported a significantly greater decrease in depressive symptoms and improvement in social functioning (Mufson, Weissman, Moreau, & Garfin-kel, 1999).

Externalizing Disorders

Conduct Problems

Evidence-based practices for conduct problems include behavioral parent training and multisystemic therapy. Behavioral parent training assumes that antisocial behavior is learned and sustained by positive and negative reinforcement, and it seeks to shift social contingencies such that children's prosocial behaviors receive positive parental reinforcement, while negative behaviors are consistently punished or ignored (Serketich & Dumas, 1996). Webster-Stratton's videotape-based parent training program is one example of behavioral parent training (Webster-Stratton & Hancock, 1998). Using videotaped vignettes of parents and children interacting in natural situations (e.g., during mealtime), group therapists discuss topics such as limit setting, using praise and incentives, and ignoring negative child behaviors. Videotaped scenes depict both negative and positive examples of parenting behaviors. One study of videotape-based parent training indicated that parents participating in the program reported significantly fewer oppositional or noncompliant behaviors and exhibited significantly fewer critical statements and more praise toward their children than a waitlist control group (Webster-Stratton, 1984).

Multisystemic therapy (MST) is an individualized family- and home-based treatment grounded in an ecosystemic framework (Henggler & Borduin, 1990; Henggler, Melton, & Smith, 1992). MST therapists implement a range of therapeutic interventions (e.g., structural family therapy, cognitive behavioral therapy) that reflect the treatment goals identified by the family. Its present-focused and action-oriented interventions target specific and well-defined problems (Henggler, Melton, Brondino, Scherer, & Hanley, 1997). Efficacy research on MST indicates that the program results in improved family functioning and significantly fewer arrests and self-reported offenses than alternative treatments (e.g., probation, individual therapy; Borduin et al., 1995; Henggler et al., 1992).

Attention-Deficit/Hyperactivity Disorder

Evidence-based practices for attention-deficit/hyperactivity disorder (ADHD) include behavior management and pharmacotherapy. Behavior management typically involves the use of positive reinforcement, where children and adolescents earn tokens or points for positive behaviors, and response cost, where negative behaviors cost tokens or points, in order to shape behavior (Pelham & Hoza, 1996). Behaviors that are commonly addressed for youth with ADHD include following rules, paying attention, and remaining on task. Pharmacotherapy involves the use of medications (e.g., methylphenidate) to control ADHD symptomatology.

An example of the combined use of behavior management and pharmacotherapy for ADHD is the summer treatment program (Carlson, Pelham, Milich, & Dixon, 1992; Pelham & Hoza, 1996; Pelham et al., 1993). The program is an intensive summer day treatment program for youth with ADHD that combines behavior management in the classroom (e.g., point system or token economy, time-out procedures), social skills training, daily report cards, and pharmacotherapy (Pelham & Hoza, 1996). Research on the separate and combined effects of behavior management and methylphenidate for youth in the program indicate that both treatments are more effective than no treatment (Carlson et al., 1992; Pelham et al., 1993). Further, one study found that the use of behavior management with lower doses of methylphenidate was as effective as the use of higher doses of methylphenidate alone (Carlson et al., 1992).

EFFECTIVENESS

Recently, critiques of the efficacy literature on evidence-based child and adolescent programs have focused on their effectiveness (i.e., clinical utility) as real-world practices. Much of this literature has focused on dissemination and implementation of these programs (Goldman et al., 2001; Schoenwald & Hoagwood, 2001), or what some have called "diffusion of innovation" (Henggler & Lee, 2002). Three factors described in the literature have been thought to influence the diffusion of evidence-based practices: (a) philosophical differences as to the importance of evidence-based practices versus effective "practice principles," (b) structural characteristics of the intervention, and (c) systemic or political issues.

Philosophical Differences

One of the issues impeding the dissemination and implementation of evidence-based practices relates to the therapeutic value of these practices compared with effective "practice principles." Rather than focusing solely on specialized protocols for specific disorders, advocates of this model suggest that it may be more important to examine the common factors that cut across these treatment protocols and contribute to their effectiveness. For example, Bickman (2002) and Drisko (2002) suggest that therapeutic alliance (i.e., agreement on clinical tasks and goals, an affective bond with the therapist) is a common factor that cuts across all therapeutic techniques for different child and adolescent disorders and has been shown to have a relationship to clinical outcomes. In fact, Drisko indicates that treatment protocol (e.g., CBT) accounts for only about 15% of the therapeutic outcome variance, while common factors, including therapeutic alliance and factors related to the characteristics of the agency and client, account for about 70% of the outcome variance. Clearly, conceptualization of evidence-based practice within this paradigm would influence the direction of clinical research and subsequent implementation in the field. As an example of research within this paradigm, Sapyta, Karver, and Bickman (2000) describe preliminary test development procedures on a therapeutic alliance measure focused on practitioners working with children, which would have relevance for measuring this construct in the practice setting. While research in the area of common factors is promising, Bickman notes that there has been very little research in this area, and therefore very little is known about its relationship to effective and efficacious practice.

Structural Characteristics

Henggler and Lee (2002) identify several characteristics of evidence-based practices that influence their probability for implementation into real-world settings. They suggest that evidence-based practices that have a perceived advantage over current practices, do not deviate far from current practices, are simple to administer, and can be implemented in stages have a higher probability for adoption. Others have suggested that the structural characteristics of evidence-based practices and their relative "fit" into the existing child and adolescent service system need much more research. In fact, well-conducted, randomized, controlled trials that are strong in internal validity are often weak in external validity. Often, serious questions emerge regarding the transportability of these studies into real-world settings. Bickman (2002) suggests that research should focus on the needs and perceptions of service providers and families in order to identify the feasibility of implementation of evidence-based practices. He suggests that there is a need to know which treatments are acceptable to clinicians, based on the ways in which they practice. Further, there is also a need to know how evidence-based practices vary according to within-subject characteristics, such as gender, ethnicity or culture, severity of disorder, and contextual factors. Thus far, research examining such differences has been minimal.

Further, evidence-based practices have been criticized for having limited applicability to youth with comorbid disorders (Bickman, 2002; Hawley & Weisz, 2002). While youth in the research samples used to establish evidence-based practices have been carefully screened for comorbid disorders, youth receiving services in the real world typically have more than one disorder. How does one implement these practices to meet the needs of the multiproblem youth who are seen in community-based agencies and institutions? Further, how do these practices hold up to other real-world practice constraints (e.g., managed care, lack of intense supervision to ensure treatment fidelity)? Clearly, much more research needs to be conducted to adapt the structural characteristics of these interventions to meet the complex needs of existing child and adolescent service systems.

Systemic and Political Issues

Henggler and Lee (2002) identify characteristics of the service system that influence the probability for the implementation and dissemination of evidence-based practices. They state that, while authoritarian decisions to adopt an evidence-based practice (e.g., directive from a CEO) result in the fastest implementation of the practice, collective decisions to adopt the practice are more likely to be sustained. Further, they suggest that the culture of an organization influences decisions to adopt evidence-based practices. These factors point to the importance of involving key stakeholders in the process of implementing evidence-based practices in order to ensure the success of the process. Further, these factors suggest that successful implementation of these practices may be a lengthy process, as it typically requires a shift in the organizational culture for the practices to be accepted. Perspectives of consumers, clinicians, and administrators will most likely influence this culture and its readiness to accept the interventions.

CONCLUSIONS

This chapter reviewed several evidence-based practices for internalizing and externalizing child and adolescent disorders and reviewed some of the issues related to dissemination and implementation of these interventions. While research has identified treatment techniques that have demonstrated clinical efficacy (e.g., CBT), there is still ambiguity as to how to best incorporate these techniques into the field. Recently, there have been documented efforts toward integrating evidence-based practices into the real world. Chorpita et al. (2002), for example, describe one state's efforts toward this goal by establishing the Empirical Basis to Services Task Force (EBS). EBS is a consortium of researchers from different disciplines (e.g., social work, psychiatry, psychology), clinicians in the field, and parents of youth receiving services, whose goal is to identify efficacious programs that have a high probability of utilization in the field. The next logical step might be for consortiums such as EBS to develop and evaluate programs for youth that have a focus on both efficacy and effectiveness. For now, however, more research is needed to examine aspects of the service system, perceptions of consumers and clinicians, and the unique clinical attributes related to diverse populations in order to successfully "fit" evidence-based practices into the field.

REFERENCES

APA Task Force on Psychological Intervention Guidelines. (1995). *Template for developing guidelines: Interventions for mental disorders and psychosocial aspects of physical disorders.* Washington, DC: American Psychological Association.
Barrett, P. M. (1998). Evaluation of cognitive-behavioral group treatments for childhood anxiety disorders. *Journal of Clinical Child Psychology, 27,* 459–468.
Bickman, L. (2002). The death of treatment as usual: An excellent first step on a long road. *Clinical Psychology, 9,* 195–199.
Borduin, C. M., Mann, B. J., Cone, L. T., Henggler, S. W., Fucci, B. R., Blaske, D. M., et al. (1995). Multisystemic treatment of serious juvenile offenders: Long-term prevention of criminality and violence. *Journal of Consulting and Clinical Psychology, 63,* 569–578.
Brestan, E. V., & Eyberg, S. M. (1998). Effective psychosocial treatments of conduct-

disordered children and adolescents: 29 years, 82 studies, and 5,272 kids. *Journal of Clinical Child Psychology, 27,* 180–189.

Campbell Collaboration. (2002). Retrieved November 16, 2002, from http:// campbellcollaboration.org

Carlson, C. L., Pelham, W. E., Milich, R., & Dixon, J. (1992). Single and combined effects of methylphenidate and behavior therapy on the classroom performance of children with attention-deficit hyperactivity disorder. *Journal of Abnormal Child Psychology, 20,* 213–232.

Center for Substance Abuse Prevention. (n.d.). Retrieved October 20, 2002, from http://www.samhsa.gov/centers/csap/csap.html

Center for the Study and Prevention of Violence. (2002). Retrieved October 20, 2002, from http://www.colorado.edu/cspv/

Chambless, D. L., Baker, M. J., Baucom, D. H., Beut-ler, L. E., Calhoun, D. S., Crits-Christoph, P., et al. (1998). Update on empirically validated therapies II. *The Clinical Psychologist, 51,* 3–16.

Chambless, D. L., Sanderson, W. C., Shoham, V., Johnson, S. B., Pope, K. S., Crits-Christoph, P., et al. (1996). An update on empirically validated therapies. *The Clinical Psychologist, 49,* 5–18.

Chorpita, B. F., Yim, L. M., Donkervoet, J. C., Arensdorf, A., Amundsen, M. J., McGee, C., et al. (2002). Toward large-scale implementation of empirically supported treatments for children: A review and observations by the Hawaii Empirical Basis to Services Task Force. *Clinical Psychology, 9,* 165–190

Christophersen, E. R., & Mortweet, S. L. (2001). *Treatments that work with children: Empirically supported strategies for managing childhood problems.* Washington, DC: American Psychological Association.

Clarke, G., Lewinsohn, P., & Hops, H. (1990). *Adolescent coping with depression.* Eugene, OR: Castalia.

Clarke, G. N., Rohde, P., Lewinsohn, P. M., Hops, H., & Seeley, J. R. (1999). Cognitive-behavioral treatment of adolescent depression: Efficacy of acute group treatment and booster sessions. *Journal of the American Academy of Child and Adolescent Psychiatry, 38,* 272–279.

Cochrane Library. (2002). Retrieved November 16, 2002, from http://www .cochrane.org

Corcoran, J. (in press). *Clinical applications of evidence-based family interventions.* New York: Oxford University Press.

Derzon, J. H., Wilson, S. J., & Cunningham, C. A. (1999). *The effectiveness of school-based interventions for preventing and reducing violence.* Nashville, TN: Vanderbilt Institute for Public Policy Studies, Center for Evaluation Research and Methodology.

Drisko, J. W. (2002, January). *Common factors in psychotherapy effectiveness: A neglected dimension in social work research.* Paper presented at the sixth annual conference of the Society for Social Work and Research, San Diego, CA.

Goldman, H. H., Ganju, V., Drake, R. E., Gorman, P., Hogan, M., Hyde, P. S., et al. (2001). Policy implications for implementing evidence-based practices. *Psychiatric Services, 52,* 1591–1597.

Hawley, K. M., & Weisz, J. R. (2002). Increasing the relevance of evidence-based treatment review to practitioners and consumers. *Clinical Psychology, 9,* 225–230.

Henggler, S. W., & Borduin, C. (1990). *Family therapy and beyond: A multisys-*

temic approach to treating behavior problems of children and adolescents. Pacific Grove, CA: Brooks/Cole.

Henggler, S. W., & Lee, T. (2002). What happens after the innovation is identified? *Clinical Psychology: Science and Practice, 9,* 191–194.

Henggler, S. W., Melton, G. B., Brondino, M. J., Scherer, D. G., & Hanley, J. H. (1997). Multisystemic therapy with violent and chronic juvenile offenders and their families: The role of treatment fidelity in successful dissemination. *Journal of Consulting and Clinical Psychology, 65,* 821–833.

Henggler, S. W., Melton, G. B., & Smith, L. A. (1992). Family preservation using multisystemic therapy: An effective alternative to incarcerating serious juvenile offenders. *Journal of Consulting and Clinical Psychology, 60,* 953–961.

Kaslow, N. J., & Thompson, M. P. (1998). Applying the criteria for empirically supported treatments to studies of psychosocial interventions for child and adolescent depression. *Journal of Clinical Child Psychology, 27,* 146–155.

Lewinsohn, P. M., Clarke, G. N., Hops, H., & Andrews, J. (1990). Cognitive-behavioral group treatment of depression in adolescents. *Behavior Therapy, 21,* 385–401.

Lewinsohn, P. M., Clarke, G. N., Rohde, P., Hops, H., & Seeley, J. R. (1996). A course in coping: A cognitive-behavioral approach to the treatment of adolescent depression. In E. D. Hibbs & P. S. Jensen (Eds.), *Psychosocial treatments for child and adolescent disorders* (pp. 109–135). Washington, DC: American Psychological Association.

Mufson, L., Moreau, D., & Weissman, M. M. (1996). Focus on relationships: Interpersonal psychotherapy for adolescent depression. In E. D. Hibbs & P. S. Jensen (Eds.), *Psychosocial treatments for child and adolescent disorders* (pp. 137–155). Washington, DC: American Psychological Association.

Mufson, L., Moreau, D., Weissman, M. M., & Kerman, G. (1993). *Interpersonal psychotherapy for depressed adolescents.* New York: Guilford.

Mufson, L., Weissman, M. M., Moreau, D., & Garfinkel, R. (1999). Efficacy of interpersonal psychotherapy for depressed adolescents. *Archives of General Psychiatry, 56,* 573–579.

Ollendick, T. H., & King, N. J. (1998). Empirically supported treatments for children with phobic and anxiety disorders: Current status. *Journal of Clinical Child Psychology, 27,* 156–167.

Pelham, W. E., Carlson, C., Sams, S. E., Vallano, G., Dixon, M. J., & Hoza, B. (1993). Separate and combined effects of methylphenidate and behavior modification on boys with attention deficit-hyperactivity disorder in the classroom. *Journal of Consulting and Clinical Psychology, 61,* 506–515.

Pelham, W. E., & Hoza, B. (1996). Intensive treatment: Summer treatment program for children with ADHD. In E. D. Hibbs & P. S. Jensen (Eds.), *Psychosocial treatments for child and adolescent disorders* (pp. 311–340). Washington, DC: American Psychological Association.

Rapee, R. M., Wignall, A., Hudson, J. L., & Schniering, C. A. (2001). *Treating anxious children and adolescents: An evidence-based approach.* New York: New Harbinger.

Sapyta, J. J., Karver, M. S., & Bickman, L. (2000). Therapeutic alliance: Significance in non-psychotherapy settings. In C. Liberton, C. Newman, K. Kutash, & R. Friedman (Eds.), *The 12th annual research conference proceedings, a system of care for children's mental health: Expanding the research base* (pp. 183–186). Tampa,

FL: University of South Florida, The Louis de la Parte Florida Mental Health Institute, Research and Training Center for Children's Mental Health.

Schoenwald, S. K., & Hoagwood, K. (2001). Effectiveness, transportability, and dissemination of interventions: What matters when? *Psychiatric Services, 52,* 1190–1197.

Serketich, W. J., & Dumas, J. E. (1996). The effectiveness of behavioral parent training to modify antisocial behavior in children: A meta-analysis. *Behavior Therapy, 27,* 171–186.

Silverman, W. K., & Kurtines, W. M. (1996). *Anxiety and phobic disorders: A pragmatic approach.* New York: Plenum.

Silverman, W. K., Kurtines, W. M., Ginsburg, G. S., Weems, C. F., Lumpkin, P. W., & Carmichael, D. H. (1999). Treating anxiety disorders in children with group cognitive-behavioral therapy: A randomized clinical trial. *Journal of Consulting and Clinical Psychology, 67,* 995–1003.

Task Force on the Promotion and Dissemination of Psychological Procedures. (1995). Training in and dissemination of empirically-validated psychosocial treatments: Report and recommendations. *The Clinical Psychologist, 48,* 3–23.

Tolan, P., & Guerra, N. (1994). *What works in reducing adolescent violence: An empirical review of the field.* Boulder, CO: University of Colorado, Institute for Behavioral Sciences.

Webster-Stratton, C. (1984). Randomized trial of two parent-training programs for families with conduct-disordered children. *Journal of Consulting and Clinical Psychology, 52,* 666–678.

Webster-Stratton, C., & Hancock, L. (1998). Training for parents of young children with conduct problems: Content, methods, and therapeutic processes. In J. M. Briesmeister & C. E. Schaefer (Eds.), *Handbook of parent training* (pp. 98–152). New York: Wiley.

17

Evidence-Based Treatment for Traumatized and Abused Children

CARLTON E. MUNSON

The basic premise of this chapter is that intervention with traumatized children must have a developmental focus, using a scientific perspective that relies on evidence that is grounded in a therapeutic relationship. There have been few efforts to link the concepts of a developmental perspective, evidence, and the science of relationship in work with traumatized children. The research literature regarding child trauma is generally not presented or described in a way that is usable for the average practitioner. This chapter provides information that can assist in specifying and measuring relationship in ways that have not been systematically applied in the past and explains uses of evidence in work with traumatized children. This chapter uses a practical but comprehensive approach to child trauma treatment that can be easily understood and applied by practitioners.

Even though awareness of childhood trauma in its modern form has been described since the late 1800s, the treatment of childhood trauma is not well validated, empirically derived, or clearly codified (Kazdin, 1998). There is no generally accepted definition of childhood trauma that can be applied to clinical situations. The American Psychiatric Association's *DSM-IV-TR* (American Psychiatric Association, 2000a) contains a general and nonspecific definition of trauma within the diagnostic criteria for posttraumatic stress disorder that is generally applied to children, but it is not sensitive to the effects of trauma on the developmental process. In order to use an evidence-based approach to child trauma practice, the intervention must be derived from a clear definition of the phenomenon that is to be treated. For this chapter, a child-focused definition of trauma is used. Reactions to traumatic events can be variable, and the criteria for deciding whether a child has met the threshold of being traumatized are based on the following definition: Child trauma can result from any event or series of events that overwhelms, overstimulates, or creates subtle or extreme fear in a child that causes temporary or permanent interruption of normal developmental processes or tasks that occur with or without physical or psychological symptoms and behavioral change (Munson, 2001). Child intervention that focuses exclusively on trauma events or reactions to trauma is limited because the treatment must address the developmental issues (Amster, 1999; Law, 2000) and the caregiver role (see, for example, Carr, 2000; Denton, Walsh, & Daniel, 2002; Reddy & Pfeiffer, 1997; Ryburn, 1999). From an evidence perspective, the effect of trauma can be established by direct measures of traumatic reactions and by developmental measures that identify levels of functioning before and after trauma.

THE SCIENTIFIC METHOD

Collins (1994) has provided a succinct definition of the *scientific method* that is an effective guide for evidence-based child trauma practice:

> Science means knowledge about the objective world that is true because that is the way things are, not just because we have imagined it. (p. 3)
> The key to the scientific method is to compare, to look for the conditions under which something happens by contrasting them with the conditions under which it does not happen. The scientific method is the search for a set of mutually consistent causal generalizations that are based on the systematic comparison of conditions associated with a varying range of outcomes. (p. 183)

Evidence is the product of science. Evidence is "something that tends to prove" and provide "grounds for belief" (McKechnie, 1983, p. 633). Evidence can be produced in nonscientific ways. For example, in the law there are specific rules for producing evidence, but these rules do not necessarily result in the evidence being true or reliable. When evidence is produced from standard scientific procedures that strive for objectivity, reliability, and validity, evidence is more acceptable and closer to reality. There is a growing trend of merging conceptions of evidence collected through scientific methods and clinical practice activity and outcomes (Monette, Sullivan, & DeJong, 2002).

RELATIONSHIP AND THE LIMITS OF EVIDENCE

Evidence to inform intervention cannot be the exclusive focus of treatment (Benbenishty, Segev, Surkis, & Elias, 2002; Shaw, 2003). The practitioner's relationship with and advocacy for the child client is a critical aspect of effective and accurate assessment and positive outcome of intervention (Proctor, 2002; Sheldon, 2001; Soldz & McCullough, 2000; Webb, 2001, 2002). In this chapter, *clinical professional relationship* is defined as a dynamic collaborative process of interaction between a clinician and a client based on openness and honesty, which is designed to explore, assess, and promote change through recognized theoretical orientations and generally accepted practical interventions derived from scientific research.

Historically, studies have shown that relationship is the key to intervention outcome (Shirk & Russell, 1996), and assessment skills have been added because they are inherently essential to successful intervention. At the same time, relationship cannot be the only measure of outcome. Clinical anecdotal case reports that cannot be replicated and have no generalizability (Wicks-Nelson & Israel, 2002) can hamper effective therapy outcomes if applied by others (for example, see Spiegelman, 2002). Relationship has been described as dealing with the "nonspecifics" of intervention that are difficult to observe, describe, and teach (Kamphaus & Frick, 2001). Research methodology is increasingly being applied to the concept of therapeutic relationship, and the research has quantified relationship-based concepts such as personal attributes, in-session activities, technical activity, alliance activities, instillation of confidence and trust, positive connectedness, therapist training, consistency, nonverbal gestures, verbal expressions, empathy, congruence, positive regard, understanding, and outcome. For a review of the empirical referent studies for these relationship concepts, see Ackerman and Hilsenroth (2003). These relationship indicators can be applied to a number of roles common to child trauma work, such as networker, broker, support provider, educator, clinician, mediator, expert witness, and advocate (Anderson, Weston, Doueck, & Krause, 2002). Through using empirical referents and role concepts, relationship concepts can be transferred from the research world to the practice arena through a practical process of systematically and scientifically assessing skills grounded in an evidence orientation that includes:

- Identifying and reviewing practitioner natural interpersonal relationship skills
- Assessing educationally acquired professional relationship skills
- Surveying for inherent lack of professional relationship skills
- Providing learning that promotes development of relationship skills when they are deficient
- Documenting strategies that connect specific intervention techniques, relationship skills, and evidence-based outcomes
- Identifying intervention strategies that promote fostering trust between client and practitioner

The assessment of relationship skills should be continuously monitored through evaluation of three critical intervention requirements essential to fostering ongoing positive, effective relationship and evidence-focused intervention. To be successful, the practitioner must demonstrate capabilities in each of these areas:

- Articulated, compassionate, and nonjudgmental attitude that is operationalized and communicated to the child and caregivers
- Acquired skill at doing evidence-based objective assessment (nonsuggestive information gathering) and subjective scientific intervention (techniques that suggest, recommend, and motivate the child and caregivers to change or achieve mastery)
- Keen ability to accurately interpret the behavior and communication of the child, caregivers, and self (countertransference) through use of evidence

These intervention requirements set the stage for change. Relationship itself does not produce change, and evidence does not produce change. The use of relationship and evidence through interaction with the child and caregivers produces change, and scientific methods are used to measure the quality of the change (outcomes).

ETHICS, RELATIONSHIP, AND EVIDENCE

Practice based on evidence-related tasks and outcomes has ethical implications. There must be a rational connection between relationship and evidence use in child treatment. The vast expansion of child trauma research and child development research requires evidence-based interventions (Jellinek, 1999). To ignore empirical evidence can be harmful to clients. At the same time, concern must be shown for how practitioners conduct tasks and how outcomes are achieved. There must be monitoring for the subtle belief that only evidence-based tasks or outcomes have value. In child therapy, ethics are central to the process, because children lack the capacity or facility to confront unwanted interventions. Children have expectations of how one should behave toward the other, regardless of expected outcomes, but do not always have the ability to express their desires in power-based relationships such as treatment. The lack of expressive capacity in children that can result from traumatic experience is a strong argument for evidence-based interventions because evidence can aid in avoiding misinterpretation of children's intentions. At the same time, lost expressive capacity in a child requires scientifically derived relationship skills in the practitioner, who must patiently provide direct and indirect forms of alternative expression.

Professional ethics mandates evidence-based, relationship-focused intervention that should be monitored. The increased emphasis on techniques and tasks requires supervisors to monitor the use of techniques to ensure that (a) techniques used are related to problem assessment and resolution, (b) the practitioner is thoroughly trained in the techniques that are being applied, and (c) the techniques are generally accepted and appropriate. Techniques that have not been subjected to empirical analysis or are not subject to regular and consistent monitoring should not be used under current child intervention practice standards. For example, statements made by children during symbolic play should not be interpreted by a therapist without corroboration through independent evidence. Nondirective child therapy and symbolic play used in child abuse cases can lead to expressions of fantasy that are often misinterpreted (Dickinson & McCabe, 1991; Guerney, 1983; Reif & Stollak, 1972), especially in the case of very young children (Hewitt, 1999). In child trauma intervention, clinical symbolic or anecdotal information should not be interpreted without supportive evidentiary information.

INTERVENTION GUIDELINES

Collins's (1994) description of the scientific method reflects the activities and analysis that promote applying the scientific model to practice activity. Therapy has not traditionally been a scientific endeavor, but increasingly interaction and content are focused on promoting the scientific method in the practice situation. General intervention guidelines for promoting evidence-based relationship-focused practice are as follows.

- An intervention can be identified by the practitioner and can be understood by the client.
- An established connection between the intervention and the problem can be articulated by the practitioner (in some cases the child can also make the connection based on developmental level).
- The practitioner and client can implement the intervention with reasonable effort.
- The client has an identifiable reason/motivation to comply with the intervention.
- Along with the proposed intervention an alternate intervention can be identified by the practitioner.
- Possible outcomes (intended and unintended, positive and negative) of intervention can be identified in advance of applying the intervention.
- The intervention can be observed and measured. (Munson, 2003, p. 5)

All the principles do not have to be met in every situation, but the higher the number met, the more likely it is that the intervention will be successful. Applying these simple guidelines clinically can be much more effective than citing a series of research studies regarding the outcome of competing theoretical orientations that can be confusing to the average practitioner.

TYPES OF EVIDENCE

In the scientific method, there are four research goals: description, prediction, explanation, and evaluation (Monette et al., 2002). These four goals also apply directly to the evidence-based clinical situation, and intervention can be conceptualized in this framework. *Description* applies to the database information gathered during the assessment phase that precedes treatment. Historically, it was held that treatment begins at the moment of first contact with the client and that problems and solutions are inseparable (Selekman, 1997). In the actual process of assessment, diagnosis, and treatment, there is a merging and interaction of these functions. The increased emphasis on evidence-based practice has produced the standard that treatment does not deliberately begin until a thorough assessment has been completed, and treatment is connected to and derived from diagnostic and assessment data with respect to exploring the connection between each of these functions (Blythe & Reithoffer, 2000; Jongsma & Peterson, 2000). This does not mean that treatment impact does not occur at the initial contact, but a logical, scientific approach to intervention consists of *conscious* acts that occur after the situation is understood and assessed, based on known events, symptoms, behaviors, and risk factors.

The extensive literature regarding children who have had trauma experience (see, for example, Wolchik & Sandler, 1997) necessitates that clinicians be familiar with and utilize risk factors in assessment and treatment protocols. The concepts of risk factors and protective factors (Rutter, 1987,1998; Vance, Bowen, Fernandez, & Thompson, 2002) are established in child trauma and relate to the second scientific concept of *prediction*. In evidence-based child treatment, there are two forms of prediction. Type 1 prediction is associated with risk factors and protective factors related to the child that occur outside the intervention process and can be compared with scientific literature to establish future risk of symptoms or behavioral outcomes for a specific child (Milner, Murphy, Valle, & Tolliver, 1998). Risk factors serve as guides for the clinician to target areas for immediate intervention and other areas with a prevention focus (Sox, 1993). Type 2 prediction occurs within the treatment and relates to the prediction of the expected outcome of a specific intervention or an intervention strategy. For example, research has shown that Type 1 prediction is associated with early- or late-onset conduct disorder. Family dysfunction, family size, and severe aggression are more prevalent in the early-onset conduct disorder subtype. Type 2 prediction is associated with the fact that research has shown a more positive treatment outcome for the late-onset conduct disorder subtype when problem-solving skills training, parental management training, and multisystemic therapy are used (Kazdin, 1998). Other general examples of Type 1 prediction are low family income, parental chronic mental illness, parental availability, parental criminality, and poor parental supervision. Other examples of Type 2 prediction are that use of anatomically correct dolls in a sex abuse treatment protocol can have interpretive value when based on existing research (Ceci & Bruck, 1995). There is research evidence that child trauma treatment takes approximately 16 to 20 sessions to produce symptom resolution (Finkelhor & Berliner, 1995) and that the use of cognitive behavioral approaches are more effective in reducing symptoms of trauma (Cohen & Mannarino, 1998). Listings of risk factors and theoretical orientation outcomes are not alone sufficient for evidence use. The relevance of theoretical orientations and a set of risk factors and their interactions must be considered in the context of the individual case (Kazdin, 1998).

The concept of *explanation* is related to the interpretations of the child's situation, symptoms, or behavior. Explanation is different from prediction in that predictions can be made without an explanation (Monette et al., 2002). Explanations should be based on empirical support. For example, in a case where a child has symptoms of posttraumatic stress disorder (PTSD) but does not meet the *DSM-IV-TR* criteria, the therapist should make reference to the literature showing that only a small portion (approximately 13%) of children who experience trauma meet PTSD criteria (Merry & Andrews, 1994; Scheeringa, Pebbles, Cook, & Zeanah, 2001; Scheeringa & Zeanah, 2001; Scheeringa, Zeanah, Drell, & Larrieu, 1995; Scheeringa, Zeanah, Myers, & Putnam, 2003; Stoppelbein & Greening, 2000). Lack of understanding of the role of evidence in disorders like PTSD can result in failure to differentially diagnose other debilitating disorders, such as major depression (Weissman, 2001). Diagnostic and treatment explanations that cannot be derived from or supported by empirical literature or standardized measures (Cohen & Mannarino, 2002) should be based on hypothesis testing. This occurs most often in child abuse investigations. Hypothesis testing is applied to the speculative information of the situation to confirm or refute the speculation.

Hypothesis testing has evolved as a standard methodology in child sex abuse allegations (Bowlby, 1988; Ceci & Bruck, 1994, 1995; Faller, 2002; Jones, 1997; Nurcombe & Partlett, 1994). Hypothesis testing has become more essential in child trauma practice since the incidence of abuse allegations has increased in the last three decades (Hobbs, Hanks, & Wynne, 1999), especially in intrafamily sex abuse. The increase of divorce and the decline of adultery as a basis for obtaining a divorce have been paralleled by increasing use of abuse allegations as grounds for divorce (Ehrenberg & Elterman, 1995; Eminson & Postlethwaite, 2000).

Hypothesis testing is used to rule out other plausible explanations once a child has made a disclosure of abuse or in the absence of a disclosure (Ceci & Bruck, 1995; Faller, 1999; House, 2002; Lamb & Johnson, 2002; Ney, 1995; Pezdek, 1994). Faller (2002) states, "The evaluator begins the assessment process with a series of competing hypotheses. . . . The process of decision-making is best described as a process of ruling out hypotheses. The goal is to arrive at one or more most likely explanations for the concerns about abuse" (p. 15). This process is the clinical equivalent of Collins's (1994) scientific principle of establishing when an event has or has not occurred. Ceci and Bruck (1995), in their detailed analysis of the literature on suggestion of abuse, view hypothesis testing as essential to accurately assess abuse allegations, and hypothesis-related questions used in establishing the credibility of abuse allegations have been identified (Adams, 2000).

The concept of *evaluation* applies to the measurement of the outcomes of the interventions (see, for example, Cohen & Mannarino, 1997, 1998). Evaluation occurs when the intervention is being contemplated, as well as postintervention. Evaluation can relate to a single technique, a single session, or a course of therapy. A model for technique intervention guidelines was described in the previous section titled "Intervention Guidelines."

SOURCES OF EVIDENCE

The sources of evidence are observed evidence, reported evidence, and research evidence. *Observed evidence* is most important during the assessment phase and includes nonintrusive informal observations to evaluate children while engaged in routine interactions, as well as formal assessment through the use of standardized instruments (Horton & Bowman, 2002; Ohan, Myers, & Collett, 2002). Observations should be compared with reported evidence. *Reported evidence* is provided by caregivers or other collateral sources, such as teachers, social service workers, or probation officers (Apel, 2001; Lynagh, Perkins, & Schofield, 2002). For example, corroborative evidence can be in the form of structured clinical interviews, standardized scales or checklists (Schaefer, Gitlin, & Sandgrund, 1991) completed by a teacher, or a nonnormed or normed checklist completed by a foster parent. Reported evidence should be compared with observed evidence. *Research evidence* is data that can be used to assess the child in comparison to scientifically accepted research reports. Included in this type of evidence are practice parameters and research reviews, such as those published by the American Academy of Child and Adolescent Psychiatry that are summary guidelines for understanding and treating various disorders or conditions (Dunne, 1997). For example, 46 review articles and 70 parameters papers have been published. Some of these have direct relevance to child trauma, such as items for child sexual abuse (Bernet, 1997; Shaw, 1999), posttraumatic stress disorder (Cohen, 1998; Pfefferbaum, 1997), oppositional defiant disorder and conduct disorder (Burke, Loeber, & Birmaher, 2002; Loeber, Burke, Lahey, Winters, & Zera, 2000), childhood depression (Boris & Brent, 1998), and language disorders (Beitchman, 1998).

Over the past five decades, there have been various efforts from an organizational and administrative perspective to develop forms of evidence-based outcomes (Manela & Moxley, 2002). These efforts have been variously called management by objectives, program planning and budgeting systems, agency accountability systems, integrated client information systems (Dobmeyer, Woodward, & Olson, 2002), and managed care (Alperin & Phillips, 1997; Austad, 1996; Stout, 2001). The tendency to equate clinical evidence-based intervention with these administrative methods has resulted in confusion about the basis of clinical evidence-based practice. The question is whether clinical evidence-based practice is an individual or organizational endeavor. The answer is that it is both (Hernandez & Hodges, 2001), but there must be a clear distinction about the individual and organizational components of evidence-based practice. Organizational guidelines for evidence-based practice are formalized, structured, procedural guidelines such as practice protocols, whereas individual clinical practice aids are compilations of information to inform clinical decision making, including practice guidelines, standards of practice, and standards of care. Concepts like best practices tend to merge individual and organizational orientations. These models are not necessarily based on evidence but are more effective and useful when grounded in evidence. These models are convenient vehicles for organizing and presenting evidence for use in clinical practice.

FORMATS FOR ORGANIZING EVIDENCE

Evidence-based measures should be applied within the context of a practice protocol. The earliest efforts to devise practice protocols for children were Gardner's (1992, 1995, 2002) in the 1980s regarding sex abuse investigations. A practice protocol is a set of standard procedural guidelines that are applied to all cases in a given area of practice (Munson, 2003). In the current environment of individual and agency accountability for all aspects of practice activity, professionals are being called upon to use standardized protocols to justify interventions (Munson, 2002). Accrediting organizations, private payers, and courts are requiring practice protocols for specific areas of practice. Each practice setting should have intervention practice protocols established by supervisors, practitioners, and agency administrators.

Practice protocols are different from practice guidelines (also referred to as *practice parameters* and *best practices*), standards of care, and standards of practice. These terms are often confused and used interchangeably in ways that can be confusing and inappropriate. Practice guidelines are a set of client care strategies and methods to aid practitioners in making clinical decisions (for more details about and examples of practice guidelines, see American Psychiatric Association, 2000b). Standards of care are precise performance expectations for the level and type of intervention that are provided to a specific child population (for example, sexually abused children) or a specific condition (for example, an anxiety disorder). Standards of care are used to manage risk for the client and liability for the practitioner (Bongar, Berman, et al., 1998). Standards of care are usually based on available clinical data and are subject to change as research and knowledge advance (American Psychiatric Association, 2000a). Standards of care are measured as the degree of care a reasonable professional should use in the same or similar circumstances, and deviations from a standard of care are usually considered negligence or gross negligence (Bongar, Maris, Berman, & Litman, 1998). Child trauma intervention based on this standard has lagged behind other practice areas, but a consensus is gradually emerging. Standards of practice are general guidelines set by professional organizations to guide practitioners in day-to-day professional activities in relation to clients. The current standards of practice use the principle of "professional expectations," which judge professional actions on the basis of the question, "Did the act of a given professional, in a given situation, conform to expectations of practice as defined by the general consensus of professionals working in that area of practice in the same locale?" This principle is also used by courts in deciding professional liability (Flach, 1998; Nurcombe & Partlett, 1994).

The concept of best practices is increasingly being used to assure others that agencies are of high quality and worthy of being considered on the forefront of practice knowledge. What constitutes best practice in organizations is not clear. Currently there are no standards for determining best practices, and they can be based on research evidence, expert testimonials, lobbying, marketing, or other efforts to promote their acceptance (Manela & Moxley, 2002). There is no standard format for establishing and describing best practices. Before the concept of best practices can be considered evidence-based, there must be clarification of the criteria and procedures for determining what constitutes a best practice in clinical settings.

EVIDENCE LIMITATIONS

The use of evidence-based practice is limited by the lack of widely accepted criteria for assessing the reliability and validity of research studies (Salzer, 1996) and the lack of standardized measures for observed and reported evidence use. No organized systems of meta-analysis of outcome research exist (Chang, Sanacora, & Sanchez, 1996). There are no methodologies in place to reconcile conflicting research findings focused on the same problem (see Bolen, 2000; Buttell & Pike, 2002). For example, two widely cited studies found significant differences in the amount of psychotherapy needed to produce effective outcomes for children with psychiatric illness (Petti, 2000). Evidence use is limited by the variation in availability of evidence. In some areas such as conduct disorder, there is limited evidence available (Kazdin, 1998), while there is an array of measures in other areas such as sexual abuse and childhood depression.

After 15 years of delivery systems basing outcomes on managed care cost criteria, professions are faced with how to orient practitioners to pursuing outcomes based on science (Coble, 2002; Jellinek, 1999; Showalter, 1995). For evidence-based practice to become the basis for child trauma intervention, there must be a more concerted effort to teach this approach in graduate training programs (Hodes, 1998), and there must be better systems for making research findings and standardized measures readily available and accessible to practitioners (Card, 2001; Kronenberger & Meyer, 2001; Randall, Cowley, & Tomlinson, 2000). Developing effective standardized intervention protocols is dependent on the dissemination of research findings. Technology has assisted somewhat in the dissemination of knowledge, but many practitioners do not have access to the evidence-based material described in this chapter that promotes empirically grounded child trauma intervention. The increase in research and knowledge about child trauma has led to some codification of evidence, but much more work needs to be done to ensure effective practice based on good evidence (Weber & Sergeant, 2003).

CONCLUSION

The main view of this paper is that evidence-based practice must be balanced with a relationship model. Practice cannot be grounded only in evidence, just as it cannot be formulated solely on relationship. Evidence-based practice is more than compiling supportive research evidence, more than setting up research centers (Iwaniec & McCrystal, 1999), and more than cataloging outcomes. Evidence-based tasks without relationship-based structure in child intervention can lead to outcome errors. For evidence-based practice to be successful, there cannot be an approach of imposing the evidence on the child, but useful evidence can be applied and generated through a facilitated and collaborative relationship with the child. In 1934, Vygotsky (1986) observed that child psychology was a method of exploring human consciousness rather than elementary behavioral acts. We now know that intervention includes both, and only when evidence and relationship are used in combination is effective, scientifically informed practice achieved.

REFERENCES

Ackerman, S. J., & Hilsenroth, M. J. (2003). A review of therapist characteristics and techniques positively impacting the therapeutic alliance. *Clinical Psychology Review, 23,* 1–33.

Adams, J. A. (2000). How do I evaluate suspected sexual abuse in the adolescent female? In H. Dubowitz & D. DePanfilis (Eds.), *Handbook for child protection practice* (p. 206). Thousand Oaks, CA: Sage.

Alperin, R. M., & Phillips, D. G. (1997). *The impact of managed care on the practice of psychotherapy: Innovation, implementation, and controversy.* New York: Brunner/Mazel.

American Psychiatric Association. (2000a). *Diagnostic and statistical manual of mental disorders* (4th ed., text revision). Washington, DC: Author.

American Psychiatric Association. (2000b). *Practice guidelines for the treatment of psychiatric disorders: Compendium 2000.* Washington, DC: Author.

Amster, B. J. (1999). Speech and language development of young children in the child welfare system. In J. A. Silver, B. J. Amster, & T. Haecher (Eds.), *Young children and foster care* (pp. 117–157). Baltimore: Brookes.

Anderson, L. E., Weston, E. A., Doueck, H. J., & Krause, D. J. (2002). The child-centered social worker and the sexually abused child: Pathway to healing. *Social Work, 47* (4), 368–378.

Apel, K. (2001). Developing evidence-based practices and research collaborations in school settings. *Language, Speech, and Hearing Services in Schools, 32,* 196–198.

Austad, C. S. (1996). *Is long-term psychotherapy unethical? Toward a social ethic in an era of managed care.* San Francisco: Jossey-Bass.

Beitchman, J. H. (1998). Summary of the practice parameters for the assessment and treatment of children and adolescents with language and learning disorders. *Journal of the American Academy of Child and Adolescent Psychiatry, 37,* 1117–1119.

Benbenishty, R., Segev, D., Surkis, T., & Elias, T. (2002). Information-search and decision-making by professionals and nonprofessionals in cases of alleged child-abuse and maltreatment. *Journal of Social Service Research, 28,* 1–18.

Bernet, W. (1997). Practice parameters for the evaluation of children and adolescents who may have been physically or sexually abused. *Journal of the American Academy of Child and Adolescent Psychiatry, 36*, 37s–56s.

Blythe, B., & Reithoffer, A. (2000). Assessment and measurement issues in direct practice in social work. In P. Allen-Meares, & C. Garvin (Eds.). *The handbook of direct social work practice* (pp. 551–564). Thousand Oaks, CA: Sage.

Bolen, R. M. (2000). Validity of attachment theory. *Trauma, Violence and Abuse, 1*, 128–153.

Bongar, B., Berman, A. L., Maris, R. W., Silverman, M. M., Harris, E. A., & Packman, W. L. (Eds.). (1998). *Risk management with suicidal patients.* New York: Guilford.

Bongar, B., Maris, R. W., Berman, A. L., & Litman, R. E. (1998). Outpatient standards of care and the suicidal patient. In B. Bongar, A. L. Berman, R. W. Maris, M. M. Silverman, E. A. Harris, & W. L. Packman (Eds.), *Risk management with suicidal patients* (pp. 4–33). New York: Guilford.

Boris, M. D., & Brent, D. (1998). Practice parameters for assessment and treatment of children and adolescents with depressive disorders. *Journal of the American Academy of Child and Adolescent Psychiatry, 37*, 46s–62s.

Bowlby, J. (1988). *A secure base: Parent–child attachment and healthy human development.* New York: Basic Books.

Burke, J. D., Loeber, R., & Birmaher, B. (2002). Oppositional defiant disorder and conduct disorder: A review of the past 10 years, part II. *Journal of the American Academy of Child and Adolescent Psychiatry, 41* (11), 1275–1293.

Buttell, F. P., & Pike, C. K. (2002). Investigating predictors of treatment attribution among court-ordered batterers. *Journal of Social Service Research, 28*, 53–68.

Card, J. J. (2001). The sociometrics program archives: Promoting the dissemination of evidence-based practices through replication kits. *Research on Social Work Practice, 11*, 521–527.

Carr, A. (2000). Evidence-based practice in family therapy and systemic consultation in child focused problems. *Journal of Family Therapy, 22*, 29–61.

Ceci, S. J., & Bruck, M. (1994). How reliable are children's statements? . . . it depends. *Family Relations, 43*, 255–257.

Ceci, S. J., & Bruck, M. (1995). *Jeopardy in the courtroom: A scientific analysis of children's testimony.* Washington, DC: American Psychological Association.

Chang, R., Sanacora, G., & Sanchez, R. (1996). The need for outcome studies. *Journal of the American Academy of Child and Adolescent Psychiatry, 35*, 557.

Coble, Y. (2002, December 27). Medicine is more than science. *USA Today,* p. A11.

Cohen, J. A. (1998). Summary of the practice parameters for the assessment and treatment of children and adolescents with posttraumatic stress disorder. *Journal of the American Academy Child and Adolescent Psychiatry, 37*, 997–1001.

Cohen, J. A., & Mannarino, A. P. (1997). A treatment study for sexually abused preschool children: Outcome during a one-year follow-up. *Journal of the American Academy of Child and Adolescent Psychiatry, 36*, 1228–1235.

Cohen, J. A., & Mannarino, A. P. (1998). Factors that mediate treatment outcome of sexually abused preschool children: Six- and 12-month follow-up. *Journal of the American Academy of Child and Adolescent Psychiatry, 37*, 44–51.

Cohen, J. A., & Mannarino, A. P. (2002). Addressing attributions in treating abused children. *Child Maltreatment, 7*, 82–86.

Collins, R. (1994). *Four sociological traditions*. New York: Oxford University Press.

Denton, W. H., Walsh, S. R., & Daniel, S. S. (2002). Evidence-based practice in family therapy: Adolescent depression as an example. *Journal of Marital and Family Therapy, 28*, 39–46.

Dickinson, D., & McCabe, A. (1991). The acquisition and development of language: A social interactionist account of language and literacy development. In J. F. Kavanagh (Ed.), *The language continuum: From infancy to literacy* (pp. 1–40). Parkton, MD: York Press.

Dobmeyer, T. W., Woodward, B., & Olson, L. (2002). Factors supporting the development and utilization of an outcome-based performance measurement system in a chemical health case management program. *Administration in Social Work, 26*(4), 25–44.

Dunne, J. E. (1997). History and development of the practice parameters. *Journal of the American Academy of Child and Adolescent Psychiatry, 36*, 1s–3s.

Ehrenberg, M. F., & Elterman, M. F. (1995). Evaluating allegations of sexual abuse in the context of divorce, child custody, and access disputes. In T. Ney (Ed.), *True and false allegations of child sexual abuse: Assessment and case management* (pp. 209–230). New York: Brunner/Mazel.

Eminson, M., & Postlethwaite, R. J. (Eds.). (2000). *Munchausen syndrome by proxy abuse: A practical approach*. Oxford: Butterworth Heinemann.

Faller, K. C. (1999). Questioning children who may have been sexually abused: An integration of research into practice. In K. C. Faller (Ed.), *Maltreatment in early childhood: Tools for research-based intervention* (pp. 37–58). New York: Haworth.

Faller, K. C. (2002, April). *Update on allegations of sexual abuse in divorce*. Paper presented at National Child Advocacy Center conference, Huntsville, AL.

Finkelhor, D., & Berliner, L. (1995). Research on treatment of sexually abused children. *Journal of the American Academy of Child and Adolescent Psychiatry, 34*, 1408–1423.

Flach, F. (Ed.). (1998). *A comprehensive guide to malpractice risk management in psychiatry*. New York: Hatherleigh.

Gardner, R. A. (1992). *The psychotherapeutic techniques of Richard A. Gardner*. Cresskill, NJ: Creative Therapeutics.

Gardner, R. A. (1995). *Protocols for the sex-abuse evaluation*. Cresskill, NJ: Creative Therapeutics.

Gardner, R. A. (2002). *Sex-abuse trauma? Or trauma from other sources*. Cresskill, NJ: Creative Therapeutics.

Guerney, L. F. (1983). Client-centered (nondirective) play therapy. In C. E. Schaefer & K. J. O'Connor (Eds.), *Handbook of play therapy* (pp. 21–64). New York: Wiley.

Hernandez, M., & Hodges, S. (Eds.). (2001). *Developing outcome strategies in children's mental health*. Baltimore: Paul H. Brookes.

Hewitt, S. K. (1999). *Assessing allegations of sexual abuse in preschool children: Understanding small voices*. Thousand Oaks, CA: Sage.

Hobbs, C. J., Hanks, H. G. I., & Wynne, J. M. (1999). *Child abuse and neglect: A clinician's handbook* (2nd ed.). London: Churchill Livingstone.

Hodes, M. (1998). A core curriculum for child and adolescent psychiatry. *European Child and Adolescent Psychiatry, 7*, 250–255.

Horton, C., & Bowman, B. T. (2002). *Child assessment at the preprimary level: Occasional paper number 3.* Chicago: Erickson Institute.

House, A. E. (2002). *The first session with children and adolescents: Conducting a comprehensive mental health evaluation.* New York: Guilford.

Iwaniec, D., & McCrystal, P. (1999). The Centre for Child Care Research at the Queen's University of Belfast. *Research on Social Work Practice, 9,* 248–260.

Jellinek, M. S. (1999). Changes in the practice of child and adolescent psychiatry: Are our patients better served? *Journal of the American Academy of Child and Adolescent Psychiatry, 38,* 115–117.

Jones, D. P. H. (1997) Assessment of suspected child sexual abuse. In M. E. Helfner, R. S. Kempe, & R. D. Krugman (Eds.), *The battered child* (5th ed., pp. 297–312). Chicago: University of Chicago Press.

Jongsma, A. E., & Peterson, L. M. (2000). *The child psychotherapy treatment planner.* New York: Wiley.

Kamphaus, R. W., & Frick, P. J. (2001). *Clinical assessment of child and adolescent personality and behavior.* Boston: Allyn & Bacon.

Kazdin, A. E. (1998). Psychosocial treatments for conduct disorder in children. In P. E. Nathan & J. M. Gorman (Eds.), *A guide to treatments that work* (pp. 65–89). New York: Oxford University Press.

Kronenberger, W. G., & Meyer, R. G. (2001). *The child clinician's handbook.* Boston: Allyn & Bacon.

Lamb, N. B., & Johnson, M. (2002, April). Combating defense strategies in child sexual abuse cases. Paper presented at the National Child Advocacy Center conference, Huntsville, AL.

Law, M. (2000). Strategies for implementing evidence-based practice in early intervention. *Infants and Young Children: An Interdisciplinary Journal of Special Care Practices, 13,* 32–41.

Loeber, R., Burke, J. D., Lahey, B. B., Winters, A., & Zera, M. (2000). Oppositional defiant disorder and conduct disorder: A review of the past 10 years, part I. *Journal of the American Academy of Child and Adolescent Psychiatry, 39,* 1468–1484.

Lynagh, M., Perkins, J., & Schofield, M. (2002). An evidence-based approach to health promoting schools. *Journal of School Health, 72,* 300–303.

Manela, R. W., & Moxley, D. P. (2002). Best practices as agency-based knowledge in social welfare. *Administration in Social Work, 26*(4), 1–24.

McKechnie, J. (Ed.). (1983). *Websters' new twentieth century dictionary* (2nd ed.). New York: Simon & Schuster.

Merry, S. N., & Andrews, L. K. (1994). Psychiatric status of sexually abused children 12 months after disclosure of abuse. *Journal of the American Academy of Child and Adolescent Psychiatry, 33,* 939–944.

Milner, J. S., Murphy, W. D., Valle, L. A., & Tolliver, R. M. (1998). Assessment issues in child abuse evaluations. In J. R. Lutzker (Ed.), *Handbook of child abuse research and treatment* (pp. 75–115). New York: Plenum.

Monette, D. R., Sullivan, T. J., & DeJong, C. R. (2002). *Applied social research: Tool for the human services* (5th ed.). New York: Harcourt Brace.

Munson, C. (2002). *Handbook of clinical social work supervision.* New York: Haworth.

Munson, C. E. (2001). *The mental health diagnostic desk reference: Visuals, guides* and more for learning to use the Diagnostic and Statistical Manual, DSM-IV-TR (2nd ed.). New York: Haworth.

Munson, C. E. (2003). Evolution and trends in supervision. In M. J. Austin & K. M. Hopkins (Eds.), *Human service supervision in the learning organization.* Thousand Oaks, CA: Sage.

Ney, T. (Ed.). (1995). *True and false allegations of child sexual abuse: Assessment and case management.* New York: Brunner/Mazel.

Nurcombe, B., & Partlett, D. F. (1994). *Child mental health and the law.* New York: Free Press.

Ohan, J. L., Myers, K., & Collett, B. R. (2002). Ten-year review of rating scales IV: Scales assessing trauma and its effects. *Journal of the American Academy of Child and Adolescent Psychiatry, 41,* 1401–1422.

Petti, T. A. (2000). Commentary: More outcome studies are needed. *Journal of the American Academy of Child and Adolescent Psychiatry, 39,* 169–171.

Pezdek, K. (1994). Avoiding false claims of child sexual abuse: Empty promises. *Family Relations, 43,* 258–260.

Pfefferbaum, B. (1997). Posttraumatic stress disorder in children: A review of the past 10 years. *Journal of the American Academy of Child and Adolescent Psychiatry, 36*(11), 1503–1511.

Proctor, E. K. (2002). Social work, school violence, mental health, and drug abuse: A call for evidence-based practices. *Social Work Research, 26,* 67–69.

Randall, J., Cowley, P., & Tomlinson, P. (2000). Overcoming barriers to effective practice in child care. *Child and Family Social Work, 5,* 343–353.

Reddy, L. A., & Pfeiffer, S. I. (1997). Effectiveness of treatment foster care with children and adolescents: A review of outcome studies. *Journal of the American Academy of Child and Adolescent Psychiatry, 36*(11), 581–588.

Reif, T., & Stollak, G. (1972). *Sensitivity to children: Training and its effects.* East Lansing, MI: Michigan State University Press.

Roberts, A. R. (Ed.). (2002). *Handbook of domestic violence intervention strategies: Policies, programs, and legal remedies.* New York: Oxford University Press.

Rutter, M. (1987). Psychosocial resilience and protective mechanisms. *American Journal of Orthopsychiatry, 57,* 316–331.

Rutter, M. (1998). Routes from research to clinical practice in child psychiatry: Retrospect and prospect. *Journal of Child Psychology and Psychiatry, 39,* 805–816.

Ryburn, M. (1999). Contact between children placed away from home and their birth parents: A reanalysis of the evidence in relation to permanent placements. *Clinical Child Psychology and Psychiatry, 4,* 505–519.

Salzer, M. S. (1996). Interpreting outcome studies. *Journal of the American Academy of Child and Adolescent Psychiatry, 35,* 1419.

Schaefer, C. E., Gitlin, K., & Sandgrund, A. (Eds.). (1991). *Play diagnosis and assessment.* New York: Wiley.

Scheeringa, M. S., Pebbles, C. D., Cook, C. A., & Zeanah, C. H. (2001). Toward establishing procedural, criterion, and discriminant validity for PTSD in early childhood. *Journal of the American Academy of Child and Adolescent Psychiatry, 40,* 52–60.

Scheeringa, M. S., & Zeanah, C. H. (2001). A relational perspective on PTSD in early childhood, *Journal of Traumatic Stress, 14,* 799–815.

Scheeringa, M. S., Zeanah, C. H., Drell, M. J., & Larrieu, J. A. (1995). Two approaches to the diagnosis of posttraumatic stress disorder in infancy and early childhood. *Journal of the American Academy of Child and Adolescent Psychiatry, 34*, 191–200.

Scheeringa, M. S., Zeanah, C. H., Myers, L., & Putnam, F. W. (2003). New findings on alternative criteria of PTSD in preschool children. *Journal of the American Academy of Child and Adolescent Psychiatry, 42*, 561–570.

Selekman, M. D. (1997). *Solution-focused therapy with children: Harnessing family strengths for systemic change*. New York: Guilford.

Shaw, I. F. (2003). Cutting edge issues in social work research. *British Journal of Social Work, 33*(1), 107–111.

Shaw, J. A. (1999). Practice parameters for the assessment and treatment of children and adolescents who are sexually abusive of others. *Journal of the American Academy of Child and Adolescent Psychiatry, 42*, 119–120.

Sheldon, B. (2001). The validity of evidence-based practice in social work: A reply to Stephen Webb. *British Journal of Social Work, 31*, 801–809.

Shirk, S. R., & Russell, R. L. (1996). *Change processes in child psychotherapy: Revitalizing treatment and research*. New York: Guilford.

Showalter, J. E. (1995). Managed care: Income to outcome. *Journal of the American Academy of Child and Adolescent Psychiatry, 34*, 1123.

Soldz, R., & McCullough, L. (Eds.). (2000). *Reconciling empirical knowledge and clinical experience: The art and science of psychotherapy*. Washington, DC: American Psychological Association.

Sox, H. C. (1993). Evidence-based practice guidelines from the U.S. Preventive Services Task Force. *Journal of the American Medical Association, 269*, 2678.

Spiegelman, C. (2002, Summer). The power of magic in working with traumatized children. *Access: Clinical Social Work Federation*, 12–13.

Stoppelbein, L., & Greening, L. (2000). Posttraumatic stress symptoms in parentally bereaved children and adolescents. *Journal of the American Academy of Child and Adolescent Psychiatry, 39*, 1112–1119.

Stout, C. E. (2001). A broadened vision of accountability for our children. *Behavioral Health Accreditation and Accountability Alert, 6*, 8.

Toppelberg, C. O., Medrano, L., Pena Morgens, L., & Nieto-Castanon, A. (2002). Bilingual children referred for psychiatric services: Associations of language disorders, language skills and psychopathology. *Journal of the American Academy of Child and Adolescent Psychiatry, 41*(6), 712–722.

Vance, J. E., Bowen, N. K., Fernandez, G., & Thompson, S. (2002). Risk and protective factors as predictors of outcome in adolescents with psychiatric disorder and aggression. *Journal of the American Academy of Child and Adolescent Psychiatry, 41*, 36–43.

Vygotsky, L. (1986). *Thought and language*. Cambridge, MA: MIT Press.

Webb, S. A. (2001). Some considerations on the validity of evidence-based practice in social work. *British Journal of Social Work, 31*, 795–800.

Webb, S. A. (2002). Evidence-based practice and decision analysis in social work: An implementation model. *Journal of Social Work, 2*, 45–63.

Weber, J. B., & Sergeant, A. J. (2003). Review of finding the evidence: A gateway to the literature in child and adolescent mental health. *Journal of the American Academy of Child and Adolescent Psychiatry, 38*(11), 55s–76s.

Weissman, M. M. (2001). *Treatment of depression: Bridging the 21st century.* Washington, DC: American Psychiatric Press.

Wicks-Nelson, R., & Israel, A. C. (2002). *Behavioral disorders in children* (5th ed.). Upper Saddle River, NJ: Prentice Hall.

Wolchik, S. A., & Sandler, I. N. (Eds.). (1997). *Handbook of children's coping: Linking theory and intervention.* New York: Plenum Press.

18

Treating Juvenile Delinquents With Conduct Disorder, Attention-Deficit/ Hyperactivity Disorder, and Oppositional Defiant Disorder

DAVID W. SPRINGER

Juvenile delinquents with externalizing disorders are a challenging, yet reward-ing, population to treat. The externalizing disorders—namely, attention-deficit/ hyperactivity disorder (ADHD), conduct disorder (CD), and oppositional defiant disorder (ODD)—are some of the most common encountered by practitioners working with juvenile delinquents (Kazdin, 2002; Kronenberger & Meyer, 2001). In studies of community and clinic samples, a large percentage of youths with CD or ADHD (e.g., 45% to 70%) also met criteria for the other disorder (Fer-gusson, Horwood, & Lloyd, 1991), and comorbidity between CD and ODD, anxiety disorders, and depression is common as well (Kazdin, 2002). In a recent epidemiological study that examined psychiatric disorders in juvenile delinquents (Teplin, Abram, McClelland, Dulcan, & Mericle, 2002), the most common dis-orders were substance use disorders and disruptive behavior disorders (ODD and CD), with more than 40% of males and females meeting criteria for a disruptive behavior disorder. Accordingly, this chapter presents a case exemplar of treating a juvenile delinquent dually diagnosed with conduct disorder and alcohol abuse.

First, it is important to highlight the difference between juvenile delinquency and CD. Many readers may be aware of the behaviors associated with a diag-nosis of CD, such as aggressive behavior toward others, using a weapon, fire setting, cruelty to animals or persons, vandalism, lying, truancy, running away, and theft (American Psychiatric Association [APA], 2000). The *DSM-IV-TR* al-lows for coding a client with one of two subtypes of CD: childhood-onset type (at least one criterion characteristic occurs prior to age 10) and adolescent-onset type (absence of any criteria prior to age 10). While an adolescent may be considered a "juvenile delinquent" after only one delinquent act, to warrant a diagnosis of CD, that same adolescent must be engaged over an extended period (at least 6 months) in a pattern of behavior that consistently violates the rights of others and societal norms. It is critical, therefore, that practitioners take painstaking care in their diagnostic assessments of conduct disorder, as both false positives and false negatives carry potentially serious consequences for both the offender and society (Springer, McNeece, & Arnold, 2003).

Part of what makes treating juveniles with conduct disorder so challenging is the multifaceted nature of their problems. Fortunately, in recent years, significant advances in psychosocial treatments have been made in treating children and adolescents with disruptive behavior disorders. Some of these evidence-based practices are applied to the case example of Matt that follows. For purposes here, Rosen and Proctor's (2002) definition of *evidence-based practice* (EBP) has been adopted, whereby "practitioners will select interventions on the basis of their empirically demonstrated links to the desired outcomes" (p. 743).

CASE EXAMPLE: MATT

Matt is a 16-year-old Anglo male who was recently picked up by a police officer and taken to the local juvenile assessment center for truancy, vandalism (graffiti), and underage drinking. Earlier that morning, Matt had beaten up a classmate at school. This physical altercation was unprovoked. His case was formally adjudicated through the county juvenile drug court. Rather than being expelled, he is now attending the alternative learning center (ALC). Following the recommendation from the multidisciplinary treatment team, the judge has ordered Matt to receive substance abuse and mental health treatment while on probation. Matt lives with his mother and stepfather. Matt's father committed suicide when Matt was 8 years old, and his mother married Matt's stepfather when Matt was 10. His mother and stepfather have been having difficulty in parenting Matt since he was 13. He does not respect the rules at home, such as abiding by curfews and completing chores. Matt often loses his temper and takes little responsibility for his behavior, and he has a pattern of stealing and lying. His IQ falls within the normal range, and his medical history is uncomplicated.

Matt's social worker was interested in helping Matt and his family by using interventions that gave them the best shot at a successful outcome. While there were many interventions from which to choose, the social worker wanted to use only those that had a solid evidence base. Vandiver (2002) outlines seven steps in applying evidence-based practices with clients: (a) Conduct a biopsychosocial assessment, (b) arrive at a diagnosis and select diagnostic specific guidelines, (c) identify problems, (d) develop goals or planned targets of change, (e) develop an intervention plan, (f) establish outcome measures, and (g) evaluate. As best as she was able, the social worker used these seven steps as a framework to guide her work with Matt and his family.

Biopsychosocial Assessment

As the first active phase of treatment, a thorough assessment is the cornerstone of a solid treatment plan (Springer, 2002a). During their initial session together, the social worker conducted a complete biopsychosocial assessment with Matt and his parents. (For a more detailed overview of the biopsychosocial interview, see, for example, Austrian, 2002; Springer, 2002a.)

As part of this initial assessment, the Child and Adolescent Functional Assessment Scale (CAFAS) (Hodges, 2000) was also administered. The CAFAS is a standardized multidimensional assessment tool that is used to measure the extent to which the mental health and substance use disorders of youth age 7 to 17 impair functioning. It is completed by the clinician and requires specialized training. A major benefit of the CAFAS in helping practitioners determine a youth's overall level of functioning is that it covers eight areas: school/work, home, community, behavior toward others, moods/emotions, self-harmful behavior, substance use, and thinking. The adolescent's level of functioning in each of these eight domains is scored as severe (score of 30), moderate (20), mild (10), or minimal (0). Additionally, an overall score can be computed. These scores can be graphically depicted on a one-page scoring sheet that provides a profile of the youth's functioning. An appealing feature of recent versions is that the CAFAS now includes strength-based items. While these items are not used in the scoring, they are useful in treatment planning (Springer, McNeece, & Arnold, 2003). The psychometric properties of the CAFAS have been demonstrated in numerous studies (cf. Hodges & Cheong-Seok, 2000; Hodges & Wong, 1996). One study on the predictive validity of the CAFAS supported the notion that this scale is able to predict recidivism in juvenile delinquents (Hodges & Cheong-Seok, 2000). Higher scores on the CAFAS have been associated with previous psychiatric hospitalizations, serious psychiatric diagnoses, restrictive living arrangements, below-average school performance and attendance, and contact with law enforcement (Hodges, Doucette-Gates, & Oinghong, 1999).

The CAFAS was selected for a few reasons. It is clinician rated (as opposed to a self-report pencil-and-paper scale), which is especially important, given that adolescents with CD often suffer from low insight and underreport problematic behavior (Kronenberger & Meyer, 2001; Teplin et al., 2002). The CAFAS is also standardized, covers several areas of functioning, provides clinical cutting scores, and includes strength-based items. For these reasons, it is used widely in communities across the United States. Of course, other scales would have also been excellent choices, such as the widely used Eyberg Child Behavior Inventory (ECBI), a 36-item parent-rating scale that measures conduct-problem behaviors in children and adolescents (Burns & Patterson, 1990; Robinson, Eyberg, & Ross, 1980).

In addition to the CAFAS, the timeline follow-back procedure (Sobell & Sobell, 1992) was used specifically to assess Matt's substance abuse history (his primary substance of choice was alcohol). This procedure is a structured interview technique that samples a specific period of time. A monthly calendar and memory anchor points were used to help Matt reconstruct daily use during the past month. Whereas adult studies have found that direct self-report measures have high levels of sensitivity in detecting substance use problems and compare favorably with biomedical measures (blood and urine tests) (National Institute on Alcohol Abuse and Alcoholism, 1990), the timeline follow-back may offer the most sensitive assessment for adolescent substance abusers (Leccese & Waldron, 1994). (As part of his probation, Matt also had to submit to random urine screens.)

Diagnose and Review Corresponding Evidence Base

After ruling out medical causes, and based upon the collective results of the biopsychosocial assessment, the CAFAS, and the timeline follow-back, the social worker diagnosed Matt as follows:

Axis I.   312.82   Conduct Disorder, Adolescent-Onset Type, Moderate
            305.00   Alcohol Abuse
Axis II.   V71.09   No diagnosis
Axis III.   None
Axis IV.   V61.20   Parent–Child Relational Problem; V62.3 Academic Problems;
                       Involvement with juvenile justice system

Once the initial assessment had been conducted, the social worker began working collaboratively with Matt and his parents to decide the best course of action. Through a search of the literature and key databases (cf. Fonagy, Target, Cottrell, Phillips, & Kurtz, 2002; Kazdin, 2002; http://www.effectivechildtheraphy.com; http://www.samhsa.gov), the social worker was able to learn the following.

Several recent meta-analyses suggest that the most effective approaches for treating juvenile offenders are those with a cognitive-behavioral component combined with close supervision and advocacy. There is evidence that more positive treatment effects are realized in community settings than in institutional settings (Deschenes & Greenwood, 1994). More recently, Lipsey and Wilson (1998) conducted a meta-analysis of experimental or quasi-experimental studies of interventions for serious and violent juvenile delinquents. They reviewed 200 programs, which were further divided into programs for institutionalized juveniles ($N = 83$) and noninstitutionalized juveniles ($N = 117$). McBride, VanderWaal, Terry, and VanBuren (1999, p. 58) nicely synthesized the findings of Lipsey and Wilson's meta-analysis.

Noninstitutionalized programs that demonstrate good evidence of effectiveness include behavioral therapies (family and contingency contracting), intensive case management (including system collaboration and continuing care), multisystemic therapy (MST), restitution programs (parole- and probation-based), and skills training. Institutionalized programs that demonstrate good effectiveness include behavioral programs (cognitive mediation and stress inoculation training), longer term community residential programs (therapeutic communities with cognitive-behavioral approaches), multiple services within residential communities (case management approach), and skills training (aggression replacement training and cognitive restructuring).

More specifically, the social worker found that expert consensus exists that treatments with the strongest evidence base (as demonstrated in randomized controlled clinical trials) for treating children and adolescents with conduct disorder include parent management training, multisystemic therapy, cognitive problem-solving skills training, brief strategic family therapy, and functional family therapy (Fonagy & Kurtz, 2002; Kazdin, 2002).

Parent Management Training

Parent management training (PMT) is a summary term that describes a therapeutic strategy in which parents are trained to use skills for managing their child's problem behavior (Kazdin, 1997), such as effective command-giving, setting up reinforcement systems, and using punishment, including taking away privileges and assigning extra chores. While PMT programs may differ in focus and therapeutic strategies used, they all share the common goal of enhancing parental control over children's behavior (Barkley, 1987; Cavell, 2000; Eyberg, 1988; Forehand & McMahon, 1981; Patterson, Reid, Jones, & Conger, 1975; Webster-Stratton & Herbert, 1994). To date, parent management training is the best treatment for youth with oppositional defiant disorder (Brestan & Eyberg, 1998; Hanish, Tolan, & Guerra, 1996), and the effectiveness of parent training is well documented and, in many respects, impressive (Serketich & Dumas. 1996).

Yet, studies examining the effectiveness of PMT with adolescents are equivocal, with some studies suggesting that adolescents respond less well to PMT than do their younger counterparts (Dishion & Patterson, 1992; Kazdin, 2002). In Brestan and Eyberg's (1998) review of studies that examined the effectiveness of psychosocial interventions for child and adolescent conduct problems, two interventions were considered to be "well-established treatments," according to the stringent criteria set forth by the Division 12 (Clinical Psychology) Task Force on Promotion and Dissemination of Psychological Procedures: the videotape modeling parent-training program (Spaccarelli, Cotler, & Penman, 1992; Webster-Stratton, 1984, 1994) and parent-training programs based on Patterson and Gullion's (1968) manual, *Living with Children* (Alexander & Parsons, 1973; Bernal, Klinnert, & Schultz, 1980; Wiltz & Patterson, 1974). These two approaches target parents with children ages 3 to 8 and 3 to 12, respectively.

Multisystemic Therapy

Multisystemic therapy (MST) (Henggeler & Borduin, 1990; Henggeler, Schoenwald, Borduin, Rowland, & Cunningham, 1998) is a family- and community-based treatment approach that is theoretically grounded in a social-ecological framework (Bronfenbrenner, 1979) and family systems (Haley, 1976; Minuchin, 1974). A basic foundation of MST is the belief that a juvenile's acting out or antisocial behavior is best addressed by interfacing with multiple systems, including the adolescent's family, peers, school, teachers, neighbors, and others (Brown, Borduin, & Henggeler, 2001). Thus, the MST practitioner interfaces not just with the adolescent but with various individuals and settings that influence the adolescent's life. Services are delivered in the client's natural environment, such as the client's home or a neighborhood center. There have been numerous studies demonstrating the effectiveness of MST with high-risk youth (cf. Borduin et al., 1995; Brunk, Henggeler, & Whelan, 1987; Henggeler et al., 1986). According to Brown, Borduin, and Henggeler (2001), "To date, MST is the only treatment for serious delinquent behavior that has demonstrated both short-term and long-term treatment effects in randomized, controlled clinical trials with violent and chronic juvenile offenders and their families from various cultural and ethnic backgrounds" (p. 458).

Problem-Solving Skills Training

Problem-solving skills training (PSST) (Spivak & Shure, 1974) is a cognitively based intervention that has been used to treat aggressive and antisocial youth (Kazdin, 1994). The problem-solving process involves helping clients learn how to produce a variety of potentially effective responses when faced with problem situations. Regardless of the specific problem-solving model used, the primary focus is on addressing the thought process to help adolescents address deficiencies and distortions in their approach to interpersonal situations (Kazdin, 1994). A variety of techniques are used, including didactic teaching, practice, modeling, role playing, feedback, social reinforcement, and therapeutic games (Kronenberger & Meyer, 2001). The problem-solving approach typically includes six steps for the practitioner and client to address: (a) defining the problem, (b) identifying the goal, (c) brainstorming, (d) evaluating the alternatives, (e) choosing and implementing an alternative, and (f) evaluating the implemented option (Kazdin, Esreldt-Dawson, French, & Unis, 1987). Several randomized clinical trials (Type 1 and 2 studies) have demonstrated the effectiveness of PSST with impulsive, aggressive, and conduct-disordered children and adolescents (cf. Baer & Nietzel, 1991; Durlak, Furhman, & Lampman, 1991; Kazdin, 2000; cited in Kazdin, 2002).

Brief Strategic Family Therapy

Brief strategic family therapy (BSFT) has developed out of a programmatic series of studies with Hispanic youths (Coatsworth, Szapocznik, Kurtines, & Santisteban 1997; Szapocznik & Kurtines, 1989). With its strong grounding in a cultural frame of reference, this approach considers factors such as family cohesion, parental control, and communication. Treatment strategies focus on changing concrete interaction patterns in the family, with the therapist challenging interaction patterns to help the family consider alternative ways of dealing with one another. A unique aspect of this approach is that Szapocznik and his colleagues assert that family therapy is a way of conceptualizing problems and interventions but that seeing the entire family may not be necessary (Kazdin, 2002). Several studies (Type 1 and 2) have demonstrated improvements in child and family functioning compared with other treatment and control conditions (cf. Coatsworth et al., 1997; Szapocznik & Kurtines, 1989).

Functional Family Therapy

Functional family therapy (FFT) (Alexander & Parsons, 1973, 1982), like MST, is an integrative approach that relies on systems, behavioral, and cognitive views of functioning. Clinical problems are conceptualized in terms of the function they serve for the family system and for the individual client. Research underlying FFT has found that families with delinquents have higher rates of defensiveness and blaming and lower rates of mutual support (Alexander & Parsons, 1982). The goal of treatment "is the achievement of a change in patterns of interaction and communication, in a manner that engenders adaptive family functioning" (Fonagy & Kurtz, 2002, p. 158). Treatment is grounded in learning theory. FFT has clinically significant and lasting effects on recidivism. In nine studies conducted on FFT between 1973 and 1997, a 25% to 80% improvement was found in recidivism, out-of-home placement, or future offending by siblings of the treated youth (Fonagy & Kurtz, 2002).

Select Intervention Plan

According to Gambrill (1999), in EBP

> social workers seek out practice-related research findings regarding important practice decisions and share the results of their search with clients. If they find that there is no evidence that a method they recommend will help a client, they so inform the client and describe their theoretical rationale for their recommendation. Clients are involved as informed participants. (p. 346)

Accordingly, the social worker shared as much as she knew about all of these approaches back with Matt and his parents, with the decision making taking place as follows. Given that Matt was 16 years old, that the outcome findings on PMT with adolescents were equivocal, and that his pattern of behavior was rather entrenched, the social worker and his parents decided against PMT as a primary treatment option. While MST is probably the most effective treatment available for treating high-risk juvenile offenders like Matt, MST was not being used in the social worker's setting, or even in the local community. Thus, this treatment was not considered an option for Matt's family. Both PSST and FFT were implemented with Matt and his family. Both of these approaches have been demonstrated to be effective with clients like Matt, and the social worker had been trained in both approaches. While BSFT was also considered, the social worker was not trained in this sophisticated family therapy approach.

Establish Treatment Goals and Targets for Change

Now that the primary interventions, PSST and FFT, had been selected, treatment goals had to be established. The following guidelines are helpful in establishing treatment goals: The goals should be clearly defined and measurable, feasible and realistic, set collaboratively by the practitioner and the client, stem directly from the assessment process, and stated in positive terms, focusing on client growth.

The practitioner worked collaboratively with Matt and his parents to come up with the following treatment goals: (a) Matt's parents will set firm and consistent limits, using natural rewards and consequences; (b) Matt and his parents will improve communication and establish a behavioral contract; (c) Matt will follow the rules at home, as spelled out in the behavioral contract, at least 90% of the time; (d) Matt will follow the rules at school, as evidenced by earning 3 points a day in every class for doing so; (e) Matt will meet all the terms of his probation; (f) Matt will learn alternative ways of dealing with his anger; and (g) Matt will abstain from using alcohol or other drugs. Matt and his family agreed to these terms for a 2-week period, at which time they would be reexamined and modified if needed. The 2-week time limit on these goals was set because doing something for 2 weeks seems more feasible to many adolescents than agreeing to such conditions indefinitely. For an example of a more detailed and comprehensive treatment plan, see Springer (2002b).

Implement Intervention Plan

With treatment goals in place, the social worker began working with Matt and his family in family therapy. In the early phase of treatment, the social worker engaged all of the family members in the therapeutic process, in part by using a "nonblaming message." The social worker stressed the need for active participation on the part of everyone in the family and addressed the effect that Matt's behavior had on the entire family system.

The patterns of blaming in the family were first addressed. Matt often got blamed for all of the family's problems. In other words, Matt has assumed (or been assigned) the family role of scapegoat. Matt's behavior was reframed; he was praised by the social worker for doing too good of a job in acting out the family's problems, and he was relieved of this responsibility for the time being. The social worker introduced cognitive aspects commonly associated with the FFT approach, including behavioral components, communication skills training, behavioral contracting, and contingency management. Positive reinforcement among family members was also encouraged.

It was also important for the social worker to provide Matt with as much one-on-one time as possible early on in treatment to help establish therapeutic rapport (cf. Todd & Selekman, 1994). By joining with Matt, the social worker did not lose him when it came time to empower his parents to set limits. To this end, she also used empathy and humor with Matt.

As Matt's family progressed through treatment, they sometimes had difficulty in translating their treatment goals into actions. For example, when Matt's behavior began to improve, issues that the family had been pushing aside began to surface. The social worker helped the family gradually shift toward more interpersonal issues. Recall that a key assumption of the FFT approach is that clinical problems are couched in terms of the function they serve for the family and for the individual. During one session, Matt shared that he sometimes wondered if his dad had the right idea (by killing himself). The family had never discussed the suicide of Matt's father. This was explored at length in the next couple of family therapy sessions, which served several purposes. It allowed all of them to express their thoughts surrounding this tragic event, and it also gave the family an opportunity to practice some of the new communication skills that they had learned by discussing a sensitive and emotionally charged topic.

As the family examined Matt's alcohol abuse, the social worker avoided the use of labels such as addict or alcoholic. Labels like this often do more harm than good when working with adolescent offenders (Todd & Selekman, 1994). Instead, during individual sessions (with Matt) and family sessions, techniques commonly used in PSST (e.g., role playing, feedback, and in vivo practice) were used to help Matt generate alternative solutions to interpersonal problems (e.g., becoming angry with others) that triggered his drinking.

To help specifically with anger management, which many of her other clients at the ALC also struggled with, the social worker started an anger management therapy group. The Substance Abuse and Mental Health Services Administration, Center for Substance Abuse Treatment (Reilly & Shopshire, 2002), has issued a 12-week cognitive-behavioral anger management group treatment manual, titled *Anger Management for Substance Abuse and Mental Health Clients: A Cognitive Behavioral Therapy*, that is available at no cost from the National Clearinghouse on Alcohol and Drug Information (NCADI) (http://www.samhsa.gov/). This treatment group is a cognitive-behavioral therapy (CBT) approach that employs relaxation, cognitive, and communication skills. The approach presents clients with options that draw on these different interventions and then encourages them to develop individualized anger control plans by using as many of the techniques as possible. The social worker used this treatment manual to successfully facilitate the anger management group with her clients at the ALC. It is important to note that only a few of the adolescents in this group had a diagnosis of conduct disorder. Having too many conduct-disordered youths in the same treatment group can actually be countertherapeutic (Feldman, Caplinger, & Wodarski, 1983).

Matt's anger management plan reflects many of the interventions used in the 12-week group therapy manual, including five primary treatment goals along with corresponding interventions. See Table 18.1 for a listing of the treatment goals and a sampling of some of the corresponding interventions related to Matt's anger management plan. Of course, this list of interventions is not exhaustive, and there is some overlap across treatment goals and interventions. For a more detailed example of an anger management plan that includes long-term goals

Table 18.1   Treatment Goals and Corresponding Interventions for Matt's Anger Management Plan

Treatment Goals	Interventions
1. Become aware of intense anger outbursts	1. Monitor anger using the "Anger Meter" 2. List positive payoffs that Matt gets from angry outbursts and aggressive actions
2. Stop violence or the threat of violence (physical and verbal)	1. Explore events that trigger anger and cues to anger 2. Explore, role-play, and practice alternative coping strategies (e.g., take a time-out, exercise, deep breathing, conflict resolution model, progressive muscle relaxation)
3. Develop self-control over thoughts and actions	1. Review the aggression cycle 2. Use Ellis's A-B-C-D model of cognitive restructuring 3. Model and practice thought stopping
4. Accept responsibility for own actions	1. Confront Matt in group when he does not accept responsibility for his actions, and reward him when he does 2. Record at least two irrational beliefs during the week and how to dispute these beliefs, using Ellis's A-B-C-D model
5. Receive support and feedback from others	1. Use the here-and-now of the group experience to provide feedback to Matt 2. Discuss Matt's progress in family therapy sessions

and corresponding short-term objectives and interventions, the reader is referred to Dulmus and Wodarski (2002).

Monitor Treatment Progress

As the termination of treatment approached, the social worker introduced longer intervals between sessions, treating the final sessions as once-a-month maintenance sessions when the family reported on how things were going. Matt and his family made considerable progress on the desired treatment outcomes, which are "the targets toward which interventions are directed" (Rosen & Proctor, 2002, p. 744). Over the course of 4 months, this was evidenced across several areas of functioning. Matt performed well enough at the ALC that he was allowed to transition back into his mainstream school. For the most part, he continued to meet the terms of probation. This included producing clean urine drug tests. However, on two separate occasions, Matt did report drinking a six-pack of beer at a party. On both occasions, Matt was angry at his parents. Using a harm-reduction approach to substance abuse treatment (cf. McNeece, Bullington, Arnold, & Springer, 2002), the social worker encouraged the family to view this as a normal part of the treatment process. She worked with Matt on identifying the anger that triggered his drinking and, using PSST, problem-solved with him on what he could do differently the next time he was feeling angry. Matt had no incidents of physical violence at school or in the neighborhood, although he did sometimes still "lose his temper" at home when his parents enforced rules.

Matt's therapeutic gains were also monitored by using the CAFAS, which was

Table 18.2 Matt's CAFAS Results: Intake and Termination

CAFAS Domain	Intake	Termination
School/work	30	10
Home	30	10
Community	30	0
Behavior toward others	30	10
Moods/emotions	20	10
Self-harmful behavior	0	0
Substance use	30	10
Thinking	10	0
Overall functioning	180	50

administered at intake and at termination (see Table 18.2). Based on the scores for each domain, Matt's impairment in functioning could be interpreted as follows: severe (score of 30), moderate (score of 20), mild (score of 10), or minimal (score of 0). The overall scores can also be computed as severe (140–120), marked (100–130), moderate (50–90), mild (20–40), or minimal to no (0–10) impairment in functioning. In sum, then, it seems that Matt made significant progress over the course of treatment, moving from "severe impairment in functioning" at intake to the low range of "moderate impairment in functioning" 4 months later.

CONCLUSION

In the treatment of adolescents, cognitive-based interventions are generally most effective when combined with behavioral contingencies in the child's natural environment (Ervin, Bankert, & DuPaul, 1996). It makes little sense to treat an adolescent in isolation from his or her natural environment. Pearson, Lipton, Cleland, and Yee (2002) encourage policy makers to consider adopting cognitive skills training programs such as those reviewed in this chapter.

The first three treatments reviewed (PMT, MST, and PSST) have more extensive (Type 1 and 2 studies) and follow-up data supporting their effectiveness. FFT has controlled clinical trials supporting its efficacy, but the scope of this evidence is not as solid as it is for the other approaches. Nevertheless, these approaches are all quite promising, and their empirical base places them ahead of other approaches available for treating children and adolescents with conduct problems (Kazdin, 2002). It is worth noting that all but PSST place a primary emphasis on the family.

Despite the promising treatment effects produced by the interventions reviewed here, existing treatments need to be refined and new ones developed. We cannot yet determine the short- and long-term impact of evidence-based treatments on conduct-disordered youths, and it is sometimes unclear what part of the therapeutic process produces change. In the meantime, practitioners can use the existing knowledge base to guide their work with this complex and challenging population.

REFERENCES

Alexander, J. F., & Parsons, B. V. (1973). Short-term behavioral intervention with delinquents: Impact on family process and recidivism. *Journal of Abnormal Psychology, 81,* 219–225.

Alexander, J. F., & Parsons, B. V. (1982). *Functional family therapy.* Monterey, CA: Brooks/Cole.

American Psychiatric Association. (2000). *Diagnostic and statistical manual of mental disorders* (4th ed., text revision). Washington, DC: Author.

Austrian, S. G. (2002). Guidelines for conducting a biopsychosocial assessment. In A. R. Roberts & G. J. Greene (Eds.), *Social workers' desk reference* (pp. 204–208). New York: Oxford University Press.

Baer, R. A., & Nietzel, M. T. (1991). Cognitive and behavioral treatment of impulsivity in children: A meta-analytic review of the outcome literature. *Journal of Clinical Child Psychology, 20,* 400–412.

Barkley, R. A. (1987). *Defiant children: A clinician's manual for parent training.* New York: Guilford.

Bernal, M. E., Klinnert, M. D., & Schultz, L. A. (1980). Outcome evaluation of behavioral parent training and client-centered parent counseling for children with conduct problems. *Journal of Applied Behavior Analysis, 13,* 677–691.

Borduin, C. M., Mann, B. J., Cone, L. T., Henggeler, S. W., Fucci, B. R., Blaske, D. M., et al. (1995). Multisystemic treatment of serious juvenile offenders: Long-term prevention of criminality and violence. *Journal of Consulting and Clinical Psychology, 63,* 569–578.

Brestan, E. V., & Eyberg, S. M. (1998). Effective psychosocial treatments of conduct-disordered children and adolescents: 29 years, 82 studies, and 5,272 kids. *Journal of Clinical Child Psychology, 27,* 180–189.

Bronfenbrenner, U. (1979). *The ecology of human development: Experiences by nature and design.* Cambridge, MA: Harvard University Press.

Brown, T. L., Borduin, C. M., & Henggeler, S. W. (2001). Treating juvenile offenders in community settings. In J. B. Ashford, B. D. Sales, & W. H. Reid (Eds.), *Treating adult and juvenile offenders with special needs* (pp. 445–464). Washington, DC: American Psychological Association.

Brunk, M., Henggeler, S. W., & Whelan, J. P. (1987). A comparison of multisystemic therapy and parent training in the brief treatment of child abuse and neglect. *Journal of Consulting and Clinical Psychology, 55,* 311–318.

Burns, G. L., & Patterson, D. R. (1990). Conduct problem behaviors in a stratified random sample of children and adolescents: New standardization data on the Eyberg Child Behavior Inventory. *Psychological Assessment, 2,* 391–397.

Cavell, T. A. (2000). *Working with parents of aggressive children: A practitioner's guide.* Washington, DC: American Psychological Association.

Coatsworth, J. D., Szapocznik, J., Kurtines, W., & Santisteban, D. A. (1997). Culturally competent psychosocial interventions with antisocial problem behavior in Hispanic youths. In D. M. Stoff, J. Breiling, & J. D. Maser (Eds.), *Handbook of antisocial behavior* (pp. 395–404). New York: Wiley.

Deschenes, E. P., & Greenwood, P. W. (1994). Treating the juvenile drug offender. In D. L. MacKenzie & C. D. Uchida (Eds.), *Drugs and crime: Evaluating public policy initiatives* (pp. 253–280). Thousand Oaks, CA: Sage.

Dishion, T. J., & Patterson, G. R. (1992). Age effects in parent training outcomes. *Behavior Therapy, 23,* 719–729.

Dulmas, C. N., & Wodarski, J. S. (2002). Parameters of social work treatment plans: Case application of explosive anger. In A. R. Roberts & G. J. Greene (Eds.), *Social workers' desk reference* (pp. 314–319). New York: Oxford University Press.

Durlak, J. A., Furhman, T., & Lampman, C. (1991). Effectiveness of cognitive-behavioral therapy for maladapting children: A meta-analysis. *Psychological Bulletin, 110,* 204–214.

Ervin, R. A., Bankert, C. L., & DuPaul, G. J. (1996). Treatment of attention-deficit/hyperactivity disorder. In M. A. Reinecke, F. M. Dattilio, & A. Freeman (Eds.), *Cognitive therapy with children and adolescents* (pp. 38–61). New York: Guilford.

Eyberg, S. (1988). Parent–child interaction therapy: Integration of traditional and behavioral concerns. *Child and Family Behavior Therapy, 10,* 33–45.

Feldman, R. A., Caplinger, T. E., & Wodarski, J. S. (1983). *The St. Louis conundrum: The effective treatment of antisocial youths.* Englewood Cliffs, NJ: Prentice Hall.

Fergusson, D. M., Horwood, L. J., & Lloyd, M. (1991). Confirmatory factor models of attention deficit and conduct disorder. *Journal of Child Psychology and Psychiatry, 32,* 257–274.

Fonagy, P., & Kurtz, A. (2002). Disturbance of conduct. In P. Fonagy, M. Target, D. Cottrell, J. Phillips, & Z. Kurtz (Eds.), *What works for whom? A critical review of treatments for children and adolescents* (pp. 106–192). New York: Guilford.

Fonagy, P., Target, M., Cottrell, D., Phillips, J., & Kurtz, Z. (2002). *What works for whom? A critical review of treatments for children and adolescents.* New York: Guilford.

Forehand, R. L., & McMahon, R. J. (1981). *Helping the noncompliant child: A clinician's guide to present training.* New York: Guilford.

Gambrill, E. (1999). Evidence-based practice: An alternative to authority-based practice. *Families in Society: The Journal of Contemporary Human Services, 80,* 341–350.

Haley, J. (1976). *Problem solving therapy.* San Francisco: Jossey-Bass.

Hanish, L. D., Tolan, P. H., & Guerra, N. G. (1996). Treatment of oppositional defiant disorder. In M. A. Reinecke, F. M. Dattilio, & A. Freeman (Eds.), *Cognitive therapy with children and adolescents* (pp. 62–78). New York: Guilford.

Henggeler, S. W., & Borduin, C. M. (1990). *Family therapy and beyond: A multisystemic approach to treating the behavior problems of children and adolescents.* Pacific Grove, CA: Brooks/Cole.

Henggeler, S. W., Rodick, J. D., Borduin, C. M., Hanson, C. L., Watson, S. M., & Urey, J. R. (1986). Multisystemic treatment of juvenile offenders: Effects on adolescent behavior and family interactions. *Developmental Psychology, 22,* 132–141.

Henggeler, S. W., Schoenwald, S. K., Borduin, C. M., Rowland, M. D., & Cunningham, P. B. (1998). *Multisystemic treatment of antisocial behavior in children and adolescents.* New York: Guilford.

Hodges, K. (2000). *The Child and Adolescent Functional Assessment Scale self training manual.* Ypsilanti: Eastern Michigan University, Department of Psychology.

Hodges, K., & Cheong-Seok, K. (2000). Psychometric study of the Child and Adolescent Functional Assessment Scale: Prediction of contact with the law and poor school attendance. *Journal of Abnormal Child Psychology, 28,* 287–297.

Hodges, K., Doucette-Gates, A., & Oinghong, L. (1999). The relationship between the Child and Adolescent Functional Assessment Scale (CAFAS) and indicators of functioning. *Journal of Child and Family Studies, 8,* 109–122.

Hodges, K., & Wong, M. M. (1996). Psychometric characteristics of a multi-dimensional measure to assess impairment: The Child and Adolescent Functional Assessment Scale. *Journal of Child and Family Studies, 5,* 445–467.

Kazdin, A. E. (1994). Psychotherapy for children and adolescents. In A. E. Bergin & S. L. Garfield (Eds.), *Handbook of psychotherapy and behavior change* (4th ed., pp. 543–594). New York: Wiley.

Kazdin, A. E. (2000). *Psychotherapy for children and adolescents: Directions for research and practice.* New York: Oxford University Press.

Kazdin, A. E. (2002). Psychosocial treatments for conduct disorder in children and adolescents. In P. E. Nathan & J. M. Gorman (Eds.), *A guide to treatments that work* (2nd ed., pp. 57–85). New York: Oxford University Press.

Kazdin, A. E., Esveldt-Dawson, K., French, N. H., & Unis, A. S. (1987). Effects of parent management training and problem-solving skills training combined in the treatment of antisocial child behavior. *Journal of the American Academy of Child and Adolescent Psychiatry, 26,* 416–424.

Kronenberger, W. G., & Meyer, R. G. (2001). *The child clinician's handbook* (2nd ed.). Boston: Allyn & Bacon.

Leccese, M., & Waldron, H. B. (1994). Assessing adolescent substance abuse: A critique of current measurement instruments. *Journal of Substance Abuse Treatment, 11,* 553–563.

Lipsey, M. W., & Wilson, D. B. (1998). Effective intervention for serious juvenile offenders: A synthesis of research. In R. Loever & D. Farrington (Eds.), *Serious and violent juvenile offenders: Risk factors and successful interventions* (pp. 313–344). London: Sage.

McBride, D. C., VanderWaal, C. J., Terry, Y. M., & VanBuren, H. (1999). *Breaking the cycle of drug use among juvenile offenders.* Retrieved October 24, 2002, from http://wwwncjrsorg/pdffiles1/nij/179273.pdf

McNeece, C. A., Bullington, B., Arnold, E. M., & Springer, D. W. (2002). The war on drugs: Treatment, research, and substance abuse intervention in the twenty-first century. In R. Muraskin & A. R. Roberts (Eds.), *Visions for change: Crime and justice in the twenty-first century* (3rd ed., pp. 11–36). Upper Saddle River, NJ: Prentice Hall.

Minuchin, S. (1974). *Families and family therapy.* Cambridge, MA: Harvard University Press.

National Institute on Alcohol Abuse and Alcoholism. (1990). *Seventh special report to the U.S. Congress on alcohol and health.* Rockville, MD: U.S. Department of Health and Human Services.

Patterson, G. R., & Gullion, M. E. (1968). *Living with children: New methods for parents and teachers.* Champaign, IL: Research Press.

Patterson, G. R., Reid, J. B., Jones, R. R., & Conger, R. E. (1975). *A social learn-*

ing approach to family intervention: Vol. 1, Families with aggressive children. Eugene, OR: Castalia.

Pearson, F. S., Lipton, D. S., Cleland, C. M., & Yee, D. S. (2002). The effects of behavioral/cognitive-behavioral programs on recidivism. *Crime and Delinquency, 48*(3), 476–496.

Reilly, P. M., & Shopshire, M. S. (2002). *Anger management for substance abuse and mental health clients: A cognitive behavioral therapy.* Washington, DC: U.S. Department of Health and Human Services, Substance Abuse and Mental Health Services Administration.

Robinson, E. A., Eyberg, S. M., & Ross, A. W. (1980). The standardization of an inventory of child conduct problem behaviors. *Journal of Clinical Child Psychology, 9,* 22–29.

Rosen, A., & Proctor, E. K. (2002). Standards for evidence-based social work practice: The role of replicable and appropriate interventions, outcomes, and practice guidelines. In A. R. Roberts & G. J. Greene (Eds.), *Social workers' desk reference* (pp. 743–747). New York: Oxford University Press.

Serketich, W. J., & Dumas, J. E. (1996). The effectiveness of behavioral parent training to modify antisocial behavior in children: A meta analysis. *Behavior Therapy, 27,* 171–186.

Sobell, L. C., & Sobell, M. B. (1992). Timeline follow-back: A technique for assessing self-reported alcohol consumption. In R. Z. Litten & J. P. Allen (Eds.), *Measuring alcohol consumption: Psychosocial and biochemical methods* (pp. 41–72). Totowa, NJ: Humana Press.

Spaccarelli, S., Cotler, S., & Penman, D. (1992). Problem-solving skills training as a supplement to behavioral parent training. *Cognitive Therapy and Research, 16,* 1–18.

Spivak, G., & Shure, M. B. (1974). *Social adjustment of young children.* San Francisco: Jossey-Bass.

Springer, D. W. (2002a). Assessment protocols and rapid assessment instruments with troubled adolescents. In A. R. Roberts & G. J. Greene (Eds.), *Social workers' desk reference* (pp. 217–221). New York: Oxford University Press.

Springer, D. W. (2002b). Treatment planning with adolescents: ADHD case application. In A. R. Roberts & G. J. Greene (Eds.), *Social workers' desk reference* (pp. 731–738). New York: Oxford University Press.

Springer, D. W., McNeece, C. A., & Arnold, E. M. (2003). *Substance abuse treatment for criminal offenders: An evidence-based guide for practitioners.* Washington, DC: American Psychological Association.

Szapocznik, J., & Kurtines, W. M. (1989). *Breakthroughs in family therapy with drug-abusing problem youth.* New York: Springer.

Teplin, L. A., Abram, K. M., McClelland, G. M., Dulcan, M. K., & Mericle, A. A. (2002). Psychiatric disorders in youth in juvenile detention. *Archives of General Psychiatry, 59,* 1133–1143.

Todd, T. C., & Selekman, M. (1994). A structural-strategic model for treating the adolescent who is abusing alcohol and other drugs. In W. Snyder & T. Ooms (Eds.), *Empowering families, helping adolescents: Family-centered treatment of adolescents with alcohol, drug abuse, and mental health problems* (pp. 79–89). Rockville, MD: U.S. Department of Health and Human Services, Center for Substance Abuse Treatment.

Vandiver, V. L. (2002). Step-by-step practice guidelines for using evidence-based practice and expert consensus in mental health settings. In A. R. Roberts & G. J. Greene (Eds.), *Social workers' desk reference* (pp. 731–738). New York: Oxford University Press.

Webster-Stratton, C. (1984). Randomized trial of two parent-training programs for families with conduct-disordered children. *Journal of Consulting and Clinical Psychology, 52,* 666–678.

Webster-Stratton, C. (1994). Advancing videotape parent training: A comparison study. *Journal of Consulting and Clinical Psychology, 62,* 583–593.

Webster-Stratton, C., & Herbert, M. (1994). *Troubled families: Problem children.* New York: Wiley.

Wiltz, N. A., & Patterson, G. R. (1974). An evaluation of parent training procedures designed to alter inappropriate aggressive behavior of boys. *Behavior Therapy, 5,* 215–221.

19

Evidence-Based Treatments for Obsessive-Compulsive Disorder

Deciding What Treatment Method Works for Whom

JONATHAN S. ABRAMOWITZ
STEFANIE A. SCHWARTZ

Effective treatments for obsessive-compulsive disorder (OCD) can be divided into two broad categories: biological and cognitive-behavioral. Biological treatments include pharmacotherapy with serotonin reuptake inhibitors (SRIs) and neurosurgery. Cognitive-behavioral treatment (CBT) includes exposure, response prevention, and cognitive therapy. These procedures can be delivered on an individual, group, or inpatient basis. Moreover, the frequency of therapy sessions may vary from weekly to daily. We begin this chapter with a brief description of the strengths and limitations of the principal treatment approaches. Next, we review the factors to be considered in deciding which treatment may be most beneficial for a given patient (Table 19.1). A brief discussion of decision factors that are less specific to OCD patients is followed by a more extensive examination of factors specifically related to OCD.

SEROTONIN REUPTAKE INHIBITORS

Although they are the most widely used treatment for OCD, SRIs produce a modest 20% to 40% reduction in symptoms (Rauch & Jenike, 1998). The major strength of a pharmacological approach for OCD is its convenience. Limitations include the relatively modest improvement, the likelihood of residual symptoms, a high rate of nonresponse (40% to 60% of patients show little response), and

Table 19.1 Considerations for Choosing a Treatment Modality for Patients with Obsessive-Compulsive Disorder

SRI Medication Alone	Individual Outpatient Cognitive-Behavioral	Inpatient Cognitive-Behavioral	Group Cognitive-Behavioral	Supportive Therapy	No OCD Treatment
• If CBT unavailable • If patient prefers medication to psychotherapy • If patient has poor insight • If noncompliance with CBT	• If residual symptoms after SRI trial • If primary OCD • If good support from family/friends • Consider intensive therapy if rituals are severe • Consider loop-tape exposure for severe obsessions • Consider cognitive therapy if hoarding • Consider personality disorders • Consider severity of comorbid anxiety or mood disorder	• If outpatient therapy unsuccessful • If patient has poor insight • If social environment is obstructive of outpatient therapy • If additional severe psychopathology (e.g., suicidal depression) • If comorbid medical condition is present • Consider costs	• Consider patient's comfort and willingness to share symptoms with others	• If symptoms persist despite adequate trials of SRIs and CBT • For long-term symptom management	• If OCD is clearly secondary to another disorder (e.g., generalized anxiety, substance abuse, bipolar disorder, psychosis), address the primary problem before beginning OCD treatment

the prospect of unpleasant side effects. Moreover, once SRIs are terminated, OCD symptoms typically return rapidly (Pato, Hill, & Murphy, 1990).

INDIVIDUAL OUTPATIENT CBT

Traditional behavioral treatment for OCD involves exposure and response prevention (ERP). Exposure entails repeated and prolonged confrontation with obsessional stimuli; response prevention means refraining from compulsive rituals. Cognitive therapy, a newer approach to OCD, emphasizes cognitive change through education and rational discourse, although "behavioral experiments" involving exposure procedures are almost always performed to reinforce accurate beliefs and assumptions about probability and risk. Because of the procedural and conceptual overlaps (i.e., ERP and cognitive methods both aim to modify dysfunctional cognitions), we collectively refer to these procedures as CBT here and differentiate between ERP and cognitive techniques only when discussing their implementation in specific circumstances.

Research demonstrates that ERP is a highly effective therapy for OCD: Typical improvement rates are in the 60% to 70% range (e.g., Franklin, Abramowitz, Kozak, Levitt, & Foa, 2000). Initial studies show that cognitive therapy is also beneficial, yet whether it is as effective as ERP is still unknown. Strengths of CBT in general include its brevity (most programs involve 16 sessions), short-term effectiveness, and long-term maintenance of treatment gains. A drawback of this approach is that patients must confront their fear-evoking stimuli and resist urges to ritualize to obtain symptom reduction. Because CBT requires compliance with such procedures, a number of patients refuse this therapy or terminate prematurely. Moreover, CBT is highly focused and does not typically directly address comorbid problems such as personality disorders that often accompany OCD. Finally, only a small percentage of mental health treatment providers are trained in the provision of CBT for OCD.

A few OCD-anxiety disorders specialty clinics offer *intensive* outpatient CBT, meaning 15 daily outpatient treatment sessions over 3 weeks. Abramowitz, Foa, and Franklin (2003) found that this intensive schedule was more effective than 15 sessions of twice-weekly ERP (delivered over 8 weeks) immediately after treatment. However, at 3-month follow-up, these differences were no longer apparent. A practical advantage of the intensive approach over less intensive schedules is that massed sessions allow for regular therapist supervision and therefore rapid correction of subtle avoidance, rituals, or suboptimal exposure practice that might otherwise compromise outcome. The primary disadvantage is the inherent scheduling demands for both the clinician and the patient.

GROUP CBT

Group CBT programs have been found effective in reducing OCD symptoms (McLean et al., 2001). Strengths include the support and cohesion that are nonspecific effects of group therapy. Potential weaknesses to a group approach include the relative lack of attention to each individual's symptoms, particularly given the heterogeneity of OCD symptoms.

INPATIENT CBT

Although most inpatient psychiatric hospitals are equipped to provide standard care for patients with OCD, programming is often limited by the short duration of stay. Therefore, the initial focus is often on stabilizing patients via medication and nonspecific psychotherapy (e.g., supportive counseling). Only a few specialized inpatient treatment programs for severe OCD exist. These residential OCD programs typically include individual and group CBT, medication management, and supportive therapy for comorbid psychiatric conditions. Length of stay may vary from a few weeks to a month or more.

One strength of specialized inpatient OCD programs is that they provide constant supervision for patients requiring help with implementing treatment (i.e., conducting self-directed ERP). This may be helpful to the patient who lacks family or friends to assist with treatment. A shortcoming of inpatient treatment for OCD is that it is often costly. Because patients with obsessions and compulsions regarding specific places or stimuli (e.g., bathrooms at home) may have difficulty reproducing these feared situations within the hospital setting for the purposes of exposure, generalization of treatment effects must be considered. The only study to directly compare inpatient to outpatient CBT for OCD found no differences in outcome between 20 sessions of outpatient and 5.4 months of inpatient treatment (van den Hout, Emmelkamp, Kraaykamp, & Grietz, 1988).

NEUROSURGICAL TREATMENT

Currently there are four different types of neurosurgical interventions for OCD: subcaudate tractotomy, limbic leucotomy, cingulotomy, and capsulotomy. These procedures involve severing interconnections between areas of the brain's frontal lobes and the limbic system. Recommended only in cases where severe OCD and depressive symptoms persist despite all other available treatments having been tried, neurosurgery has risks that include alterations in cognitive functioning and personality. Although clinical improvement has been observed in some cases, it remains unknown why these procedures are successful for only a subset of OCD patients (Jenike, 2000). There is also an increased risk of suicide following failure with this approach.

NONSPECIFIC FACTORS TO CONSIDER WHEN DECIDING ON TREATMENT

Age, Gender, and Race Age

Age

For different reasons, children, adolescents, and the elderly may have more difficulties with adherence to medication regimens than do young and middle-aged adults. Missed doses or overdoses may result in reduced benefit or unpleasant side effects. Older adults may be subject to more adverse side effects from SRIs because of reduced metabolic rates and interactions with medicine prescribed for other conditions. Thus, CBT is the best initial treatment option for younger children and older adults. Evidence that CBT is highly effective for children with OCD is accumulating (Abramowitz, Whiteside, & Deacon, 2002), and initial studies with elderly populations are encouraging as well (Calamari & Cassiday, 1999). Nevertheless, family conflict occasionally interferes with the effects of CBT in children with OCD. Also, older individuals may feel more comfortable with medication than with attending outpatient psychotherapy. This issue should be discussed openly with such patients.

Gender

Research has not identified gender as a variable to consider when making treatment decisions for OCD. Nevertheless, some patients may feel more comfortable with therapists of their same sex, especially if they have obsessions or compulsions regarding uncomfortable sexual or contamination concerns (e.g., public restrooms). For example, a same-sex therapist would be necessary to accompany the patient during exposure to public restrooms.

Race

Some members of minority groups perceive an increased stigma in presenting for mental health treatment and thus may be more likely to opt for pharmacotherapy over psychotherapy, as there is typically less stigma associated with medication treatment (Williams, Chambless, & Steketee, 1998). This sense of shame can also interfere with CBT by hindering patients' self-report of symptoms and their performance of ERP exercises in public settings. Despite these issues, Williams et al. (1998) reported clinically significant improvement for African-American patients with OCD who completed CBT.

Educational Level

Successful CBT requires that the patient comprehend a theoretical conceptual model of OCD and a rationale for treatment. Moreover, patients must be able to consolidate information learned during exposure practice and implement treatment procedures on their own. This may be difficult for individuals who are very concrete in their thinking. Because group CBT may proceed at a pace that is too rapid for individuals with cognitive impairment, individual therapy is recommended. For those OCD patients too cognitively impaired to comprehend or profit from CBT, it may be more fruitful to explore pharmacotherapy options.

Availability of Treatment

Geographic location limits the availability of CBT but not medication for OCD. Although the number of professionals trained in CBT is increasing, access to qualified therapists is limited, especially in rural areas. Thus, many patients must travel for adequate treatment. Insurance coverage may also dictate the availability of both CBT and pharmacotherapy because some providers do not adequately cover mental health treatment.

Two CBT self-help programs have been developed and tested for OCD. Fritzler, Hecker, and Losee's (1997) 12-week bibliotherapy program uses Steketee and White's (1990) self-help book, *When Once Is Not Enough,* and five sessions with a therapist to review information presented in the book. Improvement among the nine patients in this study was modest, yet three obtained clinically significant benefit. Greist et al. (2002) described an interactive (over the telephone) computerized self-help behavior therapy program for OCD (*BT Steps*). The intervention included education about OCD, treatment planning, ERP instructions, and relapse prevention. Greist et al. (2002) found that patients receiving this program improved about 25% in their OCD symptoms. These findings suggest that some degree of benefit may be obtained from self-help programs, absent a therapist. However, the lack of therapist assistance is likely to jeopardize the integrity of exposure and may compromise long-term outcome.

Patient Preference

It is important to weigh the patient's treatment preferences when considering therapeutic recommendations. We typically review the pros and cons of both CBT and pharmacotherapy and address any concerns when helping a patient decide which treatment(s) they will receive. Greater adherence can be expected if the patient is agreeable with the particular treatment plan. For example, some patients may not be willing to confront anxiety-evoking situations as in ERP.

Availability of Support System

Relatives and friends of OCD sufferers may play a role in maintaining the patient's symptoms by engaging in rituals or avoidance. In some cases family members are aware of this fact, yet in others relatives believe they are helping the patient or that they must avoid conflict over symptoms at all costs. Although it is useful for CBT to involve a support person to help with therapy exercises outside the session, it is a certain kind of support that is helpful in CBT. Several studies suggest that nonanxious, empathetic, firm family members are more successful than anxious, critical, argumentative, and inconsistent ones in providing support during CBT (Mehta, 1990; Steketee, 1993). Chambless and Steketee (1999) found that relatives' emotional overinvolvement, criticism, and hostility predicted higher rates of dropout from CBT. Thus, how individual family members interact with the patient should be assessed before requesting their assistance with CBT. If family members are not supportive and empathetic, involving them in CBT may be counterproductive and is discouraged. For patients who need additional support, group or inpatient CBT may be better options.

OCD-RELATED VARIABLES TO CONSIDER WHEN DECIDING ON TREATMENT

Symptom Presentation

Primacy and Severity of OCD Symptoms

A characteristic of CBT is that treatment methods target specific symptoms. Thus, we recommend CBT for OCD only when obsessions and compulsions are among the patient's primary complaints. Because ERP requires a fairly generous commitment, we typically do not initiate this treatment if patients are concurrently undergoing simultaneous therapies likely to compete for their time and energy. Instead, we advise patients seeking treatment who have additional therapeutic undertakings to delay therapy for OCD, or begin with SRIs, until their schedule can accommodate CBT.

For the most part, clinical severity itself should not be a factor in the decision of whether to pursue medication or CBT. We tend to recommend CBT as the first-line treatment before SRIs. However, more severe symptoms may require a more intense regimen of whichever treatment is offered: a higher dose of medicine or more frequent CBT sessions. In cases where patients are extremely impaired or present a danger to themselves or to others, inpatient treatment is recommended. Where possible, however, we recommend CBT be conducted on an outpatient basis to maximize generalizability of treatment gains to the patient's own personal surroundings.

Symptom Theme

Because of the heterogeneity of OCD, there has been interest in whether patients with different symptom presentations (e.g., checking, hoarding) respond preferentially to certain treatments. Research suggests that both ERP and SRIs are of reduced benefit for hoarding symptoms (Abramowitz, Franklin, Schwartz, & Furr, in press; Mataix-Cols, Rauch, Manzo, Jenike, & Baer, 1999; Saxena et al., 2002). Novel CBT interventions for hoarding symptoms have been developed and tested in preliminary studies (e.g., Hartl & Frost, 1999). Thus, although still experimental, we recommend consideration of these newer procedures when patients present with primarily hoarding symptoms.

Some have suggested that OCD patients with severe obsessions and mental rituals ("pure obsessionals") fare less well in treatment than those displaying overt compulsive rituals (Baer, 1994). However, recent developments in the conceptualization of obsessions have led to a highly effective form of CBT for such patients involving exposure to the obsessional thought itself (i.e., via loop tape) and abstinence from neutralizing or mental rituals. Freeston et al. (1997) found that more than 70% of patients evidenced clinically significant improvement in obsessions with this regimen.

Insight

There exists a range of insight into the senselessness of OCD symptoms (Foa et al., 1995). It appears that patients with poor insight about their symptoms improve less with ERP than those who have more insight (Foa, Abramowitz, Franklin, & Kozak, 1999). Perhaps patients with poor insight have difficulty deriving changes from exposure exercises. Alternatively, those with poor insight may be more reluctant to confront obsessional situations during therapy because of their fears. While we recommend a trial of ERP even for patients with poor insight, those who struggle with ERP may benefit from the addition of cognitive techniques (Salkovskis & Warwick, 1985). A second augmentative approach in such cases is pharmacotherapy with SRIs, and some psychiatrists even prescribe antipsychotic medication for such patients.

Comorbidity

Certain comorbid Axis I conditions may impede the effects of CBT for OCD. Major depressive disorder (Abramowitz & Foa, 2000; Abramowitz, Franklin, Kozak, Street, & Foa, 2000; Steketee, Chambless, & Tran, 2001) and generalized anxiety disorder (Steketee et al., 2001) are particularly associated with poorer response to ERP. Perhaps seriously depressed patients become demoralized and experience difficulties in complying with CBT instructions. Strong negative affect may also exacerbate OCD symptoms and limit treatment gains. For generalized anxiety patients, pervasive worry concerning other life issues probably detracts from the time and emotional resources available for learning skills from ERP treatment (Steketee et al., 2001).

Other Axis I conditions likely to interfere with ERP are those with psychotic and manic symptoms, which involve alterations in perception, cognition, and judgment. Active substance abuse or dependence is also an exclusion from CBT. These problems presumably impede patients' ability to follow treatment instructions on their own or attend to the cognitive changes that CBT aims to facilitate. Our recommendation is that patients receive treatment to bring these other conditions under control before attempting CBT for OCD.

Research also suggests that both CBT and medication are negatively affected by severe Axis II psychopathology (e.g., schizotypal personality disorder; De Haan et al., 1997; Steketee et al., 2001). Different personality disorder (PD) clusters may differentially influence the process and outcome of CBT. For example, anxious (e.g., obsessive-compulsive PD) and dramatic (e.g., histrionic PD) traits seem to interfere with developing rapport; however, if a therapeutic relationship can be developed, success is possible. If patients gain reinforcement for their OCD symptoms, CBT is unlikely to succeed because patients do not perceive themselves as achieving rewards for their efforts in therapy. In contrast, patients with personality traits in the odd cluster (e.g., schizotypal PD) present a challenge to CBT because of their reduced ability to consolidate corrective information during exposure or cognitive interventions.

Treatment History

For the most part, patients who have received an adequate length and dosage of one SRI (see March, Frances, Carpenter, & Kahn, 1997, for recommended doses) are unlikely to respond to others or to combinations of SRIs. Thus, for medicated patients who have not tried psychotherapy, CBT is the optimal next choice. If, however, patients report that they have undergone CBT, the adequacy of this therapy course should be assessed before making additional recommendations. If previous ERP was inadequate (i.e., infrequent sessions, lack of adequate exposure or response prevention), another course of CBT involving ERP should be considered. Noncompliance with prior ERP due to extreme fear may necessitate the use of cognitive techniques before initiating exposure. However, a history of noncompliance due to motivational factors may suggest the need for inpatient treatment or a supportive approach. Similarly, for patients who have failed adequate trials of both pharmacotherapy and intensive CBT, we recommend supportive therapy, OCD support groups, or, if symptoms are unremitting and insufferable, psychosurgery.

REFERENCES

Abramowitz, J. S., & Foa, E. (2000). Does comorbid major depressive disorder influence outcome of exposure and response prevention for OCD? *Behavior Therapy, 31*, 795–800.

Abramowitz, J. S., Foa, E. B., & Franklin, M. E. (2003). Exposure and ritual prevention for obsessive-compulsive disorder: Effectiveness of intensive versus twice-weekly treatment sessions. *Journal of Consulting and Clinical Psychology, 71*, 394–398.

Abramowitz, J. S., Franklin, M. E., Kozak, M. J., Street, G. P., & Foa, E. B. (2000). The effects of pretreatment depression on cognitive-behavioral treatment outcome in OCD clinic patients. *Behavior Therapy, 31*, 517–528.

Abramowitz, J. S., Franklin, M. E., Schwartz, S. A., & Furr, J. M. (in press). *Symp-*

tom presentation and outcome of cognitive-behavior therapy for obsessive-compulsive disorder. *Journal of Consulting and Clinical Psychology.*

Abramowitz, J. S., Whiteside, S. P., & Deacon, B. J. (2002). *Treatment of pediatric obsessive-compulsive disorder: A comprehensive meta-analysis of the outcome research.* Manuscript submitted for publication.

Baer, L. (1994). Factor analysis of symptom subtypes of obsessive-compulsive disorder and their relation to personality and tic disorders. *Journal of Clinical Psychiatry, 55,* 18–23.

Calamari, J. E., & Cassiday, K. L. (1999). Treating obsessive-compulsive disorder in older adults: A review of strategies. In M. Duffy (Ed.), *Handbook of counseling and psychotherapy with older adults: A review of strategies* (pp. 526–538). New York: Wiley.

Chambless, D. L., & Steketee, G. (1999). Expressed emotion and behavior therapy outcome: A prospective study with obsessive-compulsive and agoraphobic outpatients. *Journal of Consulting and Clinical Psychology, 67*(5), 658–665.

De Haan, E., van Oppen, P., van Balkom, A., Spinhoven, P., Hoogduin, K., & van Dyck, R. (1997). Prediction of outcome and early vs. late improvement in OCD patients treated with cognitive behavior therapy and pharmacotherapy. *Acta Psychiatrica Scandanavica, 96,* 354–361.

Foa, E. B., Abramowitz, J. S., Franklin, M. F., & Kozak, M. J. (1999). Feared consequences, fixity of belief, and treatment outcome in patients with obsessive-compulsive disorder. *Behavior Therapy, 30,* 717–724.

Foa, E., Kozak, M., Goodman, W., Hollander, E., Jenike, M., & Rasumssen, S. (1995). DSM-IV field trial: Obsessive-compulsive disorder. *American Journal of Psychiatry, 152,* 90–96.

Franklin, M. E., Abramowitz, J. S., Kozak, M. J., Levitt, J., & Foa, E. B. (2000). Effectiveness of exposure and ritual prevention for obsessive compulsive disorder: Randomized compared with non-randomized samples. *Journal of Consulting and Clinical Psychology, 68,* 594–602.

Freeston, M. H., Ladouceur, R., Gagnon, F., Thibodeau, N., Rheaume, J., Letarte, H., et al. (1997). Cognitive-behavioral treatment of obsessive thoughts: A controlled study. *Journal of Consulting and Clinical Psychology, 65,* 405–413.

Fritzler, B. K., Hecker, J. E., & Losee, M. C. (1997). Self-directed treatment with minimal therapist contact: Preliminary findings for obsessive-compulsive disorder. *Behaviour Research and Therapy, 35,* 627–631.

Greist, J. H., Marks, I. M., Baer, L., Kobak, K., Wenzel, K., Hirsch, J., et al. (2002). Behavior therapy for obsessive-compulsive disorder guided by a computer or by a clinician compared with relaxation control. *Journal of Clinical Psychiatry, 63,* 138–145.

Hartl, T., & Frost, R. (1999). Cognitive-behavioral treatment of compulsive hoarding: A multiple baseline experimental case study. *Behaviour Research and Therapy, 37,* 451–461.

Jenike, M. (2000). Neurosurgical treatment of obsessive-compulsive disorder. In W. Goodman, M. Rudorfer, & J. Maser (Eds.), *Obsessive-compulsive disorder* (pp. 457–482). Mahwah, NJ: Lawrence Erlbaum.

March, J., Frances, A., Carpenter, D., & Kahn, D. (1997). The expert consensus guidelines for the treatment of obsessive-compulsive disorder. *Journal of Clinical Psychiatry, 58* (suppl 4), 11–72.

Mataix-Cols, D., Rauch, S., Manzo, P., Jenike, M., & Baer, L. (1999). Use of factor-analyzed symptom subtypes to predict outcome with serotonin reuptake inhibitors and placebo in obsessive-compulsive disorder. *American Journal of Psychiatry, 156,* 1409–1416.

McLean, P. D., Whittal, M. L., Thordarson, D., Taylor, S., Sochting, I., Koch, W. J., et al. (2001). Cognitive versus behavior therapy in the group treatment of obsessive-compulsive disorder. *Journal of Consulting and Clinical Psychology, 69,* 205–214.

Mehta, M. (1990). A comparative study of family-based and patient-based behavioural management in obsessive-compulsive disorder. *British Journal of Psychiatry, 157,* 133–135.

Pato, M. T., Hill, J. L., & Murphy, D. L. (1990). A clomipramine dosage reduction study in the course of long-term treatment for obsessive-compulsive disorder. *Psychopharmacology Bulletin, 26,* 211–214.

Rauch, S., & Jenike, M. (1998). Pharmacological treatment of obsessive-compulsive disorder. In P. Nathan & J. Gorman (Eds.), *Treatments that work* (pp. 358–376). New York: Oxford University Press.

Salkovskis, P., & Warwick, H. (1985) Cognitive therapy of obsessive-compulsive disorder: Treating treatment failures. *Behavioural Psychotherapy, 13,* 243–255.

Saxena, S., Maidment, K. M., Vapnik, T., Golden, G., Rishwain, T., Rosen, R. M., et al. (2002). Obsessive-compulsive hoarding: Symptom severity and response to multimodal treatment. *Journal of Clinical Psychiatry, 63,* 21–27.

Steketee, G. (1993). Social support and treatment outcome of obsessive compulsive disorder at 9-month follow-up. *Behavioural Psychotherapy, 21*(2), 81–95.

Steketee, G., Chambless, D., & Tran, G. (2001). Effects of axis I and II comorbidity on behavior therapy outcome for obsessive-compulsive disorder and agoraphobia. *Comprehensive Psychiatry, 42,* 76–86.

Steketee, G., & White, K. (1990). *When once is not enough.* Oakland, CA: New Harbinger.

Van den Hout, M., Emmelkamp, P., Kraaykamp, H., & Grietz, E. (1988). Behavioral treatment of obsessive-compulsives: Inpatient vs outpatient. *Behaviour Research and Therapy, 26,* 331–332.

Williams, K. E., Chambless, D. L., & Steketee, G. (1998). Behavioral treatment of obsessive-compulsive disorder in African Americans: Clinical issues. *Journal of Behavior Therapy and Experimental Psychiatry, 29,* 163–170.

20

The Implications of Controlled Outcome Studies on Planned Short-Term Psychotherapy With Depressive Disorders

BERNARD L. BLOOM

KENNETH R. YEAGER

ALBERT R. ROBERTS

Depressive disorders are the major component of what are referred to in the *DSM-IV-TR* (American Psychiatric Association, 2000; see also Mays & Croake, 1997a, Chapter 4; Morrison, 1995) as mood disorders—periods of time when patients feel abnormally and pathologically happy or sad. The term *depressive disorder* is reserved to describe a person who has had multiple depressive episodes, periods of time of 2 weeks or longer when they feel depressed, cannot enjoy life, and have problems with eating and sleeping, guilt feelings, loss of energy, trouble concentrating, and thoughts about death. Most depressive disorders are recurrent and lifelong.

Depressive disorders are divided into three major subcategories: major depressive disorders, which tend to be relatively severe but relatively short in episode duration (although there is some growing belief that these disorders may also be chronic in nature); dysthymic disorders, which are less severe but chronic; and depressive disorders not otherwise specified, in which symptoms of depression are present but do not meet the criteria for depressive diagnoses or for any other diagnosis in which depression is a major feature.

Symptoms of depression are often found as a direct biological consequence of substance abuse or of a variety of medical conditions or medications, and they can accompany other psychiatric disorders such as schizophrenia, eating disorders, anxiety disorders, panic disorders, or gender identity disorders. In these cases, the depression is thought of as secondary in importance.

The term *adjustment disorder* is usually applied when some stressor (such as illness, normal aging, chronic marital tension, or occupational difficulties) can be identified that appears to serve as a psychological rather than biological precipitant of depressive symptoms. This type of depression was formerly called *reactive depression* (Goodwin & Guze, 1996, pp. 8–10; see also Hudson-Allez, 1997, p. 53; Kasl-Godley, Gatz, & Fiske, 1998).

It has been estimated that as many as 8 million individuals in the United States are afflicted with a major depressive illness in a given year and that the lifetime probability of developing a major depressive disorder may be as high as 25% for women and about half that for men (Biggs & Rush, 1999). The economic burden of depression in the United States alone exceeds $40 billion per year (Biggs & Rush, 1999). Depressive conditions are "common, costly, disabling, typically recurrent, and not infrequently chronic" (Biggs & Rush, 1999, p. 125).

A large literature—larger than for any other single diagnostic category—examines the effectiveness of brief episodes of psychotherapy in their treatment (see, for example, Bemporad & Vasile, 1999; Freeman & Oster, 1999; Mays & Croake, 1997a, 1997b; Swartz, 1999). This chapter reviews controlled outcome studies of brief psychotherapy in the treatment of depression that have been published since 1990. Readers might find it useful to read the papers that have described the results of the National Institute of Mental Health Treatment of Depression Collaborative Research Program (Elkin, Parloff, Hadley, & Autry, 1985; Elkin et al., 1989) and the National Institute of Health Consensus Development Conference on the Diagnosis and Treatment of Depression in Late Life (Schneider, Reynolds, Lebowitz, & Friedhoff, 1994).

In addition, the practice guidelines for the treatment of depressive disorders promulgated by the American Psychiatric Association (American Psychiatric Association, 1993) and the Depression Guideline Panel of the Agency for Health Care Policy and Research (Depression Guideline Panel, 1993), along with their associated commentaries (Blatt, 1995; Blatt, Quinlan, Pilkonis, & Shea, 1995; Lazar, 1997; Persons, Thase, & Crits-Christoph, 1996; Schneider & Olin, 1995; Schulberg et al., 1996; Scogin & McElreath, 1994; Scott, Tacchi, Jones, & Scott, 1997; Zeiss & Breckenridge, 1997), should be examined. Underlying these commentaries is a persistent controversy regarding the relative merits of psychological as opposed to biological approaches to the treatment of depressive disorders (Biggs & Rush, 1999; Feinberg, 1999; Markowitz, 1999).

EVIDENCE-BASED PRACTICE FOR DEPRESSION

Increasingly, practitioners are challenged to justify and improve treatment processes for those presenting with resistant and chronic mental illness. At the same time, practitioners are inundated with a flurry of information surrounding treatment approaches and new medication developments. Application of evidence-based practice can provide decision support based in current practice and outcome research. Eight questions that have been asked and answers from the current literature follow.

1. Is brief psychological treatment, regardless of type (social support, cognitive or behavioral treatment, or psychodynamic treatment), consistently superior to no-treatment or usual-care control conditions in its clinical effectiveness?
2. What happens to the client rate of improvement when treatment is time-limited?
3. Is cognitive and behavioral psychotherapy helpful in the brief treatment of depression?
4. Of all the orientations to psychodynamic psychotherapy, which is the most helpful?
5. Is the outcome of drug treatment for depression enhanced by the addition of brief psychotherapy to the treatment program?
6. Is long-term treatment superior to brief treatment in the case of some particularly severe depressions when outcome is assessed at the termination of treatment?
7. Is there is evidence that patients who do not improve significantly in brief psychotherapy respond better to longer-term treatment?
8. What is the best and most consistent predictor of outcome of psychotherapy for depression?

CONTROLLED PSYCHOTHERAPY OUTCOME STUDIES

Controlled outcome studies involve the collection of outcome data in at least two groups who differ with respect to some salient characteristics upon entry into the study. The groups may differ by demographic characteristics, diagnosis, severity of disorder, type of treatment, or duration of treatment. The important aspect of controlled outcome studies is that groups of clients who differ in some important way can be contrasted. Controlled outcome studies permit the investigator to examine whether outcome is meaningfully related to specific characteristics of the therapist, the therapy, or the client, and they are thus more informative than uncontrolled outcome studies that simply report on degree of change in a single group of treated clients.

DEPRESSIVE DISORDERS

Shapiro et al. (1994) examined the extent to which initial severity of depression, treatment approach (cognitive-behavioral or psychodynamic-interpersonal psychotherapy), and duration of treatment (8 or 16 sessions) affected treatment outcome in a study of 117 depressed clients whose degree of change was assessed at intake, at the end of treatment, and at 3-month and 12-month follow-ups. Virtually all clients made substantial overall gains that were maintained at follow-up assessments. The cognitive-behavioral and psychodynamic-interpersonal therapies yielded generally equivalent results. Clients with relatively severe depressions who participated in the longer treatment seemed to do better at the end of treatment and at the 3-month follow-up than those in the shorter treatment group, and clients assigned to psychodynamic-interpersonal treatment seemed to be doing better at the 12-month follow-up than clients assigned to cognitive-behavioral treatment.

In a subsequent replication of this study with 36 clients in more varied settings, Barkham, Rees, Shapiro, et al. (1996) found that results were in general about the same as in the first study, but the overall findings were somewhat attenuated. While initial gains were impressive, clients generally failed to maintain their gains. Cognitive-behavioral treatment and psychodynamic-interpersonal treatment yielded equivalent results. Longer therapy duration resulted in generally greater improvement at the end of therapy, but the differences at the follow-up assessments were considerably diminished in comparison with the original study. There were no significant treatment type by treatment duration by initial severity interaction effects.

In a further study of dose—effect relations in time-limited psychotherapy for depression, Barkham, Rees, Stiles, et al. (1996) contrasted outcome in 212 depressed clients randomly assigned to either 8 or 16 sessions of time-limited treatment in order to determine whether (a) there is a negatively accelerated dose—effect curve and (b) there is a differential response rate for acute, chronic, and characterological or interpersonal components of depression. Improvement was found to be negatively accelerated, with change occurring more rapidly earlier in treatment and when tighter time limits were imposed, and certain symptoms were relieved more quickly than others. Changes in remoralization (subjectively experienced well-being) occurred first, followed by remediation (reductions in symptomatology), and finally rehabilitation (enhanced life functioning)—a finding also reported by Howard, Lueger, Maling, and Martinovich (1993).

More recently, Barkham, Shapiro, Hardy, and Rees (1999) evaluated their three-session model of brief psychotherapy for depression (two sessions 1 week apart, followed by a third session 3 months later) in a sample of 116 mildly depressed adults stratified by severity of depression, type of treatment (cognitive-behavioral or psychodynamic-interpersonal), and presence or absence of a 1-month delay before inaugurating treatment. Outcome assessments took place shortly after the conclusion of the final treatment session and again about 8 months later.

Virtually all patients made significant gains between the beginning and end of treatment and final follow-up. Effects of treatment delay were short-lived, with the delay group catching up quickly. Differences in treatment modality were small and insignificant whenever assessed. There was some evidence that time alone was most helpful to the least depressed and that the third session was most helpful to the most depressed in this group.

Because panic disorders have a high relapse rate if treated by drugs alone, Wiborg and Dahl (1996) sought to determine whether adding brief dynamic psychotherapy to the drug treatment would reduce the relapse rate in panic disorder patients as compared with those treated by drugs alone. Two treatment groups of 20 patients each were formed, with one randomly selected group assigned to 9 months of drug treatment and the other assigned to the same drug treatment regimen plus 15 weekly sessions of brief dynamic psychotherapy. Anxiety and depression were assessed at intake and at 6, 12, and 18 months after beginning treatment. All patients in both groups became free of panic attacks within 26 weeks of the start of treatment. Addition of brief dynamic psychotherapy to treatment with clomipramine significantly reduced the relapse rate of panic disorders compared with the group receiving clomipramine treatment alone. Between the end of medication treatment and the 18-month follow-up, the relapse rate was 20% in the drug and psychotherapy group and 75% in the drug treatment alone group.

PROBLEM-SOLVING TREATMENT

Mynors-Wallis (1996) described and evaluated problem-solving treatment, a brief cognitive-behavioral psychotherapy for patients with mild to moderate mental disorders, particularly involving depression, in primary care. Problem-solving treatment involved three steps: (a) Symptoms were linked with their problems, (b) problems were defined and clarified, and (c) attempts were made to solve the problems in a structured way. The treatment program was conceptualized as passing through seven stages: (a) explanation of the treatment and its rationale, (b) clarification and definition of the problems, (c) choice of achievable goals, (d) generation of alternative solutions, (e) selection of a preferred solution, (f) clarification of the necessary steps to implement the solution, and (g) evaluation of progress.

After 4 weeks of treatment with explanation, reassurance, and advice, a total of 47 patients who had high scores (12 or more) on the Present State Examination were randomly assigned to three sessions of problem-solving treatment or usual care. After 7 weeks, both groups had improved significantly, but the reduction in scores was significantly greater for the problem-solving group than for the control group. At 28 weeks, the problem-solving treatment group showed nonsignificant further improvement.

In a second study, problem-solving treatment was used to treat major depression and contrasted with patients receiving antidepressant medication and standard clinical management and a third group receiving drug placebo with standard clinical management. Each treatment was given in six sessions over 12 weeks, with the first session lasting 60 minutes and all others lasting 30 minutes. With about 30 patients in each group, problem-solving treatment was found to be significantly more effective than placebo but not significantly different from amitriptyline both at 6 weeks and at 12 weeks. Average total duration of treatment was about 3 hours. Problem-solving treatment was judged to be as effective as amitriptyline and more effective than placebo, feasible in practice, and acceptable to patients.

A final study examined effectiveness of problem-solving treatment administered by community nurses. Six nurses were recruited and trained. Problem-solving treatment was found to reduce sickness-related days off work, but otherwise the outcomes were the same as those obtained by usual primary care treatment. When indirect costs were included, problem-solving treatment was found to produce significant savings. More recent studies reported by this research group—contrasting problem-solving treatment in primary care with and without accompanying use of antidepressants—demonstrate substantial improvement in all groups, with no advantage attributable to the addition of antidepressant medication to the treatment program (Hegel, Barrett, & Oxman, 2000; Mynors-Wallis, Gath, Day, & Baker, 2000).

Rudd et al. (1996) evaluated an intensive, structured, time-limited outpatient group format for the treatment of suicidal patients based on a problem-solving and social competence paradigm targeting fundamental skill development and improved social and adaptive randomized functioning and coping. These authors contrasted 143 patients randomly assigned to the treatment group and 121 patients randomly assigned to a treatment-as-usual control group. All patients were in the military, and most patients were white men. Follow-up assessments were done at 1, 6, 12, 18, and 24 months posttreatment with a variety of measures: suicidal ideation, life stress, negative expectations, depression, problem-solving behavior and attitudes, personality, symptomatology, diagnoses, intellectual functioning, and psychosocial history. Treatment took place in a day hospital format for 9 hours per day for 2 weeks, and it included three components: a traditional experiential-affective group, psychoeducational classes, and an extended problem-solving group. Treatment and control participants exhibited significant improvement across all outcome measures throughout the follow-up period.

Improvement was generally rapid at first, after which it tapered off. The experimental treatment was more effective than treatment as usual at retaining the highest risk participants. Nonsignificant superiority in clinical improvement was found for the experimental group: 64% versus 48%.

In a study conducted in the United Kingdom, Friedli, King, Lloyd, and Horder (1997) contrasted self-reported outcome and level of satisfaction in a sample of 136 depressed patients randomly assigned to either routine general practice care or to routine care plus between 1 and 12 sessions of nondirective Rogerian psychotherapy provided over a 12-week time period. The mean number of sessions per patient was 7.7.

Follow-up data were collected 3 and 9 months after inauguration of treatment. While patients assigned to the psychotherapy group were more satisfied with the help they received than those assigned to the general practitioner, there were no significant differences in judged outcome, with all patients improving significantly over time.

Weisz, Thurber, Sweeney, Proffitt, and LaGagnoux (1997) reported on the development of an eight-session, small-group, cognitive-behavioral therapeutic intervention program designed to enhance primary control (changing objective conditions to fit one's wishes) and secondary control (changing oneself to buffer the impact of objective conditions) among mildly to moderately depressed elementary school children and contrasted the results of their program with those found in an untreated control group. Scores on measures of childhood depression decreased significantly in both the treated and untreated groups, with score reductions among the treated children significantly greater (averaging two to three times greater) than among the untreated children, both immediately posttreatment and at a 9-month follow-up.

Blatt, Zuroff, Bondi, and Sanislow (2000) have examined previously unanalyzed data from the Treatment for Depression Collaborative Research Program (see Elkin et al., 1985) to determine whether any additional differences in outcome could be found other than symptom reduction. This study contrasted depressed patients who had been assigned to four treatment groups: antidepressant medication (imipramine), cognitive-behavioral therapy, interpersonal therapy, and placebo. While previous studies showed superior symptom reduction at the 8-week mid-treatment assessment for the group receiving imipramine, no significant differences in symptom reduction were found at termination or at the 18-month follow-up. Blatt et al. (2000) found, however, that significant treatment differences emerged at the time of the 18-month follow-up in patients' ratings of the effects of treatment on their life adjustment. Patients in the interpersonal therapy group reported significantly greater satisfaction with treatment at the 18-month follow-up than any of the other groups, and patients in both the interpersonal therapy and cognitive-behavioral therapy groups reported significantly greater effects of the treatment on their capacity to establish and maintain interpersonal relationships and to recognize and understand sources of their depression than did patients in either the placebo or imipramine groups.

These recent controlled outcome studies, all fairly well designed, suggest that depressive symptoms are responsive to most brief psychotherapy treatment approaches. Both cognitive-behavioral and interpersonal-psychodynamic approaches to brief psychotherapy appear to be as effective as pharmacological treatment, particularly in the case of mild to moderate depression. In addition, brief psychotherapy often has a significant additive effect when used in conjunction with psychotropic drugs.

DEPRESSIVE ADJUSTMENT DISORDERS

A number of controlled outcome studies have been reported in which depressions associated with a variety of identifiable stress-inducing precipitating events were treated. These events range from life-threatening illnesses to family caregiving, earthquakes, HIV infection, miscarriage, and infertility. A particularly interesting background paper in this area is that of Cohen, Stokhof, van der Ploeg, and Visser (1996) that describes a brief scale useful in identifying patients recovering from acute myocardial infarctions who require and would accept psychological care.

Fawzy et al. (1990; see also Spiegel, 1999) developed and evaluated a structured 6-week psychiatric intervention for cancer patients that included health education, enhancement of problem-solving skills, stress management, and psychological support. A group of postsurgical patients with malignant melanomas were randomly divided into an experimental sample of 38 patients and 28 controls. By the end of the intervention, patients in the experimental group exhibited higher vigor and greater use of active-behavioral coping. Differences were more pronounced at the 6-month follow-up, at which time the intervention group showed significantly lower depression, fatigue, confusion, and total mood disturbance, as well as higher vigor and more active-behavioral and active-cognitive coping, than did the controls. In general, the intervention program reduced psychological distress and enhanced longer-term effective coping.

Stewart et al. (1992) provided eight 2-hour weekly support group sessions to 64 infertility patients (usually couples) and evaluated their effectiveness by contrasting results with 35 similar patients not offered the support group. Patients in the support group had significantly greater entry than exit scores on several measures of psychological distress and depression. Patients in the comparison group had similar scores at the start of the program but showed no change over 8 weeks. Support groups were found to be highly acceptable and effective.

Greer et al. (1992) examined the effectiveness of adjuvant psychological therapy for patients with cancer. An 8-week course of weekly cognitive-behavioral psychotherapy that was problem focused and designed for individual cancer patients produced significant improvement in various measures of psychological distress at the conclusion of therapy and at 4 months when contrasted with a randomly selected no-psychotherapy control group. Patients receiving adjuvant psychological therapy showed significantly greater improvement than control patients—less anxiety, helplessness, fatalism, and anxious preoccupation with cancer; less depression; and a more positive adjustment toward their disease and its treatment. At 4 months, significant improvement persisted, and treated patients experienced significantly less anxiety and psychological distress than did the untreated controls.

Kelly et al. (1993) evaluated the effects of brief cognitive-behavioral or social support group therapy with depressed HIV-infected patients. A total of 68 patients were randomly divided into three groups: eight-session cognitive-behavioral groups, eight-session support groups, or a usual-care comparison condition. Group sessions lasted 90 minutes per meeting and included two coleaders. Considerable data were collected before the start of the programs, and patients were studied at the conclusion of the experimental program and at a 3-month follow-up. Both interventions produced reductions in depression, hostility, and somatization when compared with the usual-care group. Social support intervention produced reductions in overall psychiatric symptoms and tended to reduce maladaptive interpersonal sensitivity and anxiety, as well as frequency of unprotected receptive anal intercourse. While the cognitive-behavioral intervention resulted in less frequent illicit drug use during the follow-up period, the social support intervention produced greater evidence of clinically significant change. Thus, the two forms of therapy resulted in both shared and unique improvements in functioning (see also McDermut, Miller, & Brown, 2001).

Gallagher-Thompson and Steffen (1994) randomly assigned 66 clinically depressed family caregivers of frail elderly relatives to 16 to 20 sessions of either cognitive-behavioral or brief psychodynamic individual psychotherapy. Treatment was conducted twice per week for the first 4 weeks and then once per week thereafter. In cognitive-behavioral therapy, caregivers were taught to challenge their dysfunctional thoughts and to develop more adaptive ways to view problematic situations. They were also taught behavioral strategies to enhance mood. Brief psychodynamic therapy was based on the theory that caregivers' past conflicts over dependence and independence were reactivated by the caregiving situation. Therapy focused on understanding past losses and conflicts in separation and individuation.

Assessments were conducted at entry into treatment, 10 weeks later, at the end of treatment, and at 3 months and 12 months after completing treatment. At posttreatment, 71% of the caregivers were no longer clinically depressed, with no differences found between the two treatments. Clients who had been caregivers for shorter periods of time showed greater improvement in the brief psychodynamic condition, while those who had been caregivers for at least 44 months improved most with cognitive-behavioral therapies (see also Niederehe, 1994, pp. 305ff.; Steffen, Futterman, & Gallagher-Thompson, 1998).

Evans and Connis (1995) studied a group of 72 depressed patients undergoing radiation treatment for cancer who were divided into three groups: cognitive-behavioral group treatment, social support, or no-treatment control. Treatments averaged about eight sessions in duration. The cognitive-behavioral groups focused on the use of cognitive and behavioral strategies to reduce maladaptive anxiety and depression. The social support groups encouraged members to describe their feelings about having cancer, to identify and discuss shared problems, and to adopt supportive roles toward others in the group. Patients were assessed with a variety of measures of symptom distress at the beginning and end of treatment and at a 6-month follow-up. Relative to the comparison group, both the cognitive-behavioral and the social support therapies resulted in less depression, hostility, and somatization. The social support intervention resulted in fewer psychiatric symptoms and less maladaptive interpersonal sensitivity and anxiety, and it had longer effectiveness than did the cognitive-behavioral treatment group.

Lee, Slade, and Lygo (1996) tested the effectiveness of a 1-hour psychologically oriented debriefing provided in the home by a female psychologist 2 weeks after a miscarriage by contrasting two groups of women: those who received the debriefing and those who did not (total $N = 39$). Levels of anxiety and depression were assessed 1 week and 4 months after miscarriage. While women exhibited considerable anxiety and depression following the miscarriage and exhibited reduction in anxiety and depression as time went on, the debriefing program did not significantly influence emotional adaptation.

Noting that palliative care (treatment designed to reduce pain and discomfort without curing the underlying condition) involves relief of emotional symptoms as well as control of physical symptoms, Wood and Mynors-Wallis (1997; see also Mynors-Wallis, 1996) contrasted outcomes in two groups of dying patients undergoing hospice home care: patients receiving traditional hospice care and those who also were provided with three to five sessions of problem-solving treatment. This latter form of treatment was designed to help patients formulate ways of dealing with emotional and psychosocial symptoms induced by their illnesses by helping patients clarify and define the problem, set achievable goals, consider alternative solutions, select a preferred solution, implement the solution, and evaluate progress.

In a small, randomized, controlled clinical trial, the authors reported that the few patients in the problem-solving treatment group found the treatment to be acceptable and helpful. These authors hope to undertake a larger study to determine more definitively the efficacy of problem-solving treatment.

Goenjian et al. (1997) contrasted brief psychotherapy focused on trauma and grief among early adolescents exposed to the 1988 earthquake in Armenia with untreated groups on posttraumatic stress and depressive reactions. The intervention program included classroom group psychotherapy and an average of two 1-hour individual sessions (maximum of four sessions), which were conducted over a 3-week period. All treatment began 18 months after the earthquake and was completed within a 6-week period. Data collected pretreatment, posttreatment, and 3 years after the earthquake revealed that severity of symptoms decreased in the treated group and increased in the untreated group. Symptoms of posttraumatic stress disorder decreased following treatment, while depressive symptoms increased in the untreated group and remained stable in the treated group.

With the single exception of the 1-hour debriefing session provided to women who had suffered a miscarriage 2 weeks earlier, these recent studies, also quite well designed, provide consistent support for the effectiveness of brief psychotherapeutic approaches in the treatment of stress-induced depression.

DEPRESSION AMONG THE ELDERLY

The category of geriatric depression occupies some middle ground between depressive disorders of unknown origin and depressive adjustment disorders that are reactions to some identifiable psychological precipitating event. The extent to which depression can be precipitated as a psychological reaction to normal aging versus its development as a component of the physiology of the aging process is a complex question, but what is clear from the literature is that brief psychotherapeutic approaches have commonly been used in the treatment of such depressions (Coon, Rider, Gallagher-Thompson, & Thompson, 1999; Gatz et al., 1998; Nordhus, Nielsen, & Kvale, 1998).

Useful background papers have been prepared by Sadavoy and Thompson. Sadavoy (1994) contrasted three approaches to treating depression in the elderly—brief psychodynamic, interpersonal, and cognitive-behavioral therapies—and discussed the strengths of each approach. Suggesting that age, per se, is not an impediment to change and may in fact be an important asset in motivating the patient to overcome resistance and work more quickly, Sadavoy outlined an integrated treatment strategy that can help in the tasks of assessment, diagnosis, and selection of treatment modality.

Thompson (1996) provided a clinical description of cognitive and behavioral techniques used in treating elderly depressed patients. These techniques provide the older patient with a broad range of skills to use in coping with stressful life events once the therapy is completed. Thompson described and contrasted cognitive and behavioral theory and described techniques that have been used for the past decade. The paper also described the typical cognitive and behavioral therapy session, as well as the phases of cognitive and behavioral therapy, and discussed special considerations to keep in mind when working with elderly clients.

Niederehe (1994) has provided a very useful review of controlled outcome studies published between 1974 and 1990 in which depressed elderly patients were treated, objective outcome assessments were undertaken, and some comparison or control group was used for comparative analysis. Psychodynamic therapies (examined in six studies) were found to be clinically efficacious in reducing symptoms in elderly depressed patients. Effectiveness of psychodynamic therapy was found to be equivalent to cognitive-behavioral therapies, both in acute phases and in terms of its longer-term impact, with follow-up data available for as long as 2 years.

In a related review, Scogin and McElreath (1994) examined the efficacy of psychosocial treatments of geriatric depression in 17 studies published between 1975 and 1990. In each of these studies, the psychosocial treatments were contrasted with either a no-treatment comparison group or some other psychosocial treatment. Treatments were reliably more effective than no treatment, and effect sizes were significant for both major and less severe levels of depression. The psychosocial treatments averaged 12 sessions in duration. While the type of treatment could not be evaluated because there were too few studies of any specific treatment approach, psychosocial interventions for older adults experiencing depressive symptoms were found to be quite effective and about as successful as pharmacotherapy.

Another useful review of the literature on acute treatment efficacy for geriatric depression was prepared by Schneider and Olin (1995). Their review was based on 30 placebo-controlled clinical trials published between 1982 and 1994 with randomized depressed patients who were not suicidal, not severely ill, and without significant medical illness. Psychotherapy was found to be more effective than waitlist controls, no treatment, or pill-placebo and equivalent to antidepressant medications in geriatric outpatient populations with both major and minor depression. About half of the studies involved group interventions. Therapy orientations were cognitive, interpersonal, reminiscent, psychodynamic, and eclectic.

As for recent controlled outcome studies, Gallagher-Thompson, Hanley-Peterson, and Thompson (1990) contrasted three approaches to psychotherapy with a sample of 91 older adults with a mean age of 67 years initially diagnosed as cases of major depressive disorder. Patients were randomly assigned to 16 to

20 sessions over a 4-month period of either cognitive, behavioral, or psychodynamic psychotherapy and were followed for 2 years. Improvement increased with time, and treatment gains were maintained by the majority of patients. There were no significant differences in response by therapy modality.

Mossey, Knott, Higgins, and Talerico (1996) contrasted the effectiveness of 6 to 8 sessions of interpersonal counseling (IPC) versus usual care (UC) for a sample of 76 randomized subdysthymic patients age at least 60 who did not meet *DSM-III-R* criteria for major depression or dysthymia. Data from the initial assessment as well as from the 3-month and 6-month follow-ups are presented. Geriatric Depression Scale (GDS) scores, health ratings, and measures of physical and social functioning were collected at each data collection point. At 3 months, IPC group members showed nonsignificantly greater improvement than UC group members on all outcome variables. At 6 months, significant differences in the rate of improvement in GDS scores and on self-rated health measures were observed for IPC compared with UC members. The self-rated health of the IPC group members improved, while it deteriorated in the UC group.

Empirical studies evaluating treatment outcome with elderly depressed patients consistently demonstrate the effectiveness of brief psychotherapy. All psychotherapeutic treatment approaches examined in these studies appear to have equal effectiveness and to be as effective as pharmacological approaches and significantly more effective than usual-care control-group treatment.

CONCLUDING COMMENTS

This review of controlled outcome studies of planned short-term psychotherapy in the treatment of depression published since 1990 suggests that:

1. Brief psychological treatment, regardless of type (social support, cognitive or behavioral treatment, or psychodynamic treatment), is consistently superior to no-treatment or usual-care control conditions in its clinical effectiveness.
2. Rate of improvement is negatively accelerated; that is, improvement is more rapid early in treatment than later in treatment and appears to be greater when time is more stringently limited.
3. Cognitive and behavioral psychotherapy has been found to be consistently helpful in the brief treatment of depression. Of all the orientations to psychodynamic psychotherapy, the most helpful has been interpersonal psychotherapy (Bloom, 1997, pp. 100ff.; Hinrichsen, 1997, 1999; Klerman, Weissman, Rounsaville, & Chevron, 1984). These conclusions are similar to those found in the review of controlled outcome studies conducted during and before the 1980s. Marks (1999) has called attention to the fact that these two helpful approaches have both been shown to be valuable in the treatment of depressive disorders, but it is not clear whether similarities in these two approaches account for the similarities in results or whether different but equally effective treatment pathways account for the similarities of results.

4. Outcome of drug treatment for depression is generally enhanced by the addition of brief psychotherapy to the treatment program.

5. Long-term treatment has occasionally been found to be superior to brief treatment in the case of some particularly severe depressions when outcome is assessed at the termination of treatment, but that superiority is often no longer in evidence at the time of follow-up assessments.

6. Relapse rate is high among depressed patients treated by brief psychotherapy. There is evidence that some patients who do not improve significantly in brief psychotherapy do improve with longer-term treatment and that relapse rate can be reduced by providing maintenance treatment.

7. The best and most consistent predictor of outcome of psychotherapy for depression is the level of severity of depression at the start of treatment. The most severely disturbed patients at the start of treatment tend to be the most severely disturbed at the end of treatment (Luborsky et al., 1996; Shea, Elkin, & Sotsky, 1999).

Given that degree of improvement is negatively accelerated in psychotherapy and that maintenance treatment seems to be helpful in reducing relapse rate, there is continuing reason to believe that patients should be encouraged to enter or reenter psychotherapy when needed while episodes of psychotherapy are kept as short as possible. More generally, as Jarrett and Rush have suggested, "the challenge is to determine how to best use the psychotherapies that appear to reduce depressive symptoms, when to use pharmacotherapy alone or in combination with psychotherapy, and how to innovate or adapt psychosocial interventions to reduce the human suffering, as well as the economic cost, of depressive disorders" (1994, p. 128).

REFERENCES

American Psychiatric Association. (1993). Practice guideline for major depressive disorder in adults. *American Journal of Psychiatry, 150* (Suppl. 4), 1–26

American Psychiatric Association. (1994). *Diagnostic and statistical manual of mental disorders* (4th ed.). Washington, DC: Author.

American Psychiatric Association. (2000). *Diagnostic and statistical manual of mental disorders* (4th ed., text revision). Washington, DC: Author.

Barkham, M., Rees, A., Shapiro, D. A., Stiles, W. B., Agnew, R. M., Halstead, J., et al. (1996). Outcomes of time-limited psychotherapy in applied settings: Replicating the second Sheffield Psychotherapy Project. *Journal of Consulting and Clinical Psychology, 64,* 1079–1085.

Barkham, M., Rees, A., Stiles, W. B., Shapiro, D. A., Hardy, G. E., & Reynolds, S. (1996). Dose-effect relations in time-limited psychotherapy for depression. *Journal of Consulting and Clinical Psychology, 64,* 927–935.

Barkham, M., Shapiro, D. A., Hardy, G. E., & Rees, A. (1999). Psychotherapy in two-plus-one sessions: Outcomes of a randomized controlled trial of cognitive-behavioral and psychodynamic-interpersonal therapy for subsyndromal depression. *Journal of Consulting and Clinical Psychology, 67,* 201–211.

Bemporad, J. R., & Vasile, R. G. (1999). Dynamic psychotherapy. In M. Hersen & A. S. Bellack (Eds.), *Handbook of comparative interventions for adult disorders* (2nd ed., pp. 91–107). New York: Wiley.

Biggs, M. M., & Rush, A. J. (1999). Cognitive and behavioral therapies alone or combined with antidepressant medication in the treatment of depression. In D. S. Janowsky (Ed.), *Psychotherapy indications and outcomes* (pp. 121–171). Washington, DC: American Psychiatric Press.

Blatt, S. J. (1995). The destructiveness of perfectionism: Implications for the treatment of depression. *American Psychologist, 50,* 1003–1020.

Blatt, S. J., Quinlan, D. M., Pilkonis, P. A., & Shea, M. T. (1995). Impact of perfectionism and need for approval on the brief treatment of depression: The National Institute of Mental Health Treatment of Depression Collaborative Research Program revisited. *Journal of Consulting and Clinical Psychology, 63,* 125–132.

Blatt, S., Zuroff, D. C., Bondi, C. M., & Sanislow, C. A. (2000). Short- and long-term effects of medication and psychotherapy in the brief treatment of depression: Further analyses of data from the NIMH TDCRP. *Psychotherapy Research, 10,* 215–234.

Bloom, B. L. (1997). *Planned short-term psychotherapy: A clinical handbook* (2nd ed.). Boston: Allyn & Bacon.

Cohen, L., Stokhof, L. H., van der Ploeg, H. M., & Visser, F. C. (1996). Identifying patients recovering from a recent myocardial infarction who require and accept psychological care. *Psychological Reports, 79,* 1371–1377.

Coon, D. W., Rider, K., Gallagher-Thompson, D., & Thompson, L. (1999). Cognitive-behavioral therapy for the treatment of late-life distress. In M. Duffy (Ed.), *Handbook of counseling and psychotherapy with older adults* (pp. 487–510). New York: Wiley.

Depression Guideline Panel. (1993). *Clinical practice guideline No. 5: Depression in primary care, 2: Treatment of major depression* (USDHHS Publication No. AHCPR 93-0551). Rockville, MD: Agency for Health Care Policy and Research.

Elkin, I., Parloff, M., Hadley, S., & Autry, J. (1985). NIMH Treatment of Depression Collaborative Research Program: Background and Research Plan. *Archives of General Psychiatry, 42,* 305–316.

Evans, R. L., & Connis, R. T. (1995). Comparison of brief group therapies for depressed cancer patients receiving radiation treatment. *Public Health Reports, 110,* 306–311.

Fawzy, F. I., Cousins, N., Fawzy, N. W., Kemeny, M. E., Elashoff, R., & Morton, D. (1990). A structured psychiatric intervention for cancer patients: I. Changes over time in methods of coping and affective disturbance. *Archives of General Psychiatry, 47,* 720–725.

Feinberg, M. (1999). Pharmacotherapy. In M. Hersen & A. S. Bellack (Eds.), *Handbook of comparative interventions for adult disorders* (2nd ed., pp. 156–177). New York: Wiley.

Freeman, A., & Oster, C. (1999). Cognitive behavior therapy. In M. Hersen & A. S. Bellack (Eds.), *Handbook of comparative interventions for adult disorders* (2nd ed., pp. 108–138). New York: Wiley.

Friedli, K., King, M. B., Lloyd, M., & Horder, J. (1997). Randomised controlled assessment of non-directive psychotherapy versus routine general practitioner care. *Lancet, 350* (9092), 1662–1665.

Gallagher-Thompson, D., Hanley-Peterson, P., & Thompson, L. W. (1990). Maintenance of gains versus relapse following brief psychotherapy for depression. *Journal of Consulting and Clinical Psychology, 58,* 371–374.

Gallagher-Thompson, D., & Steffen, A. M. (1994). Comparative effects of cognitive-behavioral and brief psychodynamic psychotherapies for depressed family caregivers. *Journal of Consulting and Clinical Psychology, 62,* 543–549.

Gatz, M., Fiske, A., Fox, L. S., Kaskie, B., Kasl-Godley, J. E., & McCallum, T. J. (1998). Empirically validated psychological treatments for older adults. *Journal of Mental Health & Aging, 4,* 9–46.

Goenjian, A. K., Karayan, I., Pynoos, R. S., Minassian, D., Najarian, L. M., Steinberg, A. M., et al. (1997). Outcome of psychotherapy among early adolescents after trauma. *American Journal of Psychiatry, 154,* 536–542.

Goodwin, D. W., & Guze, S. B. (1996). *Psychiatric diagnosis* (5th ed.) New York: Oxford University Press.

Greer, S., Moorey, S., Baruch, J. D. R., Watson, M., Robertson, B. M., Mason, A., et al. (1992). Adjuvant psychological therapy for patients with cancer: A prospective randomised trial. *British Medical Journal, 304,* 675–680.

Hegel, M. T., Barrett, J. E., & Oxman, T. E. (2000). Training therapists in problem-solving treatment of depressive disorders in primary care: Lessons learned from the "Treatment Effectiveness Project." *Families, Systems, & Health, 18,* 423–435.

Hinrichsen, G. A. (1997). Interpersonal psychotherapy for depressed older adults. *Journal of Geriatric Psychiatry, 30,* 239–257.

Hinrichsen, G. A. (1999). Treating older adults with interpersonal psychotherapy for depression. *Journal of Clinical Psychology, 55,* 949–960.

Howard, K. I., Lueger, R. J., Maling, M. S., & Martinovich, Z. (1993). A phase model of psychotherapy outcome: Causal mediation of change. *Journal of Consulting and Clinical Psychology, 61,* 678–685.

Hudson-Allez, G. (1997). *Time-limited therapy in a general practice setting: How to help within six sessions.* London: Sage.

Jarrett, R. B., & Rush, A. J. (1994). Short-term psychotherapy of depressive disorders: Current status and future directions. *Psychiatry, 57,* 115–132.

Kasl-Godley, J. E., Gatz, M., & Fiske, A. (1998). Depression and depressive symptoms in old age. In I. H. Nordhus, G. R. VandenBos, S. Berg, & P. Fromholt (Eds.), *Clinical geropsychology* (pp. 211–217). Washington, DC: American Psychological Association.

Kelly, J. A., Murphy, D. A., Bahr, R., Kalichman, S. C., Morgan, M. G., Stevenson, L. Y., et al. (1993). Outcome of cognitive-behavioral and support group brief therapies for depressed, HIV-infected persons. *American Journal of Psychiatry, 150,* 1679–1686.

Klerman, G. L., Weissman, M. M., Rounsaville, B. J., & Chevron, E. S. (1984). *Interpersonal psychotherapy of depression.* New York: Basic Books.

Lazar, S. G. (1997). The effectiveness of dynamic psychotherapy for depression. *Psychoanalytic Inquiry* (Suppl), 51–57.

Lee, C., Slade, P., & Lygo, V. (1996). The influence of psychological debriefing on emotional adaptation in women following early miscarriage: A preliminary study. *British Journal of Medical Psychology, 69,* 47–58.

Luborsky, L., Diguer, L., Cacciola, J., Barber, J. P., Moras, K., Schmidt, K., & DeRubeis, R. J. (1996). Factors in outcomes of short-term dynamic psychotherapy for chronic vs. nonchronic major depression. *Journal of Psychotherapy Practice and Research, 5*, 152–159.

Markowitz, J. C. (1999). Interpersonal psychotherapy: Alone and combined with medication. In D. S. Janowsky (Ed.), *Psychotherapy indications and outcomes* (pp. 233–247). Washington, DC: American Psychiatric Press.

Marks, I. (1999). Is a paradigm shift occurring in brief psychological treatments? *Psychotherapy and Psychosomatics, 68*(4), 169–170.

Mays, M., & Croake, J. W. (1997a). *Treatment of depression in managed care.* New York: Brunner/Mazel.

Mays, M., & Croake, J. (1997b). Managed care and treatment of depression. In S. R. Sauber (Ed.), *Managed mental health care: Major diagnostic and treatment approaches* (pp. 244–278). Bristol, PA: Brunner/Mazel.

McDermut, W., Miller, I. W., & Brown, R. A. (2001). The efficacy of group psychotherapy for depression: A meta-analysis and review of the empirical research. *Clinical Psychology: Science and Practice, 8*, 98–116.

Miller, I. J. (1996). Time-limited brief therapy has gone too far: The result is invisible rationing. *Professional Psychology: Research and Practice, 27*, 567–576.

Morrison, J. (1995). *DSM-IV made easy: The clinician's guide to diagnosis.* New York: Guilford.

Mossey, J. M., Knott, K. A., Higgins, M., & Talerico, K. (1996). Effectiveness of a psychosocial intervention, interpersonal counseling, for subdysthymic depression in medically ill elderly. *Journal of Gerontology: Medical Sciences, 51A*, M172–M178.

Mynors-Wallis, L. (1996). Problem-solving treatment: Evidence for effectiveness and feasibility in primary care. *International Journal of Psychiatry in Medicine, 26*, 249–262.

Mynors-Wallis, L. M., Gath, D. H., Day, A., & Baker, F. (2000). Randomised controlled trial of problem solving treatment, antidepressant medication, and combined treatment for major depression in primary care. *British Medical Journal, 320*(1), 26–30.

Niederehe, G. T. (1994). Psychosocial therapies with depressed older adults. In L. S. Schneider, C. F. Reynolds, B. D. Lebowitz, & A. J. Friedhoff (Eds.), *Diagnosis and treatment of depression in late life: Results of the NIH consensus development conference* (pp. 293–315). Washington, DC: American Psychiatric Press.

Nordhus, I. H., Nielsen, G. H., & Kvale, G. (1998). Psychotherapy with older adults. In I. H. Nordhus, G. R. VandenBos, S. Berg, & P. Fromholt (Eds.), *Clinical geropsychology* (pp. 289–311). Washington, DC: American Psychological Association.

Persons, J. B., Thase, M. E., & Crits-Christoph, P. (1996). The role of psychotherapy in the treatment of depression: Review of two practice guidelines. *Archives of General Psychiatry, 53*, 283–290.

Rudd, M. D., Rajib, M. H., Orman, D. T., Stulman, D. A., Joiner, T., & Dixon, W. (1996). Effectiveness of an outpatient intervention targeting suicidal young adults: Preliminary results. *Journal of Consulting and Clinical Psychology, 64*, 179–190.

Sadavoy, J. (1994). Integrated psychotherapy for the elderly. *Canadian Journal of Psychiatry, 39*(Suppl. 1), S19–S26.

Schneider, L. S., & Olin, J. T. (1995). Efficacy of acute treatment for geriatric depression. *International Psychogeriatrics, 7*, 7–25.

Schneider, L. S., Reynolds, C. F., Lebowitz, B. D., & Friedhoff, A. J. (1994). *Diagnosis and treatment of depression in late life: Results of the NIH consensus development conference.* Washington, DC: American Psychiatric Press.

Schulberg, H. C., Block, M. R., Madonia, M. J., Scott, C. P., Rodriguez, E., Imber, S. D., et al. (1996). Treating major depression in primary care practice. *Archives of General Psychiatry, 53*, 913–919.

Scogin, F., & McElreath, L. (1994). Efficacy of psychosocial treatments for geriatric depression: A quantitative review. *Journal of Consulting and Clinical Psychology, 62*, 69–74.

Scott, C., Tacchi, M. J., Jones, R., & Scott, J. (1997). Acute and one-year outcome of a randomised controlled trial of brief cognitive therapy for major depressive disorder in primary care. *British Journal of Psychiatry, 171*, 131–134.

Shapiro, D. A., Barkham, M., Rees, A., Hardy, G. E., Reynolds, S., & Startup, M. (1994). Effects of treatment duration and severity of depression on the effectiveness of cognitive-behavioral and psychodynamic-interpersonal psychotherapy. *Journal of Consulting and Clinical Psychology, 62*, 522–534.

Shea, M. T., Elkin, I., & Sotsky, S. M. (1999). Patient characteristics associated with successful treatment. In D. S. Janowsky (Ed.), *Psychotherapy indications and outcomes* (pp. 71–90). Washington, DC: American Psychiatric Press.

Spiegel, D. (1999). Psychotherapeutic intervention with the medically ill. In D. S. Janowsky (Ed.), *Psychotherapy indications and outcomes* (pp. 277–300). Washington, DC: American Psychiatric Press.

Steffen, A. M., Futterman, A., & Gallagher-Thompson, D. (1998). Depressed caregivers: Comparative outcomes of two interventions. *Clinical Gerontologist, 19*(4), 3–15.

Stewart, D. E., Boydell, K. M., McCarthy, K., Swerdlyk, S., Redmond, C., & Cohrs, W. (1992). A prospective study of the effectiveness of brief professionally-led support groups for infertility patients. *International Journal of Psychiatry in Medicine, 22*, 173–182.

Swartz, H. A. (1999). Interpersonal psychotherapy. In M. Hersen & A. S. Bellack (Eds.), *Handbook of comparative interventions for adult disorders* (2nd ed., pp. 139–155). New York: Wiley.

Thompson, L. W. (1996). Cognitive-behavioral therapy and treatment for late-life depression. *Journal of Clinical Psychiatry, 57*(Suppl. 5), 29–37.

Weisz, J. R., Thurber, C. A., Sweeney, L., Proffitt, V. D., & LaGagnoux, G. L. (1997). Brief treatment of mild-to-moderate child depression using primary and secondary control enhancement training. *Journal of Consulting and Clinical Psychology, 65*, 703–707.

Wiborg, I. M., & Dahl, A. A. (1996). Does brief dynamic psychotherapy reduce the relapse rate of panic disorder? *Archives of General Psychiatry, 53*, 689–694.

Wood, B. C., & Mynors-Wallis, L. M. (1997). Problem-solving therapy in palliative care. *Palliative Medicine, 11*, 49–54.

Zeiss, A. M., & Breckenridge, J. S. (1997). Treatment of late life depression: A response to the NIH consensus conference. *Behavior Therapy, 28*, 3–21.

21

Evidence-Based Practice With Anxiety Disorders

Guidelines Based on 59 Outcome Studies

BERNARD L. BLOOM

KENNETH R. YEAGER

ALBERT R. ROBERTS

While the number of well-designed, controlled, clinical outcome studies is not large, brief psychotherapeutic interventions appear to play a useful role in the treatment of anxiety spectrum disorders. Such interventions not only appear to be effective in their own right but also add a significant component to the benefits of medication. This chapter summarizes and describes the time-limited interventions and outcomes from 59 studies. This database includes 11 recent outcome studies that measured the effectiveness of crisis intervention and brief therapy approaches with posttraumatic stress disorder (PTSD) precipitated by gunshot injuries, sexual assaults, terrorist attacks, vehicular accidents, and violent crimes.

REVIEW OF EVIDENCE

Several recent outcome studies reviewed in this chapter suggest that psychological approaches to the treatment of anxiety disorders are remarkably effective in their own right and usually add a significant component to the effectiveness of more traditional psychopharmacological treatments. The evidence suggests that brief psychotherapy not only helps reduce symptoms but also serves to reduce relapse rate. Controlled outcome studies are not common, however. The evidence appears to indicate the following:

- *Brief psychotherapeutic treatments of anxiety disorders*: Brief psychotherapeutic treatments of anxiety disorders usually appear to be no less effective than longer-term treatments.
- *Brief cognitive-behavioral therapy*: Generally seems to be more efficacious than brief psychodynamic therapy, supportive psychotherapy, or nondirective therapy.
- *Brief psychotherapy*: Is not invariably helpful, however. Longer-term psychotherapy may be recommended when brief symptom-focused treatment is not sufficient, although it is not yet clear whether longer treatment yields a consistently superior result (Shear, 1995).

There is need, however, for additional and better-designed controlled outcome studies to solidify our understanding of the overall effectiveness of approaches to the treatment of anxiety.

As to accounting for the effectiveness of cognitive-behavioral therapy in the treatment of anxiety disorders, Harvey and Rapee (1995) have suggested that cognitive-behavioral therapy involves treating the anxiety by "teaching patients to identify, evaluate, and modify the chronically worrisome danger-related thoughts and associated behaviors" (pp. 862–863; see also Wright & Borden, 1991).

Brief cognitive-behavioral psychotherapeutic treatment has been provided in both individual and group formats, as well as by self-help, bibliographic, and other limited therapist-contact procedures. Outcome studies indicate that:

- Therapist-directed programs are usually superior to other formats but that virtually all cognitive-behavioral approaches are superior to waitlist controls.
- There is some evidence that there is a generalized component to psychotherapeutic effectiveness in that treatment conducted with dual-diagnosis patients that include anxiety disorders appear to be just as helpful as treatments designed for single-diagnosis patients.
- Finally, there is consistent evidence that the success of physician treatment for anxiety disorders related to generalized medical conditions can be significantly enhanced by the addition of a psychotherapeutic component to the treatment program.

Significant elements in cognitive and behavioral treatment appear to include:

- Informational and educational components (understanding the disorder and the treatment rationale)
- Somatic management skills (relaxation and breathing training)
- Cognitive restructuring (understanding the role of catastrophic thoughts in anxiety development; psychological debriefing)
- Controlled graded exposure to settings that tend to precipitate symptoms.
- Cognitively based homework assignments

If these positive findings regarding the effectiveness of brief psychological treatments for the anxiety disorder spectrum are corroborated by additional controlled outcome studies, the inclusion of a psychotherapeutic component in the treatment of these conditions should become the recognized treatment standard.

ANXIETY AND EVIDENCE-BASED TREATMENT

Anxiety disorders, affecting some 16% of the population at any given moment, are divided into two subordinate diagnostic categories. The first group includes generalized anxiety disorder, anxiety disorder due to a general medical condition, panic disorder, agoraphobia, specific phobia, social phobia, and acute stress disorder. The second group includes obsessive-compulsive disorder, substance-induced anxiety disorder, and posttraumatic stress disorder (American Psychiatric Association, 1994). Patients in the first group are commonly treated by primary care physicians (see, for example, Catalan et al., 1991). In contrast, patients in the second group are usually thought of as more disabled and are more often treated by mental health professionals (Choy & de Bosset, 1992; Walley, Beebe, & Clark, 1994).

Principal symptoms of anxiety disorders include excessive anxiety and worry, self-limiting panic attacks, irrational avoidance of situations that present the possibility of embarrassment or humiliation, obsessive thoughts and compulsive behavior, cardiopulmonary symptoms (chest pain, hyperventilation, tachycardia and palpitations, tremulousness, dizziness, light-headedness, faintness, headache, and paresthesias), gastrointestinal symptoms (nausea, vomiting, diarrhea, abdominal pain, and anorexia), depressive symptoms, and sexual dysfunction.

The growing importance of treatment outcome evaluation has been recognized by most writers in the field (see, for example, Lane, 2000), and a number of overviews of empirically validated brief treatments for the anxiety disorders are now available in the literature (see Ballenger, 1999; Barlow, Esler, & Vitali, 1998; Gatz et al., 1998; Hersen & Biaggio, 2000; McCullough, 2000; Newman, 2000; Stanley & Averill, 1999).

This chapter examines recent outcome studies of brief psychotherapy treatments designed to be of help with many of these anxiety disorders. Very few empirical outcome studies have been reported in the case of the more severe anxiety disorders, with the exception of posttraumatic stress disorder, although a number of interesting reviews and clinical case reports are in the literature (e.g., Franklin, Foa, & Kozak, 1999; Marks, 1990; Marmar, 1991; Sifneos, 1985; Starcevic & Durdic, 1993; Weiss & Marmar, 1993; see also Schmidt & Harrington, 1995).

While a variety of pharmacotherapeutic agents, including benzodiazepines, azapirones, tricyclics, monoamine oxidase inhibitors, beta-blockers, and serotonin reuptake inhibitors, are employed in the treatment of anxiety disorders (see, for example, Gross & Rosen, 1997; Sutherland, Tupler, Colket, & Davidson, 1996; Warneke, 1985), psychotherapeutic interventions are being increasingly recognized as having a significant therapeutic role as well.

There are three reasons for the growing interest in alternatives to exclusively pharmacological treatment of anxiety disorders:

- First, many medications have undesirable side effects.
- Second, medications appear to have decreasing effectiveness with time.

- Third, discontinuance of medication results in relapse rates that are far higher than in the case of psychotherapeutic approaches (Harvey & Rapee, 1995; Juster & Heimberg, 1995; Otto & Whittal, 1995).

PANIC DISORDER

The synergistic effectiveness of psychological and biological approaches to the treatment of anxiety disorders is evident in the case of panic disorders. Pollack and Smoller (1995) noted that many patients treated with pharmacotherapy, while improved, remain symptomatic despite treatment. Adding cognitive-behavioral psychotherapy to the pharmacotherapy appears to improve both acute and long-term outcome.

Wiborg and Dahl (1996) studied 40 patients with panic disorders and found that 15 weekly sessions of combined dynamic psychotherapy and treatment with clomipramine significantly reduced the relapse rate, when compared with the clomipramine-only group at the 9-month blind follow-up.

Otto and Whittal (1995) suggest psychological treatments, especially cognitive-behavioral therapy. Findings suggest such treatments offer patients with panic disorders "the potential for . . . efficacy equal to pharmacologic treatment, without the risk of exposure to drug-related side effects or discontinuation effects, or the need for ongoing medication treatment" (Otto & Whittal, 1995, p. 816; see also Craske, Maidenberg, & Bystritsky, 1995).

Beck, Sokol, Clark, Berchick, and Wright (1992) contrasted focused cognitive therapy with brief supportive psychotherapy in a sample of patients with panic disorders. They found that the cognitive therapy yielded significantly superior results in terms of reductions of panic symptoms and general anxiety in comparison with those obtained by brief supportive psychotherapy, both at the conclusion of the therapeutic episode and at the time of a 1-year follow-up.

Additionally, Westling and Öst (1999) developed a four-session, 1 hour per week format that also included keeping a panic diary, reading about the treatment rationale, and thinking about how the patient's own panic problems could be explained by the cognitive treatment model presented to them. Data that were collected pretreatment, posttreatment, and at a 6-month follow-up included independent assessor ratings, self-observation, and self-report scales. A total of 10 patients were involved in this pilot study from whom complete data were obtained.

Compared with pretreatment assessments, posttreatment and follow-up assessments showed significant drops in full panic attacks and in limited symptom attacks, highly significant decreases in virtually all self-report measures, and significant decreases in levels of pathology as judged by independent assessors. All improvements noted at the time of the posttreatment assessment were maintained at the time of the follow-up.

In a similar study, Clark et al. (1999) developed a very brief (up to five sessions during a 3-month period) cognitive therapy approach for the treatment of panic disorder that included between-session self-study modules. They examined its effectiveness by contrasting results with a more traditional cognitive "full" therapy approach (up to 12 1-hour treatment sessions during a 3-month period) and a 3-month waitlist control. Patients in the 3-month waitlist control were randomly assigned to one of the two cognitive treatment programs at the conclusion of the waitlist period.

A total of 42 patients were randomly assigned to the treatment or waitlist groups and completed the treatment sequence. Total therapy and booster-session time was 11.9 hours for patients receiving traditional cognitive therapy and 6.5 hours for patients receiving brief cognitive therapy. Mean age of the patients was 34 years. Mean duration of the current panic episode was 3.7 years. About 60% of the patients were female. About three fourths of the patients were on stable doses of a psychotropic medication (either low-potency benzodiazepines or beta-blockers).

While there were no differences in assessment scores at the start of the treatment program between any of the three groups, at the end of treatment scores on all of the various assessments were significantly less pathological in both of the treatment groups than in the waitlist control, and there were no significant differences between the two treatment groups' scores. The gains made by the members of the two treatment groups were maintained at the time of the 12-month posttreatment follow-up assessment, with no difference in gain maintenance between the two treatment groups.

In these studies, brief interventions have clearly been found to be useful in the treatment of panic disorders in their own right, as well as providing significant supplementary help to patients being treated with psychotropic medication.

GENERALIZED ANXIETY DISORDERS

Crits-Christoph, Connolly, Azarian, Crits-Christoph, and Shappell (1996) have noted that generalized anxiety disorders are characterized by a high level of chronicity and a significant degree of impairment in functioning. Average duration of this disorder, which often begins in the teens or early twenties, is between 6 and 10 years. While pharmacological treatment appears to be efficacious, there are a number of adverse side effects, including attentional, psychomotor, cognitive, and memory-impairing symptoms, reduced coping and stress response capabilities, and physical dependence and withdrawal reactions.

In the case of patients with generalized anxiety disorders, brief cognitive-behavioral therapy has been found to be superior to results with waitlist controls. Treatments accentuating cognitive components have been found to be equal in effect to treatments accentuating behavioral components. Regardless of emphasis, cognitive-behavioral treatments have been generally found to be superior to nondirective treatment methods and to the use of benzodiazepines, particularly when long-term follow-up assessments have been undertaken (Harvey & Rapee, 1995), although the degree of superiority is quite modest.

Crits-Christoph et al. (1996) have explored the potential therapeutic role of interpersonally oriented psychodynamic therapy for generalized anxiety disorders. Their studies examined the effectiveness of a 16-session treatment program conducted on a weekly basis, followed by three monthly booster sessions. The treatment program was oriented toward understanding the anxiety symptoms in the context of interpersonal and intrapsychic conflicts. Initial research design involved five therapists and a total of 26 patients. Contrasted pre–post measures on a variety of self-report instruments indicated statistically significant changes on all outcome measures. Large decreases were found in interpersonal problems and in anxiety, with smaller decreases found in measures of depression. Controlled outcome studies and long-term follow-up evaluations are envisioned for the future.

In a particularly informative study, Durham et al. (1994) contrasted three brief treatments in a sample of 110 outpatients with generalized anxiety disorders who were randomly assigned to either cognitive therapy, psychoanalytic psychotherapy, or anxiety management training. The cognitive therapy and psychoanalytic psychotherapy groups were further randomly assigned to brief (8 to 10 sessions within 6 months) or longer term (16 to 20 sessions within 6 months) treatment episodes. Assessments by senior staff blind to patients' therapists and treatment conditions used a variety of assessment instruments before treatment, after treatment, and 6 months following the conclusion of treatment.

Cognitive therapy was found to be significantly more effective than psychoanalytic psychotherapy, with about 50% of patients considerably better at follow-up. There were no significant outcome differences associated with length of treatment. Patients receiving anxiety management training improved as much as patients in cognitive therapy when assessed immediately at the conclusion of the treatment episode, but their levels of improvement deteriorated somewhat by the time of the follow-up assessment. The authors suggest:

> Cognitive therapy is likely to be more effective than psychodynamic psychotherapy with chronically anxious patients. . . . The superiority of cognitive therapy at follow-up suggests that the greater investment of resources required for this approach is likely to pay off in terms of more sustained improvement. There is no evidence that 16–20 sessions of treatment is more effective, on average, than 8–10 sessions. (Durham et al., 1994, p. 315)

Noting that there is considerable overlap in the diagnoses of anxiety disorder and depression, Kush and Fleming (2000) developed a brief cognitive group therapy approach to the simultaneous treatment of depression and anxiety. Their 12-session group program met weekly for 90 minutes and was based on a curriculum that synthesized cognitive psychoeducational approaches to the treatment of depression and anxiety, cognitive modification, and problem-solving training.

Patients in this pilot program included 29 adult outpatients, of whom 26 completed the curriculum. Diagnoses included depressive mood disorder ($N = 18$) and anxiety disorder ($N = 8$), including generalized anxiety disorder. Assessments were obtained at the beginning and end of the treatment program and included the Beck Depression Inventory, the Beck Anxiety Inventory, and the Dysfunctional Attitudes Scale. Significant reductions in all three scores were found, with scores on the Beck Depression Inventory showing the most significant drop.

PHOBIAS

Two reports have documented the effectiveness of brief interventions for phobias. Hellstrom and Öst (1995; see also Öst, 1989) contrasted five cognitive approaches in a sample of 52 patients with spider phobias. One approach involved a single 3-hour session of therapist-directed graded exposure. The other approaches involved either specific or general manual-based treatments conducted in either the home or the clinic. The therapist-directed exposure was found to be significantly more effective than three of the four manual-based treatments, both immediately after treatment and at a follow-up assessment that included behavioral, physiological, and self-report measures. The specific manual-based treatment conducted in the clinic was significantly superior to the other three manual-based treatments but only at follow-up. Clinically significant improvement levels were 80% at follow-up for the therapist-directed treatment program, 63% for the manual-based treatment program conducted at the clinic, and 10% or less for the other programs.

Three cases of cognitive-behavioral treatment for choking and swallowing phobias were described by Ball and Otto (1994). This treatment was conducted for 11 to 13 sessions and involved psychoeducational, cognitive restructuring, interoceptive, and in vivo exposure techniques. All three patients responded well, as measured by their food hierarchy progressions and by weight gain.

In their recent review of cognitive-behavioral treatment programs, Juster and Heimberg (1995) reported that in the case of patients with social phobias, exposure-oriented treatments seem superior to drug treatments in terms of both degree and duration of improvement. Multicomponent treatment programs (e.g., cognitive restructuring and exposure) do not tend to be superior to single-component programs.

ANXIETY DISORDERS DUE TO A GENERALIZED
MEDICAL CONDITION

A number of outcome studies conducted in medical settings have examined the effectiveness of adding brief psychological treatment to traditional medical treatment for anxiety reactions related to medical disorders. Greer et al. (1992) found that an 8-week brief problem-focused cognitive-behavioral treatment program, added to traditional medical treatment in a sample of 174 randomized cancer patients, resulted in significantly decreased helplessness, preoccupation, fatalism, and anxiety symptoms, as well as significantly increased fighting spirit, when the experimental and control groups were contrasted. At the time of a 4-month follow-up, patients receiving the brief psychological treatment program had significantly lower scores than controls on anxiety, psychological symptoms, and psychological distress.

Baldoni, Baldaro, and Trombini (1995) found that adding short-term dynamic psychotherapy to traditional medical treatment in a sample of 13 female patients suffering from urethral syndrome resulted in dramatic superiority in treatment effectiveness when they were contrasted with a sample of 23 patients who received only traditional medical treatment.

In a sample of 68 depressed men with HIV infection randomly assigned to eight-session cognitive-behavioral treatment, eight-session social support groups, or a control group, Kelly et al. (1993) found that both the cognitive-behavioral and social support group therapies produced reductions in overall psychiatric symptoms and tended to reduce maladaptive interpersonal sensitivity, anxiety, and frequency of unprotected intercourse when contrasted with the control group. The two forms of therapy resulted in both shared and unique improvements in functioning.

Harrison, Watson, and Feinmann (1997) provided an 8-week group therapy experience to a total of 19 patients with chronic idiopathic facial pain that had ranged from 1 to 5 years in duration and that had been unresponsive to a variety of prior medical treatments. Four groups of four or five patients met in weekly 3-hour sessions. The therapeutic orientation was cognitive-behavioral and included relaxation exercises during and between group sessions. Significant reductions in reported pain, anxiety, and depression were obtained, along with improved abilities in coping.

In a particularly striking study of the use of cognitive-behavioral interventions, de Jongh et al. (1995) examined the effectiveness of this treatment in a sample of 52 patients suffering from dental phobias. These patients were randomly assigned to a cognitive restructuring group, an educational group, and a waitlist control condition. Neither of the interventions lasted longer than 1 hour. Cognitive restructuring was designed to modify negative cognitions associated with dental treatment, while the educational intervention provided information about oral health and dental treatment. Compared with the waitlist control and the educational intervention, the patients in the cognitive restructuring condition showed a significant decrease in frequency and believability of negative cognitions and in dental anxiety following the intervention. One year later, patients in the two intervention conditions were reexamined. Further reductions in dental anxiety were found in both intervention groups, and the reductions were so great in the case of the educational intervention condition that differences in treatment effectiveness between the two intervention groups no longer were found.

Two recent studies have been located in which psychoeducational interventions did not appear to be helpful with 39 women whose pregnancies had ended in miscarriages. Lee, Slade, and Lygo (1996) found no significant differences between their experimental and control groups in measures of anxiety, depression, intrusion, or avoidance 4 months after the miscarriage.

A 10-session cognitive psychotherapy program designed to reduce the 1-year recurrence rate of duodenal ulcer by helping patients cope with anxiety and dependence failed to achieve its objective in a study reported by Wilhelmsen, Haug, Ursin, and Berstad (1994).

POSTTRAUMATIC STRESS DISORDERS

Investigation of brief approaches to the treatment of posttraumatic stress disorder (PTSD) has, until recently, been largely confined to the study of war-related traumas and natural or man-made disasters. In recent years, attention has also been directed to the treatment of victims of sexual assaults, terrorist attacks, vehicular accidents, gunshot injuries, violent crimes, and other traumas (Austin & Godleski, 1999; Choy & de Bosset, 1992; Foa & Meadows, 1997). Study of the psychological consequences of such events has a special appeal because, in contrast to most psychiatric disorders, there is a recognized and unequivocal precipitating event.

Principal symptoms of PTSD include pervasive anxiety, reexperiencing, avoidance, and hyperarousal following exposure to a traumatic event. The development of PTSD involves both psychological and biological components and can produce enduring neurohormonal changes and serious long-term morbidity. Accordingly, it is generally agreed that prompt and effective treatments are urgently needed.

Most brief treatment programs that have been reported were cognitive and behavioral in nature and included some combination of psychological debriefing, education, and imagery rehearsal. Both individual and group approaches have been studied, and programs have been evaluated that involved children as well as adults.

Rose, Brewin, Andrews, and Kirk (1999) conducted a randomized controlled trial of two brief individual approaches to crisis intervention—educational and psychological debriefing—in a sample of 157 adults who had been victims of violent crimes within the past month. The educational intervention had an average duration of 30 minutes, and the debriefing intervention lasted about 1 hour. One third of the sample served as a no-treatment control in that they participated in the assessment procedures but received no specific additional intervention. Follow-up assessments were conducted for the entire sample 6 months after the intervention and for about two thirds of the sample 5 months later.

The authors reported that all three groups improved over time but that there were no significant between-group differences. Based on their analysis of their own as well as prior studies, the authors suggest that somewhat more intensive interventions that allow for the recasting or restructuring of the traumatic experience to attribute new meanings to the event may be necessary.

The effectiveness of a brief psychotherapeutic approach in the management of PTSD was examined by Gersons, Carlier, Lamberts, and van der Kolk (2000) in a sample of 42 Dutch police officers randomly divided into a treatment group and a waitlist control (subsequently treated). All officers met the diagnostic criteria for PTSD. None exhibited evidence of organic mental disorders, substance abuse, psychoses, or severe depression, and all had been medication-free for at least 6 months prior to the start of treatment. Treatment consisted of 16 1-hour sessions of brief eclectic psychotherapy (BEP) with five elements: psychoeducation, imagery guidance, writing assignments, meaning and integration, and a farewell ritual.

Blind psychometric assessments were conducted 1 week before the start of treatment, after four sessions, at termination of treatment, and 3 months after termination. No significant differences between the two groups were found at the pretest or at the end of the fourth treatment session. In contrast, at the end of treatment and at the follow-up assessment, the BEP group demonstrated significant improvement in PTSD, in work resumption, and in some comorbid conditions, notably, phobic anxiety, depression, obsessive-compulsive symptoms, and sleeping problems. Symptom checklist scores were significantly above the norm at the pretest and after the fourth treatment session for both the treated and the waitlist groups. Waitlisted police officers remained significantly above the norm on all symptom checklist scores throughout the study, while treated officers' scores dropped to normative levels at the time of treatment termination and follow-up assessment.

A psychological debriefing technique thought to be particularly useful in working with new war zone cases has been reported by Busuttil et al. (1995; see also Choy & de Bosset, 1992) using a group therapy format. Psychological debriefing was originally proposed to help groups of military personnel who had undergone the same traumatic event to process their experiences together, usually within 48 hours of the event itself. Busuttil et al. (1995) used this general strategy in working with 34 cases of posttraumatic stress disorder in a 12-day residential treatment program, followed by group outpatient sessions for up to 1 year, and found it to be remarkably effective as assessed at the time of treatment termination, as well as at 6 weeks, 6 months, and 1 year during the follow-up period.

Debriefing involved (a) initial group formation; (b) detailed descriptions of the facts, emotions, and sensory perceptions associated with the traumatic events; (c) didactic presentations regarding stress and stress management, drugs commonly used in the treatment program, supplemented by relaxation exercises to reduce stress; (d) problem solving; and (e) family reintegration. Most of the improvement occurred within the first 2 months of treatment.

The use of imagery rehearsal therapy (IRT) in the treatment of chronic nightmares in the case of sexual assault survivors with posttraumatic stress disorders was examined by Krakow et al. (2001). The patients were 168 women who had suffered rape, other sexual assaults, or repeated exposure to sexual abuse in childhood or adolescence and who were divided randomly into a treatment or a waitlist control group.

The IRT consisted of two 3-hour group sessions 1 week apart, followed by a 1-hour follow-up session 3 weeks later. At the first session, after some didactic material was presented about nightmares, their causes, functions, and control, and how imagery rehearsal can help eliminate nightmares, participants were given the opportunity to learn cognitive-behavioral tools for dealing with unpleasant images and for practicing pleasant imagery. At the second session, participants were taught how to use IRT to modify a single, self-selected nightmare and to rehearse the "new dream." At the follow-up session, the group discussed progress, shared experiences, and raised questions.

Small, nonsignificant reductions in the control group were found in frequency of nightmares, sleep disturbances, and symptoms associated with the diagnosis of PTSD. In contrast, highly significant reductions in these and other related symptoms were found in the treated group, including nightmare severity and frequency, sleep quality disturbances, and PTSD symptoms. Improvement occurred during the first 3 months after the start of the treatment program and was maintained during the next 3 months. There was no difference in degree of improvement as a function of use of psychotropic medication.

Three controlled studies of brief interventions for children and adolescents with PTSD diagnoses have been located. The effectiveness of a group-based cognitive-behavioral psychotherapy treatment program was examined in a sample of 17 children and adolescents diagnosed with PTSD by March, Amaya-Jackson, Murray, and Schulte (1998). The weekly treatment program was 18 weeks in length, and PTSD, anxiety, depression, anger, locus of control, and disruptive behavior were assessed at baseline, the end of treatment, and at a 6-month follow-up.

The treatment program included anxiety management training, muscle relaxation training, interpersonal problem solving as a way of dealing with anger, positive self-talk, cognitive training, development of an individually tailored stimulus hierarchy, narrative sharing, and graded in vivo exposure. Two groups were formed, and the second group began 4 weeks after the first group had started. Precipitating events in the development of PTSD included automobile accidents, severe illness, gunshot injuries, fires, and death of a loved one by means of criminal assault, illness, car accidents, fire, or gunshot injury.

Fourteen of the 17 children completed the treatment program. Results were significant on virtually all measures at the end of treatment and at the 6-month follow-up evaluation. Continued work by this group has resulted in revision and shortening of the treatment program with no apparent loss of program effectiveness.

A number of studies described brief trauma-related treatment following the 1988 Armenian earthquake that resulted in the deaths of some 25,000 inhabitants. The program, completed within a 6-week period, comprising both group and individual psychotherapy, was instituted 18 months after the earthquake.

Five components were incorporated into the program: discussion of the trauma event and its resulting effects, reminders of the traumatic event, postdisaster stresses, bereavement, and developmental impact. The individual sessions provided an opportunity for more in-depth explorations of trauma and its effects.

A total of 64 early adolescents who lived in Gyumri and who were significantly affected by the quake were divided into two groups: a treatment group of 35 children and an untreated group of 29 children. Eighteen months after the treatment program was completed, all children were reevaluated. Measures of PTSD reaction and of its components—intrusion, avoidance, and arousal—and a measure of depression were completed at the start of the intervention program and again 18 months later.

Analysis of the data revealed significant improvement in the treated group and significant deterioration in the untreated group in PTSD reaction scores on all three PTSD components. As to the depression scores, there was no significant change in the treated group, while the untreated group demonstrated a significant increase in depression. The treatment program appeared to have helped prevent the worsening course of PTSD and comorbid depression.

Two brief individual therapy interventions for sexually abused girls and their nonoffending female caretakers were compared by Celano, Hazzard, Webb, and McCall (1996). A total of 32 girls, aged 8 to 13, and their nonoffending female caretakers (primarily but not always mothers) were randomly assigned to either an 8-week 1 hour per week, theoretically based, structured experimental treatment program (focused on self-blame/stigmatization, betrayal, traumatic sexualization, and powerlessness) or to a relatively unstructured supportive psychotherapy program of the same length. Approximately equal time was spent with the girls and with their caretakers. Measures provided by both children and their nonoffending caretakers were obtained before and after treatment, as well as assessments by a clinician blind to the treatment condition.

Both treatment programs yielded improvement in posttraumatic stress disorder symptoms and reductions in self-blame and in powerlessness, as well as increases in overall psychosocial functioning of the child. The experimental program appeared to produce greater parental support, reduced self-blame, and reduced expectations of a negative impact of abuse on the child.

Because PTSD involves a known precipitating event, psychological debriefing constitutes a significant component of virtually all psychotherapeutic approaches to its treatment. The outcome literature suggests that this debriefing is a valuable aspect of the treatment.

CONCLUDING REMARKS

The outcome studies reviewed in this chapter suggest that psychological approaches to the treatment of anxiety disorders are remarkably effective in their own right, adding significant components to the effectiveness of pharmacological approaches. While controlled studies are not common, there is increasing interest in identifying and refining best practice psychotherapeutic treatments for anxiety disorders. It is important to note that brief psychotherapeutic treatments were found to be no less effective than long-term treatments.

Brief cognitive-behavioral therapy generally seems to be more efficacious than brief psychodynamic therapy, support psychotherapy, or nondirective therapy. Brief cognitive-behavioral psychotherapeutic treatment has been provided in both group and individual formats, and outcome studies indicate that directed programs are usually superior to other formats.

Finally, there is consistent evidence of successfully augmenting physician treatment of anxiety disorders related to generalized medical conditions through the addition of a psychotherapeutic component. If these positive findings regarding the effectiveness of brief psychological treatments for anxiety disorders are corroborated by additional controlled outcome studies, one could safely conclude that psychotherapeutic approaches should become an integrated component within the treatment of each of these conditions.

REFERENCES

American Psychiatric Association. (1994). *Diagnostic and statistical manual of mental disorders* (4th ed.). Washington, DC: Author.

Austin, L. S., & Godleski, L. S. (1999). Therapeutic approaches for survivors of disaster. *Psychiatric Clinics of North America, 22,* 897–910.

Baldoni, F., Baldaro, B., & Trombini, G. (1995). Psychotherapeutic perspectives in urethral syndrome. *Stress Medicine, 11,* 79–84.

Ball, S. G., & Otto, M. W. (1994). Cognitive-behavioral treatment of choking phobia: Three case studies. *Psychotherapy and Psychosomatics, 62,* 207–211.

Ballenger, J. C. (1999). Current treatments of the anxiety disorders in adults. *Biological Psychiatry, 46,* 1579–1594.

Barlow, D. H., Esler, J. L., & Vitali, A. E. (1998). Psychosocial treatments for panic disorders, phobias, and generalized anxiety disorder. In P. E. Nathan & J. M. Gorman (Eds.), *A guide to treatments that work* (pp. 288–318). New York: Oxford University Press.

Beck, A. T., Sokol, L., Clark, D. A., Berchick, R., & Wright, F. (1992). A crossover study of focused cognitive therapy for panic disorder. *American Journal of Psychiatry, 149,* 778–783.

Busuttil, W., Turnbull, G. J., Neal, L. A., Rollins, J., West, A. G., Blanch, N., et al. (1995). Incorporating psychological debriefing techniques within a brief group psychotherapy programme for the treatment of post-traumatic stress disorder. *British Journal of Psychiatry, 167,* 495–502.

Catalan, J., Gath, D. H., Anastasiades, P., Bond, S. A. K., Day, A., & Hall, L. (1991). Evaluation of a brief psychological treatment for emotional disorders in primary care. *Psychological Medicine, 21,* 1013–1018.

Celano, M., Hazzard, A., Webb, C., & McCall, C. (1996). Treatment of traumagenic beliefs among sexually abused girls and their mothers: An evaluation study. *Journal of Abnormal Child Psychology, 24,* 1–17.

Choy, T., & de Bosset, F. (1992). Post-traumatic stress disorder: An overview. *Canadian Journal of Psychiatry, 37,* 578–583.

Clark, D. M., Salkovskis, P. M., Hackmann, A., Wells, A., Ludgate, J., & Gelder, M. (1999). Brief cognitive therapy for panic disorder: A randomized controlled trial. *Journal of Consulting and Clinical Psychology, 67,* 583–589.

Craske, M. G., Maidenberg, E., & Bystritsky, A. (1995). Brief cognitive-behavioral versus nondirective therapy for panic disorder. *Journal of Behavior Therapy and Experimental Psychiatry, 26,* 113–120.

Crits-Christoph, P., Connolly, M. B., Azarian, K., Crits-Christoph, K., & Shappell, S. (1996). An open trial of brief supportive-expressive psychotherapy in the treatment of generalized anxiety disorder. *Psychotherapy, 33*, 418–430.

De Jongh, A., Muris, P., ter Horst, G., van Zuuren, F., Schoenmakers, N., & Makkes, P. (1995). One-session cognitive treatment of dental phobia: Preparing dental phobics for treatment by restructuring negative cognitions. *Behaviour Research & Therapy, 33*, 947–954.

Durham, R. C., Murphy, T., Allan, T., Richard, K., Treliving, L. R., & Fenton, G. W. (1994). Cognitive therapy, analytic psychotherapy and anxiety management training for generalised anxiety disorder. *British Journal of Psychiatry, 165*, 315–323.

Foa, E. B., & Meadows, E. A. (1997). Psychosocial treatments for posttraumatic stress disorder: A critical review. *Annual Review of Psychology, 48*, 449–480.

Franklin, M. E., Foa, E. B., & Kozak, M. J. (1999). Time-limited cognitive-behavioral therapy and pharmacotherapy of obsessive-compulsive disorder. *Crisis Intervention and Time-Limited Treatment, 5*, 37–57.

Gatz, M., Fiske, A., Fox, L. S., Kaskie, B., Kasl-Godley, J. E., McCallum, T. J., et al. (1998). Empirically validated psychological treatments for older adults. *Journal of Mental Health and Aging, 4*, 9–46.

Gersons, B. P. R., Carlier, I. V. E., Lamberts, R. D., & van der Kolk, B. A. (2000). Randomized clinical trial of brief eclectic psychotherapy for police officers with posttraumatic stress disorder. *Journal of Traumatic Stress, 13*, 333–347.

Greer, S., Moorey, S., Baruch, J. D. R., Watson, M., Robertson, B. M., Mason, A., et al. (1992). Adjuvant psychological therapy for patients with cancer: A prospective randomised trial. *British Medical Journal, 304*, 675–680.

Gross, D. A., & Rosen, A. (1997). The managed care of anxiety disorders. In S. R. Sauber (Ed.), *Managed mental health care: Major diagnostic and treatment approaches* (pp. 279–296). Bristol, PA: Brunner/Mazel.

Harrison, S., Watson, M., & Feinmann, C. (1997). Does short-term group therapy affect unexplained medical symptoms? *Journal of Psychosomatic Research, 43*, 399–404.

Harvey, A. G., & Rapee, R. M. (1995). Cognitive-behavior therapy for generalized anxiety disorder. *Psychiatric Clinics of North America, 18*, 859–870.

Hellstrom, K., & Öst, L.-G. (1995). One-session therapist directed exposure vs. two forms of manual directed self-exposure in the treatment of spider phobia. *Behavior Research and Therapy, 33*, 959–965.

Hersen, M., & Biaggio, M. (Eds.). (2000). *Effective brief therapies: A clinician's guide.* San Diego: Academic Press.

Juster, H. R., & Heimberg, R. G. (1995). Social phobia: Longitudinal course and long-term outcome of cognitive-behavioral treatment. *Psychiatric Clinics of North America, 18*, 821–842.

Kelly, J. A., Murphy, D. A., Bahr, G. R., Kalichman, S. C., Morgan, M. G., Stevenson, Y., et al. (1993). Outcome of cognitive-behavioral and support group brief therapies for depressed, HIV-infected persons. *American Journal of Psychiatry, 150*, 1679–1686.

Krakow, B., Hollifield, M. D., Johnston, L., Koss, M., Schrader, R., Warner, T. D., et al. (2001). Imagery rehearsal therapy for chronic nightmares in sexual assaults survivors with posttraumatic stress disorder. *Journal of the American Medical Association, 286*, 537–545.

Kush, F. R., & Fleming, L. M. (2000). An innovative approach to short term group cognitive therapy in the combined treatment of anxiety and depression. *Group Dynamics: Theory, Research and Practice, 4,* 176–183.

Lane, J. B. (2000). Overview of assessment and treatment issues. In M. Hersen & M. Biaggio (Eds.), *Effective brief therapies: A clinician's guide* (pp. 3–15). San Diego: Academic Press.

Lee, C., Slade, P., & Lygo, V. (1996). The influence of psychological debriefing on emotional adaptation in women following early miscarriage: A preliminary study. *British Journal of Medical Psychology, 69,* 47–58.

March, J. S., Amaya-Jackson, L. A., Murray, M. C., & Schulte, A. (1998). Cognitive-behavioral psychotherapy for children and adolescents with posttraumatic stress disorder after a single-incident stressor. *Journal of the American Academy of Child and Adolescent Psychiatry, 37,* 585–593.

Marks, I. M. (1990). Psychotherapie comportementale des troubles obsessionnels-compulsifs. *Encephale, 16,* 341–346.

Marmar, C. R. (1991). Brief dynamic psychotherapy of post-traumatic stress disorder. *Psychiatric Annals, 21,* 405–414.

McCullough, L. (2000). Short-term therapy for character change. In J. Carlson & L. Sperry (Eds.), *Brief therapy with individuals and couples* (pp. 127–160). Phoenix, AZ: Zeig, Tucker & Theisen.

Newman, M. G. (2000). Generalized anxiety disorder. In M. Hersen & M. Biaggio (Eds.), *Effective brief therapies: A clinician's guide* (pp. 157–178). San Diego: Academic Press.

Öst, L.-G. (1989). One-session treatment for specific phobias. *Behaviour Research and Therapy, 27,* 1–7.

Otto, M. W., & Whittal, M. L. (1995). Cognitive-behavior therapy and the longitudinal course of panic disorder. *Psychiatric Clinics of North America, 18,* 803–820.

Pollack, M. H., & Smoller, J. W. (1995). The longitudinal course and outcome of panic disorder. *Psychiatric Clinics of North America, 18,* 785–801.

Rose, S., Brewin, C. R., Andrews, B., & Kirk, M. (1999). A randomized controlled trial of individual psychological debriefing for victims of violent crime. *Psychological Medicine, 29,* 793–799.

Schmidt, N. B., & Harrington, P. (1995). Cognitive-behavioral treatment of body dysmorphic disorder: A case report. *Journal of Behavior Therapy and Experimental Psychiatry, 26,* 161–167.

Shear, M. K. (1995). Psychotherapeutic issues in long-term treatment of anxiety disorder patients. *Psychiatric Clinics of North America, 18,* 885–894.

Sifneos, P. E. (1985). Short-term dynamic psychotherapy of phobic and mildly obsessive-compulsive patients. *American Journal of Psychotherapy, 39,* 314–322.

Stanley, M. A., & Averill, P. M. (1999). Strategies for treating generalized anxiety in the elderly. In M. Duffy (Ed.), *Handbook of counseling and psychotherapy with older adults* (pp. 511–525). New York: Wiley.

Starcevic, V., & Durdic, S. (1993). Post-traumatic stress disorder: Current conceptualization, an overview of research and treatment. *Psihijatrija Danas, 25,* 9–31.

Sutherland, S. M., Tupler, L. A., Colket, J. T., & Davidson, J. R. (1996). A 2-year follow-up of social phobia: Status after a brief medication trial. *Journal of Nervous and Mental Disease, 184,* 731–738.

Walley, E. J., Beebe, D. K., & Clark, J. L. (1994). Management of common anxiety disorders. *American Family Physician, 50,* 1745–1753.

Warneke, L. B. (1985). Intravenous chlorimipramine in the treatment of obsessional disorder in adolescence: Case report. *Journal of Clinical Psychiatry, 46,* 100–103.

Weiss, D. S., & Marmar, C. R. (1993). Teaching time-limited dynamic psychotherapy for post-traumatic stress disorder and pathological grief. *Psychotherapy, 30,* 587–591.

Westling, B. E., & Öst, L.-G. (1999). Brief cognitive behaviour therapy of panic disorder. *Scandinavian Journal of Behaviour Therapy, 28,* 49–57.

Wiborg, I. M., & Dahl, A. A. (1996). Does brief dynamic psychotherapy reduce the relapse rate of panic disorder? *Archives of General Psychiatry, 53,* 689–694.

Wilhelmsen, I., Haug, T. T., Ursin, H., & Berstad, A. (1994). Effect of short-term cognitive psychotherapy on recurrence of duodenal ulcer: A prospective randomized trial. *Psychosomatic Medicine, 56,* 440–448.

Wright, J. H., & Borden, J. (1991). Cognitive therapy of depression and anxiety. *Psychiatric Annals, 21,* 424–428.

22

Psychoeducation as Evidence-Based Practice

Considerations for Practice, Research, and Policy

ELLEN P. LUKENS
WILLIAM R. McFARLANE

Psychoeducation is among the most effective of the evidence-based practices that have emerged in both clinical trials and community settings. Because of the flexibility of the model, which incorporates both illness-specific information and tools for managing related circumstances, psychoeducation has broad potential for many forms of illnesses and varied life challenges. This paper examines the research that supports psychoeducation as evidence-based practice for the professions dealing with mental health, health care, and social service across system levels and in different contexts by reviewing the range of applications that have appeared in the recent literature. We identified the psychoeducational examples included in the review by following guidelines for evidence-based practices created by the American Psychological Association's (APA) Task Force on Promotion and Dissemination of Psychological Procedures (1995). In the Discussion section, the common and unique themes and content across studies and populations are identified.

Psychoeducation is a professionally delivered treatment modality that integrates and synergizes psychotherapeutic and educational interventions. Many forms of psychosocial intervention are based on traditional medical models designed to treat pathology, illness, liability, and dysfunction. In contrast, psychoeducation reflects a paradigm shift to a more holistic and competence-based approach, stressing health, collaboration, coping, and empowerment (Dixon, 1999; Marsh, 1992). It is based on strengths and focused on the present. The patient/client and/or family are considered partners with the provider in treatment, on the premise that the more knowledgeable the care recipients and informal caregivers are, the more positive health-related outcomes will be for all. To prepare participants for this partnership, psychoeducational techniques are used to help remove barriers to comprehending and digesting complex and emotionally loaded information and to develop strategies to use the information in a proactive fashion. The assumption is that when people confront major life challenges or illnesses, their functioning and focus is naturally disrupted (Mechanic, 1995).

Psychoeducation embraces several complementary theories and models of clinical practice. These include ecological systems theory, cognitive-behavioral theory, learning theory, group practice models, stress and coping models, social support models, and narrative approaches (Anderson, Reiss, & Hogarty, 1986; Lukens, Thorning,& Herman, 1999; McFarlane, Dixon, Lukens, & Lucksted, 2003). Ecological systems theory provides the framework for assessing and helping people understand their illness or experience in relation to other systems in their lives (i.e., partners, family, school, health care provider, and policymakers). Under this umbrella, psychoeducation can be adapted for individuals, families, groups, or multiple family groups. Although psychoeducation can be practiced one-on-one, group practice models set the stage for within-group dialogue, social learning, expansion of support and cooperation, the potential for group reinforcement of positive change, and network building (Penninx et al., 1999). They reduce isolation and serve as a forum for both recognizing and normalizing experience and response patterns among participants, as well as holding professionals accountable for high standards of service. Cognitive-behavioral techniques such as problem solving and role-play enhance the presentation of didactic material by allowing people to rehearse and review new information and skills in a safe setting. These can be amplified through specific attention to the development of stress management and other coping techniques (Anderson et al., 1986; McFarlane, 2002). Narrative models, in which people are encouraged to recount their stories as related to the circumstances at hand, are used to help them recognize personal strengths and resources and generate possibilities for action and growth (White, 1989).

Recent mandates at both the federal and international levels have pushed to include psychoeducation as a focal point in treatment for schizophrenia and other mental illnesses, and are backed by national policymakers (President's New Freedom Commission on Mental Health, 2003) as well as influential family self-help groups such as the National Alliance for the Mentally Ill (NAMI) (Lehman & Steinwachs, 1998; McEvoy, Scheifler, & Frances, 1999). Based on an exhaustive review of the evidence-based literature on schizophrenia, the Schizophrenia PORT (Patient Outcomes Research Team) study recommended that education, support, crisis intervention, and training in problem solving be offered to available family members over a period of at least 9 months (Lehman & Steinwachs, 1998). Bestpractice and expert panels corroborated these recommendations (American Psychiatric Association, 1997; Coursey, 2000; Coursey, Curtis, & Marsh, 2000; Frances, Kahn, Carpenter, Docherty, & Donovan, 1998), given that remarkably positive outcomes have been observed in over 25 independent studies (Dixon, Adams, & Lucksted, 2000; Dixon et al., 2001; McFarlane et al., 2003). Several outcomes of psychoeducational interventions for schizophrenia are particularly noteworthy and have been demonstrated across studies (McFarlane et al., 2003). For persons receiving individual therapy and medication, or medication alone, the 1-year relapse rate ranges from 30% to 40%; for those participating in family psychoeducation of at least 9 months' duration, the rate is about 15% (Baucom, Shoham, Mueser, Daiuto, & Stickle, 1998). Other positive outcomes have been documented for patients and for families as well, suggesting that psychoeducation provides multiple benefits. These include decreased symptomatology and improved social functioning for the patient (Dyck, Hendryx, Short, Voss, & McFarlane, 2002; Dyck et al., 2000; McFarlane et al., 1995; Montero et al., 2001) and improved well-being and decreased levels of medical illness among family members (McFarlane, Dushay, Stastny, Deakins, & Link, 1996; Solomon, Draine, & Mannion, 1996; Solomon, Draine, Mannion, & Meisel, 1996).

In schizophrenia, any form of intervention is complicated by the symptoms of the illness, which include psychosis as well as functional and cognitive deficit or distortion, alogia, inertia, denial, and/or lack of awareness of illness (American Psychiatric Association, 1994). Patients, formal care providers, and informal caregivers are confronted not only by the severe burden of the illness, but by the distorted sense of reality by which it is characterized. To address this multifaceted set of challenges, the various psychoeducational models for schizophrenia build on a series of principles that exemplify the paradigm shift to a strengths-based approach to intervention. Key aspects of these approaches include service coordination (i.e., easy access and clarity of expectation regarding service, medication management and adherence, and crisis planning), provision of relevant up-to-date information in a timely and flexible manner, attention to family conflict, communication, loss, problem solving, and attention to social as well as clinical needs for the person with illness, along with expanded social support for the family, through multiple family psychoeducation and family support groups (e.g., NAMI) (Dixon Adams, & Lucksted, 2000; McFarlane et al., 1995; McFarlane et al., 2003).

Psychoeducational approaches also are well established as adjunctive treatment for cancer, where patients and families are struggling with different forms of challenge. Although persons with cancer typically fall into the normal range in terms of psychological processes, they inevitably struggle with the anxiety and depression following the extraordinary stress associated with the diagnosis and treatment of the cancer (Cunningham, Wolbert, & Brockmeier, 2000). Numerous randomized studies over the last two decades have shown significantly increased quality of life and decreased levels of anxiety and distress for persons with cancer who participate in professionally led psychoeducational groups (Cunningham, 2000; Edmonds, Lockwood, & Cunningham, 1999; Meyer & Mark, 1995). There is increasing evidence that psychoeducational and other forms of professionally led support groups can have an impact on the longevity of cancer patients as well (Cunningham, 2000; Cunningham, Edmonds, et al., 2000; Fawzy,

Fawzy, Arndt, & Pasnau, 1995; Richardson, Shelton, Krailo, & Levine, 1990; Richardson, Zarnegar, Bisno, & Levine, 1990; Spiegel, Bloom, Kraemer, & Gottheil, 1989). This reinforces the value and importance of emotional support and enhanced coping in the face of any form of severe illness.

Families and other informal caregivers of persons with cancer have been targeted as well. In one recent study focusing solely on partners of women with early-stage breast cancer, participants in psychoeducational groups showed less mood disturbance 3 months posttreatment than controls, and the women whose partner participated reported less personal mood disturbance and more emotional support (Bultz, Speca, Brasher, Geggie, & Page, 2000). These women also described significantly more stable marital relationships over time, suggesting that the psychoeducational groups served a preventive function.

The number of well-documented evidencebased studies on psychoeducation as an intervention for illnesses as different as schizophrenia and cancer suggests the potential for the model. There is significant evidence that psychoeducational interventions are associated with improved functioning and quality of life, decreased symptomatology, and positive outcomes for both the person with illness and family members as well.

However, there has been little attempt to examine the breadth of applications in other psychiatric, medical, or clinical settings. The aim of this paper is to review and discuss the range of psychoeducational interventions for other settings and circumstances using accepted criteria for designating a practice intervention as evidence based.

METHOD

Our approach is twofold: first, to show the breadth of application for psychoeducational interventions, and second, to include studies that follow the criteria for empirically supported psychological interventions devised by the Task Force on Promotion and Dissemination of Psychological Procedures (1995). These guidelines have been supported and amplified by other investigators and reported on by Chambless and colleagues (Chambless & Hollon, 1998; Chambless & Ollendick, 2001). Broadly defined, these criteria are grouped as:

Category I: established, efficacious, specific interventions, including two rigorous randomized trials conducted by independent investigators;

Category II: probably or possibly efficacious intervention, treatment compared with wait-list control; and

Category III: experimental treatments that do not meet the above criteria for adequate methodology.

In addition, the task force determined that Category I interventions should follow a treatment manual or clearly prescribed outline for treatments and that the characteristics of the sample should be specified (Chambless & Hollon,

1998). Nathan and Gorman (1998) extend the characteristics for Category I studies to include blind assessment of research subjects by independent raters, specific inclusion and exclusion criteria, up-to-date diagnostic assessment, and adequate statistical power.

Studies selected for inclusion in this review were retrieved through a search of PubMed and PsychInfo from 1995 until the present. This time period was selected because of increased attention to selection criteria for evidencebased practice that has emerged since 1995 (Chambless & Hollon, 1998; Chambless & Ollendick, 2001; Rousanville, Carroll, & Onken, 2001). Key search words included *psychoeducation, psychoeducational groups, randomized trial, control group, clinical trial, controlled trial, and outcome*. The intent was to identify studies that would meet criteria for Category I, as described above.

For the purposes of this review, the following criteria were used for the selection of published studies described as using a psychoeducational intervention:

The article focused on one or more interventions targeting a specific and clearly defined mental illness, medical illness, or other form of personal life challenge (e.g., partner abuse).

At least one of the interventions labeled as an active treatment was described as psychoeducational in nature, targeting either the family, the person challenged by the illness or life situation, or both.

The psychoeducational intervention was presented in person (as opposed to online or solely through written material).

The design of the study involved random assignment to the active psychoeducational treatment intervention and to a control group. (Note that in one instance, reports of randomized trials in process are included in the review as well, because they are based on a well-documented and randomized pilot study [Fristad, Gavazzi, & Mackinaw-Koons, 2003; Fristad, Goldberg-Arnold, & Gavazzi, 2003]).

The article provided enough information to assess the quality of the research design and methods and the applicability and relevance of outcome measures.

The article provided enough information to assess the nature and extent of the psychoeducational intervention, to determine whether psychotherapeutic and educational techniques were integrated. Intervention studies in which the authors referred to a seemingly straightforward educational intervention (i.e., with no psychotherapeutic component) as psychoeducational in nature were excluded.

One article was not reviewed because the term psychoeducation was referred to in the title and abstract but not in the text of the article (Shelton et al., 2000). A second was excluded because a psychoeducational group was used as a minimally defined control intervention (Latimer, Winters, D'Zurilla, & Nichols, 2003), and a third because psychoeducation was referred to as a combination placebo/usual care control with no description as to form or content (Kaminer, Burleson, & Goldberger, 2002).

APPLICATIONS FOR MENTAL HEALTH
CONDITIONS OTHER THAN SCHIZOPHRENIA

Although reports of randomized trials of psychoeducation for adults coping with schizophrenia are well represented in the literature, adaptations for children and adolescents and for adults with other serious mental health conditions are just beginning to appear (see Table 22.1). Fristad and her colleagues piloted multiple family psychoeducational groups with breakout sessions for children aged 8 to 11 with mood disorders (including both bipolar disorder and major depressive disorder/dysthymia as compared with wait-list controls [Fristad, Gavazzi, & Soldano, 1998; Fristad, Goldberg-Arnold, & Gavazzi, 2002]). These groups focused on both parent and child outcomes, including caregiver knowledge, increased caregiver concordance regarding diagnosis and treatment, decreased expressed emotion in parents and environmental stress for the child, and reduced symptom severity and duration for the child. The curriculum particularly attended to information dissemination, the building of advocacy and communication skills, both within the family and across systems, and strategies for social problem solving and symptom management. Outcomes were positive, with families engaged in the psychoeducational groups showing significantly more knowledge about mood symptoms, increased use of support services, and increased reports of parental support by children, both immediately after and 4 months posttreatment. Interestingly, parents reported increased positive family interactions, but not decreased negative family interaction.

The authors successfully included children with two different diagnoses (bipolar disorder and major depression/dysthymia) in each group. This represented an accommodation to practicality (i.e., ease of scheduling), and families appeared to benefit from learning about both disorders. Fristad and colleagues recently reported on two randomized trials to test two variations on the pilot; one that serves families through eight multiple family psychoeducational groups, and a second parallel model that includes 16 individual family psychoeducation sessions (parent-only meetings alternating with child sessions in which parents join at the beginning and end of the session) (Fristad, Gavazzi, et al., 2003; Fristad, Goldberg-Arnold, et al., 2003).

Honey, Bennett, and Morgan (2003) tested a brief psychoeducational group intervention for postnatal depression, randomly assigning 45 Welsh women scoring above 12 on the Edinburgh Postnatal Depression Scale to an eight-session psychoeducational group or to routine treatment. The partner was not involved. Although not manual based, the intervention followed a prescribed curriculum and included coping strategies related to child care and obtaining social supports, cognitive behavioral techniques, and relaxation. At posttest and 6 months posttreatment, women in the psychoeducational groups showed significantly decreased scores on the depression measure, controlling for antidepressant use. However, no differences occurred in terms of improved social support, marital relationship, or coping in analyses of effects for time, group, or Time × Group interaction.

Table 22.1. Mental Health Conditions

Study	Sample/Dx	Design	Active (PE) Treatment Protocol	Structure and Duration	Significant Outcomes for PE	Comment[a]
Colom et al., 2003	Outpatients diagnosed with bipolar I & II disorder. Conducted in Spain	Randomized trial: PE groups vs. nonstructured group meetings	Symptoms, course, communication, & coping skills	21 sessions	Reduced # total relapse & # relapses/person. Increased time to recurrence; fewer & shorter hospitalizations	Category II. Well-designed study
Dowrick et al., 2000	Adults with depression in community	Randomized trial; group PE vs. individual problem solving vs. controls. $N = 452$	Relaxation, positive thinking; social skills	12 two-hour sessions over 8 weeks w/class reunions	Both active interventions reduced caseness & improved subjective function. Problem solving more well received	Category II. Separates PE & problem solving
Fristad et al., 1998, 2002	Children with mood disorders	Pilot study; randomized trial in process	Decrease in symptoms; improve coping & communication; stress management; expanded social supports	Multiple family groups with break-out groups for children/adolescents. Late afternoon & evening	Improved family climate	Category II
Honey et al., 2003	Women diagnosed with postnatal depression	Randomized trial: PE groups for women vs. standard tx. $N = 45$	Coping strategies related to child care & obtaining social support; cognitive-behavioral techniques & relaxation	8 sessions	Tx group less depressed at posttest & 6-month fu, controlling for antidepressants No differences re social support, strength of marriage, or coping	Category II

Table 22.1. Mental Health Conditions (*continued*)

Study	Sample/Dx	Design	Active (PE) Treatment Protocol	Structure and Duration	Significant Outcomes for PE	Comment[a]
Miklowitz et al., 2003	Persons with bipolar disorder & family	Randomized trial; individual PE for families vs. crisis intervention for families. All patients received medication. *N* = 101	PE, with focus on communication & problem-solving training	21 individual sessions w/ family & patient over 9 months	Patients showed fewer relapses. Longer survival, greater reduction in mood disorder symptoms & better medication compliance	Category II. Well-designed study
Peterson et al., 1998	Women with binge eating disorder	Randomized trial; therapist-led PE vs. partial self-help vs. structured self-help vs. wait-list control. *N* = 61	Review of PE information, stress management, homework	14 one-hour group sessions over 8 weeks	All active tx showed decrease in binge eating at posttest	Category II. Small sample size per cell; group randomization. Manual based
Rea et al., 2003	Outpatients diagnosed with bipolar I disorder & their families	Randomized trial; individual family PE vs. individual tx for patient. *N* = 53	PE about bipolar disorder, communication enhancement, problem solving. As-needed crisis intervention	21 one-hour sessions	Patients less likely to be hospitalized; fewer relapses over 2 years	Category II. Well-designed study. Manual based

Note: Dx = diagnosis; PE = psychoeducation; tx = treatment; fu = follow-up.

[a]Chambless criteria for evidence-based practice (Chambless & Hollon, 1998).

Several studies addressed the needs of persons diagnosed with depression or bipolar disorder living in the community. In a three-armed study, Dowrick and colleagues (2000) compared group psychoeducation (12 two-hour sessions over 8 weeks), 6 individual problemsolving sessions conducted at home and controls. The authors found that the two active interventions reduced symptoms and improved subjective functioning. The patients particularly liked the individual problem-solving sessions. Interestingly, the authors utilized problem solving as a treatment independent of psychoeducation. This is in contrast to most of the studies reviewed, which specifically incorporated problem-solving techniques within the definition of psychoeducation.

In a study conducted in Spain of outpatients diagnosed with bipolar disorder type I and II, Colom and colleagues (2003) compared the impact of 21 psychoeducational group sessions with nonstructured group meetings. Participants in the active treatment were less likely to relapse overall, had fewer relapses per person, increased their time to recurrence of symptoms, and had both fewer and shorter hospitalizations. In a relatively small study (N = 53), Rea and colleagues (2003) compared outcomes for patients involved in 21 individual family psychoeducation sessions with standard individual treatment. Participants in the family psychoeducation sessions were less likely to relapse or be hospitalized over the 2-year study. In a separate, larger study, Miklowitz, George, Richards, Simoneau, and Suddath (2003) randomized 101 individuals with bipolar disorder to either 21 individual psychoeducational family sessions or crisis management (2 educational sessions plus crisis sessions as needed). The patients in the psychoeducational treatment showed fewer relapses overall, longer symptom-free periods, fewer symptoms, and better medication compliance. Both of these studies were manual based, with similar design, method, approach, and outcome. However, the studies together cannot be labeled as meeting criteria for a Category I evidence-based practice because they share an investigator (Chambless & Hollon, 1998).

Peterson and colleagues (1998) used a psychoeducational intervention for women with binge eating disorder, comparing it with three other treatment conditions (partial self-help, structured self-help, and a wait-list control). This was the only study reviewed in which participants in the psychoeducational intervention did not show superior outcomes over time. Rather, participants in all active treatments showed a decrease in binge eating immediately posttreatment. The authors noted several threats to the validity of their study: randomization that targeted groups rather than individuals, small sample size (N = 61), and lack of follow-up data.

APPLICATIONS FOR CAREGIVERS OF PERSONS WITH MENTAL HEALTH CONDITIONS

Two studies particularly addressed the needs of caregivers (see Table 22.2). Hebert and colleagues (2003) tested the efficacy of a 15-session series of psychoeduca-

Table 22.2.   Caregivers of Persons With Mental Health Conditions

Study	Sample/Dx	Design	Active (PE) Treatment Protocol	Structure and Duration	Significant Outcomes for PE	Comment[a]
Hebert et al., 2003	Informal caregivers of persons with dementia	Multisite randomized trial; PE groups vs. traditional support groups. $N =$ 158 stratified by sex & kinship status	Stress appraisal and coping	15 sessions	Tx group shows less reaction to behavior of patient, less frequency of reported problem behaviors. No difference in burden, distress & anxiety, perceived social support, or self-efficacy	Category II
Russell et al., 1999	Parents of children with intellectual disability. Conducted in southern India	Randomized trial; PE groups for parents vs. control group. $N =$ 57	Interactive group PE	10 sessions	Tx group showed improved parental attitude re child rearing & management of disability	Category II. Small total sample size

Note: Dx = diagnosis; PE = psychoeducation; tx = treatment.

[a]Chambless criteria for evidence-based practice (Chambless & Hollon, 1998).

tional groups for informal caregivers of persons with dementia in comparison with traditional support groups. Randomization involved 158 individuals stratified by sex and kinship status at several different sites. The psychoeducational content in the curriculum was focused on stress appraisal and coping. Primary outcome measures were blindly assessed and included frequency and response to behavioral problems among care receivers; secondary measures included patient burden, distress and anxiety, perceived social support, and self-efficacy. Immediately following the intervention, those assigned to the psychoeducational groups reported significantly less reaction to behaviors and a trend toward less frequency of reported behavior problems among the family members with dementia. The interaction between behavior frequency and reaction also showed a significant decrease for caregivers who received psychoeducation. However, there were no significant differences between groups for the secondary patient outcome measures.

In a small study conducted in southern India, Russell, al John, and Lakshmanan (1999) randomly assigned 57 parents of children with intellectual impairment to either an active psychoeducational group intervention or an untreated control group. Participants in the 10- session groups showed significantly improved parental attitude regarding child rearing and management of the disability immediately posttest.

APPLICATIONS FOR MEDICAL ILLNESS

Psychoeducational programs have also been devised for medical illnesses, including acute and life-threatening illnesses other than cancer, as well as more chronic conditions. These programs aim to help both the persons affected and their caregivers or partner weather both the physical and the psychological impact of chronic and acute illness (see Table 22.3).

In one of the cross-national studies identified through this review, researchers in Hong Kong (Cheung, Callaghan, & Chang, 2003) randomly assigned 96 women aged 30 to 55 preparing for elective hysterectomy to either individual psychoeducational sessions (information booklet plus cognitive interventions focusing on distraction and reappraisal) or a control group (information booklet without additional information). Number of sessions, duration, and intensity for the experimental group were not specified and it was difficult to tell how well integrated the educational component was with the cognitive techniques in the psychoeducational intervention. However, women receiving the active treatment reported significantly lower anxiety and pain and higher treatment satisfaction than those in the control group in the days immediately postoperative. There was no difference between the two groups in requests for painkillers postsurgery.

Two additional models addressed chronic medical problems, specifically obesity and generalized pain. Ciliska (1998) randomly assigned 78 women with obesity to a smallgroup psychoeducational intervention (6 to 8 people per group), to an education-alone group using a classroom format (16–20 people),

Table 22.3. Medical Illness

Study	Sample/Dx	Design	Active (PE) Treatment Protocol	Structure and Duration	Significant Outcomes for PE	Comment[a]
Cheung et al., 2003	Women age 30 to 35 preparing for elective hysterectomy	Randomized trial; individual PE sessions vs. control group (info booklet only). $N = 96$	Information plus cognitive intervention with attention to distraction & reappraisal of circumstance	Not specified	Tx group lower anxiety & pain; higher tx satisfaction. No difference in request for pain medicine post-surgery	Category II. Extent and nature of PE not defined
Ciliska, 1998	Women with obesity	Randomized trial comparing PE group, education alone, & control. $N = 78$	Education about obesity; problem solving, assertiveness training; body image work; group support	12 sessions over 12 weeks; 2-hour sessions; 6–8 women	Tx group increased self-esteem & restrained eating; increased body satisfaction	Category II
LeFort et al., 1998	People with chronic physical pain	Randomized trial comparing PE group w/ 3-month wait-list control. $N = 110$	Definitions of pain, myth busting; cognitive-behavioral techniques; pain management; group problem solving; communication skills & mutual support	6 weeks, 12 hours	Short-term improvement of pain severity & impact, role functioning & involvement, life satisfaction, self-efficacy, resourcefulness; decreased dependency. No difference re depression, uncertainty, general health, or physical functioning	Category II. Well-defined study
Olmsted et al., 2002	Adolescent girls with type I diabetes & disturbed eating attitudes & behavior, and parents	Randomized trial comparing PE group w/ tx as usual. $N = 85$	PE content, sociocultural influences, strategies to control symptoms	6 weekly 90-minute group sessions. Separate group sessions for girls and parents	Reduction in eating disturbance; maintained at 6-month fu	Category II. Manual based

Note: Dx = diagnosis; PE = psychoeducation; tx = treatment; fu = follow-up.

[a]Chambless criteria for evidence-based practice (Chambless & Hollon, 1998).

or to an untreated control group. The model emphasized problem solving and assertiveness training, with attention to etiology, risks and benefits; and the relationship between body image and self-esteem. Immediately posttreatment, the psychoeducational subjects showed significantly increased self-esteem, body satisfaction, and more restrained eating patterns compared with participants in either of the two other groups. Outcomes for participants in the education-alone intervention did not differ from those in the control group.

Unremitting physical pain is associated with depressive symptoms such as distress, hopelessness, and despair and contributes to disruption in both individual and family functioning. To address this set of problems, LeFort, Gray-Donald, Rowat, and Jeans (1998) devised a 12-hour psychoeducational model adapted from the Arthritis Self-Management Program (Lorig, 1986) for persons confronted with chronic pain. Curriculum was focused on facts and myths regarding pain, medication, depression, and nutrition in the context of problem solving, communication skills, and mutual support. The authors randomly assigned 110 individuals diagnosed with chronic pain (mean duration of pain, 6 years) to either the psychoeducational groups or a 3-month wait-list control. Immediately posttreatment, the group participants showed significantly reduced indicators of pain and dependency, improved physical functioning, vitality, general life satisfaction, and self-efficacy, and a trend toward improved mental health and social functioning. No differences emerged between the groups either in terms of depression and uncertainty regarding future functioning or on measures from the Medical Outcomes Short Form (Ware & Sherbourne, 1992) on physical functioning and general health. It is noteworthy that those who dropped out or refused the active treatment (8%) appeared to be more affected by pain (i.e., unable to sustain employment) than those who enrolled and participated (LeFort & Steinwachs, 1998). This suggests that the experience of severe pain may interfere with willingness or ability to participate in a group intervention. Olmsted, Daneman, Rydall, Lawson, & Rodin (2002) assigned 85 adolescent girls diagnosed with type I diabetes and comorbid disturbed eating patterns and their parents to either a series of six psychoeducational group sessions or a treatment-as-usual control group. The girls and parents participated in separate but parallel sessions. At 6-month follow-up, the girls in the active treatment continued to show significantly reduced eating disturbance compared with the controls.

APPLICATIONS FOR OTHER CLINICAL SETTINGS AND PREVENTION

Programs designed for other life concerns familiar to social service agencies, exclusive of those directly related to either psychiatry or medicine, have also begun to appear in the literature (see Table 22.4). Gibbs, Potter, Goldstein, and Brendtro (1996) created a manual-based psychoeducational program for adolescents incarcerated in a medium security youth correctional facility. The psychoeducational groups met daily and focused on mediation, skills and values en-

Table 22.4. Other Clinical Settings and Prevention

Study	Sample/Dx	Design	Active (PE) Treatment Protocol	Structure and Duration	Significant Outcomes for PE	Comment[a]
Gibbs et al., 1996	Antisocial youth/ medium-security youth correctional facility	Randomized PE group vs. control. Pilot data; N not reported	Strengths-based; peer group mediation, skills training, anger management, moral education	Daily meetings, 60–90 minutes; 7–9 youth. Duration & leadership not described	Pilot data: Active tx: 15 % recidivism at 6 mos. & 1 year. Controls: 30% at 6 mos.; 41% at 1 year	Clear summary of theory & conceptual model
Kubany et al., 2003	Women with hx of partner abuse plus PTSD	Randomized individual PE sessions vs. wait-list control. N = 37	Exploration of trauma hx, stress management, assertiveness, managing contact with batterer, strategies for self-advocacy & avoiding victimization	8 to 11 hour-&-half sessions	At posttx, 94% did not meet PTSD criteria; reduced depression, guilt, shame, increased self-esteem. Wait-list controls showed no change at second pretest	Category II. Small sample
Rocco et al., 2001	Adolescent girls in affluent high school in Italy; prevention of eating disorders	Random assignment to PE groups vs. no-group controls	Focus on normal developmental transitions, risk factors for eating disorders, social challenge, body shape, & weight	9 monthly sessions	Tx group showed reduced bulimic attitudes, tendency to asceticism, ineffectiveness, anxiety, & fears about maturity	Prevention-oriented study; nonclinical sample

Note: Dx = diagnosis; PE = psychoeducation; tx = treatment; hx = history; PTSD = posttraumatic stress disorder.

[a]Chambless criteria for evidence-based practice (Chambless & Hollon, 1998).

hancement, and peer support. Adolescents were taught to recognize negative social behavior both in themselves and among their peers and to replace these behaviors with more constructive and affirmative responses and actions. In a randomized pilot study, participants in the psychoeducational groups were described as dramatically easier to manage, with significantly improved social skills and adjustment and decreased antisocial behavior. However, sample size, duration of treatment, and time to follow-up were not specified.

In a small randomized trial conducted in Hawaii, Kubany, Hill, and Owens (2003) assigned 37 ethnically diverse women with both a history of partner abuse and a diagnosis of posttraumatic stress disorder (PTSD) to either an individually based psychoeducational program or a wait-list group. Most of the women (32) eventually completed the program. The active intervention incorporated 8 to 11 individual one-and-a-half-hour sessions, focusing on explorations of trauma history, stress management, monitoring of negative self-talk, assertiveness, managing contact with the abuser, and strategies for self-advocacy and avoiding revictimization. At posttreatment and 3- month follow-up, 94% of the women no longer met criteria for PTSD. Moreover, they showed significantly reduced depression, guilt, and shame, and increased self-esteem. In contrast, those women assigned to the wait-list group showed no changes in scores for any measure at the second pretest. Although the sample size was extremely small, the authors documented positive results across ethnic groups, suggesting that the themes addressed in the psychoeducational groups (i.e., male dominance and the status of women relative to men) were universal issues.

Another study involved groups of participants from the general population and was designed to promote health attitudes and behaviors regarding nutrition and as a preventive technique for the development of eating disorders (see Table 22.4). Rocco, Ciano, and Balestrieri (2001) randomly assigned adolescent girls from an affluent high school in Italy to receive either nine monthly sessions in intensive psychoeducational groups or no intervention. The program targeted normal developmental transitions as well as known risk factors for eating disorders, with attention to body shape and weight, social challenges, and academic achievement. Compared with the controls, participants showed reductions in bulimic attitudes, in tendency to asceticism, and in feelings of ineffectiveness, as well as lowered anxiety and fears about maturity.

DISCUSSION

In reviewing this relatively small number of studies, it is clear that all fall into Category II in terms of the APA criteria for evidence-based practice (Chambless & Hollon, 1998; Chambless & Ollendick, 2001; Task Force on Promotion and Dissemination of Psychological Procedures, 1995). None of the studies reviewed would meet the criteria for Category I, because they either are not sufficiently rigorous, have not been replicated by independent investigators, or both. However, reviewing the limitations and strengths of these studies is instructive so that potential investigators can anticipate the challenges involved in designing and conducting effective psychoeducational interventions across diagnostic groups and settings.

Limitations and Strengths of the Studies

The assessment tools and methods that are common across the studies identified in this paper extend our understanding of how psychoeducational interventions can be consistently evaluated. Several recurring parameters of measurement for assessing the impact of psychoeducation on participants and significant others can be identified from this group of studies (see Tables I through IV) and are consistent with those used in the work on schizophrenia and cancer. These include changes in symptoms (i.e., symptom reduction specific to the targeted illness or situation), decreased anxiety and depression (regardless of problem and setting), and less time between acute episodes of illness. They also include increased adherence to and overall satisfaction with medication and treatment, knowledge, self-esteem and resources, family/marital climate or adjustment, and quality of life.

However, measures of process—including attendance, dropout, turnover, training of facilitators, and fidelity of treatment—cannot be so clearly identified. Although these are more characteristic of evaluation studies than randomized trials, such data would help to inform future studies. In addition, assessment of resilience and competence, designated as integral to the strengths-based psychoeducational process, would contribute knowledge regarding the unique and irreducible aspects of the approach (Anderson et al., 1986; Cunningham, 2000; McFarlane et al., 2003). These include measures of the ability to act and change, willingness to initiate change, application to self-help work, and quality of relationships with others and everyday experience.

Other limitations can be identified in the studies reviewed in terms of both conceptual approach and research design. These include issues regarding sampling strategies, sample size, and statistical power; measurement (both process and outcome); analysis; and clinical definition. As regards sampling, several problems appear. There is almost no variability in ethnicity within the studies reviewed, with the exception of Kubany et al.'s (2003) work on women who have been battered and suffer from PTSD. In addition, only two of the studies provide information on independence and blindedness among assessment staff and describe inclusion/exclusion criteria for study participants (LeFort et al., 1998; Russell et al., 1999).

Both specificity as to follow-up and efforts to assess sustained impact of the interventions over time are lacking in some of the studies reviewed as well. Work is also needed to assess when and for whom psychoeducational interventions do *not* work. Addressing these limitations would involve identifying the multideterminant and "optimal" measures for each illness or set of circumstances for the individual, family unit, individual family members, and the community. Attending to the profiles of those who reject or drop out of this form of intervention is also critical. Qualitative approaches may be needed to assess subjective response to intervention, motivation, emotional availability, and readiness to process information or participate in a group intervention (Cunningham, 2000; McFarlane et al., 2003).

Another factor that interferes with the ability to replicate studies has to do with how the investigators understand and present the clinical determinants of psychoeducation in each study. Given the breadth of applications cited in this paper, it is inevitable that the documented interventions would vary greatly in intensity, duration, and content. However, the term *psychoeducation* is used inconsistently as well, and at least one study referred to the intervention as atheoretical (Bultz et al., 2000).

To address these inconsistencies, efforts are needed to further articulate the common and situation-specific aspects of psychoeducational curriculum where possible, as well as structure, duration, and organization of content (Cunningham, 2000; McFarlane et al., 2003). As specified in the APA task force on empirically supported practice (Task Force on Promotion and Dissemination of Psychological Procedures, 1995), access to a well-defined treatment manual is essential as a precursor to measuring fidelity of treatment and to ensure potential for efficacy and replication. Some established investigators have addressed this by providing access to their materials through the public domain. For example, Sherman's (2003) psychoeducational curriculum for families of persons with mental illness is available on the Internet, and McFarlane's work on psychoeducational multiple family groups for schizophrenia is available through the evidence-based practices project sponsored by the Substance Abuse and Mental Health Services Administration and the Robert Wood Johnson Foundation (Steering Committee, 2003).

Summary and Conclusions

In summary, this review indicates that psychoeducational interventions have been applied in a wide range of settings across system levels, although to date only those addressing schizophrenia and cancer can be considered evidence based. A breadth of programs using this flexible modality have emerged, as professional health care workers have become increasingly aware of the critical role that familial and other informal sources of support play in health outcome, successful functioning, and quality of life in several illnesses. As medical and psychiatric care have become less contiguous and all aspects of medical care have become more specialized and fragmented, continuity of care and knowledge regarding individual situations has become increasingly difficult to maintain and coordinate among professional providers (Lasker, 1997). This has been worsened by policy changes in the health care environment involving managed care and increasingly consolidated or truncated services (House, Landis, & Umberson, 1988; McDonald, Stetz, & Compton, 1996; Mechanic, 2002; Pescosolido, Wright, & Sullivan, 1995).

Psychoeducational interventions appear to be sufficiently flexible to circumvent some of the dangers. To date, they have been used successfully either as primary or adjunctive treatment, as part of a strategic program for prevention, or as an experiential training tool for patients and their families in a range of settings (Cunningham, Wolbert, et al., 2000; Lukens, Thorning, & Herman, 1999; McFarlane et al., 2003; Thase, 1997). However, additional efforts are needed to fully define psychoeducation at the clinical, community, and professional levels as applied to various settings and populations, and to further identify how emerging and state-of-the-art professional knowledge can be integrated into such programs. Existing programs that show preliminary success for conditions other than schizophrenia or cancer must be successfully replicated under rigorous conditions before they meet the stringent criteria for evidence-based practice laid out by the APA (Chambless & Hollon, 1998; Task Force on Promotion and Dissemination of Psychological Procedures, 1995).

To better establish efficacy and effectiveness, research designed to evaluate the impact of the interventions on outcomes over time and in a range of settings is critical. To conduct such studies, clear and readily available treatment goals and principles, carefully defined process and outcome measures, and curriculum and training manuals are needed to facilitate implementation and replication by mental health and health professionals, educators, and researchers. At the individual and family level, measures of outcome should include knowledge, attitudes, social and vocational function, self-efficacy and self-esteem, and other indicators of quality of life and health. At the service and community level, indicators should include knowledge and attitudes among providers, and documentation of health behaviors, service access and use, and cost-effectiveness (Dixon et al., 2000; Dixon et al., 2001; Lukens & Thorning, 1998). At the policy level there are two challenges: first, to assess readiness for implementation, and second, to determine acceptance and broad-based integration of the approach at the service level (Cunningham, 2000; Dixon, Goldman, & Hirad, 1999; McFarlane et al., 2003).

Psychoeducation has the potential to extend the impact of care provision well beyond the immediate situation by activating and reinforcing both formal and informal support systems (Caplan & Caplan, 2000; Lundwall, 1996; Pescosolido, Wright, & Sullivan, 1995) and teaching individuals and communities how to anticipate and manage periods of transition and crisis. If developed and implemented carefully, following specified guidelines for delivering and documenting evidence-based practices (Task Force on Promotion and Dissemination of Psychological Procedures, 1995), psychoeducational interventions have far-reaching application for acute and chronic illness and other life challenges across levels of the public health, social and civic services, and/or educational systems.

NOTE

REFERENCES

American Psychiatric Association. (1994). *Diagnostic and statistical manual of mental disorders* (4th ed.). Washington, DC: Author.

American Psychiatric Association. (1997). Practice guideline for the treatment of patients with schizophrenia. *American Journal of Psychiatry*, 154(4 Suppl), 1–63.

Anderson, C., Reiss, D. J., & Hogarty, G. E. (1986). *Schizophrenia and the family: A practitioner's guide to psychoeducation and management*. New York: Guilford Press.

Baucom, D. H., Shoham, V., Mueser, K. T., Daiuto, A. D., & Stickle, T. R. (1998). Empirically supported couple and family interventions for marital distress and adult mental health problems. Journal of Consulting and Clinical Psychology, 66, 53–88.

Bultz, B. D., Speca, M., Brasher, P. M., Geggie, P. H., & Page, S. A. (2000). A randomized controlled trial of a brief psychoeducational support group for partners of early stage breast cancer patients. *Psychooncology, 9*, 303–313.

Caplan, G., & Caplan, R. (2000). Principles of community psychiatry. Community Mental Health Journal, 36, 7–24.

Chambless, D. L., & Hollon, S. D. (1998). Defining empirically supported therapies. *Journal of Consulting and Clinical Psychology, 66*, 7–18.

Chambless, D. L., & Ollendick, T. H. (2001). Empirically supported psychological interventions: Controversies and evidence. *Annual Review of Psychology, 52*, 685–716.

Cheung, L. H., Callaghan, P., & Chang, A. M. (2003). A controlled trial of psychoeducational interventions in preparing Chinese women for elective hysterectomy. *International Journal of Nursing Studies, 40*, 207–216.

Ciliska, D. (1998). Evaluation of two nondieting interventions for obese women. *Western Journal of Nursing Research, 20*, 119–135.

Colom, F., Vieta, E., Martinez-Aran, A., Reinares, M., Goikolea, J. M., Benabarre, A., et al. (2003). A randomized trial on the efficacy of group psychoeducation in the prophylaxis of recurrences in bipolar patients whose disease is in remission. *Archives of General Psychiatry, 60*, 402–407.

Coursey, R. (2000). Competencies for direct service staff members who work with adults with severe mental illness in outpatient public mental health managed care systems. *Psychiatric Rehabilitation Journal, 23*, 370–377.

Coursey, R., Curtis, L., & Marsh, D. (2000). Competencies for direct service workers who work with adults with severe mental illness: Specific knowledge, attitudes, skills and biography. *Psychiatric Rehabilitation Journal, 23*, 378–392.

Cunningham, A. J. (2000). Adjuvant psychological therapy for cancer patients: Putting it on the same footing as adjunctive medical therapies. *Psychooncology, 9*, 367–371.

Cunningham, A. J., Edmonds, C. V., Phillips, C., Soots, K. I., Hedley, D., & Lockwood, G. A. (2000). A prospective, longitudinal study of the relationship of psychological work to duration of survival in patients with metastatic cancer. *Psychooncology, 9*, 323–339.

Cunningham, K., Wolbert, R., & Brockmeier, M. B. (2000). Moving beyond the illness: Factors contributing to gaining and maintaining employment. *American Journal of Community Psychology, 28*, 481–494.

Dixon, L. (1999). Providing services to families of persons with schizophrenia: Present and future. *Journal of Mental Health Policy and Economics, 2,* 3–8.

Dixon, L., Adams, C., & Lucksted, A. (2000). Update on family psychoeducation for schizophrenia. *Schizophrenia Bulletin, 26,* 5–20.

Dixon, L., Goldman, H., & Hirad, A. (1999). State policy and funding of services to families of adults with serious and persistent mental illness. *Psychiatric Services, 50,* 551–553.

Dixon, L., McFarlane, W., Lefley, H., Lucksted, A., Cohen, M., Falloon, I., et al. (2001). Evidence-based practices for services to families of people with psychiatric disabilities. *Psychiatric Services, 52,* 903–908.

Dowrick, C., Dunn, G., Ayuso-Mateos, J. L., Dalgard, O. S., Page, H., Lehtinen, V., et al. (2000). Problem solving treatment and group psychoeducation for depression: Mulitcentre randomized controlled trial. Outcomes of Depression International Network (ODIN) Group. *British Medical Journal, 321*(7274), 1450–1454.

Dyck, D. G., Hendryx, M. S., Short, R. A., Voss, W. D., & McFarlane, W. R. (2002). Service use among patients with schizophrenia in psychoeducational multiple-family group treatment. *Psychiatric Services, 53,* 749–754.

Dyck, D. G., Short, R. A., Hendryx, M. S., Norell, D., Myers, M., Patterson, T., et al. (2000). Management of negative symptoms among patients with schizophrenia attending multiplefamily groups. *Psychiatric Services, 51,* 513–519.

Edmonds, C. V., Lockwood, G. A., & Cunningham, A. J. (1999). Psychological response to long-term group therapy: A randomized trial with metastatic breast cancer patients. *Psychooncology, 8,* 74–91.

Fawzy, F. I., Fawzy, N. W., Arndt, L. A., & Pasnau, R. O. (1995). Critical review of psychosocial interventions in cancer care. *Archives of General Psychiatry, 52,* 100–113.

Frances, A. J., Kahn, D. A., Carpenter, D., Docherty, J. P., & Donovan, S. L. (1998). The Expert Consensus Guidelines for treating depression in bipolar depression. *Journal of Clinical Psychiatry, 59*(Suppl 4), 73–79.

Fristad, M. A., Gavazzi, S. M., & Mackinaw-Koons, B. (2003). Family psychoeducation: An adjunctive intervention for children with bipolar disorder. *Biological Psychiatry, 53,* 1000–1008.

Fristad, M. A., Gavazzi, S. M., & Soldano, K. W. (1998). Multi-family psychoeducation groups for childhood mood disorders: A program description and preliminary efficacy data. *Contemporary Family Therapy, 20,* 385–403.

Fristad, M. A., Goldberg-Arnold, J. S., & Gavazzi, S. M. (2002). Multifamily psychoeducation groups (MFPG) for families of children with bipolar disorder. *Bipolar Disorders, 4,* 254–262.

Fristad, M. A., Goldberg-Arnold, J. S., & Gavazzi, S. M. (2003). Multifamily psychoeducation groups in the treatment of children with mood disorders. *Journal of Marital and Family Therapy, 29,* 491–504.

Gibbs, J. C., Potter, G. B., Goldstein, A. P., & Brendtro, L. K. (1996). Frontiers in psychoeducation: The EQUIP model with antisocial youth. *Reclaiming Children and Youth, 4,* 22–28.

Hebert, R., Levesque, L., Vezina, J., Lavoie, J. P., Ducharme, F., Gendron, C., et al. (2003). Efficacy of a psychoeducative group program for caregivers of demented persons living at home: A randomized controlled trial. *Journals of Gerontology Series B Psychological Sciences and Social Sciences, 58,* S58–S67.

Honey, K. L., Bennett, P., & Morgan, M. (2003). Predicting postnatal depression. *Journal of Affective Disorders, 76,* 201–210.

House, J. S., Landis, K. R., & Umberson, D. (1988). Social relationships and health. *Science, 241,* 540–545.

Kaminer, Y., Burleson, J. A., & Goldberger, R. (2002). Cognitive-behavioral coping skills and psychoeducation therapies for adolescent substance abuse. *Journal of Nervous and Mental Disease, 190,* 737–745.

Kubany, E. S., Hill, E. E., & Owens, J. A. (2003). Cognitive trauma therapy for battered women with PTSD: Preliminary findings. *Journal of Traumatic Stress, 16,* 81–91.

Lasker, R. D. (1997). *Medicine and public health: The power of collaboration.* New York: New York Academy of Medicine.

Latimer, W. W., Winters, K. C., D'Zurilla, T., & Nichols, M. (2003). Integrated family and cognitive-behavioral therapy for adolescent substance abusers: A stage I efficacy study. *Drug and Alcohol Dependence, 71,* 303–317.

LeFort, S. M., Gray-Donald, K., Rowat, K. M., & Jeans, M. E. (1998). Randomized controlled trial of a community-based psychoeducation program for the management of chronic pain. *Pain, 74,* 297–306.

Lehman, A. F., & Steinwachs, D. M. (1998). Translating research into practice: The Schizophrenia Patient Outcomes Research Team (PORT) treatment recommendations. *Schizophrenia Bulletin, 24,* 1–10.

Lorig, K. (1986). Development and dissemination of an arthritis patient education course. *Family and Community Health, 9,* 23–32.

Lukens, E., & Thorning, H. (1998). Psychoeducation and severe mental illness: Implications for social work practice and research. In J. B. W. Williams & K. Ell (Eds.), *Advances in mental health research: Implications for practice* (pp. 343–364). Washington, DC: NASW Press.

Lukens, E., Thorning, H., & Herman, D. B. (1999). Family psychoeducation in schizophrenia: Emerging themes and challenges. *Journal of Practical Psychiatry and Behavioral Health, 5,* 314–325.

Lundwall, R. A. (1996). How psychoeducational support groups can provide multidiscipline services to families of people with mental illness. *Psychiatric Rehabilitation Journal, 20,* 64–71.

Marsh, D. (1992). Working with families of people with serious mental illness. In L. VandeCreek, S. Knapp, & T. L. Jackson (Eds.), *Innovations in clinical practice: A sourcebook* (Vol. 11, pp. 389–402). Sarasota, FL: Professional Resource Press.

McDonald, J. C., Stetz, K. M., & Compton, K. (1996). Educational interventions for family caregivers during marrow transplantation. *Oncology Nursing Forum, 23,* 1432–1439.

McEvoy, J. P., Scheifler, P. L., & Frances, A. (1999). Expert consensus guidelines series: Treatment of schizophrenia. *Journal of Clinical Psychiatry, 60*(Suppl 11), 3–80.

McFarlane, W. (2002). *Multifamily groups in the treatment of severe psychiatric disorders.* New York: Guilford Press.

McFarlane, W. R., Dixon, L., Lukens, E., & Lucksted, A. (2003). Family psychoeducation and schizophrenia: A review of the literature. Journal of Marital and Family Therapy, 29, 223–245.

McFarlane, W. R., Dushay, R. A., Stastny, P., Deakins, S. A., & Link, B. (1996). A comparison of two levels of family-aided assertive community treatment. *Psychiatric Services, 47,* 744–750.

McFarlane, W. R., Lukens, E., Link, B., Dushay, R., Deakins, S. A., Newmark, M., et al. (1995). Multiple-family groups and psychoeducation in the treatment of schizophrenia. *Archives of General Psychiatry, 52,* 679–687.

Mechanic, D. (1995). Sociological dimensions of illness behavior. *Social Science and Medicine, 41,* 1207–1216.

Mechanic, D. (2002). Improving the quality of health care in the United States of America: The need for a multi-level approach. *Journal of Health Services Research and Policy, 7*(Suppl 1), S35–S39.

Meyer, T. J., & Mark, M. M. (1995). Effects of psychosocial interventions with adult cancer patients: A meta-analysis of randomized experiments. *Health Psychology, 14,* 101–108.

Miklowitz, D. J., George, E. L., Richards, J. A., Simoneau, T. L., & Suddath, R. L. (2003). A randomized study of family-focused psychoeducation and pharmacotherapy in the outpatient management of bipolar disorder. *Archives of General Psychiatry, 60,* 904–912.

Montero, I., Asencio, A., Hernandez, I., Masanet, M. J., Lacruz, M., Bellver, F., et al. (2001). Two strategies for family intervention in schizophrenia: A randomized trial in a Mediterranean environment. *Schizophrenia Bulletin, 27,* 661–670.

Nathan, P. E., & Gorman, J. M. (1998). *A guide to treatments that work.* New York: Oxford University Press.

Olmsted, M. P., Daneman, D., Rydall, A. C., Lawson, M. L., & Rodin, G. (2002). The effects of psychoeducation on disturbed eating attitudes and behavior in young women with type 1 diabetes mellitus. *International Journal of Eating Disorders, 32,* 230–239.

Penninx, B. W., van Tilburg, T., Kriegsman, D. M., Boeke, A. J., Deeg, D. J., & van Eijk, J. T. (1999). Social network, social support, and loneliness in older persons with different chronic diseases. Journal of Aging and Health, 11, 151–168.

Pescosolido, B., Wright, E., & Sullivan, W. (1995). Communities of care: A theoretical perspective on case management models in mental health. *Advances in Medical Sociology, 6,* 37–79.

Peterson, C. B., Mitchell, J. E., Engboom, S., Nugent, S., Mussell, M. P., & Miller, J. P. (1998). Group cognitive-behavioral treatment of binge eating disorder: A comparison of therapist-led versus self-help formats. *International Journal of Eating Disorders, 24,* 125–136.

President's New Freedom Commission on Mental Health. (2003). *Achieving the promise: Transforming mental health care in America.* Rockville, MD: Author.

Rea, M. M., Tompson, M. C., Miklowitz, D. J., Goldstein, M. J., Hwang, S., & Mintz, J. (2003). Family-focused treatment versus individual treatment for bipolar disorder: Results of a randomized clinical trial. *Journal of Consulting and Clinical Psychology, 71,* 482–492.

Richardson, J. L., Shelton, D. R., Krailo, M., & Levine, A. M. (1990). The effect of compliance with treatment on survival among patients with hematologic malignancies. *Journal of Clinical Oncology, 8,* 356–364.

Richardson, J. L., Zarnegar, Z., Bisno, B., & Levine, A. (1990). Psychosocial status at initiation of cancer treatment and survival. *Journal of Psychosomatic Research, 34,* 189–201.

Rocco, P. L., Ciano, R. P., & Balestrieri, M. (2001). Psychoeducation in the prevention of eating disorders: An experimental approach in adolescent schoolgirls. *British Journal of Medical Psychology, 74*(Pt 3), 351–358.

Rousanville, B., Carroll, K., & Onken, L. (2001). A stage model of behavioral therapies research: Getting started and moving on from stage I. *Clinical Psychology: Science and Practice, 8*, 133–142.

Russell, P. S., al John, J. K., & Lakshmanan, J. L. (1999). Family intervention for intellectually disabled children. Randomised controlled trial. *British Journal of Psychiatry, 174*, 254–258.

Shelton, T. L., Barkley, R. A., Crosswait, C., Moorehouse, M., Fletcher, K., Barrett, S., et al. (2000). Multimethod psychoeducational intervention for preschool children with disruptive behavior: Two-year post-treatment follow-up. *Journal of Abnormal Child Psychology, 28*, 253–266.

Sherman, M. D. (2003). The Support and Family Education (SAFE) program: Mental health facts for families. *Psychiatric Services, 54*, 35–37.

Solomon, P., Draine, J., & Mannion, E. (1996). The impact of individualized consultation and group workshop family education interventions on ill relative outcomes. *Journal of Nervous and Mental Disease, 184*, 252–254.

Solomon, P., Draine, J., Mannion, E., & Meisel, M. (1996). Impact of brief family psychoeducation on self-efficacy. *Schizophrenia Bulletin, 22*, 41–50.

Spiegel, D., Bloom, J. R., Kraemer, H. C., & Gottheil, E. (1989). Effect of psychosocial treatment on survival of patients with metastatic breast cancer. *Lancet, 2*, 888–891.

Steering Committee. (2003). *Implementing evidencebased practices project, phase I.* U.S. Dept of Health and Human Services/Robert Wood Johnson Foundation. Retrieved May 10, 2004, from http://www.mentalhealthpractices.org

Task Force on Promotion and Dissemination of Psychological Procedures. (1995). Training in and dissemination of empirically validated psychological treatments: Report and recommendations. *Clinical Psychologist, 48*, 3–23.

Thase, M. E. (1997). Psychotherapy of refractory depressions. *Depression and Anxiety, 5*, 190–201.

Ware, J. E., Jr., & Sherbourne, C. D. (1992). The MOS 36-item short-form health survey (SF-36). I. Conceptual framework and item selection. *Medical Care, 30*, 473–483.

White, M. (1989). *Selected papers.* Adelaide, Australia: Dulwich Centre Publications.

23

Mental Illness, Substance Dependence, and Suicidality

Secondary Data Analysis

KENNETH R. YEAGER

ALBERT R. ROBERTS

Mental illness, substance dependence, and suicide are three of the most prevalent social and public health concerns throughout North America. Recent estimates indicate that every 20 minutes somewhere in the United States or Canada a suicide occurs. In the United States alone there are 30,000 suicides per year (Bush, Fawcett, & Jacobs, 2003; Institute of Medicine, 2002). This chapter seeks to explain the contributing factors leading to rehospitalization and suicide risk among the psychiatric, substance abuse, and substance dependent populations. Data from a university medical center will be reviewed regarding characteristics of inpatient hospitalization and potential contributing factors increasing the individual's risk of a suicide attempt following inpatient psychiatric/substance dependence hospitalization. In 2001 approximately 15 million adults age 18 or greater were estimated to have suffered from a severe mental illness during the previous year. The population with the highest rate of severe mental illness was the 18-to-25-year-old age group (12%). Persons ages 26–49 demonstrated a rate of approximately 8%, with the 50 or older age group demonstrating a rate of 5%. Females were more likely than males to have a diagnosis consistent with severe mental illness (9% female versus 6% male) (National Institute of Mental Health, 2001; Bush et al., 2003; Institute of Medicine, 2002).

It is important to understand this population and potential diagnostic pattern changes occurring within the population group to provide the most effective psychiatric illness management. To help facilitate such understanding this chapter outlines an emerging pattern of comorbid diagnosis that emerged in a recent secondary data set review of admissions to a metropolitan psychiatric and substance dependence treatment facility. Within this population the impact of multiple psychiatric diagnoses, dependence on multiple substances among substance dependent individuals, and comorbid psychiatric and substance dependence diagnoses were examined in the context of their contribution to rehospitalization within 31 days of initial hospitalization and the presence and severity of suicidal ideation in those rehospitalized.

Recent research has demonstrated that in many cases severe mental illness can be successfully managed if the affected individual is able to receive treatment; however, in 2001 National Institute of Mental Health data revealed that less than one half (47%) of persons with a severe mental illness received treatment or counseling intervention within the previous year. Within this population adults aged 26 or greater are most likely to receive treatment. Females were more likely to receive treatment (52%) compared with their male counterparts (38%). Whites were more likely to receive mental health treatment or counseling than were Hispanics or blacks (National Institute of Mental Health, 2001).

The National Institute of Mental Health data indicates that adults with a severe mental illness were more likely to have used illicit drugs during the previous year compared with those without a severe mental illness. Incidence of illicit drug use was more than twice as high among adults with an identified severe mental illness (27%) than among the general population without a mental illness diagnosis (11%) (National Institute of Mental Health, 2001; Jacobs, 1999).

DATA COLLECTION

Within the day-to-day function of the psychiatric facility examined in this study data is gathered on an ongoing basis. Data is collected for registration purposes, assessment purposes, and quality and operational improvement purposes. Initially, demographic information is collected during the initial call, emergency department admission, or upon intake. Data collected is utilized to create an electronic file for each patient and stored in the "information warehouse," the medical center's electronic warehousing computer.

The next step in the data collection process is completion of the patient's psychiatric screening. The screening consists of the patient's presenting problem, review of symptoms, suicidal risk assessment, current functionality status, and current life circumstances, including living arrangements, assessment of the individual's ability to care for self and potential risk for self-harm. The initial screen data is reviewed with the attending psychiatrist, and the patient is admitted to the most appropriate level of care. For most patients this process will take approximately 1 hour to 90 minutes. Again, information gathered is stored in the electronic record in the information warehouse.

If the psychiatric prescreeners and the psychiatrist determine that the patient meets criteria for inpatient admission, a complete biopsychosocial assessment is completed by a master of social work (MSW) or psychiatric nurse (RN) as part of the admission process. The patient's diagnosis as previously established during the screening and intake process is confirmed during the more complete bio-psychosocial assessment and treatment planning process, which are both electronically recorded. Once the patient's treatment is complete, the length of stay, primary discharge diagnosis, and other rank diagnoses are recorded into the information warehouse. It is important to note that the electronic medical record and categorization is monitored and updated throughout the patient's hospitalization. This provides for optimal data collection because the data is based on the actual care experience. Utilization of the electronic medical record minimizes commonly occurring errors in electronic data collection such as missing data, data entry errors, and poorly timed data entry secondary to data entry not being given top priority. In addition, data verification included but was not limited to comparing data by patient and encounter, diagnostic coding between billing ICD-9 codes and medical record rank ordering of diagnosis, and frequency analysis to facilitate elimination of multiple entries for the same patient.

Additional uses for the data collected over the length of stay include quality and operational improvement activities. Data collected throughout the patient's stay is analyzed for quality improvement processes. Among the quality indicators measured are patient falls, reported medication errors, observed to expected length of stay, restraint and seclusion episodes, and readmissions within 31 days. Tracking and reporting of this data is a requirement of mental health credentialing entities and accreditation entities such as the Joint Commission on Accreditation of Healthcare Organizations (JCAHO). JCAHO evaluates and accredits nearly 17,000 health care organizations and programs in the United States. An independent, not-for-profit organization, JCAHO is the nation's predominant health care standards-setting and accrediting body. As such, JCAHO seeks to continuously improve the safety and quality of care provided to the public through the provision of health care accreditation and related services that support performance improvement in health care organizations. Examples of quality and safety initiatives include each institution's analysis of trends within high risk areas of behavioral health care such as episodes of restraint and seclusion, patient falls, and medication errors and established action plans to address emergent quality improvement opportunities. For example, readmissions may be representative of issues with length of stay being either too short or longer than necessary given population breakouts. Finally, keeping track of readmissions within a 31-day period is helpful in monitoring psychiatrists' prescribing practices and to increase practice-based evidence designed to facilitate optimal medication management.

SECONDARY DATA ANALYSIS

This secondary data analysis demonstrates how hospital quality assurance programming can be combined with data analysis to determine the presence of an emerging pattern of increasing severity of suicide risk including acts of harm to self and others both prior to and during readmissions to the inpatient psychiatric facility within 31 days of initial hospitalization. Specifically, within the process of quality improvement initiatives three cases of remarkable patient acts of harm to self or others on the inpatient psychiatric facility led to completion of a root cause analysis, which examined potential contributing factors to the emergence of violent actions of harm to self or others in the inpatient psychiatric unit. Figure 23.1 is the simplified fishbone diagram completed as a portion of the root cause analysis documenting common factors among the three cases leading to potential harm to self and others. This analysis led to further investigation into the occurrence of comorbid diagnosis among the presenting population. The findings of this "drill-down" analysis indicated that an identifiable group of nominal variables was present in each case and may be indicative of a larger force working among the patient population. In the next step of the analysis the patient population of this facility was examined utilizing data collected in the information warehouse to determine the prevalence of high-risk behaviors such as suicidal ideation among those readmitted within 31 days and to determine if there were emerging patterns of increasing comorbid diagnostic categories. Analysis indicated a .79 correlation between the presence of comorbid diagnosis and increasing risk of harm to self and others.

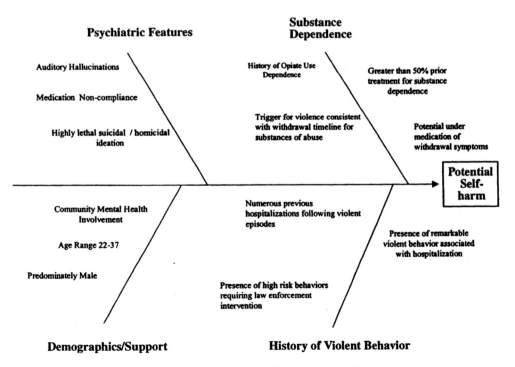

Figure 23.1   Analysis of Potential Harm to Self and Others

Table 23.1   Inpatient Psychiatric Population
Overview by Primary Diagnosis

Diagnosis	Number of Cases
Alcohol dependence	495
Drug dependence	490
Bipolar disorder	470
Anxiety disorder	436
Major depressive disorder	317
Schizophrenia group	317

Note: Substance abuse was the prevalent secondary diagnosis presenting in 740 cases. Alcohol abuse was identified in
114 cases and was considered to be under-diagnosed. Alcohol
abuse was defined as frequent consumption of more than six
drinks per occasion with the absence of physical dependence
and diagnostic criteria as defined by the DSM-IV-TR.

A study was conducted that reviewed secondary data collected over a 6-month
period examining a total of 4,467 cases evaluated for inpatient psychiatric and
substance dependence disorders. Within the population evaluated 1,942 patients
did not present with clearly identifiable diagnostic criteria on Axis 1 within a
major diagnostic category or were under 18 years of age, thus excluding these
cases from this data set. A total of 2,525 cases met criteria for inclusion in the
study, that is, cases presenting with either a substance dependence diagnosis or
a major diagnostic category for mental illness as defined by the DSM-IV-TR via
mental health assessment by licensed independent social workers and psychiatric
nurses. An overview of the primary diagnostic categories is listed in Table 23.1.
In addition, a subpopulation of 740 cases that were in the initial data set and
were readmitted within a 31-day period was examined to determine potential
trends of suicide risk factors (American Psychiatric Association, 2002).

It is important to note that criteria for inpatient admission to this facility
require presence of clear and present risk to self or others or the inability of the
individual to care for him- or herself secondary to psychosis or impending substance withdrawal requiring medical intervention. Hence the prevalence of suicidal ideation will be greater than that described above as applying to the general
population.

PREVALENCE OF SUICIDAL IDEATION AMONG THE MOOD DISORDER POPULATION

We conducted electronic case reviews of patients presenting for psychiatric and
substance dependence treatment. The first group examined was the population
presenting with depressive disorder with suicidal ideation. Within this population
72% presented with current suicidal ideation. Of the patients with current suicidal ideation 23% reported ideation without plan or intent, and 49% were able
to verbalize plan and intent (see Figure 7.2).

Not suicidal
28%

Suicidal w/
plan
49%

Suicidal w/o
plan
23%

Figure 23.2   Major Depressive Disorder Reporting Suicidal Ideation

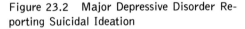

Not suicidal
12%

Suicidal w/
plan
57%

Suicidal no
plan
17%

Figure 23.3   Bipolar I and II Reporting Suicidal Ideation

Examination of the prevalence of suicidal ideation among the bipolar I and II population was conducted in much the same manner, demonstrating slightly higher rates of suicidal ideation upon inpatient hospitalization, with 86% of this population presenting with active suicidal ideation at the time of admission. Fifty-seven percent verbalized a plan with intent to carry out, 17% verbalized suicidal ideation, and only 12% were admitted without suicidal ideation (see Figure 23.3). The remaining 14% were omitted secondary to extreme manic and delusional states that made determination of suicide risk impossible.

Among the population presenting with a schizophrenia diagnosis the reporting of suicidal ideation was less than expected, and the reporting of ideation without a plan was higher than expected. In all, 29% of this population verbalized no suicidal ideation but instead were admitted secondary to an inability to care for self. Of those admitted with suicidal ideation 37% reported ideation with no specific plan, and 34% reported specific plan with intent (see Figure 23.4).

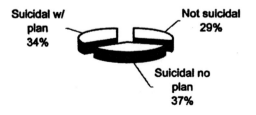

Suicidal w/
plan
34%

Not suicidal
29%

Suicidal no
plan
37%

Figure 23.4   Schizophrenia Group Reporting Suicidal Ideation

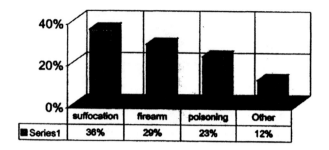

Figure 23.5   Verbalized Plan Method

EXPRESSED PLANNED METHOD

Within the population that verbalized suicidal ideation we examined the expressed suicide plan. Within the population four clear suicide plan categories emerged: poisoning (e.g., taking a known toxic substance or dose of a substance believed to create a toxic and lethal outcome; overdose was included in this area); suffocation, including hanging or suffocation by plastic bag; firearm (the use of a gun as the suicide weapon); and other, which included numerous methods, but cutting and motor vehicle accidents were prominently identified methods (see Figure 23.5).

GENDER AND RACE ISSUES

Among the population examined in this study there were more female admissions than male admissions, but only by 2%: female, 51%; male, 49%. Females had higher rates of verbalizing self-injury than males. Men and women between the ages of 18 and 45 demonstrated the highest rates of verbalizing self-harm. When examined in terms of ethnicity, females of all races and ethnicities verbalized the highest rates of suicidal ideation with plan. Black women had higher rates of verbalized desire for self-harm than white or Hispanic women.

THE IMPACT OF COMORBID DIAGNOSIS ON REHOSPITALIZATION FOR SUICIDE RISK

In this study we examined comorbid diagnosis in a population rehospitalized within 31 days following discharge to determine the impact on suicide risk of comorbid substance abuse and mental health diagnosis. The most significant findings were among the substance dependent population. Within the substance dependence population approximately one-third of initial admissions demonstrated suicidal ideation on admission via verbalization of plan or presence of suicide attempt or gesture.

Opioid-dependent persons verbalized the highest prevalence of suicide risk at 41.5%; alcohol-dependent persons demonstrated the second highest reporting of suicide risk at 39.7%, followed by sedative hypnotic and polysubstance abusers at 34.6% and 16.6% respectively.

Two significant changes occurred within the 31-day rehospitalization population. First, identified suicidal risk via plan or attempted suicide increased by 50 percentage points. The second and possibly more interesting change is that primary diagnosis upon readmission was no longer substance disorders. In fact, 56% of rehospitalizations had a primary psychiatric diagnosis of major depressive disorder (23%), schizophrenia (14%), or bipolar disorder (19%).

IMPLICATIONS FOR PRACTICE

The implications for practice stem from the percentage of those patients presenting with suicidal ideation in relation to the total admissions population. This study indicated that persons working in psychiatric intake should give strong consideration to the presence of comorbid diagnosis and the potential for suicidal ideation and risk of harm to self and others once patients are hospitalized. Patients presenting to psychiatric intake with severe levels of anxiety and agitation and a history of substance dependence demonstrated the highest risk of harm to self and others, with a 27% greater risk of violent actions in the inpatient unit versus the general admitted populations.

In addition, a cluster of symptoms emerged within the population that indicated that the following components were consistently present in those verbalizing suicidal ideation and demonstrating suicidal risk behaviors:

- Medical illness
- Impulsivity
- Anxiousness
- Irritability
- Access to weapon
- Hopelessness
- Remarkable life stressors
- Family history of suicide
- Substance abuse and psychiatric illness comorbidity

In the population examined by this study it is important to separate two stages within suicidal ideation. The first is best described as thoughts of death: frequently persons reported "fleeting thoughts of death" or thoughts of what the world would be like without them; frequently persons reported justifying the belief that others would be better off without them in the world. The second stage includes the first stage's thought process but adds the intent to die and the planning component. Within this population patients presented with vague to well-thought-out plans of how to commit suicide. It is important to note that there no distinction was made between vague plans and concrete plans because patients were frequently reluctant to reveal their suicide plan, saving it for a later "opportunity" for suicide.

LIMITATIONS AND IMPLICATIONS FOR FURTHER INVESTIGATION

This study is exploratory in nature and provides a baseline examination of psychiatric diagnosis, comorbidity, suicide ideation, and suicide attempts. It was designed to examine emergent trends among persons presenting for initial hospitalization and rehospitalization within 31 days of discharge. Nevertheless, there appears to be an increasing prevalence of comorbid diagnosis emerging among persons at acute risk for suicide. There also appear to be alarming trends demonstrating the impact of comorbid substance and psychiatric diagnosis on risk for suicidal behaviors demonstrated via verbalization of plan and intent and actual suicide attempt.

Further examination is required to document the extent of the impact of comorbid diagnosis on patient suicide risk. Application of standardized measures and statistical analysis to determine correlation and contributing and causal factors should be undertaken in a variety of settings to document national agreement on the presence of identified risk trends. In addition, examination of treatment methodology, medication management, patients' length of stay, follow-up planning, and environmental factors should be considered.

REFERENCES

American Psychiatric Association. (2002). *Diagnostic and statistical manual of mental disorders* (4th ed.). Washington, DC: Author.

Bush, K. A., Fawcett, J., & Jacobs, D. G. (2003). Clinical correlates of inpatient suicide. *Journal of Clinical Psychiatry, 64*(1), 14–19.

Institute of Medicine. (2002). *Reducing suicide: A national imperative.* Washington, DC: National Academies Press.

Jacobs, D. G. (1999). *The Harvard Medical School guide to suicide assessment and intervention.* San Francisco: Jossey Bass.

National Institute of Mental Health. (2001). *The numbers count: Mental disorders in America* (NIMH Publication No. 01-4584). Retrieved May 17, 2003, from http://www.nimh.nih.gov/publicat/numbers.cfm.

24

Cognitive-Behavioral Therapy With Posttraumatic Stress Disorder

An Evidence-Based Approach

M. ELIZABETH VONK

PATRICK BORDNICK

KEN GRAAP

Posttraumatic stress disorder (PTSD) occurs worldwide among people of all ages who experience traumatic events. The events, in which severe injury or threat of injury and death occur, may be natural disasters, such as earthquakes, or man-made, including war, automobile accidents, and crime. While most people are likely to experience some form of traumatic experience in their lifetimes, not all go on to develop PTSD. In fact, estimates of the lifetime prevalence vary widely, from 9% of the general population to 30% or more of those exposed to particular traumas such as rape, combat, or disaster (Keane & Kaloupek, 2002). In addition, several conditions are often comorbid with PTSD, including depressive and other anxiety disorders and substance abuse. Several risk factors for the development of PTSD have been identified, including female gender, history of prior psychiatric problems or abuse, and unavailability of social support (Brewin, Andrews, & Valentine, 2000). Furthermore, characteristics of the trauma itself—the severity of the trauma, the person's sense of control over the outcome and extent of injury, and the degree of actual loss—may increase the rate of PTSD development. In general, men are more likely to be exposed to trauma related to war, and women's exposure is more likely to be related to rape or assault.

Posttraumatic stress disorder involves symptoms that are organized (American Psychiatric Association, 2000) into three clusters. The reexperiencing cluster involves persistent reexperiencing of the traumatic event, including such things as intrusive images, persistent thoughts, or vivid dreams of the event. The arousal cluster includes sleep difficulties, irritability, decreased ability to concentrate, and increased startle response. The avoidance cluster includes efforts to avoid thoughts, feelings, activities, places, or persons that are reminders of the event. In addition, the person with PTSD may experience a sense of detachment or numbing.

Although trauma survivors may not meet all of the *DSM-IV* criteria for PTSD, they may still experience severe distress and trauma-related symptoms. For example, a client may appear to be experiencing PTSD related to an event that does not reach the threshold of the *DSM-IV* definition; that is, the event was not directly life-threatening. While it is not thoroughly understood why some people appear to develop PTSD symptoms related to subthreshold events, they nonetheless require specific treatment.

Fortunately, there is an available and growing evidence base for the treatment of PTSD, including systematic reviews, practice guidelines, and expert consensus guidelines. Despite the time constraints of clinical practice, there are sources available from which, with a modest time investment, social workers may find the most current reviews of treatment effectiveness research related to PTSD. Each of the sources listed in Table 24.1 helps to bridge the gap between research and practice in that they give the practitioner ready access to systematic reviews or summaries of the most recent empirical research. Practice guidelines are also useful in that they often provide more detailed instructions about particular interventions, as well as guidance for common clinical issues. For example, while a systemic review may reveal the effectiveness of exposure therapy for intrusive symptoms of PTSD, practice guidelines may help inform timing of the intervention in relation to engagement with the client, comorbidity, and other unique client characteristics. In other words, research reviews tell us "what" intervention to use with PTSD, and practice guidelines tell us "how to" apply the intervention. The guidelines are often thought to be more "user-friendly" to the practitioner, but both pieces are needed because our knowledge base is expanding so rapidly. The most up-to-date and readily available systematic reviews and practice guide-

Table 24.1   Sources of Information for Evidence-Based Practice with PTSD

Source	Web Site Address	Availability
PILOTS Database	www.ncptsd.org/publications/pilots/	Electronic searchable database of traumatic stress literature; abstracts
MedScape (from WebMD)	www.medscape.com	Summary articles of EBP; references
National Center for PTSD	www.ncptsd.org	Summary articles of EBP; references; abstracts; info about assessment tools
Expert Consensus Guidelines	www.psychguides.com	Full-text expert consensus guidelines for PTSD (and other mental disorders)
Journal of Clinical Psychiatry	www.psychiatrist.com/supplenet/	Abstracts and some full-text systematic reviews of EBP for various disorders
Journal of Clinical Psychology	http://www3.interscience.wiley.com/cgi-bin/jtoc?ID=31171	Abstracts of and references for systematic reviews of EBP

Table 24.2   Current Systematic Reviews and Practice Guidelines for EBP with PTSD

Year	Author	Title	Source	Type
2002	Yehuda, R. (Ed.)	*Treating Trauma Survivors with PTSD*	Book	Guidelines
2000	Foa, E. B., et al. (Eds.)	*Effective Treatments for PTSD: Practice Guidelines*	Book	Guidelines
2002	Vonk, M. E.	Assessment and treatment of PTSD in *Social Workers' Desk Reference*	Book chapter	Guidelines
2000	Foa, E. B.	Psychosocial treatment of PTSD	*Journal of Clinical Psychiatry*	Review
2002	Schnurr, P. P., et al.	Research on PTSD: Epidemiology, pathophysiology, and assessment	*Journal of Clinical Psychology*	Review
2002	Solomon & Johnson	Psychosocial treatment of PTSD: A practice-friendly review of outcome research	*Journal of Clinical Psychology*	Review
2002	Korn, M. L.	Recent developments in the science and treatment of PTSD	MedScape	Review
1999	E. B. Foa, et al.	Treatment of PTSD	*Journal of Clinical Psychology*	Expert consensus
2003	NCPTSD	Treatment of PTSD: A National Center for PTSD fact sheet	http://www.ncptsd.org	Overview of treatment

lines for the assessment and treatment of PTSD at this time are listed in Table 24.2.

In order to apply evidence-based practice (EBP) in the treatment setting, Corcoran and Vandiver suggest seven steps: (a) biopsychosocial assessment, (b) accurate five-axis *DSM* diagnosis, (c) valid description of the identifying problem(s) and focus of treatment, (d) description of goals and specific target(s) of change, (e) selection of a specific evidence-based treatment plan, (f) selection of outcome measures, and (g) evaluation of progress and outcome. Here a case involving rape trauma illustrates application of these steps for EBP with PTSD.

CASE EXAMPLE: JEN

Jen is a 23-year-old European American female who is an account manager with a highly regarded financial corporation. She experienced a rape at gunpoint 4 months previously and has been referred to treatment by the employee assistance program, where she had gone at the urging of her fiancé. Since the rape, Jen has coped by "not thinking about it." Although she has had to change some of her daily routines, she makes efforts to stay away from the part of town where the attack took place. Jen has become unable to concentrate at meetings or to feel connected to her friends in social settings. She frequently wonders whether she should have done more to prevent the rape from occurring. Even more disturbing to her, Jen has frequent nightmares that interfere with her sleep. On a few occasions, she has suddenly "remembered" frightening aspects of the attack while working at her desk. In addition, while she expected to experience difficulties for a week or so following the attack, she feels disappointed and angry with herself about being unable to "just get over it" now that 4 months have passed. She worries that her fiancé will be unable to tolerate her continued avoidance of physical intimacy. More than anything, she wants to return to her former high level of functioning at work, with her fiancé, and with friends. Jen reported no previous trauma, has had no medical complications, and is maintaining medical follow-up.

Assessment and Diagnosis

Hoping to help Jen as effectively and efficiently as possible, the social worker wanted to choose interventions that were supported by the evidence base. Following the recommendation of Corcoran and Vandiver, she began with a thorough biopsychosocial assessment. Through a clinical interview, the social worker allowed Jen to tell her story about the rape and its aftermath. Following suggestions by McFarlane, Golier, and Yehuda (2002) regarding initial evaluation, she was careful not to press Jen for details, but rather to lay the groundwork for future in-depth exploration of the assault, as well as to begin to tie the current difficulties to the trauma-related stress. She also explored Jen's pretrauma functioning, family history, current living situation, current methods of coping, support system, previous traumatic life events, and expectations of therapy (Vonk, 2002). The social worker also paid close attention to Jen's thoughts about the rape, noting any indications of self-blame or guilt about the assault or about how she is handling the aftermath. In addition, the social worker listened for signs and symptoms of psychiatric problems that often co-occur with PTSD, including depression, anxiety, substance abuse, and somatic complaints.

To augment her assessment and prepare for future outcome measurement, the social worker decided to use a self-report measure. After reviewing the self-report inventories described both by Keane and Kaloupek (2002) and on the Web site of the National Center for PTSD (http://www.ncptsd.org/publications/assessment/adult_self_report.html), she chose the Posttraumatic Diagnostic Scale (PTDS) (Foa et al., 1997). The PTDS is a 17-item Likert-scale instrument that measures the presence and severity of each of the 17 symptoms in the three clusters of *DSM-IV* criteria for PTSD. This provides valuable information to the social worker about Jen's particular constellation of symptoms and their severity. The PTDS also allows the client to rate her level of impairment in nine areas of life functioning (i.e., work, household duties, friendships, leisure, school, family relationships, sex life, general life satisfaction, and overall functioning). In addition, it provides a checklist of traumatic events and asks the client to endorse any to which she has been exposed and the one that is causing the greatest concern. The instrument is psychometrically sound; has been tested with men and women who have experienced a broad range of traumas, including sexual assault; and requires only a few minutes to complete. This self-report instrument was chosen over a psychometrically sound structured clinical interview such as the Clinician Administered PTSD Scale (CAPS) (Blake et al., 1995) in the interest of time.

Based on the clinical interview and the results of the PTDS, the social worker diagnosed Jen as follows:

Axis I: 309.81 Posttraumatic Stress Disorder (Chronic)
Axis II: V71.09 No Diagnosis
Axis III: None
Axis IV: Problems related to crime
Axis V: GAF = 55 (current)

Identification of Treatment Focus and Goals

The focus and goals of treatment follow directly from the results of the assessment and diagnosis. Jen presented with symptoms of reexperiencing, increased arousal, numbing, and avoidance. In addition, she reported feelings of guilt and self-blame for the rape. Among all of her symptoms, Jen reported that nightmares and intrusive thoughts of the rape were most disturbing to her. Before beginning to treat the PTSD directly, the social worker provided Jen with education about the symptoms and available treatments for PTSD. In the process, she helped Jen normalize her reactions and provided reassurance about the potential for recovery. She also encouraged Jen to share psychoeducational materials with her fiancé. (See Foa et al., 1999, pp. 69–77, for a printable handout for patient or family.) By working together, the following mutually defined, positive, feasible, and well-defined goals were established:

1. Increase Jen's ability to actively manage her anxiety at work and in social settings at least 75% of the time.
   a. Jen will increase her ability to concentrate at work.
   b. Jen will increase her enjoyment in social settings.
2. Increase Jen's ability to tolerate exposure to places, thoughts, feelings, and conversations that are reminders of the assault.
   a. Jen will be able to shop for groceries and run errands near the location of the assault.
   b. Jen will be able to share her experience, its aftermath, and her ongoing progress toward recovery with her fiancé and best friend.
   c. Jen will be able to gradually increase her enjoyment of physical intimacy with her fiancé.
3. Decrease the frequency of Jen's nightmares and intrusive thoughts of the assault.
   a. Modify Jen's beliefs about the assault that are associated with disturbing emotions.

    b. Jen will modify her belief that she is somehow to blame for the assault.

    c. Jen will identify and modify other disturbing thoughts about herself, others, and the world in relation to the assault.

Jen and the social worker agreed to work toward these goals with weekly meetings for a period of 3 months, at which time they would reassess to see what additional work might be needed. In addition, Jen agreed to follow through with a referral for a medication evaluation with a psychiatrist.

Overview of Evidence Base and Selection of Intervention

While already aware of several effective interventions, the social worker wanted to make sure she had the most up-to-date information available on which to base her treatment decisions. Following Corcoran and Vandiver's (Chapter 2 in this book) suggestions for implementing evidence-based knowledge in practice, the social worker looked to credible sources of knowledge, including systematic reviews (e.g., Solomon & Johnson, 2002), practice guidelines (e.g., Yehuda, 2002), and expert consensus (e.g., Foa et al., 1999). In addition, she quickly went to the National Center for PTSD Web site (http://www.ncptsd.org) to examine the treatment fact sheet to see if there have been recent notable developments. From these sources, the social worker learned the following about intervention with PTSD.

Empirical research has supported the effectiveness of several interventions for the treatment of rape-related PTSD. The literature most clearly supports exposure therapy, cognitive therapy, and anxiety management techniques. Eye movement desensitization and reprocessing (EMDR) and insight-oriented treatments are supported, although less conclusively than the cognitive-behavioral interventions because of the methodological rigor with which they have been studied (Rothbaum, Meadows, Resick, & Foy, 2000; Solomon & Johnson, 2002). In addition, there is growing support for the use of psychopharmacological treatment, especially with sexual assault survivors (Mellman, 2002). Expert consensus suggests that particular psychosocial interventions appear to be more effective in treating specific clusters of symptoms (Foa et al., 1999). For instance, intrusive symptoms respond particularly well to exposure techniques; avoidance symptoms respond well to exposure and cognitive therapy; numbing, guilt, and shame to cognitive therapy; and increased arousal symptoms to exposure and anxiety management.

Exposure Therapy

Exposure therapy is a behavioral intervention involving affective and cognitive activation of the trauma by using associated memories and cues. The cues may be either imaginal, such as retelling the experience of the assault, or in vivo, such as returning to a place that is a reminder of the assault. The exposure must be of significant duration to allow the client's anxiety level to substantially subside in the presence of the feared but harmless cue. Exposure therapies are effective in at least four ways (Foa & Cahill, 2002). First, they help to decrease anxiety related to the trauma. Next, they help survivors learn that thinking about the traumatic experience is not in itself dangerous. They also help survivors differentiate between the traumatic experience and other situations that may be safe, although similar in some ways. Finally, confronting through exposure rather than avoiding memories and cues of the assault helps survivors develop a sense of mastery. Because the idea of confronting or reliving the assault is frightening, survivors need to have a clear rationale and understanding of how exposure therapies work in order to be informed participants in the intervention. In addition, the development and maintenance of a trusting therapeutic relationship seems to be essential for successful completion of exposure therapies. A description of exposure therapy designed for use with sexual assault survivors can be found in Foa and Rothbaum (1998).

Cognitive Therapy

Cognitive therapy (CT) (Beck, 1995) has long been recognized as an effective treatment for anxiety and depression. The basic idea of CT is that the way one thinks about the world, others, and self influences one's interpretation of events. In turn, the interpretation influences subsequent feelings and actions. Dysfunctional beliefs following sexual assault vary, but several themes are common, including overgeneralizations about danger in the world and one's personal vulnerability, unrealistic self-blame and guilt about the rape or inability to prevent its occurrence, loss of meaning for one's life, and broken trust in others and self (Solomon & Johnson, 2002; Vonk, 2002). The goal of CT is to learn to identify specific thoughts that are causing negative emotional reactions and behaviors and then to challenge the thoughts through a process of logical examination of the veracity or functionality of the thoughts, followed by replacement of those that are dysfunctional with more reasonable ones. Cognitive restructuring in the treatment of PTSD is described by Meichenbaum (1994).

Anxiety Management

The most widely studied of anxiety management programs, stress inoculation training (SIT) was originally developed by Meichenbaum (1994) to treat a variety of anxiety disorders, including PTSD. SIT aims to help clients manage and reduce anxiety through the development of coping skills such as relaxation and breathing techniques, cognitive restructuring, guided self-dialogue, thought-stopping, and role playing. The treatment takes place in three phases. First, the client is educated about responses to trauma and PTSD. Next, the coping skills are taught to and rehearsed by the client. Finally, the newly developed skills are applied through graduated exposure to stressful cues and memories associated with the rape. Although not as well studied as exposure therapies, SIT has been studied both with groups of clients and with individuals. Foa's (2000) summary of those studies suggests that SIT is more effective when administered to individuals rather than in group treatment settings.

Eye Movement Desensitization and Reprocessing

Eye movement desensitization and reprocessing (EMDR) is a relatively new treatment that combines aspects of cognitive reappraisal and exposure techniques with guided eye movement in a specified protocol (Shapiro, 1995). Many experts remain skeptical of EMDR because of the mixed results of its effectiveness and because of questions concerning its theoretical foundation. Summaries of the results of recent effectiveness studies (Chemtob, Tolin, van der Kolk, & Pitman, 2000; Solomon & Johnson, 2002) still provide mixed results. Some studies suggest that the effectiveness of EMDR is comparable to cognitive-behavioral interventions. However, when EMDR was compared with a well-established cognitive-behavioral technique (Devilly & Spence, 1999), EMDR was not as effective in reducing PTSD symptoms either immediately following treatment or at a 3-month follow-up. In addition, the results of dismantling research spread doubt on the necessity of eye movements, without which EMDR appears to be a variation of a cognitive-behavioral intervention.

Short-Term Psychodynamic Therapy

As described by Solomon and Johnson (2002), psychodynamic treatment for PTSD was developed by Horowitz, who conceptualized trauma response in two phases: denial, in which the avoidance and numbing symptoms are prominent, and intrusive, in which the intrusive and arousal symptoms are prominent. The brief psychoanalytic treatment is geared to fit the client's phase of response. In the intrusive phase, the client is encouraged to avoid upsetting memories and to manage anxiety through the use of therapeutic relationship and other coping skills, sometimes including medication. The client in the denial phase is encouraged to confront memories until affect has subsided, at which time the client can focus on the meaning of the trauma and symptoms in order to integrate the experience into a revised sense of self, life meaning, and world image. The limited amount of research available on psychodynamic treatment of PTSD suggests that it may be more effective at reducing avoidance than intrusive symptoms; more research is needed.

Medication

While social workers and others who provide psychosocial intervention are generally not qualified to prescribe psychotropic medication, it is important to be informed of available treatments and issues related to integration of medication treatment with psychosocial intervention. Noting several limitations in the available evidence-based knowledge about medication effectiveness for PTSD, Mellman (2002) describes clear empirical support for the use of selective serotonin reuptake inhibitors (SSRIs) in the treatment of women with assault-related PTSD. He goes on to describe issues related to integrating medical and psychosocial interventions. First, he notes the importance of discussing a clear rationale for medication with the client. In some cases, it may be appropriate to augment treatment with medication following a partial response to the initial psychosocial intervention. In other cases, however, it may be appropriate to complement psychosocial intervention with medication from the outset, particularly if there are comorbid psychiatric disorders or severe symptomatology that would interfere with the progress of psychosocial treatment. Regardless of the chosen method, the client, primary therapist, and prescribing physician must maintain a close collaboration in the service of the client's recovery from PTSD.

After sharing information with Jen about the various effective interventions, the social worker and Jen decided to proceed with a combination of exposure and cognitive therapy. Both Jen and the consulting psychiatrist decided on an augmentation approach to medication, asking that the social worker monitor Jen's progress to assess the need for medication in the future.

Implementation of Treatment

Having decided on treatment goals and preferred interventions, Jen indicated that she would like to start with prolonged exposure (Foa & Rothbaum, 1998) because of its success at decreasing symptoms in all three clusters. She very much wanted to stop having nightmares, and from the information about the various interventions, Jen thought exposure would provide relief most efficiently. Knowing that the success of exposure relies on a good therapeutic relationship, the social worker spent time preparing Jen for the intervention. She carefully explained the intervention, including the potential for a temporary increase in Jen's level of distress and the potential need for sessions longer than 1 hour. Jen was encouraged to ask her fiancé and best friend for support between sessions.

Only when the social worker was confident that Jen understood the intervention thoroughly did she proceed with exposure. The first two sessions in which exposure was used were 90 minutes long; the extra time was required for Jen's anxiety to subside. In each of the following five sessions, exposure required less and less time as Jen was increasingly more able to recount the event with a more manageable level of anxiety. Between sessions, Jen was asked to listen to a tape recording of her recounting of the assault, as well as to confront concrete reminders of the assault by going back to the neighborhood where the assault took place. The social worker gave Jen lots of encouragement to do her "homework," and although she was not able to follow through the first week, Jen started listening to the tape and, accompanied by her fiancé, driving into her old neighborhood after the second session of exposure.

During the course of exposure intervention, the social worker listened carefully to Jen's narrative in order to identify beliefs about the rape, the world, others, and herself that were causing Jen pain, particularly those that indicated guilt or self-blame. Two cognitive themes emerged. First, Jen had come to believe that she was to blame for the rape, in part because she did not "fight back." Second, she had come to the conclusion that she could not trust herself to distinguish between safe and dangerous men because she had accepted the perpetrator's offer to help her with some heavy packages, providing him the opportunity to isolate and then assault her. After teaching Jen the basics of cognitive therapy (Beck, 1995), the social worker and Jen began to work toward modifying her self-blaming and other dysfunctional beliefs related to the assault.

At the end of 3 months, Jen was pleased with her progress with the presenting problems of intrusive and avoidance symptoms, but she was still experiencing more difficulty with concentration than she would like. The social worker reviewed options with Jen, including continuing with cognitive therapy, adding some education in anxiety management, or augmenting treatment with medication. Jen preferred to learn some anxiety management techniques (Meichenbaum, 1994) and to continue with cognitive work. The social worker taught Jen how to use thought-stopping, deep breathing, and guided self-dialogue techniques.

As Jen continued to make progress with her goals, the social worker increased the time between sessions. During the last session, Jen reported that she felt ready to stop treatment. She went on to describe her current thinking about being a rape survivor. Like many survivors of trauma, she was able to acknowledge personal growth along with the difficulties related to her assault (Calhoun & Tedeschi, 1999). Although she still experienced sadness, moments of anxiety, and anger that she had been victimized, Jen believed that she was a "very strong person" to have managed the aftermath of her traumatic experience. She and her fiancé had reevaluated the importance of their relationship to one another and were actively planning their wedding rather than remaining engaged without a specific date in mind. She was also reevaluating her choice of careers and was looking into taking the steps necessary to become a physical therapist, a strong interest she had set aside a few years earlier at the urging of her parents.

Ongoing Evaluation of Treatment

Throughout treatment, the social worker monitored Jen's progress, relying both on Jen's report and on clinical judgment. In addition, however, she utilized two quantitative methods. First, she utilized goal attainment scaling (GAS) (Pike, 2002). GAS is a useful tool for monitoring progress because the scales can be tailored to the individual's goals, are easy to administer, can be administered repeatedly, and can be weighted according to the relative importance of each of the goals. A 5-point goal attainment scale was developed for each of Jen's goals as they were defined in treatment, and at the start of each session, the social worker asked Jen to rate her progress on each of them. The use of the GAS method is illustrated in Figure 24.1, showing Jen's progress on the goal of decreasing the frequency of her nightmares. Finally, the PTDS (Foa et al., 1997), administered at the outset of treatment, was readministered at the close of treatment. Jen no longer qualified for the diagnosis of PTSD by the end of treatment,

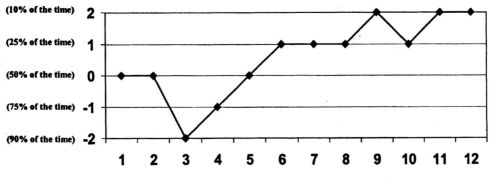

Figure 24.1   GAS self-report for occurrence of nightmares each week

although she had not reached a satisfactory level of enjoyment with physical intimacy, nor could she concentrate at work at least 75% of the time. She planned to continue working toward those goals by applying the skills learned in treatment.

CONCLUSION

The evidence base for practice with clients suffering from PTSD related to rape and other traumas is still growing. To date, the cognitive-behavioral interventions, including exposure, cognitive restructuring, and anxiety management, appear to be the most effective (Solomon & Johnson, 2002). Research on psychotropic medications has also yielded support for several drugs, including the class of drugs known as SSRIs. Yet, there are many unanswered questions regarding treatment of PTSD. Among them is the question of effective matching of a particular treatment to a particular problem or client characteristic. Another is the question of whether or when it is effective to combine psychosocial interventions. While it seems logical that two effective interventions such as exposure and cognitive therapy would complement each other to enhance treatment, some of the existing research appears to contradict this logic (Foa, 2000). In addition, more knowledge is needed about the effectiveness of psychosocial interventions in combination with psychotropic medicine (Mellman, 2002).

While the treatment of real people who suffer from PTSD is rarely as clear-cut as the case of "Jen," effective treatment is more likely when the steps of evidence-based practice are followed, from thorough biopsychosocial assessment to evaluation of outcomes. Any who fear that these steps will create a mechanized therapeutic process can rest assured that individual differences among clients will always require the use of clinical judgment; relationship-building skills to ensure engagement and continuation in treatment; and the ability to convey trustworthiness, warmth, and caring. Evidence-based practice may indeed increase the practitioner's ability to instill hope in clients with the confidence that comes from knowing that the service being offered is well supported in theory and in practice.

REFERENCES

American Psychiatric Association. (2000). *Diagnostic and statistical manual of mental disorders* (4th ed., text rev.). Washington, DC: Author.

Beck, J. S. (1995). *Cognitive therapy: Basics and beyond.* New York: Guilford.

Blake, D. D., Weathers, F. W., Magy, L. M., Kaloupek, D. G., Gusman, F. D., Charney, D. S., et al. (1995). The development of a clinician-administered PTSD scale. *Journal of Traumatic Stress, 8,* 75–90.

Brewin, C. R., Andrews, B., & Valentine, J. D. (2000). Meta-analysis of risk factors for PTSD in trauma-exposed adults. *Journal of Consulting and Clinical Psychology, 68,* 748–766.

Calhoun, L. G., & Tedeschi, R. G. (1999). *Facilitating posttraumatic growth.* Mahwah, NJ: Lawrence Erlbaum.

Chemtob, C. M., Tolin, D. F., van der Kolk, B. A., & Pitman, R. K. (2000). Eye-movement desensitization and reprocessing. In E. B. Foa, T. Keane, & M. Friedman (Eds.), *Effective treatments for PTSD* (pp. 139–154). New York: Guilford.

Corcoran, K., & Vandiver, V. L. (2004) Implementing best practice and expert consensus procedures. In A. R. Roberts & K. R. Yeager, *Evidence-based practice manual: Research and outcome measures in health and human services* (pp. 15–19). New York.

Devilly, G. J., & Spence, S. H. (1999). The relative efficacy and treatment distress of EMDR and a cognitive behavioral trauma treatment protocol in the amelioration of PTSD. *Journal of Anxiety Disorders, 13,* 131–158.

Foa, E. B. (2000). Psychosocial treatment of PTSD. *Journal of Clinical Psychiatry, 61*(Suppl. 5), 43–48.

Foa, E. B., & Cahill, S. P. (2002). Specialized treatment for PTSD: Matching survivors to the appropriate modality. In R. Yehuda (Ed.), *Treating trauma survivors with PTSD* (pp. 43–62). Washington, DC: American Psychiatric Publishing.

Foa, E. B., Cashman, L., Jaycox, L., et al. (1997). The validation of a self-report measure of PTSD: The Posttraumatic Diagnostic Scale. *Psychological Assessment, 9,* 445–451.

Foa, E. B., Davidson, J.R.T., & Frances, A. (1999). The expert consensus guideline series: Treatment of PTSD. *Journal of Clinical Psychiatry, 60*(Suppl. 16), 4–32.

Foa, E. B., Keane, T., & Friedman, M. (Eds.). (2000). *Effective treatments for PTSD: Practice guidelines.* New York: Guilford.

Foa, E. B., & Rothbaum, B. O. (1998). *Treating the trauma of rape.* New York: Guilford.

Keane, T. M., & Kaloupek, D. G. (2002). In R. Yehuda (Ed.), *Treating trauma survivors with PTSD* (pp. 21–42). Washington, DC: American Psychiatric Publishing.

Korn, M. L. (n.d.). Recent developments in the science and treatment of PTSD. Retrieved April 14, 2003, from http://www.medscape.com/viewarticle/436398

McFarlane, A. C., Golier, J., & Yehuda, R. (2002). Treatment planning for trauma survivors with PTSD. In R. Yehuda (Ed.), *Treating trauma survivors with PTSD* (pp. 1–20). Washington, DC: American Psychiatric Publishing.

Meichenbaum, D. (1994). *A clinical handbook/practical therapist manual for assessing and treating adults with PTSD*. Waterloo, Ontario: Institute Press.

Mellman, T. A. (2002). Rationale and role for medication in the comprehensive treatment of PTSD. In R. Yehuda (Ed.), *Treating trauma survivors with PTSD* (pp. 63–74). Washington, DC: American Psychiatric Publishing.

Pike, C. K. (2002) Developing client-focused measures. In A. Roberts & G. Greene (Eds.), *The social worker's desk reference* (pp. 189–193). New York: Oxford University Press.

Rothbaum, B. O., Meadows, E. A., Resick, P., & Foy, D. W. (2000). In E. B. Foa, T. Keane, & M. Friedman (Eds.), *Effective treatments for PTSD* (pp. 60–83). New York: Guilford.

Schnurr, P. P., Friedman, M. J., & Bernardy, N. C. (2002). Research on PTSD: Epidemiology, pathophysiology, and assessment. *Journal of Clinical Psychology, 58*(8), 877–889.

Shapiro, F. (1995). *Eye movement desensitization and reprocessing*. New York: Guilford.

Solomon, S. D., & Johnson, D. M. (2002). Psychosocial treatment of PTSD: A practice-friendly review of outcome research. *Journal of Clinical Psychology, 58*(8), 947–959.

Vonk, M. E. (2002). The assessment and treatment of PTSD. In A. Roberts & G. Greene (Eds.), *The social worker's desk reference* (pp. 356–359). New York: Oxford University Press.

Yehuda, R. (Ed.). (2002). *Treating trauma survivors with PTSD*. Washington, DC: American Psychiatric Publishing.

25

Recovery

Expanding the Vision of Evidence-Based Practice

PHYLLIS SOLOMON
VICTORIA STANHOPE

In 2002, President Bush created the New Freedom Commission on Mental Health to study the mental health service delivery system for persons with severe mental illness (SMI). A year later, the New Freedom Commission produced its report, Achieving the Promise: Transforming Mental Health Care in America (Department of Health and Human Services [DHHS], 2003), setting out a framework to reform a system that has often been fragmented and inadequate for persons with SMI living in the community. The rarity of federal commissions examining mental health care is an indication of their significance within the policy context. In 1955, a joint commission was instigated by the Senate and the House, and in 1977, President Carter authorized a mental health commission. The recent federal commission reflects the major shifts in the mental health policy arena during the last three decades. The most notable changes have been the National Institute for Mental Health's implementation of the Community Support Program (CSP); the consumer and family movements' growing influence in policymaking; the emergence of managed care; the Decade of the Brain's research focus on mental illness; and the Surgeon General's report addressing stigma and mental health. The report of the New Freedom Commission provides a comprehensive critique of the present system and embodies some of the most progressive and consumercentered perspectives on mental health services for persons with SMI. As a result, the report has been widely endorsed by the stakeholder community, including the National Alliance for the Mentally Ill (NAMI), the National Mental Health Association, the National Association of State Mental Health Program Directors, and the Bazelon Center for Mental Health Law. The report identified two tasks as central to reforming the mental health system: implementing evidence-based practice (EBP) and promoting recovery for all persons with severe mental illness. Some have viewed these two concepts as antithetical: EBP represents a medical-model approach to treating mental illness, while recovery represents a consumer-centered one. This paper will demonstrate how these two approaches are congruent, and, moreover, how recovery can enhance our understanding and application of EBPs to create broad-based reform within the mental health system.

EVIDENCE-BASED PRACTICES

Mental health services research has increased considerably in the last two decades, and as a result, much more is known about the efficacy of services and their effectiveness in the community. Given the limited resources available for mental health services, professionals and advocates argue that funds must be targeted at practices that are known to have improved outcomes. The commission endorsed this viewpoint and addressed the apparent disconnect between mental health research and services for persons with SMI. Specifically, the report addresses the lack of dissemination and implementation of EBPs in the services arena. EBPs are defined by the Institute of Medicine as "the integration of best-researched evidence and clinical expertise with patient values" (Institute of Medicine Committee on Quality of Health Care in America, 2001). Interventions that warrant the EBP label must have shown consistent scientific evidence that they demonstrate improvement in consumer outcomes. The Agency for Healthcare Research and Quality identified three levels of evidence: level A, good research-based evidence, with some expert opinion; level B, fair research-based evidence, with substantial expert opinion; and level C, minimal research-based evidence, with reliance primarily on expert opinion (Institute of Medicine Committee on Quality of Health Care in America, 2001). The American Psychiatric Association has released guidelines that are also based on a combination of expert consensus and research but has set the highest standard for research as meta-analysis of randomized clinical trials, comparing the practice to alternative practices or no intervention (American Psychiatric Association, 1997). The journal Psychiatric Services, in a series of articles on EBPs, has identified a core set of interventions that improve outcomes for persons with SMI. They include assertive community treatment (ACT), family psychoeducation, specific medications for specific conditions, supportive employment, and integrated treatment for co-occurring substance use disorders (Drake, Mueser, & Torrey, 2000).

RECOVERY

The commission stated that the ultimate goal for reforming the mental health system was to promote recovery for persons with SMI. This is one of the first times that federal mental health policy has adopted the language of recovery. Rosalyn Carter, a longtime mental health advocate and wife of the ex-president, summed up the most significant difference between the Bush Commission and the Carter Commission by stating that "today, we know that recovery is possible for every person with a mental illness" (Hogan, 2003). The concept of recovery, as a shaping force in mental health care, fully emerged in the 1990s. The report defines recovery as

> the process in which people are able to live, work, learn and participate fully in their communities. For some individuals, recovery is the ability to live a fulfilling and productive life despite a disability. For others, recovery implies the reduction or complete remission of symptoms. Science has shown that having hope plays an integral role in an individual's recovery. (DHHS, 2003, p. 5)

Recovery challenges the prevailing view among psychiatrists and the mental health establishment that mental illness is a chronic condition and that treatment focuses solely on symptom management and reduction. The commission takes a more inclusive approach by incorporating symptom management into its definition of recovery but emphasizes that for many, recovery means leading a fulfilling life despite having a disability and symptoms. Nevertheless, the recovery vision represents a significant shift away from the medical-model approach that was dominant in mental health care throughout the twentieth century. Instead, the focus of services moves beyond symptoms and pathology, to the individual, who may have very different treatment goals from those of the clinician.

Recovery, as a mental health concept, essentially arose out of two different strands of mental health advocacy and practice in the 1980s (Anthony, 1993). The first was the psychiatric rehabilitation movement, which drew on theories from physical disability rehabilitation to develop the idea of functionality with a psychiatric disability. Psychiatric rehabilitation brought attention to the fact that mental illness impacted all aspects of a person's life, and assessing the needs of the consumer based solely on intensity of symptoms was inadequate. The discipline defined recovery in terms of a consumer's ability to function in the major domains of life: work, housing, relationships, and recreation (Jacobson & Curtis, 2000). This approach has broadened services included in the CSP, the framework that shaped community-based services after deinstitutionalization. Psychiatric rehabilitation programs have particularly focused on the value of community and work for persons with SMI. Therefore, understanding SMI as a psychiatric disability changes how consumers and providers visualize treatment goals: they focus on moving forward while accommodating the consumer's mental health needs.

The consumer movement was the other major influence that contributed to the concept of recovery. Consumers, who had often been viewed as passive recipients of treatment, began to speak out about the experience of being mentally ill. Influenced by the civil rights movement of the 1960s and the more consumer centered approach of the CSP, consumers challenged the medical establishment and its portrayal of mental illness as persistent and hopeless. Deegan (2003), a psychologist and consumer, describes recovery as a deeply personal "process" that involves wrestling with the reality of mental illness but also includes finding a new sense of self and feeling of hope, while understanding the limitations of psychiatric disability. This more phenomenological approach to mental illness stresses that recovery is unique to the person; for some it may be striving for a reduction of symptoms through medication, but for others it may be overcoming the effects of poverty, stigma, and marginalization. The language of the consumer movement refocuses services away from sickness and cures, toward improving people's lives. Jacobson and Curtis (2000) identified the following concepts as central to recovery: hope, meaning, taking an active role, and choice. Hope involves a belief in the future and seeking to change what is possible. Meaning is intensely personal—for some it may be working at a job or craft, while for others it may be finding a spiritual center. Taking an active role involves taking responsibility for one's recovery, and choice means being able to choose from a range of possible paths to it. Consumer-based recovery does not necessarily entail collaboration with mental health professionals. Instead, the road to recovery may lie in the support of friends, family, or community.

However, for providers who are participating in the recovery process, the approach speaks directly to the manner in which services are provided. Townsend and Glasser (2003) describe the example of the consumer who wants to be an astronaut. After having two case managers who failed to take his aspirations seriously, the consumer was assigned a case manager who suggested the consumer research what it would take to be an astronaut. On finding the amount of work involved, the consumer decided that being an astronaut was not for him, but he still had a passion for space travel. The case manager then worked with him to find a placement in a company that worked with NASA. Townsend and Glasser (2003) use this story to illustrate what they call the heart and soul of treatment, where providers enter into the dreams and aspirations of the consumers of their service. The challenge for EBP is to capture this process, which, in this case, made the difference between effective case management and ineffective case management.

Creating an Evidence Base for Recovery

The commission emphasized both concepts, EBP and recovery, but there has been considerable debate as to whether the two approaches are compatible. The question arises whether the phenomenological approach of recovery is in some ways antithetical to scientific research. Many see EBP reflecting the medical-model values of disease management and symptom reduction. Consumers argue that programs based on evidence have tended to ignore consumer feedback, especially in the area of medication and its side effects. There is no doubt that the criticisms leveled by recovery advocates point to important limitations in EBP. However, whether it indicates a fundamental disconnect between the recovery approach and positivist science or just the differences between methodologies within services research is less clear. Instead, these criticisms should help us reconsider how EBP measures improvement and, as a result, which programs are identified for broad implementation. Outcome measures in mental health services research have often reflected the parameters of symptom management, such as relapse, recidivism, length of hospitalization, symptomatology, and number of days employed (Draine, 1997; Ralph, Lambert, & Kidder, 2002). None of these measures give one a sense of the consumer's quality of life, empowerment, sense of hope, or connection and functioning within the community, which is vital information for evaluating a program from a recovery perspective. There has been empirical research supporting the recovery perspective that has relied more upon qualitative methods and used a broader range of outcome measures to reflect consumercentered goals. Qualitative studies often give unique insight into the change process and the specific ingredients that bring about change both from the provider and consumer perspectives (Anthony, Rogers, & Farkas, 2003). Although the language of recovery is often at its most powerful in the personal narratives of persons with SMI, recovery advocates have strengthened their message by drawing on empirical studies.

The Well-Being Project (Campbell & Schraiber, 1989) was one of the first large-scale studies to examine what factors promote recovery in the community from a consumer perspective. The study surveyed 331 consumers and found that almost 60% were able to identify an escalation of symptoms and take steps to avert a serious episode. Over half chose strategies that did not involve mental health professionals, such as seeking out friends or using relaxation techniques. A longitudinal study in Vermont followed 262 patients who had been hospitalized for 6 years, then released into the community with supports after they completed a rehabilitation program. The study, which recontacted consumers after 32 years, found that 34% of the participants with schizophrenia made a full recovery in terms of their symptoms and their social functioning (Harding, Brooks, Asloga, & Breier, 1987). Studies on schizophrenia by the World Health Organization conducted in the 1970s and 1980s found that outcomes were better for patients in countries where they received little or no formal psychiatric care (De Girolamo, 1996). Davidson and Strauss (1992) conducted intensive interviews with 66 persons hospitalized for SMI over a period of 3 years. The interviews showed how recovery came out of taking an active role in change, understanding one's capabilities in respect to change, and using this sense of self as a resource to address stigma. Anthony and colleagues (2003a) argue that this research has marked a paradigm shift toward positive outcomes and is comparable to the increased focus on resilience within psychology. And within EBP, there has now been a move toward being more inclusive of community integration outcome measures such as quality of life, illness self-management, and housing (Drake et al., 2001).

The standards of evidence required for EBP can be problematic when applied to recovery oriented services. Randomized clinical trials, widely considered to be the highest level of evidence, are often not feasible or possible for practices that promote recovery—part of the reason being that these services are relatively new in their implementation and have not yet been subject to more rigorous studies. In response, the commission identified emerging best practices, which are defined as "treatments and services that are promising but less thoroughly documented than evidence-based practices" (p. 68). These include consumer operated services, wrap-around services, jail diversion and community re-entry programs, and multifamily group therapies. Anthony (2003a) points out that much of the basis for psychiatric rehabilitation practice has come from research employing correlational and quasi-experimental designs. Furthermore, findings from controlled studies that do not replicate clinical settings are often limited in establishing effectiveness, in comparison with findings from quasi-experimental studies in clinical settings. In applying model treatments within child mental health services, Mckay (in press) found that real-world issues (such as the diverse needs of children and limitations in provider skills) that jeopardized outcomes had not been included in the experimental setting. She argues that these real-world issues must be addressed when developing innovative treatments (Mckay, in press). In addition, randomization is not always the optimal research design. In the case of consumer-provided services, the consumer's commitment to receiving such services plays an important role in determining the service outcome. Consumers randomly assigned to these services, who would not have chosen consumer-provided services, tend to have high dropout rates. Corrigan and Salzer (2003) promote the use of preference as an important design component in researching treatment effectiveness. The issue of preference is an essential consideration for consumer-provided services. Solomon (2004) concludes that "the level of evidence for consumer-provided services is limited by virtue of a lack of research and by not very rigorous research due to this methodology being antithetical to this service element" (p. 21). Therefore, when considering how empirical studies support recovery-oriented services, applying certain types and levels of scientific evidence is not always appropriate.

The Importance of Process

As the Townsend and Glasser (2003) story illustrates, recovery's heart and soul is located in the process of change and healing, which cannot be reduced to the structural components of services or their outcomes. These social and psychological factors tend to go unstudied, and as a result contribute to the "error variance" in clinical effectiveness research (Hohmann, 1999). ACT (assertive community treatment), an EBP, has been studied extensively and manualized to ensure that the program is replicated successfully. But the manuals give no guidance in terms of process, or how the providers actually interact with the consumers in the ACT service environment. Anthony (2003b) argues that process factors may actually determine outcomes more than the structure of services. How providers relate to consumers, whether they treat them with respect and care, is key to promoting recovery for the consumer. Whereas in clinical and counseling psychology, great emphasis has been placed on the power of the relationship in determining service outcomes, community mental health continues to focus more on service models and techniques (Anthony, 2003a). Psychotherapy research has directly studied clinical relationships and nonspecific effects, or factors that contribute to change but are not considered to be the critical ingredients of the intervention (Kazdin, 2002). The nonspecific effects of interventions such as ACT may well be generated by the quality of the consumer/provider relationships.

A vital part in building successful clinical relationships is the provider's ability to communicate and connect with a diversity of consumers. The literature suggests that taking account of cultural differences is not an EBP itself but should be a key component in determining whether any practice can be deemed to be evidence based (Carpinello, Rosenberg, Stone, Schwager, & Felton, 2002; Goldman et al., 2001). The commission (DHHS, 2003) states that cultural competence is "essential to ensure . . . renewed hope for recovery among ethnic and racial minorities." However, EBPs have often failed to establish the effectiveness of interventions for racial, ethnic, and cultural minorities. The majority of research that has been used to establish EBPs has not included adequate numbers of racial or ethnic minorities to allow for evaluation of differential impacts on specific groups (DHHS, 1999; Drake et al., 2001). Therefore, by focusing on process within EBP, research can examine consumer/provider relationships and the factors—including cultural difference—that influence them.

Another important insight for EBP has arisen out of the tension between recovery and symptom management approaches. Psychiatrists have responded to criticisms from recovery advocates by suggesting that focusing on issues of self and empowerment are worthless when a person's illness is such that she is subject to acute psychotic symptoms (Peyser, 2001). What this exchange has highlighted for researchers is the importance of stage of recovery in determining service effectiveness. Frese, Stanley, Kress, and Vogel-Scibilia (2001) point out that advocates on both sides tend to represent consumers at a diversity of stages of illness, and therefore have very different agendas. The consumer perspective has often been articulated by consumers well into their recovery. These consumers are also responding to many decades of abuse and silencing and are therefore reluctant to cede decision-making power about services to the scientific community. In contrast, the NAMI (2003), which tends to represent family members with severely disabled relatives, has argued that mental illness is a brain disorder and has advocated for EBPs, specifically endorsing ACT, supported employment, and illness self-management. While agreeing that a medical approach, which communicates "biology as destiny," is countertherapeutic for consumers, Frese and his colleagues (2001) argue that persons who are very disabled by illness may benefit from evidence-based psychiatric interventions. However, as the person improves and symptoms decrease, then consumers should have more control over their treatments, and services should address a broad range of their concerns, from housing to social supports. In focusing on degree of disability, these researchers are attempting to integrate the two perspectives into a continuum of care for persons with SMI. Again, recovery can inform EBP, demonstrating that interventions are more effective when they are tailored to the consumer's recovery stage.

Implications for Mental Health Systems

The implementation of EBPs and recovery-oriented services requires profound change at the system level. Despite the progress made in services research to establish EBPs, clinical interventions still tend to rely heavily upon tradition, clinician preference, practice wisdom, and marketing practices (Drake et al., 2001). The Institute of Medicine report stated that there was on average a 15- to 20-year delay between research findings on effectiveness and their translation to routine clinical practice (Institute of Medicine Committee on Quality of Health Care in America, 2001). The findings of the Schizophrenia Patient Outcomes Research Team in its PORT study found that usual practice conforms to EBP less than 50% of the time in the area of psychopharmacology, and less than 10% in the area of psychosocial interventions (Lehman & Steinwachs, 1998). The issue remains why there is such a lag between research findings and practice. Many have pointed out the numerous intervening factors operating on the system level that determine services other than research findings; these include financing, policy, laws, and cultural norms (Goldman et al., 2001; Hogan, 2003; Minkoff & Cline, 2003). It is naïve to think that facilitating communications between researchers and clinicians about EBPs, which often require restructuring services, is sufficient to bring about change. The missing piece, therefore, in linking science and service, is the systems intervention necessary to ensure the implementation of EBPs. Minkoff and Cline (2003) argue that implementation should focus specifically on systems management such as strategic planning, management science, and quality improvement.

The commission identifies fragmentation of the U.S. community mental health system as a major barrier to systems intervention and ultimately mental health reform. EBPs such as ACT and supported employment provide services that cut across traditionally separate service domains, such as vocational rehabilitation, housing, and mental health. Recovery requires that services reflect and support the consumer as an individual. A system that has traditionally divided itself according to the different needs of persons with SMI, mental health, financial assistance, housing, and physical health is seriously challenged by a demand to treat consumers holistically. Some of the demands for a recovery-oriented system speak directly to the care provided by mental health professionals, but much of it addresses larger issues of how social service systems are structured in the United States. After deinstitutionalization, the CSP laid out a network of essential services to support persons with SMI in community, but these services emphasized minimizing symptoms and their consequences. Anthony (1993), in setting out standards for a recovery-oriented service system, stresses the importance of keeping consistent consumer outcomes across all services, which reinforces the idea of individual needs defining services.

The fragmentation of the mental health system from a recovery perspective is evidence of a system that does not reflect how mental illness and recovery involve all aspects of people's lives, or more simply expressed, does not reflect their humanity. Although research into the direct impact of fragmentation on client outcomes is hard to establish, there is no doubt that lack of coordination and inappropriate or inadequate services have a deleterious effect on quality (Anthony, 2000). Recovery is pushing systems, as well as providers, to see beyond the diagnostic and categorical services, to treating the individual consumer and his/her multiple needs. The vision of Anthony and other recovery advocates is of an external system that reflects the internal reality of its consumers (Jacobson & Greenley, 2001). However, efforts at integrating service systems without focusing on content and quality of services have not always improved outcomes at the consumer level. The Robert Wood Johnson ACCESS program provided technical assistance and funding to nine sites to implement mental health systems integration strategies. Again, although system integration was increased, the study found no additional improvement for consumer outcomes benefiting from systems integration and technical support when compared with the control group (Rosenheck et al., 2002). Similarly, an $80 million project was implemented in Fort Bragg, North Carolina, to test the effectiveness of a more continuous care system for children with mental health and substance abuse disorders. The study found no difference between the demonstration and comparison sites in terms of clinical outcomes (Bickman, 1996). Systems integration, therefore, appears to be a necessary condition for improving services for persons with SMI, but not a sufficient condition. The implementation of EBPs has reinforced the need for systems integration, but recovery reminds us that the content and quality of service delivery is also a vital part in improving service outcomes for consumers.

Several states have taken the initiative in applying the recovery approach within their mental health systems. The efforts have ranged from including the concept of recovery in their mission statements to trying to shape all their services according to recovery principles. In 1993, the Ohio Department of Mental Health (ODMH) began a series of dialogues with providers, consumers, and family members to explore the mental health recovery process. The subsequent report identified four stages, ranging from *unaware/dependent* to *aware/independent* (Hodge, Townsend, Hyde, & Hogan, 2003). The stages provided a framework for implementing recovery practices, which included clinical care, peer and family support, facilitation of employment, empowerment, stigma reduction, community involvement, access to resources, and education (Jacobson & Greenley, 2001). The ODMH then reinforced this process by offering grants to localities in order to establish comprehensive recovery centers, which offer peer support, assistance to case managers, education, and social and recreational activities. Grants were also given to agencies that adopted the recovery management plan, which allows consumers to develop their recovery process in collaboration with the provider. The Ohio recovery model is an example of tailoring a recovery vision to the specific needs of consumers and implementing change through financial incentives.

Recovery and EBP have to be compatible with existing funding systems to be successfully implemented. Managed care, with its demand for accountability, is clearly a major impetus for EBP, and as a result, there is growing pressure on providers to measure their services, in terms of both quality and outcomes (Dziegielewski & Roberts, 2004). Some have argued that there is also the potential for increased continuity of care with managed Medicaid funds (Mechanic, 2003), providing opportunities for recovery-oriented systems integration. States, including California, Massachusetts, New York, and Washington, have actually written recovery principles into their contracts with managed care organizations (Jacobson & Curtis, 2000). These principles require that organizations contract with providers who pursue recovery-oriented services, including consumer-operated services, and that consumers have an advisory role on managed care organization boards.

The support of key policymakers has been vital to bringing the recovery approach into the mainstream. The National Association of State Mental Health Program Directors in the late 1990s took on recovery-oriented mental health care as one of its major policy priorities. With funding from the Substance Abuse and Mental Health Services Administration, it established the National Technical Assistance Center, whose mission includes "fostering consumer recovery and independence through consumer-centered services" (National Association of State Mental Health Program Directors, 2003). Through conferences, meetings, and publications, the center promotes networking and information exchange about how to create recovery-oriented systems. The center has also initiated a research project to develop a set of performance indicators related to recovery. With the collaboration of several state mental health agencies, the project seeks to "devise a core set of systems-level indicators that measure critical elements and processes of a recovery-facilitating environment" and integrate them into a multistate report card to assess mental health systems (Onken, Dumont, Ridgeway, Dornan, & Ralph, 2002). Probably the most significant aspect of the work that has been done to implement recovery-oriented systems is that it has always begun by asking consumers what they need from the mental health system. The recovery approach not only determines the end goal of mental health reform, but also shapes the process.

CONCLUSION

The significance of the New Freedom Commission on Mental Health is still being debated among policy analysts. Both of the previous commissions were precursors to important mental health legislation, but the fact that President Bush required that the commission be "budget neutral" in its recommendations indicates to some that the report is powerless to bring about real change. Probably the most important aspect of the commission is the government's acknowledgement of the need to simultaneously implement EBP and recovery in order to reform the mental health system. The simultaneous endorsement of these two concepts, previously seen as antithetical, allows for a new way of thinking about how research can inform services. EBP has systematically defined the structure of effective services, but recovery gives us insight into their core, where real change is effected. Recovery advocates have challenged researchers to incorporate a more consumer-centered approach to empirical study. This approach includes expanding the aspects of services chosen for study, methodologies, outcomes measures, and standards of evidence. Recovery requires research on a micro, mezzo, and macro level to determine the system, organization, program structure, and elements that are both necessary and sufficient to activate and sustain the recovery process.

NOTE

Reprinted from *Brief Treatment and Crisis Intervention*, Vol. 4, No. 4 © Oxford University Press, 2004; all rights reserved.

REFERENCES

American Psychiatric Association. (1997). *Practice guidelines for the treatment of patients with schizophrenia*. Washington, DC: Author.
Anthony, W. A. (1993). Recovery from mental illness: The guiding vision of the mental health service system in the 1990s. *Psychiatric Rehabilitation Journal, 16*, 12–23.
Anthony, W. A. (2000). A recovery-oriented service system: Setting some system level standards. *Psychiatric Rehabilitation Journal, 24*, 159–168.
Anthony, W. A. (2003a). Expanding the evidence base in an era of recovery. *Psychiatric Rehabilitation Journal, 27*, 1–2.
Anthony, W. A. (2003b). Letter: Process, not practice. *Psychiatric Services, 54*, 402.
Anthony, W. A., Rogers, E. S., & Farkas, M. (2003). Research on evidence-based practices: Future directions in an era of recovery. *Community Mental Health Journal, 39*, 101–114.
Bickman, L. (1996). A continuum of care: More is not always better. *American Psychologist, 51*, 689–701.
Campbell, J., & Schraiber, R. (1989). *The well-being project: Mental health clients speak for themselves*. Sacramento, CA: California Department of Mental Health.
Carpinello, S. E., Rosenberg, L., Stone, J., Schwager, M., & Felton, C. J. (2002). Best practices: New York State's campaign to implement evidence-based practices for people with serious mental disorders. *Psychiatric Services, 53*, 153–155.
Corrigan, P. W., & Salzer, M. S. (2003). The conflict between random assignment and treatment preference: Implications for internal validity. *Evaluation and Program Planning, 26*, 109–121.
Davidson, L., & Strauss, J. S. (1992). Sense of self in recovery from severe mental illness. *Journal of Medical Psychology, 65*, 131–145.
De Girolamo, G. (1996). WHO studies on schizophrenia: An overview of the re-

sults and their implications for the understanding of the disorder. *The Psychotherapy Patient, 9,* 213–223.

Deegan, G. (2003). Discovering recovery. *Psychiatric Rehabilitation Journal, 26,* 368–376.

Department of Health and Human Services (DHHS). (2003). *New Freedom Commission on Mental Health: Achieving the promise: Transforming mental health care in America. Final report* (DHHS document no. SMA-03-3832). Rockville, MD: Author.

DHHS. (1999). *Mental health: Culture, race, and ethnicity: A supplement to Mental health*: A report of the Surgeon General. Rockville, MD: Author.

Draine, J. (1997). Conceptualizing services research on outpatient commitment. *Journal of Mental Health Administration, 24,* 306–315.

Drake, R. E., Goldman, H. H., Leff, H. S., Lehman, A. F., Dixon, L. B., & Mueser, K. T., et al. (2001). Implementing evidence-based practices in routine mental health service settings. *Psychiatric Services, 52,* 179–192.

Drake, R. E., Mueser, K. T., & Torrey, W. C. (2000). Evidence-based treatment of schizophrenia. *Current Psychiatry Reports, 2,* 393–397.

Dziegielewski, S., & Roberts, A. R. (2004). Health care evidence-based practice: A product of political and cultural times. In A. R. Roberts & K. R. Yeager (Eds.), *Evidence-based practice manual: Research and outcome measures in health and human services.* Oxford, UK: Oxford University Press.

Frese, F., Stanley, J., Kress, K., & Vogel-Scibilia, S. (2001). Integrating evidence-based practices and the recovery model. *Psychiatric Services, 52,* 1462–1468.

Goldman, H. H., Ganju, V., Drake, R. E., Gorman, P., Hogan, M. F., & Hyde, P. S., et al. (2001). Policy implications for implementing evidence-based practices. *Psychiatric Services, 52,* 1591–1597.

Harding, C. M., Brooks, G. W., Asloga, T. S. J. S., & Breier, A. (1987). The Vermont longitudinal study of persons with severe mental illness. *American Journal of Psychiatry, 144,* 718–726.

Hodge, M. C., Townsend, W., Hyde, P. S., & Hogan, M. F. (2003, October 16). *Practical application of recovery principles in clinical practice—the Ohio experience.* Paper presented at the Evidence Based Practices Consultative Forum, Newark, OH.

Hogan, M. F. (2003). New Freedom Commission Report: The President's New Freedom Commission: Recommendations to transform mental health care in America. *Psychiatric Services, 54,* 1467–1474.

Hohmann, A. (1999). A contextual model for clinical mental health effectiveness research. *Mental Health Services Research, 1,* 83–91.

Institute of Medicine Committee on Quality of Health Care in America. (2001). *Crossing the quality chasm: A new health system for the 21st Century.* Washington, DC: National Academies Press.

Jacobson, N., & Curtis, L. (2000). Recovery as policy in mental health services: Strategies emerging from the states. *Psychiatric Rehabilitation Journal, 23,* 333–341.

Jacobson, N., & Greenley, D. (2001). What is recovery? A conceptual model and explication. *Psychiatric Services, 52,* 482–485.

Kazdin, A. E. (2002). *Research design in clinical psychology* (4th ed.). Boston: Allyn and Bacon.

Lehman, A. F., & Steinwachs, D. M. (1998). Patterns of usual care for schizophrenia: Initial results form the Schizophrenia Patient Outcomes Research Team (PORT) client survey. *Schizophrenia Bulletin, 24,* 11–20.

Mckay, M. M. (in press). Commentary on "Increasing access to child mental services for urban children and their caregivers": A test of research/practice commitment in an urban child mental health setting. In L. Alexander & P. Solomon (Eds.), *The research process in social services: Myths and realities.* Monterey, CA: Wadsworth Group/Thomson Learning.

Mechanic, D. (2003). Policy challenges in improving mental health services: Some lessons from the past. *Psychiatric Services, 54,* 1227–1232.

Minkoff, K., & Cline, C. (2003). The missing link between science and service. *Psychiatric Services, 54,* 275.

NAMI. (2003). *Omnibus Mental Illness Recovery Act (OMIRA) brochure.* Retrieved November 11, 2003, from http://web.nami.org/update/omirabroch.html

National Association of State Mental Health Program Directors. (2003). *NTAC Mission Statement.* Retrieved November 20, 2003, from www.naspmhpd.org/ntac/about/mission.html

Onken, S. J., Dumont, J. M., Ridgeway, P., Dornan, D. H., & Ralph, R. O. (2002). *Mental health recovery: What helps and what hinders?* Alexandria, VA: National Association of State Mental Health Program Directors, the National Technical Assistance Center for State Mental Health Planning.

Peyser, H. (2001). What is recovery? A commentary. *Psychiatric Services, 52,* 486–487.

Ralph, R. O., Lambert, D., & Kidder, K. A. (2002). *The recovery perspective and evidence-based practice for people with serious mental illness.* Peoria, IL: Behavioral Health Recovery Management Project.

Rosenheck, R. A., Lam, J., Morrissey, J. P., Calloway, M. O., Stolar, M., & Randolph, F. (2002). Service systems integration and outcomes for mentally ill homeless persons in the ACCESS program. *Psychiatric Services, 53,* 958–966.

Solomon, P. (2004). Peer support/consumer provided services: Underlying process, benefits, and critical ingredients. *Psychatric Rehabilitation Journal, 27,* 392–401.

Townsend, W., & Glasser, N. (2003). Recovery: The heart and soul of treatment. *Psychiatric Rehabilitation Journal, 27,* 83–86.

Directory of Internet Resources on Evidence-Based Practice and Research in Health Care and Human Services

RESOURCES, GUIDELINES, AND TUTORIALS (LEARNING EBM)

- *Academic Center for Evidence-based Nursing (ACE):* ACE is part of The University of Texas Health Science Center at San Antonio School of Nursing and a companion entity to VERDICT (see below). As a center of excellence, its purpose is to advance cutting-edge, state-of-the-art, evidence-based nursing practice, research, and education within an interdisciplinary context. The goal is to turn research into action, improving health care and patient outcomes in the community, through evidence-based practice (EBP), research, and education. Contains some learning resources. http://www.acestar.uthscsa.edu/
- *Assessment, Crisis Intervention, and Trauma Treatment (ACT Model):* The ACT Intervention model is based on an integration of evidence-based assessment and treatment studies with persons in crisis and trauma. The ACT model presented on this website includes rapid assessment instruments, triage assessment, biopsychosocial assessment, the 7-stage crisis intervention model, and the 10-step trauma assessment and treatment protocol. http://www.crisisinterventionnetwork .com or http://www.brief-treatment.oupjournals.org
- *The Agency for Healthcare Research and Quality (AHRQ):* The United States premier evidence-based practice agency. To date, they have funded 13 Evidence-Based Practice Centers in the United States and Canada. AHRQ was established by the U.S. Congress and is the "lead agency charged with supporting research designed

to improve the quality of healthcare, reduce its cost, improve patient safety, decrease medical errors, and broaden access to essential services. AHRQ sponsors and conducts research that provides evidence-based information on healthcare outcomes; quality; and cost, use, and access. The information helps healthcare decision makers—patients and clinicians, health system leaders, and policymakers—make more informed decisions and improve the quality of healthcare services." On the AHRQ site can be found full text documents on evidence reports, clinical practice guidelines, quick-reference guides, and consumer brochures. Since 1996, AHCPR has produced evidence reports. Available free of charge via http://www.ahrq.gov

- *Bandolier:* Evaluation of systematic reviews and good quality evidence for health professionals. http://www.jr2.ox.ac.uk/Bandolier
- *Best Evidence:* This database of summaries of articles from the major medical journals, together with expert commentaries, is the CD-ROM equivalent of the combined ACP Journal Club and Evidence-Based Medicine output. Details of subscriptions are found at the BMJ site. http://www.bmjpg.com/template.cfm?name= specjou_be#best_evidence
- *BJM:* Full text of current issue, a searchable archive, collected resources, and access to Pubmed (public version of Medline) and Medline (password-controlled for BMA members). http://www.bmj.com
- *Campbell Collaboration:* A nonprofit international organization designed to assist persons in making well-informed decisions regarding the effects of interventions in the social, educational, criminology, and behavioral arenas. Objectives are to maintain, prepare, and disseminate systematic reviews of studies of interventions. http://www.campbellcollaboration.org/index.html
- *Centres of Health Evidence (CHE):* The principal task of CHE is to develop, package, disseminate, and present health care knowledge in ways that facilitate its optimum use. The website contains educational packets as introduction to EBP. http://www.cche.net/about/
- *CHID Online:* A database produced by health-related agencies of the Federal Government. This database provides titles, abstracts, and availability information for health information and health education resources. http://chid.nih.gov/
- *Clinical Evidence:* A database of clinical questions designed to help clinicians make evidence-based medicine part of their everyday practice. Hundreds of clinical questions cover the effects of treatments and interventions based on the best available research. Topics are selected to cover common or important clinical conditions seen in primary care or ambulatory settings. http://www.ovid.com/products/clinical/clinicalevidence.cfm
- *ClinicalTrials.gov:* The U.S. *National Institutes of Health*, through its *National Library of Medicine,* has developed *ClinicalTrials.gov* to provide patients, family members and members of the public with current information about clinical research studies. http://clinicaltrials.gov/
- *Cochrane Database:* Collection of databases specializing in evidence-based literature and systematic reviews. *NB Home access requires a Password—register on the NELH page to obtain a password. http://nww.nelh.nhs.uk (NHS) or http://www.nelh.nhs.uk (Home)*

- *Cochrane Database of Systematic Reviews:* A rapidly growing collection of regularly updated, systematic reviews of the effects of health care, maintained by contributors to the Cochrane Collaboration. New reviews are added with each issue of *The Cochrane Library*. Cochrane reviews are reviews mainly of randomized controlled trials. Evidence is included or excluded on the basis of explicit quality criteria to minimize bias. The Cochrane Database of Systematic Reviews is available on subscription only; the abstracts of Cochrane Reviews are available without charge and can be browsed or searched. **http://www.cochrane.org/cochrane/ revabstr/mainindex.htm**
- *Cochrane Library:* A quarterly updated electronic database containing systematic reviews and other information that will assist in making diagnostic, treatment, and other health care decisions. The Cochrane Library consists of four main databases: The Cochrane Database of Systematic Reviews, The Database of Abstracts of Reviews of Effectiveness, The Cochrane Controlled Trials Register, and The Cochrane Review Methodology Database. **http://www.cochrane.org/cochrane/cdsr.htm**
- *Cochrane Library [Abstracts]:* This facility from Update Software allows you to search the abstracts of the Cochrane Database of Systematic Reviews. The full text of the reviews is only available through the Cochrane Library (see above). **http:// www.update-software.com/abstracts/Default2.htm**
- *Consumer and Patient Health Information Section (CAPHIS):* A section of the Medical Library Association, an association of health information professionals with more than 5,000 individual and institution members. **http://www.caphis .mlanet.org/index.html**
- *CPB Infobase:* This website presents guidelines produced or endorsed in Canada by a national, provincial, or territorial medical or health organization, professional society, government agency, or expert panel. **http://www.cma.ca/cpgs**
- *Crisis Intervention, Co-morbidity Assessment, Domestic Violence Intervention, and Suicide Prevention network:* This website includes the latest abstracts on evidence-based practice articles as well as evidence-based practice handbooks published by Oxford University Press in New York. In addition, evidence-based rapid and triage assessment protocols, crisis intervention, drug treatment, and suicide prevention protocols are presented. **http://www.crisisinterventionnetwork.com**
- *Database of Abstracts of Reviews of Effectiveness:* DARE is a database of high-quality systematic research reviews of the effectiveness of health care interventions produced by the NHS Centre for Reviews and Dissemination at the University of York. **http://agatha.york.ac.uk/darehp.htm**
- *Evidence-Based Health Care—Latest Articles:* A list of the latest articles on evidence-based health care provided by the Evidence Based Resource Centre in New York. **http://www.ebmny.org/pubs.html**
- *Evidence-Based Medicine Reviews (EBMR):* Electronic information resource. Available via Ovid Online and on CD-ROM, this database from Ovid combines three EBM sources into a single, fully searchable database with links to MEDLINE® and Ovid full text journals. Sources covered include (1) the Cochrane Collaboration's Cochrane Database of Systematic Reviews, (2) Best Evidence, which consists of ACP Journal Club and Evidence-Based Medicine from the American College of

Physicians and the BMJ Publishing Group, and (3) The Database of Abstracts of Reviews of Effectiveness, produced by the expert reviewers and information staff of the National Health Service's Centre for Reviews and Dissemination (NHS CRD). http://www.ovid.com/products/clinical/ebmr.cfm

- *Evidence Based Medicine Toolkit:* (University of Alberta): Provides [something left out here?—ed.]to be applied in the implementation of evidence-based practice, including calculators and electronic resources. http://www.med.ualberta.ca/ebm/ebm.htm
- Hardin Library for the Health Sciences (University of Iowa) A comprehensive electronic resource for medical evidence. This site provides database, search, decision, and technological support. http://www.lib.uiowa.edu/hardin/electron.html
- *Health Information for the Consumer:* From the University of Pittsburgh Health Sciences Library System. http://www.hsls.pitt.edu/chi/
- *Health Information for the Consumer: Drug Information* from the University of Pittsburgh. Includes links to other drug information websites. http://www.hsls.pitt.edu/guides/chi/druginformation.html
- *Health Technology Advisory Committee Evaluation Reports:* Reports and issue briefs from the HTAC in Minnesota. http://www.health.state.mn.us/htac/techrpts.htm
- *Health Technology Assessment (HTA) Database:* The HTA Database, mounted by the NHS Centre for Reviews and Dissemination at the University of York, contains abstracts produced by INAHTA (International Network of Agencies for Health Technology Assessment) and other health care technology agencies. http://agatha.york.ac.uk/htahp.htm
- *Hospital Libraries Section of the Medical Library Association:* The Hospital Libraries Section of the Medical Library Association promotes and supports excellence in knowledge management and information resource development in the patient care and healthcare environment. http://www.hls.mlanet.org/Organization/index.html
- *InfoPOEMS:* Searchable database of POEMS (Patient Oriented Evidence that Matters) from the Journal of Family Practice. POEMS are summaries similar to ACP Journal Club articles in methodology and format, targeted at family practitioners. http://www.infopoems.com
- *JAMA—Rational Clinical Examination Series:* Provides framework for evaluation of examination of clinical evidence to be applied within evidence-based practice services. http://library.downstate.edu/resources/rce.htm
- *JANCOC—Japanese informal network for the Cochrane Collaboration:* The first systematic workshop review, held in Tokyo, Japan, in December, 1995, with 28 practitioner researchers in attendance, including physicians, pharmacists, biostatisticians, and consumers, led to a Directory of Japanese Researchers. The Chairman of JANCOC is Dr. Kiichiro Tsutani, Professor of Clinical Pharmacology at the Tokyo Medical and Dental University. For further information go to the JANCOC home page or www.cochrane.umin.ac.jp/Whats2.html
- *Lab Tests Online:* "Designed to help you, as a patient or caregiver, to better un-

derstand the many clinical lab tests that are part of routine care as well as diagnosis and treatment of a broad range of conditions and diseases." http://www .labtestsonline.org/site/index.html

- *Lamar Soutter Library Evidence-based Practice for Public Health Project:* Located at the University of Massachusetts, the purpose of this project is to examine the clinical EBM models and assess their effectiveness to the public health literature. The project will also identify any existing evidence-based projects in public health and assess their effectiveness. http://library.umassmed.edu/ebpph/
- *Making Research Count in the Personal Social Services:* A collaborative venture between six English universities (based at the University of East Anglia School of Social Work and Psychosocial Studies), offering staff in Local Authority Social Services Departments (and the NHS and voluntary organizations where joint schemes are running) the opportunity to work in partnership with their academic colleagues to develop evidence-based social work and social care practice, and to improve the dissemination of research. http://www.uea.ac.uk/swk/research/mrc/welcome.htm
- *MedlinePlus:* Provides quality health care information from the world's largest medical library, the National Library of Medicine at the National Institutes of Health. http://medlineplus.nlm.nih.gov/medlineplus/
- *Middlesex University Teaching and Learning Resources for Evidence-based Practice, Center for Transcultural Studies in Health:* Focuses on traditional and nontraditional approaches to evidence based practice. http://www.mdx.ac.uk/www/ rctsh/ebp/main.htm
- *National Guideline Clearinghouse:* The Agency for Healthcare Research and Quality (AHRQ), in partnership with the American Association of Health Plans (AAHP) and the American Medical Association (AMA), is sponsoring the National Guideline Clearinghouse (NGC). The NGC is a publicly available electronic repository for clinical practice guidelines and related materials that provides online access to guidelines. Recently, the Clearinghouse has added measures to the collection. *Note:* Only minimal criteria for quality are applied to guidelines listed in the Clearinghouse. http://www.guideline.gov
- *National Library of Medicine's Health Services/Technology Assessment Text (HSTAT):* This WWW resource contains the following collections: AHCPR Supported Guidelines, AHCPR Technology Assessments and Reviews, ATIS (HIV/AIDS Technical Information), NIH Warren G. Magnuson Clinical Research Studies, NIH Consensus Development Program, PHS Guide to Clinical Preventive Services (1989), and SAMHSA/CSAT Treatment Improvement Protocol (TIP). http://hstat .nlm.nih.gov
- *National Research Register (NRR):* A register of ongoing and recently completed research projects funded by, or of interest to, the United Kingdom's National Health Service. The current release contains information on over 57,000 research projects, entries from the Medical Research Council's Clinical Trials Register, and details on reviews in progress collected by the NHS Centre for Reviews and Dissemination. http://www.update-software.com/National/nrr-frame.html
- *NettingtheEvidence:* Introduction to evidence-based practice on the Internet. Pro-

duced by Sheffield University. Searching option offers links to evidence-based health care sites, tips on searching, how to formulate a clinical question. www .nettingtheevidence.org.uk

- *NHS Economic Evaluation Database (NHS EED):* A database of structured abstracts of economic evaluations of health care interventions produced by the NHS Center for Reviews and Dissemination at the University of York. http://agatha .york.ac.uk/nhsdhp.htm
- *NOAH (New York Online Access to Health):* Seeks to provide high-quality full-text health information for consumers that is accurate, timely, relevant and unbiased. NOAH currently supports English and Spanish. http://www.noah-health .org/
- *OMNI:* Searchable catalogue of quality health information available on the Internet. http://omni.ac.uk
- *Ovid Medline Tutorial:* Powerful tutorial for the construction and implementation of literature searches within the framework of evidence-based treatment. http:// library.downstate.edu/medtut/medtoc.htm
- *PEDro—Physiotherapy Evidence Database:* An initiative of the Centre for Evidence-Based Physiotherapy (CEBP), PEDro is the Physiotherapy Evidence Database. It has been developed to give physiotherapists and others rapid access to bibliographic details and abstracts of randomized controlled trials in physiotherapy. Most trials on the database have been rated for quality to help to quickly discriminate between trials that are likely to be valid and interpretable and those that are not. http://ptwww.cchs.usyd.edu.au/pedro/
- *Population Index:* This bibliography is designed to cover the world's demographic and population literature, including books and other monographs, serial publications, journal articles, working papers, doctoral dissertations, and machine-readable data files. http://opr.princeton.edu/popindex/
- *Primary Care Clinical Practice Guidelines:* This site will include all guidelines, evidence-based, consensus, practice parameters, protocols, as well as other resources such as primary articles, integrative studies, meta-analysis, critically appraised topics, and review articles. Compiled by Peter Sam at the UCSF School of Medicine. http://medicine.ucsf.edu/resources/guidelines/
- PubMed Tutorial: Tutorial for the development and utilization of evidence based medicine searches.http://www.library.health.ufl.edu/pubmed/PubMed2/
- *RehabTrials.org:* A new website created by the nonprofit Kessler Medical Rehabilitation Research and Education Corporation (KMRREC) to promote, encourage, and support clinical trials in medical rehabilitation. http://www.rehabtrials.org
- *RxList:* The Internet drug index search for indications, symptoms, side effects, and drug interactions. Includes the "Top 200 Prescriptions." http://www.rxlist.com/
- *SUMSearch:* A single gateway that attempts to provide references to answer clinical questions around diagnosis, etiology, prognosis, and therapy (plus physical findings, adverse treatment effects, and screening/prevention) by searching only high-quality sources. SUMSearch always searches (1) Merck Manual, (2) MEDLINE, for review articles and editorials that have full texts available, (3) National Guideline Clearinghouse from the Agency for Health Care Policy and Research (AHCPR), (4) Da-

tabase of Abstract of Reviews of Effectiveness (DARE), and (5) MEDLINE for original research. Depending on the focus requested, SUMSearch will search PubMed with the highest sensitivity filters developed by Haynes et al. **http://SUMSearch.UTHSCSA.edu/cgi-bin/SUMSearch.exe**

- *SUNY Downstate Evidence-Based Medicine Course:* Provides resources including tutorial for the development of evidence based program development. **http://library.downstate.edu/ebm/toc.html**

- *Task Force on Community Preventive Services:* The Task Force on Community Preventive Services is an independent, non-federal Task Force and consists of 15 members, including a chair, appointed by the Director of CDC. The Task Force's membership is multidisciplinary and includes perspectives representative of state and local health departments, managed care, academia, behavioral and social sciences, communications sciences, mental health, epidemiology, quantitative policy analysis, decision and cost-effectiveness analysis, information systems, primary care, and management and policy. **http://www.thecommunityguide.org**

- *Turning Research Into Practice (TRIP) Database:* This resource, hosted by the Centre for Research Support in Wales, aims to support those working in primary care. The database has 8,000 links covering resources at 28 different centers and allows both boolean searching (AND, OR, NOT) and truncation. **http://www.tripdatabase.com**

- *University of York NHS Centre for R&D:* Full text of most Effective Health Care and Effectiveness Matters publications and access to databases. Compiled by: Susan Merner, Librarian Poole Hospital NHS Trust. **http://www.york.ac.uk/inst/crd**

- *U.S. Preventive Services Task Force:* The Task Force was convened by the U.S. Public Health Service in 1984 to systematically review the evidence of effectiveness of a wide range of clinical preventive services, including screening tests, counseling, immunizations, and chemoprophylaxis. The Task Force is composed of 15 members and is closely affiliated with AHRQ. The Task Force publishes the Guide to Clinical Preventive Services. **http://www.ahrq.gov/clinic/uspstfab.htm**

- *Users' Guide to Evidence Based Practice:* Provides practical application advice for evidence-based practice. **http://www.cche.net/usersguides/main.asp**

- *Veterans Evidence-Based Research Dissemination Implementation Center (VERDICT):* VERDICT's mission is to foster a knowledge-based health care system in which clinical, managerial, and policy decisions are based upon sound information from research findings. The multidisciplinary team addresses systematic implementation of evidence in clinical practice within the Veterans Health Administration, leading to integrated models of care and improved service, quality and efficiency. Learning resources include VERDICT Briefs. **http://verdict.uthscsa.edu/verdict/default.htm**

- Widener University: Evaluating websites for evidence-based practice. **http//www2.widener.edu/Wolfgram-Memorial-Library/webevaluation/webeval.htm**

EBM AND EBP BOOKS

- *Evidence-Based Practice Manual* / edited by Albert R. Roberts and Kenneth R. Yeager
- *Diagnostic Strategies for Common Medical Problems* / edited by Edgar R. Black
- *Evidence-Based Medicine: How to Practice and Teach EBM* / David L. Sackett
- *Evidence-Based Physical Diagnosis* / Steven McGee
- *How to Read a Paper: The Basics of Evidence-Based Medicine* / Trisha Greenhalgh
- *PDQ: Evidence-Based Principles and Practice* / Ann McKibbon
- *Social Workers' Desk Reference* / edited by Albert R. Roberts and Gilbert Greene
- *Users' Guides to the Medical Literature: Essentials of Evidence-Based Clinical Practice*
- *AMA Evidence-Based Medicine Working Group* / edited by Gordon Guyatt and Drummond Rennie

EBM CALCULATORS

- UBC Clinical Significance Calculator **http://www.healthcare.ubc.ca/calc/clinsig.html**
- Stats Calculator from the University of Toronto **http://www.cebm.utoronto.ca/practise/ca/statscal/**

CLINICAL TRIALS

- ClinicalTrials.gov **http://www.clinicaltrials.gov/**

EBM COMPLEMENTARY AND ALTERNATIVE MEDICINE

- Alternative Medicine Foundation: Examines alternative medicine approaches compatible with evidence-based practice. **http://www.amfoundation.org/**
- Complementary and Alternative Therapies (from Bandolier) **http://www.jr2.ox.ac.uk/bandolier/booth/booths/altmed.html**

EVIDENCE-BASED CONSUMER HEALTH

- Ask NOAH about: Evidence-Based Medicine **http://www.noah-health.org/english/ebhc/ebhc.html**
- Cochrane Collaboration Consumer Network **http://www.cochraneconsumer.com/**
- Crisis intervention, suicide prevention, and drug-induced psychosis facts and

evidence-based assessment and treatment protocols. http://www.crisisintervention network.com
- Medline Plus http://www.nlm.nih.gov/medlineplus/
- IntelliHealth http://www.intelihealth.com/IH/ihtIH/WSIHWOOD/408/408.html
- Eccles Health Science Library's Health Brochures http://medstat.med.utah.edu/ library/refdesk/24lang.html—contains materials in 24 different languages.
- Massachusetts Health Promotion Clearinghouse http://www.maclearinghouse .com/catalog.htm—contains materials in multiple languages.

EVIDENCE-BASED DRUG INFORMATION

- UNC Health Sciences Library: Drug Information: Provides resources to assist understanding of complex nature of medication management within evidence-based practice. http://www.hsl.unc.edu/lm/druginformation/ebm.htm

EBM GERIATRICS

- Merck Institute of Aging and Health: Providing comprehensive approaches to evidence-based treatment within the practice of aging and health care. http:// www.miahonline.org/

EBM GLOSSARIES

- Clinical Epidemiology Glossary http://www.med.ualberta.ca/ebm/define.htm (from Evidence Based Medicine Working Group)
- Glossary from SUNY Downstate's EBM tutorial http://library.downstate.edu/ ebm/glos.htm
- Evidence-based Medicine Resource Center http://www.ebmny.org/glossary.html
- Medline Glossary http://www.ebmny.org/glossary.html
- Duke Medical Center Library—Evidence-based Medicine (EBM) http://www .mclibrary.duke.edu/respub/guides/ebm/overview.html
- Clinical Epidemiology and Evidence-based Medicine Glossary http://www.vetmed .wsu.edu/courses-jmgay/GlossClinEpiEBM.htm

EBM GUIDELINES

- U.S. Clinical Practice Guidelines http://www.guidelines.gov/index.asp
- Canadian Medical Association Clinical Guidelines http://www.cma.ca/cma/ common/start.do?lang=2
- New Zealand Guidelines Group includes tools for guideline development and

evidence-based health care practices and guidelines. http://www.nzgg.org.nz/tools .cfm

EBM MENTAL HEALTH

- Centre for Evidence-Based Mental Health http://cebmh.warne.ox.ac.uk/cebmh/
- Evidence-Based Mental Health http://ebmh.bmjjournals.com/
- Centre for Evidence-Based Mental Health http://www.psychiatry.ox.ac.uk/ cebmh/guidelines/
- The Royal College of Psychiatrists http://www.rcpsych.ac.uk/cru/focus/access/ access12b.htm
- Internet Mental Health http://www.mentalhealth.com/p00.html

EVIDENCE-BASED PRACTICE AND HUMAN SERVICES

- Evidence-Based Practice and the Evaluative Agenda: Providing tips and guidance and methods for application of evidence-based practice within human services. http://www.sws.soton.ac.uk/rminded/SRS3/SRS37.htm
- Evidence-Based Practice in Social Work: Providing application of evidence-based practice protocols to the field of social work. Provides specific examples to evidence-based approaches in social work. http://library.wustl.edu/subjects/sw/ebp.html
- Secondary Data in Evidence-based Practice: Providing an overview of methodologies for analysis and application of secondary database research within a framework compatible with evidence-based practice. http://www.lib.umich.edu/soc work/secondarydata.html
- Center for Technology in Social Work Education and Practice (SWTECH) is located at the College of Social Work at the University of South Carolina. The center trains human service workers in the utilization of technology for practice; examines what technologies will benefit distance education and instructional technology endeavors of schools and colleges of social work; and consults with institutions of higher education and social service agencies on implementing communication/information technologies. http://swtech.sc.edu/about.htm
- Council on Social Work Education is a nonprofit organization that sets accreditation standards and oversees and monitors site teams approximately every seven years to determine compliance with the accreditation standards by all accredited baccalaureate and master's degree programs in social work. Their long-standing goal for the past 50 years has been to promote high-quality standards in social work education throughout the United States. Each spring CSWE holds an annual conference with about 10 preconference faculty skills workshops, and numerous peer-reviewed presentations, panels, and poster sessions. The first two American universities to implement social work courses in evidence-based practice (EBP) were

Columbia University and Washington University in St. Louis, Missouri. **www .cswe.org**
- HUSITA organization is an international association dedicated to the dissemination of information technology to human service professionals. It has a listserv, mailing list, and annual conferences. The owners of the listserve are Dr. Dick Schoech and Tom Hanna of the University of Texas at Arlington School of Social Work. **HUSITA@LISTSERV.UTA.EDU**
- Formulating a Question and Effective Search Strategy: Powerful tool for development of effective evidence-based practice literature search. Provides basic and advance tips for literature searches. **http://www.lib.umich.edu/socwork/secondary data.html#form**

EBM NURSING AND ALLIED HEALTH

- Centre for Evidence Based Nursing **http://www.york.ac.uk/healthsciences/misc/ lksebn.htm**
- Evidence-Based Nursing **http://ebn.bmjjournals.com/**
- Evidence-Based Occupational Therapy **http://www-fhs.mcmaster.ca/rehab/ebp/**
- Physiotherapy Evidence Database **http://www.pedro.fhs.usyd.edu.au/**
- OT Seeker **http://www.otseeker.com/**

PREVENTION AND SCREENING

- The Agency for Healthcare Research and Quality (AHRQ) **http://www.ahcpr .gov/**
- Preventive Services **http://www.ahcpr.gov/clinic/prevenix.htm**
- U.S. Preventive Services Task Force **http://www.ahcpr.gov/clinic/uspstfix.htm**
- The Guide to Clinical Preventive Services **http://www.ahcpr.gov/clinic/cpsix.htm**
- Put Prevention Into Practice **http://www.ahcpr.gov/clinic/ppipix.htm**

EBM WEBSITES

- Canadian Centres for Health Evidence **http://www.cche.net/che/home.asp**
- Bandolier Home Page **http://www.jr2.ox.ac.uk/bandolier/**
- Evidence-Based Medicine Resource Center **http://www.ebmny.org/index.html**
- ScHARR Netting the Evidence **http://www.sheffield.ac.uk/scharr/ir/netting/**
- University of Toronto's Centre for Evidence-Based Medicine **http://www.cebm .utoronto.ca/**
- JAMA Rational Clinical Examination Series **http://library.downstate.edu/ resources/rce.htm**
- Mt. Sinai School of Medicine **http://www.mssm.edu/medicine/general-medicine/ ebm/**

- National Quality Measures Clearinghouse http://www.qualitymeasures.ahrq.gov/
- Consumer Assessment of Healthplans http://www.ahcpr.gov/qual/cahpsix.htm
- Core Library for Evidence-Based Practice http://www.shef.ac.uk/scharr/ir/core .html
- Healthlinks: Evidence-Based Practice and Guidelines http://healthlinks.washing ton.edu/clinical/guidelines.html

PDA RESOURCES

- Ectopic Brain—General Resources for both PC and Palm http://pbrain.hypermart .net/
- MedRules—Diagnosis tools for Palm only http://pbrain.hypermart.net/medrules .html
- EBM Calculator http://www.cebm.utoronto.ca/palm/ebmcalc/ Center for Health Evidence in Canada—Palm Only
- NNT Tables http//www.cebm.utoronto.ca/palm/nnt/download.htm Center for Health Evidence in Canada—Palm Only
- Healthy Palmpilot http://www.healthypalmpilot.com/ General Resources for Palm Only
- Pediatric Pilot Page http://keepkidshealthy.com/pedipilot.html Palm Only
- Medical Palm Webring—General Resources for both PC and Palm http://library -downstate.edu/resources/ebm.htm
- EBM Tools http://www.healthypalmpilot.com/Research_Tools/Evidence_Based _Medicine/ Healthy Palmpilot—Evaluation guides and calculators for both PC and Palm
- Mobile EBM Guidelines for hand-held devices http://www.ebm-guidelines.com/ mobile.html

Glossary

Compiled and Edited by Evelyn Roberts Levine

Abstinence (Detoxification) Orientation: An approach to opioid agonist therapy that views abstinence from all opioids and opioid agonists, including methadone, as the ultimate goal of therapy. A detoxification orientation among clinic staff has been linked to lower retention rates, more restrictive dosing and take-home privileges, and more punitive responses to illicit drug use.

Abstinence Orientation Scale: In 1998, Caplehorn and associates developed a 14-item scale that assesses a treatment provider's endorsement of statements reflective of an abstinence orientation toward opioid agonist therapy. The mean score across treatment providers at each clinic can be used as an indication of overall clinic philosophy. High Abstinence Orientation Scale clinic scores are predictive of poorer program retention and higher rates of illicit drug use among enrolled patients.

Abuser: A person or persons who inflict harm or threat of harm on another person. An abuser may be a family member, significant other, acquaintance, or opportunistic stranger. *See also Chronic Battering, Domestic Violence Typology, Elder Abuse, Short-Term Abuse* and *Woman Battering Continuum.*

Accounting: The process of keeping and verifying accounts and records, usually of a monetary nature.

Acculturation: A complex social process that is initiated when members of one cultural group are exposed over an extended period of time to members of another cultural group. It refers to the adoption of the values, preferences, and behaviors of the host society.

Action Factors: Interactions between the therapist and client or patient including cognitive mastery modeling and behavioral regulation.

Activities, Strategies, and Services: These refer to all operational elements of what is essentially the "effort," that is to say, the program, the initiative, the project, and so forth. Activities, strategies, and services are expected first and foremost to benefit the customer and then the service-providing organization. The "effort" expresses the hope that inputs can be converted into results. However, since this does not always happen automatically, coincidentally, or accidentally, the underlying assumptions and strategies that are expected to drive the "effort" must be articulated explicitly, executed experimentally, and tied directly to performance measures that will look for evidence of efficiency, equity, and effectiveness.

Actuarial Test: Measures designed to predict risk of future violence. These measures are designed following retrospective research looking for factors associated with recidivism in specific offender populations.

Adjectival Scale: A scale in which the respondent must select one of a series of graded adjectives (e.g., Excellent / Very Good / Good / Fair / Poor).

Age-Specific Mortality Rate (ASMR): The *mortality rate* adjusted for the age of the sample. The number of deaths from a specific disease "X" in a specific age range "Y" divided by the total number of deaths in specific age range "Y". This rate allows you to age-adjust mortality rates for a given disease.

Agoraphobia: Agoraphobia ("fear of the marketplace" in Greek) is an anxiety disorder defined by intense fear of being placed in situations where no help is available should some incapacitating or embarrassing event occur. Frequently, agoraphobia is related to or associated with repeated panic attacks. If untreated, over long periods of time agoraphobia can lead to the individual's fear of leaving his or her home altogether.

Alpha: A frequency range in the EEG, defined as 8–13 Hertz per second.

Alternate Form Reliability: Also called parallel forms, this refers to the consistency of measurement between equivalent measurement tools. It is obtained by giving two different but equivalent forms of the same measure to the same group of clients. If there is no measurement error, clients should score the same on both measures, thus yielding a high correlation coefficient (Pearson's r).

AMA (Against Medical Advice): Any discharge of a patient for any reason other than having completed the treatment process or meeting the treatment goals. Discharges against medical advice have a strong probability of being readmitted for the same or related diagnosis within a brief period of time.

American Indian: Descendants of the aboriginal people of the Americas; these persons are often called Native Americans.

Annual Incidence: The *incidence* expressed in cases per year.

Anxiety: An emotional state characterized by fear-related beliefs and/or physiological arousal. Anxiety is an adaptive emotion when experienced and responded to in proportion to the triggering event(s). Anxiety disorders are characterized by inordinately high levels of anxiety connected with an inaccurate perception of danger. They are maintained by avoidant strategies that are intended to reduce or minimize the perceived threat but which ultimately serve to reinforce the fear-related beliefs and anxiety.

Anxiety Disorders: Anxiety disorders are defined by intense feelings of anxiety and tension in the absence or presence of "real danger." Symptoms associated with anxiety disorder frequently cause significant distress. Mild to moderate symptoms frequently interfere with daily activities. Sufferers of anxiety disorders may take extreme measures to avoid situations that provoke anxiety. The physical symptoms associated with anxiety are restlessness, irritability, disturbed sleep, muscle aches and pains, gastrointestinal distress, and difficulty concentrating.

Applied Research: Research designed to solve a specific problem. It may or may not be theory based.

Area under the Curve (AUC): The AUC is a statistical measure used in a ROC analysis. In assessing sexual offenders, it is the probability that the detection method will give a randomly selected violent person a higher score than a randomly selected nonviolent person. A perfect detection method would give an AUC score of 1.0 and test that was no better than chance would give an AUC score of 0.5.

Assessment: Process of systematically collecting, organizing, and interpreting data related to a client's functioning in order to determine the need for treatment, as well as treatment goals and intervention plan.

Auditing: The process of officially examining information to ensure that it is in order. Although usually focused on financial information, audits may also be conducted on working hours, services provided, and clients of services.

Authenticity: A qualitative research term that refers to the degree to which the research process has genuinely involved key stakeholders in the phenomenon under study in the actual research process and the degree to which the study has led to a benefit for these stakeholders. Authenticity is one of a number of factors used to judge the rigor or trustworthiness of a qualitative study.

Average Days in Accounts Receivable: This phrase indicates the amount of time passed from the point a bill is submitted to a payer group until the time the account is paid. Days in accounts receivable indicates the effectiveness of collection of payment for billed services. In general, average days in accounts receivable under 60 days is considered to be very good for medical detoxification.

Average LOS (Length of Stay): Total patient days for a particular level of care divided by the total admissions for this level of care. This is utilized to determine the optimal amount of hospitalization for a given diagnostic category and degree of severity weighed against risk of rehospitalization. Utilized as a quality indicator for most medical facilities in medical detoxification.

Axial Coding: The process of coding qualitative data around a single conceptual category and drawing connections between the conceptual category and relevant subcategories.

Balanced Scorecard: An evaluation device that specifies the criteria your organization will use to rate business performance in progress toward and attaining previously established and applied strategic planning. This tool provides an at-a-glance monitor for senior administrative leaders to monitor progress made toward implementation of organizational strategic plans and specifically defined targets for rollout and ongoing rating of performance on clearly defined organizational targets, objectives, and goals.

Baseline: An initial assessment of a program at a given time to be compared with another data point or assessment in the future (ideally with an intervention or "treatment" in between the two data points).

Behavioral Exchange: A technique used in cognitive-behavioral couples therapy in which the amount of day-to-day positive behaviors between partners are increased, ameliorating partners' focus on negative parts of the relationship.

Benchmark: The best-achieved outcome score, preferably risk-adjusted, among treatment groups.

Benchmarking: A term referring to the identification of standards for performance on a particular indicator. Performance data for a given organization are compared with data from similar organizations in order to guide decision making. In order to be valid and useful, benchmarking data need to be based on similar *measures* and methods. A term utilized to describe comparison of data between a group of data points for the purpose of determining relative value. It can be utilized as a method to measure or judge quality of services provided or as a point of reference when comparing like categories, e.g., diagnostic groupings. The process of comparing one's own performance on a specific measure against a like entity. The process of taking collected data from different organizations or from different programs of the same organization and displaying that data so as to demonstrate the relative relationship of one organization to another. Benchmarking does not so much indicate what the results should be as it does display what is actually measured and allows organizations to see themselves in relationship to the other organizations.

Best Practices: Best practices are those assessment, intervention, or evaluation practices identified by authoritative review groups, such as committees set up by professional organizations, as being most appropriate for routine use in service systems. Typically, such review groups examine available scientific evidence as well as professional consensus. Feasibility and cost may also be considered.

Beta: A frequency range in the EEG, defined as greater than 13 Hertz per second.

Bipolar Disorder/Manic Depression: A serious mood disorder that involves extreme mood swings or highs (mania) and lows (depression); sometimes termed manic-depressive psychosis.

Blinding: Keeping the participants (single blind) or the participants and the researcher (double blind) ignorant of which people are in which group in a study. This is done to reduce the possibility of *placebo* or *Hawthorne* effects.

Budget: An estimate or plan of income and expenditures. It is the organization's fiscal plan, usually developed for one year but, in some cases, longer or shorter periods of time.

Buffering: The process by which an intervening or mediating variable lessens the impact of an independent variable on the dependent variable. Generally considered a protective coping factor in stressful situations.

Build Capacity: Program staff members and participants learning to conduct their own evaluations (evaluation capacity) and enhancing their ability to operate their own programs (program capacity).

Building Momentum: A three- to six-month period devoted to the establishment of executive-level support for a given project. This process involves communication and examination of processes associated with and contributing to the need for change. Frequently the establishment of a leadership team is required, as is clarification of the organization's mission and vision.

Case-Based Reasoning: A knowledge-based application in which the demographics, services, and outcomes in thousands of cases are entered into a computer software application. Practitioners can then enter the circumstances of their existing case to see how similar cases were handled and review case outcomes. A case-based reasoning system stores both successful and unsuccessful cases. A problem-solving approach is taken in which case goals are specified as well as problems that are avoided. As new cases and their outcomes are entered into the software, these cases become integrated into the "memory" of cases that are used in future case analyses.

Case-Control Study: A research design in which people with a specific outcome (e.g., a disease or syndrome) are matched with people who do not have the outcome. This is usually done to determine if the groups differ with respect to the risk of exposure to a putative causal agent (e.g., the groups could be those with and without lung cancer, with the exposure being cigarette smoking; *Compare with Cohort Study*).

Case-Fatality Rate: The proportion of people with a disorder who die from it within a specific time frame. The number of deaths from a disorder in the time period divided by the number of people with the disorder. This number focuses only on those people who have the disorder and will be higher than the more general *mortality rate.*

Case Management: Coordination of services to help meet a patient's health care needs, usually when the patient requires multiple services from multiple providers. This term is also used to refer to coordination of care during and after a hospital stay.

Casino: A single room in each casino where gaming is conducted pursuant to the provisions of the New Jersey Casino Control Act.

Casino Security Employee: A person employed by a casino to provide physical security in the gaming area, simulcasting facility, or restricted casino area. It does not include any person who also provides physical security solely in any other part of the casino hotel.

CCTV: Closed Circuit Television System (CCTV), which makes a video and, if applicable, an audio recording of, and takes a still photograph of, any event capable of being monitored on the CCTV system.

C-DISC: The Computerized Diagnostic Interview Schedule for Children (C-DISC) is a computerized version of the NIMH DISC-IV, which is a highly structured diagnostic interview, designed to assess more than 30 psychiatric disorders occurring in children and adolescents, suitable for administration by trained lay (nonclinician) interviewers. The instrument has been in development since 1979, and various versions have been produced to match different classification systems. The current version of the DISC (National Institute of Mental Health [NIMH] DISC-IV), based on the DSM-IV and ICD-10, was released for field use in 1997. Although originally intended for large-scale epidemiological surveys of children, versions of the DISC have been used in clinical studies, in prevention/screening exercises, and as an aid to diagnosis in service settings. There are parallel versions of the instrument: the DISC-P for parents (or knowledgeable caretakers) of 6- to 17-year-olds, and the DISC-Y (for direct administration to children and youths aged 9–17).

Central Tendency: The property of a distribution that refers to the extent to which there is a convergence of observations at or around a limited set of values. Statistical indices of central tendency try to assess what are the average, typical, or most likely values; they include the mean, median, and mode.

Certified Public Accountant: One who has passed state examinations and received a certificate of professional competence in accounting and who has subscribed to the state's professional expectations for accountants.

Change Levers: Motivators of change, in this chapter, discussed in an organizational context.

Chronic Battering: Victims experience numerous severe abusive incidents during their marriage. The abuse is frequently inflicted when the batterer has been drinking heavily or has explosive anger toward the victim. The chronic pattern of victimization by their intimate partners lasts from several years to several decades, and often ends when the victim or perpetrator is permanently injured, hospitalized, arrested and detained, or dead. The injuries for these victims are usually extensive and include sprains, fractures, broken bones, cuts, and head injuries that often require emergency medical attention. *See also Woman Battering Continuum.*

Chronic Suicidality: Unremittingly high suicide ideation, frequent threats of suicide, and difficulty articulating reasons for living.

Client-Centered Administrative Practice: This term was developed by Rapp and Poertner in 1992 and refers to social work practice in managing, designing, and evaluating programs that keep the realities, knowledge, and needs of the recipients of services as central to effectiveness. Along with client concern, this form of practice considers the staff implementing the services as integral to effectiveness and success.

Clinical Practice Guidelines: Clinical practice guidelines are systematically developed statements designed to structure practitioner and service recipient decisions about appropriate service for specific problems, conditions, or populations.

These guidelines prescribe how practitioners should assess and treat service recipients. Sometimes the guidelines are based on research findings. Sometimes, research is not available and, therefore, the guidelines are based on professional consensus. Professional organizations and governmental agencies have formulated practice guidelines for various conditions.

Clinical Relationship: The attitudes of a client and practitioner toward each other that develops from their personal characteristics and processes of interaction. It is widely considered to be a significant factor in the client's achievement of outcomes but is difficult to formally measure. At a basic level a positive clinical relationship should feature a bond between the parties characterized by some level of collaboration, agreement on goals, trust, and mutual comfort.

Clinical Theory: Clinical theories are systematic conceptual systems intended to explain, describe, or predict some circumscribed aspect of the empirical world pertaining to clinical practice. Such theories can purport to explain or describe a clinical problem, condition, or intervention. Theories are made up of constructs that are abstract terms representing key theoretical terms as well as propositions showing how these constructs are interrelated. These propositions may or may not have been examined in empirical research. The propositions of scientific clinical theories require empirical validation through the testing of corresponding hypotheses.

Clinical Wisdom: Clinical groups, including professional specialties, typically develop collective beliefs about their respective sphere of practice such as about the causes of typical problems or conditions seen in practice, or about which methods of assessment or intervention are most appropriate for particular problems, conditions, or populations. These beliefs emerge from the collective experience of the group; they are often codified in professional papers, manuals, and texts and are taught to new clinicians in formal training programs as well as supervision. Clinical wisdom is not verified through scientific research, but at times hypotheses derived from clinical wisdom are tested in scientific research.

Clustered Systems: Systems that use information about the provider to predetermine which information tools to present to the user. Presentation of a relevant drug database, for example, can be automated upon recognizing that a particular type of physician is logged on.

Cognitive Behavior Therapy (CBT): A form of psychotherapy that is largely present-centered and problem-oriented and which uses verbal procedures and behavioral experiments to examine and test the validity and utility of the client's perceptions and interpretations of events. A form of psychological therapy focusing on the modification of both cognitive processes and behavior. The primary focus is on current functioning and modification of maladaptive behaviors and thoughts while reinforcing positive behaviors and thoughts. CBT draws heavily on cognitive theory and research, as well as more traditional techniques of behavior modification. Therapy that involves training, discussion, and operant conditioning techniques to allow clients to recognize and change maladaptive behaviors, thoughts, attitudes, and beliefs. There are a variety of forms of CBT, but in the treatment of suicidality, they all emphasize rapid cognitive assessment and problem solving.

Cognitive Pretesting: One of many methods used to assess the thought processes of individuals responding to questionnaire items. In the current study, cognitive pretesting involved asking children questions while they answered prototype ESSP questions to determine if they understood and responded to questions as intended by the ESSP developers.

Cognitive Therapy: A form of psychotherapy used to help patients identify, challenge, and correct characteristic mistaken ideas and assumptions that lead to excessive emotional responses. In the case of anxiety disorders, patients often overestimate the probability of disastrous consequences. In cognitive therapy, patients are taught to recognize such overestimates and subject their probability estimate to logical scrutiny, leading them to reduce their estimate and hence their fears.

Cognizant Systems: Systems that use artificial intelligence to respond to clinical events, detect patterns, and determine which knowledge resources are most appropriate for problem solving. No such systems exist today.

Cohen's Kappa: A measure of the degree to which there is agreement between judges on how they rate a person or object.

Coherence: The average similarity between the waveforms of a particular band in two locations over the one-second period of time. Conceptualized as the strength/number of connections between two positions.

Cohort Study: Involves identification and selection of two groups (cohorts) of patients, one group that did receive the exposure/treatment of interest, and one group that did not, and then monitoring and evaluating these cohorts prospectively for the outcome of interest. A research design in which people who were exposed to a putative causal agent are compared to those not exposed, to determine if they differ with respect to the risk of some outcome (e.g., the groups could be smokers and nonsmokers, with the outcome being lung cancer). *See also Study Designs and Case-Control Study.*

Collaborative Evaluation: Approaches to evaluating social interventions developed by teams that include researchers, managers, and staff of agencies that serve families and children, consumers, providers of informal supports, and other stakeholders.

Collectivism: A type of social orientation held by a cultural group where deep value is placed on interdependent relationships within social groups. It is one end of an individualism-collectivism continuum onto which societies may be located.

Combined Systems: Systems that unite one or more components under a common interface. A combined drug prescription system, for example, may include menus that allow the clinician to search for dosing details or patient advice handouts before generating prescriptions.

Common Cause Variation: Fluctuation caused by unknown factors resulting in a steady but random distribution of output around the average of the data. It is a measure of the process potential, providing indication of how well the process can perform when special cause variation is removed.

Community: As defined by Boudon and Bourricaud in 1989, physical communities consist of three elements: (1) a social network that is both resilient and flexible; (2) some symbolic ties to an object of identification; and (3) an identified group that is part of a larger society.

Community Context: The state of organization or order within the community at any given time.

Community or Collective Efficacy: The belief that the community will improve over time.

Community Outreach Specialist: A community outreach specialist (COS) serves a particular role in lay health advisor (LHA) programs. The COS serves as a liaison between the LHAs, the community advisors, and the people implementing the intervention (e.g., researchers or agency staff). The COS may also participate in training the LHAs, monitoring their work, providing ongoing training, and collecting information for use in a project evaluation.

Community Quality: The physical and social state of a community.

Comorbidity: The co-occurrence of two or more conditions with related etiology and/or mechanism of maintenance. The simultaneous appearance of two or more illnesses, such as the co-occurrence of schizophrenia and substance abuse or of alcohol dependence and depression. The association may reflect a causal relationship between one disorder and another or an underlying vulnerability to both disorders. The related decisions of what, when, and how to treat any one or more of the conditions must be considered within the context of the comorbid conditions. It is also possible for the appearance of the illnesses to be unrelated to any common etiology or vulnerability.

Compulsion: A pattern of attempts to neutralize or avoid the anxiety associated with obsessions in obsessive-compulsive disorder. A symptom of obsessive-compulsive disorder involving urges to perform stereotyped ritualistic behaviors to reduce distress associated with obsessions. The words *compulsion* and *ritual* are used interchangeably. Compulsions are negatively reinforced; the function of the compulsion is simply to decrease discomfort, not to provide enjoyment. Compulsions are most often overt behaviors, such as hand washing or seeking reassurance from religious professionals. Mental compulsions are also quite common and are characterized by mental processes intended to neutralize the anxiety or discomfort associated with obsessions. Examples include repeated checking, washing, excessive praying or confessing, needless ordering and arranging, or mentally "canceling out" intrusive thoughts.

Computer-Assisted Assessment: A client assessment approach that captures assessment information via a computer software application. Computer assessment systems can be administered prospectively with the client present or retrospectively after a client interview has taken place. One example is the Client Assessment System (CAS), developed by Walter Hudson and Paula Nurius. CAS allows the client to conduct the assessment independently by keying in responses to a preset list of standardized assessment instruments. The program also scores the assessment and integrates with case management software for use by the case manager.

Computer-Assisted Personal Interviews (CAPI): A computer-assisted personal interview (CAPI) is similar to a computer-assisted telephone interview (CATI), in which a computer software program facilitates the interview process. The primary difference between a CATI and a CAPI is that the interview is conducted face-to-face, with the computer screen visible to the client or respondent.

Computer-Assisted Telephone Interviews (CATI): A computer-assisted telephone interview is a computer software program that facilitates the interview process. An interviewer follows prompts provided by the software and displayed on the computer screen to ask questions and record responses. One advantage to a CATI system is that it eliminates a separate data entry step.

Concept Map: A concept map depicts the structure of knowledge about any phenomenon of interest such as a program, organization, public policy, process or content domain. Concept maps provide guidance for evaluators to ensure that data collection is focused on key facets and relationships in the theory of the program or its implementation. The knowledge portrayed in concept maps is context-dependent. Different maps containing the same concepts convey different meanings depending upon the hierarchical relationships, linking descriptors, and arrangement of individual concepts. Related terms are logic models, systems dynamics, and implementation analysis.

Concept Paper: A short document (three to five pages) that summarizes a proposed project or research/evaluation study. The paper highlights the concepts underlying the project or study, rather than specific, technical details. The concept paper should focus on the rationale or need for the project/study, its purpose as well as its significance, and provide a limited description of the methods.

Concordant Items: The number of items upon which raters agree.

Conduct Disorder: The overriding feature of conduct disorder is a persistent pattern of behavior in which the rights of others and age-appropriate social norms are violated. This diagnosis is reached if the child demonstrates at least 3 of 15 symptoms within the past 12 months, with at least 1 symptom present within the past 6 months, and experiences impaired functioning. The symptoms of conduct disorder fall into four main groupings: (1) aggressive conduct that causes or threatens physical harm to other people or animals, (2) nonaggressive conduct that causes property loss or damage, (3) deceitfulness or theft, and (4) serious violations of rules (APA, 2000).

Confidence Interval (CI): The range of numerical values in which we can be confident (to a computed probability, such as 90% or 95%) that the population value being estimated will be found. Confidence intervals indicate the strength of evidence; where confidence intervals are wide, they indicate less precise estimates of effect.

Conjoint Therapy: Treatment that involves at least one family member in addition to the identified client.

Consensus: Substantial agreement measured by the degree of consensus that has been achieved by asking participants to agree that they can live with and support the concept both internally and externally.

Consistency/Absolute Agreement: Terminology used by SPSS to represent two different forms of the interclass correlation coefficient (ICC). Like a Pearson's r, if consistency is used, the judges' ratings can vary in a consistent manner. Absolute agreement takes into account the magnitude of the agreement, that is, how closely the judges rate the same object.

Construct: Typically used to indicate a feature of experience, behavior, etc., that has been theoretically defined and empirically measured, typically through use of several more narrowly defined variables. Higher-order general constructs may incorporate a number of lower-order specific constructs. For example, depending upon results of empirical testing of proposed quality/appropriateness items in a consumer survey, "relationship with provider" may be defined and measured as a higher-order construct incorporating more specific constructs of "responsiveness," "recovery orientation," etc.

Construct Validity: Construct validity is the highest form of validity and assures that the tool measures the client behaviors that are under assessment. This type of validity is concerned with the degree of measurement of a theoretical construct or trait.

Content Validity: Content validity refers to the evaluation of items on a measure to determine if the content contained in the items relates to and is representative of the domain that the measure seeks to examine.

Context-Sensitive Systems: Systems that are "aware" of the clinical context, allowing more efficient use of all context-compatible information systems that may be combined under a common interface. The context includes at least five elements: patient, practitioner, problem, procedure, and policy. A context-sensitive drug prescription support system, for example, would allow the user to view a laboratory result in one software application, then immediately switch to a drug database where a search for drug dosing modifications can be made based on prior knowledge of the patient's age and primary medical problems.

Contextualized: A qualitative research term that refers to taking into consideration salient aspects of a setting, such as environmental factors, interpersonal relationships, prevailing social and political structures, and/or cultural values and beliefs when investigating, describing, or analyzing a phenomenon or experience.

Contingency Management (CM): CM refers to a broad group of behavioral interventions that structure the client's environment in such a way as to encourage change. This is accomplished by setting specific, objective behavioral goals and specific, objective consequences for meeting or not meeting these goals. CM is most effective when initial behavioral goals are small and relatively easy to achieve, and consequences are provided as immediately following the demonstration of the behavioral goal as possible.

Continuous Quality Improvement: The routine collection and use of information gleaned from a program's development, implementation, and/or evaluation to improve program operations and to better achieve desired outcomes.

Control Chart: A graphical tool for monitoring changes that occur within a process, by distinguishing variation that is inherent in the process (common cause) from variation that yields a change to the process (special cause). This change may be a single point or a series of points in time—each a signal that something is different from what was previously observed and measured.

Control Group (Concurrent): A comparison group enrolled at the same time as the experimental group and treated exactly the same way, with the exception of not receiving the intervention being studied.

Control Group (Historical): A comparison group composed of people for whom data already exist (e.g., patients who were seen before a new treatment was introduced).

Coping: Adjusting; adapting; successfully meeting a challenge.

Coping Mechanisms: All the ways, both conscious and unconscious, that a person uses in adjusting to environmental demands without altering his goals or purposes.

Core: The term is used for a relatively small number of people who play a critical role in sustaining the transmission of sexually transmitted diseases in a population. Definitions vary, but they generally include people who have several sexual partners while infected and who thus transmit their infection to more than one other person.

Cost-Benefit Analysis: Converts effects into the same monetary terms as the costs and compares them.

Counterfactual: The empirical estimate of what would have happened to a client if an intervention had been withheld. The counterfactual condition can be achieved through the use of a no-treatment control group, a matched comparison group, or pre-intervention outcome estimates of a treated group.

Coupled: Systems automatically link knowledge to observations, given a specific clinical event. A coupled drug prescription system, for example, would alert the clinician to alternative, potentially cheaper, interventions just before a prescription is generated.

Covariance: The variation in a given variable that is associated with the variation in one or more other variables. For example, annual income has a great deal of variation, as has education. Education and income also co-vary, meaning that a low or high value in one is associated with a low or high value in the other.

Criminal Justice: The institution that deals with criminal violations of the law and processes alleged offenders. It includes police, courts, probation and parole, juvenile justice, and correctional agencies.

Crisis: An acute disruption of psychological homeostasis in which one's usual coping methods fail and there exists evidence of distress and functional impairment. The subjective reaction to a stressful life event or pileup of stressors that compromises the individual's stability and ability to cope or function. The main cause of a crisis is an intensely stressful, traumatic, or hazardous event, but two other conditions are also necessary: (1) the individual's perception of the event as the cause of considerable upset and/or disruption; and (2) the individual's inability to resolve the disruption by previously used coping methods. An event or situation that is experienced as distressing and challenging of human adaptive abilities and resources.

Crisis Assessment: An objective appraisal based on validated scales or measures of a client's perception of present situational or acute stressors in terms of personal threat, ability to cope, and barriers to action, as well as type of aid needed from the crisis counselor.

Crisis Intervention: A therapeutic interaction that seeks to decrease perceived psychological trauma by increasing perceived coping efficacy. It is a timely and brief intervention that focuses on helping to mobilize the resources of those differentially affected.

Criterion Validity: Criterion validity refers to the correspondence between a measurement of a variable and a measurement derived from some external standard thought to have established validity. The external standard can occur concurrently (concurrent validity) or in the future (predictive validity). Validity of a measure refers to the correspondence between the measure and how the property measured actually occurs in the empirical world. The extent to which a measure relates to an external criterion. Research is done to establish the correlations (relationships) between scores on the measure and the outcomes of the external criteria.

Critical Appraisal: Methods of critical thinking used to arrive at a key question: *How good (strong) is the evidence for that?* In the evaluation of evidence for use in the practice of clinical medicine, inquiring about and understanding the impact of evidence from clinical observations, laboratory results, scientific literature, or other sources (after answering the question *What is the evidence for that?*).

Critical Friend: An evaluator who believes in the program aims but is critical in a way that is helpful and constructive, helping define terms, clarify relationships, questioning underlying assumptions, helping to make the program theory explicit, and other activities that help program staff members and participants critically examine their goals and the strategies they implement to accomplish those goals.

Critical Thinking: The disciplined ability and desire to assess evidence. An active effort to seek a breadth of contradicting as well as confirming information, to make objective judgments on the basis of well-supported reasons as a guide to belief and action, and to monitor one's thinking while doing so (metacognition). The thought processes necessary and appropriate for critical thinking depend on the knowledge domain (e.g., scientific, mathematical, historical, anthropological, economic, philosophical, moral). Critical thinking demonstrates universal criteria: clarity, accuracy, precision, consistency, relevance, sound empirical evidence, good reasons, depth, breadth, and fairness.

Cronbach's Alpha: A measurement of internal consistency reliability with a numerical range from 1.0–0. Alpha values lower than .60–.70 are considered too weak to use except for clinical practice. Lower alpha values may be acceptable if the purpose is research rather than clinical practice.

Cross-Sectional Survey: A research design in which all of the data are collected at one time.

Culture: A social phenomenon that refers to a set of beliefs, values, attitudes, and behavioral preferences that are shared by a group of people (Barnouw, 1985). It is communicated from one generation to another or to new arrivals in a host society through socialization practices.

Current Best Evidence: As applied by the medical field, this term means to use the current best evidence in making decisions about patient care. Assessment and treatment decisions are based on empirical evidence from research studies that are published in professional literature. Current best evidence requires the use of diagnostic criteria and instruments to develop a clinical assessment and treatment plan. See chapters 2–5 in this volume for detailed discussions of best evidence and expert consensus models used in medicine and public health.

Curvilinear Relationship: A relationship in which scores on either extreme represent the same concept. For example, in the FACES clients who score on either end of the spectrum are dysfunctional, and clients who score in the middle are functional.

Data: Isolated collected measures that only indicate the actual measurement of a particular activity. For instance, the Average Length of Stay is measured data. Data also constitutes the raw observations associated with health interventions (e.g., physical examination, laboratory tests, treatment results, etc.).

Data Mining: *See Expert Systems.*

Deception: In the context of research, deception refers to withholding informed consent from research participants. Deception may occur along a continuum from participants not being made aware that research is taking place to participants not being fully informed about the nature of the research project. Deception is sometimes justified in qualitative research when the method is required to elicit authentic responses about a significant problem or phenomenon when no other method would lead to this information. Deception is not justified in clinical trials of treatments. International ethics guidelines now demand that participants be made aware that the clinical trial involves the possibility of receiving a placebo (fake treatment).

Decision Analysis: Refers to analyzing a clinical decision under conditions of uncertainty through the application of explicit, quantitative methods that numerically measure prognoses, treatment effects, and patient values.

Decision Support Systems: A computer-based software application designed to help professionals make complex decisions effectively, often in a "what-if" question format. A decision support system retrieves and records the information linked to a decision. It includes a database of case information, including the information considered critical to making a decision and some kind of statistical modeling technique that determines the decision process. The software program compares the current case of interest to its database of cases and can respond with "what if" scenarios based on available case information.

Deinstitutionalization: The process, begun in the 1950s, of moving mentally ill and mentally disabled people out of institutional settings and into community living arrangements. Although originally conceived as a way of reintegrating these persons into society, it has been used economically to justify the closing of many institutions, without commensurate funds being provided in the community settings.

Delta: A frequency range in the EEG, defined as 0–4 Hertz per second.

Depression: A mood disorder involving disturbances in emotion (excessive sadness), behavior (apathy and loss of interest in usual activities), cognition (distorted thoughts of hopelessness and low self-esteem), and body function (fatigue, loss of appetite). Symptoms extend into many parts of an individual's life and include lack of interest in daily activities, decreased motivation, feelings of worthlessness, and sometimes suicidal thoughts.

Descriptive Statistics: Statistical indices that are derived from measures that are observed on each member of the reference population or sample. As an example, defining the mean grade point average of the freshman class as a descriptive statistic implies that the mean GPA has been calculated from the GPA of each and every member of the freshman class.

Desensitization Phase: Fourth phase of EMDR where bilateral eye movements are used to activate the neural network, which typically results in the client recalling the target image and experiencing a sequence of emotions. In this phase, EMDR can be effective in minimizing or eliminating the blockage experienced through the client's traumatized neural networking system.

Design and Rollout: A six-month process in which new strategies are examined, agreed upon, and introduced at top levels of an organization. Processes are designed to address organizational needs. Within this process implementation plans are developed and implemented by direct-care practitioners across the organization.

Detained: May begin with a stop on the street by a law enforcement officer, a request by the police officer for the citizen to identify himself, and an explanation of what the suspect was doing. If probable cause exists, then the suspect may be required to stand by while the officer investigates him, searches him, or asks witnesses to identify him. Sometimes alleged lawbreakers are temporarily detained in police lockups or county detention centers pending a bail hearing before a magistrate.

Developmental Validity: A quality of an item, scale, or instrument that focuses on the degree to which it can be read, comprehended, and responded to in the intended way by respondents in the targeted age range or developmental stage. Developmental validity, like other kinds of validity, is concerned with how well items, scales, or instruments actually measure what they are intended to measure.

Dialogue: Discussing why a person assigned a specific rating to an activity during the stocktaking step.

Diffusion and Dissemination: Diffusion is the process by which an idea or practice becomes adopted by a growing number of people in a population. In some instances dissemination is considered synonymous with diffusion. Alternatively, dissemination can be considered a situation in which diffusion is actively encouraged.

Diffusion of Innovation: This is a process by which a particular innovation is communicated through certain channels over time among the members of a social system. This process results in social change also known as an alteration in the structure and function of a social system.

Dimension: Used in a nontechnical sense to refer to an aspect or component of a broader concept or domain, as in a dimension of performance or dimensions of access. In some cases, as with aspects of quality/appropriateness from the perspective of consumers, proposed dimensions may also meet the more technical criteria of *constructs*.

Disequalibrium: An emotional state that may be characterized by confusing emotions, somatic complaints, and erratic behavior. The severe emotional discomfort experienced by the person in crisis propels him or her toward action that will reduce the subjective discomfort.

Dispersion: The property of a distribution that refers to the heterogeneity of values or the degree to which there is variability in a distribution. Indices of dispersion include the variance, standard deviation, and range. As an example, there is relatively low variation in I.Q. among graduate students in physics at a major university compared to the variation in I.Q. among a group of passengers in a subway in New York City.

Domain: A group of issues, elements, or components that have some important aspects in common. For example, "access to service" is a domain; "timeliness of receipt of service" is a component or *dimension* of access. An area of individual functioning (e.g., communication, independent living, etc.).

Domestic Violence Typology: A framework for classifying information into specific categories or ideal types of woman battering that contribute to understanding the phenomenon of domestic violence. *Also see Woman Battering Continuum.*

Double ABCX Model: A model of family stress and coping, developed by Hamilton McCubbin and associates, that focuses on the interaction of a pileup of stressors (AA), present and past family resources (BB), and present and past family interpretation/appraisal process (CC) to produce the resultant level of family adaptation (XX).

Drill Down Analysis: Examination of the data within a particular case to determine potential contributing factors to the occurrence or recurrence of illness. This type of analysis may be conducted with a single case or a group of cases with a common factor. In the case of groups of cases, the drill down seeks to identify correlative factors. Statistical processes may be applied to determine the strength of relation between correlative factors.

Drug Court: A legal court, presided over by a judge, that includes an interdisciplinary team of probation officers, psychologists, social workers, and community members and handles individuals who have been arrested on offenses related to drug abuse and addiction problems.

Dual Relationships: When a professional has a relationship with one individual in two different contexts, and these contexts have different and potentially conflicting expectations and interests. A practitioner who also conducts research is said to have a dual relationship with a client when the client is involved in a therapeutic relationship and is also a participant in a study offered by the practitioner. The therapeutic relationship is focused on the needs and interests of the client and the research relationship is focused on scientific insights and discovery for the benefit of improved professional knowledge rather than the interests of the individual participant/client.

Dysthymic Disorder: The DSM-IVTR diagnosis for a person with a chronically depressed mood that occurs for most of the day, more days than not, for at least two years (APA, 2000). When depressed, the person experiences two or more of the following symptoms: poor appetite or overeating, insomnia or hypersomnia, low energy or fatigue, low self-esteem, poor concentration or difficulty making decisions, and feelings of hopelessness.

Ecological Perspective: A set of assumptions and concepts that focus on the reciprocal interactions between individuals and their environments across time to explain variations in the values, orientations, and behavior of individuals.

Ecological Survey: A survey based on aggregate data for a particular population as it exists at a specific point or points in time. The survey is conducted to study the relationship of exposure to an identified or presumed risk factor for a specified outcome.

EEG: Electroencephalogram

Effectiveness: Refers to a type of impact study where the focus is on the estimate of overall program impact, i.e., the difference between treatment and counterfactual conditions without adjustment for the fidelity of the treatment implementation. Effectiveness estimates are often referred to as lower bound estimates of treatment impact or impact that can be expected under actual practice conditions. Effectiveness studies refer to the ability of social interventions to produce desired outcomes in the lives of families and children. Also refers to the *clinical utility* of an intervention. The effectiveness of an intervention is related to the extent to which the effects of an intervention could generalize or extend to other settings, populations, etc.

Efficacy: The *potency* of an intervention. The efficacy of an intervention is related to the extent to which changes in the individual are due to the active ingredients of the intervention. This is a type of impact study where the focus is on the estimate of maximum program impact, i.e., the difference between treatment and counterfactual conditions when treatment implementation proceeds as intended. Efficacy studies are often referred to as the upper bound estimates of treatment impact or impact that can be expected under ideal practice conditions.

Efficacy Studies: Often intervention outcomes are measured in highly controlled contexts to enhance internal validity. Such studies are often called efficacy trials and they are recommended prior to examining outcomes in realistic service contexts. If the outcomes of efficacy studies merit testing in realistic service contexts, effectiveness studies are carried out.

Elder Abuse: The intentional or unintentional infliction of or threat of harm on an older adult over 60 years of age. Categories of elder abuse include physical, emotional, or financial harm, or neglect of a care-dependent older adult.

Elder Abuse Homicide: The murder of an older adult; an extreme form of physical abuse.

Elder Abuse Victim: An older person who experiences harm or threat of harm by another person.

Emotional Responsiveness: The degree to which an individual is emotionally available to another person and allows himself or herself to be empathically in touch with the inner experience of the other person.

Empirically Based Practice: Clinical services that demonstrate statistically significant effectiveness.

Empirically Supported Treatments (EST): Treatments whose efficacy or effectiveness has been supported through a program of research meeting certain scientifically established criteria.

Empirically Validated/Supported Treatments: Empirically validated/supported treatments are those that have met the rigorous criteria set forth by the American Psychological Association's Division 12 Task Force on Promotion and Dissemination of Psychological Procedures. The Task Force identified two primary categories for treatments—"well established" treatments and "probably efficacious" treatments.

Empowerment Evaluation: A collaborative evaluation process in the use of evaluation concepts, techniques, and findings to foster improvement and self-determination. This includes the evaluator, funder, program staff, and participants and community in data collection, analysis, and reporting. For example, as developed by the Kellogg Foundation empowerment evaluation utilizes ongoing communication about processes and continuous self-examination from all perspectives.

Environmental Strains: A combination of strains (i.e., ongoing stressors), which are caused by elements in an individual's social situation, over which the individual may have limited or no control (e.g., race, socioeconomic status, physical disability).

Epidemiology: The study of the distribution and determinants of various disorders in the population. *See also Incidence* and *Point Prevalence.*

Equal Probability Sampling: Any sampling method where every element in the sampling frame has an equal chance of selection. For example, a sample of households in a defined geographic area would be an equal probability sample if each household in that area had the same chance of inclusion in the sample.

Error (Type I): Error that concludes a particular cause when, in fact, this was not the cause.

Error (Type II): Acceptance of a hypothesis or statement as true when it is false.

Ethics: The branch of philosophy that deals with distinctions between right and wrong and with the moral consequences of human actions. Examples of ethical issues that arise in medical practice and research include informed consent, confidentiality, respect for human rights, and scientific integrity.

Ethnography: A qualitative research approach that involves the investigation of a culture or particular aspect of a culture, with reference to the meaning of certain behaviors or attributions for members of that culture. For example, a large group of convicted felons who are studied by members of the state parole board. A social scientific description of a people or group and the cultural basis of their identities, elicited from naturalistic, qualitative modes of inquiry (e.g., participant observation, semistructured interviews, focus groups).

Etiological Fraction: The proportion of people with a specific disease that can be attributed to a certain risk factor.

Evaluation: A systematic process of gathering and interpreting data to determine results generated by a specific set of procedures designed to meet specific goals. *See also Outcome Evaluation, Process Evaluation,* and *Program Monitoring.*

Evidence-Based Guidelines: Clinical recommendations to assist providers with managing and treating specific diseases that are based on research studies published in the scientific literature. Many consider clinical recommendations "evidence-based" if they are developed through a specific process that includes a systematic review and analyses of the scientific peer-reviewed journal literature. These professional practice guidelines are based on empirical studies preappraised for scientific validity and prescreened for clinical relevance.

Evidence-Based Health Care (EBH): The conscientious, explicit, and judicious use of current best practices and systematic reviews of evidence in making decisions about the care of individual patients. This involves all of the health professions, including health care information systems and management of health records.

Evidence-Based Medicine (EBM): The conscientious, explicit, and judicious use of current best evidence in making decisions about the care and medical treatment of individual patients. Best practices of EBM refers to integrating individual clinical expertise with the best available external clinical evidence from systematic research investigations.

Evidence-Based Practice (EBP): An approach to practice that requires the examination of research findings from systematic clinical research (e.g., randomized controlled clinical research) in making decisions about the care of a specific population with a specific problem. The process of critically identifying and employing treatment or practice approaches that have the strongest basis of empirical support for attaining desired outcomes. An evidence-based practice is considered any practice that has been established as effective through scientific research according to a set of explicit criteria. The term *evidence-based practice* is also used to describe a way of practicing in which the practitioner critically uses best evidence, expertise, and values to make practice decisions that matter to individual service recipients and patients about their care.

Evidence-based practice is the use of interventions that are based on rigorous research methods. Evidence-based practice includes the integration of different studies and establishing the combined probative value. An example of an EBP approach to supporting and serving families and children would be based on the likelihood that certain types of supports and services can be shown to be more effective than other interventions. See chapters 1 through 6 in this volume for specific definitions and discussion of the application of evidence-based practice in medicine, mental health, psychiatry, psychology, and social work settings.

Evidence-Based Practice Education: A lifelong problem-based learning approach to keep up-to-date on the scientific research and improve clinical practice and treatment outcomes. This process requires that the practitioner use theories and interventions based on empirical evidence of their effectiveness, apply approaches appropriate to the client and setting, and evaluate his/her own practice effectiveness.

Expected Nonconcordant Scores: The number of nonagreeing scores occurring by chance.

Experimental Design: A type of research design that uses random assignment of study participants to different treatment groups. Randomization provides some level of assurance that the groups are comparable in every way except for the treatment received. In general, a randomized experiment is regarded as the most rigorous and strongest research design to establish a cause-effect (treatment outcomes) relationship. These designs usually collect data before and after the program to assess the net effects of the program.

Experimental Study: One in which the independent variable is manipulated by the researcher in order to see its effect on the dependent variable(s). It is defined as a research study in which people are randomly assigned to different forms of the program or alternative treatments, including a control group and/or a placebo group.

Expert Consensus: Expert consensus is the synthesis of the evidence of treatment effectiveness using a panel of noted contributors of the field. The outcome of an expert consensus is often a treatment protocol or guideline.

Expert System: A computer program designed to draw inferences from data provided pertinent to some decision. Expert systems are developed through a process of data mining in which recognized experts in a specific knowledge domain are studied, such as through interviewing, to determine the type of information they use and the rules that they use to make decisions. Computer programs are then designed to request this information and to use the rules to draw inferences. This output is used by decision makers to support pertinent decision-making. An expert system is a form of artificial intelligence that is more sophisticated than a decision support system. An expert system is a computer software application that recommends a specific decision based on case information. Expert systems take several years to develop and typically include a knowledge base, an inference system, the facts of cases, and a question/answer system for the practitioner to interface with the expert system. Expert systems were intended to lend expert advice by capturing it in a software program that could then be accessed by staff that may not possess expert knowledge.

Exposure: A behavior therapy procedure used in the treatment of anxiety disorders to help the patient confront situations or stimuli they avoid yet which realistically pose acceptable risks of danger. During exposure, the patient gradually confronts situations in a prolonged and repeated fashion with the therapist's assistance and then on their own.

Externalizing Disorders: Also referred to as disruptive behavior disorders, this class of disorders is characterized by high rates of noncompliant, hostile, and defiant behaviors, including aggressiveness and hyperactivity. The *DSM-IV-TR* (APA, 2000) categorizes externalizing disorders into three headings: attention-deficit/hyperactivity disorder (ADHD), oppositional defiant disorder (ODD), and conduct disorder (CD).

Eye Movement Desensitization and Reprocessing (EMDR): A theoretical approach developed in 1987 by Francine Shapiro to relieve post-traumatic stress symptoms. The EMDR model is based on the hypothesis that traumatization produces neural networking that interferes with successful processing of those memories, feelings, and experiences.

Factorial Analysis: The purpose of factor analysis is to examine the interrelationships of data such as scale items, to group items together, and make it possible to identify the underlying dimension or trait for a set of items. Data can be simplified by reducing the number of items from many to the most relevant items that best capture the construct of interest.

Family Caregiving: The use of immediate or extended family members to provide services for an ill, aging, or handicapped member. Family members might choose voluntarily to provide these services out of personal connection to the needy family member, or they may be obliged to provide these services in the absence of equivalent services being provided by social agencies.

Family Educational Interventions: Nonclinical intervention with the primary objective of meeting informational and practical needs of families with a relative who suffers from severe mental illness. There are a variety of models that are delivered by either professionals and/or peers (family members).

Family Etiology of Mental Illness: The belief (now discredited) that family interpersonal dynamics and communication problems (e.g., high "expressed emotion" or "communication deviance") were responsible for causing severe mental illness (i.e., schizophrenia or bipolar disorder). It is now believed that these are biologically based illnesses, which may be exacerbated by family communication dynamics.

Family Process: The way in which members of the family interact with each other.

Family Sense of Competence: The unique appraisal of family members about how well they are managing a particular problem as a group. This may be contrasted with "locus of control" (internal control/external control) appraisal, which tends to be an individual appraisal of global functioning.

Family Status: Refers to how the family position of an adult is characterized— single, married, engaged, divorced, widowed.

Family Structure: The composition of the family, such as grandmother, mother, father, and three children.

Father Hunger: The longing desire to have an emotionally close relationship with an admiring father.

Femicide: The killing of a woman.

First-Level Coding: The first step in the coding of qualitative data, where researchers identify conceptually distinct categories of information that reflect meaningful patterns and themes.

Fiscal: The financial elements of an organization such as the year, accounting and auditing procedures, and the organization budget. The fiscal year is the 12-month period in which the organization operates financially (often July 1 to June 30 in the United States; October 1 to September 30 for federal government agencies; or the calendar year, January 1 to December 31 in some cases).

Fish Bone Diagram: Also known as a Cause and Effect Analysis Diagram, used by a problem-solving team during brainstorming to logically list and display known and potential causes to a problem. Analysis of the listed causes is done to identify root causes.

Focus Group: A focus group interview consists of a small group of individuals who are gathered together in a permissive, nonthreatening environment to discuss a topic of interest to the researcher. Focus group studies are used to gain understanding of peoples' thoughts and behaviors, to pilot test ideas, or to evaluate programs, products, or services.

Follow-Up: Observation over a period of time of an individual, group, or initially defined population whose relevant characteristics have been assessed in order to observe changes in health status or health-related variables.

Formative Evaluation: Formative evaluation seeks to change and improve programs through ongoing data collection and interpretation about program activities, structures, and short-term results. While it may include data on long-term outcomes, formative evaluation emphasizes decision-making, process, and implementation variables that need to be improved in order to effect outcomes. It is similar in purpose and practice to action research and performance improvement. An evaluation, which has the primary goal of improving the program prior to full implementation.

Frequency Matching: A method of selecting controls for case-control studies in a manner such that the distribution of extraneous factors in controls is similar to that of cases. Frequency matching is often done for age and gender so that differences in these characteristics between cases and controls do not distort the relationship between case-control status and the factor under study.

Frisk: A "pat down" based on reasonable suspicion that a citizen has been involved in criminal behavior, or is about to commit a crime.

FTE: Total organization salary hours paid 2080; also refers to full-time college enrollments.

Functional Outcomes: Measures of programmatic effectiveness based on client ability to perform in day-to-day activities (e.g., stay in school, work, avoid conflict with the law, etc.).

Generalized Anxiety Disorder: An anxiety disorder resulting in a continuous state of anxiety or fear, lasting a month or more. Defining features include but are not limited to: signs of motor tension, autonomic hyperactivity (a pounding heart), constant apprehension, and difficulties in concentration. Persons who suffer from generalized anxiety disorders often describe a chronic, exaggerated, unprovoked state of worry and tension, often accompanied by physical symptoms (trembling, twitching, headaches, irritability, sweating, hot flashes, nausea, lump in throat). Anxiety disorders, if untreated, frequently lead to the emergence of a depressive disorder.

Geographic Information System (GIS): A computer system that allows the collection, storage, integration, analysis, and display of spatially referenced data.

Global Positioning System (GPS): L Satellites constellation that allows users equipped with a GPS receiver to determine in real time their location anywhere on Earth, with an accuracy ranging from a few millimetres to several meters.

Goal: A general aim, object, or end effect that one strives to achieve.

Government Performance and Results Act: The 1993 public law that established the requirement for all federal government agencies and their programs to gauge their success on results achieved instead of activities undertaken. Specific results or outcomes are to be used to justify funding rather than activity indicators or outputs.

Grant-making: A process or system of distributing and managing resources for program implementation.

Gray Murder: A homicide of an older victim that is disguised by the perpetrator to appear as a natural death. *See also Elder Abuse, Homicide,* and *Femicide.*

Grief: A predictable series of feelings and psychological states occurring as a result of the loss, specifically death, of another.

Grief and Bereavement Counseling: Therapy, often cognitive-behavioral in nature, utilized by a psychologist, social worker, or counselor to assist in understanding and adapting to grief related to the death of others.

Grounded Theory: An inductive research method in which a theory is developed from the data. The goal of grounded theory is to explain a phenomenon by drawing on data collected from the field and generating propositions from them.

Hawthorne Effect: People's behavior may change simply because they know they are in a study or being observed. The bias is introduced when this change is erroneously attributed to specific components of the study. *See also Placebo Effect* and *Blinding.*

Health Care: Services provided to individuals or communities by a health care system or by professionals to promote, maintain, monitor, or restore health. Health care contains a broad spectrum of services and activities delivered by a team of health personnel. This contrasts with medical care, which concentrates on diagnostic and therapeutic actions performed by or under the supervision of an individual physician.

Healthy Worker Bias: People who are selected for a study through their workplace are healthier than the population at large, because the population consists of people who are unable to work for health reasons.

Heterogeneity: This takes place when there is more variation between the results in systematic research reviews than would be expected to occur by chance alone.

High-Quality Data: Specific information, either numerical or nonnumerical, that is reliable, valid, and useful for decision-making. Said another way, high-quality data are data that allow the viewer to understand more clearly the underlying reality of the situation. In the case, for example, of program management, higher data quality allows you to understand more clearly what effects your program is having, and because you have a clearer picture of reality, you are able to make better decisions about your program.

Ill Member Level of Adaptation: The functional level of a person diagnosed with serious mental illness, living in the community. It is based on Likert-scale assessments of several areas of functioning by family members (but could also be completed by the person himself/herself, case managers, or other observers). It is intended to give a broader view of community functioning than can be gained from observing symptoms alone.

Illness-Related Strains: A combination of strains (i.e., ongoing stressors) that are the direct result of a person's illness history and which subsequently affect future capabilities (e.g., number of hospitalizations, limited functioning, substance abuse complications).

Impact: The marginal change in client functioning caused by a program or therapeutic intervention. This change is measured as the difference in outcomes for clients in the treatment and counterfactual conditions.

Impact Assessments: More formal research designs, which try to determine if it was the intervention and not other factors that created a program outcome. Impact assessments usually employ experimental and quasi-experimental designs.

Impact Evaluation: A study of what changed as a result of the intervention or program under investigation. Often inherent in the definition of an impact evaluation is the idea that a judgment will be placed on the whole; the program either works (shows results) or it does not (show results), and either it should be funded or should not be funded.

Implementation Strategy: While evidence may establish a specific practice as an evidence-based practice or a best practice, it has been found difficult to move these best practices into routine practice. Accordingly, systematic plans have been developed to disseminate and facilitate the use of best practices in service systems. Top-down or macro strategies disseminate best practices for use by frontline practitioners through agency directives, guidelines, manualized interventions, accreditation requirements, algorithms, toolkits, and so forth. Bottom-up or micro strategies focus directly on individual practitioners by engaging them in or teaching them the evidence-based practice process of critical decision-making. *See also Evidence-Based Practice* and *Evidence-Based Guidelines.*

Incentives: To get people to attend a focus group interview, the recruiter offers an incentive. The incentive could be tangible, such as money, food, or gifts, or it could be intangible, such as a feeling of community service, helping a meaningful research effort, or contributing to society. Incentives are important because people need a compelling reason to give up their time to be involved in a focus group. *See also Focus Group.*

Incidence: The proportion of new cases of a disorder in the population that appear within a specified time frame. The number of new cases in a given period divided by the number of people at risk for the disorder. To make results more understandable, incidence is sometimes expressed as cases per 1,000 or 10,000 people in the time period (or even per million per year for rare disorders).

Incidence-Prevalence (Neyman) Bias: A cross-sectional survey will tend to overlook people with less serious forms of a disorder (because they would have gotten better) and more serious forms (because they would have died).

Indicator: A measure of performance based on desired or expected outcome of a specific process or activity.

Indirect Costs (IDC): A percentage of the budget (usually the overall total or sometimes the total excluding certain items) that is allocated to the grantee to cover overhead expenses, such as building space, administrative oversight and services, maintenance of facilities and equipment, insurance costs, etc. Usually a funder specifies an indirect cost rate that it allows, or negotiates with the grantee as to an acceptable IDC on a case-by-case basis.

Inferential Statistics: Estimates of population parameters based on probability sampling and theoretical distributions of sampling error. For example, an estimate of the mean GPA of the freshman class that is derived from a random sample of members of the freshman class would be classified as an inferential statistic.

Information exists when the significance of data is determined for a particular problem, patient, and practitioner (e.g., the physical examination is abnormal, laboratory test elevated, or treatment result successful). When data is displayed or analyzed in relationship to other data, it becomes information. Information becomes useful in asking the questions of why a particular organization achieves a certain result and another organization some other result. Data needs to be turned into information to become useful.

Information Management: A method used to organize information to avoid information overload and to keep information in a format that is efficient to retrieve whenever needed. Filing systems, cognitive maps, manuals, and electronic databases are examples of devices that can prove useful in information management. A network of consultants is an additional way to ensure that necessary information will be readily available.

Information-Rich: This is a term used to describe participants in a qualitative research study (including focus group interviewing) who possess the greatest information about the research topic. This concept assumes that certain people have more experience with the topic and therefore offer greater richness of insight for the purposes of the study. *See also Focus Group.*

Informed Consent: Voluntary agreement based on information about foreseeable risks and benefits associated with the agreement. In the context of research, informed consent implies that participants have been informed about the nature of the research, the benefits and risks of participating, and what will happen with the information they share or is gathered about them during the research process.

Infrastructure: The hierarchical levels of management established to support a specific process or system.

Inner City: Geographic areas within large urban centers that are usually located in the older core of the city and characterized by high population density. Although there may be a wide range of socioeconomic status among inner-city residents, in many urban areas they are severely disadvantaged and prone to poor health.

Inner-City Health Research: Research focused on the health of disadvantaged urban populations, the social, economic, and health care factors that influence individual and population health in the inner city, and the evaluation of relevant interventions.

Inputs: Inputs are the resources needed to develop deliberate efforts intended to achieve desired outcomes. There are material and nonmaterial inputs. Material inputs include: funding, personnel, volunteers, equipment, and infrastructure. Nonmaterial inputs include leadership, vision, clearly formulated and measurable goals, strategies, strategic planning, a commitment to performance measurement, competence, realistic yet challenging performance targets, social capital, appropriate technology, interorganizational collaboration, stakeholder involvement, and so forth.

Inquiry: Involves activity that a private citizen would not be expected to make but where a police officer initiated what would be labeled nonoffensive contact if it occurred between two ordinary citizens. These actions would not be considered a seizure, if questions were put in a conversational manner, demands by an officer were not made, orders were not issued, and if questions were not overbearing or harassing. It is an exchange of conversation between a police officer and a citizen that does not constitute a Fourth Amendment seizure.

Installation Phase: Fifth phase of EMDR that serves to close down the catalytic process and install more desired cognitive and affective responses. These positive, adaptive responses are elicited from the client; they illustrate how the client would prefer to think or feel about the trauma event or memory. Clients are asked to rank the validity of the new cognition as to how true it feels until it has been successfully installed. *See also Eye Movement Desensitization Reprocessing.*

Intake Interview: An initial set of in-person meetings between a clinician and a patient used to establish a working relationship and to make an assessment of client problems, symptoms, needs, strengths, and circumstances as relevant to services requested and available. The assessment can include the gathering and evaluation of biological, psychological, and social data pertaining to the patient. In mental health settings the assessment includes specification of differential psychiatric diagnoses.

Internal Consistency: The degree to which all of the items on a scale correlate with each other, indicating that they are all tapping the same attribute.

Internal Consistency Reliability: Computing the internal consistency (Cronbach's alpha) of a measure allows one to estimate how consistently respondents performed across items of a measure. The internal consistency of a measure also lends support for evidence of its content validity.

Interrater Reliability: The degree to which observations yield similar results from different judges.

Intrusiveness: The intensity of interference into a citizen's life. It can be perceived as a violation of rights if pushed too far by a police officer. However, in order to control crime and protect the public, an examination of a citizen under reasonable suspicion may be necessary. The level of intensity of the encroachment and how imposing the interruption is determines the degree of interference.

Juvenile Delinquency: Delinquency is a legal designation that includes a range of behaviors that violate the law, such as robbery, drug use, and vandalism. Some acts are illegal for both adults and juveniles (referred to as index offenses) and cover serious offenses like homicide, aggravated assault, and rape. Other acts (referred to as status offenses) are illegal only for juveniles due to their age, such as underage drinking, truancy from school, and running away from home.

Key Information Needs: These are the data required for any program to measure effectiveness and are based on the logic model design. They include data, knowledge, etc., about program performance that is necessary to make judgments about the program and manage it for positive outcomes. The information necessary to measure a program's operations may also reflect needs of the program stakeholders (i.e., funders, board members).

Kinship Care: An arrangement under which a relative or group of relatives serve on a temporary or permanent basis as substitute parent(s) for a child or sibling group whose biological parent(s) cannot ensure the safety and well-being of the child(ren).

Knowledge is abstracted from information when external evidence is used to anticipate how additional interventions could change the data (e.g., surgery will cure the physical finding, or a drug will normalize the laboratory test result and prevent disease).

Lay Health Advisor (LHA): A lay health advisor (LHA) is a person who is recognized as a natural helper and receives training to use her (or his) natural skills to raise health-related awareness and skills among her relatives, friends, and acquaintances. An LHA differs from a peer advisor or outreach work in that she does not seek to convey information to strangers. Moreover, unlike peer advisors and outreach workers, LHAs are often not employed by an agency. Rather, they share their knowledge and skills with people they know during the normal course of their lives.

Learning Factors: Interactions between the therapist and client or patient consisting of corrective emotional experiences, insight, and feedback processes.

Likelihood Ratio: This refers to the likelihood that a particular test finding would be expected in a patient with the target disorder when compared with the likelihood that this same test finding would be expected in a patient without the target disorder.

Likert Scale: Developed by Rensis Likert as a type of composite measure used to determine levels of measurement and the relative intensity of different items. For example, a bipolar scale with a neutral middle point (e.g., Strongly Agree / Agree / Neither Agree nor Disagree / Disagree / Strongly Disagree).

Line Item Budget: A fiscal plan that focuses on the monetary elements of the organization.

Literature: A written repository of knowledge pertaining to any given topic. It includes information sources such as refereed scientific journals, practice-oriented review journals, conference proceedings, trade journals, textbooks, product promotion materials, and Internet e-mail communications, literature sources vary widely in strength of evidence and can be weighted based on content and degree of rigor applied in the development of the literature.

Local Knowledge: Knowledge that is applicable to a given client or practice situation, and which derives from practitioner practice wisdom, experience, and characteristics of a practice setting. It is contrasted with knowledge that is generalized from research results.

Logic Model: An assessment/evaluation strategy used to determine the extent to which the intended outcomes of a program are consistent with the activities and resources of an agency. This is a single-page figure depicting the intended theory behind the program in terms of resources, activities, process, and outcomes. The process allows for an agency to determine the intermediate and long-term outcomes as they relate to program structure and operations.

Longitudinal Data: Involves the collection of data at different agreed-upon points in time, such as 1 month, 3 months, 6 months, and 12 months post-treatment completion. In the context of social interventions for families and children, a database that tracks the experience of families and children from their initial involvement with the formal service system through their continued involvement with that system, and which provides a valid and reliable basis for describing and assessing the experiences of families and children served by that system over time.

Longitudinal Survey: A research design in which the participants are followed at several different points in time, in comparison to a cross-sectional study, which examines participants at only one point in time.

Low-Quality Data: Information that is unreliable or invalid and does not reveal the underlying reality. These data are not useful for decision-making.

Macro: The level of results in which the organization itself is considered to be the primary beneficiary of organizational action.

Macro Results: The level of results in which the organization itself is considered to be the primary beneficiary of organizational action. Results at this level are called *outputs*, which specify the results internal to an organization that are accomplished (or not accomplished), that are *delivered* (or "put out") externally into society. A *product* becomes an *output* only when it is sold or otherwise matriculates to customers, consumers, or other external stakeholders.

Magnitude: The average absolute magnitude (as defined in microvolts) of a band over the entire epoch (1 second).

Maintenance Orientation: An approach to opioid agonist therapy that promotes long-term maintenance on an opioid agonist. Indefinite maintenance on an opioid agonist is considered a reasonable goal of treatment.

Marginalized Population: These are people in a community who do not sit in the seats of traditional power and who are often looked down upon by the people in those seats. A marginalized group is often a racial or ethnic minority but can also be the majority if the minority in power is effective in determining the social norms for the community.

Measurement: The quantification of some property or aspect of an object according to explicit rules of measurement. As an example, the mass of an object in a gravitational field is generally quantified in explicit measures of weight. The quantification of some property or aspect of an object measurement observed on each member of the reference population or measurements that are observed on each member of the reference population. In large populations, the specific values of parameters are often assumed or estimated rather than known.

Mega Results: The level of results in which external stakeholders and society are considered to be the primary beneficiaries of organizational action. Results at this level are called *outcomes*, which specify the *impact* on society of results that are accomplished (or not accomplished) by organizations, teams, and/or individuals. An out-put becomes an outcome when external stakeholders and society are impacted—positively or negatively, unintentionally or intentionally—by organizational actions.

Meta-Analysis: A study of studies, or collection and integration of experimental studies on a particular treatment or program where a statistical formula is used to measure the effect, size, and impact of the different treatment programs. Also known as a systematic literature review that utilizes quantitative methods to summarize the findings. For example, a formal synthesis of experimental research that seeks to understand how particular interventions affect specific outcomes for families and children.

Metacognition: Thinking about and documenting one's thought process; the monitoring of one's thinking for the critical thinking criteria as one acquires new information. Within the area of scientific thinking, this requires becoming aware of one's background knowledge, assumptions, and the rival hypotheses (how observing works) and assessing their validity as well.

Metric: A measure of performance.

Micro: The level of results in which individuals and teams within the organization are considered to be the primary beneficiaries of organizational action.

Micro Results: The level of results in which individuals and teams within the organization are considered to be the primary beneficiaries of organizational action. Results at this level are called *products*, which specify the results internal to organizations that are accomplished (or not accomplished) by individuals and/or teams that are produced for *other* individuals or teams *within* an organization.

Middle Range Theory: A theory that is between a total explanation of society and explaining discrete individual behavior.

Mission: The values and dreams of the group.

Mission-Based Research: Research projects whose inspiration is derived from political or social interests, in addition to purely scientific objectives.

Moderator: The term *moderator* is used to describe the individual leading a focus group interview. The moderator creates a nonthreatening environment where people feel comfortable talking, guides the discussion using predetermined questions, and keeps the discussion on track and on time.

Mortality Rate: Number of deaths from a disorder in a time period divided by the number of people at risk. When the time period is one year, this number is called the *annual mortality rate*.

Need: A gap between "What Is" (current) and "What Should Be" (required) individual, small group, organizational and/or societal performance results (not perceived shortages of personnel, resources, finances, training or service provision). Used as a noun, not a verb, a need can be represented as a simple mathematical function: required results minus current results = need.

Needs Assessment: A formal process that identifies needs as gaps in results between "What Is" and "What Should Be," prioritizes those gaps on the basis of the costs and benefits of closing versus ignoring those needs, and selects the needs to be reduced or eliminated. Needs assessments serve to identify gaps between current and desired results that occur both within an organization (at the micro level of results) as well as outside (at the macro and mega levels of results) in order to provide useful information for decision-making.

Negative Verification: A pattern of communication typical of people with depression in which they make negative remarks posed as questions for their partners ("I look terrible, don't I?"). Either way—whether the partner agrees or disagrees—the individual will not feel better, and eventually the partner may feel frustrated by these demands.

Objective: An objective is a statement of what the proposed project aims to achieve. Objectives should specify a time period and be quantifiable. For example, "within 12 months, 75% of participants will have participated in job interviews and 50% will be employed in part-time or full-time stable jobs." Ideally, a proposed project should have a manageable number of objectives (e.g., 5 to 7).

Observational Study: One in which the researcher looks at the relationship among variables but does not alter the variables in any way.

Obsession: Intrusive thoughts, feelings, urges or images that trigger intense anxiety or discomfort associated with obsessive-compulsive disorder. Obsessions occur outside of the sufferer's control, and tend to increase with attempts to control, neutralize, or suppress them. Obsessions are not excessive worries about real problems. Several categories exist, including but not limited to contamination fears, violent or horrific obsessions, superstitious obsessions; scrupulous obsessions, obsessions related to fear of responsibility for harm coming to others, and a feeling that things need to be "just right." *See also Anxiety Disorder.*

Obsessions: A symptom of obsessive-compulsive disorder involving persistent unwanted intrusive thoughts, ideas, or images that seem senseless yet evoke high levels of anxiety or distress. Examples include unwanted ideas about violence, sex, or blasphemy; senseless fears of contamination from realistically safe situations; and exaggerated fears of making unlikely mistakes (e.g., discarding important papers).

Obsessive-Compulsive Disorder (OCD): A disorder characterized by recurrent obsessions and compulsions that take at least one hour per day or cause significant distress or impairment. In discerning the differential diagnosis, OCD must be distinguished from related disorders including Hypochondriasis, Body Dysmorphic Disorder, Generalized Anxiety Disorder, Delusional Disorders, Tic Disorders, and Obsessive-Compulsive Personality Disorder. *See also Anxiety Disorders or Comorbidity.*

Odds: A ratio of events to nonevents. If the event rate for a disease is 0.1 (10 per cent), its nonevent rate is 0.9 and therefore its odds are 1:9, or 0.111. Note that this is not the same expression as the inverse of event rate.

Odds Ratio: The odds of an experimental patient suffering an adverse event relative to a control patient.

Online Groups: Online groups are therapy or support groups that are conducted via the computer in real time through e-mail, bulletin boards, or chat rooms. Online groups can also be conducted without the real-time component through e-mails. Online groups may also be referred to as "e-therapy."

OpiATE Monitoring System (OMS): A toolkit designed to assist opioid agonist therapy clinics in assessing current practices and developing quality improvement goals. The OMS contains a quick and easy method for assessing current practices and comparing these practices to best-practice recommendations as well as educational materials on best practices and multiple tools to assist in successfully carrying out quality improvement projects.

Opioid Agonist Therapy: A form of treatment for opioid (mainly heroin) dependence in which counseling and other psychosocial services are coupled with provision of a daily dose of an opioid agonist medication (methadone, levo-acetyl methadol, or buprenorphine).

Opioid Agonist Therapy Effectiveness (OpiATE) Initiative: A Veterans Administration Health Services Research and Development funded project aiming to increase access to high quality opioid agonist therapy for veterans diagnosed with opioid dependence.

Oppositional Defiant Disorder: Defined by a pattern of negativity, noncompliant defiance to authority figures (e.g., parents, teachers, and other adults), and temperamental outbursts that impair a child's ability to function effectively in home, school, and peer environments. This maladaptive pattern of behavior must have endured for six months or longer for the diagnosis to be made accurately. The DSM-IV TR (APA, 2000) is careful to note that these behaviors must occur more often than in peers of comparable age and developmental level. *See also Comorbidity* and *Externalizing Disorders.*

Organization Development (OD): Organization development (OD) is a field of study founded on principles of humanizing and improving organizations by planned change initiatives focused on individual growth, group process, and organizational culture and structure. While based on the idea of data-based change, the practice of OD has placed less emphasis on empirical procedures and focused more on the process of intervention and change. Related fields and practices include human resource management, management consulting, and training. The field of program evaluation has much to offer OD in relation to methods and processes for gathering data about change interventions and their outcomes.

Organizational Learning: Organizational learning emphasizes structures and processes by which participants share, interpret, retain, and experiment with knowledge about their work. Some practitioners emphasize the individual skills necessary to create and share knowledge, while others focus on group, resource, policy and structural aspects of organizations that impede or facilitate knowledge sharing. Related concepts include knowledge organizations, sense making, and communities of practice.

Outcome: A change in a patient's current and future health status that can be attributed to antecedent health care.

Outcome-Based Accountability: A process by which providers of supports and services are held responsible for the effectiveness of their work in terms of improved outcomes rather than conformity to prescribed standards of practice that may, in fact, not affect those outcomes.

Outcome Evaluation: A determination of the extent to which the intervention produced the intended short-term or long-term goals. Usually, outcome evaluations involve comparisons with a preintervention state and/or with comparable, untreated (control) groups. In most cases, an outcome evaluation is not very useful unless preceded by a process evaluation, which helps interpret the results. Evaluations that focus on what happens to clients as a result of the program and the program's level of success. Outcome evaluations study goals such as changes in knowledge, attitude, behavior, or improvements in client conditions. A study conducted to determine the impact of the program on the intended target(s), sometimes called impact evaluation.

Outcomes: Conditions that interventions are intended to effect or change. Specifically defined, measurable and verifiable events, conditions, states, or changes. There are two kinds of outcomes in the OPM&M framework: community outcomes, which represent improvements that the entire community desires for its well-being and livability, and service-delivery outcomes, which refer to what the service-providing organization needs to do in order to express its social commitment to accountability, efficiency, and equity. Community outcomes encompass the community's entire population and/or its environmental conditions as indicated by measures of social justice, economic prosperity, health, education, safety, recreation, aesthetics, and so forth. Service-delivery outcomes include the organization's public intention to use resources wisely and to manage operations rigorously and transparently.

Outputs: Outputs in the OPM&M framework are narrower in scope and scale than are outcomes. They refer to specific impacts that service providers actually have on the clients/customers that are actually reached. In this sense, outputs are associated with a subset of the larger population to which outcomes are linked. The "performance" of service providers is gauged by examining their outputs, in terms of how efficiently and equitably (as judged by measures of effort) and how effectively (as judged by measures of effect) they are able to reach and satisfy their clients'/customers' needs and to what extent successes and gains along these lines can be associated with the attainment or at least the approximation of the overall desired outcomes of the community.

Panic Attack / Panic Disorders: A panic attack is a stress-related feeling of intense fear and impending doom or death, accompanied by intense physiological symptoms including but not limited to rapid breathing, rapid pulse, sweaty palms, smothering sensations, shortness of breath, choking sensations, and dizziness. Panic attacks can happen very frequently and leave the individual emotionally drained. Individuals with panic disorders frequently live in fear of having another panic attack and develop avoidance (phobic) behaviors. Sufferers often consult physicians, many times thinking they are having a heart attack or asthma attack.

Parameters: Statistical indices that are assumed to be derived from measurements that are observed on each member of the reference population. In large populations, the specific values of parameters are often assumed or estimated rather than known. One can speak of the average per capita income of the United States, but actually observing the annual income of each and every person residing in the U.S. has proved impossible—even for the I.R.S.!

Paraphilia: A group of disorders characterized by recurrent, intense sexually arousing urges and fantasies or behaviors involving nonhuman objects, the suffering or humiliation of self, partner, children, or other nonconsenting person(s).

Parasuicide: Intentional acute self-injury with or without suicide intent.

Participant Incentives: Payments, whether monetary or in-kind, made to study participants for the purpose of reimbursement of expenses, compensation for time and effort, and/or as an incentive for participation in the study.

Participant Observation: A research method in which researchers observe behavior in real-life settings in which they participate.

Partnership Model: An approach to helping people with serious mental illness that relies on a triangular partnership of patient, family members, and involved mental health professionals. The model assumes that all of the "partners" have equally valid ideas and information to contribute to successful community adaptation, and it represents an alternative to the "medical model," which sees illness as an internal individual biological process that does not require attention to social context.

Paternal Bond: The degree to which an adult offspring feels attached, emotionally close, and bonded to his/her father.

Paternal Deprivation: An often overlooked form of child maltreatment most often characterized by a lack of attachment between a father and his child, emotional abandonment, indifference, failure to claim paternity, abuse, or neglect.

Paternal Involvement: The ways in which fathers are involved with their children in one-on-one activities, the degree to which they are accessible, and their level of responsibility for the care and well-being of their children.

Paternal Roles: The ways in which men carry out their roles as fathers. Major roles include breadwinner, gender role model, moral father, nurturer, and supporter of the mother.

Perceptions: Views about characteristics, based on personal prejudices, feelings, reactions and judgments. They are usually determined by race, gender, religion, socio-economic status, and other demographic and situational factors.

Performance: The results an individual or organization accomplishes in their progression toward measurable objectives of desired/required results at the societal (*see Mega*), organizational (*see Macro*), and individual/team (*see Micro*) levels. Performance is measured by the value that is added or subtracted by the results accomplished by individuals and organizations, regardless of preferred or mandated behaviors.

Performance Indicator: A specification of how well something—typically an organization—is performing. This is normally expressed as a ratio: for example, the percent of service recipients who report a certain level of satisfaction. Ratios allow meaningful comparison of groups with different sizes. Data for calculating indicators are derived from *measures*.

Performance Management: Incorporating measures of performance into management decisions on a regular, ongoing basis. A hospital manager may examine data monthly and notice after three months that one ward has lower rates of secondary infections than the others. This manager may then go and talk to the staff on the ward, find out what they are doing, then require other wards to replicate the practices.

Performance Measure/Indicator: A quantitative standard to describe performance. Usually a percentage, where the numerator represents actual performance and the denominator represents the entire population. The methodology for deriving and calculating quantitative results that may be used in a *performance measure*. Some indicators are derived from administrative data. Others may be derived from an instrument: for example, a survey that has been developed to determine consumers' perceptions regarding the quality of services they received. A multiquestion survey measure may yield one or more scores, depending upon design, and may reflect one or more *dimensions*.

Performance-Measurement Literacy: Performance measurement literacy refers to the capacity of individuals and organizations to obtain, interpret, and understand performance measurement information and the competence to use such information to benefit clients, service delivery, and the entire community.

Period Prevalence: Number of people with a disorder during the interval divided by the number of people at risk during the interval. Prevalence is the *incidence* of the disorder multiplied by the *duration* of the event.

Perpetrator: An abuser who engages in a harmful act toward an older adult when the act meets the criteria for a crime as defined by a state penal code. An *alleged* perpetrator is a perpetrator who has not been convicted of a crime by a court of law.

Personalism: The practitioner's intentional observance of informality in open displays of warmth toward a client rather than adoption of a more formal presentation. It is used as a means of engaging clients who can only feel comfortable with an informal relationship. Latino persons, for example, often value personalism in their relationships with professionals.

Pharmacotherapy: A form of treatment for obsessive-compulsive disorder involving the use of psychotropic medications. For OCD, the most effective medications are the serotonin reuptake inhibitors (SRIs). Although less is known about the exact mechanisms by which SRIs reduce OCD symptoms, one possibility is that they work by changing the way that neurotransmitters, such as serotonin, function in the brain.

Phase: The time lag between two locations of a particular band as defined by how soon after the beginning of an epoch a particular waveform at location #1 is matched in location #2.

Phenomenology: The systematic study of particular, unique states, conditions, or events for the purpose of understanding.

Phenomenologically Based Treatment: Treatment designed to assist in achieving particular goals unique to an individual condition or event that had been systematically studied.

Placebo Effect: Reacting to an inert substance or a deliberately ineffective treatment as if it were a real drug or an effective treatment. (*See Hawthorne Effect* and *Blinding.*)

Plan, Do, Check, Act (PDCA) Cycle of Improvement: (Also known as the *Plan, Do, Study, Act* cycle of improvement.) W. Edwards Deming, founder of the *Total Quality Management* movement, developed the cycle to assist organizations in making changes to improve their performances. First, an organization *plans* what it wants to improve and how to improve it. It tests the improvement in a pilot phase in the *Do* cycle. During the *Check* cycle, it analyzes performance data to determine if the change resulted in an improvement. If an improvement was made, then the organization implements the change fully in the *Act* cycle. The cycle is continuous until optimal performance is reached.

Planning for the Future: Establishing group goals and strategies (and agreeing on credible evidence to monitor change over time to determine if the strategies are working).

POEMS (Patient Oriented Evidence That Matters): Searchable databases from the Journal of Family Practice. POEMS are searchable summaries similar to journal club article summaries in methodology and format, targeted to family practitioners.

The Point-Counterpoint Technique: A cognitive intervention method for helping a client to challenge thinking patterns that are the source of his or her maladaptive emotional responses. The practitioner and client "argue" both sides of a client's arbitrary belief in a role-play. After a specified amount of time they switch roles and repeat the process. The client is thus forced to argue both sides of an issue, which is often helpful to his or her analyzing its validity and considering alternative thoughts.

Point Prevalence: Number of people with a disorder at a time divided by the number at risk. As the name implies, the point prevalence describes how many people have a disorder at a single point in time, in contrast to incidence, which describes cases over a longer time period. Prevalence is the *incidence* of the disorder multiplied by the *duration* of the event.

Population-Based Case-Control Studies: A type of epidemiological study that identifies all newly diagnosed cases of a specified disease that occur during a specified time period in a defined population. Controls are identified in a manner such that they are representative of the population that gave rise to the cases. Data related to the study hypothesis are collected from as many cases and controls as possible using personal interviews, medical record reviews, and/or biologic samples. The presence and/or degree of the hypothesized factor in cases are compared to the presence and/or degree of the same factor in controls.

Positive Paternal Emotional Responsiveness: The degree to which a father is understanding, warm, empathic, and nurturing to his children.

PQRS Objectives: A simple mnemonic device for remembering that objective statements should specify the *p*erformer who is expected to achieve the desired result, relevant *q*ualifying criteria should be delineated (typically by indicating the time frame over which the result is to be accomplished), the *r*esults (ends) to be accomplished, and the *s*tandards or conditions under which the result or performance will be demonstrated. Performance objectives never include how a result will be achieved.

Practice Evidence: Practitioners typically consider evidence of all sorts, direct and indirect, circumstantial, and even hearsay evidence when making practice decisions. Most classifications of evidence stress the likely reliability and validity of sources of evidence. Evidence derived from controlled research conducted in realistic practice contexts is typically given the most weight. Replication of such studies by independent investigators adds to the weight of the evidence. *See also Evidence-Based Practice* and *Evidence-Based Practice Guidelines.*

Practice Guidelines for Intervention: A set of systematically compiled and organized knowledge statements designed to enable practitioners to find, select, and use interventions that are most effective and appropriate for a given client, situation, and desired outcome.

Practice Theory: Explains behavior and suggests interventions to maintain or change it.

Pragmatism: A philosophy based in social democratic values and which avoids absolutes. It does not propose a total explanation of society but says that social values are enduring but manifested differently as social conditions change.

Prevalence (Period): The proportion of the population that has the outcome of interest within a specified time frame.

Prevalence (Point): The proportion of the population that has the outcome of interest at a specific point in time.

Primary Prevention: Prevention steps that reduce disease incidence; primary prevention is directed to susceptible persons before they have developed a disease. (Examples: vaccination for a variety of communicable diseases; smoking prevention)

Prison Prelease: Actions undertaken to prepare an offender for release into the community so that the chances of recidivating are reduced. Usually a minimum security program 30–90 days prior to release where the offender is transitioning through a social education program and participation in work-release.

Problem-Solving Training: Instructing couples on strategies they can use for managing problems that everyday life brings. Problem-solving involves the following steps: defining the problem; brainstorming; examining possible options; deciding on an option; implementing an option; and evaluating the implementation.

Process: Continuing dynamic interactions over time related to achieving a specific set of goals or conditions.

Process Evaluation: A determination of whether the intervention was carried out as planned, in terms of timing, service type and amount, participant eligibility, staff expertise, and so on. Process evaluations should also include an assessment of the micro- and macro-environments in which the intervention was delivered to investigate their intended and unintended effects. A process evaluation asks questions such as whether the program is being implemented as intended and whether it is reaching its target audience. Program evaluation studies conducted early in the program's development and characterized by informal types of research designs and data collection procedures such as collecting qualitative data while the program is in operation, use of agency reports, small surveys, and direct observation of the program. The purpose is to identify program targets, determine if the program fits its plan or design, and examine issues in program implementation. Applied research, which examines a program for pragmatic reasons, such as determining whether it accomplished its objectives or whether it is more efficient than comparable programs. In a nutshell, a study of the activities involved in the implementation of a program.

Process Measure: A gauge used to track the accuracy and effectiveness of implementation of a series of steps designed to achieve a certain result.

Professional Consensus: When referring to how practice guidelines or best practices are established, the term *professional consensus* refers to agreement achieved through a critical review by an authoritative group of professional experts in the review area. Typically, the review process includes a consideration of scientific evidence, collective practice experience, potential risks and benefits, relevance, problem or condition prevalence and burden, cost, and values.

Program Activities: Specific interventions that are undertaken to achieve the designated program results. Activities are "owned" by the agency offering services. For example, a program activity might include a two-hour group meeting to present and discuss contraceptives or the assignment of a volunteer to work 4 days per week with a student on homework assignments.

Program Budget: A fiscal plan that focuses on the activities of the organization and the expenditures allocated to support them.

Program Effectiveness: The extent to which program objectives have been achieved.

Program Improvement Plan: A plan designed by the program stakeholders, which considers the needs of all constituents, key information needs, and resources available to the agency. It is a collaborative effort whereby key stakeholders are engaged in a process of designing, implementing, and evaluating a program innovation for its impact on program outcome.

Program Monitoring: Evaluation studies that focus on how the program is being implemented. Questions answered in monitoring studies include: Is the program reaching its intended audience? Who is being served? What changes have been made in the program? What are the program's initial effects? Monitoring studies frequently use management information system data, available data about the program, and informal surveys about the program.

Program Results: Shorter-term outcomes for program clients or participants that result from successful interventions. These results usually represent a change in knowledge, attitudes, or behavior in the client. For example, an agency program result could include an increase in awareness of contraceptives or a higher rate of homework completion among participants.

Program Stakeholders: The group of people who are responsible for or play an important role in the administration, implementation, or consumption of services. Depending upon program structure, this group could include administrators, board members, funders, social workers, community members, and clients. Ultimately, this group must include workers and clients.

Proportional Mortality Rate (PMR): The proportion of all deaths that are due to the disorder of interest.

Prospective Study: A study in which the data are collected after the start of the study and the participants are followed forward in time.

Protective Factors: Circumstances that moderate or mediate the effects of risks and enhance adaptation. Risk factors and protective processes exist and interact on a variety of levels with individual, familial, societal, or cultural manifestations.

Psychoanalysis: An old-fashioned approach to psychology that emphasizes unconscious motives and conflicts and is based on the works of Sigmund Freud. It encompasses both a theory of personality and a method of long-term psychotherapy.

Psychoanalytic Method: In psychoanalytic therapy, the effort to bring unconscious material into consciousness, often through dream recall and free association.

Psychodynamic Theory: Four major schools of thought are encompassed by psychodynamic theory: object relations, self-psychology, drive theory, and ego psychology. In psychodynamic therapy, the patient (as opposed to the client in other types of therapy) talks, during this process the therapist acts to facilitate the discovery process providing interpretations about the patient's words and behaviors. Psychodynamic therapy may include dream analysis as a function of the therapeutic process. As with other types of therapy, some psychodynamic therapists may utilize other methods of therapy such as cognitive-behavioral techniques for specific problems.

Psychoeducation: A model for combining education with therapeutic input when dealing with problems of emotional management of an illness. It was developed as a method of engaging participants who might not otherwise commit to psychotherapy. Generally facilitated by a mental health professional, it is usually provided on a time-limited basis, and frequently in a group or multifamily context, as a way of promoting group interaction or self-help support.

Psychometric Measurement Tool: A standard way of assessing a particular aspect of human behavior. Raw scores are converted into standard scores so that statements can be made about one score as compared to the mean score. Reliability and validity are critical concepts in the development of psychometric tools.

Psychometry: The science of testing and measuring mental and psychologic ability, efficiency potentials, and functioning, including psychopathy components.

Psychopharmacology: The management of psychiatric illness using medication such as antidepressants, antipsychotics, anti-anxiety medications and more.

Psychotherapy: The treatment of mental disorders, emotional problems, and personality difficulties through talking with a therapist. There are dozens of different approaches to psychotherapy; frequently therapists choose methods based upon individual responsiveness or strengths related to a particular approach.

Q Fever: A zoonosis caused by the bacterium *Coxiella burnetii*. People become infected mainly by inhaling aerosols generated during parturition of contaminated animals. In French Guiana, an administrative French unit located between Suriname and Brazil, Q fever incidence has significantly increased since 1996. Presently, this original epidemic remains an enigma because the reservoir responsible for transmission has not yet been identified. Several facts make this epidemic different from the usual case: first, it occurs in the Cayenne region, the main urban area of the country, although Q fever is considered a rural disease. On the other hand, many facts strengthen the hypothesis of there being a wild reservoir whereas it is usually constituted by domestic ungulates.

Qualitative Data: Any information that is not numerical or quantitative in nature. Qualitative data are often obtained from in-depth interviews, direct observation of behavior, and examination of written documents.

Qualitative Research: A branch of research that is viewed as naturalistic and encompasses a range of methods that, broadly defined, describes and provides insights into naturally occurring phenomena and everyday experiences, and the meanings associated with those phenomena and experiences.

Quality Assurance (QA): A process or set of activities to maintain and improve the level of care provided to patients. (also known as quality improvement, or

QI). These activities may include review, formal measurements, and corrective actions. The QA/QI function is a standard part of health insurance plans and all institutional health care providers. Managed care often demands that providers present QA/QI findings to the sponsoring plans, especially data on the outcome of care. In the era of managed care, it has become critical to demonstrate effective outcomes in measurable terms.

Quality Enhancement Research Initiative (QUERI): A large-scale initiative funded by the Veterans Administration Health Services Research and Development Service. QUERI's goal is to improve quality of care and outcomes for patients suffering from eight prevalent chronic illnesses, including substance use disorders, through the implementation of evidence-based practice guidelines.

Quality Improvement (QI): Enhancement of products and/or services to obtain optimal levels of efficiency, effectiveness, and overall performance. Total quality management, an organization-wide approach geared to achieving better results by constantly making improvements in processes and performance.

Quantitative Research: A type of research that tests well-specified hypotheses concerning predetermined variables. It gathers information in numeric form and produces findings by statistical procedures or other means of quantification. It aims to answer questions such as whether or how much. Examples include whether cancer mortality rates are higher in different immigrant populations; what proportion of older adults in the U.S. has chronic illnesses such as diabetes.

Quasi-Experimental Designs: Experimental designs in which people are not randomly assigned to different forms of the program. Quasi-experimental designs can compare different forms of the program that naturally occur or can use procedures such as matching or waiting lists to form quasi-control or comparison groups.

Questioning Route: A questioning route is the set of questions developed for the focus groups. These questions are distinctive in that they are carefully sequenced or focused to lead the discussion into the areas of greatest importance to the researcher. In a two-hour focus group the questioning route might consist of about a dozen questions.

Quit Rate (ratio): The proportion of smokers who quit smoking during a specified time period; many more smokers attempt to quit than actually achieve the goal of quitting.

Random Digit Dialing (RDD): A technique used to generate and call random telephone numbers. If properly executed, RDD can be used to identify a sample of households or individuals that is representative of all households/individuals with residential telephones in a designated geographic area.

Randomized Control Trials (RCT): A type of research design, also called experimental design, in which participants (subjects) are randomly assigned to a control (no treatment or treatment as usual) condition or to an experimental condition. The purpose of an RCT is to minimize biases, which may compromise, confound, or obscure the results of research contrasting the treatment with the control condition. The purpose of random assignment is to test the counterfactual—that is, what would the outcome be for the treatment group if they had not participated in the treatment?

Randomized Controlled Clinical Trial: A group of patients is randomized into an experimental group and a control group. These groups are followed up for the variables / outcomes of interest.

Randomized Controlled Study (RCS): A research design, also called an *experiment*, in which participants are randomly assigned to receive a specific intervention or to be in a control group.

Randomized Field Experiment: An explanatory research study conducted in a naturalistic setting in which subjects are randomly assigned to intervention conditions. To enhance external validity, subjects are often randomly selected from a larger population. The experimental independent variable (e.g., an intervention) is actively manipulated by the researchers such as by randomly assigning active or placebo conditions to subjects. (Ideally subjects are not aware of which condition they are exposed to, e.g., an active treatment or a placebo, and information is gathered pertaining to the dependent variable in a manner that is blind to which condition the subject has experienced.)

Rapid Assessment Instruments (RAI): RAIs provide a brief standardized format for gathering information about clients. These instruments are scales, checklists, and questionnaires that are relatively brief, often less than 50 items, and easy to score and interpret. RAIs have established psychometrics and, thus, reliably and validly ascertain traits of an individual in terms of its frequency, intensity, or duration. Such instruments are useful for determining the nature and/or extent of specific behaviors, assessing the presence of psychiatric disorders, or monitoring client progress and evaluating treatment effectiveness.

Reassurance-Seeking: A pattern of negative communication typical of people with depression in which they request excessive reassurance from their partners, leading to rejection and dissatisfaction.

Receiver Operating Character Analysis (ROCA): A nonparametric test that identifies the ability of a measure to determine presence or absence of a particular trait.

Recidivism: Recurrence of criminal activity in an offender. Recidivism rate refers to the general rate of re-offense in a particular group of offenders during a specified time period. For example, re-arrest, technical parole violation, or re-conviction rate twelve months post-release from prison.

Regression toward the Mean: The phenomenon whereby people who are selected for a study because their score on some measure is significantly above (or below) the mean will, on retesting, have scores closer to the mean. This will occur simply because of the unreliability of the measure, and not because of the effectiveness of any treatment that may have been given between the two testing periods.

Relative Power: The relative magnitude of a band (absolute magnitude of the particular band divided by the total microvolt generated at a particular location by all bands).

Relative Risk Reduction (RRR): The percent reduction in events in the treated group event rate (EER) compared to the control group event rate (CER): RRR = (CER − EER) / CER * 100

Relaxation Training: A behavioral intervention in which the practitioner helps a client learn and master one or several exercises for physiological anxiety reduction. Common methods include deep breathing, progressive muscle relaxation, and imagery construction. All of these methods generally require practice by the client prior to mastery.

Reliability: The extent to which research/evaluation measures produce replicable and consistent results. Reliability is most commonly assessed between raters (inter-rater reliability), over time (test-retest reliability), or in terms of the internal consistency of a measure (e.g., split-half reliability, inter-item correlations, item-total correlations).

This concept relates to the consistency of a measure to yield the same results over multiple measures. It is assessed through test-retest reliability, alternate form reliability, split-half reliability, and internal consistency reliability. Reliability is especially important for tools used in making clinical assessments and practice decisions. When a scale is reliable, you get the same results every time. When using the term to describe a measure, it means the same thing. If the measure is a good measure, then each time you test it in the same way, you should get the same result. For example, let's say that you are a SCUBA diver. You take out your air gauge and measure that you've got 21% oxygen in your tank (that's good; it mirrors the percent of oxygen in the air we breathe). Then you immediately test the tank again with the same gauge and find that it reads 5% oxygen (that's a one-way track to brain damage). Do you go diving with the tank? Chances are you would opt to find a reliable gauge and measure again. An unreliable measure makes the data untrustworthy. In summary, reliability refers to the quality of an item, scale, or instrument that focuses on how consistently it collects information across time from the same respondents, or across raters.

A commonly reported type of reliability is internal consistency reliability, which assesses the intercorrelations among the scale indicators used to measure a latent construct.

Reliability (Inter-Rater): The degree to which two people, observing the same behavior, give similar scores on a scale.

Reliability Test-Retest: The degree to which a scale, given at two times, yields similar results (assuming that the person has not changed in the interim).

Remote Sensing: Process of acquiring information about an object from a distance. This broad definition includes Earth observations using airborne and spaceborne sensors, which measure the electromagnetic radiation reflected or radiated from the Earth's surface and store the measurements in 2D images. There is a wide range of remote sensing sensors, which provide information about sea and land surfaces. Distinctions are usually made between passive (which responds to the natural radiation incident on the instrument) and active (which generates its own radiation and measures the reflected signal) sensors; between high spatial resolution (resolution <100 m) and low spatial resolution (resolution around 1 km) sensors; between imaging and non-imaging instruments. Remote sensing systems can also be categorized according to the range of wavelengths in which they are operating: visible and near-infrared sensors, thermal-infrared sensors, microwave sensors.

Research: Scientific inquiry using the scientific method or an organized quest for new knowledge and better understanding, such as of the natural world or determinants of health and disease. Research can take several forms: empiric (observational), analytic, experimental, theoretical, and applied.

Resilience: The capability of individuals to cope successfully in the face of significant change, adversity, or risk. This capability changes over time and is enhanced by protective factors in the individual and environment. Resilience is influenced by diversity. It is expressed and affected by multilevel attachments, both distal and proximal, including family, school, peers, neighborhood, community, and society. In addition, it is affected by the availability of environmental resources.

Resiliency: Factors that are present in the lives of families and children that may offset the risks facing those families and children and help produce better outcomes for them.

Response Bias: A specific type of selection bias. It occurs when relevant characteristics of respondents who participate in a study differ from those who do not participate. Response bias is more likely to introduce error into study results if the proportion of eligible persons who are included in the study is low.

Response Prevention: A behavior therapy technique in which the patient refrains from acting on urges to perform compulsive behaviors. Response prevention is typically used along with exposure in the treatment of obsessive-compulsive disorder.

Results-Based Accountability: Program oversight that includes resource and output monitoring but emphasizes performance measures to evaluate how well programs achieve desired outcomes and impacts.

Results Management: A planning and resource allocation strategy for achieving client or participant outcomes through designing and managing program operations with a clear focus toward achieving targeted results. Program results for clients are actively monitored and used to make adjustments in program interventions and to allocate program resources.

Retrospective Study: One in which the data exist before the start of the study, as in administrative or clinical databases.

Risk: A psychosocial adversity or event that would be considered a stressor to most people and that may hinder normal functioning. Risk is understood as a dynamic process rather than a causal mechanistic one. A confounding factor causally related to the outcome under study.

Risk Assessment: Methods of determining adverse factors or events that hinder normal functioning in a particular area, such as alcohol use. Quantitative methods are used to ascertain empirical factors and qualitative methods are valuable in gaining insight into the complexity and interrelationships of these factors.

Risk-Adjustment: The process of accounting for pertinent patient characteristics before making inferences about the effectiveness of care.

Risk Factor: An aspect of personal behavior or lifestyle, environmental exposure, or inborn or inherited characteristic, which on the basis of epidemiological evidence is known to be associated with an unfavorable health-related condition and considered important to prevent, if possible. It is used as an indication of increased probability of a specified health outcome such as the occurrence of a disease but is not necessarily a causal factor. The term risk factor is further used to mean a determinant that can be modified by intervention, thereby reducing the probability of occurrence of disease or other specified outcomes.

Risk Ratio is the ratio of risk in the treated group (EER) to the risk in the control group (CER): RR = EER/CER. RR is used in randomized trials and cohort studies.

Root Cause: A factor that, if changed or removed, will permanently eliminate a nonconformance. Common to quality review process seeking to find the contributing factor to issues in service delivery.

Sample (Haphazard): A study group chosen simply on the basis of the availability of people (e.g., those who pass by a booth at a mall, or students in a class).

Sample (Random): A study group selected in such a way that everyone in the population has the same probability of being chosen.

Sample (Stratified): A study group chosen so that people are selected from different strata (e.g., by age, gender, social class). This is done either to ensure that there are a sufficient number of people in each stratum, or to ensure that the demographic characteristics of the final sample match that of the population.

Scenario: The presentation of case examples to reflect real life dilemmas of police decision-making. They allow an assessment of whether respondents are giving consistent answers by creating simulated situations and make it easier for respondents to understand the context of each encounter, so they can respond to the questions in the way they really believe they would if actually presented with the exact same encounter on the streets.

Scholar Practitioner: The term scholar practitioner expresses an ideal of professional excellence grounded in theory and research, informed by experiential knowledge and motivated by personal values, political commitments and ethical conduct. Scholar practitioners are committed to the well-being of clients and colleagues, to learning new ways of being effective, and to conceptualizing their work in relation to broader organizational, community, political, and cultural contexts. Scholar practitioners explicitly reflect upon and assess the impact of their work. Their professional activities and the knowledge they develop are based on collaborative and relational learning through active exchange within communities of practice and scholarship. Related concepts include reflective practice and wisdom.

Screens: People are selected and invited to a focus group interview because they have certain experiences or qualities in common. These criteria or qualifications are called screens. The screens could be social, demographic, geographic or the extent of exposure or use of a program or product. The screens ensure that those attending the focus groups have the characteristics or experiences that are of interest to the researcher. *See also Focus Group.*

Secondary Data Analysis: This process involves the utilization of existing data, collected for the purposes of a prior study or quality improvement process in order to pursue a research interest that is distinct from that of the original work.

Secondary Prevention: Prevention steps used for early detection and treatment; secondary prevention is directed to asymptomatic persons who have developed biologic changes from a disease. Examples: mammography; Papanicoulaou (pap) tests

Second-Level Coding: The second step in the coding of qualitative data, where researchers identify conceptually distinct subcategories within larger conceptual categories that were identified in first-level coding. *See also Qualitative Research.*

Selection Bias: Occurs when the individuals (or units) included in a study are not representative of the population of interest. Selection bias is a result of flawed selection procedures and can threaten study validity.

Self-Efficacy: One's perceived capacity to meet some challenge or perform a particular response. An individual's beliefs that particular behaviors will produce the desired outcome and the confidence in his/her ability to perform the essential tasks involved in a particular behavior.

Self-Instruction Training: A cognitive intervention technique that is intended to increase the client's control over behavior by improving the quality of his or her internal, self-directed speech. The technique assumes that many behaviors are mediated by internal, self-directed speech, and negative cues or an absence of positive cues may characterize a client's self-dialogue. The practitioner assesses the client's behavior and its relationship to deficits in subvocal dialogue, models more adaptive behavior, demonstrates how overt self-directed speech can be used to guide behavior, helps the client to rehearse new self-talk and behaviors, and helps the client make plans to risk more adaptive behavior while using covert self-directed speech.

Self Object: An individual's subjective psychological experience of an important relationship.

Self Object Functions: Empathic psychological responses that support the emerging sense of self in the child. They include mirroring, idealizing, and twinship.

Self-Psychology: A theory of how the self-structure of a person develops.

Self-Report Measure: A pen-and-pencil measurement tool designed to be completed by the client in order to measure his or her own attitudes, feelings, or behaviors.

Sense of Community: Feelings of connectedness to the physical characteristics and/or the social groups within the environment.

Sensitivity: A measure of the ability of any test to identify individuals with a selected trait. In other words, sensitivity gives us the proportion of cases picked out by the test, relative to all cases in which individuals actually have the disease. *Specificity* is the ability of the test to pick out individuals who do *not* have the selected trait. Results are reported in terms of an AUC.

Sentinel Events: Those events/incidents that the Joint Commission on Accreditation of Healthcare Organizations defines as reportable Sentinel Events (e.g., suicide, loss of limb or function, rape).

Sexual Predator: This is not a psychiatric term but rather has been defined by law. The Washington State law defines a sexual predator as anyone who seeks a relationship with another solely for the purposes of sexual assault.

Short-Term Abuse: Victimization occurs one to three times during a relatively short time period of a day to several months. The abuse victim is usually in a dating relationship and breaks the relationship off permanently with the help of parents or older siblings after a few pushes, slaps, or punches.

Single-Subject Design: The structure for studying a single unit such as one person, one family, or one organization over time is called a single-subject design. Such designs typically require the researcher to clearly identify specific interventions to be studied, operational specification of measurable outcomes or dependent variables, and establishment of a baseline rate followed by measurement of rates following the intervention.

Situation Analysis: Any process of estimating how institutional policies and actions influence the state of the neighboring universe. Examination of the current reality of the organization utilizing statistical analysis rather than speculation to assess current status.

Skill: The ability to perform a task well, usually gained by training or experience; a systematic and coordinated pattern of mental and/or physical activity.

Slot Zone: A specified area on the casino floor that contains one or more slot machines.

Snowball Sampling: This is a method to locate hidden groups such as drug abusers, incest survivors, and/or wealthy battered women who usually have no contacts with formal agencies and social institutions (e.g., hospital, police department, or prosecutor's office).

Social Environment: Collective processes in the neighborhoods, schools, families, and peer systems of children that organize, facilitate, and constrain their behavior over time.

Social Interventions: A blend of formal services and informal supports that is created with the intention of improving outcomes for a family, or the children in a family, and entails the combined efforts of professional service providers, paraprofessionals, friends, and family members.

Social Network: These are people who interact with each other on a regular basis. A social network is likely to include relatives, neighbors, coworkers, and members of one's church or faith organization. It is difficult to determine where a social network ends, particularly when considering network ties that are weak (i.e., remote acquaintances).

Social Phobia: Persistent anxiety surrounding social and/or performance situations. Symptoms are usually based in a fear of embarrassment. Social phobias often drive sufferers into self-imposed isolation resulting in dropping out of school, the tendency to avoid making friends, or job loss. Feelings induced by public speaking can provide insight into the types of issues faced by persons with social phobia when engaging in day-to-day functions such as meeting new people, going to parties, and going to school or work. *See also Anxiety Disorders.*

Social Policy: The statement of what is or should be in relation to meeting the needs of members of society.

Social Services: The help provided by the network of public and private agencies that serve the community's needs in relation to health and welfare.

Social Survey: Collection of data for the purpose of developing information to solve a specific problem. Technical criteria for collecting and handling data are the same as for hypothesis testing research.

Somatization: A process whereby psychological distress manifests as symptoms of physical illness. Specifically, it refers to complaints about or the manifestation of physical symptoms such as headaches, stomach aches, sleep problems, fatigue, and loss of concentration that have a psychological origin.

Soup Kitchen: A place where hungry people can obtain a free meal. Usually sponsored by religious organizations.

Space-Borne Remote Sensing: Process of acquiring information about the Earth by a space-borne sensor. Satellite remote sensing dates back to the early 70's, when images provided by space-borne sensors began to be used for environmental monitoring, either with wide field (e.g., NOAA AVHRR) or medium to high resolution (Landsat TM). Nowadays, wide field sensors, with resolution around 1 km have generally been designed for specific application, e.g. SeaWiFS or MeRIS for ocean colour, AATSR for sea surface temperature, or SPOT-Vegetation for biosphere monitoring. High-resolution sensors have reached performances comparable to those classically obtained with airborne sensors, i.e., resolution of 1–3 m (SPOT-5, IKONOS, QuickBird).

Special Cause Variation: A shift in output caused by a specific factor—for example, environmental conditions or process input parameters. It can be accounted for directly and potentially removed and is a measure of process control. Unlike common cause variability, special cause variation is based in known factors that result in a nonrandom distribution of output frequently referred to as "exceptional" or "assignable" variation.

Split-Half Reliability: The split-half method consists of administering one form of a scale to a group of subjects. Half of the items are used to compute one total score, and the other half to compute a second total score. To the extent that the two halves correlate, split-half reliability is established.

Stakeholder: People who will be affected by the project or can influence it but who are not directly involved with doing the project work. Examples are managers affected by the project, practitioners, who work with the process under study, and departments or businesses that support the process, e.g., suppliers, environmental management, and financial departments.

Standard: Refers to a model, example, or rule for the measure of quantity, weight, extent, value, or quality, established by authority, custom or general consent. It is also defined as a criterion, gauge, or yardstick by which judgments or decisions may be made. A meaningful standard should offer a realistic prospect of determining whether or not one actually meets it.

Standard Deviation: A statistical process to determine the expected range of responses for a particular set of collected data. Those responses that fall outside of the normal standard deviation become outliers and deserve particular attention.

Standardized Mortality Rate: Multiply the *Age-Specific Mortality Rate* by the proportion of people of a given age (compared to the rest of the general population across the United States, for example) and add up the results across the strata. The result is the mortality rate, standardized to the comparison group. This allows you to age-adjust mortality rates for a given disease and compare them to other, more general populations.

Statistical Significance: The observation of a statistical value that exceeds the explicitly stated limit of values that might occur by random chance. In most social science applications a statistical observation is considered statistically significant if its probability of occurrence simply by random chance is less than .05. The most straightforward example of this is a difference in means on a depression scale between two groups exposed to two different treatment conditions, where a difference in means is of sufficient magnitude to justify a conclusion that the observed difference is not due to random chance (i.e., random variation of the depression scale that is unrelated to the treatment conditions). Under such circumstances, it may be reasonable for the researcher to conclude that the difference in means is influenced by the difference in treatment conditions. It should be emphasized, however, that statistical significance is not proof but rather a statistical justification for the rejection of random chance as an explanation for the observed difference in means.

Strategic Planning: The process of determining an organization's long-term goals and then applying statistical analysis, review of best practice, and evidence-based approaches for identifying the best approach for achieving those goals.

Stress-Diathesis Theory: Based on the biopsychosocial model of understanding the functioning of the individual in a social context, this theory proposes that many people have a genetic or biological "weak link" or vulnerability (diathesis), which is the part of the organism that will break down first under stressful conditions. The theory advocates attention to those elements in the social context that put stress on that particular vulnerability.

Subjective Units of Disturbance (SUDS): Client self-report measure of the feelings and emotions associated with the trauma image on a scale from 0 to 7, with 7 being the most severe. The scale is done pre- and post-test for each counseling session to evaluate changes in those emotions and feelings.

Substance Abuse: Ingesting on a regular basis illegal chemical agents that alter perception, coordination, and mental and/or physical state and interfere with behaviors necessary for maintaining a healthy and prosocial lifestyle.

Suicidality: Refers to the degree and intensity of a person's desire to attempt to kill himself or herself. This includes suicidal ideas, thoughts, threats, and gestures and suicidal attempts. *See also Chronic Suicidality.*

Suicide Intent: The intensity and pervasiveness of one's wish to die.

Support Factors: Therapeutic interactions between therapist and client or patient, including therapeutic alliance, catharsis, and therapist warmth.

Surrogate End Point: A dependent variable that is measured rather than the outcome of interest (e.g., scores on a scale of proneness to suicide, rather than suicidal attempts themselves). This is usually done because the outcome of interest is either too difficult to measure directly or occurs too rarely.

Sustainable Execution: An extended period of time in which demonstration of sustained impact is documented with causation being assigned to the implementation of specific, well documented and defined strategic planning.

Symbolic Interaction: A social theory that says humans base their responses to what others do by taking account of their expectations and what they expect of themselves.

Systematic Critical Reviews: Reviews of research in a given area and/or on a given topic that are conducted according to an explicit, pre-established methodology, and which can be criticized and replicated.

Systematic Review: The process of searching for, recording, analyzing, and interpreting the evidence emanating from all valid research studies addressed to a specific question, using explicit criteria and methods, is called a systematic review. Sometimes systematic reviews use a quantitative method, meta-analysis, to analyze the data provided by the studies reviewed. Systematic reviews are often conducted by groups of researchers expert in the specific area examined. Also, the summary report of this process is called a systematic review. The process of retrieving and synthesizing empirical results in order to establish quantitative findings of the effects of an intervention.

Systems Theory: Evolved from the physical sciences as a method of analyzing complex interactions in closed systems. In family therapy, the behaviors of people cannot be understood without looking at the social system in which they live. The whole is greater than the individual parts.

Taking Stock: The prioritization of key activities a group will assess, the actual assessment of the activities on a 1 to 10 scale, and a dialogue about the ratings.

Target Results: These are longer-term outcomes toward which program activities and interventions are directed. These results are directly influenced by the interventions but are "owned" by the client or participant or community. Thus, the program cannot take full credit for their achievement or full blame if they are not achieved. For example, a program may have a target result of lowering the dropout rate or teenage pregnancy rate in a community.

Tests of Significance: *See Statistical Significance.*

Thanatology: The study of death and of actions and reactions associated with death.

Theory: A proposition, perspective, or conceptual framework for interpreting data. A series of related hypotheses.

Theory of Explanation: A theory that seeks to explain the cause of a problem.

Theory of Intervention: A theory that seeks to provide direction for intervening to solve a problem.

Therapeutic Alliance: According to L. Bickman, therapeutic alliance has generally been conceptualized as an agreement on tasks and goals between the client and the therapist, and a clients' affective bond with the therapist. Therapeutic alliance is recognized as one of the common factors related to therapeutic efficacy and effectiveness.

Theta: A frequency range in the EEG, defined as 4-8 Hertz per second.

Thought Stopping: A process of helping a client to eliminate an unwanted thought. The client is taught to concentrate on an unwanted thought and, after a short time, suddenly interrupt the thought with a vocal or subvocal command, some other loud noise, or some type of sensory jolt. The command serves as a punishment and thus inhibits the unwanted thinking behavior. The client can follow thought stopping with thought substitutions or reassuring, self-accepting statements.

Tolerance: A characteristic of substance dependence that may be shown by the need for markedly increased amounts of the substance to achieve intoxication or the desired effect, by markedly diminished effect with continued use of the same amount of the substance, or by adequate functioning despite doses or blood levels of the substance that would be expected to produce significant impairment in a casual user.

Toxicology: The branch of science concerned with the nature, effects, and detection of poisons and toxic substances.

Transportability: Transportability research examines the movement of efficacious interventions to usual direct care settings. This research examines not only the components of an intervention, but who is able to conduct the intervention and under what circumstances they can conduct it.

Trauma: This often be characterized by intrusive thoughts, bad dreams, nightmares, flashbacks, and psychological disequilibrium. Traumatic experiences involve the actual or threat of death, serious injury, or loss of physical integrity to which the person responds with fear, helplessness, or horror.

Treatment Effectiveness: Deals with issues of validity, specifically addressing whether a particular treatment works or not. Treatment effectiveness studies seek to increase understanding of the impact of a particular intervention assuring that said intervention is responsible for the identified impact.

Treatment Efficiency: Encompasses several aspects of accountability, effectiveness, efficiency, and effect. The focus is on more than a single intervention, asking the question Does more than one intervention provide an advantage for impact and change?

Treatment Manuals: Written instructions to practitioners on how to implement a particular treatment, specifying the components, dosage, and ordering of the practice approach.

Trend Lines: The establishment of the same information measured over a period of time with the intent to measure movement in a positive or negative direction over that period of time.

Type III Error: First proposed in 1968 by statistician Howard Raiffa, type III error involves giving a precise answer to the wrong question, i.e., errors in question formulation or conceptualization of the problem, rather than statistical error.

Validity: The extent to which a measurement tool accurately measures a specified concept. There are four types of validity: content validity, criterion validity, construct validity, and factorial analysis. The type of validity that should be assessed depends on the measure being used and the measure's intended use. The extent to which data collection actually measures the construct of concern, also referred to as the accuracy of the measure. Measures may be reliable but not valid; however, reliability is a precondition of validity. Validity is assessed in numerous ways. All validation studies attempt to determine whether a measure reflects the "true" situation; for example, by examining correlations with expert opinions, established measures, current state, or eventual outcome. A scale or questionnaire is valid if you are measuring what you think you are measuring. For example, many of the intelligence tests done at Ellis Island on immigrants were not valid: they purported to measure intelligence when in fact they measured the ability to speak English. If you couldn't speak English, you did not pass. Validity is tricky because it is difficult to prove; how do we really know we are measuring what we want and nothing else? In summary, validity refers to a quality of an item, scale, or instrument that focuses on how well it measures the concept it is intended to measure.

Validity (Construct): Determining what a test is measuring through a process of hypothesis testing.

Validity (Content): Ensuring that all of the items in a scale pertain to the construct of interest (content relevance), and that all aspects of the construct are tapped by a sufficient number of items (content coverage).

Validity (Criterion): The degree to which one scale correlates with other measures of the same attribute. The other measures can be given at the same time (concurrent validity) or can be an outcome observable only at some time in the future (predictive validity).

Validity of Cognition (VOC): Client self-report measure of the validity of the cognition associated with the trauma, ranked on a scale 0–7, with 7 feeling the most true to the client. The scale is done pre- and post-test for each counseling session to evaluate changes in the cognition and during the installation phase to evaluate the desired cognition(s).

Variance: The variation in the values for a given variable.

Visual Analog Scale (VAS): A scale consisting of a 10 cm line, along which the respondent places a mark to indicate the amount of the attribute (e.g., pain) that he or she has.

Volunteer Bias: People who agree to be part of a study differ from those who refuse to participate. They are generally older, more likely to be married, working, and healthier.

Wisdom: Added to knowledge when internal data and external evidence is integrated with considerations of preference, values, and costs to determine whether and how the primary intervention should have been performed in the first place. Wisdom is also referred to as practice wisdom.

Woman Battering Continuum: A range of levels of the magnitude of woman battering based on the duration, severity, and frequency of battering incidents. Also taken into account is the psychosocial and demographic pattern of variables common to each of the levels. *See also Abuser, Domestic Violence Typology, Elder Abuse, Short Term Abuse,* and *Chronic Battering.*

Index

CPSIA information can be obtained at www.ICGtesting.com
Printed in the USA
BVOW021432070512

289427BV00002B/5/P